THE LIVINGSTONS OF
LIVINGSTON MANOR

THE LIVINGSTONS

OF

LIVINGSTON MANOR

Being the History of that Branch of the Scottish House of
Callendar which settled in the English Province of
New York during the Reign of Charles the Second;
and also including an Account of Robert
Livingston of Albany, "The Nephew,"
a Settler in the same Province, and
his principal Descendants

BY

EDWIN BROCKHOLST LIVINGSTON

Author of "The Livingstons of Callendar and their Principal Cadets"
With a New Introduction by Edward Renehan

"Of the two great families which the system of manorial grants had raised
up, the Livingstone inclined to Republicanism, and, uniting activity to
wealth and ability, exercised a predominant influence."
—GEORGE BANCROFT, *History of the United States 1910*

EXCELSIOR
EDITIONS

Cover: *Chancellor Robert R. Livingston (1746–1813)* by artist John Vanderlyn (1804).
Used by permission of the New York Historical Society.

Published by State University of New York Press, Albany
Printed in the United States of America

Excelsior Editions is an imprint of State University of New York Press
For information, contact State University of New York Press, Albany, NY
www.sunypress.edu

Library of Congress Cataloging-in-Publication Data
Names: Livingston, Edwin Brockholst, 1852– author.
Title: The Livingstons of Livingston Manor : Being the history of that
    branch of the Scottish House of Callendar which settled in the English
    Province of New York during the Reign of Charles the Second ; and also
    including an Account of Robert Livingston of Albany, "The Nephew," a
    settler in the same Province, and his principal descendants / by Edwin
    Brockholst Livingston.
Description: [Albany] : [State University of New York Press], [2023] |
Series: [Excelsior editions] | Includes bibliographical references and
    index.
Identifiers: LCCN 2022050294 | ISBN 9781438494036 (hardcover) | ISBN
    9781438494029 (paperback) | ISBN 9781438494043 (ebook)
Subjects: LCSH: Livingston family. | Livingston, Robert, 1654–1728--Family.
    | Livingston Robert, 1663-1725--Family.
Classification: LCC CS71.L787 2023 | DDC 929/.20973--dc23/eng/20221122
LC record available at https://lccn.loc.gov/2022050294

10 9 8 7 6 5 4 3 2 1

𝕿𝖔

JOHN HENRY LIVINGSTON, ESQ.

OF

CLERMONT

GREAT-GRANDSON OF CHANCELLOR LIVINGSTON

IN THE ELDEST LINE

THIS VOLUME IS DEDICATED

IN SINCERE RESPECT AND ESTEEM

BY HIS COUSIN, THE AUTHOR

"People will not look forward to posterity who never look backward to their ancestors."

—Edmund Burke

PREFACE

SINCE the author completed his manuscript, and placed it in the hands of Mr. John Henry Livingston of Clermont for publication in New York, he came across some further, and quite unexpected, information concerning the family of William, the fourth Lord Livingston of Callendar, which, he considers, settles the question as to the identity of the great-grandfather of the Rev. John Livingston of Ancrum, who is stated by the latter in his *Autobiography* to have fallen at Pinkie, *anno* 1547 ; and which, moreover, completely fits in with the pedigree drawn up by the writer before he was aware of this new information.[1]

This new information is derived from the recently published volume—the fifth—of the new *Scots Peerage*, edited by Sir James Balfour Paul, Lyon King of Arms, and is to be found in the account of "Livingston, Earl of Linlithgow," contributed to this volume by Mr. W. B. Cook of Stirling,[2] who had access to some original authorities not consulted by the author. In his valuable and learned article, Mr. Cook states William, the fourth lord, had *three* sons (the two younger of these being hitherto unknown to any genealogist) namely:

1. ALEXANDER, who succeeded as fifth lord, and was the father of William the sixth lord.
2. MR. JAMES, concerning whom Mr. Cook appends the following note: "13 October 1547[3] arrestment of goods of deceased Mr. James Livingston, brother to Alexander, Lord Livingston, for behoof of his creditors." *Stirling Town Council and Court Book* (MS.), 1544–1550.
3. WILLIAM, "styled 'brother-german of Alexander, Lord Livingston,' in an action against the Earl of Huntly as to the rents of 'Pawplay' in Orkney, 28 November 1553."

The deceased Magister James Livingston, some of whose goods were seized by his creditors in October, 1547, was evidently one of those persons of "gentil bluid" who fell in battle on that "Black Saturday" in Scottish annals, when, according to the prophecy of Thomas the Rhymer: —

"There shall the lion lose the gylte,
And the libbards bear it clean away;
At Pinkie Cleuch there shall be spilt
Much gentil bluid that day."[4]

For the seizure of his goods took place during the month following the Pinkie fight, and just at a time, when, owing to the retirement of the victorious English army across the border the defeated Scots had the necessary leisure for attending to their private affairs. Moreover, some of the articles in the inventory of those arrested, such as a camp-bed[5] and quarrels or bolts for a crossbow,[6] point to the owner as being a man of war. In the account of this battle, contained in Robert Lindsay of Pitscottie's *Chronicles of Scotland*[7]— who must have been a lad at the time, and probably obtained his particulars from an actual participant—it is stated "thair was slaine that day be the Inglischmen, to wit, the lord Fleming, the maister of Erskine, the maister of Ghrame, the maister of Bouchan, the maister of Levingstoun, the maister of Ogillvie, with money great barrouns, quhilk" —he quaintly remarks—"war langsum[8] to rehearse and no fruitt nor plesour heirof." But it certainly would not have been "langsum" reading to anyone searching for the information thus unfortunately withheld by this worthy chronicler!

In this battle, so fatal to so many junior members of the Scots' nobility, it will be noted, the Lords Erskine and Livingston, the guardians of the infant Mary, Queen of Scots —and who had been personally excused, on this account, from taking the field "aganis our auld inymyis of Ingland"[9] —both lost their eldest sons and heirs. The Erskines and Livingstons, two of the most ancient families in Stirlingshire, were old friends and allies, and it is an interesting fact, that the pre-Reformation predecessor of the Rev. Alexander Livingston in the family living of Monyabroch, was a Magister Alexander Erskine, a son of the fourth lord, and younger brother of the fifth Lord Erskine, the Queen's guardian, and uncle to the Master of Erskine who fell at Pinkie.[10] This is an additional proof, if one was needed, that the rectorship of Monyabroch—now Kilsyth—was considered an appropriate living for the younger sons of these two noble families. There is no doubt, therefore, in the author's mind, that the above Magister

James Livingston, also fell at Pinkie, and that he was the father of the Rev. Alexander Livingston, Rector of Monyabroch *anno* 1561,[11] and so the great-great-grandfather of Robert Livingston, the founder of the New York Manor of Livingston.

E. B. Livingston.

LONDON, 2 October, 1908.

Notes

1. See Pedigree in Chapter I, of this work; also *Livingstons of Callendar*, p. 652. To which the author has now only to add the Christian name "James," hitherto either left blank or queried as "Robert?"
2. *The Scots Peerage*, vol v, p. 435, and note 4. This is by far the best Scots peerage ever compiled, but it will be some time before it is completed.
3. Mr. Cook kindly informs the author this date is misprinted 23 October in the *Peerage*.
4. The Lion, of course, meaning Scotland, and the Leopards, England.
5. Owing to the courtesy of Mr. David B. Morris, Town Clerk of Stirling, the author has obtained a full transcript of this interesting minute from the town archives. In the transcript this word is queried as "ane letitains(?) bed," which evidently should read "ane lettgant bed," from the French "Lit-de-camp," These beds are to be found in the inventories of the Scottish kings of this period.
6. Namely "xxvj genzeis." The rest of the goods consisted of ordinary tapestry beds, bedding, books, a lute, personal wearing apparel, etc.
7. Scottish Text Society's edition, vol. ii, p. 101. Mr. William Patten, Londoner, the pioneer of English war correspondents, who accompanied the invading army, estimated, that besides thirteen thousand of the common folk, there also fell on the Scottish side "of Lairds, Lairds' sons and other gentlemen, above twenty-six hundred." But he doubtless grossly exaggerated for the sake of praising his patron the Protector Somerset, who commanded the English army.
8. Anglo-Saxon and old Scots for "tedious."
9. Privy Council Order of 10 July, 1545.
10. The new *Scots Peerage*, vol. v, p. 609. According to charters in possession of the Earl of Mar and Kellie, he was Rector of Monyabroch, *anno* 1518.
11. William, the sixth Lord Livingston, the second son of the Queen's guardian, who presented the Rev. Alexander Livingston to Monyabroch, succeeded to the Barony of Callendar "cum advocatione et donatione ecclesie de Monyabro," in 1551. *Exchequer Rolls of Scotland*, vol. 18, p. 529.

CONTENTS

LIST OF ILLUSTRATIONS

NEW INTRODUCTION

Edward Renehan

Published on a subscription basis by the Knickerbocker Press in 1910, *The Livingstons of Livingston Manor* provides a rich history of one of the most important families in the early history of New York State as well as the fledgling nation. The book was written by a rather adoring descendant, Edwin Brockholst Livingston (1852–1929), who, though his prose might be a bit flowery at times, did his research well and appears to have left no stone unturned in revealing the long history of his clan—but with a few strategic gaps.

It is nearly impossible to overstate the role of the Livingston family in the early development of the economy and politics of early New York State and, indeed, of the country as a whole. "Livingston Manor"—granted to Robert Livingston the Elder (1654–1728) via royal charter from King George I of Britain in 1716—embraced 160,000 acres, including nearly all of what is today Columbia County, as well as much of Sullivan and Delaware Counties. The immediate successors to the Lordship were Philip Livingston (1686–1749) and Robert Livingston (1708–1790). The latter Robert Livingston, upon his death, divided the manor amongst his several children, giving each a smaller (but still substantial) fiefdom.

The primary family estate in Germantown, New York, where the leaders of the clan lived for more than 200 years starting 1728—*Clermont* on the Hudson River—is now a New York State Historic Site. Succeeding generations included "Chancellor" Robert R. Livingston (1746–1813) who served on the famed "Committee of Five" charged with drafting the Declaration of Independence (collaborating with Thomas Jefferson, Benjamin Franklin, John Adams, and Roger Sherman). The term "Chancellor" came from the prominent New York State office that he held for a quarter of a century.

Other members of the clan also played major roles in New York State as well as nationally. Philip Livingston (1716–1778, known in the family as "Philip the Signer") was a delegate to the Continental Congress from New York and signed the Declaration of Independence. William Livingston (1723–1798) was a Delegate to the Constitutional Convention and a signatory to the US Constitution.

It was Chancellor Robert R. Livingston who funded the design and building of Robert Fulton's "North River Steamboat," also known as "The Clermont," in 1809. This established a Livingston/Fulton monopoly on Hudson River steam transport which stood strong until the famous Gibbons v. Ogden Supreme Court decision (a challenge argued by Daniel Webster) eradicated it in 1824. The author gives rather short shrift to the Livingston/Fulton interpretation of the Commerce Clause of the US Constitution, with which they argued unsuccessfully that the Commerce Clause did not give total authority to regulate interstate commerce to the Federal Government. The Supreme Court's decision broke the back of the Livingston/Fulton monopoly by negating the relevant New York State statutes and opening all New York State waters to competition from Cornelius Vanderbilt and others.

The author also gives rather short shrift to the policies of various Livingston heirs—branches of the clan that had inherited individual portions of what by then was called the "Livingston Patent"—which led rather directly to the Anti-Rent Wars of 1839–1845, a key episode in the history of New York State. (Anya Seton's critically acclaimed Rent-War novel *Dragonwyck* [1944] featured a vast estate that most scholars believe was inspired by the homes, lands, and politics of the various Livingstons. Seton [1904–1990] had been born to great northeastern wealth and counted several Livingston descendants in her social circle.)

The writer of *The Livingstons of Livingston Manor*, Edwin Brockholst Livingston, was born in New York City but spent nearly all his life living abroad in London, where he pursued a career as a broker of shipping insurance. In his spare time, he appears to have devoted himself nearly entirely to researching Livingston genealogy and family history. Edwin's father was Jasper Livingston Jr. (1815–1883). He was in turn the son of Jasper Hall Livingston (1780–1835), who himself had been married to one of his Livingston cousins, Eliza Livingston (1786–1860). Edwin was the husband of Alice Mary Power (born 1850, death date unclear), daughter of the famed Irish politician Maurice Power (1810–1870) and his wife Catherine Livingston (1815–1890, yet another cousin). Edwin and his wife had two children. There are a number of descendants, all in Europe.

The first section of Edwin's book, detailing the family's Scottish roots, was actually a simple reprint of an earlier work, *The Livingstons of Callendar and Their Principal Cadets: A Family History*, published by Scott & Ferguson in 1887. In this, Edwin established that the family had been nearly as significant in Scotland as they were destined to become in the New World. The Livingstons were descended from the Callendar clan, a family prominent from medieval times with an ancestral seat called Callendar House, situated within the grounds of "Callendar Park" in Falkirk. The house—more of a castle than a house—still stands and dates back to the 1400s, although it has been extensively remodeled and expanded through the intervening years. Amongst the guests in olden times were Charles Edward Stewart (Bonnie Prince Charlie), Oliver Cromwell, and Mary, Queen of Scotts.

Previous to the building of the house, the so-called "Callendar Lands" had been granted in 1345 by King David II to a Sir William Livingston, who was married to a Callendar heiress at a time when women, for the most part, did not own lands. From there on, the Livingstons seem to have become accustomed to lordships and the overseeing of vast tracks of terrain worked by vast armies of renters and/or serfs. Through several centuries, the family thrived, moving upward in ranks through the Peerage (various members becoming Regent of Scotland, and Earls of Linlithgow, Callendar, and Newburgh). But all this came crashing down when during the early 18th century—1715 to be precise—James Livingston (5th Earl of Linlithgow, 4th Earl of Callander) chose the wrong and losing side when he backed the heir of King James II of England during the Jacobite Uprising. Away went the lands. And away went James Livingston to exile on the Continent. It was a cousin, from a branch of the clan that had relocated to Holland and thence to the New World, who received what became Livingston Manor from King George I in 1716.

Our author Edwin is (needless to say) a devout cheerleader for all things Livingston. Of course, some embarrassments were likely unknown to Edwin. For example, in 1812 Philip Henry Livingston (1769/70–1831, grandson of Philip the Signer), followed in the tradition of several of his grandfather's fellow signatories (notably Thomas Jefferson) in fathering a child by a black slave: a Jamaican woman by the name of Barbara Williams. This fact was for a long time obscure, only to be discovered in the late 20th century by several black descendants, one of them being Laura Murphy, who at the time served as the Director of the National Legislative Office of the American Civil Liberties Union, and who made something of a hobby of genealogy.[1]

Ms. Murphy and her clan were promptly and—and, for the most part, graciously—accepted by contemporary Livingston cousins. (Thirty-four black descendants received invitations to a Livingston family reunion at Clermont in 1997. Nevertheless, one of them later spoke truth when she wrote: "The Livingstons were powerful, wealthy, and influential, but instead of being instruments for change, they perpetuated slavery and grew rich using slave labor. ... The Livingstons and every other white American who has enjoyed the fruits of this system has either directly or indirectly profited from the misery of slaves."[2])

It should be noted that the Livingston line remains quite prominent in many realms. Descendants include the Bush clan, Eleanor Roosevelt (through her mother), and former New Jersey Governor Thomas H. Kean. (Eleanor's maternal grandmother was Mary Livingston Ludlow Hall [1843–1919] by whom she was raised at a family estate located on the Hudson at Tivoli, not far from Clermont.) More recently, Representative Robert Linlithgow Livingston Jr., Republican of Louisiana, was slated in 1998 to replace outgoing Newt Gingrich as Speaker of the House of Representatives. However, that otherwise likely occurrence got derailed when allegations of an extra-marital affair surfaced. The job instead went to Dennis Hastert, a man destined for his own scandal in 2015.

The value of The Livingstons of Livingston Manor is its rich detail gleaned from voluminous family archives many of which to this day remain quite private. Edwin's intimate portrait of a clan of signal importance in the history and development of both New York and the United States remains a vital resource for anyone wishing to understand the rich period of American history during which the Livingstons stood as one of the most powerful forces in the young nation.

Notes

1. David W. Chen, "A Livingston Legacy Revived," The New York Times, November 23, 1998, Section B, Page 1.
2. Madeline Wheeler Murphy, "Slavery – A Family Divided History: The Relationship of Two People Long Dead Reaches Down Through Time to Shape the Lives of Their Descendants, Black and White," The Baltimore Sun, June 29, 1997.

INTRODUCTION

W HEN consenting to the private publication some years ago, of a limited edition of *The Livingstons of Callendar and their Principal Cadets*,[1] for presentation only to near relatives and literary friends, I had no idea there would have been an outside demand for a work of this nature, or I might then have been induced to have had a larger edition printed by subscription. As, however, the reprinting of this work would be a very expensive affair, I have been precluded from acceding to the wishes of numerous kind correspondents, who wrote requesting a new edition. But understanding there would be a demand in America for that portion of my book, which treats of the branches settled in New York, I have so far gladly fallen in with their wishes, and the result is the present volume.

For some years past, I have devoted my leisure hours to fresh researches connected with this portion of the family history, and the results of these researches are incorporated in this edition. To save space, and make the book better suited for a larger circle of readers, I have, though with considerable reluctance, eliminated nearly all the explanatory notes, which were a feature of the work as privately printed. These notes I had purposely made very full, as I consider anyone engaged in compiling a family history cannot be too careful in giving chapter and verse for every statement contained therein, otherwise the truth of his conclusions might be left open to doubt.[2] I must, therefore, refer any of my readers, who may want to test any statement, and where no reference is given in this volume, to my earlier work, copies of which are to be found in the libraries of the New York Historical Society, and the New York Genealogical and Biographical Society, both in the City of New York, as well as in that of the British Museum in London. This volume, I may add, is not a mere copy of the earlier work, but has been entirely re-written; and while the historical portion has been added to, wherever possible, by the aid of my later researches, the purely genealogical parts have been much condensed, so as to endeavour to make the history of more interest to the general reader.

It may be of interest to American Livingstons to know that they have preserved the correct form of spelling the family surname, which in Scotland in modem times has been sadly spoilt by the addition of a final "e," which alters its whole meaning! For the surname of "Livingston" is derived from the name of the Saxon thane, the founder of the family, one Leving or Living, in conjunction with his lands or dwelling place, which in the earliest charters now extant, namely those of the twelfth century, is either written in the monkish Latin of those days "Villa Leving," or in the vernacular Saxon equivalent "Levings–tun." Hence the origin of the village of Livingston, in Linlithgowshire, Scotland, and the surname adopted by Leving's descendants— "de Levingstoun,"— when these came into use about a century later.

The American Livingstons have, however, with some rare exceptions, not been so careful of preserving the family arms intact; for misled by careless information furnished in 1698 to their ancestor Robert, the first lord, or proprietor, of the New York Manor of Livingston, they have borne for over two centuries, a spurious quarter in the place of one of the two Callendar quarters, to which they are legally entitled, according to the laws of heraldry, as cadets of that ancient and noble House. Surely it ought to be a matter of justifiable pride to members of this family on the other side of the Atlantic, that their right to bear the quartered arms of Livingston and Callendar, which date back to the middle of the fourteenth century, and have figured honourably in the history of Scotland, is so unquestionable!

E. B. LIVINGSTON.

LONDON, ENGLAND.

Notes

1. Issued in five parts between the years 1887–1892. A sixth, containing the Addenda, Errata, etc., still remains to be printed. This edition was limited to seventy-five sets.
2. At the end of this volume will be found a list of the authorities, manuscript and printed, made use of in writing this portion of the family history; but wherever I have quoted from *any other author*, his or her name is always given, either in the text or in a footnote; otherwise the authorities are all original, such as family charters, deeds, memoirs, journals, letters, public papers, correspondence, Journals of Legislative Council, Assembly, Provincial Congresses, Conventions, Continental Congress, and other public documents. I have, however, when making use of *new material*, given the references, as these will not be found in my earlier work.

A SHORT SKETCH OF THE SCOTTISH HOUSE OF CALLENDAR[1]

IT has been suggested to the author, that as his earlier work is practically inaccessible to the general reader, he should give, as an introduction to the present volume, a brief account of the origin and history of this once powerful Scottish family, whose romantic attachment to a "Lost Cause," led to its complete downfall in Scotland; so that to–day it is represented in the female line only, by Major Fenton-Livingstone of Westquarter, whose father, in accordance with the terms of the will of the late Sir Thomas Livingstone of Bedlormie and Westquarter, adopted the surname and arms of Livingstone in succeeding to this estate in 1853.[2] The earlier Scottish peerage writers, when at fault for the origin of a name, hid their ignorance by inventing some fabulous ancestor as the founder of the family, and that of Livingston was therefore ascribed by them to one Leving or Living, a noble Hungarian, who came to Scotland in the train of Margaret, when she and her brother, Edgar the Atheling, took refuge at the court of Malcolm Canmore about the year 1068. Margaret, who was a grand-daughter of Edmund Ironside and a great-niece of Edward the Confessor, afterwards married Malcolm, and became the mother of Scottish kings.

In the case of the Livingston family, the old peerage writers had a certain substratum of truth for their inventive tactics, for the founder of the family was a Saxon thane or landowner at this period, and his name *was* Leving, as is clearly proved by his donation of the church of his "villa" or manor[3] to the Abbey of Holyrood, which was founded by Margaret's son, King David I, in 1128. Though Leving's original charter cannot now be found, two charters confirming it are still in existence: one by Robert, the Bishop of St. Andrews, and the other by Leving's son, Thurstan, who, after his father's death "confirmed to God and to the Church of the Holy

Cross of the Castle of the Maidens—*Ecclesie Sande Cruris de Castello Puellarum*[4]—and to the canons serving God there, the Church of Leving's-tun[5]— *Ecclesie de villa leving*—with half a plough of land and a toft, and with all the rights pertaining thereto, as my father gave them—*sicut pater meus eis dednt*—in free and perpetual alms."

This ancient "villa" or manor of Leving's now forms the present parish of Livingston in Linlithgowshire, and remained in the possession of the elder branch of the family, namely the Livingstons of that ilk, until the commencement of the sixteenth century, when it became extinct in the male line. Surnames did not come into use in Scotland until about a century after Leving's time, when his descendants naturally adopted that of "de Levingstoun" from the name of their estate. The date of Leving's settlement in Scotland cannot now be ascertained. He may have entered with Margaret, or his family may have been settled in the lowlands of Scotland before her time? The name is of undoubted Anglo-Saxon origin, however. It is to be found in old Saxon charters and also in *Domesday*; and we can rest content with the fact that few families can show such an authentic and ancient origin.[6]

Thurstan, the son of Leving, had three sons, Alexander, William, and Henry, all of whom were witnesses to charters in the reign of William the Lyon 1165–1214.[7] The next member of the family, of whom any trace can be found, is Sir Andrew de Livingston, Sheriff of Lanark in 1296. He and his kinsman, Sir Archibald de Livingston, were among those of the magnates of Scotland, who rendered formal homage to Edward I of England in that year.[8] Sir Archibald was the representative of the senior line, while Sir Andrew was the ancestor of the junior, but far more important branch, as he was the grandfather of Sir William de Livingston, the founder of the House of Callendar. This Sir William was a doughty fighter, and served under Sir William Douglas at the siege of Stirling Castle in 1339, and was an active member of the patriotic party during the minority of David, the son of King Robert Bruce. David, on his return to Scotland from France, rewarded his faithful follower by the grant of the forfeited Callendar estates, and to better strengthen his title to these lands, their owner married (about 1345) Christian, the daughter and heiress of Sir Patrick de Callendar, the late proprietor. It is from this marriage that all the titled branches in Scotland, including the Barony of Callendar (*anno* 1458); the Earldoms of Linlithgow (1600), Callendar (1641), Newburgh (1660); the Viscounties of Kilsyth (1661), and Teviot (1696); and also the American branches of this family, are descended. As the Barony of Callendar became merged in the higher dignity of Linlithgow, there were five distinct Scottish peerages held by Sir William's descendants, and of these now only one is in existence, and that one—the Earldom of Newburgh—is held by an Italian nobleman, who probably has never been in Scotland in his life![9]

Sir William, the first of the House of Callendar, accompanied King David II in his unfortunate invasion of England, which resulted in that monarch's defeat and capture at the Battle of Durham or Neville's Cross, 17th October, 1346. Sir William, who had been dubbed a knight banneret[10] for his gallant behaviour during this short campaign, was also among the prisoners. He was released soon after, and at the particular request of the Scottish King was appointed one of the commissioners to treat for his ransom. These negotiations extended over a period of ten years, and as one of the six Scottish commissioners, who finally ratified the treaty, his seal is affixed to this document, which can still be seen, as it is now preserved in H. M. Record Office in London.[11] In 1362 King David II conferred on him and his wife the lands of Kilsyth, as these had also formerly belonged to the Lairds of Callendar. It was no doubt this same monarch, who granted Sir William the right to add to his family arms the royal tressure of Scqtland.[12]

The next member of this House of importance was Sir John Livingston of Callendar, whose second wife was a daughter of Sir James Douglas of Dalkeith (1381). From this marriage the line of Kilsyth is descended. Sir John fell in battle against the English at Homildon Hill in 1402, where the Scots under the Earl of Douglas were defeated by the English under the famous Hotspur and the Earl of March. By his first wife, a daughter of Menteith of Kerse, he is said to have had three sons, of whom the eldest, Alexander, who succeeded to the estate of Callendar, was the most famous. This Alexander was a man of unquestioned ability, so that James I of Scotland, on his return from his long English captivity, employed him as one of his trusted councillors, in his attempts to destroy the overgrown power of the great nobles. James perished in his attempt, being murdered in the Dominican Monastery at Perth on the night of the 20th February 1437. During the troublous years that followed the fortunes of the House of Callendar ebbed and flowed. For some time Sir Alexander Livingston of Callendar had the custody of the youthful James II, while his son and heir, James, was captain of the Castle of Stirling. His quarrels with Crichton, the chancellor, the queen-mother, and the Douglases, would take up too much space to relate here. He became later on Justice-General and Ambassador to England; but the enemies of the Livingston family, during his absence from Scotland in 1449, were successful in obtaining their temporary downfall.

Sir Alexander's second son and namesake, Alexander, ancestor of the Dunipace line, was beheaded, as also was Robert Livingston of Linlithgow, the Comptroller; while others, including Sir Alexander Livingston on his return from England, were flung into prison and their estates confiscated and distributed among the King's favourites. Though released soon after, Sir Alexander did not long survive his downfall. He was succeeded by his eldest son James, who was a great favourite of the young King's, whose custodian he had been in succession to his father, and then later (1448) had been given the post of Great Chamberlain. Probably, the young King's protection saved Sir James of Callendar from sharing his younger brother's fate, for after a short imprisonment he was received back at court, from whence he escaped to the Highlands. The downfall of the Livingstons in 1449 was quickly followed by the downfall of their powerful enemies the Douglases in 1452; whereupon Sir James was received back into the King's favour, and reinstated in his old office of Great Chamberlain. From this date his fortunes rose rapidly, he had the family estates restored to him, was made Master of the Household, and in 1458 his lands were erected into the free Barony of Callendar. His creation as a Lord of Parliament probably occurred three years earlier.

His son and namesake, the second Lord Livingston of Callendar, was under tutorship, being an idiot. He was succeeded by another James as third Lord Livingston. His father is supposed to have been Alexander, second son of James, first Lord of Callendar. He was therefore nephew of James, the second lord. He married Agnes Houstoun, daughter of Sir John Houstoun of that ilk. He was succeeded by his son William, the fourth lord (*anno* 1503). This William married Agnes, a daughter of Alexander Hepburn of Whitsome (about 1501) and had three sons. Of these, Alexander, the eldest, succeeded as fifth lord, while James, the second son, killed at Pinkie (*anno* 1547),[13] was the ancestor of the American branches treated of in this volume. Alexander, the fifth lord, was appointed by the Scottish Estates, on the death of James V, one of the two guardians of the infant Mary, Queen of Scots. In this capacity he accompanied her to France in 1548, and died in Paris two years later. His eldest son John having fallen at Pinkie, without leaving issue, he was succeeded in the title by his second son William. Two of his daughters were maids of honour to Mary, Queen of Scots. The elder of these, the queen's namesake, was one of the famous quartette known as "The Queen's Maries."

At the Reformation William, the sixth Lord Livingston, espoused the Protestant cause, and became one of its leaders, or Lords of the

Congregation. This did not prevent him and his wife being loyal to Mary, Queen of Scots, who, in 1565, was godmother to one of their children. Lady Livingston was cousin to the queen, through her grandmother Isabel Stuart, the mistress of James IV. Lord and Lady Livingston shared in the earlier years of Mary's captivity in England, and he was one of her commissioners in the negotiations with Queen Elizabeth. It was this lord who appointed the Rev. Alexander Livingston, his first cousin, to be the first reformed Rector of Monyabroch. This clergyman was the great-grandfather of Robert Livingston, the first Lord of the Manor of Livingston, New York. The sixth lord died in 1592.

He was succeeded in the title by his eldest son Alexander, as the seventh Lord of the House of Callendar. He was entrusted by King James VI in 1596 with the care and education of his eldest daughter, the Princess Elizabeth, afterwards the wife of Frederick, the Elector Palatine, and ancestress of King Edward VII. Owing to his wife being a Catholic, this arrangement gave great offence to the Presbyterian Kirk elders. But James was keen enough to know the value of trusting a family, which had been so loyal to his mother in her days of adversity, to be moved by their threats; and he still further showed his confidence in Lord Livingston by placing under his care his second daughter, Margaret, born two years later. King James VI rewarded Lord Livingston's services by erecting his lands and baronies into a free regality (anno 1600). By which act, he saved his royal purse the sum of £10,000 (Scots), due to Lord Livingston "for the support and education of his said daughters." The rent to be paid for this "free regality" was one pair of gilt spurs to be rendered at the Castle of Callendar on every Whitsunday. A few months later the King created him Earl of Linlithgow. He was also appointed Keeper of the Palace of Linlithgow and the Castle of Blackness, which became hereditary in this family, until the attainder of the fifth Earl in 1716. The first Earl of Linlithgow died in 1622; by his wife Lady Helenor Hay, he had three sons, besides daughters. The eldest John died in his father's lifetime, unmarried. Alexander, the second, became the second Earl of Linlithgow, while James, the third son became a soldier of fortune, and succeeded so well, that he was created by Charles I, Earl of Callendar.

Alexander, second Earl of Linlithgow, was created Vice-Admiral of Scotland in 1627. He was loyal to Charles I, while his younger brother James took the side of the Covenanters. He died in 1645. He was married twice. By his first wife, Lady Elizabeth Gordon, he had a son, George, who succeeded his father as third Earl of Linlithgow. By his second wife, Lady

George Livingstone, 3rd Earl of Linlithgow, 1616–1690. Etching by Robert White English, Scottish National Portrait Gallery. CCNC (Creative Commons-Non-Commercial) license.

Mary Douglas, he had another son, Alexander, afterwards to become the second Earl of Callendar. George, third Earl of Linlithgow, had had a military training abroad under the able tuition of his uncle James, afterwards first Earl of Callendar. Like his uncle, he was for a time attached to the court of the Princess Elizabeth, then Queen of Bohemia, who had a great regard for the Livingston family owing to her early days having been spent at Callendar House. So much did she regret having to quit this home of her youth, on her father succeeding to the throne of England, that at Berwick, on parting with the first Countess of Linlithgow, the little princess sobbed to her mother "Oh Madam! nothing can ever make me forget one I so tenderly loved. "[14]

On his return to Scotland, George Lord Livingston, though his father, the second earl, was a Royalist, served in the Covenanting army under the chief command of the Earl of Leven. In this, he was probably influenced by his uncle James, who was second-in-command of the Scottish forces (see later under Earldom of Callendar). He later on,— also like his uncle,—when Charles the First had become a prisoner in the hands of the English Parliament, joined the Duke of Hamilton in his disastrous invasion of England for the purpose of rescuing the King they had so lately fought against.

The third Earl of Linlithgow, after the Restoration, was given the command of the Scots Foot Guards. He subsequently became commander-in-chief of the forces in Scotland (1677), and in that capacity had to serve against the armed Covenanters until the arrival of the Duke of Monmouth, who then took over the chief command and defeated the Covenanters at Bothwell Bridge (1679). He remained colonel of the Foot Guards until July, 1684, when he exchanged it for the office of Lord Justice General of Scotland. He had also been appointed President of the Privy Council in 1682. At the Revolution of 1688 he lost both these posts. He died in 1690, and was succeeded by his eldest son, George, as fourth Earl of Linlithgow. This son had been an officer in his father's regiment, and as its lieutenant-colonel had led the Foot Guards in the attack on Bothwell Bridge. He was subsequently promoted to be captain of the King's Life Guards on the death of the Marquis of Montrose, and upon the expected landing of the Prince of Orange, he was second-in-command of the Scottish cavalry which crossed the Tweed to oppose it. He, with Claverhouse, Viscount Dundee, and a few others, remained loyal to James, when the bulk of the forces—English and Scottish—went over to the Prince of Orange. After the flight of King James, he was permitted to return home, and subsequently submitted to the Estates. He died in 1695, and having no children, he was succeeded by his nephew, James, the fourth Earl of Callendar.

This nobleman was the only son of Alexander, third Earl of Callendar. He had succeeded his father as fourth Earl of Callendar in 1692, and now by his uncle's death he became also fifth Earl of Linlithgow. In 1713, on the death of the Duke of Hamilton, who was killed in a duel with Lord Mahon in Hyde Park, the Earl of Linlithgow and Callendar was elected to fill his seat, as one of the sixteen representative Scottish peers who sat in the English House of Lords, as agreed upon at the Union of the Kingdoms in 1707. This, the last Earl of Linlithgow and of Callendar, was a strong Jacobite. He fought at Sheriffmuir, and upon the failure of the rising fled to France. He died an exile at Rome in April, 1723, aged 35 years. His only son, James, had predeceased him, unmarried. He, however, left a daughter, Lady Anne Livingston, by his wife Lady Margaret Hay, second daughter of John, eleventh Earl of Erroll. Her father had been attainted, and his estates forfeited to the Crown, but she was allowed to remain on at Callendar House on lease, as the government found considerable difficulty in disposing of the "rebel" estates. She married William Boyd, fourth Earl of Kilmarnock, and all went well with them until the landing of Prince Charles Edward in 1745, when Lady Kilmarnock's devotion to the exiled House of Stuart caused her to urge her husband, much against his own judgment, to join the young prince's army. Kilmarnock was taken prisoner at Culloden, at which battle his eldest son, Lord Boyd, was serving as an ensign in the English ranks. The unfortunate earl was one of the last of the Jacobite noblemen to lose his head on Tower Hill, and the block is still preserved in the Tower of London on which he and Lord Balmerino were beheaded. Their bodies were buried in the church within this fortress. His son, Lord Boyd, lost his right to his father's title of Kilmarnock, but became fourteenth Earl of Erroll on the death of his maternal aunt, without issue, in 1758, this peerage being in no way effected by the Act of Attainder; and thus his descendant, the present Earl of Erroll, owes his title and his office of Hereditary Lord High Constable of Scotland, solely to the fact of his being descended from the last Earl and Countess of Linlithgow and Callendar.[15]

We must now briefly treat of the creation and history of the Callendar earldom before it became merged in the older earldom of Linlithgow. The third son of the first Earl of Linlithgow, Sir James Livingston of Brighouse, started in life—as already mentioned—as a soldier of fortune, winning his spurs under the Prince of Orange and the great Gustavus Adolphus. He subsequently returned to Scotland and was created a peer by Charles I in 1633, as Lord Livingston of Almond; and eight years later was further advanced to the dignity of an earl; when, having recently purchased from the head of his family the estate of Callendar, he took his higher title from that place. Though he owed these favours to the unfortunate Charles the First, this did not prevent his accepting, after a show of reluctance, high command in the army of the Covenant. He fought with distinction in England against the Royalists, but with the surrender of Charles to the English Parliaments, his views changed, as was the case with other officers of rank in the Scottish army; and thus Callendar became second-in-command under the Duke of Hamilton in 1648, when the Scots made their disastrous attempt to rescue their king from his English prison. The earl thereupon had to flee to Holland. After the Restoration, on account of his having no legitimate issue, he obtained a fresh patent of his earldom (1660), in which his nephew Alexander, the eldest son of the second marriage of his late brother Alexander, the second Earl of Linlithgow, was named his successor. The first Earl of Callendar spent the last years of his life in improving his estate, and by rebuilding the greater part of his mansion, which had suffered heavily from the bombardment it had undergone from the cannon of General Monk, when he stormed it in 1651, on which occasion the little garrison were nearly all put to the sword.

Of Alexander, the second Earl of Callendar, there is little to relate. In his youth he was a zealous Covenanter, and after his succession to the title, his strong Whig views brought him, on more than one occasion, in conflict with the government, and he narrowly escaped being involved in the Rye House Plot. He married Lady Mary Hamilton, second daughter of William, the second Duke of Hamilton who fell at the Battle of Worcester. He having no issue by this marriage, his titles and estates were claimed by Alexander, second son of George, third Earl of Linlithgow, in accordance with the terms of the patent of 1660.

Of the third Earl of Callendar, there is also little to relate, beyond the fact that he was one of those who opposed the introduction of the Toleration Act into Scotland in 1686; and also, that he three years later retired for a time with his elder brother, Lord Livingston, to the Highlands, so as to avoid taking the oath of allegiance to William and Mary. He died in 1692, leaving by his wife, Lady Anne Graham, eldest daughter of James, second Marquis of Montrose, a son, James, who thereupon became the fourth Earl of Callendar, which title became merged in that of Linlithgow when he succeeded to his uncle George, as already related, in 1695.

The third Livingston earldom, that of Newburgh, dates its origin from the son of a successful courtier in the reign of James the Sixth (First of England), who was also raised to the peerage by Charles the First, though unlike his namesake and kinsman, the Earl of Callendar,—Sir James Livingston, Viscount of Newburgh, was loyal throughout to his royal master, and fell therefore under the displeasure of Cromwell, and had to fly to the continent. At the Restoration he received the reward for his loyalty by being created Earl of Newburgh (1660) and, in addition, the captaincy of the Scottish Life Guards was conferred on him by Charles II. The vicissitudes which befell this earldom and its possessors during the course of two centuries, until it came to be claimed by an Italian princess half a century ago, fill a romantic chapter in the family history, but require too much explanation to be recorded here.

Of the two remaining titled branches, that of Kilsyth is the oldest, and has the most interesting history, though it was not until the reign of

Charles II that it was ennobled. One of the lairds of this line fell at Flodden Field, and it was the ninth laird—Sir James Livingston—who was raised to the peerage, after the Restoration (1661), by the titles of Viscount Kilsyth, Lord Campsie, etc., as a reward for his loyalty. The third, and last, viscount of this unfortunate race was William Livingston of Kilsyth, a dashing cavalry officer at the date of the Revolution of 1688, whose unsuccessful attempt to bring his regiment of dragoons—afterwards famous in military annals as the Scots Greys—over from the service of William of Orange to that of the gallant Dundee, and his subsequent marriage to that brave leader's widow, and her sad and tragic death, together with their only child, while in exile in Holland, form another romantic episode in the history of the House of Callendar. It was not until after his first wife's death—Lady Dundee's—that Colonel Livingston succeeded to the peerage on the death of his elder brother James, the second viscount of that name. With the usual evil fortune of his House, he espoused the losing side in the rising of 1715, and like his kinsman, the fifth Earl of Linlithgow, died an exile in Rome, when this line also became extinct.

Sir Thomas Livingston, created Viscount of Teviot by William of Orange in 1696, was a descendant of the Lairds of Jerviswood, cadets of the House of Kilsyth. Reared in Holland, where his father commanded a Scottish regiment in the service of the States General; he also rose to the rank of colonel under the Prince of Orange, whom he accompanied to England in 1688. After the flight of James II he was promoted to the command of the Scottish Dragoons, the same regiment in which his kins- man, William Livingston of Kilsyth, was serving as lieutenant-colonel. He was subsequently appointed commander-in-chief of the forces in Scotland, and created a peer by William III, on account of his services against the Jacobites, whom he defeated at the Battle of Cromdale. As commander- in-chief he became involved in that disgraceful episode of that monarch's reign the Massacre of Glencoe, and dying without male issue, in 1711, his title of Viscount became extinct. He was buried in Westminster Abbey, where the handsome monument erected by his brother Sir Alexander Livingston is still to be seen.

Of the minor Scottish branches, including that of Westquarter, which estate escaped the general confiscation following the risings of 1715 and 1745, there is no need to refer to here. But while as we have seen the once powerful House of Callendar, in spite of its numerous cadets, has perished so utterly in its native land, that there is now no longer a Scottish representative left, *in the male line*, to inherit the remains even, of the numerous honours and extensive estates which formerly belonged to the Livingstons of Callendar, it fared otherwise with the branches of this House which settled in America in the latter part of the seventeenth century, and it is therefore to the history of these important cadets of the House of Callendar that the following chapters are devoted.

E. B. Livingston.

LONDON, 26 January, 1909

Notes

1. Unless otherwise stated, the authorities for the above sketch are given in *The Livingstons of Calendar.*
2. This branch of the family adhere to the modern, and erroneous, method of spelling the family surname with the final.
3. Sir Henry Ellis in his *General Introduction to Domesday Book* (vol i, p. 240) says "Vill or Villa" was "another term for a Manor or Lordship."
4. This was the ancient name of Edinburgh Castle. The canons lived there while the Abbey of Holyrood was being built.
5. The vernacular Saxon equivalent of the Latin "villa leving."
6. The two charters referring to Leving's donation are to be found in the *Liber Cartarum Sancts Crucis*, pp. 11, 15, 16. Copies are given in the Appendix to the *Livingstons of Callendar*, also a facsimile of the Bishop's confirmation. These old charters are never dated, but Robert, the second Bishop of St. Andrews, under the new Roman system established by Alexander I, filled this see between 1124–1158.
7. The third son—Henry—was discovered by the late Mr. Joseph Bain.
8. See under special chapter on the Heraldry of Livingston at end of this volume.
9. The grandmother of the present holder of the title—Princess Giustiniani-Bandini—proved her right to it in 1858. The Earldom of Newburgh was not limited to heirs-male, and has descended through the families of Livingston, Radcliffe, Clifford, Mahony of Naples, and Giustiniani.
10. "Willelmus de Levingston bannerettus" he is styled in the safe conduct granted by Edward III of England, 7 December 1347.
11. See also under chapter on the Heraldry of Livingston.
12. See also under special chapter on Heraldry.
13. See under Preface to this volume for fuller details.
14. Memoirs of the Queen of Bohemia by One of her Ladies, p. 43.
15. The Earldom of Erroll being one of those Scottish peerages, like that of Newburgh, which is not limited to heirs-male.

SEAL AND AUTOGRAPH OF WILLIAM, SIXTH LORD LIVINGSTON
*From original Charter at Callium House, dated
13th March 1560-1*

SEAL AND AUTOGRAPH OF REV. ALEXANDER LIVINGSTON,
FIRST REFORMED MINISTER AT MONYABROCH (KILSYTH)
*From original Charter at Callium House, dated
19th March 1560-1*

SEAL AND AUTOGRAPH OF REV. WILLIAM LIVINGSTON,
SECOND REFORMED MINISTER AT MONYABROCH
(KILSYTH)
*From original Charter at Callium House, dated
8th June 1607*

The Livingstons of Livingston Manor

CHAPTER I

CONCERNING THE REVEREND ALEXANDER LIVINGSTON, RECTOR OF MONYABROCH IN THE REIGN OF MARY QUEEN OF SCOTS, AND HIS DESCENT FROM THE ANCIENT HOUSE OF CALLENDAR.

"Every British gentleman entitled to bear coat-armour is noble, whether titled or not. It is only in comparatively recent times that this has been forgotten, and the term 'Nobility' exclusively appropriated to the peerage."
—LORD LINDSAY, *Lives of the Lindsays*.

"A subject of the British Empire, if he be a gentleman of coat-armour, and resident abroad, ought always to assert his nobility. He is legally a noble in the continental sense of the term, and he does wrong not only to himself, but to others similarly situated, if through a false idea of modesty, or through ignorance

he repudiates that nobility to which he is fully and legally
entitled."

—REV. JOHN WOODWARD, *Heraldry British and Foreign.*

A MONG the Livingston papers formerly belonging to the Viscounts
of Kilsyth, and still preserved in the charter room at Colzium House,
Stirlingshire, are some deeds relating to the Scottish ancestors of the
American branches of this once noble and powerful family. The most
interesting and important of these ancient documents is one bearing date
15th March, 1560,[1] and which had been executed at Callendar House,
the principal seat of the Lords Livingston—afterwards created Earls of
Linlithgow—in that county. This deed, which is in Latin, is to the effect
that Alexander Livingston, rector of the parish church of Monyabroch
(now Kilsyth), with the consent of his patron and chief, William Lord
Livingston feus[21] half his glebe to another William Livingston and Janet
Makgowin his spouse. To this document are attached the armorial seals of
both Lord Livingston and the rector, who also both signed it; and to which
this important attesting clause is added:—

> In cujus rei testimonium presentibus manu mea subscriptis sigil-
> lum meum proprium unacum sigillo et subscriptione manuali
> dicti nobilis et potentis domini Will'mi Domini Levingstoun
> de Callander patroni dicte mee rectorie in signum expressum
> sui consensus et assensus ad premissa est appensum. Apud
> Callander die decimoquinto mensis Martii anno Domini mil-
> lesimo quingentesino sexagesimo coram hiis testibus Will'mo
> Levingstoun de Kilsith, etc., etc.[3]

This Reverend Alexander Livingston, the first rector of Monyabroch after
the legal establishment of the reformed doctrines in Scotland, was the
grandfather of another and far more celebrated divine, the Reverend John
Livingston of Ancrum, whose youngest son, Robert, was the founder of the
principal branch of the American Livingstons. This document does not
state the exact degree of the relationship that the rector bore to his patron
and chief, William, the sixth Lord Livingston, but they must have been first
cousins.[4] The facts proving this connexion are briefly as follows, and are
"well ratified by law and heraldry."[5]

The Reverend John Livingston in his well-known *Autobiography*, cearly states:

> My father was Mr. William Livingston, first minister at Monyabroch, where he entered in the year 1600, and thereafter was transported about the year 1614 to be minister at Lanark, where he died in the year 1641, being sixty-five years old. His father was Mr. Alexander Livingston, minister also at Monyabroch, who was in near relation to the House of Callendar, his father, who was killed at Pinkie Field, *Anno Christi* 1547, being ane son of the Lord Livingston's which house thereafter was dignified to be Earls of Linlithgow.

It will be noticed that the Rev. John Livingston unfortunately omits to give the Christian name of his great-grandfather, who fell at Pinkie,[6] and unless younger sons in those distant days were possessed of landed estate, their *exact* position in the family pedigree is very difficult, and often impossible, to ascertain at the present time. However, in this particular case, heraldry renders us valuable assistance in confirming the truth of the Rev. John Livingston's very explicit statement; as his grandfather's armorial seal is sufficient proof that its owner was a cadet of the House of Callendar. Moreover, on closely examining the two seals attached to the above-mentioned deed, there is a remarkable similarity in the spelling of the family surname, which points to a very close connexion between the chief and the cadet, and also to a foreign origin as regards the seals themselves. For, instead of the family name being spelt "Levingstoun," in accordance with the Scottish style of that date, it appears on these two seals as "Levistoun" or "Levestoun."[7] Now Mary Queen of Scots usually wrote it "Leviston," as also did Lord Livingston's sister, the queen's namesake, and one of the celebrated quartette of "Queen's Maries," owing to their French upbringing.[8] It is therefore highly probable that the Rev. Alexander Livingston in his youth had accompanied his namesake and chief, Alexander, the fifth Lord Livingston, one of the guardians of the little Queen of Scots, and the father of William (afterwards sixth lord) and his sister Mary, to France in 1548, and that the above seals were the work of some French seal cutter.[9]

William succeeded his father in the title within two years of their arrival in Paris, which would sufficiently account for his having had his earliest seal as Lord Livingston cut in France, instead of in his native land.[10] Having been young men together in a foreign land, would have given the younger Alexander a claim on the new chief of their house on their return to Scotland, and hence his presentation to the family benefice as its first "reformed" rector; as William, Lord Livingston, had, like many another Scottish noble of his day, adopted the reformed doctrines and become a prominent Lord of the Congregation, and, subsequently, one of the Regents of the Realm of Scotland during the queen's absence. It may be worth recording here, that the patronage of the church of Monyabroch, which came into the possession of the Livingston family with the Callendar estates in the year 1345, remained in their hands until the attainder of William, third Viscount of Kilsyth in 1716, when it reverted to the crown.

A further proof of the probable French origin of the Reverend Alexander Livingston's seal is afforded by the manner in which cadency is denoted on his arms. For these bear in the Livingston quarters a *single* cinquefoil only within the double tressure, in place of the usual three. This is a mark of cadency seldom made use of by Scottish heralds—namely this diminution in the number of the charges; but in France it is much more common thus to difference the paternal arms.[11] Moreover, the rector's seal is absolutely unique in this respect, as the "single cinquefoil" was not retained by his son even, who preferred to use the quartered arms of Livingston and Callendar as customary, with the exception of a single, instead of the usual double tressure, but this may have been only the engraver's error, as *his* son, the Reverend John Livingston of Ancrum, bore the family arms without any difference whatever[12]; though as a matter of strict heraldry the two latter ministers ought to have continued to have differenced their paternal arms to have shown that they were cadets of the House of Callendar. It is quite possible that the *heir-male* of the old Lords Livingston is to be found among the descendants of the rector of Monyabroch, as the senior male lines in Scotland have long been extinct. The following rough sketch pedigree will illustrate more clearly than any written description can, the Scottish ancestry of the American Livingstons:—[13,14]

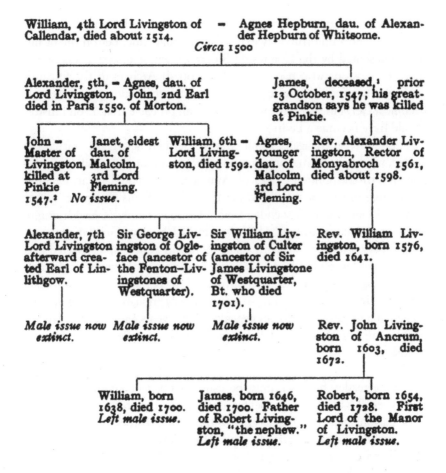

William, 4th Lord Livingston of — Agnes Hepburn, dau. of Alexander Hepburn of Whitsome.
Callendar, died about 1514.

Circa 1500

Alexander, 5th, — Agnes, dau. of   James, deceased,[1] prior
Lord Livingston,   John, 2nd Earl   13 October, 1547; his great-
died in Paris 1550. of Morton.   grandson says he was killed
                                          at Pinkie.

John — Janet, eldest   William, 6th — Agnes,   Rev. Alexander Liv-
Master of dau. of   Lord Living- younger   ingston, Rector of
Livingston, Malcolm,   ston, died 1592. dau. of Monyabroch 1561,
killed at 3rd Lord   Malcolm, died about 1598.
Pinkie   Fleming.   3rd Lord
1547.[2] *No issue.*   Fleming.

Alexander, 7th   Sir George Liv- Sir William Liv- Rev. William Liv-
Lord Livingston ingston of Ogle- ingston of Culter ingston, born 1576,
afterward crea- face (ancestor of (ancestor of Sir died 1641.
ted Earl of Lin- the Fenton–Liv- James Livingstone
lithgow.   ingstones of   of Westquarter,
                 Westquarter).   Bt. who died
                                  1701).

Male issue now *Male issue now* *Male issue now* Rev. John Living-
extinct.   *extinct.*   *extinct.*   ston of Ancrum,
                                                      born 1603, died
                                                      1672.

William, born   James, born 1646,   Robert, born 1654,
1638, died 1700. died 1700. Father died 1728. First
Left male issue. of Robert Living- Lord of the Manor
                 ston, "the nephew." of Livingston.
                 Left male issue. *Left male issue.*

The Origin of the American Livingstons has given rise to some amusing theories on the part of writers not well versed in the early history of Scottish families. For instance, Mr. Fernow, in his interesting and instructive article on early Dutch family names in New York,[15] makes the astounding assertion that "Livingston" was originally "Von Linstow," and that the family came from the Grand Duchy of Mecklenburg! But the exact reverse must have been the case, if there is any real connection between the two names. For many Livingstons during the fifteenth, sixteenth, and seventeenth centuries, left their native country of Scotland, mostly as soldiers of fortune to fight in the wars of France, Germany, and the Low Countries; or to join that famous and historical bodyguard of the ancient French kings—the Scottish Archers. Some of these wanderers from their native shores settled abroad, and founded families of note, such as the Comtes de Léviston,—now unfortunately extinct in the male line, but on the distaff side represented by the Comtes de Riocour,—whose ancestor was one of those Livingstons who had joined the Scottish Archers in the fifteenth century. Therefore, it is quite possible that a Scottish Livingston may have become a German von Linstow, but not at all probable that a von Linstow should have become a Livingston.

Quite recently again, a well-known German newspaper started the absurd, as well as untrue, argument, that there are no old families of good ancestry in the United States of America; and quoted as an example the Livingstons of New York, whom the author of this newspaper article gravely declared were descended from a German family of Jewish origin! The fact probably was that he had been misled, by some German emigrant of that persuasion, who, having made money in America, discovered that the name of Livingston had a far better sound than his own more homely patronymic, say of *Levenstein*. So without asking permission he coolly commandeered the better sounding name! Strangely enough, Mr. Holgate, who compiled a work on American genealogy sixty years ago, took the trouble to warn his readers against falling into a similar mistake. To use his own words:—

> The reader, however, must be cautious not to confound with these [Livingstons] another family, of German extraction, whose patronymic, the same as that of the Scottish stock, should be spelt *Levingsteen*, being descended from John Levingsteen, who came over to this country over a hundred years ago, settling originally in Guelderland, County of Albany, and whose posterity now reside in Montgomery County, Albany, etc.[16]

A hundred years ago the last male representative of the family in Scotland, Sir Thomas Livingstone of Bedlormie and Westquarter, fully recognised the relationship existing between himself and his American kinsmen. There is still preserved a letter written by a member of the New York branch, when on a visit to Westquarter in 1819.[17] The writer was a grandson and namesake of Peter Van Brugh Livingston, the first President of the New York Provincial Congress in 1775, and the letter was addressed to the writer's mother, Mrs. Philip Livingston.[18] In it he says:—

"I am now writing from the seat of Sir Thomas Livingstone, the only connection of our family in this country, and the nearest male representative of the noble houses of Linlithgow and Callendar. . . . He was not only perfectly aware of the existence of our family in America, and of the circumstances which obliged our ancestors to emigrate from their native home, but that they were also, after his own, the only branch in existence that remained of the Livingston family. He has frequently expressed to me his great satisfaction at making the acquaintance of a relative of the same name, while his kind treatment and attention has perfectly evinced the sincerity of his professions."[19]

But we must return to the reverend rector of Monyabroch. The lack of an adequate stipend was apparently the reason why the rector, "after due deliberation," so runs the charter, had to feu to his "beloved William Livingston and Janet Makgowin his spouse" and their heirs, the half of his glebe for the low rent of three pounds two shillings "usual money of the kingdom of Scotland," equivalent to five shillings and two pence sterling! Even in the year 1574, or thirteen years subsequent to the date of this transaction, the Rev. Alexander Livingston only had as stipend, according to the *Book of Assignation of Stipends*, "the third of the parsonage and vicarage, extending to three chaldees, five bolls, and one-third boll of meal, and the third of the vicarage pensionary of Monyabroch, three pounds, six shillings and eight pence (Scots)."

The early ministers of the Scottish Reformed Church had certainly good reason for complaining of the greed of their lay leaders, the Lords of the Congregation, who gained so much themselves by the plunder of the ancient church lands, and yet doled out such miserable pittances, as the above, to their own parsons. No wonder John Knox complained in such scathing language of the behaviour of the Scottish nobility and landed gentry for their grasping rapacity, as shown in their disposition of the confiscated church property. Which was to the effect that the ecclesiastical revenues should be divided into three parts, of which two should be given to the ejected prelates during their lives, and which afterwards were to revert to the nobility; while the remaining part was to be divided between the Court and the Protestant ministers.

"Well!" exclaimed John Knox on hearing of this arrangement, "if the end of this order be happy, my judgment fails me. I see two parts freely given to the devil, and the third must be divided between God and the devil. Who would have thought that, when Joseph ruled in Egypt, his brethren should have travelled for victuals, and have returned with empty sacks unto their families? O happy servants of the devil, and miserable servants of Jesus Christ, if after this life there were not hell and heaven."

Owing to the earlier volumes of the kirk-session Records of Kilsyth having either been lost or destroyed, probably during the civil wars of the seventeenth century, little can now be gleaned from contemporary sources concerning the long ministry of the Rev. Alexander Livingston over this parish. But from the fact of his having been appointed by the Scottish Privy Council, 6th March, 1589–[90], one of the three clerical commissioners for overseeing the maintenance of the Protestant religion in Stirlingshire, it would appear that he must have been favourably known to the government as a man of influence in his district, though his relationship to the head of his family alone, would probably have been sufficient to have got him appointed a member of this important commission. There were seven commissioners altogether—three clerical and four lay—and of these, three were members of the Livingston family, who at this period were all powerful in this county. The other Livingston commissioners were, William Lord Livingston, and John Livingston, the younger, of Dunipace. That family influence was the principal cause of his appointment, is borne out by the fact that only two years later "he was so aged and infirm, that he could neither preach, administer the sacrament, nor exercise discipline," so that the Presbytery advised him to get a helper. As he does not appear to have acted upon this advice, the Presbytery, in 1594, applied to the Synod for a helper to Mr. Livingston, but the result of this application is not recorded.

Mr. Livingston, probably owing to the fact that he "was in near relation to the House of Callendar," had been specially selected, in spite of his infirmities, by the Presbytery of Glasgow, to personally wait upon Lady Livingston, though she was not a resident of his parish[20]—Callendar House, where she usually resided, being in the parish of Falkirk,—and summon her to appear before the Presbytery upon the thirteenth of April in this same year, to answer as to her religious beliefs, which were the cause of much scandal to the kirk elders, who deemed her "a malicious papist." Failing to appear upon the date named, and her excuse for non-appearance being considered unsatisfactory, she was summoned for the second time "to give the confession of her faith under the pain of disobedience"; and Mr. Livingston was duly admonished as to the personal delivery of this summons also. The lady not deigning to take any notice of this second summons, "Mr. Alexander Livingston, parson and minister at Monyabroch" was ordered on the twenty-third of the above month to summons her for the third time, to attend before the Presbytery upon the fifteenth day thereafter "under the pain of excommunication." And that the said lady "may be won to God," the Presbytery further ordained that Mr. Patrick Sharp, Principal of the College of Glasgow, and Mr. John Cooper, should confer with her "touching the grounds of religion."

Callendar House, Stirlingshire, Scotland. Public Domain.

This attempt to bring Lady Livingston into the right path also failing, and after waiting for nearly three years for her to see the error of her
ways, the Presbytery finally, upon the first of March, 1596–[7], "ordains
every minister within the Presbytery of Glasgow to intimate next Sunday
that Dame Helenor Hay, Lady Livingston, is excommunicated, and Mr.
Alexander Livingston to do the same, under the pain of disposition." This
Lady Livingston was the wife of Alexander, seventh Lord Livingston, eldest son and successor of the Rev. Alexander's patron, soon to be created
Earl of Linlithgow. The reason why the Presbytery of Glasgow were so bitter against her religious views, was that her husband had been recently
entrusted by King James the Sixth with the care of the infant Princess
Elizabeth, in after years to become celebrated as the wife of the unfortunate
Elector Palatine, and ancestress of His Majesty King Edward VII. The worthy elders even complained to King James himself, who very diplomatically
told them in reply that his daughter was placed under the charge of Lord
Livingston, "who was a man known to be of good religion," and not under
that of his wife.[21] This dispute continued for several years, for in 1602 Lady
Livingston, now the Countess of Linlithgow, had to appeal to the king for
protection against further threats of excommunication, this time from the
Presbytery of Linlithgow. One of the charges seriously laid against her lady-
ship on this occasion, was "having dealings with midsummer fairies!"

The Rev. Alexander Livingston's conduct in this affair had, apparently, given great offence to the scandalised kirk elders, for under date 16th
of March, 1596, it is duly recorded in the Glasgow Presbytery Register, that
"as to Monyabroch neither exercise nor discipline is keepit by the minister
there." And upon the twenty-first of June in the following year—namely
a few weeks after the sentence of excommunication had been pronounced
against Lady Livingston—the rector was summoned before the Presbytery
"to hear himself deposed from the ministry at the kirk of Monyabroch for
inhability to use discipline in the said kirk as becomes." When asked if he
had anything to say in his defence, he raised no objection to the sentence of
deposition being pronounced; whereupon, again quoting from the Register,
"the moderator and brethren of the Presbytery of Glasgow by these presents
deposes the said Mr. Alexander Livingston from the ministry at the said
kirk of Monyabroch, for inhability of doctrine, and for inhability to use
discipline in the said kirk, simpliciter and for ever." The reason why the
rector so readily acquiesced in this sentence of deposition, appears to have
been owing to the fact that the Presbytery had agreed, at the same time, to
take Mr. William Livingston, his son, on trial for the living.[22]

The exact date of the Rev. Alexander Livingston's death is unknown, but a man of his great age probably did not long survive his deposition from the ministry. The last reference to him in the Colzium House deeds relating to the kirklands of Monyabroch, is an instrument stating that on the 8th of May, 1596, the William Livingston, to whom he had disposed of half his glebe in 1561, resigned the same into the hands of "Mr. Alexander Levingstoun, rector, the superior," for a new infeftment in favour of the resigner's eldest surviving son Alexander, but reserving to himself his own life-rent therein. This latter Alexander, as we shall see later, on coming into full possession of these lands at his father's death in 1607, and having meanwhile settled abroad at Treptow in Pomerania,[23] disposed of all his interest therein in favour of the Rev. Alexander Livingston's grandson John, afterwards the well-known covenanting minister, but at the date of this sale only a child of four years of age.

The Rev. Alexander Livingston had married one Barbara Livingston, "come of the House of Kilsyth," probably a daughter or a sister of the then laird, whose descendants during the next century became Viscounts of Kilsyth which title remained in this branch of the family, until loyalty to the royal House of Stuart ruined them, as it also did the senior line of Linlithgow and Callendar, and many another noble Scottish family. The issue of this marriage was a son, the William who had obtained permission from the Presbytery of Glasgow in 1597, to be taken on trial for his father's rectorship of Monyabroch.[24]

Notes

1. Old Style or 1561 N.S. Colzium House now belongs to the Edmond-stones of Duntreath. Owing to the courtesy of the late Sir William Edmondstone, Bart., of Duntreath, and his son-in-law, Mr. A. R. Duncan, the author was allowed to inspect and have copies made of these interesting family papers.
2. A Scottish term of feudal origin, signifying that property in land is held of a superior in perpetuity in consideration of an annual payment called feu-duty.
3. Which translated reads:— "In witness whereof to these presents, subscribed with my hand, my proper seal is appended, together with the seal and manual subscription of the said noble and potent lord William Lord Livingston of Callendar, patron of my said rectory, in express sign of his consent and assent to the premises. At Callendar, the fifteenth day of the month of March, the year of our Lord one thousand five hundred and sixty. Before these witnesses, William Livingston of Kilsyth, etc., etc."
4. This sixth Lord Livingston, of the House of Callendar, is thus described in a paper on the nobility of Scotland, which was sent to Queen Elizabeth in the year 1577, or sixteen years later than the date of the above document:— "Livingston, Lord Livingston, an ancient baron. His chief house, called the Castle of Callendar, lies

17 miles from Edinburgh. Of his surname are the Lairds of Kilsyth, in the Lennox, and Dynypace [Dunipace], in Stirlingshire. The living is hurt by adhering to the late Scottish Queen's party," [i. e. Mary Queen of Scots]. *Callendar State Papers Relating to Scotland and Mary Queen of Scots, 1547–1603,* voL v., p. 259.

5. *Hamlet,* Act. I, scene i.
6. This omission of the Christian name of his great-grandfather was not, by any means, a solitary case of such neglect on the part of the author of these memoirs; for though the Rev. John Livingston several times refers to his wife in his *Autobiography,* he never once mentions her by her Coristian name, which, however, we know from other contemporary evidence was Janet.
7. Facsimiles of both these seals are to be found on the plate facing the beginning of this chapter; also facing page 283 of *The Livingstons of Callendar.* For a better specimen of Lord Livingston's seal see plate facing page 14 of the latter work. A recent work on Scottish seals— *Scottish Armorial Seals* by Mr. W. R. Macdonald—contains a description of these, as well as other Livingston armorial seals, including some which are not to be found in Mr. Henry Laing's older lists.
8. In an inventory drawn up by Mary Livingston in 1566, on behalf of her royal mistress, the latter marks against each article of jewellery the name of the person to whom she, the queen, bequeaths it, in the event of her death before the birth of her expected child. Three members of the Livingston family are thus honoured, namely:—"Madame de Levinston" – Lady Livingston; "Leviston lesnee" – Mary Livingston; and "Leviston la ieusne" – Magdalen Livingston, also a maid of honour and a younger sister of the "Queen's Mary." The inventory is subscribed by the queen and Mary Livingston, the latter signing her name as "Marie Leviston." *Les Inventaires de la Royne Descosse Douairière de France.*
9. For further references to the relationship of the rector to his chief, see the concluding chapter of this volume, which treats specially of the heraldry of Livingston in connection with the New York branches of the family.
10. He was the second son, his elder brother John having died childless. This John, Master of Livingston, also fell at Pinkie.
11. Further reference to this French influence in connection with the family arms will be found in the last chapter.
12. For facsimile of the Rev. William Livingston's seal see plate already referred to. The Rev. John Livingston's seal is described by Mr. Laing in his *Supplemental Catalogue of Ancient Scottish Seals,* No. 649, but the author of this history has unfortunately been unable to obtain a facsimile of it. For description of this seal see special chapter on Livingston heraldry at end of this volume.
13. See remarks in preface to this volume.
14. Some writers have erroneously stated that the Master of Livingston, killed at Pinkie, was the ancestor of the American Livingstons, but the question of age alone proves this could not have been the case.
15. *Historic New York* (Second Series). Popular American family and local histories also abound in curious, and in some cases ridiculous, mistakes, concerning not only the Scottish ancestry of the Livingston family, but also in reference to their American history. The prettily illustrated article in Marion Harland's *Some Colonial Homesteads* is full of such errors, though only published within the last few years.
16. *American Genealogy* (edition 1851) p. 162.
17. Recently in the possession of the writer's son, the late Mr. Van Brugh Livingston of New York, to whom the author is indebted for the loan of this, as well as other

valuable family letters and papers. The letter is printed in full in the *Livingstons of Callendar*, p. 245, note 137.

18. The widow of Philip Livingston, at one time secretary to Sir Henry Moore, Governor of New York before the Revolution, and known as "Gentleman Phil" from his polished manners.

19. Sir Thomas Livingstone died, without issue, in 1853, when his great-nephew Mr. Thomas Livingstone Penton succeeded him as owner of Westquarter and assumed in accordance with the terms of his great-uncle's will, the arms and surname of Livingstone. This branch of the family always spell the name with the final "e".

20. At this date, the Eastern Barony of Kilsyth (including the parish church of Monyabroch) was still in the possession of the Lords Livingston of Callendar, while the Western Barony had been for many years owned by the younger branch of the family, the Lairds of Kilsyth. A few years later, in 1620, the then Laird of Kilsyth purchased from Alexander, Earl of Linlithgow, the Eastern Barony for the sum of 55,000 merles, when the *whole* Barony came under one ownership, until forfeited in 1716.

21. Lady Livingston was the only daughter of Andrew, seventh Earl of Erroll, and a Catholic, which was the cause of all this trouble.

22. This is a good proof that it was more on account of the Rev. Alexander Livingston's relationship to his patron, than to his orthodoxy, that had obtained for him the presentation to the family living.

23. Here is one example of a Scottish Livingston settling in Germany in the sixteenth century. In the attesting clause to the above quoted charter, which was executed at Gripswald (Greifswald), his name and description appear as "Alexandrum Leuestein ciuem Treptoniensem in Pomerania." This shows how easily the Scottish surname gets corrupted as its bearers emigrate to the continent of Europe. In France it becomes "Léviston"; in Germany "Levestein"; the latter having the very Jewish appearance of "Levenstein."

24. The Rev. Peter Anton, the present minister of this parish, says that its earliest name was "Kelvesyth," then "Monyabroch," and later, as at present, "Kilsyth"; *vide* his interesting account of his parish: *Kilsyth: A Parish History*, published in 1893.

CHAPTER II

CONCERNING THE REVEREND WILLIAM LIVINGSTON, MINISTER OF LANARK, AND HIS SON THE REVEREND JOHN LIVINGSTON, AND THEIR OPPOSITION TO THE INTRODUCTION OF EPISCOPACY INTO SCOTLAND.

"Richt trustie and weilbelovit cosines and counsellouris— Understanding of the unquiet and turbulent dispositioun of Maister Williame Levingstoun, minister, professing himselff rather a fyrebrand of discorde and dissensioun, then according to his dewtie and function, a goode instrument for the unitie and peace of the Churche, . . . oure pleasoure and will is that, by oure speciall command in oure name, you do confyne the said Maister Williame Levingstoun within the boundis of his owne parroche qhair he is preacheour, inhibiting him to transcend or come furth of the boundis thairof without oure speciall licence had and obtenit, and that under the pane of rebellioun."

—*King James the Sixth to his Scottish Privy Council, from his Court at Royston, 18th October, 1607.*

THUS wrote that sapient monarch King James the Sixth of Scotland, and First of England, from his Court at Royston in the latter kingdom, in the autumn of 1607, to his Scottish Privy Council at Edinburgh, the

King's wrath having been aroused by this young minister's sturdy opposition to his pet scheme, the introduction of Episcopacy into Scotland. The son certainly, could not be considered, as the father had been, lukewarm in the upholding of the Reformed doctrines.

The Reverend William Livingston was born, most probably at Monyabroch (Kilsyth), in the year 1576 and he completed his education at the University of Glasgow, where he was laureated in 1595. On leaving college, he was ordained to preach privately, on the 13th January, 1595–[6], licensed 27th January, instituted 10th July, and ordained 13th July in same year. As mentioned in the previous chapter, he had been permitted by the Glasgow Presbytery to have temporary charge of the parish of Monyabroch on his father's deposition; and his conduct having given satisfaction to the church authorities, they recommended, 20th February, 1598–[9], that he should be appointed to fill the vacant ministry permanently; whereupon he was duly presented to the living, upon the following first of July by the patron, Alexander, seventh Lord Livingston, admitted by the tenth, and inaugurated and instituted upon the fifteenth of the same month.

The Privy Council lost no time in carrying out the commands of the king, so that Mr. Livingston appears to have been detained a close prisoner within the bounds of his parish until his deposition six years later, for opposing the restoration of Episcopacy and not submitting to the canons and ceremonies. Whether the king considered this bold minister had been sufficiently punished by being deprived of the right of ministering to the spiritual needs of his native parish, or whether family influence had been brought to bear upon James, who was always well disposed towards the Livingstons for their unselfish loyalty to his unhappy mother,[1] it is still a rather remarkable fact that within a few weeks of his being deposed from the ministry of Monyabroch, Mr. Livingston was presented to the living of Lanark by no less a person than King James himself![2] If however that crafty monarch had ever entertained any hope that by this act of grace or policy he would not be troubled further with opposition from this quarter, he was soon doomed to be disappointed. For a very few years after receiving this appointment, one of the most outspoken of the preachers who denounced the legality of the General Assembly that passed the so-called Five Articles of Perth was this very minister of Lanark.

This conduct naturally brought Mr. Livingston to the notice of the High Commission Court, a tribunal which had been recently specially appointed for the trial of such offences. "What can you say against the Assembly?" enquired the Bishop of Glasgow, the presiding Commissioner, of the undaunted minister when the latter appeared before him. "It was neither free, nor full, nor formal, it stood not of such as had power to enact; and I thank God," he boldly replied, "I saw it and the proceedings of it, the neglecting of lawful Commissioners that got no vote, the taking in of others who had no commission." For his contumacy Mr. Livingston was deposed from his ministry and sentenced to be imprisoned, but the Court allowed him to return to Lanark before proceeding to his place of confinement. His parishioners evidently were not of the same bold type as their pastor, as upon his offering to administer the communion to them before his departure, they refused "fearing to be cut off from all benefit of his ministry."

For what length of time the people of Lanark were deprived of their pastor is not stated, but he had been restored to them prior to September, 1624, though he had not heard the last of the Court he had defied. For in the summer of 1635 he was again summoned before this tribunal to answer, this time, to the charge of having employed his Son, the Rev. John Livingston, who had been also deposed for nonconformity in Ireland, to assist him in the dispensing of the communion. Mr. William Livingston in defending his conduct on this occasion, spoke out as fearlessly as on his previous appearance before the Court; so that a clerical contemporary in writing of this event has recorded:

The Lord so assisted him with wisdom, zeal, and courage, that in defending his own deed from all just offence, he laid their heinous offences to their charge; so that they repented that they had caused summoned him, and were fain to dismiss him, skying that they would bear with him because he was an aged man.

As Mr. Livingston could barely have been in his sixtieth year, this was palpably an excuse on the part of the Commissioners to get rid of him. Clanship, moreover, in those days stood for much, and the minister probably had family connexions among the Commissioners. His age certainly did not prevent him from taking a prominent part in opposing Charles the First's disastrous attempt to introduce the use of Laud's liturgy into the Scottish Church. So much was he esteemed and respected by his fellow-ministers during these troublous times, that when they assembled to meet the King's Commissioner, the Marquis of Hamilton, on his entry into Edinburgh, on the 8th of June, 1638, they chose him to be their spokesman. The entry of the royal Commissioner into the Scottish capital, and Mr. Livingston's part in the proceedings, are thus amusingly described in a contemporary letter written by one of the ministers present on this occasion, and himself a noteworthy participator in the historical events that followed:[3]

In his [Hamilton's] entry at Leith, I think as much honour was done to him as ever to a king in our country. Huge multitudes as ever were gathered on that field set themselves in his way. Nobles, gentry of all shires, women a world, the town of Edinburgh, all at the water-gate; but we were most conspicuous in our black cloaks, above five hundred on a brae-side in the links, our alone [sic] for his sight. We had appointed Mr. William Livingston, the strongest in voice and austerest in countenance of us all, to make him a short welcome, but a good friend of yours and mine was rashly officious to inform Dr. Balcanquall [the Dean of Durham] that in the harangue were invectives against the bishops; which was not so, for you may read the speech. Upon this information the Commissioner excused himself to our nobles, and, in passing, to Mr. William himself, said that harangues in the field were for princes, and above his place; yet what he had to say he should hear it gladly in private.

Accordingly on the following day the Marquis received a deputation of ministers headed by Mr. Livingston, in the audience chamber at Holyrood House, when the latter was permitted to deliver his speech. Four months later the worthy minister was a member of the General Assembly which met at Glasgow to enquire into the evils that distressed the country, and to provide suitable remedies; and his name was placed, with four others, on the list for moderator, though he was not the one finally chosen to fill that post. He, however, took a prominent part in the proceedings of this historical Assembly, which set the king at defiance and declared that prelacy was contrary to the principles of the National Covenant and the Church of Scotland. His son, the Rev. John Livingston, at this date minister at Stranraer, was also a member.

This appears to have been the last occasion, upon which the minister of Lanark took any leading part in this great struggle between the bishops and the Presbyterian clergy; a contest which led to the outbreak of civil war very shortly after the above famous General Assembly had been dissolved. For the Rev. William Livingston only lived long enough to witness the failure of Charles's unfortunate at temps in 1639 and the year following to coerce his Scottish subjects into submission, as he died prior to October, 1641, leaving several children to mourn his loss, having been married three times.

His first wife, the mother of the Rev. John Livingston, and the only one mentioned in that divine's *Autobiography*, was, to quote her son's actual words, "Agnes Livingston, the daughter of Alexander Livingston, portioner[4] of Falkirk, come of the House of Dunipace.[5] She was a rare pattern of piety and meekness, and died in the year 1617, being about thirty-two years of age, and left three sons and four daughters." Mr. William Livingston's second wife was Nicolas Somervell, by whom he had three daughters, while the third was Marion Weir, who also predeceased her husband; by her he apparently had no issue.

The only child we need take any notice of, is his eldest Son, "Worthy famous Mr. John Livingston," as he was fondly termed by his contemporaries, and "one of the most revered names in Scottish ecclesiastical history," who was born at Monyabroch on the 21st of June, 1603; and it is an interesting fact that not only were both his parents members of the Livingston family, but also three of his grandparents (his maternal grandmother's maiden name is unknown), and his maternal great-grandmother came from the same stock! No wonder there is trouble in tracing the genealogies of a family like the Livingstons, who have been so greatly given to intermarrying among themselves, not only in their native land, but also in America. The Reverend John explains in his *Autobiography* that he was baptised by that name in compliance with the earnest wish of Lady Lillias Graham, wife of the sixth Lord Fleming of Cumbernauld, soon to be created Earl of Wigton, whose father, husband, and eldest son all bore that cognomen.

When ten years of age he was sent to a Latin school at Stirling, where "Mr. William Wallace, a good man and a learned humanist, was schoolmaster." At this school he remained until the summer of 1617, when he was summoned home to Lanark to be present at his dying mother's bedside. He subsequently entered, as his father had done before him, the University of Glasgow, whence he graduated as Master of Arts four years later. In August, 1607, when John was only four years of age, his father had re-purchased on his behalf the half of the glebe of Monyabroch that his grandfather had feued to William Livingston in March, 1561, as mentioned in the previous chapter. Shortly before his coming of age, his father wished him to marry and settle on the above land, which, owing to the absence of its owner, then living with his father at Lanark, had by ill neighbours been partly laid waste. This, however, he was loath to do, as at this period of his life he entertained the idea of devoting himself "to the knowledge and practice of medicine, and was very earnest to go to France for that purpose." The Rev. William Livingston, however, preferred that his son should remain at home and look after his property, upon which the laird, Sir William Livingston of Kilsyth, one of the Lords of Session, had cast his eye as a suitable place "to build ane burgh of barronie on at Burnsyde."

FACSIMILE (REDUCED SIZE) OF THE LATTER PORTION OF AN ORIGINAL DEED, THE LAST FOUR LINES OF WHICH ARE IN THE HANDWRITING OF,
AND SIGNED BY, THE REV. JOHN LIVINGSTON OF ANCRUM, AT LANARK, 27 JUNE 1624

From the original at Colzium House, Kilsyth.

Not knowing what was best to be done at this turning point of his life, young Livingston resolved to spend a day alone in some quiet spot, where he could pray undisturbed to God for guidance. The result of this day's meditation was his decision to lay aside all thoughts of France and medicine, and devote himself instead to the study of divinity. As a consequence of this resolution, he says he agreed to the disposal of his interest in the half glebe of Monyabroch to Sir William Livingston "although not yet major to ratify the sale." This transaction is fully borne out by the deed of sale executed on the 23d of April, 1623, and still preserved at Colzium House; which is to the effect that "Me Johnne Levingistoune sone lawfull to Maister Williame Levingistoune, sumtyme personne of Monyabroche now minister at Lanercke," with the advice of his father sells the said lands to the Laird of Kilsyth. This deed moreover bears the following confirmatory clause added by, and in the handwriting of John Livingston himself:— "As also subscryved be me the said Mr Johne Levingstone (being now major of Tuentie ane years compleet) at Lanark the XXVII day of Junii the yeer of God JAJVI^c and Tuentie four yeeres."[6]

Young Livingston was licensed, and commenced to preach the gospel at his father's and neighbouring churches in the month of January, 1625, but owing to his aversion to all Episcopal ceremonies he was regarded by the bishops with natural suspicion, so that he was prevented for several years from being ordained minister, and from obtaining the presentation to a living in Scotland, though many parishes would have gladly welcomed him as their minister. Lord Torphichen, among others, wanted to present him to the living of that parish, and invited him to be his guest at Calder, so as to assist the aged minister there, with the intention that he should be his successor. But the young preacher, who had bitterly offended the Bishop of Glasgow when at the University, by refusing to kneel at the communion table, found the Archbishop of St. Andrews would not be persuaded to consent to his ordination, though Lord Torphichen's appeal was supported by the Earl of Linlithgow, Sir William Livingston of Kilsyth, and other influential men.

While he was still waiting for ordination, and had received orders from the Presbytery of Linlithgow to desist from preaching at Torphichen, he received a pressing invitation from the younger Countess of Wigton to come to Cumbernauld, where her mother, the Dowager Countess of Linlithgow, a convert from the Catholic faith, lay dying. This is the same lady whose "papist" ways had caused such scandal to the kirk elders some thirty years before. John Livingston's godmother, the Dowager Countess of Wigton, was the younger countess's mother-in-law. At Cumbernauld he remained for some time as chaplain to the Earl and Countess of Wigton; and it was during his residence at this mansion that the memorable revival of religion at the Kirk of Shotts took place, owing to the celebrated sermon he preached there on Monday, the 21st of June, 1630. The effect of this sermon is spoken of by the Rev. Robert Fleming in his *Fulfilling of the Scripture*, as an "extraordinary appearance of God, and down-pouring of the Spirit with a strange unusual motion on the hearers," insomuch that five hundred, it was calculated, had at that time "a discernible change wrought upon them, of whom most proved lively Christians afterwards. It was the sowing of a seed through Clydesdale, so as many of the most eminent Christians in that country could date either conversion or some remarkable confirmation of their case from that day."

Finding himself precluded from ordination in Scotland, owing to the continued hostility of the bishops, Livingston was prevailed upon by his friends, in the month of August following, to accept Viscount Claneboye's invitation to come over to Ireland and take charge of the parish of Killinchy.[7] Mr. Livingston gives the following interesting and quaint account of his acceptance of this call, and the reasons for the trouble he took to travel as far as Rathmullen, in County Donegal, so that he might be ordained by Dr. Andrew Knox, Bishop of Raphoe, instead of by Dr. Robert Echlin, Bishop of Down and Connor, in whose diocese Killinchy was situated, and to whom he ought by rights have applied for his ordination:

In the summer of 1630, being in Irvine, Mr. Robert Cunningham, minister at Holywood, and some while before that Mr. George Dunbar, minister at Lame, in Ireland, propounded to me, seeing there was no appearance I could enter into the ministry in Scotland, whether or not I could be content to go to Ireland. I answered them both, that if I got a clear call and a free entry, I would not refuse. About August, 1630, I got letters from Viscount Claneboye to come to Ireland in reference to a call to the parish of Killinchy, whither I went, and got a very unanimous call from the parish; and because it was needful that I should be ordained to the ministry, and the Bishop of Down, in whose bounds Killinchy was, was a corrupt and timorous man, and would require some engagement; therefore my Lord Claneboye sent some with me, and wrote to Mr. Andrew Knox, Bishop of Raphoe, who when I came and gave him the letters from my Lord Claneboye, and from the Earl of Wigton, and some others, that I had for that purpose brought out of Scotland; he told me that he knew my errand, that I had [come] to him because I had scruples against Episcopacy and ceremonies, according as Mr. Josias Welsh and some others had done before, and that he thought his old age was prolonged for little other purpose but to do such offices, that if I scrupled to call him "My Lord" he cared not much for it; all he would desire of [me], because they got there but few sermons, [was] that I would preach there at Rathmullen the next Sabbath, and he would send for Mr. William Cunningham, and some two or three other neighbouring ministers to be present, who after sermon should give me imposition of hands; but though they performed the work, he behooved to be present, for otherwise he durst not answer [for] it to the State. He gave me the book of ordination, and desired that anything I scrupled at I should draw a line over it in the margin, and Mr. William Cunningham should not read it: but I found it had been so marked by some others before, that I needed not mark anything. So the Lord was pleased to carry that business far beyond anything that I had thought, or almost ever desired.

Having thus triumphantly obtained ordination in accordance with his own views, it is not to be much wondered at that Mr. Livingston was regarded by his own bishop with "an evil eye"; and when, certainly much against the newly ordained minister's will, he had to attend the visitation at Down in the following spring, his reply to Bishop Echlin's question as to what was his opinion of the Service Book, was so distasteful to his diocesan, that only Lord Claneboye's friendly intervention prevented the stubborn minister from being duly censured for his conduct on that occasion. It is not therefore much reason for surprise to hear that he had been barely a year at Killinchy, when he was suspended for nonconformity by his bishop, as was also his great friend Mr. Robert Blair, minister at Bangor,[8] Owing, however, to the intercession of the liberal minded primate, Archbishop Ussher, they were allowed to resume their duties after a very short suspension. Even the Rev. John Livingston, with all his hatred of prelacy and everything connected with it, bears witness to this amiable prelate's character, whom be describes as "Dr. Ussher, called Primate of Armagh, not only a learned but a godly man, although a bishop!"

The Scottish bishops, however, had not forgotten nor forgiven the former preacher of Torphichen, and were determined neither he nor Blair should get off so lightly. So they brought pressure to bear on the Irish Government through the king, and both these obnoxious ministers were again deposed for nonconformity upon the 4th of May, 1632. This suspension lasted for the space of two years. At first, John Livingston stayed on some little while at Killinchy preaching privately; but finding naturally he would not be allowed for long to evade the order of deposition in this manner, he returned to Scotland, where he travelled from place to place as he received invitations to preach. He was also frequently at Lanark with his father, and with his old friends, the Flemings, at Cumbernauld, and at other places where he had been well known before his acceptance of the call to Ireland. He did not, however, remain in Scotland all the remainder of the time previous to his restoration to his ministry; for he crossed over twice to Ireland during these two years, and it was on the last of these flying visits to his Irish parishioners, in the early part of 1634, that he took the resolve to try his fortunes in the New World. This was the first of the two attempts made by the Rev. John Livingston to cross the Atlantic, and it is a very curious circumstance, considering how numerous his descendants are at the present day in America, that both these attempts should have resulted in failure. The worthy minister himself, firmly believed he was turned back on this first occasion by Divine intervention, owing to his services still being required to carry on the Lord's work in Ireland.

To use his own quaint phraseology, he says:—

Our friends in Ireland seeing no appearance to be delivered from the yoke of the prelates' tyranny, had had a mind to transport themselves to New England, but resolved first to send a minister and a gentleman thither to the Governor and Council to try the condition of the country, and to agree for a place to settle in; and accordingly they pitched upon William Wallace and me to go straight to London, to go from thence with the first ship that went in the spring, and return with the first conveniency. Therein I perceived, howbeit I trust the Lord did accept and approve of our intention, yet wonderfully He stopped our designs; for had William Wallace come to me to Groomsport, in Ireland, at the time prefixed, we might easily have reached London before the first ships went. But he staying some two days, taking his leave of his family, all which time the wind was fair; so soon as he came the wind became contrary for a fortnight, but after that we came to Scotland, and made all the haste we could to London; but all the ships were gone, only three to go within a fortnight. The first we met with who had an interest in these ships was Mr. Humphrey, who urged much that we should go with him on his ship. We told him we would advise. After that, Mr. Bellingham having a greater ship, offered us better accommodation; yet, because, Mr. Humphrey spoke first, we agreed to go with him. Had we gone with Mr. Bellingham, we had gone forward; but Mr. Humphrey to gain time to do some business, and to eschew some tossing at sea, did not go aboard when the ship loosed, but took us with him to Dorchester, that when the ship should come over against Weymouth, we might go aboard. On a Sabbath, before noon, the ships came to Weymouth; the other two went forward with a spread sail, but Mr. Humphrey desired his ship to cast herself in stays until we should hear Mr. White of Dorchester preach. In the afternoon we went aboard; but by this means, when a storm and contrary wind came on Wednesday next, the other two ships being all past the Land's End stood to sea, while we were forced to come to anchor at Plymouth, and stayed there eight or ten days with contrary winds. During this time William Wallace fell sick, and both was averse himself and advised by doctors not to go to sea; and our friends in Ireland had condescended that I should not go alone without him, and therefore we both resolved to return. When we were coming back, I told him that I apprehended that we would get our liberty in Ireland; and accordingly, when we came, we found that we four who had been deposed, were restored by the Deputy's letter in May, 1634.

It was owing to the intercession of Lord Castlestewart, a firm patron of all Scotchmen in Ireland, that Wentworth, the newly appointed Lord Deputy, afterwards the famous and unfortunate Earl of Strafford, was persuaded this would be a politic act with which to start his rule in Ireland. He therefore sent instructions to Bishop Echlin to withdraw, for six months, his sentence of suspension, which command was promptly obeyed by the bishop. The next occurrence of importance in the Rev. John Livingston's eventful life, was his marriage to a lady of the Fleming family. This *event* took place in the summer of the following year. He *gives* the following account of his wife and her family in his *Memoirs* but curiously enough he never once mentions her by her Christian name. We, however, learn from other contemporary sources of information relating to this lady that it was Janet.

To quote again his own actual words:—

In June, 1635, the Lord was graciously pleased to bless me with a wife, who, how well accomplished every way, and how faithful a yoke-fellow, I desire to leave to the memory of others. She was the eldest daughter of Bartholomew Fleming, merchant in Edinburgh, of most worthy memory, whose brothers were John Fleming, merchant in Edinburgh, and Mr. James Fleming, minister at Bathans. Her father died at London in the year 1624, and was laid hard by Mr. John Welsh, and these two only, of a long time, had been solemnly buried without the Service Book. Her mother was a rare godly woman, Marion Hamilton, who had also three religious sisters,—Elizabeth, married to Mr. Richard Dickson, minister first at the West Church of Edinburgh, after at Kinneil; Barbara, married to John Mein, merchant in Edinburgh; and Beatrix married to Mr. Robert Blair.

This Robert Blair was Livingston's friend, the minister of Bangor; and it was owing to his introduction that the marriage came about, though not until after much searching of heart on the part of the bridegroom, who certainly, according to his own account of the courting, was no ardent suitor for the fair Janet's hand, as it took him "nine months seeking a direction from God anent that business!" And even when this laggard in love had finally made up his wavering mind, and had actually married the lady, it was above a month before the cautious minister could honestly admit he had attained the proper marriage affection for his bride. Though he candidly confesses in his simple homely way, that "she was for personal endowments beyond many of her equals," and then he only got it through prayer; but once got, he makes the quaint admission he had the "greater difficulty to moderate it."

The marriage took place on the 23d of June, 1635, at the West Church, Edinburgh, the bridegroom's father, the Rev. William Livingston of Lanark, being the officiating minister. There were reports spread about at this time that Chancellor Spottiswood had orders for the bridegroom's arrest, and that the macers were actually searching for him. This however did not prevent the ceremony from being of a public and solemn nature, and "countenanced with the presence of a good number of religious friends, among whom was also the Earl of Wigton and his son, my Lord Fleming." The newly married couple crossed at once to Ireland, where they, for a time, took up their abode at the house of Mrs. Stevenson, the bride's mother, at the iron- furnace of Milton,[9] some twelve miles from Killinchy; as Livingston was very doubtful as to his being allowed to remain much longer as minister of this parish. These doubts were soon confirmed by his fresh deposition in November of this year, followed shortly afterwards by a sentence of excommunication.

This second suspension from his ministry in Ireland led Mr. Livingston to turn his thoughts again in the direction of America. He himself says, he and some of his fellow sufferers in the cause of nonconformity, both in Ireland and Scotland, were encouraged in this resolution by letters from the governor and council of New England, "full of kind invitation and large promises of good accommodation." These letters were personally delivered to Livingston and his friends by Mr. John Winthrop, "the Younger," the eldest son of the celebrated Governor Winthrop of Massachusetts, who had come over on a mission to England in the previous year, and who was in Ireland in the winter of 1634–5.

Mr. Blair, who was to be one of Mr. Livingston's companions in this second attempt to reach New England, records in his *Memoirs* that

> about that time there came to us an English gentleman, whose name was Mr. Winthrop, from New England. This understand-ing gentleman being the son of the governor of that plantation to which we intended to join ourselves, was a man of excellent parts, being a great traveller not only in the west but in the east-ern parts of the world also—this man, I say, did earnestly invite and greatly encourage us to prosecute our intended voyage.

Livingston himself makes no mention of Winthrop by name; but in the collection of Winthrop papers published by the Massachusetts Historical Society, there is to be found an interesting letter from the Rev. John Livingston to John Winthrop, junior, proving that not only had they met at this time, but that Winthrop was indebted to Livingston for letters of introduction to various ministers and others in Scotland, to whom he could freely speak regarding matters in the New World. This letter, which is dated "Killinshie, 5th Januar, 1634–[5]," contains the wish that the writer may, at some later time, meet his correspondent "in that land where a great part of his [the writer's] heart is already." Young Winthrop returned to New England during the same year—1635—with a commission to found a new colony in Connecticut, of which planta-tion he was subsequently governor for many years; and little thought

Livingston when he penned the above letter, that he himself would never see the shores of the promised land, but that a son of his, as yet unborn, would be more fortunate, and that this son's eldest son would, sixty-six years after the date of his letter to Winthrop, marry a granddaughter of his correspondent!

Mr. Livingston gives a very full account of his second attempt to reach America, from which we learn that he and his friends had a ship built near Belfast, of about 150 tons burden, which they called *The Eagle Wing*;[10] and which, after many delays, was ready for sea in the autumn of 1636. The number of passengers was about 140 persons, rather a large complement for such a small vessel, "of whom the chief were Mr. Blair, John Stewart, Provost of Ayr, Mr. Robert Hamilton, after minister at Ballantrae, Mr. John M'Clellan, after minister at Kirkcudbright, Charles Campbell, John Somervell, Hugh Brown, and several other single persons and families, among whom was one Andrew Brown of the parish of Lame, born deaf and dumb."

Though the Reverend John Livingston states he was "abundantly clear in his mind that the Lord approved their intention," yet he also says, he often confided to his wife that he had his doubts as to their ever seeing New England. At last all was in readiness; and about September 9, 1636, they "loosed from Loughfergus, but with contrary winds were detained some time in Loch Ryan, in Scotland, and grounded the ship to search for some leaks in the Kyles of Bute." Blair, who could make some caustic remarks at times, declares they soon discovered that the only leak was in their fainthearted skipper, who grounded the vessel simply for the purpose of causing delay, as he did not wish to go to New England. They therefore dismissed him and "got another more experienced than he to take the charge." They then started with a fair wind, which continued to favour them until they were near the Banks of Newfoundland, when, to use Mr. Livingston's expressive words, they "foregathered with a mighty hurricane out of the northwest, that broke our rudder, which yet we got mended by the skill and courage of Captain Andrew Agnew, a godly passenger, who upon a tow was up to his neck in mending it. It broke much of our galleon-head, our forecross-tree, and tore our foresail, five or six of our chain plates made up, a great beam under the gunner-room door broke, seas came in over the round-house, and broke a plank or two in the deck, and wet all of them that were between decks. We sprung a leak that gave us seven hundred strokes of water in two pumps in the half-hour glass; yet we lay at hull [i. e. lay-to] a long time to beat out that storm, until the master and company came one morning and told us it was impossible to hold out any longer, and although we beat out that storm we might be sure in that season of the year we would foregather with one or two more of that sort before we could reach New England."

No wonder to men, who like Livingston, saw God's Divine will made manifest in the hurricane, this was a clear sign that the Almighty did not favour their enterprise. Still the good man was much perplexed, as he himself candidly admits, "seeing we thought we had the Lord's warrant for our intended voyage." He therefore "propounded an overture," after grave doubts as to its not being presumptuous on their part to ask for a further sign of Him, that they should continue to lay-to for another twenty- four hours, so that if in that space of time the wind should drop, they might take it God approved of their proceeding on their voyage. But instead of a calm the wind still further increased in force, so that they had the sorest storm they had as yet experienced, whereupon they doubted no longer, but under shortened sail ran before the gale until they once more found themselves back in Loughfergus.

The loss entailed on these poor ministers by this failure of their cher- ished plans was a heavy one, as they had to sell their stores, and the little merchandise they had purchased for this venture, at a great sacrifice. But what grieved them most, (as Mr. Livingston sadly confesses, who, unlike most of his contemporaries, was of a highly sensitive disposition), was that they "were like to be a mockery to file wicked." To his great relief he found instead, "the prelates and their adherents were much dismayed and feared at their return." These worthy men did not, however, altogether escape being ridiculed and mocked at on account of the unsuccessful issue of their voyage, says Dr. Reid in his *History of the Presbyterian Church in Ireland*, for Archdeacon Maxwell in the following Latin lines, prefixed to a printed sermon by Bishop Leslie, published in 1637, thus jeers at these unfortunate nonconforming clergymen:—

En navem ArcadicA properantem merce; gravatam
Mole suâ: miratur onus Neptunus, et undis
Insolitum prohibit pecus, atque remisit, et unà
Ruditus veteres, vetus in mendacia virus.
Et quasi lusa istis divina potentia nugis,
Majus in opprobrium, velis invexit eisdem

Quos simulant, ipsos per anomala dogmata asellos.
Which lines a friend of Dr. Reid rendered into English as
follows:—

Lo! this new Argos with Arcadian gear,
Hastens to reach some harbour struck with fear;
Laden and heavy with its clumsy bulk,
Neptune is moved, and wonders at the hulk;
Debars the motley crew from his domain,
And sent them hither drivelling back again;
And with them their old rant and uncouth cries,
And their inveterate hatred turn'd to lies.
And, as if mock'd by these fantastic freaks,
To raise their scorn, and bum with shame their cheeks,
The wat'ry god, with self-same sails convey'd
True genuine asses that incessant bray'd—
Which they resemble much in very deed,
By their strange dogmas and unmeaning creed.

Portrait of a man, possibly the Rev. John Livingston (1603–1672) of Ancrum,
Scotland, by Frans Hals. Public Domain.

Notes

1. Lord and Lady Livingston, the parents of Alexander, the seventh Lord and first Earl of Linlithgow, had shared Queen Mary's captivity in England. Mr. Nicholas White in reporting to Sir William Cecil from Tutbury Castle in 1569, mentions the interesting fact that "the greatest personadge in house about hir (the queen) is the Lord of Levenston and the lady his wife, which is a fayre gentilwoman; and it was told me both Protestants."

2. Deposed from Monyabroch in the summer of 1613; presented to Lanark 1 October in same year.

3. Namely, the Rev. Robert Baillie, afterwards principal of the University of Glasgow. The letter, dated as July, 1638, was written to Baillie's cousin, the Rev William Spang, minister of the Scottish Church at Campvere in Holland.

4. "Portioner," namely one who possesses part of a property which has been originally divided among co-heirs.

5. Dunipace in Stirlingshire; this line was a cadet of the House of Callender.

6. A facsimile of the latter portion of this interesting deed will be found facing this page; also page 300 of *The Livingstons of Callendar*.

7. Sir James Hamilton, Viscount of Claneboye or Clandeboye in the peerage of Ireland, was the eldest son of the Rev. Hans Hamilton, vicar of Dunlop in Ayrshire. The Marquess of Dufferin and Ava is the present representative, and senior heir-general, of this family.

8. In September, 1631, Henry Leslie, Dean of Down, writes to John Maxwell, minister at Edinburgh, regarding the "two sectaries," Livingston and Blair; the former he desired "to indite for depraving our Book of Common Prayer." The writer declares in this letter, that "there is a whole covey of birds of the feather in the diocese of Connor." *State Papers, Ireland.*

9. Dr. Reid in his *History of the Presbyterian Church in Ireland* says this place was Malone, since called New Forge, near Belfast, where a Mr. Barr had iron-furnaces. Janet Fleming's mother had married a Mr. John Stevenson as her second husband.

10. According to the authority of Blair's Son-in-law,—Mr. William Row, minister of Ceres,—this vessel was called *The Eagle Wing* from Exodus xix, 4: "Ye have seen what I did unto the Egyptians, and how t bare you on eagles' wings, and brought you Unto myself?"

CHAPTER III

CONCERNING THE REVEREND JOHN LIVINGSTON, MINISTER OF ANCRUM, AND HIS FURTHER CONFLICT WITH THE BISHOPS AND GOVERNMENT OF SCOTLAND, LEADING TO HIS BANISHMENT TO HOLLAND FOR THE CAUSE OF CHRIST.

"Chare Levistone, salve multumque valeto,
 Invidia ipsa crepit, te mea Musa canet.
Tu lachrimis madefacte tuis, nos linquis in alto
 Stertentes somno lethiferoque malo,
Sed Tralio et sociis suavis comes ibis in oras
 Quas dabit Omnipotens visere propitius, etc, etc."[1]

TO avoid arrest, Mr. Livingston, in the month of February 1637, had to flee to Scotland; where, during the stirring times that quickly followed, he took a prominent part in assisting the cause of the Solemn League and Covenant, even venturing to London in the early part of 1638, "with several copies of the Covenant, and letters to friends at Court." Here he was visited by several people interested in the cause, including some members of the English nobility, anxious to hear trustworthy particulars of the state of affairs in the sister kingdom. On his return, the Covenanters having meanwhile been partially successful in effecting a change in Church matters, he obtained the presentation to the ministry of Stranraer, which, being near to Ireland, he had preferred to other benefices offered him also at this time. He remained in charge of this parish for the next ten years.

As already mentioned, he was a member of the historical General Assembly held at Glasgow in November of this same year (1638); where his presence was objected to by the Court party, as one who was lying under the censure of the Church of Ireland. He was also a member, he says, "of all the rest of the General Assemblies, even till that in the year 1650, except only that of Aberdeen in 1640." In the invasion of England by the Covenanters in this latter year, he was deputed by the Presbytery to accompany the regiment of his friend the Earl of Cassillis[2] in the capacity of army chaplain. He was present at the skirmish at New bum, which led to the capture of Newcastle, and the short-lived Treaty of Ripon; and in accordance with the commands of "the Presbytery of the Army," he drew up a narrative "of what he saw or heard" of this affair, in which he candidly acknowledges he was assisted by the Lieutenant General. This officer was his kinsman, James, Lord Livingston of Almond, an experienced soldier of fortune, who had earned his spurs in the wars in Holland and Germany, and was soon to obtain an earldom for his services in this campaign. For King Charles the First had to reward those who had fought against him on this occasion, and Almond thereupon was created by him Earl of Callendar; which title in later years became merged in the older Earldom of Linlithgow, until they were attainted together, in the person of his namesake the last earl, in 1716.

This honest and single-hearted minister's description of the religious fervour then prevailing in the camp of the Army of the Covenant is so thoroughly characteristic of the man and of those troublous times that it is worth relating here.

> It was very refreshful to remark [he narrates] that after we came to our quarters at night, there was nothing almost to be heard throughout the whole army but singing of psalms, prayer, and reading of the scripture by the soldiers in their several huts, and as I was informed there was much more of that sort the year before when the army lay at Dunse Law. And, indeed, in all our meetings and consultings, both within doors and in the fields, always the nearer the beginning, there was more dependence on God, and more tenderness in worship and in walking, but through process of time we still declined more and more. The day we came to Newburn, the General and some others stepped

aside to Haddon-on-the-Wall, where old Mrs. Fenwick came out and met us, and burst out saying, "And is it so that Jesus Christ will not come to England for reforming of abuses, but with an army of twenty-two thousand men at His back."

Upon the termination of this brief campaign, Mr. Livingston returned to his parochial duties at Stranraer.

Want of space does not permit of more than a hasty sketch of the remaining incidents in this worthy divine's life. He was present at his dying father's bedside in the autumn of 1641, the year in which the rebellion broke out in Ireland; and in the following spring, by order of the Privy Council, he was sent over to that country in attendance on the Scots army under Major-General Monro, where he "stayed for six weeks, most part in Carrickfergus, where the headquarters were; and for six weeks, most part at Antrim, with Sir John Clotworthy and his regiment, who had obtained an order from the Council for him to do so." This was the first of a series of missions to Ireland on which this indefatigable minister was employed between the years 1642 and 1648. But all the missions subsequent to the one mentioned above were undertaken in accordance with the orders of the General Assembly, who had been petitioned by the Presbyterians in the north of Ireland for ministers to attend to their spiritual wants, as these had been sadly neglected owing to the years of persecution and subsequent rebellion. Upon the last of these visits to the "distressful country," he was specially commissioned to prevail with the Scots regiments then quartered there not to take part in the ill-fated "Engagement." In this mission he was not very successful, as his arguments did not prevent General Monro and the greater part of the Scots forces crossing the channel to assist the Duke of Hamilton and the Earl of Callendar in their disastrous attempt to rescue Charles the First from his English prison.

In the summer of this latter year (1648) he was translated by the General Assembly to Ancrum in Roxburghshire, to which place he was admitted as minister upon the presentation of the patron, the Earl of Lothian. This change of ministry is thus slightingly remarked upon by the Rev. Robert Baillie in one of his numerous and voluminous epistles to his cousin, the Rev. William Spang, detailing the doings of the General Assembly of 1648, of which he, as well as Livingston, were members.

The Assemblie [he wrote] spent diverse sessions, for small purpose, upon transportations. These I love dayly worse and worse; the most are evidently packed businesses, little for the credit either of the transporters or transported. Mr. John Livingston, refused to Glasgow, and designed to Ireland by the last Assemblie, though earnestly suted by my Lord Airds and much stucken to by my Lord Cassillis, who, for his respect, had made a constant stipend for his church, most out of his owne rent, though his parishioners had not been cited yet was, at my Lord Louthian's sute, transported to Ancrum, where the benefice was great, and the way to Edinburgh short.

At the time of his settlement at Ancrum Mr. Livingston's family consisted of six children, including an infant at the breast; and the transportation of his wife and family, four or five servants, as well as his baggage and household furniture, from Stranraer to Ancrum, a distance above one hundred miles and over bad roads, gave the worthy minister much trouble, as he duly records in his *Autobiography*.

The next important occurrence in the Rev. John Livingston's eventful life, was his nomination by the Church of Scotland as one of their three delegates on the Commission sent by the Committee of Estates, in the early part of the year 1650, to treat with the young king, Charles the Second, then at Breda, as to the conditions upon which he would be permitted to land in Scotland. This was the second Commission sent by the Estates to Holland after the execution of Charles the First twelve months previously, (the news of which tragic event had been received with mingled feelings of horror and indignation by all parties in the northern kingdom), when they at once proclaimed the Prince of Wales king, with th title of Charles the Second, though with the cautious proviso that "before being admitted to the exercise of his royal power he shall give satisfaction to this kingdom in those things that concern the security of religion, according to the national covenant, and the solemn league and covenant"; and had despatched commissioners to Holland to lay these conditions before Charles. Owing however to the influence brought to bear on the youthful and vacillating king by some of the extreme royalists at his court, including the gallant Montrose, these commissioners had returned without effecting their object.

The new Commission was composed of the following persons:— The Earls of Cassillis and Lothian for the nobility, the Lairds of Brodie and Libberton for the barons; Sir John Smith and Mr. Alexander Jaffray for the Burghs; and Messrs. James Wood, John Livingston, and George Hutcheson for the General Assembly of the Church of Scotland. On the 8th of March, 1650, these commissioners were ordered by a vote of the Scottish Parliament to embark for Holland on the following day "at two in the afternoon, wind and weather serving, without any further delay." They landed at Campvere three days later.

Mr. Livingston, in his account of the proceedings of this Commission, says:—

When it was first laid on me to go, I was most averse therefrom. My reasons were three. First, my own insufficiency, having a natural antipathy from public employment and State matters, and having some scruple that ministers meddled but too much therein, and knowing my own unacquaintedness and inability in such things, and my softness of disposition, ready to condescend too easily to anything having any shew of reason, not being able to debate and dispute any business, so that I feared I should be a grief and shame to those that sent me, besides that I could not promptly speak the Latin tongue, which was requisite among foreign divines. This first reason I expressed in the Commission of the Kirks. The other two, which weighed as much with me, I suppressed. The second was, when I considered the Commissioners sent by the State, I was not willing to embark in any business with them; Cassillis, Brodie, and Alexander Jaffray, I had no exception against; the other three I suspected would be more ready to condescend to an agreement upon unsafe terms. Lothian I had found two years before in harvest 1648, when the west rose against the engagers returning home from England, that he was very ill pleased with their rising, and he was many ways involved with the Marquis of Argyll, who of a long time had been very entire [i. e. intimate] with William Murray and Sir Robert Murray, negotiators for the king, and who it is thought, put him in hopes that the king might marry his daughter. Libberton had been long with the king at Jersey, and had brought the overture of the treaty, and in all his discourses gave evidence of an earnest desire upon any terms to have the king brought home, wherein it is like he thought he would have a chief share of the thanks. Sir John Smith had tampered with James Graham [*i. e.* Marquis of Montrose] in 1645, and was a man of no great ability, and what ability he had I suspected would not be well employed. The third reason was, when I looked upon the whole business, and the terms whereupon the king was to be admitted to his Government, upon his bare subscribing or swearing some words without any evidence that it was done from the heart, I suspected it might prove a design for promoting a malignant [*i. e.* royalist] interest to the prejudice of the work of God, and that our nobles who had power in their hands, fearing if matters went on as formerly, that they might be levelled; and knowing that many in the kingdom would be willing to receive the king upon any terms, whom possibly the malignants might bring home without them, and knowing that after so many backslidings the well-affected were but few, and many of them simple, and all of them desirous to give the king all his due, religion and liberty being secured, upon some such considerations thought it their safest [way] to have the king; not looking much what might be the consequences.

For these reasons, Mr. Livingston adds, he was "fully resolved to have gone home" and taken his chance "of any censure of the kirk for his disobedience"; but being prevailed upon by three of his fellow-ministers, to whom he had submitted his doubts, he reluctantly accompanied the other commissioners, though not before he had said in his haste, "that ere he condescended to go, and to have a hand in the consequences that he apprehended would follow, he would choose rather to condescend, if it were the Lord's will, to be drowned in the waters by the way!" This hasty speech, he quaintly admits, troubled him "many a time thereafter."

The negotiations resulted as Mr. Livingston foresaw would be the case; and he appears to have been the only one of the commissioners prepared to be outspoken before the king. But the speech he had drawn up, as the spokesman of the commissioners from the Church, containing "some things a little free, such as he thought became a minister to speak concerning the king himself and his father's house, and the counsels and ways he had followed," was so altered by the other members of the Commission—to whom he had submitted it before delivery—that as its author amusingly remarks, "it was nothing like itself." And when Mr. Livingston expostulated with his fellow-commissioners about their alterations and additions, he was promptly informed that "he was not to show his own mind, but theirs." Which made him more than ever regret he had undertaken a task "so dangerous to a man of a simple disposition," where he is compelled "to be yoked to those, who by wit, authority, and boldness can overmaster him."

For three weary months the negotiations lasted, namely, from March until the following June; and though Livingston found the king "of a courteous and tractable-like disposition," it was not until on board ship, bound for Scotland with the returning commissioners, that Charles at last consented to their most important condition, that he should before landing in Scotland, "swear and subscribe the Covenant." So cast down was Mr. Livingston with what he saw of the surroundings of the young king's Court, and with the manner in which the negotiations had been conducted by his fellow-commissioners, that he flatly refused to embark with them on their return, being of the opinion that they were taking along with them "the plague of God" to Scotland; and it was only by a stratagem on the part of his clerical associates, who were determined not to leave him behind, that he was got on board the ship in which the king was a passenger. This vessel was named the *Schiedam*; but on the following day the worthy minister "not being well, and having but very ill accommodation in that ship," where, moreover, he regarded himself "as in little other condition than a prisoner," went, accompanied by Mr. Jaffray, on board the *Sun* of Amsterdam, another of the three ships carrying the commissioners and their royal charge. Here he remained for a few days, until the vessels came to anchor off Heligoland, owing to contrary winds, when these two commissioners were summoned to return to the king's ship for the purpose of holding a consultation with their colleagues, as to bringing further pressure to bear upon Charles to induce him to agree to sign the Covenant, in accordance with the conditions prescribed by the General Assembly of the Church of Scotland. Just before their arrival in that country, Charles informed the commissioners he was willing to do as they wished. Whereupon Mr. Livingston was appointed to preach on the next sabbath, when the king should swear to keep the Covenant, and take the oath at his hands; the which day also they came to an anchor at the mouth of the Spey.

It was not, however, until earnestly pressed by the other commissioners, that Livingston reluctantly gave his consent to their wishes; for he, himself, had no great faith in this belated desire of Charles to champion their cause by subscribing the Covenant; and it was only owing to his "softness and silliness of disposition," as he characteristically expresses himself, that he agreed to perform the unwelcome duty. So dissatisfied was he with the whole business, that upon landing, after he had duly administered the required oath to the king, he hastened to get away from Charles and his Court, whom, with the exception of a chance interview at Dundee, he never saw again. At the casual meeting at Dundee of the king and the minister, the latter begged on taking leave of his majesty, that he might have "liberty to use some freedom with him." Which being granted, Mr. Livingston earnestly advised Charles to make some declaration which might pacify the English, and not for the present at least "to prosecute his title" to the crown of England by the sword. This proposition was naturally distasteful to the youthful monarch, who, in reply, said he hoped Mr. Livingston did not wish him "to sell his father's blood."

Rev. John Livingston (1603–1672) of Ancrum, Scotland. Public Domain.

Though appointed by the General Assembly one of the ministers to wait upon the army and the Committee of Estates that accompanied it, Livingston on this occasion flatly declined to go, preferring rather to run the risk of incurring the censure of the kirk, than to meddle any further in State matters. So he went home instead and thus escaped being one of the ministers present in David Leslie's camp, when Cromwell so completely defeated the Scottish army at Dunbar. And during the following winter he continued to reside at Ancrum, where on more than one occasion he was troubled by incursions of the English; who, however, did him personally no harm beyond the quartering of some of their soldiers in his manse. During these unwelcome intrusions, Mr. Livingston says "he neither eat nor drank with any of them, nor hardly spoke with them." But the fact of his having retired to his own house in despair of the proper government of Scotland under a king of the disposition of Charles the Second, led the English leaders to believe he was not unfriendly to their cause.

So that Cromwell himself, in a characteristic letter to William Lenthall, Speaker of the Parliament of England, dated at Edinburgh, 4th of December, 1650, makes the following reference to Livingston,— whom he describes as "a man as highly esteemed as any for piety and learning,"— when alluding to the unhappy dissensions among the Covenanters in connection with the employment of "malignants" in the Scottish army:—

> Those religious people of Scotland [writes the victorious English general], that fall in this Cause, we cannot but pity and mourn for them; and we pray that all good men may do so too. Indeed, there is at this time a very great distraction, and mighty workings of God upon the hearts of divers, both ministers and people; much of it tending to the justification of your Cause. And although some are as bitter and as bad as ever; making it their business to shuffle hypocritically with their consciences and the Covenant, to make it seem lawful to join with Malignants, which now they do,—as well they might long before, having taken in the Head Malignant of them [i. e. Charles II]; yet truly others are startled at it; and some have been constrained by the work of God upon their consciences, to make sad and solemn accusations of themselves, and lamentations in the face of their supreme authority; charging themselves as guilty of the blood shed in the war, by having a hand in the Treaty at Breda, and

by bringing the king in amongst them. This lately did a Lord of
the Session; and withdrew from the Committee of Estates. And
lately Mr. James [John] Livingston, a man as highly esteemed
as any for piety and learning, who was a Commissioner for the
Kirk at the said Treaty,—charged himself with the guilt of the
blood of this war, before their Assembly ; and withdrew from
them, and is retired to his own house.[3]

This unfortunate dispute among the Covenanters referred to by
Cromwell in the above letter, during the following year led to a lamentable
schism in the Church of Scotland, which for a long period split it up into
two bitterly hostile factions, who communicated the virulence of their feelings to the whole country. The incident that finally brought matters to a
crisis was the rescinding by the majority in the Scottish Parliament, with
the approval of the Commission of the General Assembly, of the Act of
Classes, "one of the most bigoted and illiberal pieces of legislation which
ever disgraced the statute book of any country."[4] This took place on the
2nd of June, 1651, and a few weeks later, on the meeting of the General
Assembly at St. Andrews (afterwards transferred to Dundee), the conduct
of the Commission in assenting to the repeal of this Act, which abolished
the restrictions hitherto in force against the employment of Royalists (or
"Malignants," as their opponents preferred to call them), in the service of
the State, was vehemently opposed by a minority of the members, and a
protest signed by twenty-two ministers was given in against its lawfulness.
The rejoinder of the majority was short, and for the time, decisive; as they
proceeded at once to depose three of their leading opponents. The minority thereupon became known as "Protesters" or "Remonstrants"; while the
majority, who voted for the acceptance of the "public resolutions," as they
were called, submitted by the Parliament for the approval of the Assembly,
went by the name of "Resolutioners." The principal ministers in the majority were David Dickson, Robert Baillie, and Robert Douglas; while in the
minority were to be found such well-known names as James Guthrie, Patrick
Gillespie, Samuel Rutherford, and naturally enough—John Livingston.
    A few weeks later the dissentient minority retaliated by holding
at Edinburgh, a meeting of the protesting members, who elected Mr.
Livingston moderator, and passed resolutions to the effect that the General
Assembly "holden at St. Andrews and Dundie" was not a legal Assembly,
and that therefore its acts were null and void. Thus this miserable conflict
between these two rival factions continued for many years, neither side

recognising the meetings of the other as lawful Assemblies of the Church of Scotland. No one among the ministers more lamented this unhappy state of affairs than did Livingston, who makes the following brief reference in his *Life* to these divisions:—

> That winter (1650) the unhappy business fell out about the public resolutions. My light carried me to join with them that protested against the resolutions and the assemblies that followed thereafter, and I was present, at the first meeting of some of the protesters in the West, at Kilmarnock, and thereafter at several other meetings. But indeed I was not satisfied in my mind that the. protesters kept so many meetings, so numerous, and of so long continuance, which I thought made the division wider and more conspicuous than otherwise it would have been, and therefore I stayed away from many meetings.

As subsequent events proved the Protesters, as their opponents were obliged to acknowledge, "had their eyes open, while the Resolutioners were blind," so that even Mr. Dickson, one of the leading Resolutioners, had to confess on his death bed that the Protesters were much the truer prophets.

Cromwell naturally favoured the Protesters, as the party opposed to the Royalists or Malignants, and endeavoured to gain them over to his interest, but with scant success, owing to the patriotism of the Presbyterian Scotch, whether of the one party or the other. For though Scotland "had in a manner been subdued" by the English, as Mr. Livingston quaintly expresses it, the Presbyterian ministers—Protesters as well as Resolutioners—continued to pray for the exiled king, being very jealous of the honour of the royal line of Stuart, and regarding the English very naturally with aversion as their conquerors, and Cromwell as a usurper. This Cromwell found to his cost, when, having invited Livingston, Gillespie, and Menzies, three of the leading Protesters, to come to London in the spring of 1654, the first of these three being called upon to preach before the Protector at Whitehall, prayed for the king and royal family thus: "God be gracious to those whose right it is to rule in this place, and unjustly is thrust from it; sanctify Thy rod of affliction unto him, and when our bones are laid in the dust, let our prayers be registrate in the book of life, that they may come forth in Thy appointed time for doing him and his family good." And for the usurpers he prayed in these terms: "As for these poor men that now fill their rooms, Lord be merciful unto them!"

The contemporary authority from whom this incident is derived, says further:—"Some would have had him [Livingston] accused for praying for the king, and calling them 'poor men'; but the Protector said, 'Let him alone, he is a good man; and what are we but poor men in comparison with the kings of England ?'"[5] The same writer also states "that about Lammas Mr. Livingston came from London, being much displeased with the English and their carriage especially in relation to Kirk affairs. The Protector was glad to be quit of him, because he spoke more plainly than pleasantly to him. But the other two ministers, Patrick Gillespie and John Menzies, abode still at London with whom the Protector was better pleased."

The Rev. Robert Baillie, one of the leading Resolutioners, sarcastically refers to these three ministers in one of his letters, as "our Triumviri, Masters Levistone, Gillespie, and Menzies."[6]

In spite of his boldness of speech, or perhaps for that very reason, Cromwell had a high opinion of Livingston's character, and had his name inserted in his ordinance of the 8th August of this year for settling the affairs of the Church of Scotland, as one of the ministers "for certifying such as were proper to be admitted to a benefice." Two years later, "the indefatigable John Livingston," once more, and for the last time, visited Ireland. He had been earnestly pressed by the inhabitants of his former parish of Killinchy to return to that charge, and "because of the present distractions in Scotland," he says, "he inclined somewhat to have gone"; but the Synod of Merse and Teviotdale refused to part with him, and some of his friends also were averse to his settling in Ireland. He was, however, in the summer of 1656, commissioned by friends in Teviotdale together with Colonel Kerr and another minister, to visit that country for making enquiries into the state of the Presbyterian Church in Ulster. While on this visit he was urged by the Council in Dublin to accept a charge in that city worth two hundred pounds sterling a year, which however he declined.

The news of the Restoration of Charles the Second, which event occurred four years later, was received by Livingston with dismay; for he, at least, clearly foresaw the danger that threatened the Reformed Church in Scotland, should the Episcopal party become once more in the ascendant. He had not long to wait before his worst fears were realised, for the members of the first Scottish Parliament held after the king's return hastened to prove their extravagant loyalty to his person, by placing the supreme power in all matters civil and ecclesiastical in his hands. Moreover, not content with this, among other measures antagonistic to the now despised Covenanters, they passed one specially sweeping edict—known in Scottish annals as the Act Rescissory—by which "all the proceedings for reformation between 1638 and 1650 were declared rebellious and treasonable; the national covenant and solemn league were condemned as unlawful oaths; the Glasgow Assembly of 1638 denounced as an unlawful and seditious meeting; and the ordering of the government of the church was declared to be an inherent right of the crown. In short all that had been done for religion and the reformation of the church during the second reformation was completely annulled."[7]

These proceedings of the Scottish Parliament were quickly followed by the trial and execution of the Marquis of Argyll, and Mr. Guthrie, minister of Stirling and a leading Protester; the re-establishment of prelacy by law, and the return of the bishops. Mr. Livingston's own time of trial was rapidly approaching, for the 29th of May, 1662, being the second anniversary of the king's restoration, it was enacted by parliament that it should be kept as "a holiday of the Lord"; and the parliament and council by proclamation ordered "all ministers, who had come in since 1649, and had not kept their holy day of the 29th of May, either to acknowledge the prelates or remove."

The worthy minister of Ancrum, like many of his compatriots, however, entertained serious doubts as to the lawfulness of honouring this anniversary as a church holy day; and he was still as stubborn as ever in refusing to recognise the authority of the bishops, though no one foresaw more clearly than he did what the result would be, if he persisted m thus disobeying the behests of the government in these matters. But Livingston was too honest a man to disguise his real feelings, or to keep silent when he judged it was his duty to speak out; and in a sermon preached on Monday, the 13th October, 1662—the day after he had held, as it subsequently proved to be, his last communion at Ancrum—he publicly stated his reasons for so doing, and boldly declared that "there are times and seasons wherein a man's silence may bring a curse upon his head."

The Privy Council being duly informed of Mr. Livingston's "seditious carriage,"—as they styled his straightforward behaviour in refusing to calmly submit to the new order of things,—lost no time in taking measures to silence this honest and brave minister; for within six weeks of the delivery of the above sermon, he received letters from friends in Edinburgh warning him that peremptory orders had been issued for his appearance, together with some other contumacious ministers, before the Council upon the 9th of December following. Being thus forewarned, and, as he naively admits, having the fear of Mr. Guthrie's fate before his eyes, he left Ancrum for Edinburgh before the arrival of the messengers conveying the summons; where he remained "close for some days," until he could ascertain through his friends what the government were minded to do in his case.

> For [to quote his own words], if they should only proceed to banishment, as they had the year before done to Mr. M'Ward and Mr. Simson, I resolved to appear, although the citation had not come to me; but if I had found they were on such a design as against Mr. Guthrie, that my life was in danger, I was minded to lurk and not appear, seeing I was not cited nor apprehended. But finding their sentence would be only banishment, and Mr. Trail having got that sentence on the 9th of December, I did, on the 11th of December, being called before the council, compear.[8]

From Mr. Livingston's account of what passed between him and the Council upon this occasion, it is apparent that he was treated with courtesy; and that when pressed to take the oath of allegiance he was informed, if he so wished, time would be given him to think over it. This offer, however, he rejected, as he considered it "would import that he was not fully cleared nor resolved in the matter, and render both himself open to many temptations, and offend and weaken many others." The reason of his refusal to take the oath was the fear, owing to its being couched in "ambiguous and comprehensive terms," that it might be regarded as a sign that he had receded "from the covenant for reformation," and admitted the lawfulness of "the bringing in of the bishops." His conscientious objections to take time to consider whether he should take the oath or not, he says, gave great offence to his examiners, and made them "sharper against him." Finding it useless to argue with him further, the Lord Chancellor ordered him to leave the council chamber, while they decided upon his sentence. Upon his return he was informed by the President of the Council that he was sentenced to banishment from his majesty's dominions within two months from that date, and that within forty-eight hours he was to leave Edinburgh for the north side of Tay, and there remain till he depart forth out of the country.[9] And though Mr. Livingston's request for permission to return home and bid his wife and children farewell was denied to him, the Council did not otherwise treat him hardily; and upon his agreeing to submit to their judgment, and signing a declaration to that effect he was permitted to depart.[10]

In accordance with this sentence Mr. Livingston left Edinburgh for Leith within the time specified; from which place he petitioned the Council a few days later, "that in regard of his age and infirmity, his going beyond Tay, in such a season of the year might be dispensed with, and he be permitted to go to the South, and see his wife and children, and dispose of his affairs; and by this means he expects, within the two months prefixed, to get a more ready and shorter passage from Newcastle, and in better vessels than can be looked for out of the Firth."

The Council, having duly considered this petition, so far consented to his prayer as to allow of his remaining at Leith "during the time that is granted him to abide in Scotland, he behaving and carrying himself peaceably in the meantime;" but they still declined to sanction his paying a farewell visit to his family. He remained at Leith, where he was constantly visited by friends from all parts of the country, until the 9th of April following, when he embarked on board "old John Allan's ship" for Rotterdam, which place he reached eight days later.

At Rotterdam Mr. Livingston found quite a colony of his fellow-countrymen, who warmly welcomed their illustrious compatriot; and the weariness of his exile he endeavoured to alleviate by literary pursuits, such as the compiling of a polyglot bible, and a new Latin translation of the old testament. But "the death of worthy John Graham, Provost of Glasgow, who was ready to have borne most of the charges of printing, stopped both these enterprises." He, however, has fortunately left us a curious and interesting *Life*, which, as the title declares, was "written by himself, during his banishment in Holland, for the cause of Christ."[11] He also found some congenial occupation in assisting the minister of the Scottish Church in that town.

During the month of December following his arrival in Holland, he was joined by his wife and two of their children; the other five then living remaining in Scotland. Mr. Livingston, with his usual carelessness as to the mention of Christian names, does not give those of the two his wife brought with her to Rotterdam; but from the list of his children to be found at the end of some of the manuscript copies of his *Life* (of which lists the most complete is the one in the MS. now in the possession of Mr. J. H. Livingston), it appears that out of a family of fifteen, the above number—seven—were alive in 1663; and of these, the two youngest were a son, Robert, born in 1654, and a daughter, Elizabeth, born in 1657. It is therefore pretty certain, that it must have been these two youngest children, whom Mrs. Livingston brought with her. This daughter, moreover, died at Rotterdam three years later, and was buried in "Zuiden Churchyard"; while the son lived to settle in New York some ten years afterwards where his knowledge of the Dutch language, acquired during his residence in Holland, was of the greatest service to him.

The Rev. John Livingston also died at Rotterdam, between the 14th and 21st of August, 1672, in the seventieth year of his age. In the Register of Deaths deposited in the archives of this town, is to be found the following entry relating to his decease:—

Janet Fleming Livingston (c. 1613–1694), wife of Rev. John Livingston.

Den 21 Augustus 1672.
Johannes Livingstone predicant uyt Schotlandt inde St:
Jacobstraet,
Is dus gestorven tussehen 14 en 21 Augustus 1672.[12]

The place of his burial is unfortunately unknown.[13] The Laird of
Brodie, one of his fellow-commissioners at Breda in 1650, thus refers to
his old friend's death in his *Diary*, under date 5th of September, 1672:—"I
heard this day from my cousin, William Brodie, that good Mr. Livingston
was at his rest in Holland." Mrs. Livingston survived her husband for over
twenty years. An interesting account of this "mother in Israel," as she was
lovingly called by a clerical contemporary, will be found in the Rev. James
Anderson's *Ladies of the Covenant*. From this we learn that she returned to
Scotland for a time after her husband's death, where, in the year 1674, she
fell under the displeasure of the Privy Council for the prominent part she
had taken in the presentation of a petition in favour of the nonconforming
ministers.[14] She subsequently returned to Holland, and in that country she
spent the remainder of her days. Mr. Anderson, however, was unaware of

the place or date of Mrs. Livingston's death, though he rightly suspected it took place in Holland. This is confirmed by an entry in her youngest son's (Robert's) journal, kept by him when on a visit to England in 1694–[5], which reads as follows:—

> 26 [July 1695] friday, I having received the sad news of my mother's death from my 2 brethren, Mr. William and James at Edinburgh, that she dyed the 13 february. 1693–[4], at Rotterdam, and [was] buried in the French Church, I prepared all things to go in deep mourning.[15]

The five children living at the date of the Rev. John Livingston's death were:— William, his second son, who, was born at Lanark, 7 January, 1638, laureated, 22 June, 1658, at the University of Edinburgh (?),[16] married Ann Veitch, 23 December, 1663. He was a merchant in Edinburgh, and was imprisoned in 1672 for corresponding with the exiled clergy in Holland. Ten years later he again got into trouble with the authorities, being accused "of distributing money to rebels and corresponding with them," but was liberated upon finding caution to appear before the Privy Council when called upon. Two of his sons—Andrew and James—served as officers in the disastrous Darien Expedition. He was at the time of his death, in 1700, Clerk to the Sessions "of the good town"—Edinburgh. He died just ten days after his younger brother James, and they were both buried in the Greyfriars Burying Ground, Edinburgh.[17]

Janet, sixth child and third daughter, was born at Stranraer, 28 September, 1643, married to Mr. Andrew Russell, a well-to-do merchant at Rotterdam. She died in August, 1696.

James, ninth child and fifth son, was born also at Stranraer 22 September, 1646; he was like his elder brother William, an Edinburgh merchant, and also fell under the displeasure of the Privy Council, and fined two hundred pounds (Scots) in 1680. He was, apparently, married twice, but only the name of his second wife is known—Christian Fish.[18] By his first wife he had a son—Robert—who went out to join his uncle Robert in America in 1687, and is known in the family annals as Robert "The Nephew," of whom more hereafter. James's death, and that of his elder brother William, are mentioned by their sister Barbara in a letter to her brother Robert in New York, in which die writes:—

I left Holland when I lost my two best friends there, my mother and my sister [Mrs. Russell], and came here [Edinburgh] to the rest of my friends, and now it has pleased the Lord also to take my two brethren. My brother James was healthful and strong, but was suddenly plucked away by a fever. . . . There were only 1 o days betwixt their deaths, and tho' my brother Mr. William had long been tender yet his death was also a surprise to us all.[19]

Barbara, eleventh child and sixth daughter, was born at Ancrum, 21 June, 1649. She is the "sister Miller," some of whose letters are also still preserved in America. Her husband was Mr. James Miller or Millar, a Scottish merchant carrying on business in Holland. He appears to have died previous to 1690, leaving his widow, with three daughters on her hands, in straitened circumstances. She resided for a time at Rotterdam, but in 1698 returned to Scotland, and took up her abode in Edinburgh.

Robert, fourteenth child and youngest son, was also born at Ancrum, 13th December, 1654, and was the ancestor of the principal branch of the New York Livingstons, of whose career a full account will be found in the succeeding chapters.

Of the remaining ten children, all of whom predeceased their parents, only two were married, namely Marion, the second daughter, born at Stranraer, 10th October, 1642, married to the Rev. John Scott, minister at Hawick, 28th September, 1658, and died at that place in July, 1667; and Agnes, the fourth daughter, who married David Cleland, chirurgeon.[20]

There are five portraits of the Rev. John Livingston, as well as two of his wife, known to be still in existence, some in Scotland and some in America. There may be also others in collections unknown to the author. The Scottish owners of the Rev. John Livingston's portraits are the Earl of Wemyss and Sir Arthur Grant of Monymusk; while the American owners are Mrs. Robert Ralston Crosby and Mrs. Charles J. Welch of New York City, and Mr. John Henry Livingston of Clermont, New York. Lord Wemyss and Mrs. Crosby also possess portraits of Mrs. Livingston.[21]

Notes

1. Lines composed by the Rev. Robert Blair, minister of St. Andrews, on hearing that his friend, the Rev. John Livingston of Ancrum, was on board ship bound for Holland, under sentence of banishment by the Scottish Privy Council in 1663. These lines have been rendered into English by a classical friend of the author's as follows:
   "Beloved Livingston, farewell, may you greatly flourish,
   Though Envy herself may carp, my Muse shall celebrate thee.
   Thou, bathed in tears, leavest us a prey to

Profound sleep and deadly misfortune,
But with thy Trail and companions, thou wilt go a pleasant fellow traveller to the shores
Which the benign Almighty permits you to see."

2. John Kennedy, sixth Earl of Cassillis, known in his day as "the grave and solemn earl."

3. *Oliver Cromwell's Letters and Speeches: with elucidations by Thomas Carlyle,* Letter CXI. In his remarks on the above letter, Mr. Carlyle thus refers to Mr. Livingston:—"Mr. James *(sic)* Livingston, the minister of Ancrum, has left a curious *Life* of himself;—he is still represented by a distinguished family in America." Livingston mentions in his *Life,* that Cromwell, about this time, sent him an invitation "to come to Edinburgh and speak with him," but that "he excused himself."

4. Cunningham *Church History of Scotland,* vol. ii, p. 73.

5. Row's *Supplement* to the *Life of Mr. Robert Blair* (Wodrow edition), pp. 313–317. According to another contemporary writer Mr. Livingston's text on this occasion was, "It is a fearful thing to fall into the hands of the living God." Lamont *Diary* (April 1654), p. 84. Mr. Livingston makes but scanty allusion to this visit. This is all he says in regard to it:—"In the summer [? spring] 1654, Mr. Patrick Gillespie, Mr. John Menzies, and I were called by letters from the Protector to come to London. I went, because he had the present power over the land, and I thought there might be some hope we might procure some good to Scotland; and I went the rather because at the time the moss-troopers were in the night time seeking for me at my house, and I was like not to be long in safety. But being in London I found no great satisfaction, and therefore I left the other two there and came home."

6. *Vide Letters and Journals,* vol. iii, p. 253.

7. M'Crie (Rev. Thos.), *Sketches of Scottish Church History,* vol. ii, p. 71.

8. From the above statement it appears that Mr. Livingston, when writing his memoirs during his banishment in Holland, was under the impression that his friend, Mr. Robert Trail, had been sentenced prior to his own appearance before the Council. The Rev. Robert Wodrow, who quotes from the Privy Council Registers, however clearly proves that Mr. John Livingston, Mr. James Gardiner, and Mr. Robert Trail were all three sentenced in the above order, and on the same day—namely the 11th of December, 1662. *History of the Sufferings of the Church of Scotland,* vol. i, pp. 313–315

9. Mr. George W. Schuyler in his *Colonial Now York* (vol. i, p. 243), in referring to the Rev. John Livingston's son, Robert, says:—"He was the son of a Scotch clergyman, who had found it expedient to seek asylum in Holland, not because of his religion, but for political reasons." It is to be presumed Mr. Schuyler could not have taken much trouble in ascertaining the true facts of the case, or he would not have distorted them in this fashion!

10. A full account of Mr. Livingston's examination by the Scottish Privy Council will be found in Addenda XXXV of *The Livingstons of Callendar.*

11. There are several manuscript copies of this *Life* still in existence. Of those, known to the author, and examined by him, one was in the possession of the late Mr. Van Brugh Livingston of New York City probably taken to America by his ancestor Robert; and another has in recent years, on the death of its former owner, the late Mr. J. E. Bailey of Stretford been purchased by the author (now in the possession of Mr. J. H. Livingston of Clermont), who has, however, been unable to discover what has become of the original. There are also several printed editions

of this autobiography, ranging in date from 1727 to 1848. A full description of all known manuscript copies and printed editions will be found in *The Livingstons of Callendar*, pp. 338–340.

12. "The 21 August 1672.

13. But as his widow was buried in the "French Church" in this city in 1694 (see latter part of this chapter), the Rev. John Livingston may also have been interred there (?)

14. References are also made to Mrs. Livingston in Wodrow's *Sufferings of the Church of Scotland*, vol. ii, p. 269; Kirkton's *History of the Kirk of Scotland*, pp. 344–346; Sir George Mackenzie's *Memoirs*, p. 273; and Row's *Supplement to Blair's Life*, p. 539.

15. From the original manuscript in the possession of Mr. Johnston Livingston of New York.

16. The date of his laureation is that given in the author's manuscript of the *life Mr. John Livingston*, but the name of the university is not mentioned. The only date that at all agrees is, however, that of the University of Edinburgh, where in the "Classis of 30 June, 1658" appears the name of "Gulielmus Livingstone." A *Catalogue of the Graduates, university of Edinburgh*, p. 78.

17. In the *Register of interments in Greyfriars Burying Ground*,1658–1700, published by the Scottish Record Society in 1902, appear these entries: James Livingston, merchant, 4 June, 1700; Mr. William Livingston, merchant, 12 June, 1700. A fuller account of these brothers will be found in the *Livingstons of Callendar*, pp. 331–334·

18. Marriage Contract dated 15th August, 1683, so she could not have been the mother of Robert "The Nephew." See also *Livingstons of Callendar*, p. 334.

19. Letter undated but endorsed by her brother Robert:—"New York, 9th October 1700, my sister Miller's letter from Edinburgh of the death of yr 2 Brethren." The original of this letter, with others from his brothers and sisters in Scotland to their brother Robert in New York, is in the possession of Mr. Johnston Livingston.

20. A full list of the Rev. John Livingston's children will be found in the Appendix B.

21. There is no space to treat of these in detail here, but for full particulars of those known to the author, see *Livingstons of Callendar*, pp. 335–338, and the *Addenda* to same work. It is the author's intention, if possible, to give reproductions of all those portraits of which he possesses photographic copies. Mrs. Welch's portrait was formerly in the possession of Mr. Van Brugh Livingston.

Robert Livingston (1654–1728), first Lord of the Manor.

CHAPTER IV

CONCERNING ROBERT LIVINGSTON, THE ELDER, AND HIS SETTLEMENT IN THE ENGLISH PROVINCE OF NEW YORK.

"Spero Meliora."
(Robert Livingston's Motto.)

ROBERT LIVINGSTON, the youngest son of the Rev. John Livingston, was born at Ancrum, Roxburghshire. on the 13th of December, 1654, of which parish his father was then minister; and he was probably one of the two children whom their mother took with her to Rotterdam in the winter of 1663. If such were the case, and there is no reason to doubt it, he would have been just nine years old at the time of his arrival in Holland, and his thorough mastery of the Dutch language sufficiently proves that he must have spent several years in that country. This knowledge of the Dutch language was later on, when he had become a person of note in the English Province of New York, made use of by his political opponents in their unsuccessful attempt to prove that he was of alien birth, and therefore debarred from the rights of a native born British subject.

At his father's death he found himself, then in his eighteenth year, thrown upon his own resources for the means of obtaining a livelihood, and, evidently not having any inclination for following in his father's footsteps and joining the church, he turned his attention to that new world of America, which had such great attractions for those who had, like his father, suffered from the effects of religious intolerance at home; or for the young and ambitious, like himself, to whom it opened up a career, which, to an industrious and active man, would be the sure road to competence, and probably to a fortune. His father, as mentioned in a previous chapter, had on two separate occasions started to cross the Atlantic, but each of those attempts had ended in failure, though, upon the second occasion, the ship in which he was a passenger had got more than half-way across before being driven back by adverse winds. Probably advancing age and infirm health had prevented the Rev. John Livingston from carrying out in his later days of exile what he had attempted in his youth, or else, instead of remaining a member of the little Scottish colony in Rotterdam, he might have joined some of his persecuted co-religionists in New England.

His son, however, had no such reasons for not proceeding to this "Land of Promise;" so after his father's death, having no further need for remaining an exile from his native country, he returned to Scotland—accompanied by his mother most probably—where he made but a short stay. For on the 28th of April, 1673, he sailed from Greenoch, as a passenger on board "the good ship called the *Catharine* of Charlestown, Captain John Phillips, commander thereof, bound for Charlestown in New England in America." So runs the entry in the, unfortunately, incomplete journal kept by the youthful Robert for the first two weeks of this, his first, voyage to America.[1]

The exact date of his landing in the New World is therefore unknown; nor is it possible to ascertain for certain the motives that influenced him to leave the New England plantations for the neighbouring province of New York. But these motives were probably his Dutch training, and his knowledge of that language, as well as the fact that during the year following his arrival at Charlestown, the Dutch colony of New Netherland had been finally transferred from the possession of Holland to that of England by the Treaty of Westminster. That Robert Livingston arrived in New York,—as the English had re-christened this colony when first conquered by them in 1664,—the year following his landing in America, is proved by his Memorial to the Lords of Trade, drawn up in 1696, in which he positively states he had then "been resident in the Province of New York for the space of twenty-two years." The energetic young Scotchman, probably not finding any suitable employment in the town of New York itself, must have proceeded up the river Hudson to Albany, the next town of importance in the colony, and owing to its proximity to the Canadian frontier a great centre of the Indian trade, then a very lucrative one. Here his knowledge of the Dutch language was of great advantage to him, for he obtained, very soon after his arrival in that town, the post of secretary to the Commissaries, who then superintended the affairs of Albany and adjacent districts. He rapidly rose in favour both with his fellowtownsmen and the English authorities at New York; so that within a very few years he was successful in obtaining the additional appointments of town clerk, collector and receiver of customs, and secretary for Indian Affairs.

According to Mr. George W. Schuyler,[2] he also lost no time in become a landed proprietor, as in March, 1675, only a few months after his settling in Albany, he bought a lot, "No. 1, on the hill." He at a later date, according to the same authority, owned the lot next adjoining, at the comer of State and North Pearl Streets. Here he lived until he removed to his manor, when he transferred this property to his eldest surviving son Philip. In private life he was also on the most friendly and intimate terms with the leading Dutch families of Albany, which he still further strengthened by marrying, in 1679, Alida Schuyler, the fair young widow of Dominie Nicholas Van Rensselaer, who was little over a year his junior in age. This marriage connected Livingston with two of the oldest and wealthiest families in the province, and is thus piously recorded by him in his Dutch family bible, a present from his mother in Holland:—

> 1679. On the 9th day of July (old style) I, Robert Livingston, was wedded to my worthy helpmeet Alida Schuyler, (widow of Dominie Nicholas Van Rensselaer), in the Presbyterian Church at Albany (America) by Domine Gideon Schaats.
> May God be with us and bless us.[3]

Mr. Livingston regularly discharged his duties as secretary to the Commissaries until July, 1686, when Albany having been created a city, the Board of Commissaries was no longer required. It was he and his brother-in-law, Peter Schuyler, who were the two commissioners, sent by the town of Albany to receive from the hands of Colonel Thomas Dongan, Governor of New York, the charter conferring on that town the dignity of a city. On their return from New York, they presented the charter to the assembled magistrates for the county of Albany, and it was received by them and the inhabitants with great rejoicings, and the bearers of the welcome document were warmly thanked for their trouble in the obtaining of it. The earliest minute in the Books of the City of Albany thus duly records this interesting event:—

In Nomine Domino Jesu Christi Amen.

Att a meeting of ye Justices of the peace for ye county of Albany, ye 26th day of July A.D. 1686.

Pieter Schuyler, gent., and Robt. Livingston, gent., who were commissionated by ye towne of Albanie, to goe to New York and procure ye Charter for this Citty, wh. was agreed upon between ye magistrates and ye right honl. Col. Tho. Dongan, Gov. Genll who accordingly have brought the same along with them, and was published with all ye joy and acclamations imaginable; and ye said two gentm. received the thanks of ye magistrates and burgesses for their diligence and care in obtaining ye same.

The diligence of the commissioners is proved by the charter having been presented to the magistrates on the fourth day after it had been signed by Governor Dongan in New York. According to one of its conditions, Peter Schuyler became the first mayor of the new city and Robert Livingston town clerk. The governor visited Albany shortly afterwards, and in writing an account of this visit to the Home Government, Colonel Dongan says:—

I alsoe went up to Albany myself on purpose to settle his Matys business there, where I made one Robert Livingston Collector and Receiver, with order to account with and into Mr. Santem[4] what money he should receive, for which he was to have is pr pound for all such monys as should pass through his hands, and alsoe made him Clerk of the Town, that both places might afford him a competent maintenance.

At a meeting of the Albany Common Council held on the 14th of September, 1686, Livingston's salary was advanced five pounds, raising it to the sum of twenty pounds per annum, "in consideration of the diverse services" which he performed as clerk. In 1693, one of his appointments, that of collector, was worth fifty pounds per annum, while that of secretary for Indian Affairs subsequently brought him in a further hundred. This last salary, however, was only granted to him in 1695, he having performed the duties of that office for the long period of twenty years without any remuneration whatever. Mr. Livingston's official duties at Albany brought him into frequent communication with the Indians, and the knowledge he thus obtained was of great assistance in after years to the various colonial governors.[5] The exposed position of Albany as a frontier town, and its close proximity to the hunting grounds of that powerful Indian confederation— the Iroquois or the Five Nations— which at this period was composed of the tribes of the Mohawks, Oneidas, Onondagas, Cayugas, and Senecas, and was later on to become known as the Six Nations on the addition of the Tuscaroras, required that all Indian questions should be treated with the greatest care, as the French governors of Canada were always actively intriguing to gain these fierce warriors over to their side. In consequence of the mutual jealousies of the French and English colonists—aggravated by the bigotry of opposing religions—constant outbreaks of the Indians had to be continually guarded against, while at the same time every inducement was held out to them, by the English governors of the colonies exposed to their destructive raids, to prevail on these savages to "bury the hatchet," and to keep "the Covenant chain" unbroken.

In reference to the religious animosities stirred up by these border disputes between the two great European nations in North America, a good story is told by William Livingston, Governor of New Jersey during the War of Independence, and a grandson of the above Robert, who spent a year of his boyhood among these Indians. He says, one of the pious frauds practised by the French missionaries in their endeavours to induce the Indians to detest the English, was "to persuade these people that the Virgin Mary was born at Paris, and that our Saviour was crucified at London by the English!"

Sir Edmund Andros, the first governor of New York after its final cession to England, as well as his successor Colonel Dongan, devoted much of their time to the study of this Indian question; and in the summer of 1684, during the rule of the latter, Lord Howard of Effingham, Governor of Virginia, came to New York for the purpose of personally conferring with Dongan on this all-important subject. These two royal governors proceeded to Albany, where they met in the city hall a deputation from the leading sachems of the Five Nations, and a long speech delivered by Dongan, on the danger of permitting the French to build forts in their territory, or to send priests to their villages, and on the advantages to be gained from an alliance with the English colonies, was listened to with great attention and respect by the assembled Indians; and their orators in reply agreed to accept the protection of the Duke of York, and to put a stop to the raids into Virginia, which had been the cause of Lord Howard's journey to Albany. During this conference Livingston was of great assistance in rendering into English the Dutch interpreter's translation of the Indian speeches; and four years later he was of still greater service to Dongan, who being out of funds had to apply to Livingston for pecuniary aid in carrying on the war against the French. This was the cause, ultimately, of the latter's first visit to England, in 1695; owing to the sums of money advanced by him on this occasion, and for the subsistence of the militia during the subsequent civil commotions, being left unpaid, he was compelled to cross the Atlantic and seek redress in London.

Before giving an account of this visit to England it will be necessary to relate briefly the cause of the civil commotions referred to above, and the part which Livingston took in them. These disturbances arose in this way. In 1688, the Duke of York, who had succeeded his brother, Charles the Second, as king, under the title of James the Second, commissioned anew Sir Edmund Andros as Governor General of "the Territory and Dominion of New England," —the fresh commission including the Province of New Jersey, as well as his old government of New York,—who, thereupon appointed Colonel Nicholson to be his lieutenant- governor at New York, while he made Boston his own headquarters. Andros, however, had never been popular in New England, and as soon as ever the news of the landing of William of Orange and the successful revolution in the mother country reached Boston, the citizens rose in arms and deposed their obnoxious governor. The spirit of disaffection rapidly spread to the neighbouring colony of New York, where Nicholson and his weak councillors found themselves powerless to cope with the popular feeling. To keep the peace and guard the fort the train-bands were called out, and under the ridiculous pretext that Nicholson had threatened to bum the town, one Jacob Leisler, a captain of one of these companies, induced most of the more ignorant of these men to sign a declaration in favour of the Prince of Orange and the Protestant succession. Six captains and four hundred men signed this document. Whereupon Nicholson weakly abandoned his government and sailed for England, which was at once usurped by Leisler, who thereupon filled the public offices with his own partisans, an early example of a principle not unknown, unfortunately, in these latter days of a far greater New York.

Though Leisler had thus successfully put a royal lieutenant-governor to flight, and made the city of New York submissive to his will, the leading colonists would have nothing to do with this "Dutch boor," as they contemptuously styled this self-made leader, but held themselves aloof, waiting for the appointment of a properly authorised successor to their late governor. This was particularly the case as regards the old Dutch families at Albany, and in their opposition to this usurper they were vigorously supported by Livingston, who, in consequence, incurred the bitter enmity of Leisler, which would afterwards have cost him dear, if he had not been successful in escaping from the officers who had been sent from New York to arrest him; and the privations undergone by Livingston in consequence of this attempt caused him to regard the author of his misfortunes with an intense hatred, which was not satisfied until Leisler had perished on the scaffold.

One of Leisler's first actions after the departure of Nicholson was to summon a Convention to meet on the 26th of June, 1689, at New York, but Albany flatly declined to send representatives to it, which refusal highly offended Leisler, who in the following autumn fitted out a small force under the command of his future son-in-law, Milborne, for the purpose of enforcing obedience. On Milborne's arrival before Albany he was refused admission to the fort, and finding the citizens were assisted by some friendly Indians, and that his own men were not numerous enough to cope with these combined forces, he returned discomfited to New York. Albany had, however, to fear a far more dreaded foe than Leisler's lieutenant, for the French were known to be fitting out an expedition for the purpose of carrying the war into the neighbouring English colonies, and in their natural anxiety to secure assistance against the common enemy, the Albanian authorities had even been obliged to call upon the hated Leisler for help, as well as on Governor Treat of Connecticut. The former in his reply, addressed to Captains Bleecker and Wendall,—as he would not recognise the civil authority as represented by the Albany Convention, which had been specially summoned to make preparations for dealing with the Indian difficulties and the threatened invasion,—said he had sent them four cannon and a small supply of powder, at the same time demanding that commissioners be sent to him at once to consult for the public good. This demand the Albany Convention paid no heed to, and their subsequent treatment of Milborne debarred them from obtaining any further assistance from New York. Governor Treat answered their call for help by sending a small force of Connecticut militia, commanded by Captain Bull, to assist in garrisoning the fort at Albany, while a detachment of twenty-four men under Lieutenant Talmadge was sent to hold the fort at Schenectady.

General Philip Schuyler (1733–1804), painted by J. Trumbull; engraved by T. Kelly. Library of Congress, Prints and Photographs Division, Public Domain.

With this slight assistance the Albanians had to rest content, and to face the chance of being attacked by a fierce foe during the long nights of a bitter winter. The storm burst at last, and, strange to say, found the garrison of the little stockaded village of Schenectady totally unprepared to meet it. This was on the night of the 8th of February, 1690, when a force of French Canadians and some Christian Iroquois silently approached the doomed settlement unnoticed, and before Talmadge and his little band were aware of the vicinity of their dreaded enemy the Indians raised their war-whoop and were inside the palisades. The usual scene of carnage and plunder ensued, and a few fugitives only carried the news of the massacre to Schuyler, the Albany commander, who sallied out in pursuit of the victorious raiders, but too late to save the unfortunate village, which was found in ashes. Robert

Livingston in an account of this massacre which he sent to Sir Edmund Andros, says the attacking force was composed of two hundred and fifty French and Indians, that they killed and destroyed sixty men, women, and children, carried off twenty-seven men and boys prisoners, and burnt the settlement, with the exception of six or seven houses which were saved "by Captain Sander,[6] whom they did not touch, having express command to meddle with none of his relations for his wife's sake, who had always been kind to the French prisoners." The Indians are said to have openly grumbled at having to spare so many people, and bitterly complained that Captain Sander had far too many relations! Mr. Livingston also informed Sir Edmund, "the people of that town were so bigotted to Leisler that they would not obey any of the magistrates, neither would they entertain the soldiers sent thither by that Convention of all; nothing but men sent from Leisler would do their turn. Thus had Leisler perverted that poor people by his seditious letters now found all bloody upon Schenectady's streets, with the notions of a free trade, &c., and thus they are destroyed."

The authorities at Albany fearing other attacks from the French, hastened to seek further aid from the New England colonies; and on the 3rd of March, the Convention of the civil and military officers of the city and county of Albany commissioned Robert Livingston and Captain Gerrit Teunisse to proceed to Connecticut and Massachusetts to ask for their assistance in an invasion of Canada, so as to carry the war into the enemy's territory. Captain Thomas Garton accompanied these two gentlemen as commissioner from the county of Ulster. An agent was also despatched to New York for the same purpose.

On receipt of the news of the destruction of Schenectady, Leisler flew into a towering rage imputing it to the machinations of his opponents, and hastened at once to lay hands on all those officers who held commissions from Governor Andros. He appears to have become more arrogant than ever since a letter from King William had reached New York, which he considered confirmed him in his usurped office. This letter, which was signed at Whitehall on the 30th of July, 1698, appointed Nicholson to be Lieutenant-Governor, and was addressed to him, or in his absence "to such as for the time being take care for preserving the peace and administering the laws." It only reached New York by way of Boston on the 9th of December. Livingston was at once signalled out by Leisler as a fit person to be made an example of,—as if he, instead of rendering all the assistance possible against the French, had aided and abetted them in this sad massacre,—and an order was issued by the Dutch dictator to have him arrested wheresoever he could be found. This order, which was addressed to the neighbouring colonies, as well as to "all persons within this Province," plainly shows the vindictive feeling which prompted Leisler in the issuing of it; the wording of it is very quaint:—

> Whereas one Robert Livingston by the instigation of the Devill did utter ye Malice of his heart in Saying that he was Enformed that a parcell of rebells were gone out of holland to England and that ye prince of Orange headed them Saying that they might see how they got of againe or words to this purpose and that they should Come to ye Same End that Monmouth did and hath Committed other high Crimes.
>
> These are in his Majesties Name to will and require all persons within this Province to apprehend ye said Livingston and bring him before me to answer for ye Same and all governors and Magistrates of ye Neighbouring Colonies are hereby advertized and desired in his Majesties King Williams behalfe to assist In apprehending ye said Livingston if within their Jurisdictions as they do tender ye King's interest, ye Welfare of ye Protestant Cause and their Allegiance, Given, &c., March the 1st, 1689–[90].
>
> *Jacob Leisler.*

To Captain Benjamin Blagge and all others whom this shall or may Concerne.

Fortunately for Livingston, he had left Albany on his mission to Massachusetts and Connecticut before Milborne at the head of Leisler's soldiers entered that city, of which he took possession this time without opposition. Disappointed at the escape of his intended victim, Leisler, on the 5th of March, despatched letters to the governors of the above colonies requesting them to have "this rebell Livingston" arrested. In reply to this demand the Governor of Connecticut expressed his willingness to have Livingston apprehended "provided any person will appear to give in sufficient security to prosecute the said complaint and make it good or answer all damages in case he fails of so doing." This does not appear to have been done, as evidently was anticipated by Governor Treat, and Livingston therefore remained unmolested during his stay in New England, and was received with great consideration by the authorities to whom he was accredited by the Convention at Albany.

Frustrated in their attempts to lay hands on Livingston's person, Leisler's agents were instructed to rake up any incriminating information they could discover concerning him, and some of the sworn depositions thus obtained are still in existence. These amount to very little beyond the fact, that some of the parties making these depositions affirmed that they had heard Livingston, during the month of February, 1689, say in his own house that "the Prince of Orange was the head of the rebels;" but this was toned down by others, who declared he had only said "that the late King James hath in his declarations against the Hollanders pronounced the prince to be the head of the rebels." The utterance of this harmless expression was however deemed by Leisler sufficient evidence to justify him to proceed against Livingston as a dangerous rebel; and warrants were accordingly issued, ordering him to deliver up his official papers, books, etc., to Leisler's agents, and also to account to them for all sums of money collected by him as Receiver of the Customs. Livingston still refusing to acknowledge the legality of such orders, he was outlawed and his property sequestrated.

This continued persecution did not hinder this energetic Scot from persevering in his endeavours to persuade the adjacent colonies to combine in an expedition against Canada, and it was through no fault of Livingston's that the attempted conquest of that country ended in failure. Major-General Fitz-John Winthrop of Connecticut was appointed to command the small confederate land force,—though against the wish of Leisler, who had desired this post for his secretary, Milborne,—and he was accompanied by Livingston, who held the local rank of colonel. The arrival of the latter at Albany, at whose house General Winthrop took up his quarters, was the occasion of a fresh outburst of wrath on the part of Leisler, who, in writing to the Earl of Shrewsbury an account of New York affairs, calls him "that Chief Instrument of those evills"; and his officers attempted to seize his person, but this was prevented by Winthrop. It was the latter part of July before that officer reached Albany,—his commission from Leisler is dated on the thirty- first of this month,—and the men at his disposal were so few in number that when he had only got as far as Lake Champlain he had to return; which so offended Leisler, that he went up to Albany himself from New York, and imprisoned "the chief actors therein," though to his great disappointment, Livingston, who had received timely warning, was again successful in making his escape. The expedition from Boston by sea under Sir William Phipps was also unsuccessful, and all the damage done to the French by this combined expedition, was effected by a small force under the command of Captain John Schuyler, who penetrated as far as the village of La Prairie, opposite Montreal, which he burnt to the ground in revenge for the destruction of Schenectady.

The friendship between Fitz-John Winthrop and Livingston led in after years to a closer connexion between their respective families, when the latter's eldest son, John, married the former's daughter, and only child, Mary. It was Fitz-John Winthrop's father, the late governor of Connecticut, who had made the acquaintnce of the Rev. John Livingston, Robert's father, when in Ireland in 1635, and this may have been the reason why this important New Englander so readily came to Livingston's assistance when threatened by Leisler's agents. Eight years after his return home from this abortive expedition Fitz-John Winthrop became also governor of Connecticut. The marriage between John Livingston and Mary Winthrop took place in 1701.

Poor Mrs. Livingston must have passed a very anxious time during her husband's absence in New England, for she had given birth to their fourth son on the very day that Mr. Livingston had been appointed by the Albany Convention commissioner to Massachusetts and Connecticut, and her natural anxiety as to his safety must have been aggravated by the fear of a fresh Indian raid into the colony. Mr. Livingston thus characteristically refers to this son's birth in the register of his children entered in the family bible already quoted from:—

> The 3rd of March (1689–90) being Monday at 5 o'clock in the morning my fourth son was born and named Hubertus [Gilbert] after my wife's brother. The Lord help him and us from this dreadful tide of war. On the fifth day he was baptised by Domine Dellius, and was carried to baptism by sister Jennilie Schuyler. The witnesses were brother Peter Schuyler the Mayor and Alderman Levinus Van Schaick. I was commissioned by the authorities to go to the colonies of New England to procure men and ammunition against the French, who had possession of Schenectady. At this time there was a usurper, Jacob Leisler by name, a merchant of New York, who assumed to rule over the Province, and who was executed in New York in May 1691.

Beyond having her house searched by the emissaries of Leisler for her husband's official books and papers, this lady appears to have been left otherwise unmolested, though owing to the arbitrary measures adopted by that ambitious personage, she must have been reduced to great straits by the sequestration of her husband's property, and Leisler's refusal to recognise as legal Mr. Livingston's loans to the Convention of Albany during the recent Indian scare. Mrs. Livingston, after the failure of the invasion of Canada, and her husband's second narrow escape from falling into the hands of the usurper's agents, joined him in the winter of 1690 at Hartford in Connecticut. She took their children with her, and at this place they remained until the fall of Leisler made it safe for them to return to Albany. They, however, left John, their eldest son, at Hartford to be educated under the care of their friend Fitz-John Winthrop. So it is not surprising under these circumstances that this son should have formed an attachment for his little playmate Mary Winthrop, which led to their marriage ten years later.[7]

We must now retrace our steps a little, to treat of matters relating to the fall of the New York usurper. The majority of the inhabitants of the Province had for some time been getting heartily tired of being ruled by a man of Leisler's temperament, and the laws which had been enacted by his Assembly which met at New York in the autumn of 1690, certainly did not err on the side of mercy towards his political opponents. One of these arbitrary acts declared that all persons who had left the Province must return within three weeks from the time of its publication, under penalty of "being esteemed disobedient"; while by another any person who refused to accept either a civil or military commission from Leisler, was to be fined seventy-five pounds; and, moreover, anyone leaving Albany or Ulster without his permission incurred a fine of one hundred pounds, while all persons who had already left those counties were ordered to return within fourteen days "at their utmost perils." No wonder then that people longed for the arrival of letters from the king to settle the dispute as to the governorship of the Province, and for an answer to their numerous petitions for a proper person to rule over them, one appointed by royal authority.

Such a person, one Colonel Sloughter, had been appointed by William the Third,—who entertained strong objections to allowing any revolutions against the royal authority, unless sanctioned, of course, in the first place by himself,— as early as the 4th of January in this year; but the new governor did not sail from England until the 1st of December following, when he left the Isle of Wight on board the *Archangel* frigate, accompanied by three smaller vessels carrying troops. He had to call at the Bermudas on his way, and owing to stormy weather and the *Archangel* getting on the rocks near those islands, he did not reach New York until sixteen weeks after his departure from England. Meanwhile, the three smaller vessels under the command of Major Richard Ingoldsby, Sloughter's lieutenant, arrived at New York on the 29th of January, 1691, nearly two months before his senior officer put in an appearance. Unfortunately Major Ingoldsby could not produce any written authority from the king or governor, and so Leisler, had an excuse for not delivering up the fort when summoned by this officer. Whereupon Ingoldsby called Leisler's refusal flat rebellion against the royal authority, and mounted cannon to fire on the fort. To this action Leisler responded by training the guns of the fort on the houses occupied as quarters by Ingoldsby's troops; but beyond a gun fired by Leisler's men at a boat containing some of the newly arrived soldiers, no actual fighting took place until just before Sloughter's arrival, when Ingoldsby refusing to disband his men as demanded by Leisler, the latter had the audacity to fire on the royal troops, killing two and wounding several others. Fortunately, before much more mischief was done, the long-expected governor from England arrived, who leaving his ship in the Narrows, proceeded up to the city in his pinnace, where he received a warm welcome from the friends of order, and at once, that same evening,— 19th of March, 1691,—took the oath of office. Which being done, he lost no time in sending Ingoldsby to demand in the king's name the surrender of the fort. But this the obstinate Dutchman refused to do, until he had satisfied himself that Colonel Sloughter was the person named in the royal commission, and alleged further, as an excuse for delay, that it was too late at night for the handing over of a military post. Three times that night did Major Ingoldsby demand its surrender in vain; and these repeated refusals of Leisler to submit to the royal authority naturally only confirmed Sloughter in his opinion that the Dutch usurper was "in actual rebellion," and that the anti-Leislerian party really represented the loyal portion of the inhabitants.

This obstinate conduct on the part of Leisler, therefore, damaged his case considerably, which he probably became aware of himself when too late; for on the following morning he wrote an apologetic letter to Sloughter offering to render "an exact account of all his actions and conduct." But by this time his men had begun to desert, on Sloughter promising pardon to all save Leisler and his principal officers; and when Ingoldsby at last obtained admission to the fort, he had the leaders arrested and brought before the governor and his council, by whose orders they were committed to prison. Thus the ambitious and rampant Protestantism of Leisler had brought him no better fortune than a prison cell, and he must have bitterly mused over the irony of fate which had led to his being treated as a rebel by an officer of that very Dutch king for whom, he considered, he had saved New York! His enemies, however, were now triumphant, and, considering the contemptuous treatment they had received at the hands of the "Dutch usurper" when in power, who had stigmatised his political opponents as nothing better than "popish dogs," it is not to be wondered at that on his fall they loudly clamoured for his punishment as a traitor.

The prisoners were duly brought to trial before a special court of oyer and terminer, on the charge of treason and murder "for holding by force the king's fort against the king's governor after the publication of his commission, and after demand had been made in the king's name, and in the reducing of which lives had been lost." Eight of the prisoners pleaded "not guilty" to the charge, but Leisler and his son-in-law Milborne refused to plead, and were therefore tried as mutes. After a trial lasting eight days, the jury found Leisler, Milborne, Abraham Gouverneur, Dr. Gerardus Beekman, Johannes Vermilye, Thomas Williams, Myndert Coerten, and Abraham Brasher guilty, while the remaining two—De Lanoy and Edsall—were acquitted. Chief Justice Dudley then pronounced sentence of death upon the eight condemned criminals in accordance with the barbarous law against high treason.

These unfortunate men at once petitioned Governor Sloughter for a reprieve, and he, not being a hard-hearted man, was willing enough to grant it, subject to the king's pleasure. In his letters to the home authorities he therefore interceded for all the prisoners except the ringleaders—Leisler and Milborne—whom he also would rather not have executed if the peace of the country would not have been jeopardised by this act of mercy. The enemies of the condemned men, however, angrily protested against any mercy being shown towards the principal offenders, and it being urged upon the governor that the Indians would not rest satisfied until Leisler had been executed; Sloughter, upon the 14th of May, brought the matter before his councillors, who thereupon "unanimously resolved that as well for the satisfaction of the Indians as the asserting of the Government and authority residing in his Excellency, and preventing insurrections and disorders for the future, it is absolutely necessary that the sentence pronounced against the principal offenders be forthwith put in Execution."

The governor had a minute of council to this effect sent down to the Lower House of Assembly then sitting, which was duly returned to his Excellency on the following day endorsed as follows:—

House of Representatives for ye Province of New York. Die Veneris, May 15th P. M. 1691.

This house according to their opinion given: doe aprove of what his Excell^y and Councill have Don.

By ord. of ye house of Representatives,

Ja. Graham, Speaker.

This approval by the House of Assembly left the governor no further choice in the matter, and he thereupon reluctantly signed the death warrant. The vulgar tradition that the leaders of the Anti-Leislerian party invited the governor to a grand banquet, and when they had got the king's representative into such a state of intoxication that he did not know what he was doing, put a pen in his hand and forced him, then and there, to sign the order for Leisler's execution, who thereupon, together with Milborne, was at once hanged before Colonel Sloughter had time to recover his senses, is hardly borne out by the above clearly expressed minute of council.

No time was, however, lost in carrying out the sentence of death on Leisler and his son-in-law, after the above-quoted approval of the House of Assembly had been obtained. And on Saturday, the 16th of May, 1691, this written approval was duly entered in the Legislative Council's Minute Book, and on the same day, in a downpour of rain, the two wretched men were conducted to the place of execution, and were there hanged. Both Leisler and Milborne made short speeches from the scaffold in vindication of their conduct, though confessing they had erred in many ways; and on the latter recognising Livingston in the crowd, who had hastened to New York on hearing of Sloughter's arrival, called out to him "You have caused the king that I must now die, but before God's tribunal I will implead you for the same." Sloughter was humane enough not to allow the barbarous sentence to be carried out in its entirety, so after they were hanged the bodies were cut down and beheaded, but not quartered as was customary with criminals condemned to death for high treason. In after years Leister's family and friends, when party passions had cooled down, were successful in getting the English Parliament to reverse the sentence of attainder passed on these two victims of their own lust for power. But as we shall see later on, the conflict between Leislerians and Anti- Leislerians, did not subside with these executions, and Robert Livingston's part in this sad affair had a considerable influence on his subsequent fortunes. Jacob Leisler and Jacob Milborne also bear the unenviable notoriety of being the only persons ever executed in New York for a political offence.

Notes

1. For a copy of this incomplete journal see *Livingstons of Callendar*, Appendix No. XXXVIII. The existence of this journal—which settles the date of Robert's departure from Scotland, and his port of landing in America—had never to the author's knowledge been noticed in print before the publication of his earlier work. His attention was drawn to it by Mr. Johnston Livingston, to whom he is also greatly indebted for a sight of the original journals kept by the same Robert on his voyage to England in 1694–1695. "Unfortunately," Mr. Johnston Livingston wrote, when forwarding the author a copy of the earlier journal of 1673, "the original, in my possession for many years, has mysteriously disappeared."
2. *Colonial Now York*, vol. i, p. 243.
3. The first two enteries in the above family record are in English, while all the others are in Dutch. Robert Livingston was accustomed to correspond in both languages; his letters to his wife being in the latter.
4. Collector at New York.
5. Mr. J. A. Doyle in a recent volume—*The Middle Colonies*—of hie history *The English in America*, speaks very highly of Robert Livingston's capabilities.
6. Namely, Captain Johannes Sanderse Glen.
7. A list of this boy's clothes, when at school in New England, is still preserved, and win be found printed in Mrs. Earle's *Home Life in Colonial Days*. John Livingston was born on the 26 April, 1680.

CHAPTER V

CONCERNING ROBERT LIVINGSTON, THE NEPHEW, AND HIS SETTLEMENT IN THE SAME PROVINCE.

"I think there be six Richmonds in the field."
—*Shakespeare, King Richard III.*

THE author considers he might well paraphrase King Richard's famous complaint, by exclaiming "I think there be six Roberts in the field!" as novelty in family nomenclature was certainly not a Livingston virtue. In Scotland, the favourite names were Alexander and William, with a James flung in, now and again, to vary the dreary monotony; while in America, not content with starting with two Roberts, the confusion is still further increased by their continuing to perpetuate this, far from uncommon name, even unto the third and fourth generation! No wonder mistakes constantly occur through confounding one Robert with another; so before proceeding further with the history of Robert, the Elder, it may be as well to give some particulars concerning another, and less known Robert, his contemporary, usually known in family annals as "Robert, the Nephew."

As soon as Robert, the uncle, had become firmly settled in the New World, and about the time when Albany had received its civic charter from Governor Dongan, he wrote to his elder brother James, advising him to send his son Robert out to him, and promising "that nothing should be wanting on his part to secure the lad's fortune." The exact age of this younger Robert, when he left his father's house at Edinburgh to join his uncle in America, is unknown. He was sent to London to embark for New

York, where he was placed under the care of Mr. Jacob Harwood, the senior Robert's English agent, who gave him a letter of introduction to his uncle in America, which is still in existence, and is dated London, August 12, 1687. In this letter Mr. Harwood remarks, the youthful bearer "hath wit enough." He reached Albany in the month of November following.

The senior Robert faithfully kept his promise, and through his influence his nephew was so well received by the old Dutch families of Albany, that ten years later he married Margaretta Schuyler, the eldest daughter of his uncle's great friend and brother-in-law, Colonel Peter Schuyler.[1] In 1699, his uncle requiring assistance in carrying on his duties as town clerk, and none of his sons being of an age to be of use, appointed Robert, junior, to be his deputy, subject to the approval of the Common Council, which was readily granted. From the council minutes we learn that five years afterwards, on the 23rd May, 1704, his services were remunerated with the magnificent annual salary of five pounds and ten shillings, which included "the supplying of paper," but which was to commence from the 14th of June, 1703. On the same day in which this salary was granted, he was sworn to keep a true minute book of the Mayor's Court. He acted as his uncle's deputy until the 6th of May, 1707, when his cousin Philip, being of age, was appointed in his place.

Robert, the Nephew, however, kept up his public connection with the city of Albany, and in the month of January following he was elected alderman of the first ward of that city. He must have fully possessed the confidence of his fellow citizens, for having been appointed by Governor Hunter, Mayor of Albany in 1710, he held that office for nine years continuously, "a longer term but one than any other, in colonial times or since."[2] He also sat in the House of Assembly, as one of the representatives of Albany, from 1711 to 1715. He was also one of the Commissioners for Indian Affairs, and in that capacity, like his uncle, he was brought into frequent official intercourse with the natives. In the spring of 1720 he accompanied Myndert Schuyler, another Commissioner, on a mission to the Senecas' "castle" or village, for the purpose of persuading the Five Nations to put a stop to some threatened hostilities with some other Indians, who were in alliance with the English. Also to throw obstacles in the way of the French, whose increasing encroachments on the Indian territories had given rise to a feeling of uneasiness in New York. The two commissioners were absent from Albany close upon six weeks, and from their report of the negotiations with the sachems of the Five Nations, it appears their commission was a successful one, as the Indians promised to perform all that "Brother Corlaer"[3]

N. B.   Offices, Commissions, etc., held under the Crown are printed in

Robert Livingston, The Neph

b. —

Deputy Town Clerk, Albany, N. Y., 1699-1

Alderman, 1708

James Livingston ═ Maria Kierstede   Jan
m.   1725   b. 170
b. 1701; d. ——   d. 172

Robert James ── Susan Smith, dau.   Janet ═ Chief Justice Wil-   Marga
Livingston   of Judge Wil-   m. 1752 liam Smith, Jr.,
m.   1747 liam Smith,   b. 1730   "The Historian."   b. 1738
b. 1725; d. 1771   Member of   d. 1819   d. 1809
Council (New
York), etc.

Mary ═ (1) Gabriel Maturin,   William Smith   Robert James Livingston   Peter R. Livin
m.   of the British Army and   Livingston,   b. 1760; d. 1837   b. 1766; d. 1847
b. 1748   private secretary to Sir   b. 1755; d. 1794   Fought and was wounded at   Member of New
d. 1830   Guy Carleton.   Lieutenant - Colo-   Trenton, as a Volunteer in   sembly 1823. Sp
nel Continental   American Army.   State Senator a
(2) Dr. Jonathan Mal-   Army, War of   1826-1829. Pr
lett, of the British   Independence.   Senate 1828, etc.
Army.

retta Schuyler
    dau. of Colonel Peter Schuyler

of Albany, 1710-1719
sioner of Indian Affairs, 1715-1720
r of General Assembly for Albany, 1711-1715

1 Henry Beekman
Rhinebeck, N. Y.

John Livingston — Catharine, eldest dau. of
                m.   1739   Dirck Ten Broeck,
    b. 1709; d. 1791   Mayor of Albany.

el Peter R.   **Richard Livingston**   **James Livingston**   **Abraham Livingston**
ngston, of   b. 1744; d. 1784   b. 1747; d. 1842   b. 1754; d. 1803
Manor.   *Lieutenant - Colonel in* *Colonel in Continental*   *Captain in Continental*
nded Manor   *Continental Army dur-*   *Army during War of*   *Army during War of*
ingston Regi-   *ing War of Independ-*   *Independence.*   *Independence.*
10th Albany   *ence.*
a, War of In-
lence, etc.

anna, dau. of Judge   **Maturin Livingston = Margaret,** dau. of General   **John P. Livingston**
Robert R. Livingston,   m. 1798   Morgan Lewis.   b. 1793; d. ——
f Clermont.   b. 1769; d. 1847   *Governor State of New*   *Captain in United States*
                       Recorder New York 1804-7.   *York, etc.*   *Army during the War*
                       Judge of the Court of   *of 1812-1815.*
                       Common Pleas, 1823.

required; and if in the future any emergency should arise, they promised to come to New York for advice, instead of going to the governor of Canada, as they had hitherto been in the habit of doing.

Of this Robert there is nothing further of interest to relate. He died in 1725, in the lifetime of his uncle, and was buried in the Dutch Church at Albany on the 21st of April in that year. By his wife, Margaretta Schuyler, he had the following children, namely four sons and two daughters:—

James, born in 1701, and who married 18th May, 1723, Maria Kierstede. One of their daughters, Janet, married in 1755, William Smith, Chief Justice of New York, afterwards of Upper and Lower Canada, and the author of a history of New York. Another daughter, Margaret, married in 1758, Peter R. Livingston, eldest surviving son of Robert, Third Lord of the Manor. It is from this James that the well known branch of the Maturin Livingstons is descended.

Peter, born in 1706; he was killed by Indians, near where the town of Geneva, New York, now stands.

John, born in 1709; he married Catharine, daughter of Dirck Ten Broeck, Mayor of Albany, and resided for some years at Montreal, Canada, but after the Revolution removed to Stillwater, New York. His second son, Colonel James Livingston, commanded a regiment of Canadian refugees under General Montgomery in his unsuccessful invasion of Canada in 1775, in which he greatly distinguished himself by the capture of Fort Chambly; and subsequently, a Continental Battalion of New York troops during the war of Independence; in which regiments, two other sons, Richard and Abraham, were also officers.[4] They took part in the assault of Quebec, which resulted in the death of their commander the gallant Montgomery, and also served under General Gates in the victorious campaign against Burgoyne in 1777. It was Colonel James Livingston who commanded the little American garrison at Verplanck's Point at the time of Benedict Arnold's treason.

Thomas, who died young.

The daughters were:—Angelica, born in 1698, who married in 1734, Johannes Van Rensselaer of Greenbush, and their daughter Catharine— "Sweet Kitty Van Rensselaer"— married General Philip Schuyler of Revolutionary fame. Janet, the youngest daughter, was born in 1703; die married Colonel Henry Beekman of Rhinebeck, and their only daughter and heiress, Margaret, married Judge Robert R. Livingston of Clermont, the father of another and better-known Robert R., the first Chancellor of the State of New York. For not content with repeating the same Christian names from one generation to another, the Livingstons in America like their kinsmen of Scotland, were also given to further complicating matters genealogical by their numerous intermarriages![5]

Notes

1. Marriage license dated 26 July, 1697, but the marriage did not take place until exactly a month later.
2. Schuyler, *Colonial New York*, vol. i, p. 289.
3. "Brother Corlaer" was the Indian name for the Governor of New York.
4. For further particulars of these officers see Chapter XIII and Appendix A.
5. A fuller list of Robert, the Nephew's family, will be found in the Appendix.

CHAPTER VI

Concerning the Compact made by Robert Livingston, the Elder, with certain Whig Noblemen at the Court of William the Third, for the Suppression of Piracy in the North Atlantic, the Failure of his Scheme, and the Consequences Thereof.

"My name was Robert Kidd,
When I sailed, when I sailed."

Old Sea Ballad.[1]

W e must now return to the far more interesting career of the senior Robert, whom we had left in New York, where he had gone to welcome the new governor. Colonel Sloughter having settled affairs in that city went up to Albany to pacify the Indians, who had become very restive under the governorship of Leisler, who had slighted them in many ways, as in depriving the Christian, or "praying Indians" of the services of their revered pastor Dominie Dellius; while their agent, Robert Livingston, had been unable to conduct their affairs during the last two years, owing to the persecution of the late government. Several sachems of the Christian Mohawks met Sloughter in the Albany town hall on the 26th of May, 1691, and expressed their pleasure at seeing a governor "come from our great king of England" and thanked him for his kindness in allowing Dominie Dellius to return to his ministry; and after the usual presents had been exchanged the Indians left perfectly satisfied with their new governor.

A more important meeting, between Sloughter and the chiefs of the Iroquois, took place six days later in the presence of the chief magistrates of the city, when the governor thanked them for their past services to the loyal gentlemen of Albany during the late troubles, and hoped they would prosecute the war against the French with renewed vigour. The Indians listened to his speeches with great attention, and their chiefs in their replies pointed out their inability to fight the French without the assistance of the English. These speeches of the Iroquois chiefs, which were rendered into English by Robert Livingston, are interesting as showing the Indians were fully alive to the disadvantages as well as the advantages of their position as a barrier between the contending European Powers. Nor did they see any reason why their English friends should expect them to do the fighting, while their white allies remained at home, safe behind their fortifications. A joint expedition into Canada was the result of this meeting, which was placed under the command of Livingston's brother-in-law, Peter Schuyler, in whom the Indians had great confidence. Schuyler succeeded in reaching La Prairie, but his force was not powerful enough to capture the fort there, though his little band created much consternation among the French, and materially assisted in raising the prestige of the English among the savage warriors of the Five Nations.

Governor Sloughter's rule was of short duration, for he died on the 23rd of July, 1691, after an illness of only two days, and within a month of his return to New York from Albany. The council thereupon appointed Ingoldsby to be commander-in-chief until the king's pleasure should be made known. He followed the late governor's example in encouraging the Indians to resist the encroachments of the French, while also calling the attention of the Home Government to the defenceless state of the province, and the necessity for adding to its strength by connecting it with the adjacent colonies of Connecticut, New Jersey, and Pennsylvania. The Lords of Trade lost no time in laying this statement of the affairs of the province before the king, who, on the 18th of March, 1692, granted a commission under the Great Seal to Colonel Benjamin Fletcher, another soldier of fortune, appointing him governor in the place of the late Colonel Sloughter. He took less time than his predecessor in arriving at his destination, for on the 30th of August of the same year in which he obtained his appointment he landed in New York, with instructions from the Lords of

Trade to use every exertion in providing for the security of the province, and for establishing his government on a firm basis.

The new governor was an energetic man, but of a hasty temper, which soon involved him in disputes with many of the leading men in the colony. Among those who considered themselves aggrieved by Colonel Fletcher was Robert Livingston, who had as yet received no recompense for his great services in supplying money and stores to the troops during the recent wars; and though he had obtained a bond from the late Albany Convention for some of his disbursements, he had never received a penny back from the colonial government, and thus his estate was impoverished by debt undertaken for the public good. Fletcher was apparently unable to assist him, owing to the exhausted state of the country, but Livingston took his refusal to render him justice as a personal matter, and much bitter feeling was thereupon engendered between these two. Finding there was no chance of obtaining a settlement of his claims in New York, Livingston decided to proceed to London and lay his case, as well as his complaints against Fletcher, before the Lords of Trade in person.

He thereupon, together with his eldest son John, then a youth of fifteen years of age, sailed from New York on the 10th of December, 1694, in the ship *Charity*, Captain Lancaster Symes in command. The voyage was a disastrous one, as is duly recorded in the journals kept by Robert Livingston on this occasion, and still in the possession of one of his descendants.[2] Shortly after leaving America they met with very tempestuous weather, and on the 3rd of January the *Charity* lost her rudder, from which date until she was driven ashore on the coast of Portugal they endured great hardships, both father and son having to assist the crew in manning the pumps, and keeping the necessary watches; and before the disabled vessel fortunately finally drifted ashore at Pedemeira[3] on the 9th of May, 1695, they had nearly perished from hunger and thirst. For they had been five months at sea, the last seventeen weeks of which period they had been reduced to a daily ration of a pint of water and a little cocoa-nut. To commemorate their providential escape Mr. Livingston adopted as his crest a ship in distress, in lieu of the well-known demi-savage borne by his Scottish ancestors, while he also altered the family motto from *Si Je Puis*—If I can— to *Spero Meliora*—I hope for better things,—which was certainly prophetic as regards his future career.

From Pederneira they proceeded via San Martinho to Lisbon. This city they left on Saturday the 22nd of June (old style), and travelling by easy stages,—a full list of which is given in the second journal,—they reached

Corunna on the 9th of July. Here they took ship for England a week later, landing at Falmouth on the eighteenth, whence they journeyed by coach to London, which place they finally reached on the afternoon of the 25th of July, 1695, or over seven months from the date of their sailing from America! Robert Livingston with his usual energy lost no time in bringing his case to the notice of the Privy Council, who, on the 22nd of August, referred his petition to the consideration of the Committee of the Lords of Trade. This Committee certainly also lost no time, for six days after the receipt of the order from the Privy Council, five of their number met in the Council Chamber at Whitehall and summoned Livingston to lay his case and produce his witnesses before the Board. Among the witnesses examined on this occasion was the master of the brigantine *Antigua*, one William Kidd, who afterwards turned pirate, and whose supposed hidden treasures have given rise to so many romantic stories.[4] His evidence, as well as that of some other sea captains, was to the effect that Fletcher had been guilty of illegal practices in endeavouring to get their sailors to vote for his partisans at the recent election of members to the New York General Assembly. Other charges against Fletcher were also brought forward at this and the subsequent inquiry held on the 14th of September, but none of the witnesses were able to swear that the governor was personally cognisant of these malpractices.

In spite of the failure of Livingston's witnesses to prove that Fletcher had been guilty of the specific charges alleged against him, still reports of some of the governor's arbitrary acts had reached England through other channels, and the Lords of Trade therefore had reason for believing that there might be some truth in them. They, moreover, treated Livingston with great consideration, and were probably prepossessed in his favour by his intimate knowledge of New York affairs, the real hardships of his case, and his social standing in the province. He had also a friend at Court in the person of ex-Governor Dongan, who willingly bore witness to Livingston's services on behalf of his government in being instrumental in securing the alliance of the Five Nations with the English, and to the efficient manner in which he had discharged his various offices. While on the other hand, the friends of Governor Fletcher, highly indignant at his accusations against that officer, roundly accused Livingston of having been "the person that protested against the proclaiming their Majesties at Albany." This was flatly denied by Livingston, who affirmed that he had "proclaimed their Majesties in person, but that indeed he had protested with others against the proceedings of Jacob Leisler and others at New York."

The examination of his accounts was a work of time, and Livingston was naturally getting anxious to return to his family, for in the month of December we still find him in London petitioning the Lords of the Treasury—to whom the king had referred the reports of the Lords of Trade—for a favourable answer to his prayer for a quick settlement of his claims, and that they would allow him the interest, as well as the principal, of the sums of money advanced by him; and on the 2nd of January, 1696, the Lords of the Treasury issued their report, in which they "conceive it reasonable [interest] to be allowed, as well as in justice to the petitioner (who alleges he might have made advantage of his money in trade or otherwise), as for the encouragement of others to be serviceable to your Majesty on the like occasion; the said interest of £8 per cent (being as we are informed the usual rate allowed there) amounts to £868—16—0." This money they also advised should be paid in London in sterling according to Mr. Livingston's desire, but at a discount of £30 per cent. which they were informed would be the value of the equivalent sum in New York currency. The remaining amounts, principal as well as interest, they advised should be satisfied out of the revenues of the province of New York. The Lords of the Treasury wound up their report by stating: "Lastly in consideration of the long and faithful services of the said Mr. Livingston in all the treaties and negotiations with the Indians in those parts, he having been (as is certified) at great trouble and charge therein, and having not hitherto had any salary for the same; we think he may deserve as a reward for the time past, and to encourage him in your Majesty's service for the time to come, a salary of one hundred pounds sterling per annum to be settled upon him out of the revenues of New York, during his life, to commence as your Majesty shall think fit. And we have no objection against his being in the offices of Collector of the Excise and Quit Rents, Town Clerk, Clerk of the Peace, and Clerk of the Common Pleas at Albany, with the usual salaries during his life as desired."

This report was signed by Godolphin, Ste: Fox, and J. Smith.

The king having given his consent, the necessary instructions were transmitted to New York to have the above report acted upon. Thus Mr. Livingston, after some months of delay, was at last successful in carrying through the object of his long and hazardous journey. His was not a nature, however, to care about leading an idle existence while the Board of Trade and the Treasury were investigating his claims; and one of the colonial difficulties at this period being the prevalence of piracy, his active mind was bent upon finding a remedy for the evil, as the French war kept the English naval forces fully employed, and thus the pirates were pretty well left to their own devices. Among the courtiers at St. James's was an Irish nobleman who took a great deal of interest in New York affairs, and knew something about them, having been a member of the Parliamentary Committee appointed to inquire into the petition of Leisler's family for the reversal of the attainder. This gentleman was Richard Coote, Earl of Bellomont and Baron of Coloony, and treasurer to Queen Mary. He had many conversations with Livingston on colonial matters, and the subject of the best method for suppressing the curse of piracy was naturally the one most discussed. The king could spare no man-of-war, and Parliament would grant no supplies for this purpose, so the only alternative was to try and suppress it by private enterprise.

Bellomont actually interested the king himself in the project, who expressed his willingness at one time to invest the sum of £3000 in the adventure. Some of the leading Whig politicians, including Somers, the Lord Chancellor; Admiral Russell, Earl of Orford, the victor of La Hogue; and the Duke of Shrewsbury, one of the Secretaries of State, were also willing to provide funds for such a laudable, as well as what was hoped to be lucrative undertaking. These influential noblemen, together with Lord Bellomont and some others, ultimately subscribed £6000 towards the expense of fitting out a suitable vessel, but the king withdrew his own offer of £3000, though he gave his royal sanction to the enterprise, and reserved to himself a one-tenth share in all the profits, as was customary with privateers.

Bellomont not knowing of a suitable person to command the privateer, Livingston introduced to him the Captain William Kidd already mentioned as having borne witness to Governor Fletcher's misgovernment in New York, and spoke highly as to his respectability and fitness for the post. This merchant captain is first mentioned in New York annals during the Leislerian troubles, when this "blasphemous privateer," as he has been called by a recent American writer, brought his vessel up to the town to assist Ingoldsby in his attack on the fort, for which service he afterwards obtained a grant of £150 from the New York Assembly. He was considered to be a man of fair means, and had a wife and child residing in New York, so that it is not surprising Livingston should have recommended Kidd as a responsible person, and one to be trusted in such a command. Moreover he was a brother Scot. What greater recommendation than this could be needful!

Accordingly, on the 10th of October, 1695, Livingston drew up with his own hand the Articles of Agreement, by which Lord Bellomont on the one side, on behalf of himself and fellow-subscribers, and Livingston and Captain Kidd on the other, settled the conditions on which the *Adventure Galley*, as the vessel was to be called, afterwards to become so notorious in the annals of piracy, was to be fitted out. The chief conditions of this agreement were briefly as follows:

The preamble to the agreement recites that Captain Kidd is desirous to obtain a commission as commander of a privateer, in order to be empowered to take prizes from the king's enemies, as well as "to fight with and subdue" certain pirates, who had sailed from ports in the American plantations "with the intention of committing spoils and depredations against the laws of nations in the Red Sea or elsewhere" the parties to this agreement therefore promise that "a good and sufficient ship to the liking of Captain Kidd shall be forthwith bought, whereof the said Captain Kidd is to have the command."

By the first article, the Earl of Bellomont covenants at his own charge to procure from the king, or from the Lords of Admiralty (as the case shall require), one or more commissions authorising Kidd to act against the king's enemies in the usual manner, as well as "to fight with, conquer, and subdue pyrates, and to take them and all their goods." Bellomont further binds himself in the next article to obtain, within three months after Captain Kidd's departure from England, "a grant from the king to be made to some indifferent and trusty person, of all such merchandises, goods, treasure, and other things as shall be taken from the said pyrates or any other pyrates whatsoever by the said Captain Kidd, or by the said ship or any other ship or ships under his command."

By articles three, four, five and six, this nobleman also agrees to provide four-fifths of the purchase money of a suitable vessel, and to bear the same proportion of the cost of fitting her out; the remaining fifth to be found by Livingston and Kidd. Bellomont furthermore also promises to pay sixteen hundred pounds by way of advance "on or before the sixth day of November next ensuing"; while by the same date the other parties to the agreement, namely Livingston and Kidd, are to "pay down four hundred pounds in part of the share and proportion which they are to have in the said ship." The balance of the total amount required to be paid within seven weeks of the date of the agreement, so anxious were the parties interested to get the vessel completed.

According to the seventh article Captain Kidd was bound to procure one hundred sailors or thereabouts, and to make what reasonable speed he can in prosecuting his intended voyage, and if successful in capturing prizes, "to make the best of his way to Boston in New England, and that without touching at any other port or harbour whatsoever, or without breaking bulk, or dimininshing any part of what he so take or obtain on any pretence whatsoever, of which he shall make oath in case the same be desired by the Earl of Bellomont, and there to deliver the same into the hands of the said earl."

The said captain further agrees in the next article to enlist his crew on the "no cure no pay" principle; and that their share of the prize money was not to exceed at the most one-fourth part, or less, "if he can so contract with them." By the terms of the ninth clause, Livingston and Kidd jointly stipulated that in the event of Kidd being unsuccessful in taking either prizes from the king's enemies, or in capturing any pirates or their plunder, that they shall "jointly and severally" refund to the Earl of Bellomont all monies advanced by him on behalf of the said adventure "on or before the twenty-fifth day of March, 1697, the danger of the seas and enemy, and mortality of the said Captain Kidd always excepted, upon payment whereof the said Robert Livingston and Captain Kidd are to have the sole property in the said ship and furniture, and this indenture to be delivered up to them, with all other covenants and obligations thereunto belonging."

The tenth and last article provides for the division of the profits, if any, arising out of the undertaking. The crew were in the first place to get their quarter interest, unless Kidd could manage to arrange better terms with them, and the balance was to be divided into five equal shares, of which Bellomont was to have four, leaving the remaining share to be equally divided between Livingston and Kidd. This clause contains the proviso that any prizes taken from the king's enemies "are to be lawfully adjudged prizes in the usual manner, before any division or otherwise intermedling therewith according to the true intent of the said commission to be granted in that behalf." The final paragraph in this article is to the effect that if the total value of the said prizes, goods, treasure, etc., shall amount to the sum of one hundred thousand pounds, then Captain Kidd shall receive "as a reward and gratification for his good services" the vessel which is to be fitted out under this agreement. Here follow the seals and signatures of Robert Livingston and Captain Kidd; but before signing the deed a memorandum was added by which it was arranged that within eight days after the grant had passed the Great Seal of England, the person to whom the king made the grant, as arranged in the above articles, shall assign and transfer unto Livingston and Kidd their stipulated share of all the (to be) captured goods. On the same day these two executed bonds in favour of the Earl of Bellomont, under penalties of £10,000 and £20,000 respectively; for the faithful carrying out of their obligations under this agreement.[5]

Bellomont was not behindhand in fulfilling his part of the contract; and on the 11th of December, or two months after the execution of this agreement, he obtained from the Admiralty the usual commission authorising Captain Kidd to command the *Adventure Galley* privateer; but as the terms of this letter-of-marque only empowered him to act against the French, a special commission under the Great Seal, dated 26 January, 1696, was granted by the king, in which it was stated that "whereas information had been given to the king, that the four persons above-named—viz: Thomas Tew, William Maze, John Ireland, and Thomas Wake—and other of his majesty's subjects, had associated themselves with many wicked persons, and committed piracies in the parts of America and elsewhere, in violation of the Law of Nations, to the discouragement of trade, and to the dishonour of his royal authority, in case any of his subjects guilty of such detestable enormities should go unpunished; his majesty did therefore give power to Captain Kidd, Commander of the *Adventure Galley*, and to the commander of that ship for the time being, to apprehend and seize the persons above-named, and all other pirates whom he should meet with on the coast of America, or other seas, with their ships and goods; and in case of resistance to fight with and compel them to yield, and to bring them to a legal trial, in order to suffer the punishment of the law."

This commission also required Kidd to keep an exact journal of his proceedings, and a complete inventory of all ships, with their arms, ammunition, and cargoes, which he should take from the pirates. At a later date, the king ordered a warrant to be prepared, as promised, for the benefit of the owners of the *Adventure Galley*, in which he had at first intended to have had it declared that he reserved to himself a tenth part of all captures, but the Lords of the Treasury holding the opinion that it would not be legal to have that right mentioned in the grant, it was omitted; the king protecting himself instead by obtaining a covenant to that effect from the grantees. In accordance with this warrant a bill was drawn up by Sir Henry Hawles, the Solicitor-General, "which recited the commission and took notice that the *Adventure Galley* was bought and fitted out for the Expedition by the King's Royal Encouragement, and at the sole charge of the persons named, and that his Majesty being desirous that so charge-able an undertaking for so good ends should meet with encouragement, did grant to them all ships and goods and other things which after the 30th of April, 1696, had been taken or should be taken with the persons above-named, or any other pirates, by Captain Kidd or other commander of the *Adventure Galley*, as far as the same might belong to the king, or were grantable by him, or in his power to dispose in right of his crown or as perquisites of the Admiralty or otherwise."

Before this bill passed the Great Seal the Earl of Bellomont and his co-adventurers in the undertaking gave security that they would account to his Majesty or his representative, on oath if required, of all prizes and captures made under the above commissions, and that they should be per-sonally liable to the king for his tenth. Certainly King William the Third showed himself a true Dutchman in this transaction!

The shareholders in this curious "joint-stock" enterprise for the sup-pression of piracy, probably indulged in hopeful anticipations as to the suc-cess of a venture started under such tokens of royal approval and favourable auspices, and with such full powers; but there were a few wise people who shook their heads over the whole affair, and even expressed the opinion that the king had no legal right to dispose of the property of innocent mer-chants, which might have fallen into the hands of pirates, or to offer grants of the ships and effects of these same pirates before their legal condemna-tion. The stipulations in the agreement between Bellomont and Livingston also contained the seeds of future trouble, as for example in the clause by which Kidd was bound to enlist his crew on the "no cure no pay" principle; well enough in its way when plenty of lawful prizes could be taken, but a strong inducement for a crew, composed of the usual rough elements to be found on the books of a privateer, to turn pirate in bad times rather than to go empty handed. Precautions were certainly taken at first to procure a responsible class of officers and seamen, by obtaining men who had fami-lies settled in England, but these sensible precautions were unfortunately frustrated before the vessel got clear of the river, owing to the pressgangs forcing the greater part of these men into the Royal Navy.

By the 20th of February, 1696, the *Adventure Galley* was fully equipped and ready for sea, but as this date was much later than was at first contemplated, a memorandum was attached to the original agreement, and signed by Kidd, in which it was stated, that though the vessel had not been completed, nor the sums of money due by the parties to the contract paid within the time stipulated, yet, as now all was in order, money paid, and the commissions obtained, it was declared that this delay should in no way prejudice the *Articles of Agreement*, which were to remain in full force "as if the said ship had been despatched and all sums of money had been actually paid within the time limited and directed by the said Articles." Captain Kidd left London within a few days of this date, but owing to the loss of many of his men from the press-gangs and other reasons he did not finally sail from Plymouth until the month of April, when he steered his course for New York. Livingston was also back in New York on the 2nd of August of this year,[6] and on his arrival at Albany was very coldly received by Fletcher, who refused point blank to recognise the king's orders to reinstate him in his various posts, or to reimburse him for his outlay on the public service.

The governor had gone to Albany to look after the Indians, and having transacted what was required returned to New York, where he was followed by Livingston, in the hope of inducing that irate personage to listen to reason. But Colonel Fletcher remained obdurate; and when Livingston petitioned him and his Council to be reinstated in his various offices, and the sums of money advanced by him refunded, in accordance with the instructions of the Home Government, the governor absented himself from the discussion which took place over this matter, on the artful plea that he was unwilling that it should be supposed he influenced the Council in their decision, though he well knew this body was composed of men mostly subservient to himself, and inimical to Livingston.

As was to be expected under such circumstances, the Council, which sat on the 15th of September, 1696, passed an adverse vote on Livingston's petition, one of the reasons. given for this decision being that, "the said Livingston is an alien, born of Scotch parents in Rotterdam, and no native born subject of his Majesty's kingdom of England or Ireland, or of his Majesty's territories or dominions in America, and so consequently disabled from executing any place of trust relating to the Treasury."

This was of course false, and Livingston in his Memorial to the Board of Trade complaining of Fletcher's conduct, very properly remarks on this objection that, "it is true I am of Scotland by birth, but born after King James the First came to the Crown of England, and as all others of that nation living and purchasing lands in England and the Plantations have always been esteemed upon all trials where that has been controverted as native English, now after my living in the Province of New York 22 years with a Commission in the Government, and owner of a great many tracts of land and buildings of a considerable value; if, after all this, I must become an alien, what must those be that are in the Council and all other places of trust throughout the Government, that are of French and Dutch birth, and have not that naturalization I have, they at the same time being by the Act of Parliament as incapable to be concerned in the Courts and Treasury as I am; and if the interpretation of the law be such that none can officiate in those stations but such as are native English, according to the liberal [literal?] construction, then there must be a new colony of English natives transplanted here to officiate in those stations."[7]

Fletcher did not rest content with having deprived Livingston of all the benefits he had expected to have derived from the commission he had been at such pains to obtain, but tried hard also to blast his sturdy opponent's character with the Lords of Trade, by asserting openly in a letter to Messrs. Brook and Nicolls, the agents for the Province in London, that he (Livingston) had got it solely "by false insinuations to the Lords of his sufferings"; and he piously expressed the hope that they would be successful in persuading the Home Government to prevent "a man of such vile principles from sucking any more the blood of the province, for he has been a very sponge to it." He, moreover, further spitefully declared, that the object of his bitter attack, "is known by all men here to have neither religion nor morality, his whole thirst being at any rate and by any ways to enrich himself, and has said—as he [the governor] had been credibly informed by many persons—he had rather be called knave Livingston than poor Livingston."

But while Colonel Fletcher was using his best endeavours to crush Livingston, his own character was being as violently assailed by the Leislerian party in the province, who had recovered much of their former influence in New York, and whose cause Livingston is said to have furthered while in London, his animosity against their former leader being probably forgiven and forgotten in favour of an alliance against their present obnoxious governor. Among the charges preferred against Fletcher, the most damning was his supposed encouragement of the notorious pirates or "Red Sea men," as they were usually called, such as Captain Tew and others, who at this period overawed New York, and for whose capture Captain Kidd had been specially commissioned. Fletcher could not deny his intimacy with Tew, but he solemnly declared that at the time he knew him he had foresworn piracy, and that he had cultivated his acquaintance solely on account of his interesting conversation, as he was "a very pleasant man," so that when his day's work was done "it was some divertisement as well as information to hear him talk." He had also been anxious, he naively declared, "to make him a sober man, and in particular to reclaim him from a vile habit of swearing." For this purpose he gave this bold bad buccaneer, of all things, a book! but considering probably, on second thoughts, a gift of this nature would not be much appreciated by a man of the amiable Tew's disposition, the governor presented him also with a valuable gun. Of course, Tew felt compelled to reciprocate such civilities, and gave Colonel Fletcher in return "some curiosity," as a present, which the governor modestly averred was of little value. Nevertheless, the governor's enemies swore the pirate gave the ladies of his powerful protector's family gifts of jewellery, in acknowledgment of services rendered him in the disposal of his ill-gotten gains.

In consequence of these serious charges, the king, on the 16th March, 1697, gave instructions to the Lords of Trade to issue the usual commissions to the Earl of Bellomont, appointing him governor of the Provinces of New York, Massachusetts Bay, and New Hampshire, as well as to have the command, during the war, of his Majesty's forces in the neighbouring colonies of Connecticut, Rhode Island, and the Jerseys; while Colonel Fletcher was ordered to come home to be examined as to his alleged malpractices. Poor governor! evidently the Lords of Trade did not properly appreciate his pious attempts to convert his ruffianly protégé from "his vile habit of swearing." So wroth was the ex-govemor with the Secretary of Indian Affairs, to whose influence at Whitehall he attributed his recall, that on their meeting one day accidentally, after Bellomont's arrival in the latter's lodgings, he shook his fist in Livingston's face, and would have fought their quarrel out there and then, *vi et armis*, but for the fact that the latter happened at the time to be unarmed.[8]

Bellomont, who sailed from England during the winter of 1697, did not reach New York until April, 1698, owing to the ship on which he was a passenger having to put into. Barbadoes in distress. Before leaving England he received very full instructions from the Privy Council as to the course of conduct he was to pursue on taking possession of his new office; and he was particularly charged to inquire personally into Livingston's case, and to foward the result of his examination to London at the earliest date possible. The new governor, unlike many of his predecessors in the office, was not a needy soldier of fortune, sent out to the colonies for the purpose of enriching themselves at the expense of the colonists, but an honest and straightforward nobleman, whose sole wish was to govern these provinces to the best of his ability, and to suppress the curse of piracy, which was increasing at an alarmingrate, in despite of the late governor's missionary efforts. Bellomont received on landing a warm welcome from the leading inhabitants of New York, and by the Leislerians in particular, who regarded him as the champion of their cause, he having sat on the parliamentary committee, whose report had led to the reversal of the attainder, and the return of the confiscated estates to the family of their late chief.

Livingston, whose fortunes had again been brought to a very low ebb by the arbitrary decision of Fletcher and his council, was much gratified at the appointment of the Earl of Bellomont to the governorship and the latter did not lose much time in holding an inquiry into his case. In fact, so energetic was Bellomont, that within three months of his arrival in New York, he had forwarded to the Lords of Trade, in accordance with his special instructions, the result of his investigation into Mr. Livingston's affairs. This inquiry was held on the 16th of May, 1698, only six weeks after his landing, and took place in the presence of the same members of the Council, who had, under Fletcher, reported adversely on Livingston's claims. On this occasion, however, though they declared that they did not consider "they could properly be judges of what they themselves had objected against the said Livingston," they reluctantly admitted that they knew of nothing to offer or urge against him more than formerly, and that "he was the fittest man in the province" for the duties he had to perform, particularly as victualler of the forces; and they declared, moreover, their willingness to refer the consideration of his case entirely to Bellomont, and to leave him to report the same to the king as he should think fit. The new governor thereupon, after careful examination of Livingston's proofs and vouchers, found that he was justly entitled to all the amounts claimed, and that he was a fit and proper person to execute the commission granted him by the king. He concluded his report by declaring that "nothing hath been offered against him to render him undeserving of his Majesty's grace and favour." Thus Livingston, though for a short time only, triumphed over his enemies.

Bellomont had a high opinion of Livingston's character and ability, and finding it necessary to suspend some members of the Council for their hostile behaviour towards himself, recommended him to the Lords of Trade as a fit person to fill one of the vacancies. He pointed out to their lordships that if Livingston had not come to the government's assistance, in providing funds for paying and victualling the troops, many of the men would have been driven to desert, and much harm thereby caused to his Majesty's service. His knowledge of the Indians was also of great use to the governor, who was quick enough to appreciate the value of employing such men as Colonel Schuyler and Robert Livingston as his chief agents in dealing with these people, as owing to their social position at Albany, the border city, and their personal popularity with the tribes composing the Five Nations, the Indians were always ready to listen with respect to their representations as to the advantages to be derived from an English alliance; and there is no reason to doubt but that these two men, by their considerate and wise treatment of these formidable warriors, saved the English government from the necessity of retaining a much larger force than was at this time quartered in New York.

In spite of these great services rendered by Schuyler and Livingston, Bellomont had to complain again and again to the Home Government of their neglect in not forwarding to New York the long arrears of pay due to the four companies of soldiers then stationed in the Province, and thus keeping these two gentlemen out of the large sums of money, amounting in the year 1700 to no less than seven thousand pounds, disbursed by them in the king's service. At this latter date the governor declared that though both men of good estate, they had spent so much of their private means in victualling the soldiers, that they were "almost if not quite broke," and that he dare not tell them he had been informed it was the government's intention to cut off the arrears of pay due to these four companies for the last two years or more.

During one of Bellomont's flying visits to Albany to look after the Indians, Mrs. Livingston gave birth to a daughter, Catherine,[9] and from an entry in her husband's family bible we learn that the infant was held to baptism by the Countess of Bellomont; an additional proof, if one were needed, of the respect which the governor bore towards Livingston.

As has already been mentioned, Bellomont had received strict instructions to use every exertion to stamp out the crying evil of piracy, which at this period of New York colonial history was so prevalent in American waters. Bellomont was just the person suitable for the task, being both honest and energetic; and he had learnt a great deal relative to the subject before his arrival in New York, for it was he who had assisted Livingston, when in London three years before, in fitting out the *Adventure Galley.* He, however, found it no light task, and while actively bent upon doing his best to put a stop to this scourge to commerce, he received the terrible news that the vessel, which had been fitted out by him and Livingston with so much care and at such great expense, had hoisted the black flag in the Indian seas, where she was reported to have committed great depredations on the merchant vessels trading between India and other eastern countries.

This rumour, which was soon confirmed, was a great shock to the governor, who was of a proud and sensitive disposition, and could not bear the idea that he should have contributed in any way, however innocently, towards promoting the very evil which he had been ordered to suppress. Livingston also became alarmed at the startling intelligence; for he not only ran the risk of losing all the money he had invested in the venture, but would also be liable to Bellomont for his bond of £10,000, which would become forfeited if the original enterprise turned out a failure. It had certainly falsified the sanguine hopes of its promoters, but neither Bellomont nor Livingston were to blame for Kidd's having turned pirate; and there can be no reason for thinking, when the latter finally sailed from New York, on the 5th of September, 1696, he had any other intention in his mind than that of carrying out the orders contained in his commissions.

Before leaving New York, Governor Fletcher had allowed Kidd to beat up for volunteers in that port, and in consequence "many flocked to him from all parts, men of desperate fortunes and necessitous, in expectation of getting vast treasures." With a crew composed of such unruly elements, it is no wonder that he subsequently lost all control over his men; and even Fletcher remarked, in the letter quoted from above, "that it is generally believed here, they will have money *per fas aut nefas*, and that if he miss of the design intended, for which he has commission, 't will not be in Kidd's power to govern such a horde of men under no pay."[10]

Livingston afterwards informed Bellomont he had heard it whispered about that " there was a private contract between Colonel Fletcher and Kidd, whereby Kidd obliged himself to give Fletcher £10,000 if he made a voyage." Bellomont considered this story was probably true, as Fletcher had allowed Kidd to obtain nearly a hundred recruits from among the sailors of New York; but there is not the slightest proof of such a bargain ever having been made, and Bellomont was so prejudiced against his predecessor that he did not always examine very closely into any tales which were unfavourable to that officer. As for example in this case, where he deplores in a letter to the Home Government the loss of so many able sailors to the province, when the men thus recruited were notoriously the scum of New York.

Before arriving at New York, Kidd had fallen in with a small French merchant vessel, which he took possession of and brought into that port, where she was legally condemned as a prize, and appraised at £350; whereupon Fletcher claimed the "king's tenths," which he informed the Lords of Trade he held at the disposal of the Admiralty. So far Kidd had acted within the terms of his commissions, but it was not until just two years afterwards—about August, 1698—that any reliable news of his further movements reached New York, when it was reported he had taken a Moorish or native East Indian merchant vessel, called the *Quedah Merchant*. It appears, after leaving America, Kidd cruised about for several months in the Atlantic without coming across any of the pirate ships he had been specially commissioned to capture; he then set sail for the coast of India in the hopes of better fortune, but was still unsuccessful. His crew now began grumbling at their ill-luck, and though apparently at first reluctant to turn pirate himself, Kidd appears to have found that something must be done to quiet his men, and while in this humour he came across and attacked some Mocha merchant ships at the entrance to the Red Sea, but these vessels being protected by an English and Dutch convoy, he was driven off. Shortly afterwards Kidd plundered some native as well as some small Dutch traders, and one of these prizes he conveyed to St. Mary's in Madagascar, a favourite resort of pirates in those days, where he divided the spoil.

Captain Kidd now found himself fairly embarked on the lucrative but perilous career of a pirate, and whatever scruples he had hitherto entertained regarding the adoption of such a course, he appears by this time to have thrown to the winds, and to have entered heart and soul into the very business he had been commissioned to put down. A few weeks after the committal of the above piratical exploit, he took a much richer prize, the *Quedah Merchant*, a vessel of some 400 tons burthen; when some of his men leaving him to take service under another pirate, Kidd with the remainder embarked on board his new capture, and having first burnt the *Adventure Galley*, set sail for the West Indies. Meanwhile the news of these piracies, as well as other crimes committed by Kidd, had reached England, where the East India Company hastened to press on the Government the necessity for despatching ships in quest of this bold buccaneer; so that by the time Kidd reached his destination he found shelter and supplies denied to him, while he had the greatest difficulty in disposing of any of his ill-gotten plunder. He, however, had the audacity to venture into Delaware Bay with forty of his men in a sloop, and having obtained some supplies, he sailed from thence "into the Sound of New York, and set goods on shore at several places there, and afterwards went to Rhode Island, from whence he sent one Emmet to the Earl of Bellomont at Boston, who told him that Kidd bad left a Moorish ship which he took in India, called the *Quedak Merchant*, in a creek on the coast of Hispaniola, with goods in her to a great value. That he was come thither to make his terms in a sloop, which had on board goods to the value of £10,000, and was able to make his inno-cence appear by many witnesses."[11]

Bellomont was overjoyed to hear that Kidd was so near, and having first of all consulted the Massachusetts Council, he sent an answer by one Campbell, a fellow-countryman of Kidd, to the effect that "if he would make his innocence appear, he might safely come to Boston." Whereupon Kidd, to his undoing, boldly sailed for that place, where he landed on the rst of July, 1699. Livingston, also, on hearing of Kidd's arrival off the coast, hastened at once to Boston, and peremptorily demanded of Bellomont the surrender of his bond for £10,000, hinting at the same time that unless this was given up Kidd would never bring in the *Quedah Merchant* and all the wealth she contained. Bellomont, very naturally, was highly incensed at Livingston's conduct, which he construed as a threat; and fearing besides, probably, that Kidd might escape, he had the latter arrested on the 6th of July, five days after his landing, and had him confined in Boston gaol until the receipt of instructions from England. Also owing to the marked sympathy shown towards piracy in the colonies, where much of the plunder obtained in eastern seas was freely bought by New York merchants and others, many of whom, moreover, were openly spoken of as being in league with Tew, Shelley, and other well-known pirates, Bellomont deemed there was no chance of obtaining a fair trial in Boston, where the law even did not punish piracy with death.

Kidd was detained in Boston gaol for many months, as the vessel sent by the Admiralty to convey him to England met with such boisterous weather that, after being at sea for several weeks, she was compelled to put back to Plymouth so badly damaged that she was unable to proceed on her voyage, so that another ship had to be sent out in her place. While in prison Kidd proposed to Bellomont that he should be allowed to proceed, under a proper guard, to the West Indies, for the purpose of securing the most valuable portion of the plundered goods and treasure which he had left behind on board the *Quedah Merchant*. If Bellomont granted him the desired permission, he promised faithfully to bring all he could recover back with him to Boston; but Bellomont, distrusting Kidd's promises, and hearing also that the men left in charge of the vessel were reported to have carried off the goods and burnt the ship, refused to entertain his request. The governor was, however, successful in seizing some of the goods which Kidd had brought with him to Boston in the sloop, or had landed at various places on the coast, and these goods Bellomont retained posses-sion of until the receipt of instructions from England as to their disposal.

The uncertainty as to what became of the greater portion of the treasure, known to have been left by Captain Kidd on board the *Quedah Merchant*, has given rise to many a tradition and romantic story as to its supposed hiding places, the search after which by credulous fortune hunters has even taken place within quite recent years.

Kidd was ultimately taken as a prisoner to England on board a vessel sent from the West Indies for that purpose, and his arrival in London was eagerly awaited by the Tories, his crimes having been made use of by that political party as an excuse for discrediting Lord Somers, the Chancellor, and the other great Whig politicians, who had taken shares in the *Adventure Galley*. To effect this purpose, the following motion was brought forward in the House of Commons, on the 6th of December, 1699:

> That the Letters Patent granted to the Earl of Bellomont and others were dishonourable to the King, against the law of nations, contrary to the law and statutes of this realm, invasive of property, and destructive of trade and commerce.

A long debate ensued, in which the Tories strove their hardest to prove that Lord Somers and his colleagues had knowingly embarked in a criminal adventure, in order to enrich themselves by the profits arising out of Kidd's piracies. They further declared the king had no power to grant away the goods, even of pirates, before legal conviction, and therefore that the grant to Bellomont and his friends was illegal and contrary to the Bill of Rights. Well might a contemporary writer remark "that a heavier charge could not possibly be framed, and persons guilty to such a degree could not be punished too severely." But no unprejudiced person could for a moment have entertained the idea that an enterprise promoted by some of the highest ministers in the government, and encouraged by the king himself, was ever intended to have turned out in the way it did, and therefore the motion was negatived by a large majority.

The Tories, however, in their great anxiety to turn their political opponents out of office, did not mind what means they employed to accomplish that desirable object as long as they were successful, and therefore did not let this charge drop after their motion was defeated on the first attempt, but brought it forward again as soon as they heard Kidd's arrival was daily expected. This time they presented an address to the king, praying "that he might not be tried, discharged, or pardoned until the next session of Parliament, and that the Earl of Bellomont might transmit over all commissions, instructions, and other papers relating to him." The motive of this address, which was granted by the king on the 25th of March, 1700, was to cunningly convey the impression that "great things would appear when those papers were produced"; and the Tories also insinuated there was another commission and secret instructions of a dangerous nature not yet discovered.

Kidd was brought to London on the 12th of April, the day after the prorogation of Parliament, and two days later was privately examined in the presence of the Commissioners of the Admiralty. He was then sent to Newgate, where he remained a close prisoner for nearly a year, until the following spring, when the Commissioners of the Admiralty were ordered by the House of Commons to produce all the original documents forwarded by the Earl of Bellomont to Secretary Vernon, as well as the notes of the preliminary examination held by them in the previous year. Kidd was also brought to the bar of the House, and closely examined as to his knowledge of Lord Somers, the Duke of Shrewsbury, and the other ministers attacked by the Tories; and according to Bishop Burnet, the most nefarious attempts were made to induce the pirate to inculpate these persons.

> Their enemies [he says] tried again what use could be made of
> Kidd's business, for he was taken in our northern plantations in
> America, and brought over; he was examined by the House, but
> either he could not lay a probable story together, or some rem-
> nants of honesty, raised in him by the near prospect of death,
> restrained him; he accused no person of having advised or
> encouraged his turning pirate; he had never talked alone with
> any of the Lords, and never at all with Lord Somers; he said
> he had no orders from them, but to pursue his voyage against
> the pirates in Madagascar; all endeavours were used to persuade
> him to accuse the Lords; he was assured that if he did it, he
> should be preserved; and if he did it not, he should certainly die
> for his piracy; yet this could not prevail on him to charge them.
> So he, with some of his crew, were hanged, there appearing not
> so much as a colour to fasten any imputation on those Lords;
> yet their enemies tried, what use could be made of the grant of
> all that Kidd might recover from the pirates, which some bold
> and ignorant lawyers affirmed to be against law. So this matter
> was for the fourth time debated in the House of Commons, and
> the behaviour of those peers in it appeared to be so innocent,

so legal, and in truth so meritorious, that it was again let fall. The insisting so much on it served to convince all people that the enemies of these Lords wanted not inclinations, but only matter to charge them, since they made so much use of this; but so partial was a great part of the House, that the dropping this was carried only by a small majority.[12]

Livingston's unfortunate choice of a captain for the *Adventure Galley* had not only, as we have seen, gravely imperilled the existence of the Whig ministry, but also very nearly led to his own political ruin. For, on the Lords of Trade receiving Bellomont's report of Livingston's highhanded proceedings in demanding with threats the delivering up of his bond for £10,000, they wrote to him asking whether, after Mr. Livingston's conduct as reported by him, it would be wise to continue him in the Council and other public employment; and also expressed their wish to be informed as to "what proof has since been given of his in-nocency." Livingston's quarrel with Bellomont was, however, of very brief duration, for though the latter declined to deliver up the bond, which was despatched to England with the other documents connected with this unfortunate affair, he took no other measures against Livingston, whose services he still highly valued; and as long as Bellomont lived Robert Livingston retained the possession of all his numerous offices. So beyond the loss of his share of the money invested in the fitting out of the *Adventure Galley*, he lost nothing, as the payment of his bond was never demanded.

Notes

1. Though given as Robert in this sea ballad, Kidd's real Christian name was William.
2. Namely Mr. Johnston Livingston of New York. Unfortunately these journals are nearly undecipherable, except by an expert in handwriting, and they are also for the most part written in Dutch, which was the language preferred by Robert Livingston in his private correspondence. They have also suffered naturally from exposure and age. There are two journals. The first, all in Dutch, and mostly written in a cramped hand on twenty-one pages of foolscap paper in loose sheets, appears to have been compiled entirely at sea, having been commenced on the 11th of January, 1694–[5], over a month after leaving New York, and completed on the 9th of May, 1695, on the writer's landing in Portugal. The second Journal is written partly in Dutch and partly in English, and covers the period between the 9th of May and 3rd of October, 1695. See also next note.
3. The name of this place is nearly undecipherable in Mr. Livingston's journal, but is apparently as given in the text. The second journal, which commences on his landing in Portugal, bears the following title in Robert Livingston's handwriting:— *Journael van myn arrivement | in Portugal 9 May 1695 | Myn Reys nae d greyn, etc,*

etc, and is endorsed Dyary from ye 9 | May 1695 till ye 3 Octob. in Portugal and England. The diary however really terminates on the 12th of August, though at the end a few lines are devoted to his proceedings at Whitehall up to 3rd October, 1695.

4. Notably Poe's romantic tale *The Gold Beetle.*

5. The original of this curious document was forwarded by the Earl of Bellomont to Secretary Vernon in October, 1700, and though the author has searched for it in the Public Record Office, London, he has been unable to come across it. There is, however, a MS. copy, as well as copies of the other papers connected with it, still preserved in this institution, all of which will be found printed in extenso in *New York Colonial Documents,* vol. iv, pp. 762–5.

6. Robert Livingston to the Duke of Shrewsbury, New York, 20th September, 1696. Letter preserved among the Duke of Buccleuch's papers at Montague House, Whitehall.

7. It was in connection with the above charge of alienism that Robert Livingston wrote to his elder brother William in Edinburgh, for proofs of his Scottish birth and ancestry. The original of William's reply is still in existence, and the author has to thank Mr. Johnston Livingston—already mentioned for similar kind services—for a copy of this interesting letter. It is dated "Edinburgh, 13th December, 1698," and was printed by Mr. Sedgwick in his *Life of William Livingston,* from a copy made by him in 1811; but his version contains numerous misprints. Mr. Sedgwick, however, very truly remarks that the original letter "undoubtedly contains genealogical as well as heraldic blunders." It will be referred to again in the last chapter of this work, in connection with "The Heraldry of Livingston."

8. *Vide* Mr. Livingston's sworn deposition, dated 19th April, 1698, among the Colonial Records in Public Record Office, London.

9. Born 22nd May, 1698, and baptised two weeks later, died in infancy. This child died in infancy.

10. The *Adventure Galley* was a vessel of about 287 tons burthen, mounted 30 guns, and had quarters sufficient for a crew of 150 men.

11. From a contemporary account of this buccaneer's doings, entitled *A Full Account of the Proceedings in Relation to Captain Kidd,* as printed in the third volume of *State Tracts of William III.*

12. *Bishop Burnet's History of His Own Times,* vol. ii., pp. 265–266.

CHAPTER VII

Concerning the Founding by Robert Livingston, the Elder, of the Lordship and Manor of Livingston.

"Granted to be Purchased according to Law And upon a Survey thereof duly returned a Pattent to be graunted him for a Bowery or farme there as desired.

"New Yorke the 12th of Novembr. 1680.

"*E. Andross.*"

WITH the above words did Sir Edmund Andros, knight, and Governor-General under his Royal Highness, James, Duke of York, of New York and Dependencies in America, endorse "the humble petition of Robert Livingston of Albany," for permission to purchase some Indian land "lying upon Roelof Jansen's kill or creek, upon the east side of Hudson's River, near Catskill." From this petition of 1680 originated the historical Manor of Livingston. So before proceeding to relate the further fortunes of this cadet of the House of Callendar, it may be as well to give here a brief sketch of his career as a landowner, and the history of the founding of his manorial estate, with which he and his descendants have been so closely identified for such a length of time.

On his arrival at Albany in 1674, Livingston found the largest landed proprietors in the newly acquired Province were a few of the leading Dutch families, who held their immense estates by patents obtained from the former rulers of New Netherland, and which had been confirmed to them by the succeeding English governors. The largest of these estates was the celebrated colony of Rensselaerwyck, which had been founded as far back as the year 1630, and under the new government was erected into an English manor fifty-five years later. The Lord of the Manor, or Patroon as he was designated in the Dutch patents, possessed in the early days of the colony nearly all the feudal privileges of an ancient baron. According to Mr. Holgate he was by his charter "endowed with baronial honours." To quote from this writer's *American Genealogy*.

> The patroon's tenants owed him fealty and military service as vassals; all adjudications in his courts were final, with the exception of civil suits amounting to 50 guilders and upwards, when an appeal lay from the judgment of the patroon to the Director-General and Council, and it is probable that a similar remedy was also afforded in all criminal offences affecting "life and limb"; this being one of the modifications already engrafted upon the feudal sovereignties of Europe. The whole, as a political machinery, was admirable. The tenant on the manor acknowledges fealty to the patroon, while the latter acknowledged the same to the Director-General and Council, and the last to the Central Government. We thus have a subordinate sovereignty within a more extensive domain, and working in harmony with it, and the whole in harmony with the General Government.

The patroon also possessed the power of appointing his own civil and military, as well as judiciary officers, and had magazines, fortifications, and all the equipment of a feudal chieftain. All game, fish, minerals, etc., were the property of the patroon, and he held despotic sway over his little principality. When New Netherland was finally ceded to England, the original owners of these estates were left undisturbed by their new rulers; and though some of their feudal rights were not recognised by English law, still the privileges left to them were very extensive, as we shall see later on when describing the patents granted by the royal governors to Robert Livingston.

This individual, who, as we have already seen, was of an ambitious and enterprising disposition, quickly noticed the power conferred on these large landowners by their manorial privileges, and so hastened to lay the foundation of his own fortune by becoming a landed proprietor himself. Most of the lands in northern New York were at this period a wilderness, the portions most sought after being those bordering on the river Hudson, the great highway of communication between New York and Albany. Livingston therefore, in his constant journeys to and fro between these places, noticed that about forty miles south of the latter town and adjoining the colony of Rensselaerwyck, there was a tract of land possessing a valuable river frontage still unclaimed by any white man; and finding that the Indian owners were willing to part with the same for a consideration, he, in November 1680, petitioned Sir Edmund Andros, then Governor of New York, for the necessary permission, without which no land purchases from the natives were recognised.

From some cause or other, Livingston did not avail himself of this permission until the 12th of July 1683, when a deed of sale was executed by the Indian proprietors in the presence of the Commissioners at Albany, conveying to Livingston a tract of land amounting to 2000 acres in all, of which two hundred faced the Hudson, while the remaining and larger portion extended back into the woods. In payment for this estate, Livingston gave the Indians previous to the eighteenth of that month, when the sale was finally ratified by the vendors acknowledging themselves to be fully satisfied, the following goods:—

To wit, three hundred guilders in zewant, eight blankets, and two childrens' blankets, five and twenty ells of duffels, and four garments of Strouds, ten large shirts and ten small ditto, ten pairs of large stockings and ten pairs of small, six guns, fifty pounds of powder, fifty staves of lead, four caps, ten kettles, ten axes, ten adzes, two pounds of paint, twenty little scissors, twenty little looking-glasses, one hundred fish hooks, awls and nails of each one hundred, four rolls of tobacco, one hundred pipes, ten bottles, three kegs of rum, one barrel of strong beer, and twenty knives, four stroud coats and two duffel coats, and four tin kettles.

From Governor Dongan, Andros's successor, Livingston obtained, on the 4th of November 1684, a patent confirming to him and his heirs this purchase from the Indians, on the payment of an annual quit-rent of twenty shillings New York currency; which patent was the foundation of the future Manor. The desire to possess property in land when once indulged in, is a case of the old French saying that "the appetite comes with eating," and Livingston was no exception to this phase of the land hunger craze. It is therefore not surprising to find that the very day on which he obtained the above patent, he, in conjunction with some of his wife's relatives, the Schuylers, and others, also obtained from Dongan the grant of the celebrated Saratoga patent. Livingston had a one-seventh share in this last patent, which he subsequently made over to his son Gilbert. He later on acquired an additional fourteenth share, which he bequeathed under his will to his daughters, Mrs. Vetch and Mrs. Van Horne. In the following year he was granted permission by the governor to add to his estate on the banks of the Hudson a further six hundred acres, and from the list of the articles presented by him to the Indian owners as the purchase consideration for this additional acreage, called by the Indians Taghkanick, it appears the price of real estate had either risen considerably in value since his first purchase, or that the Indian vendors had become more astute in driving a bargain. Eight shillings current money of the Province of New York, payable annually on the twenty-fifth day of March at the town of Albany, was the small amount of quit-rent fixed as the royal dues on these additional six hundred acres.

Livingston was now as much entitled to claim manorial rights as any Dutch landowner; and he therefore applied to Dongan, and had no difficulty in obtaining from that governor a patent of the Lordship and Manor of Livingston. This patent, which is dated the 22nd of July, 1686, first of all recites the contents of the two former patents for the lands on Roelof Jansen's kill and Taghkanick, giving a list of all the boundaries as enumerated in those grants; and it then goes on to declare that, "whereas the said Robert Livingston hath been at vast charges and expense, in purchasing the said tracts and parcels of land from the native Indians, and also in settling and improving the same, and for encouraging the future settlement, the said Robert Livingston hath made application unto me [Dongan] that I might constitute and erect the said tracts or parcels of land within the bounds and limits aforesaid, to be a Lordship and Manor, and confirm the same unto him, his heirs and assigns, by patent under the seal of the Province."

Governor Thomas Dongan of New York (1634–1715). The Miriam and Ira D. Wallach Division of Art, Prints and Photographs: Print Collection, New York Public Library Digital Collections, Public Domain.

By this new patent Livingston was confirmed in the possession of all the rights of a freeholder as to timber, game, fishing, minerals, gold and silver mines excepted; while he was further granted, as Lord of the Manor, the privilege of holding a Court-Leet and a Court-Baron from time to time, with the right of issuing writs, levying and receiving fines; and all goods of felons forfeited within the limits of his manor became his property. He had also the right of patronage and advowson of all churches erected or to be erected on his lands; and his tenants also were allowed to choose assessors of taxes. In fact the remaining feudal privileges of the old country were by these patents transplanted to the new, where they existed for just a century, until swept away with other old customs when the colonies became independent of Great Britain. The only royalty Livingston had to pay for these valuable privileges was the before-mentioned annual quit-rent of twenty-eight shillings New York currency, equal to rather less than one pound sterling!

The uncertainty as to the original boundaries of his manor, owing to the difficulty in identifying the Indian landmarks, led Mr. Livingston, in 1713, to petition the government for a new patent. In this petition he asks permission "to amend any of the Indian names mentioned in the said [Dongan's] patent, where they are misspelled, and to make the limits and bounds of the said tract of land more perfect, and particularly by adding to the natural boundaries the courses and differences of the several lines comprehending with Hudson's river the whole of the said Manor of Livingston."

Governor Hunter, with the consent of his Council, had this petition and the former patents laid before the Attorney-General erf the Province for his opinion, and in due course, a confirmatory patent was drawn up, and received the royal assent; to which document the great seal of the Province of New York was affixed in the presence of the governor, on the 1st of October, 1715, and in the second year of the reign of His Majesty King George the First.

According to a survey held in 1714 to ascertain the exact extent of the manor lands, these were ascertained to cover 160, 240 acres. Six thousand acres included in this total, however, had been purchased by the government in 1710, as a settlement for the Palatines, and is now known as Germantown. This estate, under the terms of the new and royal patent, extended for nearly twelve miles along the eastern bank of the Hudson, and nineteen miles or more back into the woods, until it reached the Massachusetts boundary line, with which it marched for nearly twenty miles, having increased considerably in width as it receded from the river.[1]

In later years, the political opponents of the Livingston family used every endeavour to upset the validity of these manorial patents. And even after the Independence of the United States had become an accomplished fact, several of the tenants on the old manor petitioned the Legislature of the State of New York for an investigation into the then owners' title to the property, but the committee to whom the petition was referred reported against its being granted, and the House thereupon promptly dismissed it.[2] Since this date—1795—the validity of the Livingston title has successfully withstood all attacks; but owing to the Revolution having abolished the law of entail this extensive estate was divided fairly among his children by the will of the third proprietor, who died in 1790. Robert, the first Lord of the Manor, before entailing the bulk of this large estate on his eldest surviving son, Philip, bequeathed about thirteen thousand acres of it to his third son, and namesake, which went to form the estate of "Clermont," of which more hereafter.

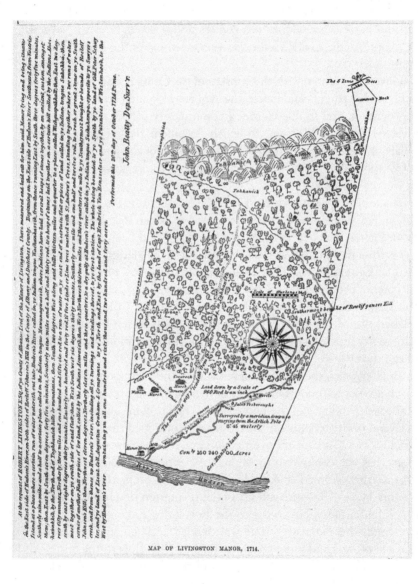

MAP OF LIVINGSTON MANOR, 1714.

Map of Livingston Manor, 1714, John Beatty, surveyor. Lionel Pincus and Princess Firyal Map Division, New York Public Library Digital Collections, Public Domain.

The later patent of 1715 also conferred on "the freeholders of the said Lordship and Manor" the great privilege of electing a "freeholder and inhabitant within the said Manor to be their representative and to sit and vote in the General Assembly of this Colony," and to rank in this respect of representation with the manors of Rensselaerwyck and Cortlandt, the former having been granted this right in 1685, and the latter in 1697.[3]

And thus did these three great manors under these grants become nothing better than "pocket boroughs"; as the freeholders, though nominally "free and independent electors," had no chance ever afforded them of returning a candidate of their own choice, but on all occasions dutifully sent the representative nominated by the Lord of the Manor to sit in the colonial House of Assembly. The representative thus elected was either the Lord of the Manor himself or some near relative; and for the sixty years the Manor of Livingston was represented in the House, its representatives, without a single exception, all bore the family surname. Another privilege allowed the inhabitants of the Manor by the Hunter Patent, was the annual appointment by them of "two constables for the said Manor, who shall use and exercise all the powers and authoritys of a constable during the year for which they shall be so chosen."

The value of this immense estate for many years did not amount to more than a few thousand dollars. In 1710, Livingston had received only £400 New York currency for the six thousand acres purchased of him by the government for the use of the Palatines. In reference to this sale, Mr. Sedgwick remarks in his *Life of William Livingston*, that, "though as the result of a government transaction it was probably a high one, gives the whole manor a value of between twenty-five and thirty thousand dollars. This is to be looked upon, however, as a nominal estimate; for even a generation after this, the dower of the widow of Philip, the second proprietor, in this extensive estate is said to have been but £90 currency per annum or about two hundred and fifty dollars. Governor Livingston, speaking of it in a letter to a son of the last proprietor, dated 10th November 1755, says, 'without a large personal estate, and their own uncommon industry and capacity for business, instead of making out of this extensive tract of land a fortune for their children, it would have proved both to your and my father but a competent maintenance.'"

No doubt, Robert Livingston, when applying for the above manorial patents, had pleasant dreams of founding in the new world a feudal estate fit to vie with that of his ancestors in the land of his birth. However "man proposes, but God disposes," and it is certainly a curious co-incidence that the year (1715) in which he obtained the last of these patents, was also the year so disastrous to the chiefs of his race in Scotland. And it is also a remarkable fact that while the Scottish Livingstons lost their titles and estates through abetting an unsuccessful rebellion, their American cousins were deprived of their manorial rights, by the very success of the revolution which they had so warmly espoused!

But more fortunate than their Scottish cousins, the American members of the Livingston family still own a fair share of their ancestral acres, which have directly descended to their present owners from the first Lord of the Manor. These acres, moreover, embrace the finest and most picturesque portion of this old estate, on the bank of the river facing the beautiful Catskill Mountains.[4]

Notes

1. The original patents of the years 1686 and 1715 are now in the possession of Mrs. Geraldyn Redmond. A reduced facsimile of the former one faces page 108. Mr. Beatty's original written report on his survey of the manor, dated 20th October, 1714 (but without the plan), as well as some field notes in the handwriting of Robert Livingston, are in the possession of the author. A facsimile of Mr. Beatty's plan is opposite this page.
2. For an account of the long dispute between the colonies of New York and Massachusetts concerning the boundary line, which ultimately resulted, in 1786, in the running of a new line reducing somewhat the manor acreage, see Chapter XIV.
3. The Manor of Livingston was the last of these New York manors to obtain this special distinction.
4. When writing his former work, the *Livingstons of Calendar*, the author was unaware that so large a portion of the manor estate was still in the possession of the first lord's descendants.

CHAPTER VIII

Concerning the Further Adventures and Death of Robert Livingston, the Elder, First Lord of the Manor of Livingston.

"A man that fortune's buffets and rewards
Hast ta'en with equal thanks."

—*Hamlet, Act. III., Scene ii.*

HAVING thus seen how Robert the Elder, the first of his race in America, had, with laudable ambition, become a Lord of the Manor with all the privileges appertaining thereto, we can now take up the narrative of his chequered career from the date of his arrival in Boston in the summer of 1699, for the purpose of demanding of the Earl of Bellomont the return of his bond for £10,000 liable to forfeiture through Captain Kidd's betrayal of his trust. Failing to persuade Bellomont to give up the bond, Livingston returned to Albany, where his services as Secretary for Indian Affairs were soon to be again in great request.

Owing to the Peace of Ryswick, there was for a brief period a cessation of the usual state of war between the two great European powers in North America; but Count Frontenac, the able Governor of Canada, considered this truce a splendid opportunity for bringing pressure to bear on the warlike Iroquois, so as to compel them to give up their alliance with the English. To counteract these French intrigues, Robert Livingston and his brother-in-law Colonel Peter Schuyler, together with one Hendrick

Hansen, were sent by the Governor of New York in the spring of 1700, on a special mission to the Indian village or castle of Onondaga. Mr. Livingston, in his report of this mission, says they found the Maquas much weakened by the late war, and daily being drawn under French influence to take shelter in Canada. He also states he much feared the great power exercised over the Indians by the Jesuit priests, while he lamented the fact that the English colonies neglected to send Protestant ministers to counteract their evil influence. The bitter, and one might say also bigoted, hatred which the Puritan colonists entertained towards these, for the most part, self-sacrificing French missionaries, many of them men of dauntless courage and simple faith, who willingly suffered the most horrible of martyrdoms in their praiseworthy attempts to win the natives from heathenism, is plainly shown in this report. For Livingston declares in all honesty of belief, that he had heard, "the Jesuits of Canada are so cunning as to have their share of whatever an Indian hunts, which is brought and laid before the image of the Virgin Mary in the church, and this being done they have not only remission of their sins, but her prayers to the bargain for good luck when they go a hunting next time."

He also remarks that "it's strange to think what authority these priests have over their Indian proselytes; they carry a chain in their pocket, and correct the Indians upon the commission of any fault, which they bear very patiently." He also further adds that if "ministers were once settled among them it would not only be a pious work in converting them to the Christian Faith, which honour would redound to his Majesty and the English nation in general, but would keep those whom we have firm to us, draw the rest home that have gone to Canada, and prevent *that diabolical practice which they have got of late in poisoning one another, by which means most of those that were true to the English interest are dispatched out of the way.*"[1]

The Earl of Bellomont highly approved of the manner in which Livingston and his fellow-commissioners had fulfilled their duties during these difficult negotiations, and frankly acknowledged to the Home Government that the result of their mission was "the hindring the Indians from a revolt to the French."

To confirm the Indians in their alliance with the English colonies, Bellomont paid, what turned out to be his last visit to Albany, in the month of August in this year; and in his report of his conference with the Indian sachems the hard-worked governor pathetically laments over the hardships he had to undergo on this occasion. The conference, he says, "lasted seven or eight days and was the greatest fatigue I ever underwent in my whole life.

I was shut up in a close chamber with 50 sachems, who, besides the stink of bear's grease with which they plentifully daub'd themselves, were continually either smoaking tobacco or drinking drams of rum. They seem'd sullen and out of humour at first, but by degrees I brought 'em to perfect good temper. I am told there never appeared so many sachems at any conference as at this. There were about 200 men, women, and children, and't was with some difficulty we could find 'em in victuals."

On his return to New York, Bellomont found fresh troubles awaiting him; for what with his enemies in England trying to disgrace him in the eyes of the King by charging him with a guilty knowledge of Kidd's piracies, and the opposition raised in New York by a small but powerful party against his crusade for "the breaking" of the large land grants, the harassed governor found little rest. There is no doubt but that his end was hastened by all these worries, as he died on the 5th of March 1701 from an attack of gout, after a very brief illness.[2] The earl's death proved an immense misfortune to Livingston, and was also a cause of a split in the Council, which, for a time, owing to the absence of Lieutenant-Colonel Nanfan, the lieutenant-governor, brought on a renewal of the old quarrel between the two political factions in the province—Leislerians and Anti-Leislerians. The former party, which had four of its members on the Council, insisted that the government during the lieutenant-governor's absence devolved of right upon the majority in the Council; while the latter maintained that Colonel William Smith, as the senior member on the Board, was the person properly entitled to act as governor until the return of Nanfan from Barbadoes, whither he had gone on private business. Livingston, his relative Colonel Peter Schuyler, and Colonel Smith, the president, were the minority members. These appealed to England for a decision in their favour; but the Lords of Trade, as well as the colonial House of Assembly, decided that the right of government under the above circumstances belonged to the majority of the Council. Thus Livingston found himself once more in opposition to his old enemies, who lost no time in abusing their accession to power by taking proceedings to crush him, and other individuals obnoxious to the new government.

One of their first proceedings, therefore, was to call upon Livingston to account to them for the public money, which he had received in his capacity as Commissioner of Excise. This he flatly declined to do, not considering that the majority of the Council had any authority over him, and rightfully regarding their interference with his affairs as a settled plan of the Leislerian faction to discredit him with the Home Government.

The Leislerians were however successful in obtaining a majority also in the new House of Assembly, which met on the 19th of August, and two days later persuaded Nanfan to appoint a Committee of Council to audit the public accounts in conjunction with a Committee, which had already been nominated by the Assembly. Before this tribunal Livingston at first indignantly refused to appear when summoned; and when at last he was induced to attend, he was unable to produce all his accounts and vouchers, as most of these had been delivered up to the late Earl of Bellomont in 1698, who had omitted to return them. But he offered to exhibit to any member of the joint Committees who would call upon him, the papers still in his possession; and asked for time to enable him to obtain copies of the other accounts demanded. This the Committee of Inquiry refused to grant, deeming his excuses "frivolous," and considering his conduct "a determination not to render an account," and thereupon recommended to the Assembly the confiscation of his estate.

Not content with having accused him of dishonesty in his accounts, Livingston's enemies further charged him with having abused his office of Secretary for Indian Affairs, by alleging that he had privately solicited the Indians to obtain permission for his being sent to England to advocate their interests before the King; and being without any proofs of this serious accusation the Committee coolly called upon him to clear himself "by taking a voluntary oath before some person authorised to administer the same." To this insolent demand Livingston contemptuously replied "that he thought it not worth his while to do the same."

So determined, however, were the Leislerians in the Assembly that he should not escape punishment, that on finding he was not to be intimidated by the proceedings of the Committee of Inquiry, they drew up a petition, which was duly presented to Nanfan, praying him to advise the King to have the obstinate and fearless Scotchman deprived of his secretaryship; and not to lose time in securing his disgrace, being probably afraid of the influence he possessed at Court, they urged upon the lieutenant-governor the necessity of having him "suspended from the same until his majesty's pleasure shall be known."

Even these extreme proceedings did not satisfy the rancorous hate of his political opponents; for, influenced by the fear that either the King might disregard their petition, or aware that Nanfan did not share their opinion as to Livingston's guilt,[3] they hastened to introduce in the House of Assembly, on the 12th of September 1701, the day after Livingston had so scornfully declined to take the desired oath, a special act aimed against the object of their vindictive pursuit, entitled "An Act to oblige Robert Livingston to account." This Act, which having passed through all its stages received the reluctant lieutenant-governor's assent on the 18th of October, certainly did not err on the side of mercy. For by its conditions Livingston's estate was made liable for the sum of £17,000; while in the event of his not being able to render a full and satisfactory account of his public expenditure by the 25th of March following, his whole estate, real and personal, was to be confiscated. It was entirely owing to Nanfan's personal intercession that this slight extension of time was granted. But these few months of grace were of little avail, as Livingston, for the reasons already given, was utterly unable to comply with the terms of this harsh and stringent Act within the time named,—as his persecutors were perfectly well aware of,—and in consequence he was remorselessly deprived of the hard-earned fruits of nearly thirty years' incessant toil, and found himself brought to the verge of ruin, and his character disgraced through the machinations of party malice.

Many men in his position would have despaired of ever again retrieving their shattered fortunes, but the adventurous and shrewd secretary was made of sterner stuff, and only awaited a favourable opportunity to triumphantly clear his character from the aspersions cast upon it by his enemies; and to recover by the means of his English friends, the offices and estate of which he had been so unjustly deprived. A proof of his energetic character and remarkable aptitude for business is to be found in the fact, that within a few weeks of Bellomont's death, and while his foes were using every endeavour to crush and disgrace him, he had drawn up a lengthy and interesting report on the state of the province for the guidance of the Lords of Trade. From this document we learn that at this period the provincial currency had still further depreciated; that clothing and drink cost double the prices paid in England; that a pot of beer in New York cost $4\frac{1}{2}$ d; and that while a labouring man could earn three shillings currency as daily wages, a soldier's weekly pay only amounted to six pence more, so that in consequence it was difficult to prevent the latter from deserting. He pointed out, moreover, that European soldiers were unsuited for Indian warfare, as their training spoilt them for the system of fighting that had to be adopted for use in the American forests; and he strongly advised the Home Government not to augment the forces already in the province by the addition of fresh companies from England; but that instead, one-half of the number of the soldiers already in the province should be disbanded, and the men thus released from their military duties, granted lands on the frontier and encouraged to settle, so that they would soon learn, under the guidance of the youth of Albany, the art of Indian fighting. Then their places in the ranks could be filled by fresh recruits from the mother-country; and that this should be repeated every two years, by which means the Canadian frontier would be materially strengthened by these new settlements. He also expressed the opinion that forts should be built in the Indian country for the protection of trade, and to prevent the natives from dealing with the French. Livingston's practical knowledge of the all-important Indian question was undoubted, and his report, therefore, must have been of considerable use to the Lords of Trade.[4]

During the summer of this year he also rendered great services to Nanfan, while the latter was engaged in treating with the Indians; and it was during one of these conferences, held by the acting governor at Albany, that the Indians expressed their desire that their secretary might be sent to "Corachoo, the great King of England," to acquaint him as to how the French were steadily encroaching on their territories, and which request, as already mentioned, led the Leislerians to accuse Livingston of having used undue influence with the natives to advance his own selfish aims. Nanfan's rule was not to be of long duration, for the King, on the 13th of June in this same year (1701), informed the Lords of Trade through Secretary Hedges, that he had been pleased to appoint Lord Cornbury to the vacant post, and that he wished them to draw up the necessary commission and instructions for the new governor. This nobleman was a grandson of the great Earl of Clarendon, the celebrated Chancellor and historian of the Civil War; but he possessed none of his grandfather's genius, and obtained the appointment solely through his having deserted the service of James II for that of his more fortunate son-in-law, William of Orange. While on his voyage to New York his royal patron died, but Queen Anne on her accession to the throne, immediately confirmed his commission. The new governor landed in New York on the 3rd of May 1702.

His arrival was a most fortunate circumstance for Livingston, as Lord Cornbury strongly objected to the proceedings of the Leislerian majority on the Council, and almost immediately after his arrival, out of deference to the wishes of the principal inhabitants of the province, had their most prominent members deprived of their seats at the Council Board, until receipt of instructions from home. He also interested himself directly in Livingston's case, by calling upon the widowed Countess of Bellomont to deliver up all his vouchers and papers in her possession, which were at once, on the 18th of June, submitted to a committee for examination; and on this committee expressing themselves satisfied that the papers were in order, his estate was restored to him on the 2nd of February following. Though so much justice was meted out to him through the influence of Lord Cornbury, Livingston still found himself suspended from his various official appointments, and thus was not only deprived of the salaries in connection with those offices, which in spite of his suspension he continued to fill, but he was also owed for salaries due before the Leislerians had procured his dismissal, besides liabilities incurred on behalf of the troops, which were still unsettled. To procure his proper re-instatement in these offices, and the payment of the large sums of money still owing, Livingston set out on his second visit to England, where he landed in July 1703, after another adventurous voyage.

On this occasion, Livingston did certainly escape the horrors of starvation and shipwreck suffered by him on his former voyage to England eight years before, but only to undergo perils of another description. For when within sight of the island of Lundy at the entrance of the Bristol Channel, and thus close to his journey's end—as the vessel he was on board, the *Thetis*, a sloop of 50 tons, was bound for Bristol,—a French privateer gave chase, and after a brief fight soon compelled the little *Thetis* to strike her flag. The noise of the firing, however, fortunately for Livingston and his companions, attracted the notice of an English frigate cruising in the vicinity, which, giving chase, quickly compelled the Frenchman to abandon his prize, but not until he had plundered his victims of everything that was worth carrying off. In a letter to the Lords of Trade, written the day after his adventure with the privateer, Livingston bitterly complains of the manner in which he had been treated by his captors, who had even carried off with them the chest containing his accounts and books, which he had brought with him from America for the purpose of submitting to their Lordships in substantiation of his claims. As this letter may be of some interest to his descendants, as a reminiscence of an adventure which was not of uncommon occurrence when the Atlantic trade was carried on by vessels of the *Thetis* class, which had little chance of escaping from the hungry privateers, that during the constant wars between England and France swarmed in the narrow seas, it is given here as copied from the original in the Public Record Office, London.

May it please Your Lordships.

This is to accompany Your Lordships' packet from my Lord Cornbury, Govemr. for N. Yorke, which we, with much difficulty sav'd from being taken by the French, who took ye sloop I came in called the Thaetis, burthen 50 tuns Nicolas Tien—hove commandr. in sight of ye Island Lundye, yesterday, wch is 25 leagues from Bristoll, whither we were bounde. We sailed from N. York ye a June and on ye 8 July being yesterday morng made ye Island of Lundye, but happened to see a saile to winderd asson as we spy'd ye land, who chas'd and came up with us about 9 o'clock in ye morning, we being a small vessel and but 11 hands gave ye privateer severall gunns, but he having 6 guns, 4 patter-eroes, and 50 men, soon master'd us with his small shott, being one Capt. Francois la Marque, belonging to Rochecaux in France, and after he had taken us, us'd us very barbarously, for we redeemed ye sloop for £450 sterlg; and gave a pledge, and after yt he had pass'd his word of honor not to meddle with us, not only plunder'd ye sloop and took every thing he could carry, away, but search'd our pockets and took all from us, and turn'd us adrift, there being a saile in sight, wch prooved ye Rye Frigat, who is gone after him. I wish he may be so fortunate to take him, for he is a great plague to these parts, and besides all I have lost he hes got several books and accounts in my chest, that trouble me much.

My Lords, I have been a servant to ye Crowne 28 yeares in that Province and have launched out all ye small fortune I have, and run my self deeply in debt for victualling Her Majes. forces and other Publick Services, and was now constrained to leave my family and concerns to come for England to gett those debts due to me from ye Crowne, and have unfortunately met with this disaster; but I hope your Lordships will, after you are throwly inform'd of my circumstances, be my intercessors to Her Majesty for releefe. We lye here for a winde to goe to Bristoll, from whence I make haste to wait upon your Lordships to give an account of ye affaires of our Province. We have had no disturbance from ye French of Canada, yet, they having had a great mortality amongst them, both Christians and Indians. Our Indians of ye 5 nations prove true hitherto, but are much tamper'd withall by ye French, wch causes many to waver. I shall not trouble yr Lordships any further at present, but remain with great respect,

May it please your Lordps,
>   Your Lordships most humble
>   and most obedient Servant,
>   Robt. Livingston.

Clovally in ye
>   County of Devon,
>   near Lundy, 9 July 1703.
>   For the Right Honble the Lords

Commissioners for Trade and Forreign Plantations. At Whitehall.

Livingston on his arrival in London was well received by the Lords of Trade, but he had to undergo the usual wearisome delays entailed on any claimant, who in those days, or even in these for that matter, seeks justice at the hands of a Government Department. His claims having been examined by the Board of Trade, were referred to Lord Godolphin, Lord High Treasurer of England, who in turn submitted them to the Attorney General for his consideration. They were also referred to the Paymaster-General of the Forces—the Earl of Ranelagh—and to the Secretary-at-War. The result of all these various examinations and reports was favourable to the pertinacious claimant, who not only obtained—on the 11th of January 1705—an Order in Council restoring to him his office of Secretary for Indian Affairs; but he was also ultimately successful in having the greater portion of his claims against the Government for victualling the troops, etc., allowed by the Treasury. And further, on the 29th of September following, Queen Anne granted "To our Trusty and Well-beloved Robert Livingston," from her Court at Windsor, a fresh commission reinstating and confirming him in all the offices previously held by him, "with the said respective fees, salaries, perquisites, and advantages."

Apparently, if it had not been for needless obstructions thrown in Mr. Livingston's way by some of the junior clerks of the Treasury, of which he makes complaint in a letter to his friend Governor Fitz-John Winthrop, he would probably have obtained a quicker settlement, as both Lord Godolphin and Mr. Lowndes were friendly disposed towards him. During his stay in London Livingston impressed upon the Government the great advantages to be derived from the conquest of Canada, and expressed the opinion that a small naval expedition, consisting of a few frigates and a single regiment to be provided by England, would be sufficient, in conjunction with a force composed of colonists and friendly Indians, to effect this desirable object. The memorial, stating his ideas as to this contemplated expedition, was forwarded by the Lords of Trade to Lord Cornbury, who, however, did not consider the force mentioned by Livingston would be sufficient, as since the failure of Phipps' unfortunate attempt the French had considerably strengthened the fortifications of Quebec. The projected invasion of Canada was therefore postponed for a time. Mr. Livingston also interested himself during this visit, in calling the attention of the Lords of Trade to the scarcity of missionaries among the Indians, and by the advice of the Bishop of London he saw the Society for the Propagation of the Gospel in Foreign Parts, who at once provided two clergymen for the work at a salary of £100 per annum each, but were unable to send four others, as requested by Livingston, owing to their lack of funds.

On his return to America in 1707 Livingston caught a complaint then very prevalent in New York, which prevented him from taking immediate steps to reap the benefit of his journey to England. He found that during his absence Lord Cornbury had become most unpopular, and his foolish habit of dressing up in female attire is noticed by him in a letter to Mr. Lowndes, of Her Majesty's Treasury, in which he describes some of the reasons for the governor's unpopularity. "Most people," Livingston writes, "were then very uneasy under this gentleman's administration"; he was said to have misappropriated public money for his own use, and "that he was wholly addicted to pleasure and enriching himself with strange and unheard of methods, having some few creatures about him whose counsel he pursued, to the great grief of the principal inhabitants. His dressing himself in women's clothes was so unaccountable that if hundreds of spectators did not daily see him it would be incredible. After dinner till twelve at night was spent at the bottle."

The people, he also wrote, complained of his relationship to Queen Anne, "but they hoped," he rather quaintly added, "God would send a deliverance."

Lord Cornbury's reception of Livingston on his return from London was not at all a friendly one, and quite different from what the latter had expected to receive. On his presenting the governor with his new royal commission his lordship declined to act upon it, and also refused to return the document when requested; so that Livingston was compelled to write to London for fresh instructions, and to complain of Cornbury's conduct; "who," he declared, "regarded no order from Court," and treated the queen's commands as if they had been but so much "waste paper." Fortunately for the writer, Queen Anne did not consider that the governor's relationship to her royal person was any reason why he should continue thus to disgrace the governorship of New York by such extravagances, and therefore had him removed and Lord Lovelace appointed in his place. The latter nobleman dying soon after his arrival, the administration again passed for a time into the hands of Colonel Ingolds-by, the then lieutenant-governor.

Ingoldsby filled the office until the arrival of the new governor from home, which event took place in the following June twelvemonth (1710), when Colonel Robert Hunter, bearing the royal commission, landed in New York. Colonel Hunter was a governor of quite a different stamp to his predecessor Lord Cornbury, and he brought with him to America the character of a gentleman and a brave soldier to boot. The new governor quickly discovered his office was no sinecure, but he was not the type of man to idle away his time in New York, when his presence was urgently needed at Albany, where the Indians were getting restive, and required a firm hand to quiet them. While at Albany Hunter first became acquainted with his fellow-countryman, the Secretary for Indian Affairs, who not only rendered him great assistance in quieting the Indian sachems, but was also able to help the governor in another matter, which was causing him much anxiety at this time, and which was subsequently to cause him still greater embarrassment.

It appears that before leaving England Colonel Hunter had received special instructions to provide suitable lands in his government for some three thousand unfortunate German refugees, or "Palatines," as they were called, who, having been driven from their native villages by the French army of invasion, had sought assistance from their English allies. The English government agreed to send them to America, on the condition that these refugees were to be employed in the production of masts, tar, and other ships' stores for their naval dockyards; and for this purpose Governor Hunter was instructed to secure suitable lands for these poor emigrants, where they could obtain the necessary materials for carrying on the required work. As the ships with these unfortunate exiles had left England about the same time as himself, Hunter had very little leisure in which to select a suitable site for this purpose; and if Livingston had not placed at his disposal a tract of land consisting of six thousand acres on the banks of the Hudson, he would have found it very difficult to have obtained what he required, as nearly all the best land on the banks of this river had already been taken up by private owners. For this large tract of land Hunter paid £400 New York currency, equal to about £266 sterling—not a very high price, even in those days of cheap land; and owing to its proximity to the river and its pine woods, as Hunter informed the Board of Trade, it was very suitable for the purpose for which it had been purchased. These six thousand acres were taken off the western portion of the manor, and now comprise the town of Germantown.

Besides purchasing of Livingston this estate, Hunter subsequently arranged with him to victual the Palatines for six months "with bread and beer." He was also appointed one of the Commissioners for managing these new arrivals, and as these people were not at all inclined to fulfil their part of the bargain with the English government, much trouble ensued, and the poor governor was nearly driven distracted in his endeavours to bring them to reason, and by his having also to advance the necessary cash for their victualling out of his private purse, as the home authorities, owing to political changes, calmly disregarded the drafts he had drawn on them for this purpose. To keep the peace a guard of soldiers had to be kept at the manor; and during his constant journeys up and down the river between New York and Albany, the governor was often the guest of Robert Livingston, under the hospitable roof of the old manor house. During one of these visits the Palatines formed a plot to seize him, but having received timely warning Hunter sent an urgent message to the Mayor of Albany to have him furnish the soldiers garrisoning that place with the necessary sloops, boats, and canoes, for their conveyance at once to Livingston Manor. The arrival of these reinforcements enabled the governor to turn the tables on the riotous Germans, who were thereupon followed to their settlement by the soldiers and disarmed. This salutary lesson restored order for a time, and the work of making pitch and tar was resumed, but this German colony never ceased to be a thorn in Hunter's flesh.

The Home Government eventually discovered, that their plan for producing naval stores for the royal dockyards by the assistance of these German emigrants was a very expensive business, for it is said, their subsistence for several years cost £20,000 beyond what the produce of their labour realised; and so orders were finally given to have their indentures cancelled, and the entire system of forced labour abolished. The change from compulsory service to that of freedom to work for themselves had its natural effect, so that the discontented Palatines soon became hardworking and thriving colonists.

Hunter was not ungrateful to Livingston for his assistance, and one of his earliest measures, after assuming the government, was to forward, with his strong recommendation, to the Lords of Trade, an Act in favour of the latter, which had been passed by the colonial House of Assembly during the previous year. This Act was the outcome of the strong personal influence now wielded by Robert Livingston in the lower House, for since April 1709, he had sat therein, as one of the two representatives for the city and county of Albany. Its purport was the repeal of the "Act to oblige Robert Livingston to account" passed eight years previously. For though his estates, which had been sequestrated under the authority of the Act of 1701, had been restored to him by the action of Lord Combury, yet the Act itself remained on the statute book, and Livingston was naturally enough anxious to obtain its removal. Hunter, moreover, confidently expressed the opinion, that after reading this later Act, their lordships themselves "would think it reasonable to offer it to Her Majesty for her approbation."

This governor's friendship did not end here, for it was owing to his influence that the confirmatory patent of the Manor of Livingston—already referred to in the previous chapter—was granted to Robert Livingston in 1715. It was in virtue of the powers conferred by his last patent, that he was elected in the year following to a seat in the New York Assembly, as the first representative for his own manor, which from this date until the Revolution, became a regular "Pocket Borough." Livingston was not a stranger to the House, as he had already sat in it for two years,— from the 5th of April 1709 until the 20th of April 1711,— as one of the representatives for the city and county of Albany, as mentioned above. In the occupation of this latter seat, he was succeeded by his nephew and namesake Robert Livingston, the Younger. Though the seventeenth Assembly, to which the senior Robert had been returned as the representative of his manor, met on the 5th of June 1716, he did not put in an appearance until the 10th of May following, when, after some debate, he was allowed to take his seat on the next day as a duly qualified member, on his taking "the oaths and signing the test according to law." He, however, with his usual energy soon became one of its most active members, and on the retirement of Mr. William Nichol from the office of Speaker twelve months later, Livingston was chosen by a plurality of votes to be his successor. For seven years Mr. Livingston discharged the duties of this honorable office with dignity and credit, until failing health compelled him to retire from active life, whereupon the House "desired he would nevertheless assist them as a member as often as his state of health would admit him, during his stay in town."

Governor Hunter had made his farewell speech to the House of Assembly on the 24th of June 1719, prior to his return to England, and in reply, Livingston, as Speaker, expressed the grateful thanks of the House for the great services he had rendered to the province during his term of office. This reply, though written and read by Livingston, is said to have been the joint production of the Speaker and the Chief-Justice—Colonel Lewis Morris,—and was as follows:—

Sir, when we reflect upon your past conduct, your just, mild, and tender administration, it heightens the concern we have for your departure, and makes our grief such as words cannot truly express. You have governed well and wisely, like a prudent magistrate, like an affectionate parent; and wherever you go, and whatever station the Divine Providence shall please to assign you, our sincere desires and prayers for the happiness of you and yours, shall always attend you. We have seen many governors, and may see more; and as none of those, who had the honour to serve in your station, were ever so justly fixed in the affections of the governed, so those to come will acquire no mean reputation, when it can be said of them, their conduct has been like yours. We thankfully accept the honour you do us, in calling yourself our countryman; give us leave, then, to desire, that you will not forget this is your country, and, if you can, make haste to return to it. But if the service of our sovereign[5] will not admit of what we so earnestly desire, and his demands deny us that happiness, permit us to address you as our friend, and give us your assistance, when we are oppressed with an administration the reverse of yours.

As William Smith, the colonial historian, truly remarks in his account of this incident, that "whether Mr. Hunter deserved the eulogium they bestowed upon him, I leave the reader to determine, it is certain that few plantation governors have the honour to carry home with them such a testimonial as this."[6]

Colonel Hunter's successor was William Burnet, a son of the celebrated bishop, who took such a leading part in the proceedings which secured the Protestant succession to the throne of England, and of which he was also the historian. Burnet assumed the government on the 17th September 1720, and found as usual a capable and willing adviser in Robert Livingston; but the latter, owing to advancing age, found himself not strong enough to continue to perform all the numerous duties attaching to his various offices, and therefore placed his resignation as Secretary for Indian Affairs, Town Clerk of Albany, etc., in the hands of the new governor, at the same time expressing the wish that those offices might be conferred on his eldest surviving son Philip, who had acted as his deputy for many years. This natural desire of Livingston to secure the reversion of these posts to his son, met with Burnet's warm approval, who considered, as he wrote to the Lords of Trade, that as Robert Livingston had been of the greatest use to him, both in the House of Assembly and in explaining to him on his arrival the true position of Indian affairs, and that as his son is "a worthy capable man," he thought the latter fully deserved, and he could earnestly recommend him for these offices.

The Lords of Trade fully endorsed Governor Burnet's opinion as to the elder Livingston's services, and in addressing the king, George the First, concerning the appointment of his successor, expressed the hope that his majesty "would be graciously pleased to grant the said places to his son Philip, in the same manner as he enjoyed them." In their report the Lords of Trade laid stress on the fact that the father had been "very serviceable ever since the year 1675, in all the transactions and treaties with the Five Nations of Indians at New York." The king, duly granted Mr. Livingston's request, though the latter's enemies in New York freely grumbled at the preference shown to "Old Livingston" by the Home Government.

For the next few years Livingston, as Speaker, was very regular in his attendance at the House of Assembly, until his increasing infirmities obliged him also to be relieved of this honourable office. This happened, as already related, in the autumn of 1725, and three years later he died at the ripe age of seventy-three.[7] By his will, executed at the Manor on the 2nd of August 1728, and proved in New York on the 15th of October in the same year, the first Lord entailed the bulk of his large estate, together with the Manor House, on his eldest surviving son Philip; while that portion lying to the south-west of Roelof Jansen's Kill, which, after the deduction of the six thousand acres sold to the government, consisted of about thirteen thousand acres, was settled on his third son, "Robert Livingston jun. of New York, merchant"; and to Gilbert, his fourth son, was bequeathed his seventh part (Lot No. 5) in the Saratoga land grant. There were also other bequests, but these were only of minor importance.[8]

Notes

1. The words printed in italics in the text are underlined by Mr. Livingston in his report.
2. Bellomont held the opinion, that the immense grants of land conferred by some of his predecessors on a few favoured individuals, greatly retarded the progress of the colony. In one of his despatches he refers to Livingston's "great grant of 16 miles long and 24 broad"; on which he has "but four or five cottages, men that live in vassalage under him, and work for him, and are too poor to be farmers, having not wherewithal to buy cattle to stock a farm."
3. Nanfan reported to the Lords of Trade, under date 21 August in this same year, that he found Livingston of great service to him, and fully deserving of his salary

as Secretary for Indian Affairs, and that he knew of "no person in the Town and County of Albany so capable and well qualified as he is for this post."

4. Letter dated 13th May 1701. In this same letter Robert Livingston submitted a scheme for the union of the colonies for mutual defence.

5. George the First.

6. Smith, *History of Now York*, p. 227.

7. Robert Livingston is said to have died at Boston, Mass., on 1 October, 1728. He was buried in his family vault on the manor, over which the Livingston Memorial Church has been erected in recent years.—See *Livingstons of Callendar*, p. 396.

8. The original will is in the possession of Mr. John Henry Livingston of Clermont.

CHAPTER IX

Concerning the Family of Robert, First Lord of the Manor of Livingston, and his Immediate Successors.

"Like leaves on trees the race of man is found,—
Now green in youth, now withering on the ground;
Another race the following spring supplies:
They fall successive, and successive rise."

—*Pope.*

ROBERT, the Elder, was the father of nine children, of whom five survived him.[1]

Johannes or John, the eldest son, was born on the 26th of April 1680, and was baptised on the following Sunday, when, in accordance with an old Scottish custom, he was so named after his paternal grandfather, the celebrated Rev. John Livingston of Ancrum. Though the eldest son, he has received very scant notice in any hitherto published accounts of the American Livingstons. By many writers he has been ignored altogether, while others have credited his younger and better-known brother Philip with some of his exploits, probably owing to the fact that, though twice married, John left no issue, and dying within his father's lifetime he never became identified with the Manor of Livingston.

The first mention of this son after the record of his birth, so duly entered as above in the family Bible, occurs in the autumn of 1690, when his father had to fly for the second time to the neighbouring colony of Connecticut, so as to escape from the persecutions of the dictator Leisler. He took refuge in Hartford, where he was joined later on by his wife and children; and on their return home on the downfall of Leisler, as already related in a previous chapter, their eldest son was left behind under the care of his father's staunch friend, Fitz-John Winthrop, in the hope that the boy, then ten years of age, would benefit from the better education to be obtained in those days in the New England colony. This hope, however, does not appear to have been realised, for on John's return home, after spending a year at Hartford, Winthrop writes to the lad's father,

> Noe consideration but ye sence of his mother's sorrow for his absence should perswade me to venture him thus late in ye yeare, being yet under ye distemper of a feavour and ague, but, I thank God, pretty moderate, and I am sure Mr. Young will be careful of him. I have allsoe to tell you, to my sorrow, that his improvement in his learning is not soe much as I expected, and can only blame the carelessness of ye master, and since his goeing out of towne here has been noe opportunity for his advantage.

Three years later John accompanied his father to England, on which voyage, as already related, they were shipwrecked on the coast of Portugal. After their return to America, John paid further visits to his New England friends, and as Fitz-John Winthrop had an only daughter, these visits naturally resulted in a closer alliance between the families. Among the Winthrop family papers is still preserved the letter which Governor Fitz-John Winthrop wrote to Mrs. Robert Livingston after the marriage of their children had been celebrated, and which letter the newly married couple are supposed to have carried with them on their wedding journey to Albany. It is addressed "For Madam Alida Livingston, at Albany," and is as follows:

> Deare Madam, —Since it hath pleased God by his providence to dispose the affections of your son and my daughter to each other, and that by your concurrence they are now joyned together in marriage, let us pray that they may be a blessing to one another, and to yourselves and us allsoe, and I am sure noething will be wanting in her to contribute to it with all dutyfull respects. You will find in her a temper fit for the impression

of all good, and your dictates and insinuations will be commandos to her; and being now your owne and most deare to us, we doe earnestly recommend her to your love and affection, which will be soe much the more generous, as she is a stranger and far from her relations. I have great hope of their happiness from their endeared affection to each other, and from the many good qualifications which I have observed in your son, which has greatly endeared him to me, and soe much soe, that I have but one affection for them both. And now, Madam, being related to you in a neerer than the neere relation of friendship, I will take all opportunity to express my sence of it, and that it will very much please me to be called—your most affectionate Brother, J. Winthrop.—New London, Aprill, 1701.

Young Livingston's connection with the Winthrop family must have been the cause of his obtaining a commission in the Connecticut militia, instead of in that of his native colony. In 1704, while holding the rank of captain in that service, he accompanied Nathan Gold on a mission to the Five Nations, in conjunction with the commissioners sent by Governor Dudley of Massachusetts. This mission evidently did not meet with the approval of Lord Cornbury, the Governor of New York, who was not only jealous of the neighbouring New England colonies, but who also dreaded any outside interference with this Indian Confederation, which probably accounts for his bitter attack on the Connecticut commissioners in a letter of complaint concerning them, which he sent to Governor Winthrop. In this letter he accuses Captain Gold of "pretending to preach and cant in our streets here." While of Captain Livingston, who had fallen foul of the irate governor on a former occasion by recruiting New York militiamen for his own regiment, he wrote:

> Mr. Levingston had best take care how he manages himself upon this journey. I have given him fair warning, and I hope he will be wiser than he has been; for it is certainly true that nothing should have saved him this time from the punishment he deserves, but purely the respect I shall be always ready to shew you upon all occasions.

Lord Cornbury's complaints apparently did Captain Livingston no harm with the New England authorities, as shortly after his return from this journey he was entrusted with a far more important mission to Canada, for the purpose of negotiating with the Marquis de Vaudreuil for an exchange of prisoners. In this he was eminently successful, and among those of the English prisoners he got released from their French prison, were some of the survivors of the Deerfield massacre, including the minister of that place, the Rev. John Williams. This gentleman on his release, wrote from Quebec, a warm letter of thanks to Mrs. John Livingston, expressing the obligations he and the other poor captives were under to herself and her "beloved consort." Five years later John Livingston, now risen to the rank of major, served in the expedition against Port Royal, and on the surrender of that place to the New England troops (in October, 1710), he was ordered by General Nicholson to accompany the Baron de Castine to Quebec, for the purpose of communicating the articles of capitulation to the Marquis de Vaudreuil. In accordance with his instructions, Major Livingston started on the fifteenth of that month for Penobscot by water, where on his arrival he was kindly entertained by the Baron de Castine at his own house. From thence the Baron and Major Livingston proceeded up the river in canoes, but owing to the lateness of the season, and the hostility of the Indians, they only reached Quebec after a most hazardous and fatiguing journey; for having been compelled through ice to abandon their canoes, they had to finish the latter part of it on foot, "through a country so thick with spruce, cedar, pine wood, and underwood, as to be scarce passable, and the greater part of the way broken and mountainous land. They were above a fortnight without a sight of the sun, the weather being stormy and foggy the whole time. They had spent their provisions six days before they came to the French settlements, and lived wholly upon moss, leaves, and dried berries."

If it had not been for De Castine's presence of mind, his companion would never have reached Quebec alive, for at one part of their journey they came to an island, where a great number of Indians were encamped, and on their landing, "an Indian being in a rage because some English prisoners had run away with his canoe, seized Livingston by the throat, and would have dispatched him with a hatchet if De Castine had not thrown himself between them, and rescued him." They reached Quebec at last on the 16th of December, or exactly two months after Major Livingston had left Port Royal.[2]

After a few weeks' sojourn in Canada, Major Livingston returned to New England by way of Albany, but one of his servants being too ill to travel, he had to leave him behind under the governor's protection. On this man's recovery, the Marquis de Vaudreuil being naturally anxious to gain information concerning the further movements of the English forces, seized upon the opportunity thus afforded him of obtaining some reliable news as to General Nicholson's plans. For, as he wrote to Monsieur de Pontchartrain, the minister in Paris, rumours of a further contemplated invasion of French territory after the arrival of the expected reinforcements from England had reached his ears; and he adds: "this information, furnished by persons in whom I could not fail to have confidence, caused me to adopt the resolution to send back again to Orange [Albany], and as I required a pretext, I had recourse of restoring a servant that Major Livingston had left behind sick when returning to Three Rivers. I even added to this servant another English prisoner, whom I sent back on his parole, in order to obtain Sieur de Beaunny, whom they have detained since three or four years from me in the Boston Government."

On his return from Quebec, Major Livingston was summoned to New London to appear before the Council of Colonial Governors, who had met for the purpose of arranging a combined attack upon Canada. He received a very flattering reception from the assembled governors, and his commission from General Nicholson as "Major and Commander of a scout drawn out of the forces employed on the late expedition against Port Royal" was fully approved by them; and they gave expression to the opinion "that the office and service was very necessary," and Governor Hunter was desired to give him a commission accordingly.

This attempt of the English colonies to conquer Canada by a combined attack by sea and land, however, ended in disastrous failure. For owing to the loss of a large portion of the English fleet in the St. Lawrence, De Vaudreuil had no further need of guarding against an attack from the sea, and thus was enabled to devote his attention entirely to defending himself from a land attack on the side of New York. So General Nicholson, who led the latter, finding his forces too weak to attempt the conquest of Canada without the expected aid from the fleet, was compelled to retreat. The failure of this attempt delayed the final conquest of Canada for many years, but the English retained Port Royal, as by the Treaty of Utrecht the French province of Acadia was ceded to that country.

The garrison of this new possession having been greatly reduced, Colonel Vetch, the lieutenant-governor, granted permission to his brother-in-law, Major Livingston, to raise a company of Indians for the defence of Annapolis Royal, as the late capital of Acadia had been re-christened by its conquerors in honour of Queen Anne, while the province itself had been re-named Nova Scotia. This company was subsequently disbanded, when it was found, owing to the peace, there was no immediate fear of a French invasion. Of Major Livingston there is little further to relate. He rose to the rank of colonel in the colonial service, and died on the 19th February 1720.[3] He was twice married. His first wife, Mary Winthrop, died on the 8th of January, 1713, on the Livingston Farm at Mohegan, seven miles from New London, but was not buried until nine days later, owing to the state of the weather. The bier was escorted to the town of New London by a procession of men on snowshoes.[4]

He took as his second wife, Elizabeth, daughter of the Mrs. Sarah Knight whose travels in New England were published in 1825. From an original letter from Major Livingston to his father, still in existence,[5] dated New London, 13th July, 1713, it appears this second marriage, then just decided upon, did not meet with the approval of the writer's family, who blames "Sister Vetch" for the fact of his father entertaining an ill opinion of the lady he had chosen for a second spouse. This lady survived her husband some fifteen years, dying on the 17th of March, 1736, and on her tombstone in the New London Burial Ground, she is described as "The Relict of Colonel John Livingston of New London."

Philip, the second son, but fourth child, of Robert, the first Lord of the Manor, was born on the 9th July, 1686. At the time of his birth at Albany, his father was absent from home on the mission to Governor Dongan, which resulted in the granting of the charter raising that town to the rank of a city. He was named after his maternal grandfather, Philip Schuyler, and his two godfathers were members of that family.

The second Lord of the Manor was in many respects unlike his father. He was a much handsomer man, as his portrait clearly shows, and in his youthful days is said to have been "dashing and gay"; while a recent lady historian declares he had "a winning way with women, and went about breaking hearts promiscuously"! Whether the handsome Philip did as much mischief among the New York belles of his day as this talented authoress credits him with, the writer of this volume knoweth not; but in accordance with the simple habits of the Albanians, he married, on coming of age, Catharine, the only daughter of Peter Van Brugh, a leading citizen, and who had been Mayor of Albany in 1699. This lady was a granddaughter of the famous Anneke Jans, whose name has become notorious, owing to the claims raised by some of her descendants in modem times, to the Trinity Church Estate in New York.

He appears, after his marriage, to have studied for the law, and to have been admitted a member of the New York Bar on the 31st December,

1719. In the following year he was appointed one of the Commissioners for the management of the Indian Affairs, and a few months later he succeeded his father as Secretary to that Board. Governor Burnet entertained a high opinion of Philip's character and capabilities, and on a vacancy occurring in the Legislative Council by the decease of Gerardus Beekman, he wrote to the Lords of Trade (7th November, 1724), recommending Mr. Philip Livingston to be appointed a member in his room. Besides this letter to the Board of Trade, the governor, a fortnight later, in another letter addressed to the Duke of Newcastle, Secretary of State for the Colonies, repeated his recommendation of Livingston, and expressed the hope that "his Grace will be favourably pleased to name him to his Majesty, that he may be appointed for that purpose." The King approving of his nomination, Philip was duly called to the Council in the succeeding year.

In the summer of the year following this appointment, Governor Burnet despatched the new member of Council on a special mission to Monsieur de Longueil, who was acting as temporary Governor of Canada, owing to the death of Vaudreuil. In his letter to the French governor, Burnet refers to the bearer "as a member of the King's Council, and one of his (Burnet's) particular friends." The purpose of this mission was to put a stop to the French building a fort at Niagara, which the Governor of New York considered an infraction of the Treaty of Utrecht. The answer of Monsieur de Longueil deferred the matter in dispute until the arrival of the new Governor-General from France, and was considered by Burnet a very unsatisfactory reply.

On the death of his father two years later, Philip succeeded to the entailed and largest portion of the Manor Estate, and to all the manorial privileges; and for many years the new Lord of the Manor took a prominent part in the political affairs of the province, and his family connexions and personal attractions always made him a person of note in New York City, where "he lived in a style of courtly magnificence." As, besides his town house in Broad Street, he had his Manor House, as well as another establishment at Albany to keep up, his open-handed hospitality must have entailed heavy expenses on him.

In 1737, he was appointed one of the commissioners to settle the boundary between the colonies of Massachusetts and New Hampshire, and being the senior member he presided over the Court. A similar duty was assigned him three years later, when he sat on the commission to determine the line to be run between the former colony and Rhode Island, "on which occasion," Hutchinson says, "he had great influence."[6]

Philip Livingston did not find all British governors so easy to work with as Burnet, for in 1745 he became involved in a serious quarrel with the then governor—Admiral George Clinton—concerning the best method of dealing with the ever recurring Indian question; and the "unlettered British Admiral," as Bancroft calls him, quickly lost his temper in the dispute, and made use of some strong sailor language in referring to the Secretary of Indian Affairs. Besides calling the Livingstons in general "a vile family," he also accused Philip personally of supplying the French Indians with arms and ammunition for use against the New England colonies. This quarrel induced Clinton to pay greater attention than was warranted by the facts to some Mohawk Indians, who declared Philip Livingston had illegally possessed himself of some lands of theirs, and prayed that the patent, which Mr. Livingston had obtained for these lands, might "be broke." Clinton, nothing loath to damage his enemy, made the most of the Indians' complaints, and wrote home begging the government to have Livingston removed from the Secretaryship, and also suspended from all his other employments in the Province as "a dangerous person," and one who has not only "been formerly a trader with the enemy at Albany," but who also "neglects his office and supports the neutrality." These accusations, even if only partially true, would brand Philip Livingston's character with infamy; but beyond the fact of there being some misunderstanding with the Indians, who apparently imagined that Livingston, had obtained their lands by some unfair means, there is not a tittle of evidence to support their complaint, or the vindictive attacks made on him by Governor Clinton—who hated the Dutch party in the province; and the Home Government probably took this view of the matter, as they disregarded Clinton's repeated requests for the suspension of this obnoxious member of the Council.

Philip Livingston was not the only member of the Council with whom Clinton had quarrelled, for the choleric sailor's despotic ideas of government kept him constantly involved in disputes with the Legislative Council and the House of Assembly; and when the latter body declined to pass some money bills as required by the governor; and, moreover, had the audacity to accuse him, the royal governor, of having misappropriated public money for his own use, he dissolved the House (25th November 1747), after a long speech, in which he taunted the members with encroaching on the royal prerogative, and by their unruly conduct encouraging disobedience throughout the colony. Owing to the fresh outbreak of hostilities between England and France, the New England colonies were planning another invasion of Canada, and New York was called upon to furnish her share towards the cost. This was agreed to by the Assembly, but with reluctance; and some of the Indian traders grumbled at the interruption the war would occasion in their lucrative traffic with the French Indians, and talked of "a neutrality" with Canada, which idea some of the principal citizens are said to have also favoured. Clinton declared that his opposition to this neutrality idea caused a faction to be formed against him, and that all the members of the Council were concerned in it. This is therefore what he meant when he accused Philip Livingston of supporting "the neutrality."

In spite of Governor Clinton, Philip retained his seat at the Council Board, and continued to take a leading part in the public affairs of his native province until his death, which event took place upon the 4th of February, 1748/9. In accordance with the extravagant ideas as to the manner of conducting funerals, then prevalent among the gentry of New York, the obsequies of the second Lord of the Manor cost his family five hundred pounds—a large sum in those days. And owing to his having died in New York, a double funeral service had to be held, one at his mansion in the city, and the other at the manor. "In the city," says Mr. Sedgwick in his *Life of William Livingston*, "the lower rooms of most of the houses in Broad Street, where he resided, were thrown open to receive the assemblage. A pipe of wine was spiced for the occasion, and to each of the eight bearers, with a pair of gloves, mourning ring, scarf, and handkerchief, a monkey spoon[7] was given. At the manor the whole ceremony was repeated; another pipe of wine was spiced, and besides the same presents to the bearers, a pair of black gloves and handkerchief were given to each of the tenants."

By his wife, Catharine Van Brugh, Philip had eleven children; seven sons and four daughters.[8] Of these the most notable were, his eldest son Robert, who succeeded him as third Lord of the Manor; the second son Peter Van Brugh; the fifth son Philip; and the youngest son William. The last three became prominent leaders on the American side in the War of Independence, and their respective careers, as well as that of their eldest brother Robert, will be fully dealt with in the succeeding chapters. The fourth son, John, was the only member of his family, of any importance, who adhered to the king during the Revolutionary War. Of the daughters, Sarah, the second, married William Alexander, titular Earl of Stirling, and one of the American generals in the fight for independence.

But to return to Robert, the first Lord of the Manor, whose other children were Robert, the third son, bora 24th July, 1688, and who subsequently became the first proprietor of "Clermont"[9]; Gilbert or Hubertus, fourth son, born 3d March, 1689/90; and William, fifth son, who died in infancy. Of his four daughters, only two survived their childhood: Margaret, the eldest, born 5th December, 1681, and married, 20th December, 1700, to Colonel Vetch, afterwards the first English governor of Annapolis Royal; and Johanna, the third, born 10th December, 1694, and who became the wife of Cornelius Van Horne.[10]

Notes

1. For complete list see Appendix C.
2. The original of Major Livingston's journal of this expedition, or what is claimed to be the original, is in the possession of the Chicago Historical Society, *vide* *Historical Magasine* for November, 1861, p. 338.
3. According to *Musgrave's Obituary* (Harleian Society's Publications vol. xlviii, p. 56). This authority says he died in America; while according to a note in 'the *Mass. Hist. Soc. Collections*—Sixth Series,—vol. iii, p. 268, "he died in England about the year 1720." Probably this should read "*New* England."
4. The author is indebted to Mrs. Harold Wilson of Clermont Town-ship, Columbia Co., New York, for the above particulars relating to the death of Colonel Livingston's first wife, and also for the information that both his wives are interred in the same grave in the Burial Ground at New London, Connecticut.
5. In the possession of Mr. Johnston Livingston.
6. History of the Province of Massachusetts Bay, edition 1764, vol. ii, p. 386.
7. The monkey spoon took its name from the figure of a monkey which was carved *in solido* at the extremity of the handle. It was used for liquor, and had a circular and very shallow bowl.
8. For full list of his children see Appendix D.
9. See next chapter.
10. See also Appendix C.

CHAPTER X

CONCERNING THE EARLY HISTORY OF THE LIVINGSTONS OF CLERMONT.

"On the 24th of July, being Tuesday at 5 o'clock in the afternoon my worthy spouse was delivered of my third son, Robert. May the Lord bless him that he may grow up in the Presbyterian religion. He was baptised on Sunday, the 29th, by Dominie Dellius. The witnesses were Uncle David Schuyler and brother Johannes Schuyler. I was at New York with Governor Dongan on business."

—*Extract from Family Record in Robert Livingston's Bible, 24th July 1688.*

THUS runs the record of the birth of this son, who, under the will of his father, the first Lord of the Manor, inherited thirteen thousand acres or thereabouts of the original manorial grant, which were settled on him and his "heirs—male lawfully begotten." This bequest to "Robert Livingston, junior, of New York, merchant," as he is designated in the will, became the estate of "Clermont," or the Lower Manor as it is sometimes erroneously called. According to a family tradition, it is said to have been left by the elder Robert to his second surviving son and namesake, as a reward for the latter's cleverness in having discovered and frustrated a plot, which some negroes are said to have planned, for the massacre of the white inhabitants of the district.

Mrs. Delafield, in her *Biographies of Francis Lewis and Morgan Lewis*, thus describes the discovery of the alleged plot, and the origin of the name "Clermont" bestowed on this estate by its first proprietor:—

> The first summer that young Robert passed with his father at the Manor [after his return from England, where he had been sent to complete his education] his attention was attracted one afternoon by what seemed to be an unusual number of negroes skulking around and keeping within the shadow of the woods. That night after he was in bed he heard a noise in the chimney. He lay quite still and watched; presently a pair of legs descended upon the hearth. Robert sprang from his bed, seized the fellow before he could extricate himself, exclaiming at the same time, Villain confess!' The man, utterly confounded, confessed that he was one of a gang who had fixed upon that night to rob and murder the whites. His father was so much pleased with his intrepidity that he gave him the lower end of the manor, a tract consisting of about thirteen thousand acres. In time Robert built a house upon the tract, and called it "Callendar." The name was easily articulated, agreeable to the ear, and associated with the mediaeval history of his race. Some of his cousins of the Manor objected. "Callendar" was an historical name, and therefore ought to belong to the estate of the elder brother. Robert yielded, and changed it to "Ancram," the name of the parish where his grandfather, John Livingston, had laboured so long and so successfully. This name was also found fault with as too ambitious for the second son. Robert, like a man of sense, would dispute neither about words or straws, and yielded again. This time he made all farther difficulty impossible by going to France for the name of his estate, and called it "Claremont," since shortened into "Clermont."

As regards Robert junior's boyhood, the first eleven years were passed at home with his mother, but soon after attaining his eleventh birthday, his father, at the invitation of his brother William, sent him, in October, 1699, to Scotland to be educated. The vessel in which he was sent over was the *Caledonia*, Captain Drummond commander, bound from New York to Glasgow, which latter port he reached about the end of November, but owing to his uncle William only receiving advice of his nephew's arrival at Glasgow some five weeks later, the boy had to remain on board ship in port all this time. The *Caledonia* was one of the fleet of the unfortunate Darien Company, and William Paterson, its founder (who was also the founder of the Bank of England), was likewise a passenger on board. According to Paterson's report of this voyage, presented to the Court of Directors in December this year, they had had "a tempestuous, stormy passage," and were, at one time, in great danger of being wrecked, "under God, owing our safety, and that of the ship, to the great vigilancy and industrie of the Commander, Robert Drummond." Robert arrived at his uncle's house in Edinburgh on the third of January, 1700, where he remained until it was burnt down, exactly a month later. He then took up his abode, for a short time, with his other uncle, James; but on both these uncles dying during the following summer—within ten days of each other—his aunt Barbara Miller took charge of him. A letter from this lady, still in existence, written to her brother Robert, describes her youthful nephew at this period, as being very like his father at the same age, "a well-disposed and witty boy." In another, and later, letter, she writes, "he loves to be fine and to have his things genteel."

His uncle William had placed him at a Latin School at Leith, but upon this uncle's death Mrs. Miller sent him to the High School, Edinburgh, for a time, as a day scholar. From Edinburgh the lad subsequently went to London to complete his education, and while there he is said to have studied law in the Temple. Apparently, it was his father who settled the younger Robert in London, as in a letter written by the elder Robert, in May, 1705, to his friend Governor Fitz-John Winthrop of Connecticut, while he was engaged—as previously related—in pressing his claims upon the English Government, he mentions his intention of going to "Scotland speedily to fetch up his son, who is there at ye Colledge." The younger Robert must have spent about eight years therefore in London, if it is true that he did not return to America until he was about twenty-five years of age. He is also said to have brought with him from England a quantity of law books, and to have opened a law office at Albany. This profession he, however, soon abandoned for the more lucrative occupation of a merchant in New York. Four years after his return home, he married Margaret Howarden, the daughter of a wealthy English merchant in New York, and "granddaughter of Captain Bethlow, a Huguenot, after whom is named Bedloe's Island. Mrs. Delafield states that owing to some financial complications with the Governor, Lord Cornbury, and from the refusal of the latter to render any account, the Bethlow family, and consequently the Howardens, were deprived of, and were unable to regain, a large fortune to which they were entitled. She also states that later there appeared in the colony a Captain Howarden, who claimed kinship with those of his name in America."[1] The marriage ceremony took place on the nth of November, 1717, at the Reformed Dutch Chinch in that city. The only offspring of this marriage was a son, also named Robert, who was baptised on the 31st of August, 1718[2]

Robert Livingston, on the death of his father, Robert of the Manor, came into the possession of the great tract of land already mentioned, upon which he built a large stone house. According to the late Mr. T. S. Clarkson, the author of *Clermont or Livingston Manor*, he, afterwards, in his old age, gave this house to his son, Judge Robert R. Livingston, "in whose family he lived beloved until his death." He took a great deal of interest in the dispute between the colonies and the mother-country, and he is said to have foretold to his family the coming independence of the former, in the following prophetic words:—"I shall not see America independent, and Robert," addressing his son "you will not." "Montgomery," speaking to the British officer who had married his granddaughter, and was later on to become a general in the American service and die in an attempt to capture Quebec, "you may." "Robert," turning to his grandson, afterward Chancellor Livingston, "you will!"

His grandson, Edward Livingston, thus describes him at the advanced age of eighty-four:

> Never was man better entitled by his manners, his morals, and his education to the appellation of gentleman. His figure was tall and somewhat bent, but not emaciated by age, which had marked, but not disfigured, a face once remarkable for its regular beauty of feature, and still beaming with the benevolence and intelligence that had always illuminated it. He marked the epoch at which he had retired from the world by preserving its costume: the flowing well-powdered wig, the bright brown coat, with large cuffs and square skirts, the cut velvet waistcoat, with ample flaps, and the breeches scarcely covering the knee, the silk stockings, rolled over them with embroidered clocks, and shining square-toed shoes, fastened near the ankle with small embossed gold buckles. These were retained in his service, not to affect a singularity, but because he thought it ridiculous, at his time of life, to follow the quick succession of fashion.

While his granddaughter, Mrs. Montgomery, adds to her brother's description by relating that her grandfather always rose at five in the morning, and read without ceasing until near breakfast. The year before his death he learned the German tongue, and spoke it fluently. On the breaking out of the war, he was in raptures. In beginning with the Bostonians he said, they had taken the bull by the horns. His sanguine temper made him expect with confidence our independence. He seemed to begin life again, his eye had all the fire of youth, and I verily believe the battle of Bunker Hill, of which such a disastrous report was made, was his death. He took to his bed immediately, lay a week without a pain, and died.

His last words, addressed to his daughter-in-law, are said to have been, "Peggy, what news from Boston?"[3]

His only son, and successor to his estate of Clermont, Robert R. Livingston, had also been brought up to the law, and what with his own talents and powerful family connections, soon acquired a good practice and a prominent position in New York society. This he further strengthened in 1742 by marrying Margaret, the only surviving child and heiress of Colonel Henry Beekman of Rhinebeck; and thus, in course of time, this couple would inherit the two large landed estates of Clermont and Rhinebeck.

Judge Robert R. Livingston (1718–1775), attributed to Gilbert Stuart. Public domain.

This lady was a granddaughter, on her mother's side, of Robert Livingston, "the nephew," and his wife Margaretta Schuyler. This marriage was a very happy one, and many years afterwards, Mrs. Livingston, in describing her husband's character, wrote as follows:—

> At the age of eighteen I was made the happy wife of Robert R. Livingston; to say that my best friend was an agreeable man would but ill express a character that shone among the brightest; his finely cultivated understanding, his just and wise decisions as a judge, a patriot ever attentive to the interests of his country, and a discerning politician. These were all brightened by an unequalled sweetness of disposition, and a piety that gilded every action of his life.

Mrs. Livingston's affection for her husband was fully reciprocated by the latter, who thus refers to her, in a letter written in July, 1755, thirteen years after their marriage, and when she had borne him seven children:—

> My last letter was written in a melancholy mood. To you I am not used to disguise my thoughts. Indeed, I have for a long time been generally sad, except when your presence and idea enliven my spirits. Think then, with how much pleasure I received your favours of 30th June and 3rd instant. This I did not till last Sunday, and I have been happy ever since. You are the cordial drop with which Heaven has graciously thought fit to sweeten my cup. This makes my taste of happiness in the midst of disappointments. My imagination paints you with all your loveliness,—with all the charms my soul has for so many years doated on,—with all the sweet endearments past and those which I flatter myself I shall still experience. I may truly say, I have not a pleasant thought (abstracted from those of an hereafter) with which your idea is not connected; and even those of future happiness give me a prospect of a closer union with you.

Livingston's position and great capabilities soon brought him into public notice, and on two vacancies occurring in the Legislative Council in 1756, owing to the deaths of James Alexander and Edward Holland, Sir Charles Hardy, then Governor of New York, wrote to the Lords of Trade submitting Mr. Livingston's and two other names for their approval, in answer to their request for those "of three persons inhabitants of this Province, whom I shall esteem best qualified to supply the vacancys that may happen in the Council." Governor Hardy resigned his office in the following year, and Chief-Justice James De Lancey, the lieutenant-governor, was temporarily appointed to act in his place. This probably accounts for the fact that though John Watts and William Walton, the other two gentlemen recommended by Governor Hardy, obtained the coveted distinction, Livingston did not; for at this period the DeLancey and Livingston parties in the province were bitterly opposed to each other.

Though denied a seat in the Upper House of the provincial Legislature, Mr. Livingston easily obtained one in the popular or Lower House of Assembly, for on the lieutenant-governor dissolving, on the 16th of December, 1758, the Assembly elected six years previously, a fresh election took place in the following month, when Robert R. Livingston and his cousin Henry Livingston were returned as the two members for Dutchess County. Besides these two Livingstons, two other members of the family were returned on this occasion, namely Alderman Philip Livingston, as one of the city members, and the latter's younger and talented brother William, the fearless leader of their party, by the freeholders on their elder brother Robert's manor. In the new House of Assembly the Livingston party formed the majority, but as this fight for political power between the De Lancey and Livingston factions will be fully dealt with in the succeeding chapter, there is no need to refer to it further here.

During the following year Robert R. Livingston was appointed to be a judge of the Admiralty Court; and on the death of Chief-Justice Pratt, in January, 1763, Governor Monckton promoted David Horsmanden to that office, while David Jones, William Smith, and Robert R. Livingston[4] were raised to the colonial bench as puisne judges of the Supreme Court of New York. These appointments did not please the new lieutenant-governor, that ultra-royalist Cadwallader Colden,[5] who wished to have the judges chosen by the king, to sit at his pleasure, and to be paid by him. The new judges soon justified Colden's fears, for, as early as the following year, they utterly refused to allow the right of appeals from the common law courts of the province to the governor and council, and finally to the king, as claimed by the lieutenant-governor. Moreover, Judge Livingston, whose liberal views were notorious, took a prominent part in protesting against Colden's interference with their duties, and his desire to introduce innovations in their method of procedure, which he deemed unconstitutional and contrary to the laws of England. This opposition to his cherished scheme for strengthening the prerogative of the crown bitterly offended Colden, who earnestly petitioned the Home Government to dismiss both Chief-Justice Horsmanden and Justice Livingston from the bench.

Of the latter, he wrote to the Lords of Trade, under date 22d January, 1765,

> I thought at first that Chief-Justice Horsmanden had gone further than any other of the judges were willing to follow him; but to what lengths Justice Livingston has gone will best appear from his harangue, which he industriously intruded on the last day of the hearing, without being desired to speak on this occasion. It requires no comment. I only beg your Lordships will peruse it. He is heir to one of the greatest Landed Estates, dispersed in several parts of the Province, and involved in disputes with the poor industrious farmers, who have settled and improved the adjoining lands. [In another letter written five days later, he expressed it [desirable that Justice Livingston, who has distinguished himself on this occasion, be removed from his office, as no cause of any consequence can come before him, in which, or in similar cases, he or the Livingston family are not interested.

This quarrel between Colden and the judges was soon eclipsed by the far more famous dispute between England and her American colonies, caused by the unfortunate attempts made by the British Parliament to tax the latter without their consent. The merchants of New York, at an early date, took alarm at the news from England, and on the 18th of October, 1764, the General Assembly of that province appointed a Committee, consisting of the members of the City of New York and Robert R. Livingston, to correspond with the other colonial Assemblies or their committees regarding their mutual grievances, and the best means to be adopted for obtaining their redress. In spite of the remonstrances of the various colonies, the now historical Stamp Act was passed by the two Houses of Parliament, and on the 22nd of March, 1765, it received the royal assent. By this Act it was provided that all bills, bonds, leases, notes, ships' papers, insurance policies, and other legal documents, to be valid must be written on stamped paper, and certain public officers were to be appointed in the different colonies for the sale of the same On receipt of the news that this Act had been passed there arose a general outburst of indignation from the colonists, who regarded the new impost as a tyrannical measure, and one that should be firmly resisted as an attempt to impose on them an internal tax without their consent. The "gentle Robert R. Livingston," says Bancroft, "had, in the summer of the previous year—1764—on receipt of the news of the intention of the English Parliament to tax the colonies, declared that 'it appears plainly that these duties are only the beginning of evils. The stamp duty, they tell us, is deferred till they see whether the colonies will take the yoke upon themselves, and offer something else as certain. They talk, too, of a land tax, and to us the ministry appears to have run mad.'" The judge evidently anticipated a general resistance to these new taxes, for he added: "We in New York shall do as well as our neighbours; the God of heaven, whom we serve will sanctify all things to those who love Him and strive to serve Him."

Margaret Beekman (1724–1800), wife of Judge Robert R. Livingston.
Public Domain.

Judge Livingston was elected by the members of this Committee of Correspondence to be their chairman; and as such he attended with his colleagues the Congress which met at New York in October, 1765, in response to a circular issued by the Massachusetts House of Assembly. This Congress, known in history as the Stamp Act Congress, consisted of twenty-eight delegates from nine of the colonies. The New York delegates were Robert R. Livingston, John Cruger, Philip Livingston, William Bayard, and Leonard Lespinard. The Congress was formally opened on the seventh of October in the City Hall, and after eleven days, debate, the members agreed upon a Declaration of Rights, and ordered it to be inserted in the journals. In this Declaration, while expressing "the warmest sentiments of affection and duty to the king," they claimed "all the inherent rights and privileges of natural-born subjects within the kingdom of Great Britain"; and "they affirmed that it is inseparably essential to the freedom of a people, and one of the undoubted rights of Englishmen, that taxes cannot be imposed on them without their own consent, given personally or through their representatives; that the colonists could not be represented in the House of Commons and could be represented only in their respective Legislatures; and that no taxes could be constitutionally imposed on them but by these Legislatures. They declared that the trial by jury is the inherent and invaluable right of every British subject in these colonies; and they arraigned the recent Acts of Parliament as having a manifest tendency to subvert the rights and liberties of the people."[6]

The judge took an active part in the deliberations of this Congress, and at the end of a long letter to his aged father—written on the nineteenth of October—with whom he was in the habit of corresponding on every matter of public importance, however occupied his time might be, he says:—

> See the three great points we have to contend for, and of what importance they are: trials by juries, a right to tax ourselves, and the reducing Admiralty Courts within their proper limits. If you, Sir, consider my situation, you will excuse my not writing to you before. Yesterday I had the whole Congress to dine with me. In one place or another we dine every day; so that, besides business, this engrosses much time. I am now obliged to drive my pen over this as fast as I can.

Unfortunately the debates of this Congress have not been preserved; but in a discussion which ensued on some of the members pleading, as the foundation of their liberties, charters from the Crown, it is recorded by Bancroft, that "Robert R. Livingston of New York, 'the goodness of whose heart set him above prejudices and equally comprehended all mankind,' would not place the hope of America on that foundation." According to the same authority, "the too gentle Livingston" expressed the opinion that it would not be wise "to insist upon a repeal of all Acts laying duties on trade, as well as the Stamp Act," as was the wish of some of the more extreme members, for, he argued, "if we do not make an explicit acknowledgment of the power of Britain to regulate our trade, she will never give up the point of internal taxation." The Congress finally approved of an Address to the King, a Memorial to the House of Lords, and a Petition to the House of Commons, which were ordered to be engrossed. The first of these important papers, praying for "the invaluable rights of taxing ourselves and trial by our peers," was drawn up by Judge Livingston, and was adopted by the Congress on the twenty-second of this month[7]; while his cousin Philip was a member of the committee appointed to draft the Memorial to the House of Lords. Three days later, the Congress having fulfilled the purpose for which it was called together, dispersed.

The arrival, on the twenty-third, at New York, of the first ship from England with the hated stamps, led to a serious riot, of which the judge was an eye-witness, and of which he wrote, on the eighth of the following month—November, 1765,—an interesting account to his friend and correspondent, General Monckton, the late governor. This is, however, much too long to give here, but the writer concludes his letter with these words:—

> Your Excellency will see by this account, that the enforcing the Stamp Act will be attended with the destruction of all Law, Order, and Government in the Colonies, and ruin all men of property, for such is the temper of people's minds, from one end of the Continent to the other, that whoever carries his opposition to this Act, to the greatest excess, will be most followed, and will force the rest into their measures. Therefore, we beg, as for life and all its comforts, from every person that can aid us, that this Act may be repealed. If it be not, it is impossible for the wisest man on earth to tell how far its mischievous consequences will extend. Britain will suffer more by it, in one year in her trade, than this tax, or any other,—should others

be imposed,—can ever recompense. Merchants have resolved to send for no more British manufactures, Shopkeepers will buy none, Gentlemen will wear none,—our own are encouraged, all pride in dress seems to be laid aside, and he that does not appear in Homespun, or at least in a turned coat, is looked on with an evil eye. The Lawyers will not is sue a writ. Merchants will not dear out a vessel. These are all facts not in the least exaggerated; and it is of importance they should be known. But the worst of all is this; that should the Act be enforced there is the utmost danger, I speak it with the greatest concern imaginable, of a civil war.

Judge Livingston's powerful description of the spirit of universal opposition aroused in the colonies against the introduction of the obnoxious Act was not at all overdrawn; and the English Government was very soon forced to acknowledge its truth, as on the eighteenth of March in the following year it was repealed. The news of the repeal of the Stamp Act was received in America with an outburst of joy, which was, however, to be of very brief duration; as the short-sighted ministers of George III, though disappointed in their attempt to force the Stamp Act on the colonists, were still obstinately determined that the right of Great Britain to tax her colonies should be insisted upon, and thereupon measures were passed through the British Parliament, which ultimately led to the overthrow of the dominion of the mother-country over the greater portion of the North American continent.

The arrival of the new governor, Sir Henry Moore, three weeks after the above-mentioned riots, led to the temporary retirement of the unpopular lieutenant-governor, and New York settled down again to a short period of quiet from political brawls. Colden appears to have been bitterly offended with Judge Livingston for the part he had taken in this dispute; for in a letter written to Secretary Conway, announcing the arrival of Sir Henry Moore, he accuses the judge of having been "a principal director in opposition to the execution of the Act of Parliament for a Stamp Duty in the Colonies and of all the consequences of that opposition.' Colden was soon to be still further incensed against Livingston and the other judges, on account of their behaviour in taking proceedings to suppress a pamphlet, which had been printed in London[8] in defence of the lieutenant-governor's conduct during the late disputes between that gentleman and the judges of the Supreme Court, and the recent Stamp Duty troubles; and which had been reprinted in New York. For at the sitting of the Supreme Court, held in October, 1767, the judges took care that the Grand Jury should not be dismissed before expressing an opinion as to the libellous character of this pamphlet, which they did by bringing in a presentment to the effect that the publication in question was *"a very vile, false, infamous, and libellous reflection on His Majesty's Council, Assembly, Courts of Justice, and the whole Body of the Law of this province."*

Colden, on hearing what the Grand Jury had done, flew into a violent passion, and wrote home in no measured terms concerning the conduct of the judges, and particularly of his old opponent, Livingston, on this pamphlet question. The latter, moreover, two months later, moved in the house of Assembly for a Committee to be appointed to inquire further into this matter, which was agreed to; and Judge Livingston himself was the bearer of a message from the Assembly to the Council, desiring them to appoint a Committee to join the Committee nominated by the Assembly to take this pamphlet under consideration. This was granted, and on the 30th of December, 1767, the Report of the Joint-Committee was read in the Lower House of Assembly. It condemned the pamphlet in severe terms, and proposed that the House should appoint a Committee "to examine and report [on] the unjust charges, with an ample and satisfactory refutation, to discover the Author and Publisher; and declare what they conceive to be the most prudent and effectual measures for applying a suitable punishment, and deterring others from so iniquitous and dangerous an Offence."

The angry lieutenant-governor, however, had his revenge, as he was successful in persuading the Home Government, that Judge Livingston was not a suitable candidate for the vacant seat on the Council, which the governor, Sir Henry Moore, wished the Lords of Trade to bestow upon him. The liberal minded judge had also incurred the displeasure of the Tory or De Lancey party, which led to his losing his seat in the Assembly for Dutchess at the elections held in the spring of 1768; but as his future career, as well as the further history of his branch of the family, will be fully dealt with in the succeeding chapters, it is not necessary to say more here.

Notes

1. From information kindly supplied by their descendant Mr. John Henry Livingston, the present owner of "Clermont."
2. He subsequently assumed after Robert, the initial "R."—equivalent to "Robert, the son of Robert"— so as to distinguish him from the numerous other Roberts in the family. This method was also adopted by other members of the American

Livingstons; thus Philip "the Signer's," eldest son Philip became "Philip Philip"; and several of Gilbert's descendants were known as Gilbert R.; Gilbert J.; and so on.

3. He died on the 27th June, 1775. In the obituary columns of the London *Gentleman's Magasine* for August, 1775, his death is recorded as follows:— "July 27. Robert Livingston, Esq., of Claremont, in America, aged 88." The "July" here is obviously a misprint for "June."

4. The latter's appointment is dated 10th August, 1763.

5. Chief-Justice De Lancey, his predecessor, had died during the summer of 1760.

6. Frothingham, *Rise of the Republic*, pp. 186, 187.

7. The members of the committee on the Address to the King were Robert R. Livingston, William Samuel Johnson, and William Murdoch, but it was drafted by the first of these.

8. *The Conduct of Cadwallader Colden, Esq.; Lieutenant-Governor of New York relating to Judges' Commissions; Appeals to the King; and the Stamp Duty.* London; 1767, 8 vo.

CHAPTER XI

Concerning the Political History of an American Pocket Borough, and of the Livingston Party in the New York House of Assembly Prior to the War of Independence.

"And we do further give and grant unto the said Robert Livingston, his heirs and assigns for ever, that from henceforth it shall and may be lawfull to and for the freeholders of the said Lordship and Manor to assemble and meet together, and to elect, choose, and send some fit person being a freeholder and inhabitant within the said Manor, to be their representative, and to sitt and vote in General Assembly of this Colony."

—*Extract from the Royal Patent for Manor of Livingston of the First of October, 1715.*

BY the above clause in George the First's confirmatory patent of the Lordship and Manor of Livingston, Robert Livingston, the shrewd and persevering Secretary of Indian Affairs, obtained the great desire of his lifetime. For the principal motive that influenced Livingston to urge his friend Governor Hunter to obtain for him this royal confirmation of his earlier manorial patent, was his ambition to have conferred on the freeholders of his Manor the privilege of electing a representative to sit in the colonial House of Assembly, so as to rank on an equality with the neighbouring Manor of Rensselaerwyck, which had obtained this right in 1685, and the Manor of Cortlandt, which had been granted the same privilege twelve years later. The Manor of Livingston was the last of these large landed estates to obtain this special mark of distinction. Thus these three great manors, under these grants, became nothing better than "pocket boroughs," for the freeholders, though nominally "free and independent electors," had no chance ever afforded them of returning any other candidate than the one nominated by the Lord of the Manor. The representative thus elected was therefore either the Lord of the Manor himself, or a near relative. For the sixty years the Manor of Livingston was represented in the House, the members, without a single exception, bore the family surname.

List of the representatives for the Manor of Livingston elected to serv in the General Assembly of the Province of New York, a.d. 1715–1776.

Date of Service.	Number of Times Elected.	Name of Representative as Entered in the Journals of General Assembly.	Brief Biographical Notices.
A.D. 1716–1726	Once	Colonel Livingston or Mr. Robert Livingston, sen.	First Lord of the Manor of Livingston. Member of Assembly for City and County of Albany from 1709–1711. Speaker of the House from 1718–1725 Born 1654. Died 1728.
1726–1727	Twice	Robert Livingston, jun., Esq.	Second surviving son of above. First proprietor of Clermont Born 1688. Died 1775.
1728–1737	Twice	Gilbert Livingston, Esq.	Third surviving son of Robert, First Lord of the Manor. Born 1690. Died 1746.
1737–1758	Seven	Captain Robert Livingston	Eldest son of Philip, Second Lord of the Manor. Succeeded his father as Third and Last Lord of the Manor in 1749. Born 1708. Died 1790.
1759–1761	Once	William Livingston, Esq.	Seventh son of Philip; Second Lord of the Manor. First Governor of the State of New Jersey Born 1723. Died 1790.

(Continued)

(*Continued*)

Date of Service.	Number of Times Elected.	Name of Representative as Entered in the Journals of General Assembly.	Brief Biographical Notices.
1761–1769	Twice	Peter R Livingston, Esq,	Eldest surviving son of Robert, Third Lord of the Manor. President of the Convention of the State of New York in 1777 Born 1737. Died 1794.
1769	Once	Alderman Philip Livingston *or* Philip Livingston, Esq.	Fifth son of Philip, Second Lord of the Manor. Member of Assembly for City and County of New York from 1759–1769. Elected Speaker, 28th Octobe 1768. Unseated 12th May 1769 for "non-residence." One of the Signers of the Declaration of Independence. Born, 1716. Died 1778.
1769–1774	Five	Captain Robert R. Livingston *or* Robert R. Livingston, Esq.	Only son of Robert Livingston, First proprietor of Clermont Member of Assembly for Dutchess County from 1759–1768. Appointed Judge of the Supreme Court of the Province of New York in 1763. Though elected on five successive occasions to represent the Manor in General Assembly, he was never permitted to take his seat, owing to Judges being excluded from the House by a Resolution passed in 1769. Born 1718. Died 1775
1774–1776	Once	Peter R. Livingston, Esq	For particulars see under years 1761–1769. After Judge Robert R. Livingston's election had been declared null and void for the fifth time, he retired from the contest, and Peter R. Livingston was returned in his place. He sat in the General Assembly until the outbreak of the War of Independence

The total number of representatives returned to the General Assembly at this date, including the Manor of Livingston and the newly enfranchised township of Schenectady, was twenty-seven. The members, while on duty, received payment for their services at rates regulated according to a scale fixed by sundry acts of Assembly, and which varied in amount from six to ten shillings per diem; the representatives from the more distant districts—including the manors of Rensselaerwyck and Livingston—receiving the higher rate of pay. The members of the Council, on the other hand, which, when full, consisted of twelve members who received their appointments direct from the crown, were unpaid; though their duties were quite as arduous as those performed by the members of the Lower House. The Councillors, however, were allowed to bear the title of "honourable" before their names. They composed the Upper House in the provincial Legislature.

At the date of the grant of the confirmatory patent there was no House sitting, Governor Hunter having dissolved the sixteenth Assembly on the seventh of August in that year, and the elections for the new one did not take place until the following summer. On the fifth of June in this year (1716), twenty-two of the newly elected members met at the City Hall, New York, and chose Mr. William Nicoll to be their Speaker; but Robert Livingston, who had been duly returned for his Manor, did not put in an appearance until the tenth of May in the following year, when, after undergoing the usual formalities required upon the admission of a representative from a new constituency, he was allowed to take his seat.

Mr. Livingston was, however, no stranger to the procedure of the House, for he had sat in the Assembly from 1709 to 1711 as one of the two representatives for the City and County of Albany, when, with his usual energy, he had devoted his attention m the former year to obtaining the repeal of a vindictive Act aimed against himself, and which had been passed by his political opponents eight years previously. On this occasion also he was not backward in looking after his own interests, for on the third day after taking his seat, he brought in a bill, entitled "An Act for making the Manor of Livingston, which is now part of the County of Albany and Dutchess County, wholly to be annexed to the County of Albany," which Act was read a third time and passed on the 22d of May, only eight days after it had been introduced! A characteristic proof of its author's promptitude in pushing his own affairs.

The first Lord of the Manor of Livingston, however, did not confine his attention solely to the promotion of his own interests in the Assembly, as some of his detractors would like us to believe; as he also devoted the same energy, which had made his fortune in private life, to the prosecution of public affairs, and his intimate knowledge of everything connected with the ever absorbing Canadian and Indian questions made his services and advice simply invaluable to the constantly changing series of royal governors. William Smith, in his *History of New York*, refers to him as one of "the members most distinguished for their activity in the House." His services were thus often required on various committees, and he also took a leading part in the debates; so that on the resignation of the office of Speaker by Mr. Nicoll, he was naturally chosen by a plurality of votes to fill that important post. This occurred on the 27th of May, 1718, and Mr. Livingston held this dignified and responsible office for the next seven years, until advancing age and failing health compelled him to retire, as "the severity of his indisposition" prevented him from devoting as much of his time to the business of the House as the duties of this office required. Mr. Philipse was therefore elected, at the opening of the fourteenth session of the seventeenth Assembly on the 31st of August, 1725, to be Speaker in the place of Mr. Livingston; and on the latter appearing in the House a fortnight later, he apologised for his absence through ill-health on the opening day of the new session, and expressed himself well pleased "that the House had proceeded to a new choice." Whereupon the House desired "he would nevertheless assist them as a member, as often as his state of health would admit him, during his stay in town."

It was during Livingston's term of office as Speaker that Governor Hunter left New York, when it fell to his duty, as the mouthpiece of the Assembly, to express the thanks of that body to the popular governor, in their reply to his farewell address. This task must have been a pleasant one for Livingston, who owed much of his prosperity to Governor Hunter's friendship and appreciation of his public services. The last notice of Livingston in the Journals of Assembly occurs on the 17th of June, 1726, when he is mentioned as being a member of one of the committees on that date. The House was adjourned on the same date by Governor Burnet, who subsequently dissolved it on the 11th of August following, so this was the last appearance of the first member for Livingston Manor in the Assembly; for in the next election he did not stand for the Manor, but retired in favour of his second surviving son and namesake, Robert of Clermont, his eldest son Philip, who had succeeded his father as Secretary for Indian Affairs, being debarred from sitting in the Lower House, as he had been appointed in the previous year to fill a vacancy on the Council Board.

Robert Livingston of Clermont represented his father's Manor during the short-lived eighteenth and nineteenth General Assemblies, but he does not appear to have taken much interest in colonial politics, for on the dissolution of the last named Assembly he did not offer himself again for re-election; whereupon his younger brother Gilbert was returned to the twentieth General Assembly as the representative for Livingston Manor. Gilbert's occupation of the family seat appears to have been intended as a temporary arrangement only, until his nephew Robert, the eldest son of his brother Philip, the second Lord of the Manor, should have come of age. For at the date of the elections for this last Assembly, this Robert was only nineteen years old; while, as already mentioned, his father could not sit in the lower House owing to his being a member of the King's Council, a position which he held until his death.

If Robert of the Manor was waiting for a fresh election, before taking his seat in the House as his father's heir, he had to wait a long time, as the twentieth Assembly was not dissolved until the 3d of May, 1737! On writs being issued for a new one to meet in the following month, Robert was duly returned, and took his seat as the Manor representative on the first of September in this year. During the next twenty-one years Captain Robert Livingston—as the heir to the Lordship and Manor of Livingston is designated in the Journals of the House, owing to his having held that rank in the provincial militia—sat uninterruptedly through seven General Assemblies, being dutifully returned at every fresh election by the Manor freeholders. But on writs being issued for the twenty-eighth Assembly to meet on the 31st of January, 1759, the Lord of the Manor[1] retired in favour of his talented younger brother William, then recognised as the leader of the Presbyterian or opposition party in the province, of which the Livingstons had become the champions, and which at this period had become so identified with this family that it was generally known as "the Livingston party"; while the Episcopalian, the party in power, took the name of "the De Lancey party" from their leader, the lieutenant-governor—the Honourable James De Lancey. These factions in after years developed into the Whig and Tory parties of the Revolution.

The new member for the Manor of Livingston was born at Albany in November, 1723, and was thus in his thirty-sixth year at the date of his election. He was the youngest son of Philip, second Lord of the

Manor, and according to his biographer, Mr. William Sedgwick, "the first fourteen years of his boyhood were spent at Albany, under the protection of his maternal grandmother, Mrs. Sarah Van Brugh." A year out of this period, however, was apparently spent among the Mohawk Indians, with a missionary of the Society for Propagating the Gospel, when he had the opportunity of studying native manners and customs. In 1737 he was entered a freshman at Yale College, where three of his elder brothers, namely Peter Van Brugh, John, and Philip, had also been students. In 1741 young Livingston graduated at the head of his class, upon which event Mr. Sedgwick remarks he "was unaware whether, in those days, this implied any distinction"; and he was therefore in ignorance of the fact that, until the year 1767, the Class Lists of Yale College gave the names in the order of family rank.[2] "To the discredit of our ancestors," to again quote from Mr. Sedgwick's work, "it must be remembered that at this time there were only six persons in the Province besides himself [viz., William Livingston] and his brothers, those in orders excepted, who had received a collegiate education."

William Livingston (1723–1790), governor of New Jersey. The Miriam and Ira D. Wallach Division of Art, Prints and Photographs: Print Collection, New York Public Library Digital Collections, Public Domain.

After leaving college William Livingston studied law in the office of Mr. James Alexander in New York, and intended to have continued his studies in England, and carried his purpose so far as to obtain admission to the Middle Temple, but for some reason or other he gave up the idea and did not leave America. In 1748 he was admitted to the Bar of New York as an attorney, and he soon became well-known in his profession. Two or three years before this date he had taken unto himself a wife. This lady was Miss Susanna French, a granddaughter on the mother's side of Major Anthony Brockholls (commonly spelled nowadays "Brockholst"), one of the early English governors of New York. Mr. Livingston's love of a quiet domestic and rural life is shown in" his earliest literary publication of any note—*Philosophic Solitude*—written in imitation of Pope, in which occur the following lines:—

> Let ardent heroes seek renown in arms,
> Pant after fame, and rush to war's alarms;
> To shining palaces, let fools resort,
> And dunces cringe to be esteemed at court;
> Mine be the pleasures of a rural life,
> From noise remote, and ignorant of strife.

The youthful poet little anticipated when he penned these lines, what years of political strife, as well as "war's alarms," lay before him, and how little of the quiet country life he so enjoyed would fall to his lot!

During the seven years prior to his election as member for the Manor, William Livingston had been actively engaged in waging open war with his pen, against all forms of official corruption and abuse in the government of the province; and had boldly proclaimed in his paper—the *Independent Reflector*—that "the Reflector," namely the editor, himself, "is determined to proceed unawed and alike fearless of the humble scoundrel and the eminent villain. The cause he is engaged in is a glorious cause. 'T is the cause of truth and liberty: what he intends to oppose is superstition, bigotry, priestcraft, tyranny, servitude, public mismanagement and dishonesty in office. The things he proposes to teach are the nature and the excellence of our constitution, the inestimable value of liberty, the disastrous effects of bigotry, the shame and horror of bondage, the importance of religion unpolluted and unadulterated with superstitious additions and inventions of priests. He should also rejoice to be instrumental in the improvement of commerce and husbandry. In short, anything that may be of advantage to the inhabitants of this province in particular, and mankind in general, may freely demand a place in his paper." Certainly a bold and ambitious programme for a young man, then only in his thirtieth year, to publish to the world; and one not lacking in self confidence, and the glorious hopefulness of youth! But the writer was as good as his word, and he soon surprised both friends and foes by a remarkable series of essays on the abuses of the day. The youthful editor, naturally, was fiercely attacked by all those persons who were likely to suffer from his exposure of their delinquencies; but nothing daunted he steadfastly continued on the course he had marked out for himself, which required no little courage in those early days before the liberty of the press had become a recognised institution in a free land. One of the earliest uses he made of his paper was an unsuccessful attempt to prevent the control of the contemplated college[3] for New York falling into the hands of the Episcopalians. For shortly before the publication of the Independent Reflector, an agitation had been set on foot in New York to obtain a college for that city, and various sums of money had been raised for this purpose by means of lotteries, which had been placed in the hands of ten trustees, of whom William Livingston was one. It soon transpired that the majority of the trustees being Episcopalians, were anxious to have the college placed under the control of members of their own denomination, and that they were using their influence to obtain from the governor a charter, in which one of the clauses was to be to the effect that the president must always be a member of the Church of England; while another was to make it a rule that the common prayer-book must be used by the students in their religious exercises.[4] The great injustice of devoting funds contributed by persons of all denominations for this purpose, at once aroused Livingston's ire, and in a series of scathing articles, published in the Independent Reflector, he exposed the gross unfairness of the proposed plan. The following are the titles of some of the numbers of his paper published during this controversy:—

> No: XXXI. Primitive Christianity, short and intelligible—
> Modern Christianity, voluminous and incomprehensible.
> No: XXXVI. The Absurdity of the Civil Magistrates interfering
> in Matters of Religion.
> No: XXXVIII. Of Passive Obedience and Non-resistance.
> No: XLVI. Of Creeds and Systems, together with the Author's
> Own Creed.

The last of these articles was partly an attack on the sectarian character of the Church of England, and partly a humorous reply to those of
his opponents who had represented the editor of The Reflector,—to use his
own words,— "some as an Atheist, others as a Deist, and a third sort as a
Presbyterian." "My creed will show," he adds, "that none have exactly hit
it. For all which reasons, I shall cheerfully lay before you the articles of
my faith." Then follow thirty-nine articles written in William Livingston's
lighter vein of satire; but as it would take up too much space to give them
all here, the following brief extracts must suffice:—

1. I believe the Scriptures of the Old and New Testament, without any foreign comments or human explanations but my own:
   for which I should doubtless be honoured with martyrdom, did
   I not live in a government which restrains that fiery zeal which
   would reduce a man's body to ashes for the illumination of his
   understanding.
5. I believe that the word *orthodox*, is a hard, equivocal, priestly
   term, that has caused the effusion of more blood than all the
   Roman Emperors put together.
7. I believe that to defend the Christian religion is one thing, and
   to knock a man on the head for being of a different opinion is
   another thing.
13. I believe that riches, ornaments, and ceremonies were assumed
    by churches for the same reason that garments were invented by
    our first parents.
15. I believe a man may be a good Christian though he be of no sect
    in Christendom.
17. I believe that our faith, like our stomachs, may be overcharged,
    especially if we are prohibited to chew what we are commanded
    to swallow.
37. I believe that, were it in the power of some gentlemen I could
    name, the Independent Reflector had long ago been cropped and
    pilloried.
38. I believe that the virulence of some of the clergy against my spec-
    ulation proceeds not from their affection to Christianity, which
    is founded on too firm a basis to be shaken by the freest inquiry,
    and the Divine authority in which I sincerely believe, without
    receiving a farthing for saying so; but from an apprehension of
    bringing into contempt their ridiculous claims and unreasonable

pretensions, which may justly tremble at the slightest scrutiny, and which I believe I shall more and more put into a panic, in defiance of both press and pulpit.

These outspoken opinions naturally created "a notable stir" in New York, and a friend of the author, then in town, in forwarding a copy of the above number to a correspondent in the country, wrote:

I send you the forty-sixth number of the *Independent Reflector*, which is making a notable stir here. The clergy and all church-men are in arms against it, and our friend Will. Livingston, who is the principal writer, is thought by some to be one of the most promising men in the province.[5]

The Church party, however, raised such "a mighty clamour" against this bold challenger of their right to domineer over all the other Christian sects in the province, that after the publication of the fifty-second number, which completed the first year's issue, his printer flatly refused to continue it. He fared no better with other printers to whom he applied, both in Boston and Philadelphia, who all firmly declined to have anything to do with the obnoxious articles. He, therefore, a few weeks after the issue of the last number, had the fifty-two numbers already published reprinted and bound in a volume, to which he added a long preface, containing a list of the subjects he had intended to have discussed, if his paper had been continued. The title-page to this volume bears the inscription: "printed (until tyranni-cally suppressed) in 1753." This wording certainly expresses very forcibly the editor's natural disappointment at his failure to continue the printing of his paper, but it is hardly correct to call such failure, arising probably from the printer's fears of incurring legal liability, tyrannical suppression!

Though Livingston was the principal contributor to the *Independent Reflector*, and sole editor, other able pens were also employed in writing articles for its columns, but owing to the fact that none of these contribu-tions bear the real names of their authors, it is impossible to identify, with any amount of certainty, his fellow-workers. It is, however, highly probable that two other young lawyers of New York, well-known friends of William Livingston, namely William Smith, junior, the historian, and John Morin Scott, afterwards one of the most active "Sons of Liberty," were contribu-tors to his paper. These two gentlemen and Livingston formed the famous "triumvirate" of New York lawyers, of whom the Rev. Samuel Johnson, first

President of King's College—now Columbia—wrote in 1759, that they were "all bitter enemies to our Church and College, and were believed to be the chief writers of the *Reflectors* and *Watch Towers.*" In a subsequent letter the same writer calls them "the wicked triumvirate of New York"; while the royalist Lieutenant-Governor Colden, who was sore troubled in his time by the actions of the popular party in the province, had good reason to complain to the Board of Trade that "for some years past three popular lawyers educated in Connecticut, who have strongly imbibed the independent principles of that country, calumniate the administration in every exercise of the prerogative, and get the applause of the mob by propagating the doctrine that all authority is derived from the people."

The fact that William Livingston's contributions to the *Independent Reflector,* like those of the other contributors already referred to, were published anonymously, though easily distinguishable from those of his fellow-writers by their editorial character, led to his being lampooned in the following doggerel verses.

> Some think him a *Tindal,* some think him a *Chub,*
> Some think him a *Ranter,* that spouts from his tub;
> Some think him a *Newton,* some think him a *Locke,*
> Some think him a *Stone,* some, think him a *Stock*—
> But a *Stock* he at least may thank Nature for giving,
> And if he's a *Stone,* I pronounce it a *Living.*

In spite of Livingston's spirited opposition, the Episcopalian majority among the trustees was successful in obtaining the insertion of the sectarian clauses in the charter for King's College, and he was the only member of the dissentient minority bold enough to lodge a strongly worded protest, against the governor granting a charter containing these obnoxious conditions. It was, of course, disregarded, though, probably in the vain hope of conciliating, or silencing, his opposition, he was appointed one of the governors, but as he could not conscientiously take the oath of office, he never frequented the meetings.

Mr. Livingston still fretted under the defeat he had sustained through his failure to obtain a printer for his paper, but though unsuccessful in this direction, his was not a nature to calmly submit to being—if one may be permitted to make use of a modem figure of speech—boycotted. Therefore, failing a separate paper of his own, he and his allies, after considerable persuasion, prevailed upon Hugh Gaine, the editor of the *New York Mercury,* to admit their essays into his columns, which had hitherto been monopolised by writers in the Church interest. These essays were published under the title of the *Watch Tower*. The first appeared in the *New York Mercury* of the 25th of November, 1754, and the last on the 17th of November of the following year; so, like its predecessor, the *Watch Tower* existed also for just twelve months.

Not long after the series of *Watch Towers* had become extinct, there was published in London an anonymous pamphlet dealing with the conduct of the recent English military operations in the war then raging—after a short lull—for the last time between England and France for the supremacy of the North American continent. This pamphlet, of which William Livingston is generally credited with the authorship, contained a slashing attack on the characters of some of the leaders of the Episcopalian party in New York, and on the favouritism shown to Sir William Johnson, one of the principal colonial officers, owing to his connection with that faction.[6] The controversy raised by this pamphlet and the college dispute materially assisted in helping the Livingston party to obtain a majority in the twenty-eighth General Assembly, summoned to meet in January, 1759, to which—as already mentioned—William Livingston had been returned for his brother's Manor. Three others of the name were also elected on this occasion; namely, Alderman Philip Livingston, an elder brother of William, as one of the members for the city and county of New York; and Robert R. Livingston of Clermont, his cousin, as one of the members for Dutchess County, while the second member for this family stronghold was another cousin, the amiable Henry Livingston, clerk for that county, and a son of the Gilbert Livingston who had sat for the Manor from 1728 until 1737.

Of the newly-elected representatives, outside the famous "triumvirate," Philip Livingston was the most prominent and popular member of the Whig or Livingston party in the House. He was a native of Albany, having been born in that town on the 15th of January, 1716 [? old style], and was the fifth son of Philip, the second Lord of the Manor. He was a graduate of Yale, of the year 1737, and soon after settled down as a merchant in New York, where he rapidly acquired a fortune; and became closely identified with the commercial progress of that growing seaport, so that Governor Sir Charles Hardy could write of him in 1755, that "among the considerable merchants in this city no one is more esteemed for energy, promptness, and public spirit, than Philip Livingston." During the French war he was extensively engaged in privateering, as were also other members of his family, which was sometimes a lucrative, as well as a popular, adjunct to a New York merchant's business in those days, and a good training school for the future Paul Joneses of the Revolutionary War.

Philip Livingston (1716–1778), signer of the Declaration of Independence.
Library of Congress, Prints and Photographs Division, Public Domain.

His close attention to business, however, did not prevent him from devoting some of his leisure time to public affairs, and in 1754 he was elected Alderman for the East Ward, which office he held until 1762. He and his brother William were among the founders of the New York Society Library in the former of these years; and when a president had to be chosen in 1756 for the newly-founded St. Andrew's Society—one of the oldest benevolent institutions in New York—Philip Livingston was the citizen selected for the post. In subsequent years he became one of the founders of the New York Chamber of Commerce—in 1770—and one of the first governors of the New York Hospital chartered during the following year. He had a great regard for the spread of education, which in his day was very much neglected in his native province; he was therefore one of the earliest advocates for the establishment of King's—now Columbia—College, and he also assisted in founding the professorship of divinity that bears his name in his *alma mater*—Yale. Like his father and grandfather before him, he intermarried with one of the oldest and principal Dutch families of New York. His wife was Christina, third daughter of Dirck Ten Broeck [mayor of Albany from 1746 to 1748], and Margarita Cuyler. They were married on the 14th of April, 1740.

The first session of the new Assembly was opened on the 31st of January, 1759, when the members present elected William Nicoll to be their Speaker.[7] According to Mr. Sedgwick, William Livingston appears to have drafted the reply of the House to the Lieutenant-Governor's Address,[8] in which he had congratulated the members of the Legislature on the recent success of the British arms in the capture of Fort Duquesne. As the vigorous prosecution of the war against the French in Canada was a matter of paramount importance at this period to the inhabitants of New York, even party feeling subsided for a time before the common danger of the threatened invasion of their province. No time therefore was lost in appointing a committee composed of members from both parties in the House, to act as a joint committee with the one appointed by the Council, for the purpose of deciding upon a plan for the defence of the unprotected northern frontier. Both Philip Livingston and his brother William served on this joint committee; and during the whole of this and the following sessions the two brothers were actively engaged in legislatorial duties.

This year—1759—witnessed the capture of Quebec by the British forces, in which decisive engagement the commanders on both sides,— the gallant Wolfe, and the equally brave, but unfortunate, Montcalm,— perished. The news of this great victory of the British arms was received with wild delight in New York and the adjacent colonies, as the ultimate conquest of Canada could now be reckoned upon as a certainty; and hence for the future, the constant nightmare of invasion by their ambitious neighbour would be at an end. While, on the other hand, far-seeing French statesmen prognosticated, that the fall of French dominion on the North American continent would, before many years had passed over, lead to the English colonies becoming independent of the mother country.

In the summer of the following year, during the prorogation of the Assembly, Lieutenant-Governor De Lancey died suddenly. As Chief Justice of the Province of New York, as well as its acting governor for many years, he had exercised great influence, and certainly was very popular with his fellow-citizens.[9] One of his descendants has pointed out as "a very remarkable fact, and as true as it is striking, that neither he nor his brothers, Peter and Oliver, who, together with their father, wielded during the British rule the strongest political and social power and influence in New York, *had a single drop of English blood in their veins*."[10] The above is, however, no exceptional case in the annals of the British Empire, whose laws have for centuries afforded shelter and protection to the persecuted peoples of other lands, and whose rulers have reaped their reward in the devotion of these fugitives and their descendants to their adopted country. The De Lanceys are a good proof, but very far from being a solitary proof, of the great benefit Great Britain has derived from her just and wise treatment of her alien-born subjects.

It is, however, certainly a curious fact, that while the leaders of the Episcopalian or Tory party in the province were of French Huguenot ancestry, and fugitives from their native country for. conscience' sake; the leaders of the Presbyterian or Whig party were also descended from one who had suffered from the persecuting spirit of that age, with this great difference, however, that, while the ancestor of the De Lanceys had been granted asylum and protection by one English sovereign,[11] the ancestor of the Livingstons had been banished from his native land by the Scottish Ministers of another English monarch.[12] This important fact therefore helps to explain, why the former family should have shown such warm attachment to the royal House of England and to the Home Government, and the latter as equally a strong aversion to the interference of the Crown and the English Ministers with the internal affairs of their adopted country. It should also be borne in mind that the majority of the Livingstons at this period, like their great rivals the De Lanceys, had no *English* blood in their veins, their principal alliances by marriage having been, since their settlement in the New World, contracted with the old Dutch families in the province.[13]

De Lancey's place was filled, until the arrival of the new governor from England, by the President of the Council, Cadwallader Colden, whose anxiety to increase the prerogative of the Crown at the expense of the liberties of his fellow-citizens was the cause of so much ill-feeling between him and the Livingstons, whom he always regarded with dislike as the leaders of the popular party in the province. On the 21st October, 1760, the third and last session of the twenty-eighth Assembly met at New York, and on the following day Colden delivered his first speech to the members, congratulating them on the conquest of Canada by the British forces. William Smith, the New York historian, says "William Livingston penned the address [in reply] offered in these triumphant moments of joy, and made the congratulatory echo louder than the first sound."[14],[15]

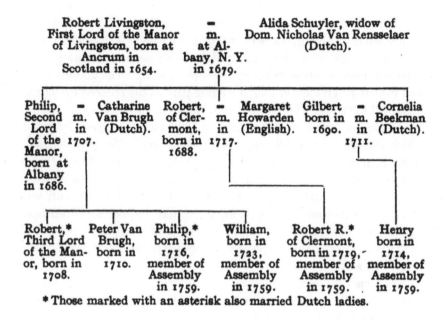

Robert Livingston,
First Lord of the Manor
of Livingston, born at
Ancrum in
Scotland in 1654.

— m. at Al- bany, N. Y. in 1679.

Alida Schuyler, widow of
Dom. Nicholas Van Rensselaer
(Dutch).

Philip,
Second
Lord
of the
Manor,
born at
Albany
in 1686.

— Catharine
m. Van Brugh
in (Dutch).
1707.

Robert,
of Cler-
mont,
born in
1688.

— Margaret
m. Howarden
in (English).
1717.

Gilbert
born in
1690.

— Cornelia
m. Beekman
in (Dutch).
1711.

Robert,*
Third Lord
of the Man-
or, born in
1708.

Peter Van
Brugh,
born in
1710.

Philip,*
born in
1716,
member of
Assembly
in 1759.

William,
born in
1723,
member of
Assembly
in 1759.

Robert R.*
of Clermont,
born in 1719,
member of
Assembly
in 1759.

Henry
born in
1714,
member of
Assembly
in 1759.

* Those marked with an asterisk also married Dutch ladies.

This session only sat until the eighth of the following month, when
the House was adjourned, to meet again after Christmas; but the news of
the death of George the Second reaching New York during the recess, the
Assembly thereupon had to be dissolved; and fresh writs issued—21st of
January, 1761—for representatives to be returned to serve in the General
Assembly summoned to meet on the third of March in that year.

Though the Livingstons were again successful at the polls, and added
to their previous gains, the leader of their party did not seek re-election on
this occasion, as his increasing legal practice prevented him from sparing
the time that would be necessary for attending to legislative duties as well.
His nephew, Peter R. Livingston, the eldest surviving son of his brother
Robert of the Manor, was therefore returned in his place, while his brother
Philip retained his seat as one of the city members, and his cousins, the two
members for Dutchess, were re-elected for that county. It was during the
sessions of this Assembly that the British Parliament attempted to introduce stamp duties into America. The universal opposition aroused in the
colonies against this obnoxious impost led to a meeting of a Congress in
the City Hall at New York, on the 7th of October, 1765. To this Congress,
known in history as the Stamp Act Congress, nine of the colonies sent delegates, to the number of twenty-eight in all. New York was represented by

its city members in the General Assembly, with the addition of Robert R. Livingston of Clermont, one of the members for Dutchess, in defiance of the governor's disapproval, who considered the Congress unconstitutional, and what was perhaps worse in his eyes—unprecedented! The cousins Philip and Robert R. Livingston took a leading part in the proceedings of this historical Congress.[16] The former had, twelve months previously, drafted the address of the General Assembly to Lieutenant-Governor Colden, in which the hope was boldly expressed that he would "heartily join with them in an endeavour to secure that great badge of English liberty of being taxed only with their own consent, to which they conceive all his majesty's subjects at home and abroad, were equally entitled." On the twenty-fifth of October this Congress concluded its labours, having agreed upon an Address to the King, a Memorial to the House of Lords, and a petition to the House of Commons. These proceedings led to the repeal of the Stamp Act in the following year.[17]

Though William Livingston, the late representative for the Manor, was not actually engaged, like his brother and cousin, in concerting measures for obtaining the repeal of the Stamp Act, his sympathies were naturally entirely with those who resisted its being forced upon an unwilling people; and in a striking article contributed by him at this critical period to Holt's *New York Weekly Post-Boy*, entitled "A New Sermon to an Old Text,"[18]—which was written in reply to the churchmen of New York who preached loyalty to the king, as they claimed was demanded by the Scriptures under the text "Touch not mine anointed"—he boldly asserted this text had been wrongly interpreted by the commentators, for the people and not monarchs, Livingston daringly argued, are "the Lord's anointed." And he also hinted that they must be very tenderly handled, "for though named 'mob' and 'rabble,' the people are the darling of Providence." Three years later—1768—be again entered the lists in defence of the dissenting interests in the province against the increasing encroaching disposition of the Church of England; and in "A Letter to the Right Reverend Father in God, John Lord Bishop of Llandaff," he defends the colonies from the undeserved reproach cast on them by some passages in his lordship's sermon preached on the 20th February, 1767. This pamphlet is couched in language of honest indignation aroused by an unjust attack, and sarcastic contempt of the bishop's ignorance of the subject upon which he preached. It created a great sensation at the time, and was immediately republished in London; and on the 21st of June, 1768, he received from the associated churches of the colony of Connecticut, assembled at Coventry, a vote of thanks "for vindicating the New England Churches and plantations against the injurious reflections in the Bishop of Llandaff's sermon." On the other hand, he was bitterly attacked by the partisans of the Church party in the province; one of whom wrote some doggerel lines in parody of the above vote of thanks, which he entitled "Reviving Cordial for a fainting Hero," and which closes thus:—

March on, brave Will, and rear our Babel
On language so unanswerable,
Give Church and State a hearty thump,
And knock down truth with falsehoods plump;
So flat shall fall their churches' fair stones,
Felled by another *Praise God Barebones*,
Signed with consent of all the tribe,
By No[a]h W[elle]s, our fasting scribe.[19]

Before leaving this subject mention must be made of an article, said to have been written by William Livingston, and published in the *New York Gazette*[20] of the nth of April, 1768, which contains the following remarkable prophecy concerning the future of America, in allusion to a plan then being discussed for a union of the colonies as part of the British Empire:—

Never was there such a phoenix state. Liberty, religion, and science were on their wing to these shores. The finger of God pointed to a mighty empire. The mother and her sons would again be collected in one house, and in proportion to the abatement of national glory would be the brightness of its resurrection in America. The day dawns in which the foundation of this mighty empire is to be laid by the establishment of a regular American Constitution. All that has hitherto been done seems to be little beside the collection of materials for the construction of this glorious fabric. 'T is time to put them together. The transfer of the European part of the great family is so swift, and our growth so fast, *that before seven years roll over our heads the first stone must be laid.*

Though this idea of a union of the British colonies in North America was not a new one, it having occupied the minds of thinking men for many years anterior to this date,[21] still William Livingston could little have foreseen when he wrote the above article, that *within the time named by him the first stone would be laid, but of an independent America!*

Two months prior to the date of this article, the governor, Sir Henry Moore, who had been sent out from England to assume the government of the province at the time of the Stamp Act Riots, dissolved the twenty-ninth Assembly, which had been in existence its full term of seven years, and had held during that period thirteen sessions.[22] The writs for a new Assembly were returnable on the 2 2d March, 1768, but on the members meeting in the Assembly Chamber on that day, they found the governor had adjourned the opening of the session until the 27th of October. The Whig or Livingston party had been again victorious at the polls, though it was not so strongly represented in the new House as it had been in the one recently dissolved, and only two members of the family were returned on this occasion, namely Philip, elected for the third time as one of the representatives for the city and county of New York, and Peter R. Livingston, re-elected for his father's Manor; while Robert R. Livingston, the judge, and his kinsman Henry Livingston, lost their seats for Dutchess. Among the other adherents of this party returned to the new Assembly, were several members whose names also became historical during the stirring times of the War of Independence, such as George Clinton, member for Ulster, afterwards first Governor of the State of New York; Pierre Van Cortlandt, member for the Manor of that name, to be in time State Lieutenant-Governor; Philip Schuyler, member for Albany, and Abraham Ten Broeck for the Manor of Rensselaerwyck, both subsequently generals in the American army; and Charles De Witt, Clinton's colleague for Ulster, and Henry Wisner, one of the representatives for the Tory county of Orange.

Twenty-six of the newly-elected representatives were in attendance at the opening of the first and only session of the thirtieth General Assembly on the 27th of October, 1768, and on the following day they "unanimously chose Philip Livingston, Esq., as their Speaker," which selection met with the approbation of the governor. Though Sir Henry Moore was on very friendly terms with the Livingstons,— his private secretary being a member of this family,[23]—it is very doubtful whether his approbation would have been so freely accorded, if he could have foreseen the trouble this sturdy opponent of the interference of the British Parliament in the internal affairs of the colony was to cause his government. For this Assembly only sat for the short space of sixty-seven days, owing to the Whig majority in the House having passed sundry resolutions asserting the rights of the colonists to be allowed to attend to their own internal affairs themselves, and protesting against the interference of the British Parliament in matters which ought, they maintained, only to be the concern of their own Legislature. These resolutions naturally gave great offence to the governor, who replied to the demands of the Assembly by dissolving it upon the second of January, 1769; and in his speech on this occasion he severely reprimanded the House for "the extraordinary nature of certain resolves lately entered on their Journals, some flatly repugnant to the laws of Great Britain, and others with an apparent tendency to give offence where common prudence would avoid it, [which] have put it out of his power to continue the Assembly any longer."

One of these resolutions contained the bold declaration that "this Colony lawfully and constitutionally has, and enjoys an internal Legislature of its own, in which the Crown and the people of this Colony are constitutionally represented, and the power and authority of the said Legislature cannot lawfully or constitutionally be suspended, abridged, abrogated, or annulled by any power, authority, or prerogative whatsoever; the prerogative of the Crown ordinarily exercised for prorogations and dissolutions only excepted." As Speaker, Philip Livingston had signed this resolution on the 31st December 1768, by which action he had not only offended the governor, but also the Tory minority in the House.

Philip Livingston, being a man of peace, was desirous of effecting a coalition between the two political parties at this critical juncture, and thus to avoid the harm that, he foresaw, would ensue from a hotly contested election under the then conditions. He therefore publicly declared he would only come forward as a candidate for the city, if he were asked to do so by the moderate men of both parties in the constituency. Political passions, however, were too much inflamed for such a combination to be arranged, though the Tories had no objection to him personally as a candidate; whereupon, finding he would fail in effecting the desired junction of parties, Philip Livingston withdrew from the contest. This, however, did not suit his own supporters, who were aghast at the withdrawal of their champion. They thereupon sent a deputation to ask him whether, if they were successful in getting him elected, he would decline the seat? To this deputation he returned the answer, "that as he had declined, he had not the least expectation of being elected; but if he were elected, he should think it his duty to serve."[24]

As Philip Livingston had feared, the canvass for the new election was conducted with a great deal of warmth on both sides, especially in the city, where party feeling at this date ran very high. The resolutions passed by the late 1 Assembly had greatly alarmed the official and mercantile classes, and they therefore used every means in their power to return the friends of the De Lancey or Tory faction. The writs were returnable on the 4th of February, so that no time was lost by the governor in having matters brought to an issue. The following extract from a letter, written at this time by Peter R. Livingston, the late representative for the Manor, to his friend Colonel Schuyler, will show what great excitement this election was causing in the city, and that some partisans of the Livingstons, in spite of their liberal views, were actually prepared to use force, if necessary, so anxious were they that their candidates should, be successful at the polls:—

> Since my last I have only to acquaint you that we are all hard at work. I think the prospect has a good aspect, and at all events Jauncey must go to the wall this time. I make no doubt, if we can keep the people to the promise they have made, that Philip [Livingston] and Scott will be two, and if the opposite party push old John Cruger, I am of opinion that they will push one of the other two out. Our canvass stands well, but there will be a vast deal of cross-voting. The two they all pitch on are Philip and Scott, which will put them in. But there is a great deal in good management of the votes. Our people are in high spirits, and if there is not fair play shown there will be bloodshed, as we have by far the best part of the Bruisers on our side, who are determined to use force if they use any foul play. I have engaged from the first day, and am determined to see it out. Lewis Morris certainly comes in for the Borough [Westchester]. Henry Holland is obliged to resign for Richmond, as young Browne and young Farmer set up in opposition to each other.[25]

Peter R. Livingston's predictions, however, were not all verified by the result of this hard-fought contest, as both Philip Livingston, the late Speaker, and John Morin Scott were defeated by the De Lancey voters, who returned "old John Cruger" in the former's place in spite of the "Bruisers"; while the Church party were also triumphant in other parts of the province, even Judge Robert R. Livingston of Clermont failing to recapture his old seat for Dutchess County. The "Churchmen" were loud in their rejoicings over the defeat of their Presbyterian opponents; and a shrewd eyewitness of this election, wrote to his brother in the country, the following interesting and amusing account of what happened in New York City when the result became known:—

> Our election is ended, and the Church triumphant. Messrs. Cruger, Delancey, Walton, and Jauncey are the members, in spite of all the efforts of the Presbyterian interest combined with some other dissenting sects. This is what the Churchmen call a complete victory; 't is a lasting monument of the power of the mercantile interest. It is impossible there ever could be a more decently conducted election, but it will add fuel to a flame of party spirit, which I believe will never be extinguished.... Mr. Kissam, who summed up the evidence for Mr. Scott in the late charge against Mr. Jauncey, happened to say that the passions of the Germans were like firebrands;—a whole congregation were, in consequence of that, resolved to vote with them in their hands; but being dissuaded, they however distinguished themselves by the name of the *Firebrands*.
>
> These gentlemen have also made themselves remarkable by a song in the German language the chorus of which is:
>
> > "Measter Cruger, Delancey,
> > Measter Walton and Jauncey."
>
> It was droll to see some of the first gentlemen in town joining in singing this song, while they conducted the members to the coffee house; on which occasion it was observed that there was a greater concourse of people than was ever seen on any former occasion in town.[26]

Though rejected by the city, Philip Livingston was returned for his brother's Manor, owing to the self-denial of his nephew, Peter R. Livingston, who retired in his favour. This was the second occasion upon which the owner of this "pocket Borough," had placed it at the disposal of a leader of the family party, when a seat elsewhere was unobtainable. The new Assembly met on the 4th of April, when owing to the popular party being in a minority, Philip Livingston was passed over for the Speakership in favour of his successful opponent at the New York polls—"old John Cruger."

Eight days later he experienced a further proof of the intention of the Tory majority to punish him for his championship of the popular cause; for a Mr. Thomas, one of the members for the Borough of Westchester, and a bigoted Tory, brought forward on the 12th of April a motion to vacate Mr. Livingston's seat on account of non-residence. This motion having been written out by Mr. Thomas in the usual way, was found to contain "so much false spelling and bad English," as to cause Mr. Clinton to sarcastically remark "that it would reflect great dishonour on this House, as well as on himself [Mr. Thomas] should it be entered as it now stands; he therefore moved that Mr. Thomas be ordered to correct his said motion, at least as to spelling, before it appears on the journal of this House." Thereupon it was ordered "that Mr. Thomas correct his said motion"; which he having corrected accordingly, is in the words following:—

> Mr. Speaker,
> I find by an Act passed by the general assembly of the colony of New York, the 8th May 1769 (sic) it is amongst other things enacted, for regulating elections in this colony, that no non-resident should have a right to a seat in the House of Assembly. I find that Mr. Philip Livingston is returned for the Manor of Livingston, in the county of Albany; I move that for the aforesaid reasons, his not being a resident, according to the Act of Assembly, that he may be dismissed from his attendance of this House.

On a debate arising on this motion, and it being put to the question, "whether Mr. Thomas's motion should be rejected or not, it was carried in the negative," by a majority of eight votes, sixteen voting in favour of the motion and only eight for its rejection; the voting being strictly on party lines. It was then ordered "that the consideration of Mr. Thomas's motion be postponed till Thursday the 27th inst." Whereupon Mr. Clinton rose and moved "that an order of this House be made charging Mr. Thomas with the payment of costs in case it should appear that his motion for dismissing Mr. Livingston (the member returned for the Manor of Livingston) from his seat in this House, is vexatious and frivolous." This, of course, was negatived by the Tory majority in the House.

On the 27th of April, the consideration of this motion was again postponed until the following day, when Colonel Schuyler, one of the leading Whig members, called the attention of the House to the fact that the Act quoted by Mr. Thomas as having been passed on the 8th of May 1769, could never have been passed on that date; but apparently on the 8th of

May 1699. He therefore moved "for the sense of the House thereupon." His objection was, however, overruled, but the date was corrected in accordance with his motion and the consideration of Mr. Thomas's further postponed until the 12th of May next.

Nothing daunted by the evident determination of his political opponents to use every means in their power to procure his expulsion from the House, Mr. Livingston, on the very day that Mr. Thomas brought forward his motion, still further inflamed the anger of the Tories by moving a resolution to the effect that the House, to prevent reports being spread abroad to the detriment of the cause of American liberty, should confirm the resolutions passed by the late Assembly, and entered in the Journals on the 31st of December last. As the passing of these resolutions was the cause of Sir Henry Moore dissolving the late Assembly, the friends of the government in the House could only deem this a further proof of his republican principles; and his motion was, as he probably foresaw would be the case, postponed from time to time, and never acted on. Not content with moving the above resolution, this daring advocate of American liberty obtained leave five days later—17th April—to lay before the House a bill, entitled "An Act to vacate the seat of any present or future member of General Assembly, who shall accept of any post or place of honour, profit, or trust, under the Crown, after his being elected a member to serve in General Assembly."[27] The bill was read a first time and ordered a second reading; but on the second reading, which took place on the 24th of April, it was referred to the consideration of a Committee of the whole House, by whom it was, on the 17th of May shelved until the next session.

Meanwhile, upon the twelfth of this month, the question "whether Mr. Livingston be dismissed from his attendance on the service of this House, on Mr. Thomas's motion, for not being a resident, agreeable to the Act of Assembly for regulating elections, passed on the 8th of May 1699," was carried in the affirmative by a majority of eleven votes out of a total of twenty-five,[28] in spite of a petition presented to the Assembly by "Robert Livingston, junior,[29] Robert R. Livingston,[30] Peter R. Livingston,[31] Dirck W. Ten Broeck, Dirck Jansen, and twenty-two other freeholders of the Manor of Livingston," to the effect that "the petitioners did unanimously elect Philip Livingston, Esq., to serve in this present General Assembly, as their representative," and that as regards non-residents they were not excluded from the British Parliament, and the Act quoted by Mr. Thomas was never intended to apply to such a case. Moreover, it was well known that non-residents were permitted to represent counties, for out of twenty-four cases only three instances have ever occurred of members being deprived of their seats on this account, and these arose solely out of party spite. The petitioners also declared that for the last fifty-three years, except in three instances, the Manor had been represented by non-residents; besides, though not actually residing on the Manor, Mr. Livingston was, as a freeholder, duly qualified to vote for a member to represent it in General Assembly, and should therefore be fully entitled also to serve himself in that capacity, if elected. The hostile majority having gained their point, the clerk was instructed, on the following day, to see that a new writ was issued for a member to be returned to represent the Manor of Livingston in that House. Five days after the dismissal of Philip Livingston, and on the very same day that the Committee of the Whole House postponed the third reading of his bill to vacate the seat of any member who shall accept of any post under the Crown, Mr. De Noyelles, member for Orange County, an ardent Tory, and one of the bitterest opponents in the Assembly of the Livingston family, moved a resolution to the effect that as it was not constitutional in England for judges to sit or vote in the House of Commons, so "no judge of the supreme court shall be allowed to sit or vote as a member of this House." Whereupon it was agreed, *nemine contradicente*, that this resolution should be entered on the journals. The only reason that can be assigned for the haste with which this resolution was introduced and rushed through the Assembly, on the vacancy occurring in the representation of the Manor by the dismissal of Philip Livingston, was the desire to debar another talented member of this family from also making use of this "pocket borough," as a means for gaining admission into the House. For it was well known that Judge Robert R. Livingston of Clermont, who had sat for Dutchess from 1759 to 1768, but who had failed to secure his return at the elections held in 1768 and 1769, was anxious to become an assemblyman again; while the Tories were determined to prevent its accomplishment, if possible.

Because the judge by his conduct during the Stamp Act riots, and his firm refusal to acknowledge the right of appeal from the provincial law courts to the King, had highly incensed Lieutenant-Governor Colden, who also owed the liberal-minded judge a personal grudge for his share in the prosecution of a pamphlet, which had been recently published in defence of this official's conduct during the late troubles; but which, it was alleged by those opposed to the lieutenant-governor's policy, contained charges against the Courts of Justice in the province of a "false, infamous, and libellous character."[32] Colden had complained to the Home Government over and over again about the trouble Judge Livingston gave him, and had denounced him as "the most violent man, both in the Supreme Court and in the Assembly, in the malicious prosecution of the pamphlet wrote in his (Colden's) vindication"; and he moreover asserted that the reason why he had failed to be returned to the Assembly in the late elections was on account of his having become so unpopular owing to his opposition to him. Sir Henry Moore, the governor, however, did not share his lieutenant's opinion as to Judge Livingston's character, for at the very time that Colden was fulminating his complaints against him to the Secretary of State, he, the governor, had written to the Lords of Trade, urging on them the advisability of appointing the judge to fill a vacancy in the Council, now that he was no longer a member of the Lower House.

Governor Moore's recommendation, owing to Colden having poisoned the minds of the English officials against Judge Livingston, was received very coldly in London, and it was more than hinted that the governor had been influenced by motives of private friendship in submitting his name as a candidate for the vacant seat at the Council Board. This slander upon his reputation the governor repelled in a warm and long letter to Lord Hillsborough written in January 1769, in which he declares that his "connections in point of acquaintance and private friendship with Mr. Robert Livingston are by no means so strong as with many Gentlemen of this province, whose names he had never mentioned to his Lordship." He then gives in detail his reasons for his recommendation of him as a suitable person to fill the vacant seat:—namely

He is a branch of the most considerable family in this Province; his father (who is very advanced in years) possessed of a very great landed Estate, which will come to him undivided as he is an only son. He is married to the richest Heiress in this Country, whose Father is likewise very old and infirm; so that in all human probability he must very shortly be the greatest Landholder without any exception in this Province; the very large Estate which must centre in him, cannot fail of giving him great weight here, and puts it very much, in his power to support Government, which all my letters to His Majesty's Ministers have shewed to be very weak and to stand much in need of every assistance which can be obtained. Mr. Livingston is a Member of the Church of England as by Law established and very well effected to His Majesty's person and Government. He is at this time one of the Judges of the Supreme Court, and has there given frequent proofs of his abilities to serve his Country. He has likewise been for several years a member of the House of Assembly, where I must acknowledge myself indebted to him, for his readiness and assistance in some difficulties I laboured under during the troubles I was engaged in, on my first arrival here, and from the whole tenor of his conduct I thought he deserved [the] recommendation I had given him, being at this time fully persuaded that if he had been a Member of Council during the last Session of Assembly I should have been better supported than I was by that Board when the resolves of the late Assembly were laid before them, which brought on the dissolution.

In his reply to the above recommendation of Mr. Livingston, the Secretary of State wrote, that it is not considered necessary to fill up the vacancy caused by the resignation of Lord Stirling, and that what he urges "in favour of Mr. Livingston must remain for the consideration of the Board of Trade when another vacancy happens"; but in another letter written a few months later (15th July 1769), Lord Hillsborough refers to the king's annoyance at the conduct of Mr. Livingston and others in giving public thanks to the merchants on account of their behaviour in forming an association to prevent the importation of merchandise from Great Britain during the late troubles, and he expresses his surprise that the governor should not have thought fit to have alluded to this fact in his official correspondence. This evidently, coupled with the governor's death, which event took place in the autumn of this year, settled all further chance of Judge Livingston ever becoming a member of His Majesty's Legislative Council for the Province of New York.

Finding he had little chance of being nominated to fill the vacancy in the Council, the judge accepted his cousin's off er of the family seat in the Lower House,—as his political opponents had anticipated he would do,—and, of course, was duly elected by "the free and independent" voters on the Manor. Owing, however, to the Assembly having been prorogued on the 20th of May, namely three days after the resolution excluding judges from the House had been passed, he was unable to claim admission as a member until it met again six months later. On the 24th of November, three days after the opening of the new session, Judge Livingston duly appeared in the Assembly, and having produced "an indenture of his being elected and returned a representative for the said Manor," claimed his seat in accordance with the same. This at once brought Mr. De Noyelles to his feet, for on the Speaker putting the question "whether two members should wait upon one of the commissioners appointed to qualify the representatives to serve in this present General Assembly and see Mr. Livingston qualified," that gentleman made a motion "that the question be put, whether this House will enter into examining the propriety of the resolution entered on the journals of the last session against the judges of the supreme court, or not." This led to a debate, which resulted in the House by a majority of eight votes out of a total of twenty-two, refusing to recognise the judge as a properly qualified representative for the Manor; and it was therefore "*Ordered,* That Mr. Speaker issue his warrant to the clerk of the Crown, to make out a new writ for electing a representative to serve in the present General Assembly for the Manor of Livingston, in the room of Robert R. Livingston, Esq. declared disqualified by his being a judge of the supreme court." As, in the division on the "non-residence" question, the voting was strictly on party lines; the Whig minority in this, as on later occasions, stedfastly voting in favour of the judge's admission, who refused to acknowledge that the Assembly had any legal right "to exclude any person they think proper without the concurrence of the other branch of the Legislature," and appealed to the Home Government for a decision in his favour.

During the next three years Judge Livingston, like another Wilkes, who was regarded as a popular hero in America as in London, was re-elected again and again by the voters on his cousin's Manor only to be as persistently excluded by the hostile majority on each fresh occasion that he appeared in the House of Assembly to claim his seat. On the third occasion of his thus presenting himself, on the 25th of January 1771, his friend Mr. Clinton, one of the members for Ulster, brought forward a resolution to have the matter at issue referred to a committee of the whole House; and in his speech he questioned the right of the Assembly to exclude "any officer under the Crown, or other persons not qualified by law, from seats in this House, by a bare resolve of the House," which he considered would be "a high invasion of the fundamental rights of our constituents, in the freedom of elections, an abridgement of the authority of the other branch of the Legislature, subversive of our happy constitution, and *tending to the erection of a republic in this colony.*" How surprised Mr. Clinton would have been, if he could have been informed at this time, that within the short space of six years he would be elected by the people of this colony to be the first governor of the independent State of New York, then battling for its very existence as a nation, but which he would live to see become the leading commonwealth in the Republic of the United States of America! His resolution was, as a matter of course, negatived by the Tory majority, and the usual vote passed declaring the judge disqualified.

As yet refusing to confess himself beaten, Judge Livingston, on a new writ being issued, presented himself for the fourth time as a candidate to the voters on the Manor, to be returned unopposed as on the three previous occasions; to be again rejected on presenting himself before the House on the 5th of February in the following year (1772); and to be again re-elected, for the fifth time, on claiming anew the suffrages of "the freeholders of the Manor of Livingston." The judge was, however, now getting tired of the unequal and monotonous struggle, and in a letter to the Earl of Dartmouth, the new English Secretary of State, written on the 5th of November, 1772, he expressed his disappointment that though "this dispute between the Assembly [and himself] has lasted now about three years, the several governors we have had in that time, to wit, Lieutenant-Governor Colden, Lord Dunmore, and Mr. Tryon, have not thought proper to do anything decisive in the matter without His Majesty's particular orders." He also in the same letter, pointed out that he had been "five times chosen Representative for the Manor of Livingston in General Assembly; four times he had been refused admittance, and on the fifth Election he had not yet presented himself." But though the English ministers strongly disapproved of the New York Assembly's action in this matter, as they regarded with a jealous eye the power claimed by that body "*to exclude any person they think proper without the concurrence of the other branch of the Legislature*,"[33] they could not obtain the withdrawal of the resolution excluding judges from the House, though in other matters, this, the last of the Colonial Assemblies, was willing enough to meet the wishes of the Home Government. Mr. Livingston allowed over a year to elapse from the date of his letter to Lord Dartmouth, before claiming his seat for the fifth and last time, and upon receiving the customary adverse vote against his admission, he retired from the unequal contest;[34] whereupon the eldest son of the Lord of the Manor, Peter R. Livingston, who had sat as the representative of his father's Manor between the years 1761–1769, was returned in his room, and was allowed to take his seat in the House of Assembly upon the 21st of February 1774, just about a month after the judge had been dismissed for the last time. Thus for nearly five years the Manor of Livingston had been practically disfranchised through the action of the De Lancey or Tory majority in the General Assembly.

Peter R. Livingston took a leading part in the later proceedings of this, the last of the Colonial Assemblies, whose days were now numbered, as its powers were being rapidly usurped by the Provincial Conventions and Congresses summoned by the popular party, in the interests of the "common safety." One of his last proceedings in the House was to move, on the 21st of February 1775, a vote of thanks "to the merchants and inhabitants of this city and colony, for their repeated, disinterested, public spirited, and patriotic conduct, in declining the importation or receiving goods from Great Britain, and for their firm adherence to the association entered into, and recommended by the Grand Continental Congress, held at Philadelphia, in the months of September and October last." This motion, after some debate, was negatived, by a vote of fifteen to ten, and the Assembly, after drawing up a petition to the King, a Memorial to the House of Lords, and Remonstrance to the House of Commons, was adjoined on the following 3d of April, to meet a month later. But its members never came together again after this date, for the governor on the 1st of May prorogued it to the following 7th of June, and then kept on proroguing it from date to date until the 17th April 1776, when the thirtieth General Assembly of the Province of New York expired through effluxion of time, and no new one was summoned to take its place.

Paper appointing Peter R. Livingston as a Colonel of the Militia in the County of Albany by George Washington, August 4, 1778. Thomas Addis Emmet Collection, New York Public Library Digital Collections, Public Domain.

Thus Peter R. Livingston was the last of the representatives returned to the New York Assembly by the freeholders of the Manor, under the terms of Governor Hunter's confirmatory patent of 1715, for on the downfall of British rule in the North American Colonies, the feudal privileges conferred by these manorial patents were completely abolished, and though the Manor of Livingston belonged to that "pernicious class of institutions, close boroughs,"[35] its representatives were always, as we have seen, foremost in the cause of liberty and the staunch defenders of the rights of the people. The descendants therefore of these worthy representatives may be honestly proud of the fact that their ancestors, in spite of their social position, their wealth, their immense landed estates, and the exceptional privileges, conferred on their family by the manorial patents, were to be found arrayed on the popular side in the great struggle between Great Britain and her revolted colonies. For on the outbreak of the War of Independence, six out of the eight representatives, who had been elected to represent the family Manor in the General Assembly during the past sixty years, were still living, all of whom heartily espoused the cause of freedom.

Of these six survivors, two died at the very commencement of hostilities; namely, the aged Robert Livingston of Clermont, who prophetically predicted that "America must and will be independent," and whose death is said to have been hastened by the news of the fight at Bunker Hill; and his only son, Judge Robert R. Livingston, who died suddenly six months later, and whose liberal principles were inherited by his famous son and namesake—Chancellor Livingston. Of the remaining four representatives, the brothers Philip and William Livingston were both members of the First and Second Continental Congress, and while the former's name is attached to the Declaration of Independence, the latter has also become celebrated in American history as the "War Governor" of New Jersey, and as one of the signers of the Federal Constitution; and though Robert, the third and last Lord of the Manor, did not personally take an active part in the War of Independence, still he encouraged his sons to do so, for his eldest son Colonel Peter R. Livingston,[36] the last of the Representatives of the Manor, served both in the Provincial Congress of the Colony of New York, and in the Convention of the State of New York—as that body was called after the Declaration of Independence—as one of the deputies from the City and County of Albany; as did also another son, Walter. Peter R. Livingston held the office of President of the Convention during the latter part of the famous year 1776, and he also acted for some time as chairman of the New York Committee of Safety. Here, therefore, worthily ends the political history of the old colonial Manor of Livingston, which became, by the new order of events, absorbed into the electoral district of Albany.

Notes

1. Robert had succeeded his father Philip, as third Lord of the Manor, in 1749.
2. Thus Peter Van Brugh Livingston was head of his Class in 1731; while John Livingston was second in 1733, owing to the first place on this List being assigned to Samuel Talcott, the fourth son of Joseph Talcott, Governor of the Colony of Connecticut; and Philip Livingston was also placed second in his year (1737), the first graduate on this occasion being John Still Winthrop, of the old New England family of that name. This classification of the Livingstons is the more significant, as, with few exceptions, the students were from the New England Colonies, Connecticut naturally supplying the greatest number; and thus the few New York students would be looked upon as strangers by their fellow-classmates, who would not be likely to regard with favour the prominent position assigned to this particular family.
3. King's College, since the Revolution re-christened Columbia College.
4. Though the members of the Church of England were in a minority in the province, seven of the ten trustees were of that persuasion. Of the remainder, two represented the Dutch Church, and one—William Livingston—the Presbyterian.
5. The writer of this letter was a youthful member of the Schuyler family; in later years to become celebrated as the Major-General Philip Schuyler of the Revolutionary War.
6. The above pamphlet bears the following lengthy title:—A Review of the Military Operations in North America, from the Commencement of the French Hostilities on the Frontiers of Virginia in 1753, to the Surrender of Oswego, on the 14th of August, 1756; in a Letter to a Nobleman. Dated 20th September, 1756. It is also claimed to have been written by William Smith, the historian, who, after the War of Independence, became Chief-Justice of Canada.
7. A son of the former Speaker of the same name.
8. Life of William Livingston, pp. 119, 120. But according to an entry in the Journals of Assembly the reply to the Address was drawn up by a committee; still William Livingston may have drafted it as its principal member.
9. Though his services to the Home Government were fully recognised, he never obtained a commission as governor, owing to the policy that did not permit of the appointment of a native of any colony to its highest office.
10. Namely Mr. Edward Floyd De Lancey in his sketch of his family in Judge Jones's History of New York during the Revolutionary War. The words in italics are so given by Mr. De Lancey.
11. James II in 1686.
12. Charles II in 1662.
13. With one notable exception all the leading members of this family in America, at the period we are treating of, were of Dutch extraction on the female side. The exception was Robert R. Livingston of Clermont, whose mother was English.
14. History of New York, edition 1829, vol. ii, p. 286. According to the Journals of Assembly, this address was read in the House by Captain Livingston, who is evidently William Livingston's cousin Robert R. Livingston of Clermont, who held that rank in the provincial militia. The Journals simply state it was drawn up by a

committee, but probably Mr. Smith is correct in ascribing the actual drafting of it to his friend William Livingston.

15. Those marked with an asterisk also married Dutch ladies.

16. Mr. Frothingham in his *Rise of the Republic of the United States*, has twice represented the two Livingston members of this Congress to have been *brothers* instead of cousins—*vide* pages 172 and 186 of his work. This error probably arose from his having mistaken Robert R. Livingston of Clermont for Philip's elder brother Robert of the Manor. Between the years 1709 and 1759 *five* different Robert Livingstons sat in the New York Assembly:—1. Robert, first Lord of the Manor; 2. Robert junior, "the nephew," of Albany; 3. Robert, the first proprietor of Clermont; 4. Robert, the third Lord of the Manor; 5. Robert R. of Clermont, and only son of No. 3.

17. For further particulars of this Congress and the Stamp Act Riots see the previous chapter.

18. One of a series of papers written by William Livingston between February and August, 1765, under the name of "The Sentinel."

19. Namely the Rev. Noah Welles, secretary to this convention, and a classmate of William Livingston.

20. As No. V of *The American Whig*, of which series of papers William Livingston was the editor, and principal contributor.

21. William Livingston's grandfather, Robert, first Lord of the Manor, was strongly in favour of such a union for mutual defence, and drew up a scheme for this end which he forwarded to the Lords of Trade in May, 1701. A copy of this letter will be found in *New York Colonial Documents*, vol. iv, pp. 870–879.

22. Before the law regulating the duration of Assemblies passed in December, 1743, which limited each Assembly to seven years unless previously dissolved, there had been no special term fixed, as the Triennial Act passed in 1737 had been vetoed by the king during the following year.

23. Namely Philip, the eldest son of Peter Van Brugh Livingston, and therefore a nephew of the Speaker.

24. *Vide* Philip Livingston's explanatory Address to the Electors. When writing of this event in the *Livingstons of Callendar*, pp. 445, 446, and note 101, the author had not seen this address, and was therefore puzzled at the statement made by Mr. DeWitt Clinton in his sketch of Philip Livingston in Sanderson's *Lives of the Signers*, that he (Philip) had declined to stand on this occasion, when all the evidence went to prove he was one of the defeated candidates.

25. Letter dated 16th January 1769. The writer, an energetic political partisan, was the eldest surviving son of Robert, the third Lord of the Manor. The prominent part he took in pushing the affairs of his party, and in aiding and abetting the often violent acts of the well-known "Sons of Liberty" brought down on his head the abuse of his opponents, by whom he was dubbed "Jew Peter"; *vide* Lossing's *Life of Philip Schuyler*, vol. i, p. 236.

26. Letter from Peter Van Schaack to Henry Van Schaack, dated New York, Friday, 27 January 1769.

The following was the result of the City Poll:—

James DeLancey	received	936	votes.
Jacob Walton	"	931	"
John Cruger	"	888	"
James Jauncey	"	872	"
Philip Livingston	"	666	"
John Morin Scott	"	646	"
Peter Van Brugh Livingston	"	535	"
Theodore Van Wyck	"	518	"

27. Since the reign of Queen Anne, a member of the British Parliament has to vacate his seat, and seek re-election, on being appointed to "an office or place of profit under the crown."
28. As the total number of representatives was twenty-seven, only two members, out of the whole House, were either absent or abstained from voting.
29. The Lord of the Manor.
30. Judge Livingston of Clermont.
31. The late member for the Manor.
32. See previous chapter.
33. The words in italics are underlined by the judge in his letter.
34. The following are the dates of the five separate occasions on which Judge Livingston presented himself to the House as the Representative for the Manor of Livingston:—(1) 24th November 1769; (2) 21st December 1769; (3) 25th January 1771; (4) 5th February 1772; (5) 26th January 1774.
35. *Vide* Sedgwick's *Life of William Livingston*, p. 39.
36. He was colonel of the Manor of Livingston, or Tenth Albany, Regiment of Militia, during the War of Independence.

CHAPTER XII

CONCERNING THE DECLARATION OF INDEPENDENCE, AND THE REASONS WHY ONLY ONE OF THE THREE LIVINGSTON MEMBERS OF THE SECOND CONTINENTAL CONGRESS SIGNED THE SAME.

"Now meet the fathers of this western clime,
　No names more noble graced the roll of Fame,
When Spartan firmness braved the wrecks of time,
　Or Rome's bold virtues fann'd the heroic flame."
　　　　　—*From Trumbull's* Elegy on the Times.

THE retaliatory measures directed against Boston in 1774 by the British Government naturally greatly alarmed the other colonies, who rightly deemed an attack upon one of their number, an attack upon all. In New York, in particular, the extreme radical party, which had been represented for some years past by an association known as the "Sons of Liberty," the turbulent conduct of which, had, on more than one occasion of popular excitement, brought its members into blows with the authorities, and disgraced the cause they had at heart, did, however, good service at this time by corresponding through their Vigilance Committee with their allies in Boston, as to the necessity of calling together a "General Congress." For upon this correspondence getting known, the more moderate men on the popular side in New York were aroused to action, as they did not wish the control of affairs at this critical juncture to fall into the hands of noisy and unscrupulous demagogues, like ex-privateersman "King Sears"[1] and his associates. They therefore summoned by advertisement a meeting of "the merchants and other inhabitants of the city of New York" to be held in the Exchange on the 16th of May 1774, "in order to consult on measures proper to be pursued on the present critical and important occasion."

The citizens convened by this notice, duly met and elected from among themselves, a Committee of Fifty Members to correspond with the other colonies upon all matters of moment. This Committee was composed of men of all shades of opinion, including the brothers Peter Van Brugh and Philip Livingston, and three days later it was increased to fifty-one by the admission of Mr. Francis Lewis. Among its other duties, this Committee had to arrange for the election of five delegates to represent New York in the First Continental Congress, summoned to meet at Philadelphia on the 1st of September in this year. Upon the 4th of July—a prophetic date!— Isaac Sears,[2] who was a member of the Committee of Fifty-one, thereupon moved "That Messrs. Isaac Low, James Duane, Philip Livingston, John Morin Scott, and Alexander M'Dougall be nominated," in the hope that the two latter gentlemen, close friends of his own and ardent "Sons of Liberty," might be elected. Strange to say, in this he was seconded by Peter Van Brugh Livingston,[3] a rich merchant, and certainly not an extremist like the proposer of these nominations. It must be mentioned that the popular party at this date was divided into two factions, namely, the moderate men, such as merchants and other well-to-do citizens, nicknamed the "Patricians"; while the other section, composed principally of mechanics, was known as the "Tribunes"—each, of course, striving to obtain the lead. This motion, however, came to nothing, for the Tories and the more moderate members of the Whig party united, and Sears was outvoted by two to one. Mr. John De Lancey then moved "That this Committee immediately proceed to nominate five persons to be held up to this city and county as proper persons to serve them as delegates in a General Congress"; when the following gentlemen were nominated, viz., Philip Livingston, John Alsop, Isaac Low, James Duane, and John Jay.

The mechanics, enraged that their nomination had not been approved by the Committee of Fifty-one, summoned a meeting of their partisans to be held in the Fields on the evening of the 6th of July; where, under the chairmanship of Mr. Alexander M'Dougall, a most violent demagogue and "Son of Liberty," they passed several resolutions, by which they endeavoured to commit the New York delegates to the line of action advocated by their section of the popular party. This was followed two days later by the resignation of eleven of the dissentient members of the Committee, including Francis Lewis and Peter Van Brugh Livingston. Finding, however, the majority were firm in their resolve to support their nomination at the election to be held in the city on the 28th of July, and that they also had the sympathy of the more respectable portion of the inhabitants, so that a contested election would only demonstrate more forcibly their own weakness, the leaders of the mechanics reluctantly withdrew their opposition to the members nominated by the majority of the Committee, who thereupon were unanimously confirmed as delegates to the Continental Congress by the votes of the citizens upon the above date. Thus, fortunately for New York, her destinies from this date onward, and during the coming struggle, were to be controlled and directed by men of standing and position in the colony, instead of by violent agitators and mob orators of the Sears type, those "stormy petrels" of every revolutionary movement.

Two years previous to this date William Livingston, who had for so many years so ably advocated the popular cause by his pen, had left New York to settle in the neighbouring colony of New Jersey, where he had purchased some years previously a small estate near the town of Elizabeth; and this new home he had named appropriately enough "Liberty Hall." He had left his native province for the purpose of spending the remainder of his days in retirement, being always fond of a country life; and also apparently "in despair of the attainment of that civil and religious freedom for which he had so long contended."[4] If he had remained in New York his inclinations would probably have led him to have thrown in his lot with the extreme wing of the popular party, as his brother Peter Van Brugh had done, rather than with the more conservative merchants, of whom his brother Philip had now become one of the recognised leaders. As it was, his dreams of a rural life were quickly dissipated, for his was not a temperament to rest idly at home, when there was the slightest chance of serving his country in her hour of need, and at the election of the New Jersey delegates for the First Continental Congress, which took place at the city of New Brunswick in that colony on the 25th of July, or three days prior to the New York election, his name was second on the list of the five gentlemen appointed to represent that province.[5]

On the 20th of August there arrived in New York the delegates from Massachusetts on their way to Philadelphia. The most notable of these gentlemen was John Adams, then a New England lawyer with a small practice, imbued with feelings of the bitterest animosity towards the mother country for her treatment of his native colony; soon to become one of the leading statesmen on the American side, and the future second President of the United States. From his Diary we glean some interesting particulars concerning his opinions on the leading politicians in New York, by the more moderate of whom he was regarded with suspicion on account of his pronounced views. For few people in New York in the summer of 1774 entertained any idea of a revolt from English rule; that was only to come later, when the colonists found to their grievous disappointment that war was unavoidable. The New England delegates, moreover, were socially looked down upon at this time, by the richer and more aristocratic merchants of New York, so that with the exception of politicians of the M'Dougall class, who received them naturally with open arms, their reception in that city was decidedly a cool one.

John Adams notes in his Diary (under date 15th August), that when at Hartford they were met by Mr. Silas Deane, one of the Connecticut delegates to the Congress, who informed the Massachusetts delegates that the New York delegation consisted of two lawyers, Duane and Jay, and three merchants, Livingston, Low, and Alsop, and that Livingston was very popular. He also said that Jay, a name to become celebrated in New York annals, had married a daughter of Peter Van Brugh Livingston. In this, however, Silas Deane was mistaken, as the lady in question, was a daughter of William Livingston.[6] By John Morin Scott, and Alexander M'Dougall, John Adams and his friends received a hearty welcome, when they reached that city five days after leaving Hartford. From the "talkative" M'Dougall they received an insight into New York politics, and learnt from him that "the two great families in this province, upon whose motions all their politics turn, are the Delanceys and Livingstons." And Adams adds "according to him" (M'Dougall), "there is virtue and abilities as well as fortune in the Livingstons, but not much of either of the three in the Delanceys."

Mr. M'Dougall acted as the cicerone of the Massachusetts delegates during their stay in New York, and it is amusing to read the naïve remarks of the New England lawyer on the "elegant" establishment kept by one of his new radical friends, and also a member of the legal profession, namely, John Morin Scott, to whose house he and his fellow-travellers were taken one morning by M'Dougall for breakfast, and to meet some of the New York delegates. Before the arrival of these latter gentlemen, M'Dougall warned his New England friends "to avoid every expression which looked like an allusion to the last appeal." He impressed upon them also that there was a powerful party in that city, "who were intimidated by fears of a war"; and that many people were also afraid "lest the levelling spirit of the New England colonies should propagate itself into New York." Concerning three of the New York delegates, who called to pay their respects to their New England colleagues, that indefatigable diarist John Adams duly records the following particulars:—"Mr. Livingston is a downright, straightforward man. Mr. Alsop is a soft, sweet man. Mr. Duane has a sly, surveying eye, a little squint-eyed, between forty and forty-five, very sensible, and very artful."

The same day some of these gentlemen met again at the house of a Mr. Platt for dinner, where they were joined by Mr. Peter Van Brugh Livingston, to whom John Adams had also been introduced on the previous day. This member of the Livingston family pleased Adams far more than his "downright straightforward" brother Philip, whose manners were decidedly brusque. For of the former he duly notes, that "P. V. Livingston is a sensible man and a gentleman. He has been in trade, is rich, and now lives upon his income." While immediately afterwards he bitterly complains that, "Phil Livingston is a great, rough, rapid mortal. There is no holding any conversation with him. He blusters away; says, if England should turn us adrift, we should instantly go to civil wars among ourselves, to determine which colony should govern all the rest; seems to dread New England, the levelling spirit, etc. Hints were thrown out of the Goths and vandals; mention was made of our hanging the Quakers, etc." In fact, the well-to-do New York merchant had snubbed the New England lawyer, and hence these complaints. For the more aristocratic leaders of the popular party in New York were naturally much alarmed, as Adams had been rightly informed by M'Dougall, lest his known extreme views on the state of affairs between England and her American colonies, and also his New England notions of equality, should still further inflame the mob against the mother country, and thus materially increase the risk of civil war, for which public opinion in New York was not then prepared. It required still further and bitter experience of the infatuated folly of George III and his ministers, before the New York Whigs were most reluctantly compelled to relinquish the hope of a peaceful termination to the dispute.

Both the Livingston brothers invited the New England delegates to dinner at their respective houses; but while Adams and his colleagues all went to dine at Peter Van Brugh's town mansion, on the afternoon of the 23d of August, he and Samuel Adams excused themselves, on the following day, from crossing over to Long Island for the purpose of paying a visit to Philip's home on the Brooklyn heights.[7] Two days later these gentlemen left New York for Philadelphia, and on their passage through New Jersey they paid a visit to the college at Princeton, where they made the acquaintance of Dr. Witherspoon,[8] its president, a friend and colleague of William Livingston in the cause of liberty; who, in the course of conversation, informed his guests that "Livingston is very sincere and very able in the public cause, but a bad speaker, though a good writer." John Adams, on his arrival at Philadelphia, a few days afterwards, met this youngest member of this famous trio of brothers, and duly remarks in his journal upon his personal appearance, as being "a plain man, tall, black, wears his hair, nothing elegant or genteel about him. They say he is no public speaker, but very sensible and learned, and a ready writer." Certainly William Livingston's appearance would not impress a stranger favourably, and he himself was perfectly well aware of this fact, for Sedgwick relates that when "speaking of himself, in the language of one of his opponents in the *American Whig*, he says 'The Whig is a long-nosed, long-chinned, ugly-looking fellow.'" The same writer also states: "He[William Livingston] was considerably above the middle stature, and in early life, so very thin as to receive from some female wit of New York, perhaps in allusion to his satirical disposition, the nickname of the 'whipping post.' In later years he acquired a more dignified corpulency."

The First Continental Congress held its first meeting at Philadelphia upon the 5th of September 1774, and both the Livingstons were present on the opening day. The labours of this Congress were confined to drawing up petitions and remonstrances to be laid before the Home Government; in drafting addresses to the people of Great Britain and the neighbouring British province of Canada; and in agreeing to support a Non-Importation Association; by which measures the members hoped to obtain from the mother country a satisfactory settlement of their grievances. Having done its work the Congress dissolved itself on the 26th of October William Livingston appears to have filled a more prominent position in this assembly than his elder brother Philip, as the former, at the commencement of the proceedings of this Congress, when a committee was appointed of two members from each colony, was chosen as one of the two to represent New Jersey; and he was also on the Committee of Three to prepare the draft of the Memorial to the people of British America, and an Address to the people of Great Britain. The other two members of this last committee were Richard Henry Lee of Virginia and John Jay of New York. Both brothers signed the Non-Importation Association on the 20th of October, and the Address to the King six days later.

One of the resolutions passed by the above Congress fixed the 10th of May following for the meeting of another Congress, "unless the redress of grievances, which we have desired, be obtained before that time." It did not take many weeks to demonstrate that another Congress would be a necessity, unless the colonists were prepared to give way without a struggle. This the majority of them were not prepared to do, and so the different colonies had soon to take the necessary steps for electing delegates to represent them in the Second Continental Congress. The New York Assembly having refused to meddle in the matter, the duty of seeing to the election of proper persons to represent the colony in the new Congress was taken up by the Committee of Sixty, which Committee had been appointed on the 22d of November 1774, upon the dissolution of the original Committee of Fifty-one, "to superintend the execution of the Association entered into by the Congress."[9] This new committee, which like its predecessor contained members from all parties, and, of course, the two Livingston brothers, Peter Van Brugh and Philip, was to continue in office until the 1st of July next. Therefore, to quote from Mr. Bancroft,[10] "under the auspices of the Committee of Sixty,... the rural counties co-operate with the city, forty-one delegates meet in convention (20th April 1775) and choose Philip Livingston unanimously as their president, re-elect all their old members to Congress, except 'the lukewarm Isaac Low'[11]; and unanimously added five others, among them Philip Schuyler, George Clinton, and Robert R. Livingston[12]; 'to concert measures for the preservation of American rights; and for the restoration of harmony between Great Britain and the colonies.'"

The Livingston members in this Convention numbered four in all; namely, Philip, as one of the city members; the above Robert R. Livingston, junior, the eldest son of Judge Robert R. Livingston of Clermont, from Dutchess; and the brothers Peter R. and Walter of the Manor, from Albany. Peter R. Livingston, however, did not attend. This Convention only sat for the short space of three days, for having performed its allotted task in appointing the delegates to represent the colony of New York in the Second Continental Congress, it dissolved itself on the 22d of April.

Robert R. Livingston, junior, one of the new delegates, was at this date only in his twenty-ninth year, but a young man of great promise, who was soon to make his mark as a statesman of no common order. Before proceeding further, it may be as well to give here the contents of a letter written by the judge to his son, on the occasion of the latter starting for Philadelphia to take his seat in the General Congress, as this letter very clearly expresses the policy of the Livingston family *at this date,* to the effect that the colonies should have, what now-a-days is called "Home Rule"; but not to be *"wholly independent of the mother-country."* The judge was prepared, be it noted, to be more liberal in the matter of colonial contributions to the military necessities of the Empire than Canada is, for example, at the present day!

5th May 1775.

Dear Son:

You, I suppose, are now on your way to Philadelphia, and will soon make one of that important body which will engage the attention of all America and a great part of Europe. May Heaven direct your counsels to the good of the whole empire. Keep yourself cool on this important occasion. From heat and passion, prudent counsels can seldom proceed. It is yours to plan and deliberate, and whatever the Congress directs, I hope will be executed with firmness, unanimity, and spirit. Every good man wishes that America may remain free. In this I join heartily; at the same time, I do not desire that we should be wholly independent of the mother country. How to reconcile these jarring principles, I profess, I am altogether at a loss. The benefit we receive of protection seems to require that we should contribute to the support of the navy, if not to the armies of Britain. I would have you consider whether it would not be proper to lay hold of Lord North's overture, to open a negotiation and procure a suspension of hostilities. In the mean time, the check General Gage has received, and our non-importation, will perhaps have a good effect in our favour on the other side of the water. This seems to be the thought of our Council here, as Mr. Jay and Mr. Livingston[13] will inform you.[1] I should think, if you offered Britain all the duties usually paid here by our merchants, even those paid since the disturbances began, those on tea excepted, which seem to be too odious, and all other duties they may think convenient to levy for the regulation of trade, shall be lodged in the treasury of each colony, to be disposed of by their respective assemblies and legislatures, on an engagement on their side that no other taxes shall be imposed on them but by their own representatives, we ought to be contented. Some specious offer should be made, to increase our friends in England. This, or some other of that kind, if Lord North meant anything by his motion, but to deceive the people of England, ought to put a stop to his proceedings for the present; otherwise the odium he lies under must increase. The Boston Charter ought by all

means to be restored, and were the tea paid for, as a *douceur*, by the whole continent, it would be no matter. But this you will not insist on except you are well supported. These are my present thoughts; however, judge for yourself, and unite by all means, for on this all depends. As to what relates to war, after agreeing on *quotas*, the manner of levying men and money will, I suppose be left to each Colony. May God direct you in all things. A dependence on him will inspire both wisdom and courage; and if his Providence interfere in anything, as I firmly believe it does in all things, it certainly does in the rise and fall of nations.
Your most affectionate father,
R. R. LIVINGSTON.[14]

Inquire whether I can have a quantity of saltpetre. I hear there is a large quantity imported at Philadelphia.[15]

No time was lost by the majority of the newly elected delegates in hastening to the scene of their labours, for it is reported in one of the contemporary New York journals[16] that upon the 8th of May,—only sixteen days after the dissolution of the nominating Convention,—"the delegates from the eastward, together with Philip Livingston, James Duane, John Alsop, and Francis Lewis, delegates for New York City; Colonel William Floyd for Suffolk, and Simon Boerum for King's County, in New York, set out for Philadelphia, attended by a great train to the North River Ferry, where two or three sloops and a number of other vessels were provided. It is said about five hundred gentlemen crossed the ferry with them, among whom were two hundred militia under arms."

Philip Livingston found his brother William, who had also been unanimously re-elected a delegate for New Jersey by the Assembly of that colony, awaiting him at Philadelphia. The Second Continental Congress commenced its proceedings on the 11th of May, and both brothers took a prominent part in its deliberations, as is proved by their names appearing constantly on its numerous committees.

Meanwhile events in New York were tending more and more in favour of resistance towards Great Britain. A few days before Philip Livingston and his fellow delegates had left that city, a meeting of the citizens had been held, at the instance of the Committee of Sixty, for the purpose of appointing a fresh and larger Committee with more extended powers. This new Committee consisted of one hundred members, and held its first meeting on the 1st of May. On the same day twenty-one gentlemen were chosen deputies for the City and County of New York, to meet deputies of the other counties in Provincial Congress, on Monday, the 21st of May. Philip and Peter Van Brugh Livingston were both members of the Committee of One Hundred as they had been of the previous committees; while the latter was also appointed one of the deputies to serve in the first Provincial Congress of the colony of New York. This Congress commenced its proceedings by unanimously electing Peter Van Brugh Livingston to be president, and Volkert P. Douw, vice-president. As usual, the Livingston family was well represented in this, the first legislative assembly convened by the popular vote in New York, for besides its president, returned as one of the deputies for the city, two other Livingstons were sent up from the country districts; namely, Walter Livingston from Albany, and Gilbert Livingston from Dutchess.[17]

Walter Livingston of Teviotdale (1740–1797), 3rd son of the 3rd Lord of the Manor Born 1740 Died 1797. The Miriam and Ira D. Wallach Division of Art, Prints and Photographs: Print Collection, New York Public Library Digital Collections, Public Domain.

Though this Provincial Congress had usurped to itself the powers, and more than the powers, of the legally constituted General Assembly,— whose actions had been antagonistic to the popular party in New York,— its members were not yet prepared to come to open conflict with the royal authority; and hence some of its actions in the anxious endeavours of the members to keep on friendly terms with both the Continental Congress, then sitting in Philadelphia, and the Government officials, were somewhat contradictory. For while engaged in their deliberations, at the instance of the Continental Congress, upon the necessity of erecting fortifications and otherwise preparing for the approaching struggle, the news was received that both the newly appointed leader of the Continental troops, General Washington, and the royal governor, Mr. Tryon, were expected to reach New York on the same day. The former on his way to Boston to take command of the American forces in that town, and the latter to resume his governorship. This was certainly a most perplexing situation for the *de facto* government of New York to be placed in, namely, as to which of these gentlemen their official welcome should be accorded! But this was rather smartly surmounted by a resolution of the Congress passed upon the 25th of June—the day of their arrival—by which it was ordered, that a company of militia should be sent to receive both the general and the governor "*with equal honours*," and that the colonel should "*wait on both as well as circumstances will allow*." Poor colonel!

No wonder Governor Tryon, who had been absent for rather more than a year from his post, bitterly complained to the Home Government of "the diminished authority the lieutenant-governor [Colden] had to transfer to him." In the same letter he also alludes to the determined opposition of the now united colonies against taxation without their consent; and he adds these pregnant words: "If it were the wish it is not in the power of any one Province to accommo-date with Great Britain, being overawed and controlled by the General Confederacy, oceans of blood may be spilt, but in my opinion America will never receive parliamentary taxation."[18]

Of the three Livingston members in the Second Continental Congress, William Livingston of New Jersey undoubtedly took the lead, for his name appears far oftener on the earlier committee lists, than that of his elder brother Philip, or his cousin Robert of Clermont. And though all three were warmly opposed to the interference of the British Parliament in the internal affairs of the colonies, they had no wish, at the period we are treating of, to force matters to a climax. In this, their views were similar to those expressed by Judge Livingston to his son Robert. But the continual

disregard of the Home Government of the repeated petitions and remonstrances of the united colonies, and the attack by the British troops on
the armed colonists at Bunker Hill, were hastening events on to that goal
so ardently desired by the Adamses and their allies; so that just thirteen
months after the assembling of the Second Continental Congress, when
Richard Henry Lee of Virginia, upon the 7th of June 1776, rose to move his
famous resolution regarding Independence, the majority of the members
had lost all hope of a peaceful reconciliation with the mother-country.

There was still, however, a powerful minority, consisting principally
of the delegates from the middle colonies, including some of the most talented members of this Congress, strongly opposed to the adoption of this
resolution, which they considered premature; and great pressure was therefore brought to bear on these members for the purpose of obtaining a *unanimous* vote in favour of the resolution. Among these dissentient colonies,
New York was the most prominent. So far, she had suffered little from the
horrors of civil war, but from her geographical position, exposed to attacks
upon her northern frontier from Canada, and upon her southern counties
from the sea, she would naturally become the greatest sufferer in a lengthy
conflict with a naval Empire like Great Britain; while she had among her
varied population a greater proportion of loyalists or "Tories" than any of
the other colonies. Moreover her members were delegates, not representatives; and so some of them even hdd the opinion that they were strictly
"bound by their instructions not to vote on that question."

Lee's motion was to the effect,

That these United Colonies are, and of right ought to be, free
and independent States, that they are absolved from all allegiance to the British Crown, and that all political connection
between them and the State of Great Britain is, and ought to
be, totally dissolved.

That it is expedient forthwith to take the most effectual
measures for forming alliances.

That a plan of confederation be prepared and transmitted to
the respective colonies for their consideration and approbation.

It was duly seconded by that other irreconcilable, John Adams of
Massachusetts, and naturally gave rise to an animated debate; but as the
journals purposely only recorded the bare result of the business transacted
by the Congress, no authentic report of the speeches made at this important

crisis has been preserved. The debate was commenced on Saturday, the 8th of June, the day following the submission of the above resolutions, and adjourned to Monday, the 10th, for further consideration, when, after some discussion, it was resolved by a Committee of the whole House, "That the consideration of the first Resolution be postponed to Monday, the first day of July next; and, in the meanwhile, that no time be lost, in case the Congress agrees thereto, that a Committee be appointed to prepare a Declaration to the effect of the said first Resolution." According to Jefferson, it was owing to "it appearing, in the course of these debates, that the colonies of New York, New Jersey, Pennsylvania, Delaware, Maryland, and South Carolina were not yet matured for falling from the parent stem; but that they were fast advancing to that state, it was thought most prudent to wait a while for them, and to postpone the final decision," as mentioned above, "to July the first."

From the same authority we also learn that the principal speakers in favour of the postponement of the final decision upon this irrevocable step were James Wilson and John Dickinson of Pennsylvania, Robert R. Livingston of New York, and Edward Rutledge of South Carolina, who argued "that though they were friends to the measures themselves, and saw the impossibility that they should ever again be united with Great Britain, yet they were against adopting them at this time. That the conduct they [the members of Continental Congress] had formerly observed was wise and proper now, of deferring to take any capital step till the voice of the people drove them into it."

Philip Livingston during this important debate was absent from Philadelphia, attending to his duties in New York as a member of the Third Provincial Congress, then also in session in the latter city[19]; and was present at the morning sitting of this Convention on Monday, the 10th of June, when the following letter from his colleagues at Philadelphia to the President of the New York Congress, asking for specific instructions as to the course they were to pursue in this emergency, was read within closed doors:—

PHILADELPHIA, June 8, 1776.

Dear Sir:
Your Delegates here expect that the question of Independence will very shortly be agitated in Congress. Some of us consider ourselves as bound by our instructions not to vote on that question, and all wish to have your sentiments thereon. The matter

will admit of no delay. We have, therefore, sent an express, who will wait your orders.

We are, Sir, with the greatest respect, your most obedient, humble servants,

William Floyd,
Henry Wisner,
Robert R. Livingston,
Francis Lewis.

To Nathaniel Woodhull, Esq.
President of the Honourable the Convention of New York.

During the afternoon sitting on the following day, the subject of Independence was fully discussed by the members present, when it was:—

Resolved unanimously, That the good people of this Colony have not, in the opinion of this Congress, authorised this Congress, or the Delegates of this Congress in the Continental Congress, to declare this Colony to be and continue independent of the Crown of Great Britain.

But whereas the perseverance of the British King and Parliament, in an unjustifiable attempt to subjugate and enslave these United Colonies, may render a determination on that and many other important points highly necessary and expedient, and a recurrence to the people at large for their sentiments on every great question that may occur in the course of the present contest would be very inconvenient to them, and probably be attended with dangerous delays:

Resolved unanimously, therefore, That it be, and is hereby, earnestly recommended to all the Freeholders and other Electors in this Colony, at the ensuing election, to be held in pursuance of a Resolution of the Congress of the 31st day of May last past,[20] not only to vest their Representatives or Deputies with the powers therein mentioned, but also with full power to deliberate and determine on every question whatsoever that may concern or affect the interest of this Colony, and to conclude upon, ordain, and execute every act and measure which to them shall appear conducive to the happiness, security, and welfare of this Colony, and that they hold and exercise the said powers until the second Tuesday of May next, or until a regular form of Government for this Colony shall be established, in case that event shall sooner take place; and it is further recommended to the said Freeholders and Electors by instructions or otherwise to inform their said Deputies of their sentiments relative to the great question of Independency, and such other points as they may think proper.

On motion, *Agreed,* That the publishing of the aforegoing Resolves be postponed until after the election of Deputies, with powers to establish a new form of Government.

Ordered, that Mr. Jay and Colonel Remsen be a Committee to draft an answer to the Letter of our Delegates at Continental Congress, received the 10th inst., on the subject of Independency.

The above resolutions of the New York Provincial Congress are here given in full, so as clearly to explain the action of their delegates in the Continental Congress in declining to vote on this all-important question. Curiously enough, upon the same day as the above resolutions were unanimously agreed to by the Provincial Congress, Robert R. Livingston of Clermont was chosen by ballot to be one of the historical Committee of Five, to whom the task of drafting a Declaration of Independence was entrusted. Probably, it was thought advisable by the irreconcilables in the Continental Congress to have a delegate from the important, but doubtful, Colony of New York, on this Committee;—and that Robert R. Livingston the youngest delegate should be chosen, was, probably, not only owing to his having been the spokesman for his colony, but also in the desire to have the powerful Livingston family committed to this irrevocable step. The other colonies represented on this Committee were Virginia by Thomas Jefferson, Massachusetts by John Adams, Pennsylvania by Benjamin Franklin, and Connecticut by Roger Sherman. Livingston was also, upon the following day, appointed the member to represent New York upon the Committee nominated to draw up a plan of confederation between the colonies. When we remember he was only twenty-nine years of age, these appointments prove, young as he was, he had already in these few months made his mark in this Congress.

Upon the seventeenth of this month, the New York Delegates duly acknowledged the receipt of the reply to their letter of the eighth asking for instructions from the Provincial Congress, and expressed to its president, Nathaniel Woodhull, their "great pleasure from knowing the sentiments of the honourable the Convention relative to the important subject on which we thought it our duty to ask their opinion." They also has-tened to add, "we are very happy in having it in our power to assure them that we have hitherto taken no steps inconsistent with their intention, as expressed in their letter, by which we shall be careful to regulate our future conduct."[21] To this rule of conduct they strictly and honourably adhered, so that when the adjourned debate on Mr. Lee's motion was resumed upon the first of July before the Committee of the whole Congress, the New York delegates read their instructions, as contained in the letter from their Provincial Congress of the eleventh of June, and were thereupon excused from voting.

Owing to the fact that the colony of South Carolina, as well as a majority of the delegates from Delaware and Pennsylvania, were still deter-mined to vote in the negative,—for it must be borne in mind that though the voting was by colonies, it sometimes happened, as in this instance, that delegates were not always unanimous as to how their particular colony should vote; in such cases, of course, the majority of the delegates of that colony present in the Congress would control the vote,—the debate was still further adjourned, "at the request of a colony," until the next day, when by the arrival of Mr. Rodney, who had been summoned to Philadelphia for this purpose, the vote of Delaware was secured, and by the absence, also purposely, of two of the Pennsylvania delegates this vote was also gained; whereupon South Carolina, though somewhat reluctantly, gave her con-sent to secure unanimity. The adherence of the other doubtful colony, New Jersey, had already been secured by other means, which will be treated of more fully later on, as it concerns the reason why William Livingston was not present in the Congress at this critical period.

So that, as Elbridge Gerry could triumphantly write to General Warren three days later:—

A determined resolution of the Delegates from some of the Colonies to push the question of Independency has had a most happy effect, and, after a day's debate, all the Colonies, except-ing New York, whose Delegates are not empowered to give either an affirmative or negative voice, united in a declaration long sought for, solicited, and necessary—the Declaration of Independency. New York will most probably, on Monday next, when its Convention meets for forming a constitution, join in the measure and then it will be entitled THE UNANIMOUS DECLARATION OF THE THIRTEEN UNITED STATES OF AMERICA.

While his colleague John Adams, on the third of July, had also written, in jubilant spirits to his wife:—

Yesterday the greatest question was decided which ever was debated in America, and a greater, perhaps, never was, nor will be decided among men. A resolution was passed without one dissenting colony "that these United Colonies are, and of right ought to be, free and independent States, and as such they have, and of right ought to have full power to make war, conclude peace, establish commerce, and to do all other acts and things which other States may rightfully do."

He then enthusiastically goes on to declare that "the second day of July 1776 will be the most memorable epocha in the history of America. I am apt to believe it will be celebrated by succeeding generations as the great anniversary feast." In this John Adams was mistaken, for the date which is, and has always been honoured in America as the birthday of the United States, is the fourth and not the second of July. The reason for this being that though the vote of the second of July turned the United Colonies into United States, the form of the Declaration itself was not approved and passed by the Congress until two days later, when it was "*Ordered*, that the Declaration be authenticated and printed."

According to popular ideas, the Declaration was thereupon signed by all the members present, amid jocular remarks by some of the signers, the pealing of the "Liberty Bell," and the joyful huzzas of a populace freed from an insufferable tyranny![22] When as a simple matter of fact the Declaration was, upon the 4th of July, only authenticated, like other papers of the Congress, by the signatures of the president and the secretary—the document now preserved in the office of the Secretary of State at Washington, not then being in existence[23]; and it is also highly improbable, that an act of such momentous consequence to all the British colonies in North America, should have been made the subject of unseemly jesting by any of the delegates present upon this most eventful day in their country's annals. Moreover, it was not until the 8th that the Declaration was read from the State House to the assembled citizens of Philadelphia; and still another eleven days were allowed to elapse before Congress, "*Resolved*, That the declaration passed on the 4th be fairly engrossed on parchment, with the title and style of 'The Unanimous Declaration of the Thirteen United States of America,' and that the same, when engrossed, be signed by every member of Congress." And, it was in consequence of this resolution, that "the Declaration of Independence being engrossed, and compared at the table, was, upon the second of August, signed by the members."[24]

As already mentioned, the New York delegates had, on the first of July, excused themselves from voting, either for or against the Declaration, on account of their instructions not to commit their colony to any decided course of action until the election of a new Provincial Congress. But they naturally felt the awkwardness of this position of affairs, for on the following day they wrote again to their local Convention pressing for definite orders; in which letter they state:—

> The important question of Independency was agitated yesterday in a Committee of the whole Congress, and this day will be finally determined in the House. We know the line of our conduct on this occasion: we have your instructions, and will faithfully pursue them. New doubts and difficulties, however, will arise should Independency be declared, and that it will not, we have not the least reason to expect; nor do we believe that (if any) more than one Colony (and the Delegates of that divided) will vote against the question, every Colony (ours only excepted) having withdrawn their former instructions, and either positively instructed their Delegates to vote for Independency, or concur in such vote, if they shall judge it expedient. What part are we to act after this event takes place?... Our situation is singular and delicate, no other Colony being similarly circumstanced, with whom we can consult. We wish, therefore, for your earliest advice and instructions, whether we are to consider our Colony bound by the vote of the majority in favour of Independency, and vote at large on such questions as may arise in consequence thereof; or only concur in such measures as may be absolutely necessary for the common safety and defence of America, exclusive of the idea of Independency. We fear it will be difficult to draw the line; but, once possessed of your instructions, we will do our best endeavours to follow them?[25]

Upon the ninth of July, exactly a week after the date of this letter, the Provincial Congress of the colony of New York, which had been specially called together for the purpose of settling a new form of government, and deciding upon the important question of Independence, met at the Court House in the town of White Plains, county of Westchester, instead of as heretofore in the city of New York, owing to the expected occupation of that place by the British troops. And as soon as the usual formalities had been hurried through in connection with the production of their credentials by the newly-elected deputies, and the appointment of the various officials, including the re-election of General Woodhull to the post of president, no time was lost in bringing the engrossing subject of Independence before the House, by the reading of the letter from their delegates at Philadelphia of the second of July, requesting instructions, and also a later one containing a copy of the Declaration itself, which was also read to the assembled deputies, and referred for consideration to a Committee, of which John Jay was the chairman. And the following report, drawn up by this Committee, was submitted to the House during the afternoon sitting of the same day, and unanimously agreed to:—

In Convention of the Representatives of the State of New York, White Plains, July 9, 1776.

Resolved unanimously, That the reasons assigned by the Continental Congress for declaring the United Colonies free and independent States, are cogent and conclusive; and that while we lament the cruel necessity which has rendered the measure unavoidable, we approve the same, and will at the risk of our lives and fortunes, join with the other Colonies in supporting it.

Resolved, That a copy of the said Declaration, and the aforegoing Resolution, be sent to the Chairman of the Committee of the County of Westchester, with orders to publish the same with beat of drum, at this place, on Thursday next, and to give directions that it be published with all convenient speed in the several Districts within the said County, and that copies thereof be forthwith transmitted to the other County Committees within the State of New York, with orders to cause the same to be published in the several Districts of their respective Counties.

Resolved, That five hundred copies of the Declaration of Independence, with the two last-mentioned Resolutions of this Congress for approving and proclaiming the same, be published in handbills, and sent to all the County Committees in this State.

Resolved, That the Delegates of this State in Continental Congress be and they are hereby authorised to consent to and adopt all such measures as they may deem conducive to the happiness and welfare of the United States of America.

Ordered, That copies of the aforesaid Resolutions be transmitted to the Continental Congress.[26]

Upon the following day it was "*Resolved* and *Ordered*, that the style or title of this House be changed from that of 'The Provincial Congress of the Colony of New York,' to that of 'The Convention of the Representatives of the State of New York.'"

Having thus briefly related the principal incidents connected with the part taken by the colony of New York in the adoption of the Declaration of Independence, it may be of interest to trace, as far as it is possible to do so, the personal share that the three Livingston members of Continental Congress had in this historical event, and to ascertain the reason why the name of only one of the three is attached to the parchment document now preserved in the Secretary of State's office at Washington. This is far from being an easy task to perform, owing to no account having been kept of the debates in the Congressional journals, and unless a delegate happened to be placed on any of the numerous committees, between whom the work of the Congress was divided, it is very difficult to learn whether he was, or was not, present in the House on a certain date.

To commence with the two New York delegates of this family. Of these, the senior, Philip Livingston, was absent from Philadelphia attending to his duties in the Provincial Convention, when Richard Henry Lee's famous resolution was moved in the Continental Congress; and being naturally anxious to return to his seat in that assembly at such an important crisis, he, upon the 14th of June, applied for permission to do so. But as his services were then also greatly needed in the Convention, his request was rather brusquely refused; and instead, it was "*Ordered*, that Mr. Philip Livingston be, and is hereby, appointed a Member of the Committee constituted by this Congress for the hearing and trial of disaffected persons, and persons of equivocal character." This Committee, of which John Jay was also a member, had a very onerous and delicate task conferred on them by this resolution; and when on the following day his colleagues unanimously chose Philip Livingston to be their chairman, he declined the honour. He, however, attended its sittings regularly up to the 29th of this month, when he was released from his attendance in the Provincial

Congress, having on the 26th obtained the desired permission to return to Philadelphia upon the following Sunday, the 30th. As it was usually about a three days' journey between New York and Philadelphia in those days it is not likely that he was present when the Declaration was adopted by the twelve colonies on the second of July; but that he was in his seat upon the fourth, when the form of the Declaration was finally agreed to, is proved by a letter from one of the New Jersey delegates, Dr. Witherspoon, to the President of his local Convention, written on the third, in which he refers to a conversation he had had with Mr. Philip Livingston of New York on that afternoon. The earliest mention made of him in the journals after his return is upon the sixth of this month, when he was one of the three members elected by ballot to serve on the Committee on Indian Affairs "in the room of those absent." One of his colleagues upon this Committee was Mr. Jefferson, just released from his labours of drafting the famous Declaration. Nine days later Mr. Livingston, for the same reason, was appointed a member of the Board of Treasury; and upon the second of August he attached his signature to the engrossed parchment copy of the Declaration of Independence, after it had been compared at the table with the one authenticated by the President and Secretary of Congress on the fourth of the previous month. He was constant in his attendance in Continental Congress up to Christmas in this year, when having applied for and obtained the requisite permission from the New York Committee of Safety, then sitting at Fishkill, to visit his family from whom he had been long separated, he left Philadelphia for Esopus (Kingston),[27] some time prior to the 28th of December.

The younger Livingston member on the New York delegation at this date was Robert R. Livingston of Clermont, who, as already mentioned, was present in Congress during the debates on Lee's resolution of the seventh of June, in which, according to Thomas Jefferson, he was one of the leading speakers in opposing the adoption of this resolution until it could be proved that the majority of the inhabitants of the colonies were anxious to be independent of the mothercountry, and who were successful in obtaining the adjournment of the debate until the first of July. On the eleventh of June he was elected by ballot to be one of the Committee of Five, to whom was appointed the task of drafting the Declaration, and who made their report to the House seventeen days later. And, as a member of this Committee, he must have been present on the fourth of July when after some slight amendments, it was finally agreed to by the House, as already related. He did not remain long in Philadelphia after his duties on this important committee had terminated. For having been elected a member of the Provincial Congress of his native colony, summoned to meet on the second Monday in July, he returned home for the purpose of taking his seat in the latter assembly; which he did on the morning of the fifteenth of this month, after "the general oath of secrecy" had been administered to him, in accordance with the rides, as he had not sat in the previous Convention. Thus he was absent from Philadelphia when the parchment copy was signed on the second of August, as was also another prominent New Yorker, George Clinton, who also was present in Congress when the Independence resolution was passed. It is strange that these two delegates, one to be the first governor of the infant State of New York, and the other its first chancellor should neither have signed the Declaration![28]

We now come to the remaining member of the Livingston trio in the Second Continental Congress, this was William Livingston, who, as already noticed, took a prominent part in the earlier sittings of this Assembly. But shortly after the Virginia delegates, had, in accordance with instructions from their Convention, forced the question of Independency upon the General Congress, he had been recalled to fill a military post in his adopted colony, and hence was not present when Mr. Lee's resolution was finally agreed to upon the second of July. William Livingston always bitterly resented his recall at this critical period; an event, which gave rise, long after his death, to a most unjust sneer from his former colleague in Congress, John Adams, who, in writing to Mr. Jefferson in September 1823, says: "I have no doubt, had he [Mr. Jay] been in Congress at the time, he would have subscribed the Declaration of Independence; he would not have left Congress like Governor Livingston and others." And as this plainly infers that William Livingston left the Continental Congress *of his own free will*, in order to shirk the responsibility of voting on such a delicate question, it may be as well to give here the true facts relating to this incident.

As far back as the month of October in the preceding year (1775), "a commission of Second Brigadier-General of the Militia forces of New Jersey," had been bestowed upon Mr. Livingston by a unanimous resolution of the Provincial Congress of that colony; and he appears to have acted in that capacity for a brief period, upon the transfer of General Lord Stirling from that command to the neighbouring province of New York in February 1776. This military appointment, however, did not prevent his re-election, for the third time, as a delegate to the Continental Congress by the New Jersey Convention upon the fourteenth of this same month of February. According to the resolution, by which he and his fellow-delegates were empowered to represent New Jersey in the General Congress, their term of office was limited to one year, "*or, until others shall be legally appointed in their stead.*" When Lee's resolution was moved in Congress, not quite four months had elapsed since Livingston's last re-appointment as one of the New Jersey delegates; but owing to the pressure put on the doubtful colonies by the irreconcilables in the Continental Congress, the Provincial Congress of New Jersey was induced to appoint a fresh set of delegates, *with special instructions to vote in favour of Independence.*[29] This appointment of new delegates took place on the twenty-second of June, which happened to be the day after this Convention had authorised "the president to write to General Livingston, and inform him, that it is the desire of Congress that he would take the command of the militia destined for New York," then threatened by the British fleet. It is therefore highly probable that the members of the Provincial Congress,—knowing William Livingston held the opinion that the Independence agitation was premature,—wished to make his military appointment an excuse for his non-election on this occasion, as they did not give him the opportunity of either accepting or declining this command, before nominating their new delegates to the Continental Congress. For upon the twenty-fifth of June, a letter from him was read in the Provincial Congress declining the New York command,—as was probably anticipated, seeing that Mr. Livingston knew absolutely nothing of military matters—and the Congress thereupon appointed Colonel Nathaniel Heard in his place.[30]

William Livingston never made any secret of his views on Independence, and in a letter to his friend Henry Laurens, dated 5th of February 1778, he says "as to the policy of it, I then thought, and I have found no reason to change my sentiments since, that if we could not maintain our separation without the assistance of France, her alliance ought to have been secured by our stipulation to assert it upon that condition. This would have forced her out into open day, and we should have been certain either of her explicit avowal or of the folly of our depending upon it." But the Rubicon having been crossed, he loyally accepted the decision of the Continental Congress as final; as in the same letter he writes "we must endeavour to make the best of everything. Whoever draws his sword against his prince must fling away the scabbard. We have passed the Rubicon, and whoever attempts to recross it will be knocked on the head by one or the other party on the opposite banks. We cannot recede, nor should I wish it if we could." He, however, keenly felt the slight thus put upon him, and in a letter written to the President of the Provincial Convention, on the 9th of August 1776, after denying some imputations as to his having made some disrespectful remarks about the Convention in a previous letter, he continues:—

> With respect to what was said about the delegates for the Congress, I did really mean to resent the conduct of those of your members, who assigned the [fact of] my being appointed to the command of that brigade as a reason against my being eligible as a member of Congress, when I had plainly refused that command in the presence of the Convention.

His fellow-citizens evidently felt that his strictures were just, for only three weeks after the date of this letter, he was elected "in joint ballot of the Assembly and Legisla-five Council," to the honourable and responsible post of first republican governor of the State of New Jersey,[31] which office he held, moreover, until his death. Thus Mr. Adams's most unfair aspersion upon the character of a dead political opponent is proved to be utterly false!

Sarah Johnson Livingston (1749–1802), wife of Philip Philip Livingston (1741–1787). National Portrait Gallery, Smithsonian Institution; gift of Mr. and Mrs. Paul Mellon, CC0 (Creative Commons) License.

Notes

1. This man was Isaac Sears of Connecticut, master mariner in the coasting trade and ex-privateersman, a notorious demagogue, who had first come into public notice as one of the leaders of the mob during the Stamp Act Riots of 1765.
2. "This man, referred to already by his nickname of "King Sears," has been ridiculously overrated as a patriot by most popular American historians of the War of Independence.
3. He had made a great part of his wealth during the late French wars as a government army contractor. At this date he was in partnership with his brother-in-law William Alexander, titular Earl of Stirling, afterwards the General Lord Stirling of the War of Independence. It was owing to the latter's influence, that Peter Van Brugh Livingston had obtained the contract for supplying General Shirley's army in 1755; vide Judge Jones's History of New York during the Revolutionary War. This writer, though bitterly opposed to these gentlemen in politics, admits, however, that "in the way of their business, they bore the character of fair traders and honest men."
4. Sedgwick Life of William Livingston, pp. 155–159.
5. The New Jersey delegates to the First Continental Congress were James Kinsey, William Livingston, John De Hart, Stephen Crane, and Richard Smith.
6. Perhaps Mr. Deane fell into this error owing to Mrs. Jay's maiden name having been Sarah Van Brugh Livingston. She was a great beauty, and had married John Jay on the preceding 28th April.
7. Exactly two years after the above date, there was held under this roof the celebrated council of war, whereat the American generals decided to retreat from Long Island to New York City. The owner was then absent in attendance on the Second Continental Congress at Philadelphia. This historic mansion has long disappeared, having been accidentally destroyed by fire some years ago.
8. Dr. Witherspoon, later one of the signers of the Declaration of Independence, is said to have been lineally descended from John Knox.
9. The Non-Importation Association was naturally enough not at all popular in the city of New York.
10. History of the United States (Centenary Edition) vol. iv, p. 513.
11. Apparently Mr. Bancroft is wrong here, as Isaac Low was elected but declined to serve. Another delegate of the previous year, John Herring of Orange also declined re-election.
12. The New York delegates to the Second Continental Congress were:—Philip Livingston, James Duane, John Alsop, John Jay, Philip Schuyler, George Clinton, Francis Lewis, Henry Wisner, Simon Boerum, Lewis Morris, William Floyd, and Robert R. Livingston, junior.
13. Namely Philip Livingston, his cousin.
14. From Hunt's Life of Edward Livingston, pp. 23, 24.
15. The postscript is in reference to his powder mill, which was then in course of erection.
16. Namely Holt's Journal of May 11, 1775.
17. Walter Livingston has already been referred to as a delegate for Albany in the nominating Convention of the previous month. He was the third son of Robert, third Lord of the Manor. Gilbert Livingston was the grandson of that Gilbert Livingston who represented the Manor in the Assembly from 1728 to 1737.
18. Governor Tryon to the Earl of Dartmouth, New York, 4th July, 1775.

19. Philip and his cousin Robert R. were both members at this time of the Provincial as well as of the Continental Congress, and they appear to have arranged between them that while one was attending the sittings of the former in New York, the latter should be in attendance in Philadelphia, and *vice versa*.

20. This was in response to the resolution passed by the Continental Congress on the 15th May, 1775, calling upon the different colonies to adopt new forms of government.

21. Letter dated Philadelphia, 17th June 1776, and signed by Francis Lewis, Robert R. Livingston, John Alsop, William Floyd, and Henry Wisner.

22. Here is a good example, from many, of this class of "Fourth of July" literature:— "The weighty importance of these vital questions had all been settled, and an expression of cool determination rested on the brows of those noble patriots. They were listening with earnest attention to the reading of the Declaration, by Secretary Charles Thompson as amended, while scarcely a breath was audible except the voice of the Secretary. A holy calm pervaded the room, and the white-winged angel of peace came as a messenger from heaven to set God's approving signet upon their actions. . . . We see them in imagination, as they gather in their representative capacity, with high and holy resolves upon their brows, advance to the Secretary's table, for the purpose of recording their votes in favour of adopting the Declaration. When that eventful moment arrived; when the deed was consummated, old Independence Bell rang out the glad tidings to the inhabitants of a disenthralled land. Then went up shouts of joy from the friends of the measure... and quaked more convulsively traitors to the cause of freedom, etc." Belisle, *History of Independence Hall*, pp. 119–121. What the "angel of peace" had to do with a deed which meant relentless war for nearly seven years, only a "Fourth of July orator" is competent to explain!

23. To show how deceptive memory may serve even the most able men, Thomas Jefferson, who actually drafted the Declaration, states in his *Memoirs*—written though many years after the events treated of above—that it was signed on the 4th "by every member present except Mr. Dickinson." While, on the other hand, John Adams, in a letter to Samuel Chase of Maryland, written on the 9th of July 1776, or only five days after the adoption of the accepted draft says: "As soon as an American seal is prepared, I conjecture the Declaration will be subscribed by all the members, which will give you the opportunity you wish for, of transmitting your name among the votaries of Independence." The New York delegates could not have signed on the fourth, even if the others had; but the *Secret Journals of Congress* quoted from in the text, clearly prove that John Adams was right and Jefferson wrong.

24. So runs the entry in the *Secret Journals*, meaning of course those members *actually present*; as some of the signatures, it is notorious, could not have been affixed until a later date even!

25. The above letter is signed by George Clinton, Henry Wisner, William Floyd, Francis Lewis, and John Alsop. What the reason was why Robert R. Livingston did not also sign it is unknown. His time may have been too much engaged as a member of the drafting committee, but there is no official mention of his name later in date than the previous letter of the 17th of June.

26. These Resolutions were read in Continental Congress on the 15th of July.

27. Philip Livingston had evidently moved his family from Brooklyn to Esopus just twelve months previous to this date; for in a letter written by Harris Cruger of New

York on the 3rd November 1775, he says: "Old Pill Livingston loaded a sloop with furniture, horses, cows, negroes, and children; away they are all gone to Sopus."

28. Robert R. Livingston is the only member of the Committee of Five, whose name is not subscribed to the parchment copy.

29. None of the then delegates were re-appointed. Dr. Gordon in his *Rise, Progress, and Establishment of the United States of America*, which was published in 1788, says (vol. ii, p. 277), in reference to this matter, "On the 21st [? 22d], however, before they could know the plot as a body, they proceeded to elect delegates for the Continental Congress, whom they empowered to join in declaring the united colonies independent of Great Britain. In this election they left out William Livingston, Esquire, under a strong persuasion that he was not favourable to independency; and chose the Rev. Dr. Witherspoon, the president of the College at Princeton, from a conviction that he would support it with all his abilities."

30. Mr. Sedgwick in his *Life of William Livingston* (pp. 182, 183, and note), owing to his having, apparently, misread the date on a letter from General Washington to General Livingston, was under the impression that the latter might have left the Continental Congress on the fifth of June 1776. But the above particulars, derived from the *Minutes of the New Jersey Provincial Congress*, show that he was still in Philadelphia in the latter part of that month.

31. If William Livingston had been returned to Congress, with the definite instructions given to the new delegates to vote for Independence in unison with the other colonies, he would have done so; in which case the author of this family history could have claimed *two direct ancestors of the same name among the "Signers,"* instead of only one. Because, while he is descended in the direct male line from Philip Livingston, who was his great-great-grandfather, he is also directly descended from William Livingston, through his paternal grandmother, who was the eldest daughter of Judge Brockholst Livingston by his first marriage—his grandparents were therefore first cousins. The author's children, moreover, are doubly descended from William Livingston, as their mother is a granddaughter of Judge Brockholst Livingston by his third marriage.

Strange to say the only son of Philip Livingston, who left descendants, remained a British subject, having settled in the British island of Jamaica, and married an Englishwoman resident there, prior to the outbreak of the War of Independence. This was Philip "the Signer's" eldest son—Philip P. Livingston—and one of *his* sons, Edward P. Livingston returned to New York, married the eldest daughter of Chancellor Livingston, and, in time, became Lieutenant-Governor of that State. It is to his grandson, the present owner of "Clermont," that this volume is dedicated.

CHAPTER XIII

CONCERNING THE WAR OF INDEPENDENCE, AND THE PART THE LIVINGSTON FAMILY PLAYED THEREIN.

"If you imagine I expect this Declaration will ward off calamities from this Country, you are much mistaken. A Bloody conflict we are des-tined to endure. This has been my opinion from the beginning."

Extract from letter of John Adams to Samuel Chase of Maryland, dated Philadelphia, 1st July 1776.

"Then with one voice thy country call'd thee forth,
Thee, WASHINGTON, she call'd:—with modest blush,
But soul undaunted, thou the call obey'd,
To lead her armies to the martial field.
Thee, WASHINGTON, she call'd to draw the sword,
And rather try the bloody chance of war
In virtue's cause, than suffer servile chains,
Intolerable bondage! to inclose
The limbs of those whom God created free.
Lur'd by thy fame, and with thy virtues charm'd,
And by thy valour fir'd, around thee pour'd
AMBRICA's long injur'd sons, resolv'd
To meet the veteran troops who oft had borne,
BRITANNIA's name, in thunder round the world."

—From Ode to General Washington by Governor Livingston of New Jersey, anno 1778.

THE adoption by the Continental Congress of the Declaration of Independence, which has been aptly described as a Declaration consisting of "glittering generalities," certainly amply fulfilled the ardent desires of its most prominent promoters, as the immediate result was the abandonment of any hopes, that had been hitherto entertained by the more moderate patriots, of a reconciliation with the mother-country. Its authors plainly intended it should be a defiant challenge to Great Britain. To use sturdy John Adams's own forcible, one might even say, brutal words, "a Bloody Conflict" was clearly foreseen would be the outcome of the vote of the second of July.[1] It meant, moreover, not only a continuance of the hostilities with Great Britain, but the worst sort of war, civil war, in which relatives are ranged against relatives, neighbours against neighbours, and a whole continent set in a blaze from the Gulf of Mexico to the River St. Lawrence! The irreconcilables, however, considered that this was a case in which the end justified the means. To men of this intolerant disposition, sympathy with those members of the Congress like Dickinson, Rutledge, and the Livingstons, who differed as to the wisdom of pressing this Declaration through Congress before the colonies were ripe for such an extreme measure, was quite out of the question. But these more moderate men plainly showed during the "Bloody Conflict" of the next seven years, that they were quite as good patriots as the most irreconcilable of their colleagues. It is doubtful whether any other family in the whole thirteen colonies had so much at stake as the Livingstons. There were richer men individually, for instance Charles Carroll of Carrollton; but considering the number of the Livingstons, their united wealth, and immense landed estates, no single family could have put more to the hazard of civil war than they! Certainly the concluding sentence of the famous Declaration, in which the signers "with a firm reliance on the protection of Divine Providence, mutually pledge to each other our *Lives*, our *Fortunes*, and our sacred *Honour*," must have brought home to these worthy men, that failure meant ruin to them and their dear ones, and probably also the block or the gallows for themselves.[2]

Before proceeding to give an account of the part played by the more prominent members of the family during the War of Independence, it may be as well to start with a list of the various civil and military[3] appointments held under Congress, or under the local State Conventions and Legislatures during this eventful period, by Livingstons, as well as by men who had married daughters of this House, which will alone prove that the above statement is no mere idle boast.[4]

To commence with four sons and one daughter of PHILIP LIVINGSTON, SECOND LORD of the MANOR, and their respective families:—

(1) ROBERT, the eldest son and third Lord of the Manor, filled no official position himself under the revolted colonies, probably because of his age, and his large estate which occupied all his time. But he proved his loyalty to the cause by placing his iron mines and foundry at the disposal of the New York Committee of Safety; and the following members of his family were actively employed on the American side:—

   i, Peter R., Member of Provincial Convention 1775; Member of Provincial Congress 1775, 1776; President of Provincial Congress 1776, 1777; Member of Assembly 1780, 1781; and Colonel of Militia, Manor of Livingston Regiment, during the war.

   ii, Walter; Member of Provincial Congress 1775; Member of Assembly 1777, 1778, 1779; Speaker of Assembly 1778; Commissioner of United States Treasury 1785; and Deputy Commissary General, Northern Department 1775, 1776.

   iii, John; Aide-de-Camp to Governor Clinton 1778.

   iv, Henry; Lieutenant-Colonel of Militia, Manor of Livingston Regiment, fought at Saratoga.

   v, Mary; wife of James Duane, Member of Continental Congress 1774–1784; State Senator etc., etc.

(2) PETER VAN BRUGH; Member of Committee of One Hundred 1775; Member of Provincial Congress 1775, 1776; President of same 1775; and Treasurer 1776.

His sons were loyalist in their sympathies, and neutral during the war. One of his daughters married, after the war John Kean, Member of the United States Congress 1785–1787.

(3) PHILIP; Member of Committee of One Hundred 1775; President Provincial Convention 1775; Member of Continental Congress 1774–1778; Member of Provincial Congress 1776, 1777; State Senator 1777, 1778; and a Signer of the Declaration of Independence.

   i, Abraham; Commissary of Provisions to the American Army 1776 *et seq.*:

   ii, Henry P., Officer in Washington's Corps of Guards.

iii, Sarah; wife of Rev. John H. Livingston, D.D., Chaplain to Provincial Congress 1775; and after the war President of Queen's College, New Brunswick, N. J.

(4) WILLIAM; Member of Continental Congress 1774–1776; Brigadier-General, New Jersey Militia 1775, 1776; Governor of the State of New Jersey, 1776–1790; and a signer of the Federal Constitution, 1787.

i, William; Registrar New Jersey Court of Admiralty; and Secretary to his father, Governor Livingston, 1777.

ii, Henry Brockholst; Lieutenant-Colonel in the American Army, and Aide to General Schuyler 1776, 1777; Volunteer Aide to General Arnold at Battle of Freeman's Farm, 19 September 1777; Private Secretary to John Jay in his Mission to Spain 1779; after the war, Judge of the Supreme Court 1802–6, and Judge of the Supreme Court of the United States 1806–1823.

iii, John Lawrence; Midshipman in the Continental Navy 1780, 1781, and lost in the *Saratoga* in the latter year.

iv, Sarah Van Brugh; wife of John Jay, Member of Continental Congress 1774–1777; Member of Provincial Congress 1776, 1777; Minister to Spain 1779; a signer of the Treaty of Peace 1783, etc., etc.

Another daughter, Susannah, after the war, married John Cleve Symmes, member of New Jersey Convention 1776, etc., etc.

(5) SARAH; wife of William Alexander, Earl of Stirling, Major-General in the American Army. His right to this title was never recognised by the British Government, but, as a matter of courtesy, he was always addressed, during the war, as "Lord Stirling." He died just before its close.

i, Catherine, married in 1779, Colonel William Duer, Member of New York Convention 1777, etc., etc.

(1) JUDGE ROBERT R. LIVINGSTON OF CLERMONT, who died soon after the outbreak of hostilities in December 1775:—

i, Robert R., junior; Member of Continental Congress 1775, *et seq.*; Member of Provincial Convention 1775; Provincial Congress 1776, 1777; Chancellor 1777–1801; Secretary for Foreign Affairs 1781–1783; after the war,

Member of New York Convention 1788; Minister to France 1801–3, etc., etc.

ii, Henry Beekman; Colonel Fourth New York Line; fought at Saratoga, etc., etc.

iii, John R.; Major of Militia; Army agent, etc., etc.

iv, Janet; wife of General Richard Montgomery, who fell at Quebec, 31 December 1775.

v, Margaret; wife of Dr. Thomas Tillotson of the American Army, etc., etc.

vi, Gertrude; wife of General Morgan Lewis of the American Army, etc., etc.

vii, Alida; wife of General John Armstrong of the American Army, etc., etc.

GILBERT LIVINGSTON, the fourth son of Robert Livingston, first Lord of the Manor, had the following sons and grandsons occupying official positions, civil and military under the American government during the war:—

(1) ROBERT GILBERT; he was too old himself to take an active part in the war, besides he was a loyalist in his sympathies, but he had three sons holding commissions in the American Army:—

i, Robert Gilbert, junior; Colonel and Deputy Adjutant-General to the Northern Army 1775; Major of Minute Men for Dutchess County 1775; Member of Provincial Congress 1775, 1776.

ii, Henry G.; Captain in Colonel John Lasher's Regiment of Militia 1775; Brigade-Major to Lord Stirling 1776.

iii, Gilbert R.; Volunteer with Colonel Wind's New Jersey Regiment in Canadian campaign 1776; Ensign and Second-Lieutenant, Third New York (Continental) Regiment 1776, 1777. Probably at Saratoga (?)

(2) HENRY; County Clerk of Dutchess under the Crown 1742; continued to hold this office under the State Government until 1789.

i, Gilbert; Member of Provincial Congress 1775–1777; Member of Assembly 1777, 1778; after the war, Member of Assembly 1788, 1789; Delegate to New York Convention of 1788, etc., etc.

ii, Rev, Dr. John H.; Chaplain to Provincial Congress 1775; after the war, President of Queen's College, New Brunswick, N. J.

iii, Henry, junior; Major Third New York (Continental) Regiment 1775.

iv, Robert H., Lieutenant New York (Continental) Artillery; after the war, County Clerk of Dutchess in succession to his father 1789.

(3) JAMES; Member of Provincial Congress 1776, 1777. Chairman of Committee of Safety 1777.

i, Gilbert J.; Ensign and Second-Lieutenant, Second New York Continental Regiment 1776, 1777; Captain in Local Levies under Colonels Weissenfels, Malcom, and Pawling; fought at Saratoga in Colonel Van Cortlandt's Regiment (Second New York).

Also a daughter:

(4) JOHANNA; wife of Pierre Van Cortlandt, President Council of Safety, and first Lieutenant-Governor State of New York, 1777, etc., etc.

The following grandsons of ROBERT LIVINGSTON OF ALBANY, THE NEPHEW, held commissions in the American Army:—

(1) JAMES; Colonel Regiment of Canadian Refugees 1775, 1776; Colonel Additional Battalion New York Line, 1776–1781; fought at Saratoga, etc., etc.

(2) RICHARD; elder brother of the above James; Lieutenant-Colonel in the same regiments; fought at Saratoga, etc.

(3) ABRAHAM; another brother; Captain in the same regiments; fought at Saratoga, etc., etc.

The following great-grandson of ROBERT LIVINGSTON, THE NEPHEW, also served in the American Army:—

(1) WILLIAM SMITH; a son of Robert James Livingston, merchant of New York, and nephew to William Smith, the Chief Justice and Historian; Major in Colonel Lasher's Regiment of Militia 1776; Aide-de-Camp to General Greene; and Lieutenant-Colonel in Colonel S. B. Webb's Additional Battalion of Connecticut Line 1777, 1778.

One of the most important duties, which the first New York Provincial Congress was called upon to perform, was the raising of their colony's proportion of the troops required to form "a part of the army of the United Colonies for the defence of American Liberty, and for repelling every hostile invasion thereof." This Congress met on the 23rd of May 1775, and as already mentioned Peter Van Brugh Livingston was unanimously elected to be its first President. By the end of the following month it had sanctioned the formation of four regiments as their quota of the continental or regular Army, and had selected the names of the persons suitable to hold commissions therein. These four regiments were to be recruited from the following districts, namely:—The First Regiment from the City and County of New York and vicinity; the Second Regiment from the County of Albany; the Third Regiment from the County of Ulster; and the Fourth Regiment from the County of Dutchess. As it was in the latter county that the Livingston influence was strongest at this period, it was natural that in the first lot of warrants issued, should be three commissions conferring the rank of captain in the last named regiment, upon three youthful members of this family. These young men were Henry Beekman Livingston, John R. Livingston, and Henry G. Livingston. The first of these was, however, the only one of the three who accepted the proffered commission; though Henry G. Livingston shortly afterwards became a captain in Colonel Lasher's regiment of militia, known as the First Battalion of New York Independents.

This Henry Beekman Livingston was the second son of Judge Robert R. Livingston of Clermont, and was then in his twenty-fifth year. He must not be confounded with his cousin Henry Brockholst Livingston, a son of William Livingston of New Jersey, whose initials are the same, and who was soon to be appointed an aide-de-camp to General Schuyler with the rank of major. Henry Brockholst was only eighteen years of age when he obtained this appointment, but the War of Independence was the young man's opportunity. Colonels at twenty, statesmen under thirty, were not at all uncommon at this momentous period in American history.[5]

Henry Beekman Livingston was a young man of spirit, and as he had held a commission in the militia under the crown, of a higher grade than the one offered him by the Provincial Congress, he naturally, when writing to his relative President Livingston accepting the warrant, protested "it was not without surprise he had received a commission inferior to that he had been honoured with."[6] He, however, at once set to work to recruit his company, and by the 8th of August, he was able to inform the Provincial Congress, he had "enlisted upwards of seventy-two men." But he was early to experience the neglect, or inability, of the local convention to supply their soldiers with proper necessaries, as in another letter to the same body, written a couple of days later, he complains that the "clothes issued to the troops are utterly insufficient."[7] In this latter letter he also refers to a rumour that "a person inexperienced in his profession is to be advanced over his head"; and he again reminds the Congress that some two years previously he had been considered "fit for a majority under the Crown." This rumour probably referred to his cousin and namesake Henry Livingston, junior,[8] who, upon the second of this month, had, by a large majority of votes in the Provincial Congress, been nominated Major of the Third Regiment, which commission was then vacant. Major Livingston was nearly two years older than his cousin, which may have been the reason why the former obtained the higher rank, The other candidate for the vacant majority was yet another cousin, Robert G. Livingston, junior, who, however, only got the votes of one county, that of Albany, in his favour. But he got his compensation three weeks later, when the same Congress appointed him to be "Deputy Adjutant-General with the rank of Colonel in the place of William Duer, Esq., and that he be directed to join the army under the command of General Schuyler, with all possible despatch."

It would, however, be tedious work to give here a list of all the commissions, Continental or Militia, bestowed on various members of the family during the war; so we must confine ourselves to relating what is of most interest, concerning those who bore a prominent part in the struggle.[9] Of these military Livingstons, Captain Henry Beekman Livingston's career is of the greatest importance. His first campaign was with the Northern Army under Generals Schuyler and Montgomery in the invasion of Canada, which the Continental Congress considered would be a good counter-stroke to the British occupation of Boston. General Richard Montgomery, a former British officer, who had retired from that service, and having bought some land near the Hudson had made New York his home, was Captain Livingston's brother-in-law.[10] General Schuyler having to return to Albany on account of ill health, the command of this unfortunate enterprise fell to his second-in-command, Montgomery.

General Richard Montgomery (1737–1775), married Janet, eldest daughter of Judge Robert R. Livingston of Clermont. The Miriam and Ira D. Wallach Division of Art, Prints and Photographs: Print Collection, New York Public Library Digital Collections, Public Domain.

Judge Livingston went to Albany to see his soldier son start on his march to Canada, and there is still in existence a portion of the first letter Captain Livingston wrote to his father after he had joined the American army. From this interesting fragment, dated from "Canada, Camp before St: John's, 6th October 1775,"[11] are derived the following extracts:—

Dear Sir, I just received your letter. Your illness gives me great uneasiness. I hope it will be of no duration.[12] After you left me at Albany we marched to Fort George in three days, where I was obliged to stop till Colonel Gates[13] who commanded there would please let us cross the lake, which was in about three days. We had a favourable passage across, being but one night by the way; the next morning we came to Ticonderoga. As soon as we came there, I waited upon Colonel Hinman, commanding officer at that place and begged leave to be permitted to proceed with the first boats for the army, then at Ile au Noix; this I obtained for myself but not for my company, there not being a sufficiency of boats to carry them off. I therefore took my departure and ordered my lieutenants to follow, the first opportunity. When I'came down'I found all in health at the army, except General Schuyler.[14] A party of them, about five hundred, had been sent down the lake as far as we now are, under the command of General Montgomery. They were attacked upon their landing by a party of Indians, who were beat off by our people with the loss of about nine killed and wounded; the enemy had fifteen of their number killed upon the spot and some wounded. Our people intrenched themselves in two places about a mile apart, along the banks of the river Sorel (this part of the lake takes that name.) The next morning they went back to the Isle, having made the discoveries they thought necessary. All this happened before I came down.

When I came there, Colonel Ritzema[15] was detached with a party of picked men to take possession of La Prairie, a village fifteen miles the other side of St: John's, in order to cut off the communications between Canada and that place, from his own and a Connecticut regiment. General Montgomery followed with another party, consisting of the same number, to see us safely landed (I obtained leave to come in character of aid-de-camp to Col. Ritzema upon this occasion, as my company was not yet come.) We landed safely at the upper breastworks about a mile from this we now occupy; and marched then within two hundred yards of this place, where was another breastwork. A flanking party having been sent out from the front to scour the woods, while we were coming, we, who were in front, found ourselves deserted of a sudden by nine-tenths of our party; upon going back to learn the cause we found they had been affrighted by our flanking party, who came suddenly out of the woods upon them in order to join us. The panic was so great that it was with difficulty we prevailed upon them to proceed on their march; we had not advanced a hundred yards farther, before we were attacked with musketry a little ahead of us, and some cohorns thrown from a boat upon the water. Our men were again affrighted and retreated with great precipitation, except about thirty who entered the breastworks, where they found some Indians, soldiers, and French, about fifteen in number, who they fired upon; an Indian and a Frenchman were killed of their number, the rest made their escape.

Next day the general, who came to see us land safely, was obliged to proceed upon his way back with us all to the Isle, not being able to prevail upon the detachment to go forward. However, a few days after he brought down the same detachment (having first made peace with the Indians), that they might have an opportunity of retrieving their honour. This they effected. After staying a day or two to complete our breastworks, General Montgomery marched round St: John's with this party, and as he came out of the woods popped very unexpectedly upon a body of about four hundred of the enemy, who attacked him with field pieces, but he obliged them to retreat into the fort. This they did in good order, carrying their field pieces with them, the loss trifling on both sides. The general having effected his purpose ordered a party to intrench themselves about two miles below St. John's, upon the only two roads that lead from that place to the inhabited parts of Canada. Another party was dispatched to La Prairie. . . . Mr. James Livingston has been exceedingly active, he had several skirmishes, since we came down and before. We have now nine hundred men the other side St: John's strongly intrenched, about a thousand on this side at the main camp in the same situation.

This James Livingston was a grandson of Robert Livingston "the nephew," and was also a close connection of Captain Livingston, whose maternal grandmother was Janet, a daughter of this same Robert Livingston, and wife of Colonel Henry Beekman of Rhinebeck, after whom he had been named. James Livingston's father was John Livingston, who had married Catherine, eldest daughter of Dirck Ten Broeck of Albany, and who had been settled for some years in Montreal, Canada. His sons, James, Richard, and Abraham, took an active interest in rousing the Canadians to arms in aid of their fellow colonists, but with the exception of the *habitants* living in the district of the Richelieu, the Canadians mostly held aloof. The Continental Congress certainly hoped the majority of them would rise *en masse*, and welcome their liberators with open arms, but the French seigneurs and clergy either remained neutral, or rendered active assistance to the British governor, that fine gentleman and able soldier, Sir Guy Carleton. Why should they throw off "the Yoke of Britain," which protected them in their religion, laws, and customs, to oblige their historic, and former bigoted enemies, *Les Bastonnais*, as the Canadians somewhat contemptuously called the revolutionists?

With the Canadians he had enlisted, James Livingston joined General Montgomery, who bestowed upon him the command of this force with the local rank of major, and his two brothers, Richard his senior, and Abraham his junior in age, held commissions under him. About a fortnight after the date of Captain Henry Beekman Livingston's letter to his father, this James, with about three hundred of his Canadians, and aided by Major Brown of the Continental army captured Fort Chambly,[16] thus materially assisting General Montgomery in his siege of St. John's, which also fell into American hands the first week of November. As a reward for his services in the capture of Fort Chambly, Continental Congress, on the eighth of the following January (1776), "*Resolved,* That this Congress does approve of the raising of a Battalion of Canadians, and of the appointment of James Livingston, Esquire, Colonel thereof."[17]

But patriotism in some quarters at this period was at a very low ebb. For while General Washington in his camp before Boston, disgusted with the New England notions of equality and self interest, which permitted the privates to elect their own officers, was having, what he called, "a pretty good slam" among these gentry, breaking colonels and captains freely for cowardice, peculation, and other military crimes; Montgomery was also complaining in the bitterest terms of the conduct of many of his own subordinates and asking Schuyler "why cannot we have gentlemen for officers?"[18] Many of General Montgomery's despatches at this date are pitiable reading; the one thought of many of these "patriot soldiers" being to return home at once on the expiration of their limited term of service, their "homesickness" increasing by leaps and bounds the nearer they got to the enemy! General Schuyler was quite as heartbroken as his lieutenant over the conduct of some of these soldiers; for in a letter to Congress, written on the twentieth of November from his headquarters at Ticonderoga, he remarks, with biting sarcasm, that he has discovered a cure for "this prevailing disorder," and that is to discharge the invalids! Whereupon, to use his own words, "no sooner is it administered, but it perfected the cure of nine out of ten, who, refusing to wait for boats to go by the way of Fort George, slung their heavy packs, crossed the lake at this place, and undertook a march of two hundred miles with the greatest good-will and alacrity!"[19]

In spite of such serious drawbacks, Montgomery, with the brave men who still adhered to their general—though even many of these he had "to coax"—advanced on Montreal, which place surrendered to him on the twelfth of November, and was occupied by his little force on the following day. He sent his brother-in-law with the despatches announcing the good news to General Schuyler, and in his letter to his chief, covering these, he wrote: "I will take it as a favour if you will send Harry Livingston with your despatches for Congress."[20] A few days later, General Schuyler speeded him on his way to Philadelphia, and in his letter to President Hancock, he recommended the bearer "Captain Livingston (who brought me General Montgomery's despatches) as a gentleman whose alertness and zeal has caused him to be distinguished in the army."[21] Brother-in-law to the, so far, successful general, and brother to one of the prominent members of the Continental Congress, the bearer on his arrival in Philadelphia was received with marked favour, and "a sword of the value of one hundred dollars," was voted him by Congress on the twelfth of December, "as a testimony of their sense of his services to this Country," with a promise he should be promoted "on the first opportunity."[22]

Meanwhile, Montgomery was continuing his march on to Quebec, in the face of the fearful hardships of a winter campaign in such a climate, only, however, to find a soldier's death at the head of a forlorn hope! It is strange the level-headed Washington should have countenanced such a scheme as this, for even if Montgomery, with the assistance of Benedict Arnold, had taken Quebec, the Americans could never have held it against the British fleet. Colonel James Livingston's regiment of Canadian refugees took part in the unsuccessful assault on Quebec, but their work was confined to making a demonstration against the St. John's Gate. They also served during the rest of the campaign, until with the remainder of the American army, they were driven out of Canada by Sir Guy Carleton in the following summer. Being now without a command, Congress presented James Livingston with a commission, of the same rank he had held in Canada, in the Continental Service, and he was granted permission "to recruit his regiment in any of the United States."[23] He finally raised a battalion in his native State, which he commanded—as an Additional Battalion of the New York Line—until the regiment was reduced in 1781.[24]

But we must now return to Captain Henry Beekman Livingston, who, on receipt of the sword of honour, wrote to President Hancock the following letter, which was read in Congress on the 22nd December 1775:—

The compliment paid me by Congress does me great honour. Their present is amazingly genteel, and their promise very flattering to a young man who wishes to acquire a reputation. These distinguished marks of their approbation deserve my warmest acknowledgments and most cordial thanks. These I could beg leave to present in person, did not my affection for my late father render me unfit to appear before them.[25]

Early in the following year Congress was busy reorganising its little army, and New York was called upon to see that her regiments were put upon a proper war footing. Therefore, on the twenty-eighth of February 1776, the New York Congress forwarded to the Continental Congress the names of certain field officers proposed by them for the, to be, reorganised New York battalions, and among these Livingston's name appeared in the list of majors. The Continental Congress was, however, more generous in their treatment of him, for on the eighth of March that body elected him Lieutenant-Colonel of the new second New York Battalion, which was to be commanded by Colonel James Clinton, and even were willing to give him precedence in rank over Lieutenant-Colonel Philip Van Cortlandt, a matter which, unfortunately subsequently led to much bickering and ill feeling between these two young men.[26] Upon the twenty-seventh of April the Congress approved of eight companies for Colonel Clinton's regiment, and "ordered, That a copy of this appointment be given to Lt. Colo. Henry B. Livingston."

Henry Beekman Livingston did not return to Canada, as part of his new regiment was employed in garrisoning the forts on the Hudson, while three of its companies were stationed on Long Island. On the fourth of May, the Commander-in-Chief, General Washington, wrote to Lieutenant-Colonel Livingston, from his headquarters in New York City, instructing him to proceed to Forts Montgomery and Constitution, where four of his companies were stationed,[27] and should no superior officer be there, to take over the command and push on with energy the construction of the works then in progress. The lieutenant-colonel certainly lost no time in acting upon these orders, for on the ninth of this month he was at Fort Constitution, and five days later reported to General Washington that the fortifications were in a most deplorable condition. While in command here, he firmly declined to continue the system of putting to hard labour on these fortifications—unless specially ordered to do so by his superior officer or Congress—"those unhappy wretches made prisoners by the

County Committees"; as he conceived, and rightly too, "those commands to be rather a tyrannical exercise of power in these gentlemen, which they have no right to exercise, and such as no Continental officer is bound to conform to without a particular direction from Congress or a superior officer."[28]

A few weeks later he was detailed on special duty again, this time to patrol the eastern portion of Long Island, so as to protect the farmers from raids from the British ships of war, then cruising off the coast, and also to intimidate the Tories from rendering assistance to the British forces. On the defeat of the American main army at the battle of Long Island,[29] Lieutenant-Colonel Livingston found himself and his detachment cut off from New York, but he managed to retreat across the sound to Connecticut and from there he ultimately got safely back to the Hudson. His soldierly behaviour under these difficult circumstances so pleased Washington that he sent a message to William Duer of the New York Convention, on the 8th of October, in which he says:—

> He has ever avoided recommending officers to preferment, lest he should be taxed with partiality, but that he cannot pass by the merit of Lieutenant-Colonel Livingston, of Colonel Clinton's regiment, he having upon every occasion exhibited proofs of his activity and zeal for the service. He therefore wishes he may not be overlooked in the preferments that must naturally take place upon the new establishment of your forces.[30]

Great praise indeed coming from a commander-in-chief of Washington's character; and which naturally led to this officer's promotion to the rank of colonel, and the command of his old regiment—the Fourth,—upon the twenty-first of the following month.

For the next few months Colonel Livingston was stationed at Peekskill on the Hudson, his regiment forming part of Brigadier-General M'Dougall's command. One of his duties during this period was to act as president of a Court-Martial appointed for the trial of State prisoners. But, as we have seen on a former occasion, Colonel Livingston strongly objected to army officers being employed in such political matters; so he, and the other officers sitting on this Court-Martial, formally protested against civilian prisoners being brought to trial before a purely military tribunal. It was while stationed at this place that the colonel quarrelled with his superior officer, ex-privateersman and "Son of Liberty" M'Dougall, owing to the garrison having to retreat before a British detachment sent to destroy some stores which they were there to protect; and which Colonel Livingston is said to have called "A Damned Scandalous Retreat!" Evidently, there was no love lost between these two officers, both of whom were possessed of a fiery temper, and the brigadier plainly showed his animus by his reference to the colonel of the Fourth as that "poor boy."[31] Colonel Livingston was court-martialled on account of this quarrel, but got off with a reprimand. One of the findings of the Court, which sat on the 1st of June 1777, was to the effect "that though the colonel appears to this Court to be guilty of great imprudence and indiscretion in some parts of his language and conduct towards the general, yet his conduct was not such as will warrant the appellation of being unbecoming a gentleman and an officer." Strangely enough, five years later, General M'Dougall was tried and censured for exactly the same offence, namely for using disrespectful language to his superior officer.

A few weeks after this episode, the regiments of Colonel Livingston and Colonel Van Cortlandt were detached from General M'Dougall's brigade,[32] and sent north to reinforce General Schuyler then close pressed by the British army from Canada under General Burgoyne.[33] These regiments on their arrival at the American camp on the 21st of August, or two days after Schuyler had been superseded by General Gates, were brigaded with the command of General Poor, to be transferred to the division of General Benedict Arnold on that officer's return from the relief of Fort Stanwix.[34] Colonel Livingston took part in the Battle of Freeman's Farm, nineteenth of September 1777[35]; and in this, as well as in the subsequent battle of the seventh of October, the Fourth New York distinguished themselves by their dash and bravery, particularly in the latter engagement in which they earned special praise from General Arnold, who declared "great part of our success on that day was owing to the gallant part they acted in storming the enemy's works, and the alertness and good order they observed in the pursuit."[36] After the surrender of Burgoyne's army, the Fourth was one of the first of the line regiments ordered south by General Gates to the assistance of Governor Clinton, who entrusted its colonel with a mission to the British commander in New York City, Lieutenant-General Sir Henry Clinton, a namesake, but no connexion, of the "rebel" governor.

Colonel Livingston left Albany for the south, prior to the 29th October 1777, "in the bateau that carried Lord Viscount Petersham, aide-de-camp to

Lieutenant-General Burgoyne;"[37] and upon his return, in accordance with his instructions, he reported himself to Governor Clinton, then at New Windsor. The governor, in forwarding his report to General Gates, sarcastically remarks:—

> Inclosed you have the Report[38] made to me by Colo. H. B. Livingston on the Commission with which he was charged by you to Lieut-Genl. Sir Henry Clinton. I fancy with the Colo. that my Namesake found himself incapable of Justifying on any Sound Principle the Villainies committed by the Troops under his Command and therefore has evaded answering your Letter. In this at least he has discovered a Degree of Prudence beyond Mr. Burgoyne who seemed pleased with those Literary Productions which now add to his Confusion.[39]

Probably, Colonel Livingston was entrusted with this commission, owing to the fact that the residences of his mother and eldest brother had suffered from "the Villainies" complained of.[40]

The Fourth New York Regiment shortly after joined the main army under Washington, and shared in the hardships of Valley Forge. In a letter, written from this camp on Christmas Day 1777, Colonel Livingston bitterly complains to Governor Clinton regarding the destitution and sufferings of his unfortunate regiment, "wholly destitute of clothing, the men and officers perishing in the field."[41] In the year following he took part in the battle of Monmouth or Freehold, where he again distinguished himself by his dashing bravery. In a letter written by a fellow-combatant, Colonel John Laurens to his father, describing this affair, he concludes by remarking:—

> Our officers and men behaved with that bravery which becomes freemen, and have convinced the world that they can beat British grenadiers. To name anyone in particular would be a kind of injustice to the rest. There are some, however, who came more immediately under my view, whom I will mention that you may know them. B. Genl. Wayne, Col. Barber, Col. Stewart, Col. Livingston, Col. Oswald of the artillery, Capt. Doughty deserve well of their country, and distinguished themselves nobly.[42]

According to another contemporary account published in the *Pennsylvania Packet*, Colonel Livingston "behaved very handsomdy" on this occasion[43]; while in yet a third, sent to Governor Clinton, his name appears among those officers mentioned as slightly wounded in this engagement.[44]

A few weeks later, he was again actively engaged under General Sullivan and the Marquis de Lafayette, in the attack on Newport, Rhode Island, and again he attracted the attention of his fellow-officers by his conduct "on the field." For at the battle of Quaker Hill, 29th August 1778, General Greene in a letter to Washington mentions him as follows:—

> On the evening of the 29th [?28th] the army fell back to the north end of the Island. The next morning the enemy advanced upon us in two columns upon the East and West road. Our light troops commanded by Colonel Livingston and Colonel Lawrens, attacked the heads of the columns about 7 o'clock in the morning but were beat back; they were reinforced with a regiment upon each road. The enemy still proved too strong. General Sullivan formed the army in order of battle, and resolved to wait their approach upon the ground we were encamped on, and sent orders to the light troops to fall back. The enemy came up and formed upon Quaker Hill, a very strong piece of ground within about one mile and a quarter of our line. . . . General Sullivan ordered Colonel Livingston with the light troops under his command to advance. We soon put the enemy to the rout, and I had the pleasure to see them run in worse disorder than they did at the battle of Monmouth. Our troops behaved with great spirit. . . . Lieutenant-Colonel Livingston,[45] Colonel Jackson, and Colonel Henry B. Livingston did themselves great honour in the transactions of the day.[46]

While General Sullivan, himself, in his despatch to Congress, specially commends the conduct of "Colonel Livingston, and all the officers of the light corps [who] behaved with remarkable spirit."[47] But in spite of this gallant stand Sullivan had to continue his retreat, and abandon Rhode Island to the British.

This was the last campaign in which Colonel Henry Beekman Livingston took part, as upon the 20th of November following he wrote to

Congress, "requesting leave to resign his commission," and his letter having been read to the House upon the same day, was referred to the Board of War. And on the 13th of January 1779, Congress "*Resolved,* That the resignation of Colonel Henry B. Livingston of the 4th New York Regiment be accepted"; and "*Ordered,* That the president inform Colonel H. B. Livingston, that Congress have a high sense of the services he has rendered to his country."[48] No reason is given for his thus leaving the army, but, probably, like others in his position, he resigned because he did not obtain that further promotion, which he naturally considered his due. His rival Colonel Philip Van Cortlandt, however, solemnly declares he resigned in a fit of pique, because General Washington would not allow him leave of absence, when he (Cortlandt) and Livingston happened to apply for it at the same time![49] But then the colonel of the Second New York Regiment so palpably shows his dislike of his fellow-colonel of the Fourth, that all his statements concerning the latter in his *Autobiography* must be taken *cum grano salis.*[50]

Judge Henry Brockholst Livingston (1757–1823). The Miriam and Ira D. Wallach Division of Art, Prints and Photographs: Print Collection, New York Public Library Digital Collections, Public Domain.

Henry Brockholst Livingston, who was just seven years younger than his cousin of the similar initials,[51] had an early experience of warfare, but on water instead of on land. He was living at home—Liberty Hall, Elizabethtown, New Jersey,—during the winter of 1775–1776, when news arrived that his uncle, Colonel Lord Stirling, wanted volunteers for a cutting-out expedition he had planned for the capture of a British transport, which was supposed to have a cargo of arms and ammunition on board, of which the patriots of New Jersey stood much in need. This vessel, the *Blue Mountain Valley*, was lying off Sandy Hook in distress, awaiting assistance from the men-of-war at New York, when Lord Stirling seized a pilot boat at Perth Amboy, and joined by three other boats with militia and volunteers from Elizabethtown, captured her in the early hours of the morning of the 23d January 1776. The skipper's surprise at this unexpected bit of privateering must have been great! She was, to the disappointment of Lord Stirling, only laden with stores and provisions for the "ministerial army" at Boston; no ammunition or arms as expected.[52] All the same, the Continental Congress was mightily pleased at the success of this adventure, and at once, on receipt of the news, passed a resolution, "That the alertness, activity, and good conduct of Lord Stirling, and the forwardness and spirit of the gentlemen and others from Elizabethtown, who voluntarily assisted him in taking the ship *Blue Mountain Valley* were laudable and exemplary."[53] An elder brother of Henry Brockholst, William Livingston, junior, was also a "gentleman volunteer."

The next occasion we hear of Henry Brockholst Livingston is as aide-de-camp to General Schuyler, with the Continental rank of major[54]; and when that much maligned and shamefully ill-treated commander tendered his resignation to Congress—14th September 1776,—he recommended to the president that certain officers of his staff, including Major Livingston, should be provided for. Of the latter he wrote:—"I also beg leave to recommend to the attention of Congress, as a gentleman of a most amiable and deserving character." Whereupon that body, eleven days later, passed a resolution to the effect that "Major Henry Brockholst Livingston, aide-de-camp to General Schuyler be provided for by Congress in a station equal to his merit, when a proper vacancy happens, he being recommended by the general as a very deserving officer."[55] This promotion, apparently, did not come quick enough to suit the temper of this ambitious and high-spirited young officer[56]; who also felt deeply the unmerited disgrace which had befallen his beloved commander, whose resignation, however, was not accepted by Congress until some months later. For upon the 14th of

September 1777 —exactly a year after Schuyler had first offered to resign the northern command—Major Livingston writes to his father, Governor Livingston, from Stillwater:—

> We shall not decamp for Philadelphia as soon as I had expected. General Schuyler is at Albany preparing for trial. As he had not much business for me at that place, I obtained his permission to visit this army, and General Arnold having given me an invitation to spend a few weeks in his family,[57] I did myself the pleasure to join him on the ninth instant. Though my duty did not require my presence in camp, my general being at Albany, yet I scorned to take advantage of that privilege at a time when a battle is hourly expected, and joined the army as a volunteer. This is not the first time I have offered my services, trifling as they are in that capacity. My stay at Ticonderoga was entirely voluntary, as General Schuyler was absent. Skenesborough, Fort Anne, and other places can witness the same. I never screened myself under the cloak of duty. I mention not this by way of boasting, but only to convince you I have been neglected. General Schuyler's recommendations in my favour have been repeatedly neglected. I am happy that I shall soon have the opportunity of leaving the army with honour to myself and family, it being my fixed determination, the moment my general resigns, to leave a service where promotion goes by favour and not by merit.

The writer was evidently smarting under recent disappointment, for he had only lately returned from Philadelphia, where he had been sent by Schuyler with his despatch announcing the defeat of the British-German detachment under Colonel Baum at Bennington; and he naturally expected the coveted promotion as his reward for the welcome news. He probably had heard, moreover, that the question of his promotion had actually been put to the vote in Congress, 22d August 1777, but lost, the necessary majority of votes not having been obtained owing to the antagonism of the New England members. Whereupon, after debate, the resolution was ordered to be expunged from the journals, and the matter referred to the Board of War.[58]

When at Ticonderoga Major Livingston was attached to the staff of General St. Clair, and shared in the hardships of the retreat from that place, on its abandonment before the advancing British army under Burgoyne. General St. Clair was subsequently court-martialled for not making a firmer resistance, but was acquitted; as was also General Schuyler for his conduct in this campaign, in which General Gates, the protégé of the New England coterie in Congress, "reaped where others had sown." Livingston gave evidence in favour of both these generals, before these two courts-martial held during the following year. While attached to General Arnold's staff he had a dispute with a Major Chester, arising out of Gates's marked animosity to both Schuyler and Arnold, which resulted in a duel with pistols but, fortunately, without any serious result.[59] Three days after this duel was fought the expected battle took place.

It was at this time that Major Livingston exultingly and feelingly wrote to his old commander, General Schuyler:—"Burgoyne is in such a situation that he can neither advance nor retire without fighting. A capital battle must soon be fought. I am chagrined to the soul when I think that another person will reap the fruits of your labours." In this battle,[60] the first of the engagements known as the Battles of Bemis's Heights, Stillwater, or Saratoga, Major Livingston took part as volunteer aide to General Arnold,[61] that fiery commander who was the real hero of the day, while General Gates took all the credit to himself, entirely ignoring his subordinate general's dashing bravery, which resulted in the repulse of the British. Apparently, Major Livingston's services were not also overlooked, as upon the 4th of October, or fifteen days after this battle, Congress resolved "That Major Henry Brockholst Livingston, aide-de-camp to Major General Schuyler, be promoted to the rank of lieutenant-colonel as a reward for his merit and services in the American army."[62]

Major Livingston in his letters to General Schuyler, written immediately after this battle, boldly championed the neglected Arnold's cause, and thus incurred the bitter enmity of the American commander-in-chief. In one of these letters, dated from "Camp, Bemis's Heights, 23d September," he says "Believe me, Sir, to him [Arnold] alone is due the honour of our late Victory."[63] General Gates did not hide his vexation at Major Livingston's championship of his rival, so that in another letter written three days later, Livingston informs Schuyler, "I find myself under the necessity of returning to Albany, merely to satisfy the caprice and jealousy of a certain great person. It has been several times insinuated by the Commander-in-chief to General Arnold, that his mind has been poisoned and prejudiced by some of his family, and I have been pointed out as the person who had this undue influence over him."

Evidently therefore Major Livingston was not present at the second of these battles,[64] in which General Arnold again demonstrated his military genius and reckless courage. This last battle led to Burgoyne's capitulation a few days later. In the victorious American army, besides Henry Brockholst Livingston, there were six, if not seven, other officers of his surname. These were Colonel Henry Beekman Livingston, whose military career has just been related; Colonel James Livingston, formerly of the Canadian Regiment, now also commanding a Battalion of New York Continentals,[65] and the latter's two brothers, officers in their brother James's regiment[66]; Lieutenant-Colonel Henry Livingston of the Manor,[67] who commanded the regiment of militia from that place, and who had joined General Gates's army just in time to share in the final victory over Burgoyne; Lieutenant Gilbert James Livingston of Colonel Van Cortlandt's regiment; and lastly, the doubtful one, Lieutenant Gilbert R. Livingston of Colonel Gansevoort's Regiment, whom Governor Clinton had, on the 19th of September, sent to General Ten Broeck with a letter recommending him warmly for the post of brigade major on his staff. Surely a record for any one family! It was Lieutenant-Colonel Henry Livingston of the militia who accompanied Colonel Wilkinson, Gates's favourite aide, when he was sent to meet Major Kingston, the British envoy with a flag of truce, on the 14th October 1777.[68] This was the opening of the negotiations which resulted in the Convention of Saratoga.

To assist Burgoyne, Sir Henry Clinton, the British commander in New York City, had advanced up the Hudson and taken by storm, on the 6th of October, Forts Montgomery and Clinton. This British force, however, after wasting much valuable time in the burning of Kingston, and some private houses on the banks of the river, including the residences of Chancellor Livingston and his mother, returned to New York upon hearing the news of the surrender of the army they had hoped to have joined hands with. This was the second occasion upon which the British commanders had lost a great opportunity through their dilatory tactics. The first was missed by General Howe after the battle of Long Island, when, if he had pushed his victory he might have captured General Washington and the remnants of his army, and thus probably ended the war! In Sir Henry Clinton's case, the Home Government, apparently, was principally to blame in not having sent the necessary instructions in time.

Governor George Clinton, who with his brother James, commanded these two forts at the time of their capture, in his despatches[69] giving particulars of their fall, says after his outlying forces had been driven in, and when "the sun was an hour high," the British general sent a flag to demand their surrender, so as to "prevent the effusion of blood." To meet the flag, Governor Clinton sent Lieutenant-Colonel William S. Livingston,[70] of Colonel Samuel B. Webb's Additional Battalion Connecticut Line, who had "accidentally" arrived at Fort Montgomery a few minutes before the attack commenced.[71] In answer to the British Lieutenant-Colonel Campbell's summons to surrender, Livingston replied "he had no authority to treat with him, but, if they would surrender themselves prisoners of war, they might depend upon being well treated; and if they did not choose to accept of these terms they might renew the attack as soon as he should have returned within the fort, he being determined to defend it to the last extremity."

Certainly, Governor Clinton's description of this interview between his envoy and that of the British general is quite appropriate to the character borne by the former, who was known among his comrades by the sobriquet of "Fighting Bill!"[72] The British reply to this scornful refusal of their terms was a general and desperate assault, which terminated, after about three hours' stubborn fighting in the capture of the American works. The two Clintons, owing to their knowledge of the locality, were able in the dusk of the evening to break through the attacking forces and make good their escape; but "Fighting Bill" was among the prisoners, and with some companions in misfortune, sent in a schooner to New York. The British lost heavily, and among their killed was Lieutenant-Colonel Campbell.

One of Livingston's fellow-prisoners was an ensign, one Abraham Leggett, an illiterate "soldier of the Revolution," who has, however, left behind him an interesting, though badly spelt, account of their captivity.[73] From his narrative we learn that on their arrival at New York, they were confined "in the Main Guard, in the Old City Hall, at the head of Broad Street." At first they were roughly treated, until the receipt of the news of Burgoyne's surrender, when their captors thought it advisable to be more lenient in their treatment of them. The gallant ensign thus relates how they received the glad tidings in their prison, before even the news was known in the city, except by some of the higher officers. "The way the news was conveyed to the prison," he explains, "was in a large loaf of bread; the statement [written] on paper and placed in a loaf and baked, and was sent [to] Colonel William Livingston, who was taken with us. As soon as that was read in the Congress Room, the whole prison resounded with three cheers. The keeper was alarmed with such an uproar, as he called it. Hastened to the second floor to know what was the uproar. Then he was informed, he denied it, and said it was a D— Rebel lie."

Soon after this, however, most of the prisoners, including Lieutenant-Colonel Livingston, were released on parole and sent to Long Island; but towards the end of this year, when a landing of American troops was feared, the British authorities had Livingston and some other officers transferred to one of their gun-ships[74] or transports,[75] from which he and two of his companions in misfortune managed to escape, within a few days of their transfer, by seizing a boat lying "alongside the ship *Martel*."[76]

After his escape, William S. Livingston went to his home in New Jersey—the escaped prisoners probably landed on the New Jersey shore—and from there he wrote to Governor Clinton that he had lost his horse when captured at Fort Montgomery, but as soon as he could procure one, he would report himself. This does not appear to have been an easy matter, as a few weeks later, he was still claiming $300 from the State for the loss of this horse and accoutrements. This claim was endorsed by Governor Clinton, on the 20th May 1778,[77] and the next mention made of the Lieutenant-Colonel is in connection with Sullivan and Lafayette's unfortunate expedition to Rhode Island in the following month of August.

During his captivity, his friend and chief, Colonel Samuel B. Webb, had also fallen into the hands of the British, having been captured at sea with most of his regiment while attempting a landing on Long Island. This will account for Livingston being in command of his old regiment in General Varnum's brigade, during the following summer, in the attack on Rhode Island.[78] This brigade formed part of General Greene's division, on whose staff Lieutenant-Colonel Livingston had served two years previously on Long Island.[79] General Greene, in writing to his wife, on the evening of the 29th August 1778, a brief account of the battle of Quaker Hill, R. I., says:—"I write upon my horse and have not slept any for two nights, therefore you'll excuse my not writing very legible, as I write upon the field. Col. Will. Livingston is slightly wounded. My aids all behaved with great gallantry."[80] While in his letter to Washington, of two days later date—already quoted from—he refers to Lieutenant-Colonel Livingston as one of those officers, who "did themselves great honour in the transactions of the day."[81] According to another account of this action, written by John Trumbull to his father Governor Trumbull of Connecticut, "Major Shireburn of Portsmouth has lost a leg, and Major Walker of Boston is killed; several other officers are wounded. Lieut.-[Col.] Wm. Livingston was touched by two spent balls in the breast, and had his horse's head shot off by a 12lb. shot."[82] For some reason not mentioned, Lieutenant-Colonel Livingston resigned his commission, on or about, the tenth of October in this year.[83]

Before leaving the military Livingstons, it is only right to refer in a little more detail to Colonel James Livingston's cannonade of the *Vulture*, British sloop-of-war, at the time of General Arnold's treason, as credit for this exploit has been awarded in some quarters to the wrong officers. On the 3d of August 1780, Washington wrote to Major-General Arnold, commanding at West Point, that "Colonel James Livingston's regiment is, till further orders, to garrison the redoubts at Stony Point and Verplanck's Point." During the following month Colonel Livingston applied to Colonel Lamb, who had charge of the batteries at West Point for some ammunition for a four pounder, the only cannon he had at Verplanck's Point, as he wanted to try a shot at the sloop, whose movements had aroused his suspicions. He got the powder, also a short lecture from the artillery colonel upon the folly of "firing at a ship with a four pounder."[84]

But Colonel Livingston was not to be baulked of his desire by this reproof, for he did try a shot, which had the desired effect, for it "raked the vessel fore and aft"[85] and compelled her to shift her berth, and thus led to important results. For if Major André had returned to New York in the *Vulture*, he would not have been captured, and Arnold's treason would have remained undiscovered probably, until too late! On receiving the news of André's capture and Arnold's flight, Washington at once sent for Colonel James Livingston to come to his Headquarters, at Robinson House, that night—25th September 1780,—[86] when the commander of these important posts was able to satisfy his commander-in-chief of his loyalty, and his entire ignorance of these treacherous negotiations. He was still in charge of these redoubts in the month of November of this year, when the Marquis de Chastellux breakfasted with him one morning,— the second breakfast he had had that day he duly remarks in his journal,—and says "il consista en *Beef-Stakes*, accompagné de thé au lait et de quelque bowls de grog, car la cave du Commandant n'etoit pas mieux fournie que la garde-robe des soldats." The marquis was very pleased with his host, whom he describes as "un jeune homme aimable et instruit."[87]

We must now return to the three Livingston statesmen, and resume our account of their respective careers from where it was discontinued in the previous chapter. To start with William Livingston—who had more to do with military matters than the other two—he, having left Philadelphia for Elizabethtown at the end of June 1776, at once, on his arrival at the latter town, took over the command of the New Jersey militia, and energetically exerted himself to get that force into a proper state of discipline before the daily expected arrival of the British army of invasion. Upon the twenty-eighth of this month Colonel Reed, Washington's Adjutant-General, wrote to the New Jersey Convention asking for their assistance, and informing them of General Howe's arrival off the coast; and upon the following day Washington wrote direct to General Livingston, begging him to hurry forward the forces promised towards the defence of New York. In his reply to the commander-in-chief, dated Elizabethtown, 4th July 1776, General Livingston candidly writes:—

> Your Excellency must be sensible that as the department I now act in is to me entirely new, I must be desirous of every aid that can possibly be obtained. If you, sir, could spare a few experienced officers to assist me in this important business it might be of essential service. Our men are raw and inexperienced, our officers are mostly absent, want of discipline is inevitable, while we are greatly exposed for the distance of twelve or fourteen miles.

While in a letter to a friend in the Continental Congress, written a few weeks later, he thus amusingly describes his appearance in the military rôle of a Brigadier-General:—

> I received yours of yesterday's date just after I had got into my new habitation, which is a markee tent in an encampment here. You would really be astonished to see how grand I look, while at the same time I can assure you I was never more sensible (to use a New England phrase) of my nothingness in military affairs. I removed my quarters from the town hither, to be with the men, and to enure them to discipline, which by my distance from the camp before, considering what scurvy subaltern officers we are like ever to have while they are in the appointment of the mobility,[88] I found it impossible to introduce. And the worst men (was there a degree above the superlative) would be still pejorated, by having been fellow soldiers with that discipline hating, good-living loving, "to eternal fame damned," coxcombical crew we lately had here from Philadelphia. My ancient corporeal fabrick is almost tottering under the fatigue I have lately undergone; constantly rising at two o'clock in the morning to examine our lines, which are very extensive, till daybreak, and from that time perpetually till eleven in giving orders, sending despatches, and doing the proper business of Quartermasters, Colonels, Commissaries, and I know not what!

While General Livingston was thus employed in his hard task of bringing the raw material under his command into a better state of discipline, the first republican Legislature of the State of New Jersey assembled on the twenty-seventh of August at Princeton, and four days later, in joint ballot of the two houses he was chosen governor of the new born commonwealth. A fact which speaks highly for Mr. Livingston's popularity in New Jersey, of which colony he had only been a resident for the short space of four years; and proves conclusively, that in spite of his well-known opinion as to the prematureness of the Declaration of Independence, his fellow-citizens fully appreciated his great services in the cause of American freedom, rendered mostly at a time when few persons could be found willing to incur the risk of offending the officials of a powerful government. The position to which he was thus raised made him, in the eyes of the loyalists, one of the most obnoxious rebels on the continent, owing to the energy and zeal with which he entered upon his new duties. His official title ran as follows:—"His Excellency William Livingston, Esquire, Governor, Captain General, and Commander-in-chief in and over the State of New Jersey and Territories thereunto belonging, Chancellor and Ordinary of the same." A very surprising and formidable array of dignities for the chief magistrate of a struggling republican state to bear! It is therefore not so much to be wondered at that the royalist newspapers in New York nicknamed him, "The Despot-in-Chief in and over the rising State of New Jersey, Extraordinary Chancellor of the same, etc." He was also spitefully dubbed by them, "Spurious Governor"; "Mock Governor"; "Don Quixote of the Jersies"; "Knight of the most honourable Order of Starvation"; "Itinerant Dey of New Jersey"; and many other opprobrious epithets of a similar nature were freely showered on his devoted head during the next seven years.

Everything naturally being in confusion in the newly created government at the date of his election, there was no Great Seal ready for the infant commonwealth, and so, until one could be prepared, a resolution was passed by the New Jersey Legislature that "the seal at arms of his Excellency William Livingston should be deemed, taken, and used, as the great seal of the State until another could be procured." Certainly a strange vicissitude in the history of the family coat-armour!

Upon the 11th of September Governor Livingston delivered to the Council and Assembly of the State of New Jersey his first speech, in which he alluded to the causes which had led to the separation of the American colonies from the mother-country, and the earnest need for all patriotic citizens to exert themselves manfully in this time of peril for the common weal. His high flown style of oratory was much appreciated in his day; so much so, that one admirer wrote from Philadelphia, suggesting that one paragraph in this speech "ought to be printed in letters of gold, that it might engage the attention of the most heedless American." An expression which he made use of, that the citizens should set their faces "like a flint against that dissoluteness of manners and political corruption which will ever be the reproach of any people," gained for him in his own State the nickname of "Doctor Flint."[89]

And well and nobly through the anxious years that followed, years of civil war with all its accompanying horrors, with a price put upon his head, and his life actually several times attempted by the emissaries of unscrupulous enemies, did Governor Livingston steadfastly adhere to the line of conduct laid down by him in this, his maiden speech, to the Legislature of New Jersey. A French officer, a few months later, enthusiastically and tersely summed up Mr. Livingston's character, in a report to his government, in these few words:—"The Governor, Livingston, is a Roman!"

Though General Livingston had relinquished his command in the field to take up his higher duties as governor, he had not relaxed his efforts with the Assembly and the people to have the Line regiments and militia put in a state of readiness to oppose the enemy, who were now in the occupation of the city of New York, and even part of New Jersey itself. His troubles in his endeavours to achieve this object, may be ascertained from glimpses into General Washington's correspondence with him at this date. In one letter, Lord Stirling, writing at the request of the commander-in-chief, says, "there is an absolute necessity of a new arrangement of the officers of your quota of the troops for the continental service. As things now stand, no man of spirit will serve, nor will any one exert themselves in the recruiting service until the appointments of officers is altered; if this is not immediately done the force of New Jersey is lost. Come, for God's sake, and see these matters regulated, let merit in service, and not dirty connections, take place. Excuse all this freedom; I write this at the request of General Washington with a very lame hand. . . ."[90]

While Washington himself, writing from Morristown[91] a month later, is just as bitter in his remarks as to "the irregular and disjointed state of the militia of this province [which] makes it necessary for me to inform you, that unless a law is passed by your Legislature to reduce them to some order, and oblige them to turn out in a different manner from what they have hitherto done, we shall bring very few into the field, and even those few will do little or no service. Their officers are generally of the lowest class of people and instead of setting a good example to their men, are leading them into every kind of mischief, one species of which is plundering the inhabitants under pretence of their being Tories. A law should, in my opinion, be passed to put a stop to this kind of lawless rapine, for unless there is something done to prevent it, the people will throw themselves of choice into the hands of the British troops."

But the governor and his defenceless Legislature at this time were in no condition to pay heed to these letters, as in spite of the former's exertions, they were now fugitives themselves, wandering "from Princeton to Burlington, from Burlington to Pitt's Town, from Pitt's Town to Haddonfield, and there finally, at the utmost verge of the State, dissolved themselves on the second of December, leaving each member to look for his own safety, at a moment when the efforts of legislators could be of no avail, and when there was no place where they could safely hold their sessions."[92] The victory Washington gained over the Hessian troops at Trenton on Christmas night, quickly followed by that at Princeton, helped to infuse a little more spirit into the demoralised inhabitants of New Jersey and its Legislature, which body was thereupon able to reassemble at Haddonfield during the following month; when the governor, acting upon Washington's advice, urged upon the members the absolute necessity for the passage of a law dealing with the formation of an efficient militia, as theirs had become the laughing stock of the whole American army!

If all the patriots in New Jersey had been as enthusiastic in the cause of Liberty, as one juvenile member of the Livingston family proved himself to be at this very affair of Trenton, the governor would have had no cause for anxiety. This lad of sixteen years, whose name was Robert James, a younger brother of Lieutenant-Colonel William Smith Livingston, "accidentally learned that the American army was in motion and was secretly moving upon the enemy. He left home to join the vanguard of the Americans and fell severely wounded at the victory of Trenton. Tradition states that he was wounded in the first onslaught and that for a few moments he was in the power of the Hessians, by whom he was roughly used. A lady, whose name unfortunately has not been preserved, had the lad removed to her house, sent for his mother and kept them until he could be carried in safety to his home at Princeton."[93]

At length, upon the 15th of March 1777, the wished for act was passed, but its conditions did not fulfil the expectations either of Washington or Livingston; and on the 5th of April the latter wrote to the commander-in-chief, "the act is extremely deficient, and it has cost me many an anxious hour to think how long it was procrastinated, and how ineffectual I had reason to apprehend it would finally prove. My only consolation is, that my messages upon their minutes will show my sense of the matter, and that I was not remiss in the strongest recommendations to construct it in such a manner as would have had effectually answered the purposes intended."[94]

Though loath to grant a proper Militia Bill, which was a great deal owing to the strong Quaker element in the State, the Legislature was induced by Governor Livingston's arguments to delegate certain powers to a Council of Safety, so as to enable the Executive to act with greater promptitude and vigour against the common enemy during the recess of the Assembly. During the summer of this year, the governor procured the passage of another act through the Legislature, which brought down on his devoted head an outburst of wrath from the adherents of the mother-country in his State, and which also culminated in more than one attempt upon his life. This was an edict confiscating all the personal estates of the refugees within the British lines, unless they should, within a certain period, take the oath of allegiance to the State of New Jersey. This was no doubt an extremely harsh measure, and one which even the strain of civil war can hardly excuse. Livingston was, however, no believer in half measures, and at this date, when the fortunes of the revolutionists were at the lowest ebb; with a great portion of his government in the possession of the British troops; with a militia not to be depended upon; surrounded with lukewarm friends to the cause; and with the illegal and injurious traffic carried on with the enemy by a considerable number of the "patriotic" inhabitants of the State, it was certainly a bold and daring stroke, to declare thus openly, that no mercy would be shown to those who did not come in and submit to the new order of events, arising out of a Declaration of Independence then barely a year old!

It was about this time also, that some refugee Jerseymen having been captured while serving with the British army, Livingston wrote to Washington asking him for his advice, as to having these men tried for High Treason. The cooler tempered commander-in-chief in his reply, pointed out to the irate governor that "two could play at that game"; and that if he were to start trying and hanging men for treason, the British authorities could, and would probably, retaliate with a greater show of justice, on their American prisoners. He therefore gave the wiser counsel, that they should be treated as "prisoners-of-war." This advice, Governor Livingston followed as regards the majority of his prisoners, but he absolutely refused to treat otherwise than as criminals, those who were of notorious bad character.

From this date his life was constantly threatened by the furious refugees, a price was placed upon his head, and he had several narrow escapes from falling into their hands. In connection with these attempts upon his person, he wrote to Henry Laurens, President of Congress, on the 25th June 1778,—"They certainly overrate my merit, and I cannot conceive what induces them to bid so extravagant a sum, having now raised my price from 500 to 2000 guineas, unless it be that General Skinner[95] intends to pay his master's debts as he has long been used to pay his own." His re-election for governor for the third time in October 1778,[96] caused great disappointment to the loyalists, and one of these gentry wrote to a correspondent in London, "Livingston is reappointed Governor of New Jersey, and more wantonly pursuing his career of barbarity and wickedness than ever." While another refugee, wrote at the same date, "Livingston is re-elected Governor. . . . You know the man, and will with me pitty the poor people that fall under his displeasure."

Captain (afterwards Major) André of the British army, whose sad end as a spy is so well known, read on the 7th January 1779, a sort of parable, or what he called an "extempore dream," to an appreciative loyalist audience in New York, in which he compared the leading rebels to different wild beasts! This is his charitable description of the hated Governor of New Jersey:—

> The black soul of Livingston, which was "fit for treason, sacrilege, and spoil," polluted with every species of murder and iniquity, was condemned to howl in the body of a wolf; and I beheld with surprise that he retained the same gaunt, hollow, and ferocious appearance, and that his tongue still continued to be red with gore. Just at this time Mercury touched me with his wand, and thereby bestowed an insight into futurity, when I saw this very wolf hung up at the door of his fold, by a shepherd whose innocent flock had been from time to time thinned by the murdering jaws of this savage animal.

Poor André little thought he was forecasting in these words his own sad fate!

If, however, a British officer could be permitted to publicly denounce the Governor of New Jersey in such terms, it is not surprising that the partisan leaders should consider he was fair prey. A few weeks after Captain André's amiable parable, an attempt was made by a British regular officer to capture the obnoxious "rebel governor," but when the troops reached Livingston's private residence "Liberty Hall," it was only to find that its owner was "not at home."[97] Chagrined at the ill-success of this enterprise, Governor Livingston was informed, a British general officer had offered a large sum of money to an inhabitant of New Jersey, to induce him to assassinate the head of his State, should he not be able to take him alive. This led to a correspondence between the governor and Sir Henry Clinton, then commanding in New York, in which the latter, in very brusque and discourteous language, denied that "he had ever harboured such an infamous idea."[98] The above attempt, however, was not the last by any means; but the immediate effect of this correspondence was, that wherever the regular army was concerned, orders were given to the officer in command "not to offer any violence to his person" in the event of his capture; which in spite of Sir Henry Clinton's assertion to the contrary, was ardently desired by the British authorities. The following order, a copy of which was found among Governor Livingston's papers, clearly proves this desire on their part:—

> To Ensign Moody,
>   First Battalion, New Jersey Volunteers,
>   Head-Quarters, New York, May 10th, 1780.
>   Sir:
>   You are hereby directed and authorised to proceed, without loss of time, with a small detachment into the Jerseys, by the most convenient route, in order to carry off the person of Governor Livingston, or any other acting in public stations whom you may fall in with in the course of your march, or any persons you may meet with, and whom it may be necessary to secure for your own security and that of the party under your command.
>   Should you succeed in taking Governor Livingston, you are to treat him according to his station, as far as he's in your power, nor are you upon any account to offer any violence to his person. You will use your endeavours to get possession of his papers, which you will take care of, and upon your return deliver at head-quarters.
>   By order of his Excellency, Lieutenant-General Knyphausen.[99]
>   Geo. Beckwith,
>   *Aide-de-Camp.*

Ensign Moody, however, failed in this attempt, and was himself captured by Captain Lawrence, of the New York State Levies, who sent a copy
of the above order to Governor Livingston.

In April of the following year (1781), Governor Livingston was warned
by General Washington, that "Intelligence has been sent me . . . that four
parties had been sent out to take or assassinate Your Excellency."[100] This
coupled with the escape of the partisan leader Moody, who had recommenced committing fresh depredations in New Jersey, led Governor
Livingston, upon the 3rd of August in this year, to issue the following
Proclamation:—

> *Whereas* it has been represented to me that the persons
> hereinafter mentioned have been guilty of atrocious offences,
> and have committed divers robberies, thefts, and other felonies
> in this State. I have therefore thought fit, by and with advice
> of the Honorable Privy Council of this State, to issue this
> Proclamation, hereby promising the rewards herein mentioned,
> to any person or persons who shall apprehend and secure in
> any gaol of this State, any or either of the following persons or
> offenders, to wit: Caleb Sweesy, James O'Hara, John[101] Moody,
> and Gysbert Eyberlin, the sum of two hundred dollars of the
> bills of credit issued on the faith of this State.
>
> Given under my hand and seal-at-arms, at Trenton, the third
> day of August, 1781, and the fifth year of the Independence of
> America.
>
> WIL. LIVINGSTON.

This Proclamation appears to have sorely offended the gallant ensign,
who retaliated by publishing in Rivington's *Royal Gazette* of the 25th of
August (under Governor Livingston's Proclamation), the following scurrilous counter-proclamation of his own:—[102]

> HUE AND CRY : *Two Hundred Guineas Reward.*
> *Whereas* a certain William Livingston, late an Attorney-
> at-Law, and now *a lawless usurper* and *incorrigible rebel*, stands
> convicted in the minds of all honest men, as well as in his own
> conscience, of many atrocious crimes and offences against God
> and the king, and among many treasonable practices, has lately,
> with malicious and murderous intention, published a seditious

advertisement in a rebel newspaper,[103] offering a reward, of what he calls two hundred State dollars, to an assassin who shall take and deliver me and three other loyalists into the power of him, the said William Livingston.

I do therefore promise to pay the sum of two hundred guineas, *true money*, to the person or persons who shall bring the said William Livingston alive into New York, and deliver him into the custody of Captain Cunningham, so that he be duly lodged in the provost, till the approaching extinction of the rebellion, then to be brought to trial for his numerous crimes and offences aforesaid. In the meantime, if his whole person cannot be brought in, half the sum above specified will be paid for his EARS and NOSE which are too well known, and too remarkable to be mistaken. Observe, however, that his life must not be attempted, because that would be to follow his example of exciting the villainous practice of assassination, and because *his death* at present would defraud Jack Ketch of a future perquisite.

Given under my hand and seal-at-arms, in New York, this twenty-third day of August, 1781 (a style of which I have surely as much right to assume as William Livingston, or any other rebel usurper).

J. MOODY.

The several printers on the Continent are requested to insert the above in their newspapers.

The partisan leader's sarcastic reference to "State dollars" in comparison with "true money," unfortunately hit a very weak spot in the condition of the American finances, for the depreciation in the Continental and State currencies was something enormous at this period. Governor Livingston himself was personally a great sufferer from this cause. His salary for the previous year (1780) "was fixed," says Mr. Sedgwick, "at £8000 Continental money which not amounting to more than £150 in silver, the Legislature added £300 of what was called lawful money, emitted by the State; but this 'lawful' being itself about 50 per cent below par, his salary and perquisites together did not exceed a thousand dollars; and at this time he had a large family, was constantly travelling, and every article of consumption was exorbitantly high."

But a greater sufferer than even Governor Livingston from this cause, and from the ruinous war taxes, was his elder brother Robert of the Manor. The letters written about this time by the Lord of the Manor to his brother, Peter Van Brugh Livingston, are full of complaints concerning the excessive taxation, and the harsh and unfair manner of its collection.[104] In one, dated 4th April, 1780, he says "my burden is heavy, am taxed 43,890 dollars, which is a 23d part of the whole City and County of Albany, and a 53d of the whole State of New York, by much too high but not to be helped."[105] But taxes were heaped upon taxes, and in another letter written a few months later, he writes:—

> Our Country in this and the Upper Counties, have suffered more this year than in all the former years of this or any other war . . . scarcely a family but is suffering one way or other, even myself am in a great measure reduced, could you believe it that I cannot command this day one hundred pounds, in hard nor soft money together, I was obliged to blow out my Furnace in the midst of her blast for want of money to pay workmen, all I had to make money of is taken to supply the army, such as iron, wheat, and flour; without money of any kind my Taxes for this year will run up to £100,000. O Monsterous! its not in my power to discharge them, however, willing I am to assist my poor Country.[106]

In another letter to the same brother written six months later,[107] he begs him "to write as often as opportunities may offer, *but not by post as we have no money left of any kind amongst us.*"[108]

In spite of the Manor being reduced to such straits for want of money, fresh taxes and contributions in kind were continually being levied; and for the month of September 1781, the unfortunate Lord of the Manor was called upon to pay a wheat tax of 881 ½ bushels, besides two new emission taxes and one hard money tax! Patient as he had been under all his previous misfortunes, these last taxes were evidently the proverbial last straw, and in another letter to his brother, dated 28th January, 1782, the poor landowner complains bitterly of the unfair manner in which these latter taxes had been assessed. "For mine," he writes, "are nearly three times as much as Patroon Stephen and John's together,[109] monsterous and cruel indeed; to wit, 881 ½ if bushels of wheat, £118 in hard and £380 in new emission, and another tax just on hand. I should not complain of my tax had I neighbours fair, but to run me up so that all my cattle, about 60 in number, and all my horses about 40 in number, will not pay this tax, when the others can pay theirs and retain half of their stock is too unreasonable."

And those taxes were demanded at a time when, as the writer had explained in a previous letter—dated 1st October, 1781—it was simply impossible "to sell any of our produce, nor buy any necessaries for our families, we are really in want of winter clothing, and how or where I shall procure it I know not." Even in an earlier part of the war, Chancellor Livingston had to complain to Governor Clinton of the oppression of the Manor. "No part of the State," he writes in one letter, "has suffered half so much by the oppression of Quartermasters and Commissaries, or done more duty."[110] But there were other troubles to vex the Lord of the Manor besides taxes, these arose from his neighbours, as the majority of the inhabitants of the district were decidedly loyalist in their sympathies, and on more than one occasion, force had to be used by the State government to reduce them to a state of quietude. Even the Manor Regiment was not to be depended upon, and in August 1777, when under orders to march to Stillwater, John R. Livingston writes to his brother the chancellor, "it seems impossible to get any of them to go. They say that the Oath which they have taken to the State is not any longer binding."[111] He advises "a few examples" being made of the ringleaders; probably his advice was followed, as the regiment, under the command of Lt.-Col. Henry Livingston, did reach General Gates in time to participate in the battle of the seventh of October. But these troubles did not exhaust Robert of the Manor's anxieties, for though situated at such a distance from the Canadian frontier, marauding parties of Tories penetrated to within three miles of his Manor House, carrying off a neighbour, with his son and two negroes, into captivity.[112]

The enormous depreciation in the currency also gave rise to a very serious peril, arising from the officers in the Continental army finding their rate of pay totally inadequate to meet their expenses, particularly those who were so unfortunate as to have families to support as well. The New York Line officers considered they were not so well treated in the rate of their pay, as was the case with their fellow officers in regiments from other States, and at last their grievances found vent in a Memorial to the Commander-in-Chief, in which they explain "with the most painful sensations," that their "wants and the sufferings of their distressed families, loudly call on them to quit a service, which although of the utmost necessity promises nothing better than an increase of misery, already scarce supportable." They therefore inform Washington that they have sent in their resignations to their State government, and express the hope that their successors "being possessed of independent fortunes may be able to render their country more eminent services."[113] Sixty-four officers in all signed this memorial, among their names being that of Gilbert James Livingston, second lieutenant in Colonel Van Cortlandt's regiment.

One more instance of the financial distress caused by the war, an incident which also illustrates Governor Livingston's dislike to the granting of passes permitting of visits being made to the city of New York while in the occupation of the British. For some time, the British authorities themselves were far from being stringent in this respect, but the system of passes was one certainly liable to be abused by unscrupulous persons. In the early years of the war ladies living outside New York, within the American Lines, were often allowed to visit their relatives in the city under cover of a flag of truce. Lady Stirling, though the wife of one of Washington's favourite generals, and the sister of Governor Livingston of New Jersey, was thus permitted by the British authorities, in the summer of 1778, to visit her eldest daughter, Mrs. Watts, then in delicate health, whose husband resided in the city. She was accompanied by her youngest daughter, Lady Kitty, who enjoyed "our jaunt" immensely, as she wrote to her father, and found the British officers very civil, and the baby "one of the most charming little creatures I ever saw." The mother and daughter had old acquaintances among the military; but in spite of the civility they experienced, Lady Stirling on her return to New Jersey, complained to her husband, that though "General Clinton[114] sent a card to Mr. Watts, desiring him to let him know when we arrived in town, for he intended to show us all the civility in his power. We never heard from him again until I applied for a pass to leave town; then Mr. Elliot came with Sir Henry's compliments that he was sorry he had not had it in his power to call on us before, but that he would endeavour to do it before we left town, for old acquaintance sake; but we heard no more of him. So much for that."[115]

Governor Livingston's opinion concerning the granting of such passes was, evidently, the principal reason that influenced Lieutenant-Colonel William S. Livingston— though he ascribes it to the fact of his friend Mr. Samuel Ogden having quarrelled with the governor—to appeal to Governor George Clinton of New York in March 1781, when he and his friend Mr. Ogden were desirous of obtaining permits to visit the city on private business. It is this private business, that throws a side-light on the privations endured by refined and cultured ladies and their families during these sad times. In his letter, which is dated from Bever-wyck, near Morris Town, 12th March, 1781, he says:—

> On my return from Maryland from whence I am just come, I stopped at my mother's[116] in Princeton, whose peculiar situation and at present distressed condition, has induced me to lay before you a state of facts and in consequence thereof to make application to your Excellency for a favour, which nothing but her wants, and a consciousness of your friendship, could ever induce. She has hitherto been struggling hard with difficulties innumerable to support her little flock. Her two sons, Peter [R.] and Maturin,[117] have just entered College [Princeton] and bid fair to be an ornament to society.[118] By taking in young gentlemen to board with her, and some little assistance which she received from her father's estate,[119] she has been able, heretofore, to support them in their education and to surmount in a great measure the difficulties of the times. But Dr. Witherspoon.[120] who was her landlord, by renting the house in which she lives over her head without previous notice, because he could get a little more from some other person, has entirely cut off her resources; and where she and her family will put their heads after the first of May next, God only knows!

The writer then formulates his plan for his mother's relief, which is to go to New York, and sell some property in land he and his family possess there, and with the proceeds purchase the only house in Princeton that is for sale, as there is not another in the place to be rented. The house that is for sale being "large and commodious," will enable his mother to take in a dozen young gentlemen to board, and by this means "pay for the education of her children, free her from all incumbrances and finally place her above want." He explains further that it is absolutely necessary for him to go in, as "representation after representation has been made to her brother in New York, he has from time to time given promises of relief, but the day of her distress is now near at hand, and something more than empty promises is necessary." The reply of Governor Clinton, as was to be expected, was a friendly refusal to grant the pass, unless "it could be done consistent with his duty and the respect which he owes the State [New Jersey] in which she at present resides."[121]

But we must now return to Governor Livingston and Ensign Moody's mock proclamation in Rivington's *Royal Gazette*. The printer of this ultra-loyalist paper was never weary of publishing the most infamous charges against the public and private life of the "spurious governor," as he was fond, among other opprobious epithets, of designating Governor Livingston.[122] So that the latter jokingly remarked in a letter written about this time, "If Rivington is taken I must have one of his ears; Governor Clinton is entitled to the other; and General Washington, if he pleases, may take his head." To counteract the effects of this journal, one Isaac Collins, a Quaker,—whom Rivington with a sneer dubbed "Mr. Livingston's printer,"—had started at Burlington, on the 5th of December 1777, a paper which he named the *New Jersey Gazette*, and which continued to be the leading New Jersey journal on the American side during the war. The governor, who had not lost his talent for writing essays on the principal topics of the day, contributed to its columns for some months under the *nom-de-plume* of "Hortentius," until some members of the Legislature expressed their dissatisfaction that the chief magistrate should, as they considered, thus lower himself in the eyes of the public; whereupon he discontinued these articles until some years after the peace, when he recommenced writing again under the name of "Scipio." As to that ultra-loyalist, Rivington, he would have made a very good modem politician, for upon the evacuation of New York, and the flight of his old patrons to England, the *Royal Gazette* simply altered its title to the *State of New York Gazette;* and as Chancellor Livingston jocularly wrote to his friend John Jay, four days after the departure of the British garrison, "Rivington himself goes on as usual, the *State of New York Gazette* is as well received, as if he had never been printer to the king's most excellent majesty."[123]

It is now necessary to take up the narrative of the two other Livingston statesmen, from the date of the Declaration of Independence. William's elder brother Philip, as related in the last chapter, remained in Philadelphia, attending to his congressional duties until Christmas of this year, when he was granted leave of absence to enable him to spend it with his family then residing at Kingston. After a short and hard earned rest we find him back again in Continental Congress, and upon the 29th April, 1777, he was appointed a member of the Marine Committee. His services in Congress were so much appreciated by the members of his State Convention, that when it was resolved upon the thirteenth of the following month by that assembly, then sitting at Kingston, "that five delegates be elected by ballot to represent this State in Congress until the Legislature of this State shall, at their first meeting, make further provision," he was one of the five chosen.[124] Sixteen days later he presented his new credentials to Congress, together with the resolution of same date thanking him and his former colleagues "delegates of this State, in the honourable the Continental Congress, for their long and faithful services rendered to the colony of New York and the said State."

On the eighth of this same month—May 1777—a further mark of his fellow citizens' regard for Philip Livingston was shown by the Convention appointing him one of the Senators under the new Legislature, for the Southern District. He was appointed by the Convention, it being impracticable for the inhabitants of that district to vote for Senators or Assemblymen, as it was in the occupation of the British troops. He was also, upon the fifth of July, elected by Continental Congress a member of the Committee of Commerce; and six days later he was appointed one of a Committee of three members commissioned "to proceed immediately to the army under the command of General Washington," for the purpose of making an inquiry into its condition. As senior member of this Commission, he reported the result of their visit of inspection to the Congress, upon the twenty-fourth of this month.

The first Legislature of the State of New York met at Kingston during the following September, and Philip Livingston attended its sittings in the capacity of senator for the southern district. His cousin Robert R. Livingston had been a member of the Convention of the Representatives of the State of New York, which had met at White Plains, Westchester County in July of the previous year, and had taken an active part in the framing of the new Constitution. This Constitution was adopted on the 20th April, 1777; and among the state appointments ballotted for on the 3rd of May, Robert R. Livingston obtained the Chancellorship, and his great friend John Jay the post of Chief Justice. These appointments were duly confirmed to them by the New York Legislature, and Robert R. Livingston held his office of Chancellor for the long period of twenty-four years. In the House of Assembly also two members of the Livingston family had seats; namely Walter Livingston as one of the representatives for Albany, and Gilbert Livingston for Dutchess. The former of these two gentlemen was elected to be its first Speaker, which office he held during this and the succeeding session. Thus was the Livingston family well represented in this, the first independent Legislature of their native State.

But the Legislature was rudely interrupted in its labours, and obliged to precipitately abandon Kingston, owing to the approach of a British force under General Vaughan, which had been despatched by Sir Henry Clinton for the purpose of effecting a diversion in favour of General Burgoyne, then completely hemmed in by the American army under General Gates at Saratoga. Instead, however, of pushing on to Albany, where he might have rendered some much needed assistance to that unlucky commander by capturing or destroying the American supplies stored in that town, General Vaughan lost most valuable time in landing troops from the flotilla under Sir James Wallace, for the purpose of burning Kingston and some "rebel houses" on the other side of the river. One of these was Clermont, the residence of Mrs. Margaret Livingston, the widow of Judge Robert R. Livingston, while another on the same estate, was that of her son, the newly appointed chancellor.

On the 19th of October, 1777, a day or so after the destruction of the Livingston mansions, the New York Council of Safety—with whom were associated those members of the recently elected Legislature, who had been brave enough to remain in the neighbourhood of Kingston, on the chance of their services being needed—held a meeting at the house of Andrew Oliver at Marbletown, under the presidency of Pierre Van Cortlandt, and for the next few weeks the government of the State practically devolved upon this Council. One of the duties which thus fell to this body was that of keeping up a correspondence with the New York delegates in the General Congress; while another was to see that a quorum of these delegates was always in attendance at Philadelphia, or wherever the Congress might be sitting for the time being. At this time Mr. Duer, one of the delegates, was anxious to obtain leave of absence, and in the natural course of events Philip Livingston,[125] who was, as we have seen, also a State Senator, would have taken his place, but owing to the dispersal of his family by the sack of Kingston, he had asked permission to be excused from this duty "until things wear a more settled aspect in this part of the country"; meanwhile he regularly attended the sittings of the Council of Safety. Whereupon, the Council addressed a letter to their delegates at Philadelphia, explaining Mr. Livingston's position; and, as this letter also contains an interesting official American account of this raid of the British flotilla up the Hudson, in which a contemporary reference to the burning of the residences "of the chancellor and his mother" is to be found, it is given here in full:—

COUNCIL OF SAFETY, 22nd October, 1777.

GENTLEMEN, This Council are extremely anxious to have a proper representation in Congress, and for that purpose have made the resolution and order, copies whereof are enclosed. The Council, fully sensible of the necessity of gratifying Mr. Duane with leave of absence, do not desire to delay his return after the arrival of Mr. Morris or Mr. Lewis at Congress; in which case we shall have a quorum of two, as the concurrent resolutions of the Senate and Assembly previous to the appointment of the Delegates, a copy whereof, and of the resolutions are also enclosed, absolutely require.

The loss of Fort Montgomerie, after a gallant defence, and for want of a proper and seasonable reinforcement, having opened Hudson's river to the enemy, they improved the opportunity, advanced up to Kingston, and on the sixteenth instant, about two hours before the Governor's troops, who made a forced march, could arrive, gained the Landing; and faintly opposed by about 150 militia only, marched, immediately up to Kingston, and reduced the whole town to ashes. You can easily conceive the consternation and dispersion of the inhabitants of the town and its environs on this lamentable occasion. Mr. [Philip] Livingston's family being among the refugees, it will be impossible for him to attend Congress, until things wear a more settled aspect in this part of the country, and he shall have properly provided for his family. He assures the Council that as soon as this can be effected, he will repair to Congress to relieve Mr. Duer.

The enemy now lie opposite Sagherties. As their decision to extricate General Burgoyne has proved abortive, we apprehend they are waiting for orders from General Clinton, at New York, respecting their further destination. In their passage from Kingston to that place, they landed and destroyed several buildings and improvements; among others those of the chancellor and his mother. The Governor now lies with his little army at Hurly, waiting for expected succours from General Gates, and determined to move with the enemy in such manner as will best serve the purpose of annoying them, should they land, and covering the country against their further attempts. Notwithstanding the depredations of the enemy along the river, the total reduction of their northern army affords us great comfort. We wait impatiently for an account of something as decisive from the southward, which will most amply compensate for all our losses.

Ordered, That a copy thereof be engrossed, and signed by the President, and transmitted to the Delegates of this State in Congress.

The following extract from the Journal of the British Deputy Adjutant-General in New York, Lieutenant-Colonel Stephen Kemble, though not mentioning the house destroyed as being that of the chancellor, must also refer to this same spiteful act of vandalism. The British landing parties certainly did not get as far north as the Manor House, though the flotilla may have lain in the river near by.

> Sunday, Oct. 19th to Saturday, 25th. Nothing extraordinary. Informed this evening by an officer from General Vaughan that he had been as far as Livingston's Manor; that he had burnt Livingston's House, and some others.

Colonel Kemble's informant may have confused "the upper" with "the lower manor," as Clermont is sometimes designated, though claiming no right to that title. Even in an official communication relating to the disaffection in the Manor, of a few months earlier date than the above raid, and which was signed by Robert R. Livingston, as one of the committee sent by the New York Convention to enquire into the state of affairs in the Manor of Livingston, it is referred to as "the upper manor, as it is sometimes called."[126]

The following interesting account of the burning of these two mansions, as preserved in the family by tradition, is derived from the late Mr. Thomas Streatfeild Clarkson's *History of Clermont or Livingston Manor:*—

> There was intense excitement at Clermont when the news arrived of Burgoyne's surrender. Margaret, afterwards Mrs. Tillotson, was knitting a long stocking for an old family servant, which, for a wager, she was to finish in a day. It was near midnight, the stocking was rapidly approaching its completion, when black Scipio rushed in with the joyful news of Burgoyne's surrender. The stocking was at once thrown aside and the wager lost.

The enemy, however, were steadily approaching from the south, lighting their way by burning towns and private dwellings. Clermont might have been untouched, as at that time two British officers, a wounded captain named Montgomery,[127] and his surgeon, had been for some time very hospitably entertained by Mrs. Livingston, at Clermont. They proposed to extend their protection to the house and family, but Mrs. Livingston and her son both refused to have their property protected by the enemies of their country, and her son, the future Chancellor,[128] sent them to the house of a Tory neighbour. The preparations for the quick departure of the family were made. All were busy; the females of the household all giving a hand, to assist the general packing, for the removal of clothing and all movable valuables. Silver and the articles of value were buried in the wood, books were placed in the basin of a dry fountain and covered with rubbish; wagons and carts were piled up with baggage, and all necessary articles required by so large a family, both for immediate use as well as for preservation. Even at this hour, Mrs. Livingston burst into a hearty laugh, at the odd figure of an old black woman perched upon this miscellaneous assortment of trunks and bundles.[129] There was not much time to spare, for as the last load had disappeared, and when the carriages containing the family had reached the top of the hill overlooking the house, they beheld the smoke already arising from its walls. It had been fired as soon as entered by the British soldiers, one party of whom had arrived by land from Rhinebeck, which place they had burned, and another party landed from the British ship-of-war, which lay south of the point.

Large looking-glasses had been carefully hung in an outhouse by the family before their departure and an inside frame made to conceal them from view, but the soldiers discharged their muskets at the building, and reduced to splinters the valuable mirrors. With heavy hearts the family left a home endeared to them by all the associations which makes a home one of cheerfulness, happiness, and contentment. They took refuge in the town of Salisbury, in Berkshire, just beyond the border of Massachusetts, where they made a temporary home, in a house which is still standing; a stone house near a picturesque lake; here they remained but a short time. The hasty retreat of Vaughan's forces rendering Clermont a safe residence again, Mrs. Livingston and her family returned to her farm-house, and at once commenced to rebuild the mansion-house, and in about a year removed into it.[130]

A few days after the destruction of his home, the chancellor wrote from Salisbury,[131] apologising to the President of the Council of Safety for his temporary absence from the duties of his office, which arose from the fact of his having been on the eastern side of the Hudson at the time of this raid:—

> I thought [he wrote], it improper when the enemy came up the river to leave this side of the water, which was unfortunate, in wanting both yours and the Governor's direction. I therefore remained with the militia[132] till the enemy left us. I am just now arrived at this place in order to inquire into the situation of my family, which has hitherto been left to shift for themselves. I am therefore unacquainted with the measures adopted by the Council, but doubt not that they are such as are best suited to the present distressing occasion.

He then goes on to propose that to prevent such raids for the future, as "the enemy have in their late ravages effected to distinguish between their friends and those who are attached to our cause," a means should be found to fix the losses arising from any further depredations on those inhabitants who are hostile to the new government. "In order to carry this into execution," he suggested, "an inquest should be taken in each county of the damage done, as well as of all Tory property," and then tax the latter "by a general assessment, upon which the loss should be repaid." He also thought "Congress should be pressed to make retaliation."

Considering how barbarously the chancellor and his family had been treated by the enemy, his proposed plan for putting a stop to such a savage system of warfare certainly did not err on the side of harshness, but some of his fellow-citizens held far stronger views on this subject, and cherished bitter feelings of revenge against the British and their friends—the hated Tories—for their wanton destruction of private property on this occasion. This feeling was shortly to find expression in the New York Legislature by the introduction of a vindictive Confiscation Act, which would have immediately become law if it had not been for the opposition of Chancellor

Livingston, who, supported by a strong minority in the Senate, used his powerful influence as a member of the Council of Revision in obtaining its rejection, though unfortunately only for a brief period. But before treating of this matter in more detail, we must return to Philip Livingston, whose career was now nearing its close.

Upon the return of the raiders to New York, and the restoration of confidence as to the security of their families, Philip Livingston and his fellow delegates to the Continental Congress proceeded to York, Pennsylvania, where that body was then sitting owing to the temporary occupation of Philadelphia by the British forces. On the 14th November 1777, these gentlemen presented their credentials and took their seats. There is no record preserved as to how much of the next six months was devoted by Philip Livingston to his congressional duties, but he must have been absent for a short time, previous to the 5th of May 1778, on a final visit, as it turned out to be, to his family; for upon that date it is entered in the Journals of Congress, that he took his seat "as a delegate from the State of New York," which proves he had been absent on leave. When he said farewell to his family on this occasion, Mr. Livingston had a presentiment that he would never see them again, as he was in feeble health when he started to resume his place in Congress at the urgent request of the State government; but he patriotically devoted the last few weeks of his life, as well as a portion of his personal estate, to the service of his country, then passing through a most critical period of her existence.

Philip Livingston literally "died in harness," for upon the 27th of May, or only three weeks after his return, Gouverneur Morris was appointed in his place as the New York member on the Marine Committee, on account of his failing health; and, upon the twelfth of the following month, his death is thus recorded in the Journals:—

Friday, 12th June 1778.

Congress being informed that Mr. P. Livingston, one of the delegates for the State of New York, died last night, and that circumstances require that his corpse be interred this evening:

Resolved, That Congress will, in a body, attend the funeral this evening, at six o'clock, with a crape round the arm, and will continue in mourning for the space of one month.

Ordered, That Mr. Lewis, Mr. Duer, and Mr. G. Morris, be a committee to superintend the funeral, and that the Rev. Mr. Duffield, the attending chaplain, be notified to officiate on the occasion.

His death was caused by dropsy on the chest, and he did not die on the night of the eleventh of June, as the above entry might seem to imply, but during the early morning of the twelfth. This is borne out by a letter from Gouverneur Morris to Governor Clinton, dated "York Town, 16th June 1778," in which the writer says "I am sorry to have to inform your Excellency of the Death of our friend and my very worthy Colleague Mr. Livingston. He was from the moment almost of his arrival here confined to his room, and on Friday [12th June] last at 4 o'clock in the morning paid the last debt to nature." This is confirmed by his youngest son Henry, a youth of eighteen, who immediately upon hearing of his father's critical state of health, obtained leave from General Washington, and hastened to his father's bedside. The young man was at this date a lieutenant in the commander-in-chief's Corps of Guards, and was the only member of the family present when Philip Livingston breathed his last. He was buried in what is now the Prospect Hill Cemetery, where a monument to his memory was subsequently erected by his grandson, General Van Rensselaer.[133]

This son Henry, or Henry Philip, as he was usually designated, to distinguish him from the numerous other Henry Livingstons, was upon the fourth of the following December promoted, by a resolution of Congress, "to the rank of captain in the corps of General Washington's guards, in the room of Captain Gibbes, lately promoted to the rank of major."

Henry was only eighteen when promoted to the rank of captain in General Washington's Life Guards, and had already seen some sharp fighting. A letter from him to his father written from Philadelphia, on the 13th of September, 1777, two days after the battle of the Brandywine, fell into the hands of the British, and was published in one of the loyalist papers with some sarcastic remarks on the writer's claiming it as an American victory![134] In it he says:—

> Our loss in killed, wounded, and missing, as near as any judgment can be formed (for no return has yet been made) may amount to between five and six hundred at most. . . . The enemy sustained a much greater loss; you may at least rate it at the double of ours. I was myself a witness to the havock which General Maxwell made among them in the morning, being directly on the opposite side of the Brandywine. Had it not been for the incongruous information which General Washington received, concerning the movement of the enemy's main body to our right; had we been apprised of it in time

to bring up our whole army, and form, I believe, in my soul, that day would have put an end to the British army in America. ... It was, however, thought preferable to retire, and the whole army, at present, occupy their old ground near Germantown. . . . The next will be an important week. I am persuaded that our men can fight them upon equal terms, and I hope we shall not wait for them to attack us again. Our troops are in high spirits, and will march towards the enemy with much greater cheerfulness than they did from them.[135]

We have already alluded to the disgraceful Confiscation Act or Bill of Attainder. This was introduced into the Senate, upon the 24th June, 1778, by Mr. John Morin Scott —an extreme Whig, and formerly one of the triumvirate of New York lawyers referred to in a previous chapter,—during the second meeting of the First Session of the State Legislature, then sitting at Poughkeepsie.[136] It passed in the affirmative by a bare majority; but the Session then being on the point of terminating, nothing further could be done with it at this time. One of the first acts of the Second Session, which commenced its sittings upon the following 13th of October, was to choose a senator in the place of Philip Livingston, and Sir James Jay, an elder brother of Chief Justice John Jay, but a far less able man, was the person chosen. Sir James Jay was very bitter in his feelings against the Tories, and at once sided with Mr. Scott in favour of his Bill. But nothing was effected either on this occasion before the Legislature adjourned until the 27th of January, 1779, when upon reassembling no time was lost by its abettors, and it was introduced into the Lower House of Assembly on the day following. It went through the usual procedure, and was duly reported to the Senate; passed by the Upper House with some amendments, and returned to the Assembly. There is no need to discuss the proceedings in full, except to mention that two of the honourable members of the Senate, who opposed the Bill becoming law were Mr. Yates and Mr. Richard Morris, and that the latter proposed an amendment to the effect "that the names of such persons in the Bill, as are not known to have taken up arms against us, or been guilty of High Treason, be expunged."

This amendment was lost by one vote only. Finally ten members voted in the Bill's favour and six against. Five of these six minority senators were so indignant, that they had entered in the Journals over their names a severe and forcible "dissent," in which the terms of this partisan Bill were held up to richly deserved ridicule.[137] The Bill having been returned to

the Assembly with the Senate's amendments, was, after some little bickering between the two branches of the Legislature, finally agreed to by the
majority in both Houses on the eleventh of March, 1779; and on the same
day the Assembly had it presented to the Council of Revision.

Two days later, which happened to be a Saturday, the Legislature
adjourned to "4 o'clock on Sunday afternoon, the 14th," and as the only
business to detain them in session was the receipt of the answer from the
Council of Revision, therefore, presumably, to show the Council they were
in a hurry, they adjourned from a Saturday to a Sunday. Possibly, these
patriotic legislators considered such a Christian act deserved to be consummated on the Sabbath! These worthy men had, however, misjudged
the character of the chancellor and his fellow councillors. For at the hour
named, four o'clock on Sunday afternoon, Chancellor Livingston appeared
in the Assembly, and delivered to the angry House the Council of Revision's
veto of the Bill,— entitled "An Act for Forfeitures and Confiscations, and
for declaring the Sovereignty of the People of this State, in respect to all
the Property within the same,"— which being read twice was postponed
for further consideration. The next morning the Council's objections were
thrown out by a vote of twenty-eight to nine, and the Bill sent up again to
the Senate. This being a vote of more than the required two-third's majority, the Assembly, as far as it could, thus declared for its legality.

In the Senate, however, the voting was nearly equal-eight for and
seven against, so that here the necessary two-thirds majority was not
obtained, naturally to the intense disgust of Messrs. John Morin Scott and
Company. But so determined were the implacables in the Legislature to
attain their object, that as soon as it was known that the Bill was lost they
passed a resolution in. both Houses, "that a [similar] Bill be brought in at
the next meeting of the Legislature"; and there and then appointed the
necessary committees to see that this was done. So energetic, moreover,
was the majority in the Legislature in their craving for revenge on their
political foes, that a few months later they finally attained their purpose,
and this most abominable act became a law of the State of New York.

It was to the chancellor himself that the Council of Revision,—
now no longer in existence,—owed its origin.[138] The original draft of its
Constitution is in his handwriting. After stating that "laws inconsistent
with the Spirit of this Constitution, or with the public good, may be hastily and unadvisedly passed," it ordained "that the Governor, for the time
being, the Chancellor and the Judges of the Supreme Court, or any two of
them, together with the Governor, shall be, and hereby are, constituted a

Council to revise all bills to be passed into Laws by the Legislature." The veto of the 14th of March, 1779, which has been described as one of the ablest documents of that day,[139] was also evidently drawn up by Chancellor Livingston. Considering the cruel manner in which he and his family had been recently treated by the British authorities, it shows that Robert R. Livingston stood upon a much higher plane than the great majority of his fellow-citizens, and that he was a true patriot and lover of his country. He, at least, "did not wish that one of the leading acts of the newly-born State, should be a perpetual monument of private revenge, selfish greed, patent injustice, and bad law."[140]

Another true lover of his country was John Jay, who had recently resigned the post of Chief Justice on being appointed Minister to Spain. When he read an account of this Confiscation Act in an English newspaper, he at once wrote to Governor Clinton from "Aranjuez, 21 miles from Madrid," in terms of honest indignation. In this letter he says,

> An English paper contains what they call, but I can hardly believe to be, your Confiscation Act. If truly printed, New York is disgraced by injustice too palpable to admit even of palliation. I feel for the honour of my country, and therefore beg the favour of you to send me a true copy of it; that, if the other be false, I may, by publishing yours, remove the prejudices against you occasioned by the former.[141]

Mr. Jay never altered his opinion as to the disgrace caused to his native State by the passage of this revengeful act. Like most fair-minded people, he considered "the dispute with Great Britain as one in which men might conscientiously take opposite sides; and while he was ever ready to adopt all proper measures for preventing the Tories from injuring the American cause he abhorred the idea of *punishing* them for their opinions. His wish was that no estate should be confiscated except such as belonged to those who had either been perfidious or cruel. By the act alluded to, many were attainted who had been perfectly inoffensive; and he believed motives of avarice had led to their proscription."[142]

What John Jay's thoughts must have been when he heard of his elder brother's share in this disgraceful transaction, may be easily imagined!

In the same letter Mr. Jay writes: "I wish to know who are your members in Congress. I find Livingston is one, and am glad of it." This refers to the appointment of Chancellor Livingston, by a joint vote of the

Legislature, on the 18th October 1779, as special delegate to the General'
Congress. It appears from the Assembly Journals, that upon the tenth of
this month, after notice had been received of Mr. Jay's resignation as a
member of Congress, owing to his appointment as Minister to Spain, and
arrangements made to have an election held shortly to appoint another
person in his place, the following resolutions were agreed to:

> Whereas several matters will shortly be depending before
> Congress in which this State is greatly interested:
>
> Resolved, That in the opinion of this House, a special occa-
> sion does now exist, on which the Chancellor and Judges of
> the Supreme Court may be elected Delegates to the General
> Congress.
>
> Resolved, That of the Chancellor and Judges of the Supreme
> Court, one be elected a Delegate on this occasion, and to con-
> tinue in office until the first Day of April next.
>
> Ordered, That Mr. Benson and Mr. Palmer carry a copy of
> the two last Resolutions to the Honorable the Senate, and
> report their concurrence.

Under these resolutions, Chancellor Livingston was unanimously
elected a special delegate eight days later; while General Schuyler was
chosen, though not unanimously, to fill the vacancy among the annually
elected delegates caused by Chief Justice Jay's resignation. The chancellor took his seat in the General Congress on the following twentieth of
November, and at once, as on former occasions, took an active part in its
proceedings. On the seventh of March in the following year he produced
a resolution of the Legislature of the State of New York, extending his
delegation "until the first day of October next," and this was subsequently
again extended until the first of March, 1781.

Upon the tenth of January, 1781, the committee of Congress appointed
to consider and report upon a plan for the creation of a special department
for the conduct of foreign affairs, made their report: whereupon it was

> Resolved, That an office be forthwith established for the
> Department of Foreign Affairs, to be kept always in the place
> where Congress shall reside;
>
> That there shall be a Secretary for the despatch of the
> business of the said office, to be styled "Secretary for Foreign
> Affairs."

Chancellor Robert R. Livingston (1746–1813) of Clermont. The Miriam and Ira D. Wallach Division of Art, Prints and Photographs: Print Collection, New York Public Library Digital Collections, Public Domain.

The resolution then goes on to define the duties appertaining to this new office, as hitherto all the foreign correspondence of Congress had been very loosely carried on by means of a Committee of Secret Correspondence. On account of the mutual jealousies existing among the various newly confederated states, no Secretary of Foreign Affairs was appointed until seven months later, when, on the tenth of August 1781, upon the nomination of Mr. Floyd, one of the New York delegates, Chancellor Livingston, was elected by ballot to fill this important office. On the seventeenth of the following month he wrote accepting the post, and his letter of acceptance was read in Congress on the first of October, and upon the twentieth of this latter month he took the oaths of office and commenced his new duties.

The American ministers abroad soon found a great change for the better had arisen, through the appointment of such a capable man as Secretary of Foreign Affairs, and they all wrote, in answer to his circular letter announcing his acceptance of this office, expressing the great satisfaction this news had given them. To quote from two of the most prominent of these ministers' letters, Benjamin Franklin, writing from Passy, 28th January 1782, says:

> Sir, I received, at the same time, your several letters of October 20th, 24th and November 26th, which I purpose to answer fully by the return of the *Alliance*. Having just had a very short notice of the departure of this ship, I can only at present mention the great pleasure your appointment gives me, and my intention of corresponding with you regularly and frequently, as you desire. The information contained in your letters is full and clear; I shall endeavour that mine, of the state of affairs here, may be as satisfactory.

While John Adams writes from Amsterdam, 14th February, 1782:

> DEAR SIR, Yesterday the duplicate of your letter of the 23rd October was brought to me, the original is not yet arrived. It is with great pleasure I learn, that a Minister is appointed for foreign affairs, who is so capable of introducing into that department an order, a constancy, and an activity, which could never be expected from a Committee of Congress, so often changing, and so much engaged in other great affairs, however excellent their qualifications or dispositions, etc., etc., etc.

The foreign correspondence of the War of Independence has been twice printed within the last century. The first edition, under the title of the *Diplomatic Correspondence of the American Revolution*, was edited by Mr. Jared Sparks; while, within recent years, a fuller and more correct version has been published at the cost of Congress, under the editorship of the late Dr. Francis Wharton, and entitled *The revolutionary Diplomatic Correspondence of the United States*. Both these editors are loud in their praises of the first Secretary of Foreign Affairs. Mr. Jared Sparks says:

> From this date [20th October 1781] a salutary change found its way into the management of Foreign Affairs. To abilities and other qualifications well suited to the station, Mr. Livingston added energy, diligence, and promptitude, as his numerous letters on a great variety of topics abundantly testify. We hear no

more complaints from the Ministers abroad, that their letters are forgotten and unanswered, or that they receive no intelligence nor instructions from home.

Dr. Wharton's description of the newly-appointed Secretary is as follows:

Livingston, though a much younger man than Franklin, possessed in his dispassionateness and his many sidedness, not a few of Franklin's characteristics. From his prior administrative experience as royalist recorder of New York he had at least some acquaintance with practical government in America; his thorough studies as a scholar and jurist gave him a knowledge of administrative politics in other spheres. As Secretary of Foreign Affairs in 1781–1783, he did more than any one in the home government in shaping its foreign policy. But the system he indicated was, as will be seen, not the "Militia" system of unsophisticated impulse, but that which the law of nations had at the time sanctioned as the best mode of conducting international affairs. His course as secretary was based on the law of nations as thus understood by him. He at once accepted Franklin's position, that it was unwise, as well as against international usage, for the United States to send ministers to foreign courts without some intimation that they would be received. He saw that from the nature of things the then neutral courts of Europe would not throw away the advantage of their neutrality by entering into an alliance with the United States, which, as a revolutionary republic, they, as absolutists, could have no desire to encourage. He therefore advised the recall of Dana, and he opposed any further efforts being made to send ministers to European courts by whom such missions were not invited. Acting also on the principle that a minister to a foreign court must be a *persona grata*, and aware of Franklin's transcendent gifts as a negotiator, as well as of his great acceptability to France, to Franklin he gave his unwavering support.

On the eighth of May 1782, Secretary Livingston submitted to Congress a report concerning the annual expense of his office, which was read in that House on the twentieth, and in which he gave, among other matters, the following interesting particulars as to the mode of living adopted by their ministers abroad:

> Dr. Franklin[143] has a part of Mr. Chaumont's house at Passy; he keeps a chariot and pair, and three or four servants; and gives a dinner occasionally to the Americans and others. His whole expense, as far as I can learn, is very much within his income. Mr. Adams[144] lives in lodgings, keeps a chariot and pair, and two men-servants. He has hitherto retained a private secretary, who will in the absence of Mr. Dana,[145] it is to be presumed, be paid by Congress. I have lately heard that Mr. Adams was about to take a house. Mr. Dana's salary, even if he should assume a public character in a country where the relative value of money is so high, that, if I am well informed, an elegant house may be hired for fifteen guineas a year, is very ample. Of Mr. Jay's[146] manner of living, I have been able to obtain no account; but I should conclude from the price of the necessaries of life in that part of Spain in which he lives, from the port the court and the people about it maintain, and above all, from its sitting in different parts of the kingdom, that to live in the same style with Dr. Franklin or Mr. Adams, his expenses must amount to nearly the double of theirs. But as every conjecture of this kind must be very uncertain, all I can do is to lay before Congress the relative expense, as far as I can learn it, between the different places at which the ministers reside, taking Philadelphia for a common standard. Paris, if wine, clothing, and the wages of servants are included, is about twenty per cent, cheaper than Philadelphia; Amsterdam, ten; and at Madrid the expenses of a family are somewhat higher than at this place. But the unsettled state of those who follow the court, their travelling equipage and charges, must greatly enhance this expense.

From this report we also learn that the salary of the Secretary of Foreign Affairs was four thousand dollars per annum, but this only covered a little more than half Mr. Livingston's expenses; while the three principal ministers abroad, Messrs. Franklin, Adams, and Jay, were allowed to draw the sum of two thousand five hundred pounds each, and these payments were reluctantly granted by the Congress, then at their wits' end to provide the necessary funds for prosecuting the war. Robert Morris, the able Superintendent of Finance—whom Governor Livingston coupled with Washington as a saviour of his country—had the greatest difficulty in providing the requisite salaries, as his correspondence at this date clearly shows. In a previous part of this chapter, reference has been made to the enormous burdens the unhappy land-owners were groaning under during the later years of the War of Independence. Chancellor Livingston, owing to his large landed estate, was one of the heaviest sufferers also from this cause. In a letter to Governor Clinton, dated 29 June, 1780, he states in that year his "annual tax amounts to upwards of £50,000" while his income for that period did not amount to £10,000.[147] This was, however, only half the tax his cousin Robert of the Manor had to pay during the same year.

Owing to pressure of work arising from his occupation of the dual offices of Secretary for Foreign Affairs and Chancellor of the State of New York, Mr. Livingston, towards the close of 1782, saw that he would have to relinquish one of these posts; and he therefore decided to send in his resignation of the secretaryship. Before so doing he, upon the 28th of November, called upon Mr. Madison,[148] who gives the following account of what passed at this interview:

> Mr. Livingston, Secretary of Foreign Affairs, called upon me, and mentioned his intention to resign in a short time his office; observing, that as he ultimately was decided to prefer his place of Chancellor in New York to the other, and the two had become incompatible by the increase of business in the former, he thought it expedient not to return to Philadelphia, after a visit to New York, which was required by this increase. In the course of conversation, he took notice that the expense of his appointment under Congress had exceeded his salary by about three thousand dollars per annum. He asked me whether it was probable Mr. Jefferson would accept the vacancy, or whether he would accept Mr. Jay's place in Spain, and leave the vacancy to the latter. I told him I thought Mr. Jefferson would not accept it himself, and doubted whether he would concur in the latter arrangement; as well as whether Congress would be willing to part with Mr. Jay's services in the negotiations of peace; but promised to sound Mr. Jefferson on these points by the first opportunity.

Four days later Mr. Livingston formally resigned this office, but intimated that he was willing to carry on the duties of Secretary of Foreign Affairs till the first of January 1783, so as to give time for the choice of a successor. Whereupon Congress, on the following day, passed a resolution

> That Thursday the 19th inst: [December] be assigned for
> electing another person to fill the office of Secretary for Foreign
> Affairs; and that Mr. Livingston be informed that Congress do
> approve of his proposal of continuing to perform the duties of
> the office until a person shall be appointed to succeed him.

Mr. Madison states, that in the course of the debate arising out of
Mr. Livingston's resignation, "the expediency of augmenting the salary was
suggested, but not much supported." When, however, the time came for
the election of his successor, it was found that some of the States were
unwilling to agree to the appointment of any of the persons proposed, and
a committee was thereupon empowered to confer with Mr. Livingston, and
ask him to withdraw his resignation until this difficulty could be overcome. This he willingly complied with, on the condition that he should
be allowed "to make a short visit to the State of New York in the month of
January," which was agreed to by Congress upon the 21st of December, the
date on which the committee delivered their report of the result of their
interview with Mr. Livingston, and it was also resolved to postpone the
election of his successor "until the first Monday in May next."

The Prince de Broglie, who was on a visit to America at this time,
made the acquaintance of the various Ministers while in Philadelphia,
and he thus describes, in the narrative of his travels, his impression of
the Secretary of Foreign Affairs, whom he met at the house of Mr. Robert
Morris, the celebrated Superintendent of Finance: "Mr. Livingston,
Minister of Foreign Affairs," says the prince, "is quite as lank as the other
two gentlemen (Morris, Comptroller-General, and Lincoln, Secretary of
War) are rotund. He is thirty-five years of age, his face is very fine, and it is
generally conceded that he is a man of talent."

During his remaining term of office, Mr. Livingston was busily
employed in corresponding with the American plenipotentiaries, then
engaged at Paris in negotiating a treaty of peace with Great Britain; and
upon the 26th of February, 1783, he had the pleasure of informing General
Washington, "that our last despatches, dated in October, announce a disposition in the belligerent powers to terminate the war by a general peace.
The Court of London, whose sincerity was most suspected, because it was
to make the greatest sacrifices, appears to have smoothed the way by the
commission to Mr. Oswald (which your Excellency has seen) empowering
him to treat with the Thirteen United States of America." And a fortnight
later, he joyfully dashes off a hurried despatch, to let the Commander-in-
Chief know that "the *Washington* packet arrived this morning."

I have not had leisure [continues the Secretary of Foreign Affairs] to read all my letters, but as an express is ready to go early to-morrow, I rather choose to rely upon your goodness to excuse a letter in extreme haste, than to hold myself inexcusable, by not informing you of what we yet know of the state of the negotiations. None of my letters is of later date than the 25th of December. All difficulties had then been removed with respect to us, and the preliminaries were signed; they consist of nine articles:

The *first* acknowledges our Independence.

The *second* describes our boundaries, which are as extensive as we would wish.

The *third* ascertains our rights as to the fishery, and puts them upon the footing that they were before the war.

The *fourth* provides that all British debts shall be paid.

The *fifth* and *sixth* are enclosed for your perusal, as they are likely to be the least satisfactory here.[149]

The *seventh* stipulates that hostilities shall immediately cease, and that the British troops be withdrawn without carrying off any property, or dismantling fortifications; that records and archives shall be restored.

The *eighth* stipulates that the navigation of the Mississippi shall be open to us and Great Britain.

The *ninth* that all conquests made in America after the ratification shall be restored.

These preliminaries are only provisional upon the determination of a peace with France, whose negotiations have not made such progress as ours. I believe they find themselves very much embarrassed by the demands of their other allies.

Mr. Livingston hated the idea of any deception being practised upon his country's allies, and he considered the American Plenipotentiaries in Paris had acted wrongly in not always consulting the wishes of the French Court, during their prolonged negotiations with the English envoy, Mr. Oswald. He felt so strongly upon this point, that on the 18th of March 1783, namely six days after the date of his last quoted letter to Washington, he wrote a long despatch to the President of Congress, in which he fully set forth his objections to this conduct on the part of the American Commissioners, and to the introduction of the secret article in the Preliminary Provisional Treaty of Peace, which had to be withheld from the knowledge of the French Court.[150] He proposed, therefore, that

Congress should empower him to divulge the secret article relating to West Florida "to the Minister of his most Christian Majesty in such manner as will best tend to remove any unfavourable impression it may make on the Court of France, of the sincerity of these States or their Ministers." And he ended his arguments in favour of this course of action, by expressing the hope that "Congress will easily believe, that I offer these sentiments with the utmost diffidence; that I see many and powerful arguments that militate against them; that I feel extreme pain in advising a measure which may hurt the feelings of ministers, to whom we are indebted for their continued zeal and assiduity, all of whom I respect, and with one of whom I have had the closest and most intimate friendship from our earliest youth.[151] But, Sir, it is a duty that my office requires; and I am happy in reflecting that this duty is discharged, when I have proposed what I think right, and that the better judgment of Congress is to determine."

The above letter was read in Congress on the same day; but the consideration of it was postponed until the following one, when it became the subject of an important debate, which was adjourned on that day after the appointment of a committee of five, of whom Alexander Hamilton was one, to inquire more fully into all the circumstances connected with the adoption of the secret or separate article complained of. The committee's report, submitted to Congress on the twenty-second of March, was entirely in favour of the course of action advocated by the Secretary of Foreign Affairs, and is worded as follows:

1. That our ministers be thanked for their zeal and services in negotiating the preliminary articles.
2. That they be instructed to make a communication of the separate article to the Court of France, in such way as would best get over the concealment.
3. That the Secretary of Foreign Affairs inform them that it is the wish of Congress that the preliminary articles had been communicated to the Court of France before they had been executed.

This report led to further debates, as a large proportion of the members were "predetermined against every measure which seemed in any manner to blame the ministers, and the eastern delegates, in general, extremely jealous of the honour of Mr. Adams." Congress therefore adjourned to Monday, the 24th of March, without any vote on the motion before it. When the debate was again resumed, the general opinion apparently prevailing among the members was, that though the ministers had committed a mistake in agreeing to a concealment of the separate article from their French allies,

THE WAR OF INDEPENDENCE | 269

it would be as well now to let bygones be bygones, and bury in oblivion the whole transaction. This appears to have been acted upon, as no vote is recorded in the congressional journals; and the Secretary on the following day,[152] in his strongly worded despatch to the commissioners at Paris, in which he expresses his own opinion of what he considers their "want of candour and fidelity" in their treatment of the Court of Versailles, thus refers to this incident, and the failure of Congress to come to any official decision:

> I intended to have submitted this letter to Congress, but I find there is not the least prospect of obtaining any decision upon it in time to send by this conveyance, if at all. I leave you to collect their sentiments, as far as I know them, from the following state of their proceedings. After your joint and separate letters and journals had been submitted to them by me, and had been read, they were referred back to me to report upon, when I wrote them a letter, and when it was taken into consideration, motions were made and debated a whole day. After which the letters and motions were committed, and a report brought in. This was under consideration two days, when the arrival of a vessel from Cadiz with letters from the Count d'Estaing and the Marquis de Lafayette, containing accounts that the preliminaries were signed, induced many members to think it would be improper to proceed in the report, and in that state it remains without any express decision. From this you will draw your own inferences. I make no apology for the part I have taken in this business. I am satisfied you will readily acquit me for having discharged what I conceived to be my duty upon such a view of things as you presented to me. In declaring my sentiments freely, I invite you to treat me with equal candour in your letters. . . .

The Secretary's outspoken despatch naturally gave great offence to the American Plenipotentiaries in Paris; and John Adams, in particular, bitterly resented his action in this matter. In his letter in reply, he sarcastically remarks, "Your late despatches, sir, are not well adapted to give spirits to a melancholy man, or to cure one sick with a fever"[153]; while, the commissioners in their joint reply, explaining their reasons for keeping the separate article concealed from their allies, which practically amounted to a confession that they could not trust the French Court, wrote: "We perfectly concur with you in sentiment, sir, that 'honesty is the best policy.' But until it be shown that we have trespassed on the rights of any man, or body of men, you must excuse our thinking that this remark, as applied to our proceedings, was unnecessary." They then went on to say:

(Circular) Office for foreign affairs, Philadelphia
24 March 1703

Sir

I have the honor to enclose
an abstract of the preliminary Articles for a general
peace, signed the 20th January 1783 — They were
brought by a Vessel that arrived last night from
Cadix, dispatched by Count d'Estaing to recall the
cruizers & privateers of his most Christian Majesty
& his subjects — Tho' not official, they leave no
room to doubt this happy event, on which I
sincerely congratulate Your Excellency — When
the wisdom of the United States shall have re-
established their credit, & strengthened their bond
of union, which will doubtless be the first work
of peace, we shall have every reason to hope that
this will be a happy & a flourishing Country
I have the honor to be, Sir
With great respect
Your Excellency's
most obedient humble servant
R R Livingston

(REDUCED SIZE) OF CIRCULAR LETTER TO THE GOVERNOR OF GEORGIA FROM ROBERT R.
LIVINGSTON, SECRETARY OF FOREIGN AFFAIRS, ANNOUNCING PEACE WITH
GREAT BRITAIN, 24 MARCH 1783

We are persuaded, Sir, that your remarks on these subjects resulted from real opinion, and were made with candour and sincerity. The best men will view objects of this kind in different lights even when standing on the same ground; and it is not to be wondered at, that we, who are on the spot, and have the whole transaction under our eyes, should see many parts of it in a stronger point of light, than persons at a distance, who can only view it through the dull medium of representation.[154]

Though the Definitive Treaty of Peace between Great Britain and the now recognised United States of America was not signed until the third of September 1783, a suspension of hostilities was to take place, as soon as the former country had arranged the preliminary terms of peace also with France and Spain. News of this event, *a general peace*, reached Philadelphia on the twenty-third of March, 1783, and one of Mr. Livingston's last acts as Secretary of Foreign Affairs, was to send a circular letter to the various State governors, enclosing "the preliminary articles, for a general peace,"[155] and to endeavour to persuade Sir Guy Carleton and the English Admiral on the American station, to at once order a cessation of arms, so as "to stop the further effusion of blood." This the British officers very properly declined to do without specific orders from their own government, but Sir Guy Carleton, in his reply to the Secretary for Foreign Affairs, pointed out he had "hitherto abstained from all hostilities," and this conduct he meant to continue so far as his "own security would admit." Thirteen days later Sir Guy also received the welcome news, whereupon he hastened to inform Mr. Livingston, that he intended to have the king's proclamation ordering a cessation of arms, published in New York on the eighth of April, and he finished his letter by stating,

Upon this great occasion, Sir, I am to offer my strongest assurances, that during the short period of my command here, I shall be ready and earnest to cultivate that spirit of good will, which between the United States of America and the King of Great Britain, and the subjects and citizens of both countries, will I trust always remain.

To which the Secretary of Foreign Affairs replied, on the twelfth of April,

I give the fullest credit, Sir, to your assurances, that you are ready to cultivate the spirit of harmony and good will between the subjects and citizens of his Britannic Majesty and these States, since I find them warranted by the humanity which has uniformly distinguished your command in America.[156] But, Sir, time only, with liberality in those that govern in both countries, can entirely efface the remembrance of what has passed, and produce that perfect good will, which I sincerely concur with you in wishing to cultivate.

On the same day, Mr. Livingston despatched another circular to the governors of all the States, announcing the cessation of hostilities.

The Committee of Congress to whom had been referred the question of the appointment of a new secretary to take Livingston's place, found this no easy task, and he was therefore approached by those gentlemen to know whether he could not be persuaded, by an increase in salary, to continue to fill this important office. In his reply to the Chairman of this Committee, dated Philadelphia, 19th of May, 1783, he says,

The inquiries that the Committee were pleased to do me the honour to make this morning, relative to my continuance to exercise the office of Secretary of Foreign Affairs, were extremely embarrassing to me, because on the one hand, I find it impossible to continue in the office on the present establishment, without material injury to my private affairs, and, on the other, to propose the terms on which I would stay would be to overrate my own importance, and to suppose that others could not be had upon such conditions as Congress have been pleased to consider as sufficient. Having given my whole time, and a considerable part of my property, to the public during the war, I see, with pleasure, that the affairs of the United States are not now in such a situation as to render the contribution of an individual necessary. It is my wish to endeavour to repair the injuries my estate has sustained by the ravages of the enemy, and my own neglect, by the offices I have held. From my former letter, Congress will be able to judge how far my expenses in the office exceed the salary. But as it by no means follows, that another by greater economy, and humbler, but perhaps more just ideas of the importance of this office, could not live at less expense, I do not think that mine should be any reason to induce Congress to make other changes, than such as they shall of themselves deem necessary. And in this view I requested the Committee, that called upon me last winter, to keep the matter of emoluments entirely out of sight in their report, as I then considered 'my stay only as a temporary inconvenience.

On the fourth of June, Mr. Livingston definitely signified to Congress his decision to resign this office, whereupon Mr. Hamilton moved that "Mr. Livingston having signified to Congress his desire of relinquishing the exercise of the office of foreign affairs, and his intention of returning to the State of New York, the Secretary of Congress be directed to receive the papers of the said office into his care till a successor to Mr. Livingston can be appointed; and that next Wednesday be assigned for the election of a secretary for the department of foreign affairs." Upon this being put to the House Mr. Peters moved, "in order to detain Mr. Livingston in office, that it be declared by the seven states present, that the salary ought to be augmented. To this it was objected—first, that it would be an assumption of power in seven states to say what nine states ought to do; second, that it might insnare Mr. Livingston; third, that it would commit the present, who ought to be open to discussion when nine states should be on the floor. The motion of Mr. Peters then being withdrawn, that of Mr. Hamilton was agreed to."
It was thereupon

> *Resolved* unanimously, that the thanks of Congress be presented to Mr. Livingston for his services during his continuance in office; and that he be assured, Congress entertain a high sense of the ability, zeal, and fidelity, with which he hath discharged the important trust reposed in him.

When his old friend John Jay heard of his resignation of his office under Congress, he wrote to him from France, expressing the hope that in so doing he had not acted too hastily.

> Dear Robert [he wrote], at your form with your family, in peace, and in plenty, how happy is your situation! I wish you may not have retired too soon. It is certain you may do much good where you are, and perhaps in few things more than in impressing by precept, influence, and example, the indispensable necessity of rendering the Continental and State governments vigorous and orderly.[157]

There is no doubt Livingston's preference for his State office over that held under the Confederation, caused great annoyance in some quarters; but the choice appears natural enough when we consider his home, his immense estate, and all his great family influence were to be found in New York; while the, perhaps, very human, but highly injurious, jealousies, then existing between the delegates from the confederated states in Congress, were beginning to make that body a laughing-stock throughout America. Besides the reasons given by him to Congress, as to the necessity for his resigning this office, there was another one arising out of the complaints of an extreme faction in his native State, who grumbled loudly against Mr. Livingston holding these two offices at the same time, which these grumblers averred was against the spirit of the Constitution; so that, according to their contention, by his acceptance of the post of Secretary of Foreign Affairs in 1781, he had virtually disqualified himself for the chancellorship. To get over this difficulty he was reappointed to the latter office upon the 27th June 1783.

We will close this chapter on the War of Independence, with a quotation from Governor Livingston's address to the New Jersey Legislature announcing its welcome termination: "Let us," he said, "show ourselves worthy of freedom by an inflexible attachment to public faith and national honour; let us establish our character as a sovereign State on the only durable basis of impartial and universal justice!"

Notes

1. See quotation from John Adams's letter to Samuel Chase at head of this chapter. How grimly this patriot would have chuckled, could he have read Mr. Belisle's effusion about the "white-winged angel of peace," being present in the room, when the voting took place! A few years later, towards the end of the war, when peace negotiations were in progress, John Adams wrote to Franklin, "Congress have done very well to join others in the commission for peace who have some faculties for it. My talent, if I have one, lies in making war."
2. The Livingstons in particular had an object lesson in the downfall of their family in Scotland, through their share in the abortive risings against the House of Hanover in 1715 and 1745.
3. For instance at the battles of Saratoga at least seven, probably eight, Livingstons held commissions in the victorious army, and three of these officers commanded regiments in action, either in both or in one of these engagements. It is doubtful whether any other family can show as many members commissioned officers in the American army on this eventful occasion. For particulars see later on in this chapter, also Appendix A at end of this volume.
4. See also the frontispiece. Wherever the name of Colony or State is omitted "New York" is meant.

5. For example, the above Henry Brockholst Livingston was a major at eighteen, and lieutenant-colonel at nineteen! John Armstrong, who subsequently, married a sister of Henry Beekman Livingston, was also a major at the same age, and adjutant-general at twenty-one. Robert R., Henry Beekman's elder brother, was a leading member of Continental Congress when twenty-eight, chancellor at thirty, and secretary for Foreign Affairs at thirty-four. While Alexander Hamilton was only thirty years of age, when he so ably led the Federalists to victory in 1787.

6. Letter dated "Claremont 6 July 1775," and read before the New York Committee of Safety in the City Hall, New York, upon the eleventh of the same month. Misprinted "6 June" in the Journals of the Provincial Congress.

7. On the 28th August, his senior officer, Lt.-Col. Philip Van Cortlandt, writes to President Livingston from Albany, the place of rendezvous, that he found Captain Livingston's company required "shoes, stockings, shirts, underclothes, haversacks and cash"; and that the captain had "advanced all himself that has been paid as yet."

8. A son of Henry Livingston of Poughkeepsie, Clerk of Dutchess County.

9. A rough list of the various commissions granted during the war, drawn up as accurately, as is possible from the various scattered original authorities available, will be found in the Appendix.

10. The marriage of Captain Montgomery to Janet Livingston took place on the 24th July 1773. It is thus chronicled in the London *Annual Register* of 1773, in the list of marriages published in its columns between 19th August and 9th September:— "Lately, Richard Montgomery, Esq., brother to the Right Hon. the Countess of Ranelagh, to Miss Livingston eldest daughter of the Hon. R. Livingston, Esq. one of the Judges of the Supreme Court of Judicature for New York."

11. Contributed by Mr. Marturin L. Delafield to the *Magazine of American History*, vol. xxi., pp. 256–258. In the above extracts the orthography has been modernised, as is the case of other contemporary letters. The captain was especially fond of using capitals.

12. The judge died a few weeks later, as will be noticed farther on.

13. Afterwards the General Gates of Saratoga fame.

14. General Schuyler had rejoined the army, though still in bad health, on the 30 August 1775.

15. Lieutenant-Colonel Ritzema of the First New York Regiment.

16. Articles of surrender were arranged on the 18th October, and the place occupied by the Americans on the following day. Among the military spoils which were of great service to Montgomery were the colours of the Seventh Regiment, which were sent to adorn President Hancock's house in Philadelphia.

17. Force, *American Archives*, Fourth Series, vol. iv, p. 1636.

18. General Washington to Richard Henry Lee, 29 August 1775. *Correspondence of General Washington*, vol. iii, pp. 96–98. General Montgomery to General Schuyler, November 13th, 1775. Force, *American Archives*, Fourth Series, vol. iii, pp. 1602, 1603.

19. General Schuyler to the President of Congress, Ticonderoga; 20 November 1775. Force, *American Archives*, Fourth Series, vol. iii, p. 1617.

20. General Montgomery to General Schuyler, Montreal, 13 November 1775. Force, *American Archives*, Fourth Series, vol. iii, pp. 1602, 1603.

21. General Schuyler to the President of Congress, Ticonderoga, 18 November 1775. Force, *American Archives*, Fourth Series, vol. iii, pp. 1595, 1596.

22. Force, *American Archives*, Fourth Series, vol. iii, p. 1950. The fact that Captain Livingston received the sword of honour as the bearer of General Montgomery's despatches, is duly noted by Mr. Richard Smith, a New Jersey delegate in Congress, in his Diary, under date 20th December, 1775. Printed in *American Historical Review*, vol. i, pp. 296, 297.
23. Force, *American Archives*, Fifth Series, vol. iii, p. 1566.
24. *Journals of Congress* (original edition), vol. x, p. 71. References will be made to his serving at Saratoga under General Gates, etc., later on. See also under Appendix A.
25. Judge Livingston died on the 9th December 1775 from a fit of apoplexy.
26. The following is the wording of this commission. As Philip Van Cortlandt had obtained this rank in June 1775, when the New York regiments were first organised, he certainly had a grievance; but as a matter of fact, when they both became colonels later in the year 1776, Van Cortlandt obtained the seniority.
27. The eighth company, Washington tells him, he must order to join him at the forts with all convenient speed. These instructions were sent to Lt.-Col. Livingston as Colonel James Clinton had not as yet returned from Canada.
28. Lieutenant-Colonel H. B. Livingston to General Lord Stirling, 11th June 1776.
29. Though Henry Beekman Livingston took no part in the Battle of Long Island two of his cousins did: namely, Henry G. Livingston, who was Brigade-major and aide-de-camp to Lord Stirling; and William S. Livingston, who acted in the same capacity to General Greene. See also Appendix A.
30. Force, *American Archives*, Fifth Series, vol. ii, p. 948.
31. General M'Dougall uses this contemptuous expression in a letter to General, soon to be Governor, George Clinton, dated 18 June 1777. *Public Papers of George Clinton*, vol. ii, p. 38.
32. When writing *The Livingstons of Callendar* (*vide* page 531 of that work), the author was under the impression that Colonel Livingston served under General M'Dougall at Germantown (3rd October 1777), whose brigade was then attached to the main army under Washington; but later researches have satisfied him that the statement in the text is the correct one.
33. On the 14th August 1777, General Putnam informs Governor Clinton, that he has "ordered Col. Courtland's and Col. Livingston's Regiments to march immediately to the Northward." *Public Papers of George Clinton*, vol. ii, p. 225.
34. General Gates to General Washington, 22 August 1777. *Correspondence of the American Revolution*, vol. i, p. 427.
35. Colonel Philip Van Cortlandt in his *Autobiography* (*Mag. Am. Hist.* May 1878), says Colonel Livingston arrived in camp two days before the battle of nineteenth September, and declares he disobeyed General Poor's orders on that day, which were to reinforce him (Cortlandt). But owing to the unfortunate feud between these officers, Colonel Van Cortlandt takes every opportunity he can in his *Autobiography* to belittle his rival. On the other hand, Colonel Varick, writing from the camp at Stillwater to General Schuyler, on the very evening of the battle says:— "At 3, Colonel Cook's regiment of militia was ordered out. At about 4, Colonel Courtland was ordered to support them, At 4 1/2, Colonel Livingston was ordered on the right of the enemy; both these soon fell in with and furiously attacked the enemy." In the same interesting letter he writes:—"Almost the whole of Arnold's division, except James Livingston's regiment, was engaged." Arnold's *Benedict Arnold at Saratoga*, p. 3.

THE WAR OF INDEPENDENCE | 277

36. Quotation from a letter dictated by General Arnold, when his wounds prevented him using the pen himself, and sent to Colonel H. B. Livingston. Chancellor Livingston quotes from it in a letter to General Washington, dated 14 January 1778. The chancellor's object was to obtain Washington's interest in favour of his brother. *Correspondence of the American Revolution*, vol. ii, pp. 550–553. Owing to the somewhat loose wording of Arnold's letter, his detractors have made use of it as an argument that he was not in command of the attacking force, nor "on the field," during the battle of the nineteenth of September; *vide* Bancroft's *History of the United States*, vol. x, p. 410. See also *Benedict Arnold at Saratoga* for full particulars of this controversy.
37. General Gates to Governor Clinton, Albany, 29 October 1777. *Correspondence of the American Revolution*, vol. ii, p. 546.
38. Not now to be found.
39. Governor Clinton to General Gates, New Windsor, 13 November 1777. *Public Papers of George Clinton*, vol. ii, p. 517.
40. See later on for an account of the destruction of these two private mansions by the British troops under General Vaughan, Sir Henry Clinton's second-in-command.
41. Public Papers of George Clinton, vol. ii, pp. 605, 606.
42. Dated Headquarters, English Town, 30 June 1778. *Army Correspondence of Colonel John Laurens*, 1777–1778, pp. 198, 199.
43. *Pennsylvania Packet* of 16th July 1778.
44. Public Papers of George Clinton, vol. iii, p. 508.
45. Namely Lieutenant-Colonel William Smith Livingston, a great-grandson of Robert "the Nephew," of whom more anon.
46. General Greene to General Washington, Camp Tiverton, 31 August 1778. Greene, *Life of Nathanael Greene*, vol. ii, pp. 130, 131.
47. General Sullivan to Congress, Headquarters, Camp Tiverton, 31 August 1778. As printed in Dawson's *Battles of the United States*, vol. i, p. 440.
48. *Journals of Congress*, vol. iv, p. 479; vol. v, p. 15.
49. *Autobiography of Philip Van Cortlandt* (*Mag. Am. Hist.*, vol. ii, pp. 288, 289). Jealousy of Colonel Van Cortandt may have had something to do with Colonel Livingston's resignation, in so far, that the latter officer objected to having to serve under the former. Chancellor Livingston in his letter of 14th January 1778 to Washington (already quoted from), mentions in it his brother's dispute with Colonel Van Cortlandt as to ranking, and explains he has endeavoured to prevail with his brother "to yield up that preference to which he conceived Colonel Cortlandt's seniority entitled him, though it may, in some measure, be superseded by the resolutions of Congress."
50. For some further particulars relating to Colonel Livingston's military career see Appendix A.
51. This similarity of their initialshas led to numerous mistakes. See under Appendix A. Henry Brockholst Livingston had graduated at Princeton College in 1774.
52. Duer, Life of Lord Stirling, pp. 124–126. Hatfield, History of Elisabeth, New Jersey, pp. 421–425.
53. Continental Congress, 29 January 1776. Force, *American Archives*, Fourth Series, vol. iv, p. 1658.
54. Force, *American Archives*, Fourth Series, vol. vi, pp. 415, 416.
55. Force, *American Archives*, Fifth Series, vol. ii, pp. 334, 1378. *Journals of Congress*, vol. ii, p. 366.

56. As Major Livingston was born on the 25th November 1757, he was not quite nineteen years of age at this date!

57. Namely, his military family or staff.

58. *Journals of Congress* (new edition, in course of publication), vol. viii, p. 665.

59. In a letter to General Schuyler written after this duel, and dated 26 September, 1777, Major Livingston refers to his antagonist as "an impertinent pedant" Arnold, *Life of Benedict Arnold*, p. 183.

60. Fought on the 19th September, 1777, and also known as the Battle of Freeman's Farm.

61. His colleague on Arnold's staff, Colonel Varick, in a letter to General Schuyler, written on the evening of this battle says, "In this action, Major Livingston being sent out with orders, remained a spectator till the close." Arnold, *Benedict Arnold at Saratoga*, p. 3.

62. *Journals of Congress* (new edition), vol. viii, p. 769.

63. Mr. Isaac N. Arnold in his *Life of Benedict Arnold* (pp. 178–185), as well as in his pamphlet *Benedict Arnold at Saratoga*, deals very fully with Major Livingston and Colonel Varick's defence of Arnold.

64. Fought on the 7th October 1777. On the 25th September, Colonel Varick writes to General Schuyler, "Livingston will go down to-morrow." *Life of Benedict Arnold*, p. 184.

65. It was this Colonel James Livingston who commanded the garrisons of Stony Point and Verplanck's Point, and cannonaded the *Vulture*, at the time of Arnold's treason in September, 1780, and not Colonel Henry Livingston as erroneously stated by Dr. Lossing in his *Field Book of the Revolution*. Cf. *Livingstons of Callendar*, p. 529, note 71.

66. Namely Lt.-Col. Richard Livingston and Captain Abraham Livingston.

67. Upon the 20th October 1775, the New York Provincial Congress issued the following commissions for field officers in the District of Manor Livingston, Tenth Albany Regiment: Peter R. Livingston, Colonel; Robert R. Livingston, junior, Lieutenant-Colonel; Henry Livingston, First Major. The colonel was the eldest surviving son of Robert, third Lord of the Manor, and the first major was his youngest son. Robert R. Livingston, junior, afterwards the chancellor, could not serve, so his cousin Henry was subsequently promoted to be lieutenant-colonel in his place. See also under Appendix A.

68. General James Wilkinson, *Memoirs of My Own Times*, vol. i, p. 299.

69. To the New York Council of Safety, Legislature, and General Washington, dated respectively 7th, 8th, and 9th October 1777. The forts were captured on the sixth. *Public Papers of George Clinton*, vol. ii, pp. 380–404.

70. He became a lieutenant in Colonel Lasher's Regiment of Militia, the New York Independents, in September 1775 and in June 1776 was elected by the Battalion to be their major. He served as aide-de-camp to General Greene on Long Island in August that year. In January 1777 his friend Colonel S. B. Webb, then raising an Additional Battalion of Connecticut Line, appointed him to be his lieutenant-colonel. This regiment was, at the time of the attack on Fort Montgomery, under General Putnam's command guarding the Hudson, but was not near enough to take part in the fighting. For authorities see under Appendix A. Mr. H. B. Dawson, usually a very careful writer on military subjects, in his *Battles of the United States* (vol. i, p. 338), commits the mistake of saying the Colonel Livingston at Fort Montgomery was Colonel Henry Livingston, who was, at that date, at Saratoga.

71. So Governor Clinton informs General Washington. *Public Papers of George Clinton*, vol. ii, p. 404.
72. According to Mr. Maturin L. Delafield in his account of Judge Smith's descendants in the *Magazine of American History*, vol. vi, p. 277. He says the name of "Fighting Bill" was "preserved in a doggerel erse of the period."
73. Ensign Leggett subsequently rose to the rank of major. His narrative is printed in Mr. Charles I. Bushnell's *Crumbs for Antiquarians*.
74. The Provincial Congress had sat in this room before the British occupation of the city.
75. In December 1777, William Ellery wrote from York, Pa., to General William Whipple:—"Col. Rollins, who was taken at Fort Washington; Lieut.-Col. Livingston, at Fort Montgomery; and Major Steward at Staten Island, lately made their escape from a gun-ship on which they had been but a few days confined." *Penn. Mag. Hist. Biog.*, vol. xxii, pp. 502, 503.
76. "Diary of Captain Andrew Lee" in *Penn. Mag. Hist. Biog.*, vol. iii, lc. 173.
77. Public Papers of George Clinton, vol. iii, pp. 90, 91, 311.
78. New York Journal, 14 September, 1778, vide Moore's Diary of the American Revolution, vol. ii, p. 89. American Historical Review, vol. v, pp. 719, 720.
79. Force, *American Archives*, Fifth Series, vol. i, p. 967.
80. Camp near Bristol Ferry, 29 August, 1778. Greene, *Life of Nathanael Greene*, vol. ii, p. 129.
81. Camp Tiverton, 31 August, 1778. *Ibid.*, vol. ii, p. 131.
82. Head Quarters on Butts Hill, Rhode Island, 30 August, 1778. *Mass. Hist. Coll.*, Seventh Series, vol. ii, pp. 261–263. Cf. *New York Journal* of 14th September, 1778.
83. *Correspondence and Journals of Samuel Blatchley Webb*, vol. i, p. 341; and vol. ii, p. 264. See also Appendix A for further particulars of Lt.-Col. William S. Livingston.
84. Washington's Writings, vol. vii, p. 139. Magazine of American History, vol. xxi, pp. 71–74. Cf. Livingstons of Callendar, p. 529, note 71.
85. So Colonel Livingston informed the Marquis de Chastellux on his visit in November this year.
86. *Magazine of American History*, vol. xxi, p. 74. Colonel Lamb was Washington's messenger.
87. Voyages de M. Le Marquis de Chastellux dans L'Amérique Septen trionale, tome i, p. 84.
88. This is exactly the same complaint Washington had made at Cambridge the year before, but it sounds stranger coming from General Livingston, who was far more democratic in his ideas than Washington ever was.
89. This nickname, owing to his inflexible impartiality, so stuck to him, that at a dinner in New York after the war, one of the guests "set the table in a roar" by addressing Governor Livingston inadvertently as "Dr. Flint."
90. Letter dated 28 December 1776, written a few days after "our little expedition to Trentown."
91. Letter dated 24 January 1777.
92. Sedgwick, *Life of William Livingston*, pp. 210, 211.
93. Mr. Maturin L. Delafield, *Descendants of Judge William and Mary Smith* (*Mag. Am. Hist.*, vol. vi, p. 277). An anonymous correspondent in same magazine says the name of this good Samaritan was Mistress Beckie Coxe.
94. Governor Livingston to General Washington, 5th April 1777. Sedgwick, *Life of William Livingston*, p. 230.

95. The commander of a refugee corps, whose name became a by-word during the war.
96. Livingston was re-elected every year to this post, until his death in 1790. The author of this work, has in his possession Governor Livingston's autograph acceptance of his last re-election, dated 2d November, 1789.
97. Mrs. Livingston and some of her daughters, however, were residing in the house at the time, and received polite treatment from the British officers. An account of this raid will be found in Chapter XVIII.
98. Sir Henry Clinton wrote: "Had I a soul capable of harbouring so infamous an idea as assassination, you, sir, at least, would have nothing to fear; for, be assured I should not blacken myself with so foul a crime to obtain so trifling an end."
99. Lieutenant-General Knyphausen commanded the German troops in New York, and during Sir Henry Clinton's absence, as upon this occasion, acted as commander-in-chief. A month after the issuing of this order, General Knyphausen himself invaded New Jersey, and a part of his force passed through Elizabethtown. An account of their visit to Liberty Hall will be found in a later chapter.
100. Letter dated New Windsor, 8th April, 1781.
101. "John" is a mistake, should be "James."
102. The words printed in italics and capitals are so printed in the original.
103. Namely Governor Livingston's paper the *New Jersey Gazette*.
104. Quotations from the original letters lent the author by the late Mr. Van Brugh Livingston of New York.
105. Robert Livingston to Peter V. B. Livingston, Manor Livingston, 4 April 1780.
106. Robert Livingston to Peter V. B. Livingston, Manor Livingston, 13 December, 1780.
107. Robert Livingston to Peter V. B. Livingston, Manor Livingston, 5 June, 1781.
108. It must be borne in mind, however, that Continental currency was so depreciated at this date that it became a byword "not worth a continental!" All the same the taxes were crushing!
109. The Van Rensselaers.
110. Chancellor Livingston to Governor Clinton, Clermont, 23 September, 1778. *Public Papers of George Clinton*, vol. iv, pp. 75, 76.
111. John R. Livingston to Chancellor Livingston, Clermont, 12 August, 1777. *Journals of Provincial Congress*, vol. i, p. 1039.
112. Robert Livingston to Peter V. B. Livingston, Manor Livingston, 4th September 1781. In this letter the writer mentions "the return of his neighbour Mr. David Abeel from Canada with 120 others on parole, he having been taken with his son and two negroes this spring out of his house, not 3 miles distance from me."
113. Dated from Camp, February 1st, 1780. *Public Papers of George Clinton*, vol. v, pp. 478–480.
114. Sir Henry Clinton, then commanding the British forces in New York.
115. Duer (W. A.), *Life of Lord Stirling*, pp. 200–204. These were Lady Stirling's only children. The youngest daughter married during the following summer, Colonel William Duer, a meipber of the New York Convention, etc., who had in his youth been an ensign in the British army, and had served under Lord Clive in India.
116. This lady was a sister of Chief-Justice William Smith.
117. Peter R. was born 3 October 1766, and graduated at Princeton College in 1784. Maturin was born 10 April 1769, and graduated with the highest honours in 1786. Maturin L. Delafield, *Descendants of Judge William and Mary Smith*.
118. These lads, when they grew up, amply fulfilled their elder brother's forecast. Peter R. became a member of the New York Senate, Speaker, and finally President of

the same, besides filling other official positions; while Maturin became a Judge of the Court of Common Pleas in the same State. Both were well-known members of New York society in their day. Peter R. married Joanna, a daughter of Judge Robert R. Livingston of Clermont; while Maturin married Margaret Lewis, a granddaughter of Judge Livingston.

119. Her father was Judge William Smith.

120. President of Princeton College, and one of the signers of the Declaration of Independence.

121. Public Papers of George Clinton, vol. vi, pp. 680–683.

122. The *Royal Gazette* in retaliation was dubbed "Jemmy Rivington's royal, loyal, lying Gazette."

123. Robert R. Livingston to John Jay, New York, 29th November, 1783.

124. The other delegates elected upon this occasion were: General Philip Schuyler, James Duane, William Duer, and Gouverneur Morris.

125. Prior to the dispersal of the Legislature it had appointed, upon the 3d of October, five delegates to represent the State in the General Congress; of these, four, including Philip Livingston, had served in the provincial delegation elected on the preceding 13th of May; while Philip Schuyler was temporarily replaced by Francis Lewis.

126. *Journals of Provincial Congress*, vol. i, pp. 918, 919.

127. Said to have been a relative of Mrs. Livingston's son-in-law, the late General Montgomery.

128. Mrs. Delafield, in her account of the destruction of Clermont, says Edward, the youngest, was the only one of the sons then with his mother. The chancellor, in his letter to the Council of Safety, quoted from later on, would certainly seem to corroborate this view.

129. Mrs. Delafield also differs from Mr. Clarkson in her account of this incident, for she says it was Gertrude, afterwards Mrs. Lewis, who laughed as she looked out of the back window of the family coach as they drove off, and saw an overgrown negress rolling helplessly from side to side perched on the top of a feather bed; and that her mother turned to her and said, "Oh, Gertrude, can you laugh now!" Mrs. Delafield declares hers is the correct version, and it certainly sounds the more probable one. *Biographies of Francis and Morgan Lewis*, vol. i, p. 151.

130. For some further references to "Clermont" see Chapter XVIII.

131. Chancellor Livingston to the Honble. Pierre Van Cortlandt, Salisbury, 28 October, 1777.

132. A commission as lieutenant-colonel of the Manor of Livingston Militia had been conferred on him by the Provincial Congress on the 20th October 1775.

133. This monument bears the following inscription:—

Sacred
To the memory of the Honble.
Philip Livingston
who died June 12th, 1778,
aged 63 years,
while attending the Congress
of the United States at York
Pa. as a Delegate from the
State of New York.
Eminently distinguished for

his talents and rectitude, he
deservedly enjoyed the confidence
of his country and the
love and veneration of his
friends and children.

134. The loyalist newspaper—*The Pennsylvania Ledger*—considered the writer was Henry Brockholst Livingston, the son of the "usurped" governor of New Jersey, who was then at Saratoga. But the letter is signed "Henry P. Livingston" clear enough, and was intended for *his* father—Philip Livingston. The editor of the volume, *New Jersey Archives*, Second Series, vol. i, p. 484, in which it is reproduced, also commits the same error.

135. This letter was republished by the *New York Gazette and Weekly Mercury* of 10th November, 1777.

136. For a full account of the proceedings connected with this Bill of Attainder, see Judge Jones's *History of New York during the Revolutionary War*, and the editor's article upon the same. *Cf.* also Street's *Council of Revision of the State of New York*.

137. The names of these five just men deserve preserving; they are Richard Morris, Isaac Roosevelt, William Smith of Suffolk, Isaac Stouten-burgh, and Abraham Yates, junior.

138. The council was abolished by the Constitution of 1821.

139. By Mr. De Lancey in his article in Judge Jones's *History of New York*.

140. *Ibid.*

141. Letter dated 6th May, 1780.

142. From Judge William Jay's comments on the above letter in his *Life of John Jay*, vol. i, p. 113.

143. Minister to France.

144. Minister to Holland.

145. Mr. Francis Dana had been recently appointed by Congress their minister to the court at St. Petersburg, but the Empress Catherine flatly declined to recognise the revolutionary envoy. He had left Amsterdam for St. Petersburg during the summer of 1781. Secretary Livingston had nothing to do with this appointment, and finding he was not wanted in St. Petersburg advised Congress to have him recalled.

146. Minister to Spain.

147. Of course Continental currency is meant here.

148. Chairman of the Committee for Foreign Affairs.

149. These two articles related to the Loyalists or "Tories."

150. The Provisional Articles of Peace, nine in number, had been signed at Paris by the English and American Commissioners, on the 30th November 1782. The secret article was signed separately, and related to the boundary to be fixed between West Florida and the United States "in case Great Britain, at the conclusion of the present war, shall recover or be put in possession of the same." It was then held by Spain.

151. This reference was to John Jay, who subsequently wrote to his friend from Paris, on the 19th July 1783, explaining the reasons of the American Cmmissioners for keeping this article a secret from the French Court. The American Commissioners were, John Adams, Benjamin Franklin, John Jay, and Henry Laurens.

152. Secretary Livingston to the American Commissioners, Philadelphia, 25th March, 1783.

153. John Adams to Robert R. Livingston, Passy, 9 July, 1783.

154. The American Commissioners to Secretary Livingston, Passy, 18 July, 1783.

155. A facsimile of this circular, from the original addressed to the Governor of Georgia, now in the possession of Mr. John Henry Livingston of Clermont, faces this page.
156. Sir Guy Carleton, afterwards Lord Dorchester, richly deserved this compliment. He was, without exception, the most humane commander on the British side during the war.
157. John Jay to Robert R. Livingston, Passy, 12th September, 1783.

CHAPTER XIV

CONCERNING THE POLITICAL HISTORY OF THE LIVINGSTON FAMILY FROM THE EVACUATION OF NEW YORK BY THE BRITISH, UNTIL THE ELECTION OF THOMAS JEFFERSON AS THIRD PRESIDENT OF THE UNITED STATES OF AMERICA.

"Party divisions, whether on the whole operating for good or evil, are inseparable from free government."

—*Edmund Burke.*

THE departure of the last redcoat from New York, and the dismissal of the American soldiers to their homes, did not end the labours of the Revolutionary statesmen. Rather these events only accentuated their difficulties, as it is a well-known axiom that it is easier to destroy than to rebuild. Two great dangers the wisest of these men foresaw had to be surmounted; the one that, now the outside pressure had been removed, the various states would fly apart and become each an independent republic; and the other, that, should a federal republic be established, it would become too democratic.

The leaders of the Federalists, including such men as Hamilton, Madison, John Jay, and Chancellor Livingston, certainly were not believers in the *vox populi* doctrine,[1] a doctrine which often results in a popular leader being torn to pieces one day, to have his virtues acclaimed by his destroyers the next. Few statesmen would care to acquire such posthumous glory!

Even Governor Livingston, good democrat as he was, and who had in the past preached from the text "Touch not mine anointed," to the effect that these words referred to the people and not to their rulers; began to discover, now his country had become independent, that these "Lord's anointed" could show the cloven hoof, as well as the worst of those "devils" of red-coated monarchists who had so recently been driven back to Old England.[2] For three years had not elapsed since the departure of the British troops, when the effigy of the aged governor was carried through the streets of Elizabethtown, and drawn up to a stake for burning,[3] by those very patriots for whom he had suffered so much during the late war. Because, forsooth, he had dared to vote against the popular demand for a large emission of paper money!

No wonder he gave vent to his feelings, after the emission had become legalised, in an article contributed by him to the *New Jersey Gazette*.[4] In this article, he remarks on what "I Have Seen and I Have not Seen": and says, among other things,

> I have seen our soldiers marching barefoot through snow and over ice: I have *not* seen them duly recompensed for it; nor America so grateful for such the inexpressible hardships they suffered, as I thought she would have been. I have seen Congress recommending to the several States such salutary measures as would have been of infinite benefit to the Union to have adopted; I have *not* seen the States adopt these measures. I have seen justices of the peace, who were a burlesque upon all magistracy. Justices illiterate, justices partial, justices groggy, justices courting popularity to be chosen assemblymen, and justices encouraging litigiousness. But I have *not* seen any joint-meeting sufficiently cautious against appointing such justices of the peace. I have seen paper money emitted by a Legislature that solemnly promised to redeem it, that afterwards depreciated it themselves—and I therefore believe that I shall never see the honest redemption of it. I have seen Assemblies enacting laws amending the practice in the court of justice, but I have *not* seen that practice really amended by them. I have seen, since our revolution, Tories promoted to offices of trust and profit, to the exclusion of Whigs; but I have never seen the man who dared to avow either the propriety or the justice of such promotion. I have seen hundreds paying their debts with Continental money at the

depreciated rate of above sixty to one; but how many have I seen that had too much integrity to avail themselves of the subterfuge for dishonesty which the law unintentionally afforded them; and instead of infringing the golden rule, though protected by the chicanery of human edicts to sin against it, nobly disdained to violate the dictates of their consciences, and against light, and knowledge, and gospel, to defraud their neighbour of his due! How many? Not enough to constitute a legal jury.

Though the governor and his council had to yield to the pressure brought to bear upon them, the former had hopes that the emission of this paper currency would be kept within reasonable limits. But "No Acts of Assembly," he declared, "have hitherto been able to reconcile him to cheating according to law, or convinced him that human legislators can alter the immutable duties of morality." He also amusingly ridiculed the acts of the "silver men" of his day in the following lines:

> For useless a house-door, e'en if we should lock it,
>   When an insolvent legislative brother
> Can legally enter into a man's pocket,
>   And preamble all his cash into another.

As Governor Livingston never took advantage of this "new way of paying old debts," it is not surprising that he died a poor man; and that his last years were embittered by the idea, that he might he unable to leave sufficient even to keep a roof over his widow's head.[5]

The city of New York was evacuated by the British troops on the 25th November, 1783', and exactly two months later, Chancellor Livingston writes John Jay a letter[6] in which he describes the state of the local political parties as follows:

> The quiet, which in my last[7] I mentioned to have prevailed here, still continues with very few interruptions, though the imprudence of the Tories has, in some instances, given disgust to the warm Whigs. . . . Our parties are, first, the Tories, who still hope for power, under the idea that the remembrance of the past should be lost, though they daily keep it up by their avowed attachment to Great Britain. Secondly, the violent Whigs, who are for expelling all Tories from the State, in hopes, by that means, to preserve the power in their own hands. The third are

those who wish to suppress all violences, to soften the rigour of the laws against the royalists, and not to banish them from that social intercourse which may, by degrees, obliterate the remembrance of past misdeeds; but who, at the same time, are not willing to shock the feelings of the virtuous citizens, that have at every expense and hazard fulfilled their duty, by at once destroying all distinction between them and the royalists, and giving the reins into the hands of the latter; but who, at the same time, wish that this distinction should be rather found in the sentiments of the people, than marked out by the laws. You will judge to which of these parties the disqualifications contained in our election bills has given the representation, when I tell you that the members for this city and county are Lamb, Harper, Sears, Van Zandt, Mallone, Rutgers, Hughes, Stag, and Willet. I must, however, do all parties the justice to say, that they profess the highest respect for the laws, and that, if we except one or two persons, they have as yet, by no act contradicted that profession.

A few days later, Governor Livingston, who was now enabled to return to his home near Elizabethtown, thus amusingly describes his impressions of this place after his long and enforced absence, in a letter to his friend Dr. John Beatty: "Solitary indeed is Queen Elizabeth's namesake to me at present, when instead of my quondam agreeable companions, the village now principally consists of unknown, unrecommended strangers, guilty-looking tones, and very knavish whigs."[8] Perhaps some of these "very knavish whigs" represented those patriotic gentry, who had carried on during the war, such a flourishing and lucrative contraband trade with the British in New York, in despite of all the exertions of Governor Livingston to stamp it out. It was this class of "patriot," which had led the governor, in the autumn of 1779, to sarcastically complain to President Huntington, that "Our Patriotism is as much depreciated as our currency."[9]

On the 24th of July, 1784, John Jay landed at New York on his return from Europe, and the chancellor wrote from Clermont to welcome him home:

Permit me, my dear friend [he wrote], to congratulate you on your return to your native shore, and to the friendly embraces of those who love you in every situation in which you have been or can be placed. My impatience to see you led me to New York about three weeks since, where, from the time you had set for sailing, I had thought it probable that you must have arrived before this. An unfortunate accident which has happened to my eldest daughter, who a few days ago broke her arm, obliges me to send you these cold expressions of my friendship, rather than comply with my wishes in offering them and receiving yours in person. Having, as I hope, concluded my political career, I have no other wish left but that of spending the remainder of my life with those who have contributed so much to the happiness of its gayest period. Whether you entertain the same moderate wishes, whether you content yourself with the politics of this State, or whether you will engage in the great field that Congress have opened again to you, I shall still have the consolation to reflect that seas do not roll between us, that I may sometimes see you, and frequently hear from you. If you are not cured of your ambition, you have every thing to hope for, both in the State and Continental line. I need not tell you that I only wish to know your objects that I may concur in them.[10]

From the tone of this letter it would appear Mr. Livingston at this date had taken a distaste to public life, probably owing to the ascendency in his State of the second political party mentioned in his previous letter, as well as to his real love of a country life. But this did not last for long, as before the close of the year, he had been sent by the State Legislature, for the fourth time, as a delegate to Congress, while he still retained the chancellorship for several years to come. The reference to the "great field" opened by Congress to his old friend, was the latter's election by that body, on the previous seventh of May, when Congress had been informed of his approaching return, to fill the office of Secretary of Foreign Affairs left vacant by Livingston's final resignation eleven months before. Thus, Congress, after innumerable delays, had decided upon one of the two persons named to them by the retiring secretary, as being most suitable for the office: the other person mentioned— Jefferson—having declined the nomination. Mr. Jay held this post, the most important office under the Confederation, until the establishment of the Federal government in 1789.

The chancellor took his seat in Congress on the seventh of December, 1784, and at once resumed the prominent position he had always held when a member of that assembly. On the 31st of January, 1785, we find him proposing the appointment of a minister plenipotentiary "to represent the United States of America at the court of Great Britain," in which he was seconded by Mr. Pinckney, and John Adams was a few weeks later selected by Congress to fill this office. Mr. Livingston was also employed at this time, as one of the New York agents on the Boundary Commission, appointed to settle the old standing dispute between that State and Massachusetts. His colleagues were James Duane, John Jay, Egbert Benson, and his kinsman Walter Livingston of the Manor.

The source of this friction between these two States dated back to the middle of the century, when Robert third of the Manor, nearly immediately after his succession to the estate, found himself involved in serious disputes with squatters, who crossing the border line separating Massachusetts from New York coolly settled on his land. These squatters refusing to pay rent or to be ejected, the matter Digitized by at last assumed such a dangerous phase, that the Lord of the Manor had to petition Governor Clinton[11] for protection from these unpleasant land-grabbers. This petition having been read in Council on the 4th of May, 1752, was submitted to the Attorney-General, as well as to the Surveyor-General of the province, for their opinions as to what was most expedient to be done in the matter. The former expressed the opinion, that the lands mentioned properly belonged to the petitioner, and that they were "lands claimed as part of this Province of New York," and that a representation in accordance with the true facts of the case, should be laid before the "Government of his Majesty's Province of Massachusetts Bay," but that meanwhile no forcible means should be used against the offenders. Mr. Cadwallader Colden, the Surveyor-General, reported that he was also of the opinion that the lands claimed by the Massachusetts government, on behalf of these squatters, really belonged to the Manor, and were evidently within the boundaries of the Province of New York.

In consequence of these opinions, the New York government had the matter brought under the notice of the General Court of the neighbouring colony, and a committee was appointed to confer with commissioners to be appointed by Massachusetts, "to agree upon measures for settling the bounds of the two provinces in an amicable manner." Unfortunately this arrangement did not settle the dispute, for before these commissioners had been appointed, matters had assumed a more serious aspect, owing to one William Bull and others, including some of Livingston's tenants, having petitioned the General Court of Massachusetts for a grant of a tract of land which lay within the Manor boundaries. Instead of telling these petitioners to wait until the joint commission had decided as to the boundaries of the two provinces; the General Court hastened to appoint a special committee of their own, to make a full enquiry into the ownership of the said tract of land, without communicating with the government of New York, which was in direct contradiction to the agreement as to the appointment of a joint commission.

By the Honourable
JAMES DE LANCEY, Esq;
His Majesty's Lieutenant-Governor and Commander in Chief, in and
over the Province of New-York, and the Territories depending thereon
in America.

A Proclamation.

WHEREAS it appears, That certain Persons residing on or near the Eastern Borders of this Province, have entered into a Combination to dispossess *Robert Living Ston*, jun. Esq; Proprietor of the *Manor of Living Ston*, within this Province, and the Tenants holding under him, of the Lands comprised within the said Manor, under Pretence of Title from the Government of the *Massachusetts Bay*, as also of an Indian Purchase lately made by the said Persons; altho' 'tis most notorious that the said Manor hath, 'til very lately been peaceably held and enjoyed by the said *Robert Living Ston*, and His Ancestors for Seventy Years last past. And ...... the said Government can legally ... their Claim. Notwithstanding which clear and manifest Right on the Part of this Government, the said Persons, not content with their former Intrusions on His Majesty's Lands within the same, first began to carry their Designs into Execution, by endeavouring to corrupt and turn Mr. *Living Ston's* own Tenants against him, in which they so far succeeded, that several Persons, who 'til within a few Years held Lands as Tenants under ... and paid their Rents to him, now keep Possession of the Lands in Defiance of, and set up a pretended Right against him, under the Government of the *Massachusetts Bay*, and the aforementioned Indian Purchase; by which illegal Proceedings, supported with force, the Course of Justice hath been obstructed, the Lives of several of his Majesty's Subjects lost, and private Property ... and greatly injured. And Whereas Thirty One of such evil minded Persons, in order to prosecute their unjust Designs, in the 7th Day of *May* last, armed and riotously assembled themselves at *Taghonuk*, at the House of *Jonathan Darby*, which ... the Distance of not more than Eighteen Miles from *Hudson's River*, among whom were the said *Jonathan Darby*, also *Johannes Rese, Hendrick Brush, Joseph Pangelder*, and his Brother, said to be *Andries Pangelder, Samuel Taylor, Ebenezer Taylor*, and *Andries J. Rese*; and being to riotously assembled, were commanded to disperse by the Deputy Sheriff of the County, in the presence of one of His Majesty's Justices of the Peace, two Constables, and other Persons who came thither with the said *Robert Living Ston*, to suppress the Riot, and disperse the Rioters; four only of whom went off, the others shutting themselves up in the said *Darby's* House, in which there were Loop Holes, fired through the same, and before they dispersed, several were wounded on both Sides, one of whom died in about an Hour thereafter, and another ... some Time after, of the Wounds they then received. IN Order therefore to put a Stop as much as may be to Proceedings, the Consequences whereof have already been fatal to some, and which if not timely prevented, may still be productive of the worst Evils to ... ; and to establish and keep up Peace and a good Understanding among the Borderers, till this unhappy Controversy shall be decided in a legal Course: I HAVE thought fit, with the Advice of His Majesty's Council, to issue this Proclamation, Hereby in His Majesty's Name, strictly enjoining all His Majesty's good Subjects in this Province, to forbear and refrain from such violent and unjust Proceedings, as every Instance of that Nature will be punished with the utmost Rigour of the Law. AND that the Offenders before named may be brought to Justice, the Sheriffs of the Counties of *Albany* and *Dutchess*, and all other Officers therein, are hereby commanded and required to apprehend the said *Jonathan Darby, Johannes Rese, Hendrick Brush, Joseph Pangelder, Samuel Taylor, Ebenezer Taylor*, and *Andries J. Rese*, and all and every of their Associates, who shall appear to have been aiding or abetting in the said Offenders in the Riot aforesaid; and them and every of them to keep, or cause to be committed, in safe Custody, in the County Goal, until delivered by due Course of Law: And in like Manner, to apprehend and keep in safe Custody all and every other Person and Persons who shall hereafter be guilty of the riotous and illegal Practices, And all His Majesty's Subjects in the said Counties of *Albany* and *Dutchess*, are to give due Assistance to the said Sheriffs within their respective Counties, who are hereby empowered and required, if necessary, to summon the Posse, or whole Power of the County, for putting the Premises in Execution.

GIVEN under my Hand and Seal at Arms, at Fort-George, in the City of New-York, the Eighth Day of June, One Thousand Seven Hundred and Fifty Seven, in the Thirtieth Year of the Reign of our Sovereign Lord GEORGE the Second, by the Grace of GOD, of Great-Britain, France and Ireland, King, Defender of the Faith, and so forth.

By His Honour's Command,
Gw. Banyer, Dep. Secry.

JAMES DE LANCEY.

GOD Save the KING.

REDUCED FACSIMILE OF BROADSIDE PROCLAMATION WARNING RIOTERS OFF THE MANOR OF

Though this committee had no proper authority for deciding the point at issue, Robert Livingston thought he might help to an amicable arrangement of the dispute by appearing before them, when summoned to show proof of his claim to the lands in question, instead of refusing to acknowledge their right to interfere in the matter, as he was perfectly entitled to have done; and he pointed out to the Massachusetts Commissioners that he not only held the Manor lands through purchase from the original native owners, but that his title to the same had been ratified by patents under the crown granted by former governors of New York. This Committee of Inquiry, however, did not consider these facts sufficient proof of title, and flatly denied the right of New York to grant the lands in dispute. This strange behaviour of the Massachusetts commissioners led to a vigorous remonstrance being addressed to their government by Governor Clinton, who wrote that "it cannot with any appearance of reason be imagined that this Government will tamely suffer yours to go on in settling the lands claimed on both sides, but, on the contrary, it behooves us to take every measure and expedient to prevent so extraordinary a proceeding." And, as the interference of this committee had encouraged these claimants, and some malcontents among the Manor tenants, to resist Mr. Livingston's agents when sent to regain possession of the disputed lands, which had led to rioting, and, ultimately to loss of life, Governor Clinton issued a proclamation commanding the sheriffs of the counties of Albany and Dutchess to assist the proprietor of the Manor in having the rioters apprehended.[12]

Mr. Livingston, thereupon, lost no time in taking proceedings against the leading rioters; and in consequence for several months his life was in great danger, for these rough New England squatters would have had not the slightest compunction in shooting the unpopular Lord of the Manor, if they had got the chance. As it was, on one occasion, he only escaped by the receipt of timely warning from his relative and neighbour, Mr. Van Rensselaer of Claverack, who sent him a hurried note begging him to be on his guard, as he had been credibly informed that the New England people intended to carry him off either "dead or alive."[13] While on another, some three years later, one Nicholas Koens travelled twenty miles to advise him to keep good watch, as some of the malcontents had secured the services of the Stockbridge Indians for the purpose of murdering him, and burning his house over his head; so that the New-York government had to send a military force to keep guard over the Manor and iron works.[14]

These unfortunate disputes regarding the unsettled boundary line caused Robert, the third proprietor, infinite trouble and expense; and even the last and final struggle between the English and French during the Seven Years' War, did not cause any abatement in the rioting on the Manor; for on the 30th July, 1757, De Lancey wrote to the Lords of Trade, deploring the continual strife occasioned by these disputes, when the united energies of the English colonies in North America were required for the conquest of Canada. It would, however, be a tedious as well as an unprofitable task, to relate here all the various incidents in this long and wearisome contest between the Lord of the Manor and these unwelcome intruders on his lands, which, even as late as the summer of 1766, gave rise to the issuing of another proclamation by Governor Moore of New York, for the arrest of one Robert Noble and other rioters and disorderly persons on Livingston Manor. The outbreak of the War of Independence interfered with an arrangement, agreed to by these colonies in 1773, regarding the running of a proper boundary line; and thus, one of the first duties that fell to the Confederation, after peace was concluded with Great Britain, was the settlement of a question, which had even during the late war, been a cause of constant and bitter quarrels between New Yorkers and New Englanders. The boundary line finally decided upon by the commissioners appointed by Congress, somewhat reduced the immense acreage of the Manor as contained in the patent of 1715; yet the proprietor could not have been entirely a loser by the running of this line, owing to its settlement of this long outstanding dispute, and thus leaving him in peaceful possession of the rest of the Manor lands.[15]

On the sixteenth of March, 1785, Congress voted Chancellor Livingston the sum of fifteen hundred dollars, "the amount of the extra expenses beyond his salary for the last six months he continued in office as Secretary of Foreign Affairs." It was during this month that the Council of Revision, of which, as chancellor, Robert R. Livingston was still the principal member, vetoed an act passed by the New York Legislature in the spring of this year, "for the gradual abolition of slavery within this State." It seems strangely inconsistent, that Chancellor Livingston, who like his cousin Governor Livingston was in favour of the abolition of slavery within the confederated states, and even was a member of an abolition and manumission society, of which Alexander Hamilton was secretary, and Jay and Duane were also associates, should agree to veto such an act. But the Council of Revision's objections to this bill, as ably reported to the New York Legislature on the 21st of March, 1785, were, however, thoroughly sound and legitimate ones, and a strong protest against denying to one class of citizens, solely on account of their colour, rights that all should share in common. This bill, right enough in principle, contained one clause, which practically cancelled all the benefits it claimed to confer on a despised race. This clause read as follows:

> And be it further enacted by the authority aforesaid, that all negroes and those of any description whatsoever, commonly reported and deemed slaves, shall forever hereafter have the privilege of being tried by a jury, in all capital cases, according to the course of the common law; *and be it further enacted by the authority aforesaid, that no Negro, Mulatto, or Mustee shall have a legal vote in any case whatsoever.*

Though accustomed to the ownership of household slaves themselves, the leaders of the Livingston family did not share the views of those members of the Continental Congress, who objected to Jefferson's clause in the original draft of the Declaration of Independence rightly condemning the iniquitous slave trade, and who succeeded in getting it cancelled in committee. The clause, as it stood, was another highly coloured denunciation of that unlucky monarch, George the Third, though, as the Americans, particularly the planters in the southern colonies so largely profited by this diabolical traffic, it was hardly justice to assign *all the blame* to Great Britain![16] Even during the war, and while occupied by far more pressing matters, Governor Livingston,—who fully recognised the glaring anomaly created by a Declaration of Independence, which, in spite of its noble platitudes concerning the Rights of Man, had no word to say in condemnation of the laws which retained in slavery thousands of Americans because they happened to be of another colour,—had found time to send a message to the New Jersey Legislature, during a session held in the year 1777, in which he recommended a scheme for the gradual manumission of the negroes. This message, however, he was asked to withdraw, as that assembly did not think they could deal with this question at such a critical time. "But," as he wrote to a Quaker correspondent a few months later, "I am determined, as far as my influence extends, to push the matter till it is effected, being convinced that the practice is utterly inconsistent with the principles of Christianity and humanity, and in Americans, who have almost idolised liberty, particularly odious and disgraceful."[17]

Some years later, when this great question, as we have seen above, began to be seriously discussed in the Northern States, Governor Livingston expressed his ardent wish to become a member of the New York manumission society to which his cousin the chancellor belonged. In the letter, in which he expresses this wish, dated Elizabethtown, 26th June, 1786, he wrote:

> If elected I can safely promise that neither my tongue, nor my pen, nor purse shall be wanting to promote the abolition of what to me appears so inconsistent with humanity and Christianity, and so inevitably perpetuating of an indelible blot, with all the nations of Europe, upon the character of those who have so strongly asserted the unalienable rights of mankind, and whose conflict in the defence of those rights it has pleased Providence to crown with such signal and (to all human experience) triumphant success. May the great and equal Father of the human race, who has expressly declared his abhorrence of oppression, and that he is no respecter of persons, succeed in a design so laudably calculated to undo the heavy burdens, to let the oppressed go free, and to break every yoke.

Governor Livingston was as good as his word, for during the same year he got the New Jersey Legislature to pass an act to prevent the importation of slaves into that State; and a few month later, "in consideration," as the manumission document reads, "of my regard for the natural liberties of mankind, and in order to set the example, as far as my voluntary manumission of slaves may have any influence on others," he emancipated the only two slaves he had, and made a resolution never to own another.

The cousins also shared the same strong views regarding the folly of flooding the States with a depreciated paper currency. According to the historian of the formation of the Constitution:[18]

> New York successfully extricated itself from the confusion of Continental and State paper money, but in April of the fatal year 1786,[19] its Legislature, after long debates, made remarkable by the remonstrances of Duer, voted to emit two hundred thousand pounds in bills of credit. The money so emitted was receivable for duties, and was made a legal tender in all suits. In the Council of Revision, the Chancellor set forth that a scarcity of money can be remedied only by industry and economy, not by laws that foster idleness and dissipation; that the bill, under the appearance of relief, would add to the distress of the debtor;

that it at the same time solicited and destroyed credit; that it would cause the taxes and debts of the State to the United States to be paid in paper. Hobart, one of the justices, reported that it would prove an unwarrantable interference in private contracts, and to this objection Livingston gave his adhesion. Morris, the Chief Justice, objected to receiving the bills in the custom-house treasury as money, and held that the enactment would be working iniquity by the aid of law; but a veto was not agreed upon.[20]

The year previously, on the 23rd June 1785, to be exact, upon the nomination of Mr. Stewart, one of the New Jersey delegates in Congress, Governor Livingston had been elected by that body to succeed Mr. Adams as Minister Plenipotentiary at the Hague, in opposition to Benjamin Harrison and Edward Rutledge, whose names had also been put forward for this post. Governor Livingston was naturally highly gratified by this proof of the confidence that the confederated states had in his patriotism and abilities, and as he was proficient in the Dutch language, and had friends in that country, his appointment was a very judicious one. But advancing age and his reluctance to leave New Jersey, whose people had placed so much confidence in him, led Mr. Livingston to decline the mission. Mr. Stewart afterwards informed him that he had proposed his nomination for this post, because he had thought him "chalked out by God Almighty as the most proper person to be their minister at the Hague," and without any design to compliment or flatter him.

His years were no doubt numbered, but he lived long enough to witness the triumph of the Federalists, with whose views regarding the formation of a constitution for the United States, to replace the unworkable confederation then in existence, he was in cordial agreement. In this matter the governor certainly differed from the great majority of the people of his State, who were very jealous of parting with any of their cherished rights of government to a central authority. There is no need here to dwell on the well-fought battle between the Federalists and Anti-Federalists in the drafting of the new constitution. The result was a compromise, the larger and more populous States gaining in one branch of the new legislature (the House of Representatives), while in the other branch (the Senate), all the States were placed on an equality. The new constitution finally agreed upon by the majority in the Convention of 1787, also put such checks upon the powers of the lower house, that no legislation of a revolutionary nature could become law without an alteration in the constitution. Hamilton would have gone further, if he had had his way, because he sincerely dreaded the power of the mob. Certainly none of the framers of this constitution carried the "Rights of Man" doctrine to extreme lengths. That was good enough for the Declaration of Independence, but practical politics required safeguards! Even such an ardent patriot as John Jay was fond of saying, that "from Absalom down there had never been an honest demagogue," and he was not alone in this opinion.

Governor Livingston attended this famous Convention as one of the delegates from New Jersey[21]; but owing to his official duties he was unable to take his seat as one of its members, until the fifth of June. According to Mr. Madison, who was the principal personage there, "Mr. Livingston did not take his seat in the Convention till some progress had been made in the task committed to it, and he did not take any active part in the debates; but he was placed on important committees, where it may be presumed he had an agency, and a due influence. He was personally unknown to many, perhaps most of the members, but there was predisposition in all to manifest the respect due to the celebrity of his name. The votes of New Jersey corresponded generally with the plan offered by Mr. Paterson,[22] but the main object of that being to secure to the smaller States an equality with the larger in the structure of the government, in opposition to the outline previously introduced, which had a reversed object, it is difficult to say what was the degree of power to which there might be an abstract leaning. The two subjects, the structure of the government, and the quantum of power for it, were more or less inseparable in the minds of all, as depending a good deal the one on the other. After the compromise which gave the small States an inequality in one branch of the Legislature, and the large States an inequality in the other branch, the abstract leaning of opinions would better appear. With those, however, who did not enter into debate, and whose votes could not be distinguished from those of their State colleagues,[23] their opinions could only be known among themselves or their particular friends."[24]

It was upon the 17th of September, 1787, that, "the engrossed Constitution being read, it was moved that the Constitution be signed by the members"; whereupon thirty-nine of the delegates present, including Governor Livingston, subscribed their names to this historical document.[25] But the battle was not nearly over; the bitterest and hardest fighting had yet to come, as this draft Constitution required the ratification of the conventions of nine States for its legal establishment as the Government of the

United States of America, in the place of the now decrepit confederacy. The fiercest battle-ground was in the State of New York; but though the Federalists here had the governor— George Clinton—and a majority of the people against them, they were fortunate in having three such notable champions as Alexander Hamilton, John Jay, and Robert R. Livingston for leaders, who were worth a host in themselves, and who, after a gallant fight, were victorious by the narrowest of majorities.

The New York Convention, summoned to decide as to the acceptance or rejection of the new Constitution, met at Poughkeepsie on the 17th June 1788. The number of delegates was sixty-seven, and of these three were members of the Livingston family: Chancellor Livingston from the city of New York; Philip Livingston[26] from the county of Westchester; and Gilbert Livingston from the county of Dutchess. The two former were warm Federalists, but Gilbert Livingston was sent to the Convention as an Anti-Federalist, though he finally voted in favour of ratification. Alexander Hamilton, whose watchword was "Learn to think continentally,"[27] a member of the late Federal Convention, and an enthusiastic champion in defence of the Constitution which he had helped to frame, was also a leading member of this State Convention. His enthusiasm was not of a nature to be damped by the fact that "two-thirds of the Convention and four-sevenths of the people" were against them. When we consider, that forty-six out of the sixty-seven members of this Convention were elected pledged to vote against the adoption of the new form of government, we can realise what formidable odds faced the undaunted believers in a strong "national government." The debate was opened by Chancellor Livingston on the nineteenth of June, "with an eloquent sketch of the advantages enjoyed by the American people in forming a national Union; of the effects of the confederation, showing the necessity of a change of government, and of the peculiar importance of Union to New York, from the nature of her products and her geographical position. Having lamented that this superiority of position had excited an improper confidence, and produced an inflexibility, which had rendered her regardless of the wishes of other states, he described her exposed situation, stated at large the impracticability of preserving an efficient league, and urged the necessity of establishing a well-ordered government. A resolution was then offered, that no question should be taken on the Constitution, or any part of it, or on any amendment to it, until each clause had been considered. It was the policy of the governor [Clinton] to take the vote upon it in mass; that of its friends, to protract the debate until intelligence should be received from New Hampshire.[28] This resolution was discussed and prevailed."[29]

The discussion of the various clauses of the Constitution continued for the next three weeks, during which time several important amendments were proposed and adopted by the majority. Thereupon, on Friday, the eleventh of July, Mr. Jay moved "That the Constitution under consideration ought to be *ratified* by this Convention," and further, "that such parts of the said Constitution as may be thought doubtful ought to be explained, and whatever amendments may be deemed useful ought to be *recommended*." These resolutions were warmly supported by the chancellor and the chief justice (Morris), while Mr. Melancthon Smith as warmly opposed their adoption by the Convention, as the mouth-piece of the Anti-Federalists, who contended that unless the proposed Constitution should be materially altered, they would have to vote for its rejection. The debates on Mr. Jay's resolutions continued until the Tuesday following, when Mr. Smith moved to amend the first resolution, so that it should read "*upon condition*" that certain specified amendments should be made. After another long debate, the Federalists, on the twenty-third of this month, were successful, by the narrow majority of two votes, in obtaining the insertion of the words "*in full confidence*," instead of "*on condition*" in the ratification, so that Mr. Jay's resolution would now read: "*Resolved*, That the Constitution be ratified in full confidence that the amendments proposed by this Convention will be adopted."

The following day, one of the Anti-Federalist members— Mr. Lansing—actually moved to adopt a resolution, "that there should be reserved to the State of New York *a right to withdraw herself from the Union* after a certain number of years unless the amendments proposed should previously be submitted to a general Convention." This motion was, of course, negatived, and upon Saturday, the 26th of July 1788, the final vote was taken, when the Constitution was ratified by a bare majority of three votes! And even this slender majority might not have been obtained, if the recent ratification of the new Constitution by the ninth State— New Hampshire,—had not proved to the New York Anti-Federalists that, the required number of States having now given their adherence to the new form of government, it would therefore be adopted whether New York agreed or not.[30]

To his friend the Marquis de Lafayette, the chancellor wrote a few weeks later,[31]

In many of the States the new plan has met with great opposition, and more particularly in this, where the governor headed the opposition with all the weight arising from his office. However, after six weeks laborious debate, we were happy enough to bring over such a number of our opposers as to carry the question for the adoption of the new constitution, which has now been acceded to by all the States but North Carolina and Rhode Island, both of which are at present convulsed by the paper money epidemic of which the other States have been so lately cured. The plan will now be carried into effect, and I cannot but hope from it such consistency as will give us the weight which our situation and increasing numbers entitle us to.

Probably owing to Governor Livingston's great influence in New Jersey, the Convention specially summoned in this State, to decide whether the new Constitution should be adopted or not, had, on the previous 18th of December, ratified it by a unanimous vote to his unbounded delight. And in his message to the Legislature, on the 29th August 1788, after the necessary number of States had given in their adhesion, he gave expression to his feelings in the following passage:

I most heartily congratulate you, gentlemen, on the adoption of the Constitution proposed for the government of the United States, by the Federal Convention, and it gives me inexpressible pleasure that New Jersey has the honour of so early and so unanimously agreeing to that form of national government which has since been so generally applauded and approved of by the other States. We are now arrived to that auspicious period which, I confess, I have often wished that it might please Heaven to protect my life to see. Thanks to God that I have lived to see it.

It is interesting to note how Governor Livingston and his kinsman, the chancellor, were in such thorough agreement on three important matters concerning their country's welfare, namely, the Constitution, the currency, and slavery. They evidently thought alike in spite of the great difference in their ages and temperaments. Apparently, they rarely corresponded with one another, and, probably, had never met since they were fellow-members of the Second Continental Congress in 1776, so that their thorough accord is the more remarkable. Previous to the adoption of the new form of government, Governor Livingston had been very despondent as to the future of his country. In a letter, written in the winter of 1786, he says, "I hope I am neither enthusiastic nor superstitious, but I have strange forebodings of calamitous times, and that those times are not very remote"[32]; while in another, written two months later, he states:

> I am really more distressed by the posture of our public affairs, than I ever was by the most gloomy appearances during the late war. We do not exhibit the virtue that is necessary to support a republican government; and without the utmost exertions of the more patriotic part of the community, and the blessing of God upon their exertions, I fear that we shall not be able, for ten years from the date of this letter, to support that independence which has cost us so much blood and treasure to acquire. I pray for the disappointment of my forebodings, but God will not smile upon public iniquity, nor upon that astonishing ingratitude wherewith we requite his marvellous interposition to deliver us from the bondage to which our enemies meditated to reduce us. . . . Our situation is truly deplorable, and without a speedy alteration of measures, I doubt whether you and I shall survive the existence of that liberty for which we have so strenuously contended.[33]

His labours in securing the ratification of the Constitution he had assisted in drawing up, were nearly his last in the service of his country; but *now* he considered he could sing his *Nunc dimittis* in a far happier frame of mind, than he could have done before the establishment of a national government. His last days were, however, saddened by the death of his wife, which event took place upon the 17th of July 1789; and this fatal termination to her illness probably hastened his own end. But he lived long enough to be re-elected governor for the fourteenth time in succession, in the autumn of this year, dying from an attack of dropsy during the following summer.[34] Mr. Sedgwick, his biographer, winds up an appreciative notice of his character by applying to him, with but a trifling alteration, the high eulogium of the Roman historian: "Citizen, senator, husband, father, friend; equal in all stations of life, contemning riches, pertinacious in well-doing, unmoved by fear."[35]

While a contemporary poet contributes the following lines to his memory:

> O! frail mortality, behold thy doom!
> Heroes and sages crowd the narrow tomb,—
> The vet'ran Putnam bows his laurell'd head,
> And beckons sages to the mighty dead.
> Franklin obeys and treads the shadowy shore,
> And the good Livingston is now no more.
> His mighty soul, unwilling to remain,
> Elated, rush'd to join th' illustrious train.

The year before Governor Livingston died, Washington was installed as the first President of the United States of America. The inauguration took place in New York, the temporary seat of the new government, on the 30th of April 1789; and Robert R. Livingston, as Chancellor of the State, had to administer the oath of office. This historical event is thus described by Washington Irving in his *Life of George Washington*:

> At nine o'clock in the morning there were religious ser-
> vices in all the churches, and prayers put up for the blessing
> of Heaven on the new government. At twelve o'clock the city
> troops paraded before Washington's door, and soon after the
> committee of Congress and heads of departments came in their
> carriages. At half-past twelve the procession move forward, pre-
> ceded by the troops; next came the committees and heads of
> departments in their carriages; then Washington in a coach of
> state, his aide-de-camp, Colonel Humphreys, and his secretary,
> Mr. Lear, in his own carriage. The foreign ministers and a long
> train of citizens brought up the rear.
>
> About two hundred yards before reaching the hall,
> Washington and his suite alighted from their carriages and
> passed through the troops, who were drawn up on each side,
> into the hall and Senate chamber, where the Vice-President,
> the Senate, and House of Representatives were assembled. The
> Vice-President, John Adams, recently inaugurated, advanced
> and conducted Washington to a chair of state at the upper end of
> the room. A solemn silence prevailed; when the Vice-President

rose and informed him that all things were prepared for him to take the oath of office required by the Constitution.

The oath was to be administered by the Chancellor of the State of New York, in a balcony in front of the Senate chamber, and in full view of an immense multitude occupying the street, the windows, and even roofs of the adjacent houses. The balcony formed a kind of open recess, with lofty columns supporting the roof. In the centre was a table with a covering of crimson velvet, upon which lay a superbly-bound Bible on a crimson velvet cushion. This was all the paraphernalia for the august scene.

All eyes were fixed upon the balcony when, at the appointed hour, Washington made his appearance, accompanied by various public functionaries, and members of the Senate and House of Representatives. He was clad in a full suit of dark brown cloth, of American manufacture, with a steel-hilted dress sword, white silk stockings, and silver shoe-buckles. His hair was dressed and powdered in the fashion of the day, and worn in a bag and solitaire. His entrance on the balcony was hailed by universal shouts. He was evidently moved by this demonstration of public affection. Advancing to the front of the balcony he laid his hand upon his heart, bowed several times, and then retreated to an arm-chair near the table. The populace appeared to understand that the scene had overcome him, and were hushed at once into profound silence. After a few moments Washington rose and again came toward. John Adams, the Vice-President, stood on his right; and on his left the Chancellor of the State, Robert R. Livingston; somewhat in the rear were Roger Sherman, Alexander Hamilton, Generals Knox, St. Clair, the Baron Steuben, and others.

The Chancellor advanced to administer the oath prescribed by the Constitution, and Mr. Otis, the Secretary of the Senate, held up the Bible on its crimson cushion. The oath was read slowly and distinctly; Washington at the same time laying his hand on the open Bible. When it was concluded, he replied solemnly, "I swear—so help me God!" Mr. Otis would have raised the Bible to his lips, but he bowed down reverently and kissed it. The Chancellor now stepped forward, waved his hand and exclaimed, "Long live George Washington, President of the United States!" At this moment a flag was displayed on the cupola of the hall, on which signal there was a general discharge of artillery on the Battery. All the bells of the city rang out a joyful peal, and the multitude rent the air with acclamations.

In spite of his great services to the nation, and in securing the ratification of the Constitution, the chancellor did not obtain the recognition from the president that he rightly deserved; which can only be accounted for by the fact that Washington at this time was much hampered by the great number of applicants for the principal posts, such as the heads of the various departments of state, under the general government, which were few in number; while each State expected that one of its citizens, at least, should benefit by the creation of these necessary and coveted offices. According to Madison, Livingston desired to be Secretary of the Treasury.[36] There is, however, apparently, no direct evidence to prove that the chancellor ever solicited Washington for this particular post; but from a letter from the president to him, written exactly a month after his inauguration,[37] it appears the chancellor must have made some allusion to his willingness to hold some office under the national government; and as he had amply proved his fitness for such a position, by his successful administration of the secretaryship of Foreign Affairs under the late confederacy, there is no reason why his natural ambition should not have been gratified.

Washington, however, had already two New York statesmen to provide for,[38] and he therefore probably considered that that State had got its full share of these appointments, for he writes from New York to Livingston, in the letter referred to above:

The new and busy scenes in which I have been constantly engaged since my arrival in this place, and which will not allow me to pay that pointed attention to the favours of my friends that my inclination would lead me to do, will, I trust, apologise for this late acknowledgment of your letter of the 15th instant. To you, Sir, and others who know me, I believe it is unnecessary for me to say that when I accepted of the important trust committed to my charge by my country, I gave up every idea of personal gratification that I did not think was compatible with the public good. Under this impression I plainly foresaw that the part of my duty which obliged me to nominate persons to offices would, in many instances, be the most irksome and unpleasing; for, however strong my personal attachment might be to anyone,—however desirous I might be of giving a proof of my friendship,—and whatever might be his expectations, grounded upon the amity which had subsisted between us, I was fully determined to keep myself free from every engagement that could embarrass me in discharging this part of my administration. I have, therefore, uniformly declined giving any decisive answer to the numerous applications which have been made to me; being resolved whenever I am called upon to nominate persons for those offices which may be created, that I will do it with a sole view to the public good, and shall bring forward those who upon every consideration, and from the best information I can obtain, will, in my judgment, be most likely to answer that great end. The delicacy with which your letter was written, and your wishes insinuated, did not require me to be thus explicit on this head with you; but the desire which I have that those persons whose good opinion I value should know the principles on which I mean to act in this business, has led me to this full declaration; and I trust that the truly worthy and respectable characters in this country will do justice to the motives by which I am actuated in all my public transactions.

According to Hamilton's son and eulogist,—who is, however, not always a reliable guide to follow, when he is writing of any of his celebrated father's political opponents with whom the chancellor was shortly to be numbered,[39] Washington had intended at one time to have conferred the office of Postmaster-General on Livingston, but for some reason or other this was not done. Some writers[40] think Hamilton's jealousy of the political power exercised by the chancellor in the State of New York, led him to use his great influence with the president against a possible rival, and his conduct at this time certainly gives a certain amount of probability to this supposition. For not only had Livingston's wishes been totally disregarded in the appointments of the heads of the great national government departments, and the office of Chief Justice of the Supreme Court bestowed upon another New York citizen,—namely John Jay, the chancellor's old school-fellow, who had held for a short time a similar position in his own State,—but even in the election of United States Senators during the following summer, Hamilton, in his usual imperious way, desired these seats to be filled by his nominees. The Livingston family, however, wanted one of those senator-ships for one of their friends, and though perfectly willing to agree to the election of General Schuyler—Hamilton's father-in-law—they demurred to Rufus King, then a comparative stranger in the State, being preferred to their candidate. Hamilton, nevertheless, persisted, and King was chosen in spite of the Livingston opposition. The chancellor and his friends, however, did not forget, and Hamilton lived to rue his headstrong conduct upon this occasion.

At this period, Hamilton's scheme for funding the State debts and the creation of a national bank, met with much opposition from the Republicans or Democrats,—as the Anti-Federalists were beginning to be indifferently designated,—in New York, and the chancellor is said to have shared their views. At any rate, so the story goes, "*the family* one evening had a meeting for the purpose of deliberating on the subject, and the result of their deliberations was such, that the next morning every member of it took a position in the ranks of the Republican party."[41] This is, however, true only as regards that portion of the Livingston family who were intimately connected with the chancellor, and including Brockholst Livingston. The result of this coalition was most disastrous to the Federalists, its first-fruits being the rejection of General Schuyler by the New York Legislature upon his renomination for United States Senator in January, 1791,—the general having drawn the shortest term, on casting lots, at his election of the previous year,—and the appointment of Hamilton's great rival, Aaron Burr, in his place.

This clever but unscrupulous political adventurer, who taught the New York Republicans not only how to organise their forces for victory, but how to abuse that victory when gained, was then merging to the front in the stormy times that marked the early years of the independent history of this State, when rival factions disputed for political ascendancy. As the son of Governor Livingston's old friend, the Reverend Aaron Burr, first President of the College of New Jersey, he was naturally on friendly terms with the members of this family at this period of his eventful career, before disappointment, at the frustration of his ambitious hopes led to the intrigues which caused his ultimate political ruin.[42] In 1791, he had, however, done nothing to forfeit any man's just esteem; and as John Adams wrote of him some years later, "connected by blood with many respectable families in New England. The son of one president, and the grandson of another president of Nassau Hall, or Princeton University; the idol of all the Presbyterians in New York, New England, New Jersey, Pennsylvania, Maryland, Virginia, and elsewhere. He had served in the army, and came out of it with the character of a knight without fear, and an able officer. He had afterwards studied and practised law with application and success. Buoyed up on those religious partialities, and this military and juridical reputation, it is no wonder that Governor Clinton and Chancellor Livingston should take notice of him."[43]

In the State of New York at this time were three distinct political parties, and herein lay Burr's great opportunity. To quote the words of Colonel Burr's able defender, though by no means blind apologist of his hero's great faults, the late Mr. James Parton:

> There were, first, the *Clintons*, of whom George Clinton, Governor of the State, was the important person. He was the undisputed leader of the popular party. He had been governor since 1777, and was re-elected, every other year, to that office for eighteen years. The Clintons, as a family, were not, at this time, either numerous or rich; but George Clinton, an able, tough, wary, self-willed man, wielding with unusual tact the entire patronage of the State, and dear to the affections of the great mass of the people, is an imposing figure in the politics of the time, and must ever be regarded as the chief man of the State of New York during the earlier years of its independent existence. De Witt Clinton, a nephew of the governor, was a student in Columbia College at this time.
>
> Then there were the *Schuylers*, with General Schuyler at their head, Alexander Hamilton, his son-in-law, for ornament and champion. General Schuyler was formed for unpopularity. Rich, of an imposing presence, austere in manners, a very honest, worthy man, he had no real sympathy with the age and country in which he lived. No more had Hamilton, as Hamilton well knew, and bitterly confessed. But not to anticipate, it is

enough here to say that the Schuyler party, as used and led by Alexander Hamilton, was the one most directly opposed to the Clintons. General Schuyler had been a competitor with George Clinton for the governorship in 1777, and his disappointment, it was thought, was still very fresh in the general's recollection.

But there was a third family in the State, which, merely as a family, was more important than the Clintons or Schuylers. This was the *Livingtson* family—rich, numerous, and influential. At the time we are now considering, there were nine members of this family in public life—politicians, judges, clergymen, lawyers—of whom several were of national celebrity. And besides those who bore the name of Livingston, there were distinguished and aspiring men who had married daughters of the family. The Livingstons had been rooted in the State for more than a hundred years, and the circle of their connections embraced a great proportion of the leading people. Robert R. Livingston, a member of Congress in 1776, one of the Committee who drew up the Declaration of Independence, a conspicuous framer of the Constitution, afterwards its stanch supporter, in later years the patron of Robert Fulton, and therefore immortal, was at this period the head and pride of the Livingston family.

These were the three families. The Clintons had *power*, the Livingstons had *numbers*, the Schuylers had *Hamilton*. Neither of the three was strong enough to overcome the other two united, and any two united could triumph over the third. Such statements as these, [continues Mr. Parton] must, of course, be taken with proper allowance. A thousand influences enter into politics, and general statements are only outline truths. Nevertheless in a State where only freeholders have a vote, and where there are not more than twelve or fourteen thousand freeholders, the influence of great families, if wielded by men of force and talent, will be, in the long-run, and in great crises, controlling. It was so in the State of New York for twenty years after the Revolution.[44]

It was the union of the second and third of these parties that gave to the Federalists in the late convention the victory over the Clintonians;

and now, the freshly-formed alliance of the Livingstons with the latter, led to the defeat of General Schuyler in the New York Legislature, and the election of Burr as United States Senator in his place, by which the latter's office of Attorney-General of the State of New York became vacant. Whereupon, the Council of Appointment, in which the governor was all-powerful, upon the 8th of November in this year, promoted Morgan Lewis, Chancellor Livingston's brother-in-law, to be his successor. Twelve months later, this gentleman resigned this office on being appointed a judge of the Supreme Court of the State.

Early in the year 1794, Washington found "it expedient to recall Mr. Gouverneur Morris from his mission to the Republic of France," and looking about for a suitable person to be his successor, thought of Chief Justice Jay, who had just been appointed envoy to Great Britain. He, thereupon, wrote a letter marked "secret and confidential" to Jay, offering him this mission also; but as he had doubts as to his correspondent accepting it, he enclosed in it another letter of the same date—29th April, 1794—addressed to Chancellor Livingston making him the same offer.

> If you answer in the affirmative [he wrote to the former], be so good as to return the enclosed letter to me, and corresponding arrangements shall be made. If in the negative, I pray you to forward it through the penny post, or otherwise, according to circumstances, to the gentleman to whom it is directed, without delay; and in either case to let the transaction be confined entirely to ourselves.

The reason why the president made the offer in the first place to Jay, was that he was a member of the party in power, while the chancellor belonged to the opposition, which was therefore all the greater compliment to the latter. Jay, as Washington had rightly anticipated, did not care about undertaking the French mission; and in his reply declining the offer, he says: "The gentleman, to whom your letter is addressed, is not in town. To obviate delay and accidents, I sent it to his brother, who will doubtless forward it immediately, either by a direct conveyance or by the post."[45]

Facsimiles of Autographs
OF SOME
Historical American Livingstons.

FIRST LORD OF THE MANOR OF LIVINGSTON.
8TH APRIL 1700.

SECOND LORD OF THE MANOR.
5TH JANUARY 1744.

THIRD LORD OF THE MANOR.
5TH AUGUST 1751.

PRESIDENT OF NEW YORK PROVINCIAL CONVENTION 1775.
SIGNER OF THE DECLARATION OF INDEPENDENCE.
26TH FEBRUARY 1752.

FIRST GOVERNOR OF THE STATE OF NEW JERSEY, ETC.
19TH OCTOBER 1749.

PRESIDENT OF THE FIRST NEW YORK PROVINCIAL
CONGRESS 1775.
9TH JULY 1763.

PRESIDENT OF THE CONVENTION OF THE STATE OF
NEW YORK 1776.
12TH SEPTEMBER 1759.

JUDGE OF THE SUPREME COURT OF THE UNITED STATES.
14TH JANUARY 1823.

FIRST PROPRIETOR OF THE CLERMONT MANOR.
4TH JANUARY 1772.

JUDGE OF THE SUPREME COURT OF THE PROVINCE OF
NEW YORK.
10TH FEBRUARY 1767.

FIRST CHANCELLOR OF THE STATE OF NEW YORK, AND
FIRST UNITED STATES MINISTER OF FOREIGN AFFAIRS.
28TH JULY 1791.

AUTHOR OF THE "LIVINGSTON PENAL CODE," STATESMAN
AND JURIST.
4TH OCTOBER 1831.

. The following is a copy of the enclosure addressed to Robert R. Livingston, in which Washington explains the reason why no time should be lost in appointing a successor to Mr. Morris:

(Private)

Philadelphia, 29th April 1794.

Dear Sir:

Circumstances have rendered it expedient to recall Mr. Gouverneur Morris from his mission to the Republic of France. Would it be convenient and agreeable to you to supply his place? An affirmative answer would induce an immediate nomination of you for this appointment to the Senate; and the significa-tion of your sentiments relative thereto, as soon as your deter-mination is formed, would oblige me particularly, as it is not expected that that body will remain much longer in session. With my great esteem and regard, I am, dear Sir, etc., etc.,

Geo. Washington[46]

The president must have been anxious, after hearing from Jay, that Chancellor Livingston should not also decline. Otherwise, it is difficult to understand why, only ten days after Washington's "secret and confidential" communication to the chief justice, one of his—the president's— most influential opponents in the Senate, James Monroe of Virginia, an ardent Republican, should have written to the chancellor strongly advising him to accept this mission. He could not have done so without Washington's sanction, who probably had thought it advisable to sound the Senate in this matter, owing to his nomination of Jay as minister to Great Britain having caused such an outburst of feeling among the Republican senators. In this letter Monroe writes:

I need not mention to you that the favorable inclination of the President to y^r mission to France is seconded and wished by the republican interest here. You would, of course, conclude this, and that y^r acceptance is earnestly desired, as it will put us at ease with respect to our ally [France], and with an arrange-ment in which in every view we are deeply interested. What will be the consequence of your refusal we know not. You know well the difficulty of succeeding in a republican nomination at all. Some will probably decline if nominated, others in the course of political transactions have created irritation and will not be thought of, so that what may be the effect of your declining cannot be perceived. I therefore hope you will accept, if any way compatible with those arrangements formed for the welfare of y^r family, and y^r permanent tranquillity.[47]

Livingston, however, who of course knew nothing of his old friend John Jay having had the refusal of this post, also declined it, and Monroe was subsequently appointed to take charge of this important mission. Mr. John C. Hamilton, who never misses an opportunity of making derogatory remarks concerning his famous father's political antagonists, asserts that Edmund Randolph, the then secretary of state, was adverse to Livingston's appointment, owing to his deafness,[48]—a complaint which was, as we shall see later on, also brought forward on another important occasion, as an argument against his fitness for being nominated as a candidate for the vice-presidency.

Though the chancellor's reasons for declining Washington's offer are unknown, they probably arose from the state of ferment the country was in over the foreign policy of Washington's administration. For the American Republicans at this period had apparently lost their heads over the French Revolution; and in their enthusiasm for the sister republic, they considered their government was betraying the cause of freedom by not espousing the side of France in her quarrel with Great Britain. The Federalists were also considered by their opponents to be only too anxious to slavishly please the latter country; so that when the president demanded the recall of Genet, the French minister to the United States, owing to his extraordinary proceedings while in that country, there was an outburst of wrath from the Republican party, and it was plainly insinuated by some of its extreme partisans that his recall had originated in foreign influence. Livingston probably, under these circumstances, thought it would not be advisable to accept such a difficult task, disagreeing as he did with Washington's policy on this occasion.

In his views as to the proper foreign policy to be pursued by the United States, the chancellor was strictly consistent, for while foreign secretary under the late confederacy, he had steadfastly upheld the propriety of considering French interests before those of Great Britain. Holding these ideas, it is not to be much wondered at, that he vigorously opposed the ratification of the treaty with Great Britain which Jay had been sent to negotiate, and this minister's return, after the accomplishment of his labours, had still further inflamed the wrath of the Republicans, whose journals bitterly denounced the treaty before even the writers were aware of its contents! When these became known the Republican press was filled with shamefully abusive articles on the treaty and its negotiator, and meetings were held all over the country by the Republicans for the purpose of expressing their disapproval, and in the hope, possibly, of intimidating the president from ratifying it.

Though Chancellor Livingston was strongly opposed to the ratification of the treaty, and wrote essays against it over the pen-names of "Cato" and Decius,"[49] he did not stoop to the level of the Republican press in its disgraceful abuse of Washington and Jay. As a last resource, he sent a written remonstrance to the president himself; who, in his reply, dated 20th August, 1795, namely, five days after he had signed the obnoxious treaty, says:

> Aiming only to promote and secure the true interests of my country, I willingly receive information concerning those interests from my fellow-citizens. The opinions and reasonings of enlightened men are particularly acceptable; but, as it happens in other matters, so in this, they are extremely variant. You deem the Treaty palpably defective and pregnant with evils; others think it contains substantial good. For myself, I freely own that I cannot discern in it the mischiefs you anticipate. On the contrary, although it does not rise to all our wishes, yet it appears to me calculated to procure to the United States such advantages as entitle it to an acceptance. My final act, of course, conforms to this opinion. I feel myself greatly obliged by your expressions of respect, esteem, and attachment, and, if the unvarying integrity of my views have deserved them, they will not now be withdrawn; for I can merit your good opinion, and the general approbation of my fellow-citizens, only by a conscientious discharge of what I conceive to be my duty.[50]

That objections coming from such a quarter must have had some weight with the president, is proved by the fact that, before writing the above reply, nearly six weeks after the receipt of Livingston's letter, he had forwarded the latter to the secretary of state, with another document connected with the treaty, for his consideration. And in the letter, accompanying these papers, he wrote in a post-script,

I add to the paper sent, Chancellor Livingston's letter, and wish, if it is best to give it an answer, that one may be prepared. Although this letter is a hurried, as well as a private one, I have no objection to the confidential officers seeing it, and wish them to prepare their minds on the several subjects mentioned therein by the time I arrive.[51]

This last letter was written to Randolph from Washington's home at Mount Vernon.

The chancellor, who had still entertained hopes that Washington would not have consented to sign the British Treaty, wrote to a friend after receiving the president's letter:

Alas! that hope is frustrated. He has ratified the fatal instrument, alike hostile to our liberties, and the good faith we owed to France, and to our own Constitution, which confines to Congress many of these powers which are bartered away by the Executive . . . In the papers you will find a full discussion of the treaty, and your respect for Hamilton will doubtless be greatly increased by knowing that he is the author of Camillus.[52]

Though Washington had acted perfectly correctly in thus ratifying this much disputed treaty, the Republicans continued to regard this act of the president as a direct insult to their old ally; and at a banquet given in the city of New York on the following 6th of February, in honour of the ninth anniversary of the treaty of alliance between France and America, which was attended by several distinguished members of that party, as well as a considerable number of French citizens, this feeling found full vent in the toasts drunk on this occasion. Brockholst Livingston[53] is said to have eloquently addressed the assembled company, and while no toasts were proposed in honour of the president or national government, one of those given was "The British Treaty—May it be an awful lesson how to trust to the justice and magnanimity of those who ever have, and still do, seek the ruin of our commerce, and destruction of our liberty." While another, proposed by Chancellor Livingston, was—"May the present coolness between France and America produce, like the quarrels of lovers, a renewal of love."[54]

A sadder proof of the effects of the violence of party feeling at this period was soon to occur. For in May, 1798, when the foreign policy of the

314 | THE LIVINGSTONS OF LIVINGSTON MANOR

government, in connection this time with France, gave rise to another outburst of political excitement in New York, Brockholst Livingston, who had not as yet been elevated to the bench, wrote a humorous account of a rival political meeting for the *Argus* newspaper, which led to the writer being publicly assaulted while promenading one evening on the Battery, by a Mr. Jones. Mr. Livingston thereupon, had no option left him but to challenge his assailant. The duel took place at Hoboken on the following afternoon. They both fired at the same time, and Mr. Jones being shot in the groin died in a few minutes. The verdict of the coroner's jury, at the inquest held on the tenth of May, is thus laconicly recorded: "Doth agree on there Verdick that the said man Jemes Jones accepted a challenge from Brockholst Livingston, fought and fell."[55] Of course, the Federalist news-papers held Mr. Jones up as a martyr to their cause, while denouncing his opponent as a murderer.[56] But in those days duels were of constant occur-rence, and no man was considered to have suffered in reputation because he had "killed his man."[57]

This unfortunate quarrel between the Federalists and Republicans over the foreign policy of the national government, led to a deplorable break in the life-long friendship between John Jay and Robert R. Livingston. For the former, who had shortly before his return from England been elected by the Federalists governor of the State by a large majority, was upon the expiration of his term of office, nominated by his party for re-election, whereupon the Republicans, who were in search of a strong candidate, per-suaded the chancellor to stand in opposition to his old friend. A good, but sad, proof of the bitterness of party feeling in New York a hundred years ago! The Republicans were, however, badly beaten on this occasion, as the Federalists re-elected Jay by the large majority of two thousand three hun-dred and eighty votes.[58] And it was not until two years later (1800) that the efforts of Burr and his "*myrmidons*," as his immediate followers were styled by Alexander Hamilton—"*The Tenth Legion*," they were proudly called by Theodosia, his daughter—were at last crowned by success. But this success would probably not even then have been obtained, if the Republicans had not been greatly assisted by the errors committed by their opponents. The greatest of these was the stringent enforcement of the Alien and Sedition Laws, against whose passage through the House of Representatives, the chancellor's youngest brother Edward[59] had, on the 19th of June, 1798, made one of his greatest speeches,[60]—a speech which "was printed on satin and hung up in thousands of the taverns and parlours of the Democratic States."[61]

Burr, moreover, was still further assisted in his far from light task of disciplining the Republican voters, by the quarrels between the Federalist leaders, arising out of Hamilton's contempt for that old Revolutionary veteran, John Adams—the then president; and also from the former's carelessness in not selecting men of position, as the Federalist candidates for election as representatives for the city of New York in the State Legislature, upon whom would fall the task of choosing electors of the new president and vice-president. According to Mr. Parton, Hamilton had "fixed upon a list of his own friends, people of little weight or consideration in the city or the country. Burr, who had friends in all circles, had a copy of this list brought to him immediately. He read it over, with great gravity folded it up, put it in his pocket, without uttering another word, said, 'Now I have him hollow.' And he really had him hollow. In a moment, the means of carrying the city, upon which all depended, flashed upon his mind, and he proceeded forthwith to execute the scheme."[62] Colonel Burr's scheme was simply to checkmate his rival Hamilton, by securing a ticket containing the names of the most prominent men in the city, so as to make the insignificance of the Federalist candidates all the more apparent. He therefore carefully selected the names of thirteen men, "whose wealth, and talents, and weight of character were probably greater than any other equal number of Republicans then to be found in the city, or perhaps any other equal number of citizens. But this was not all. At that time some degree of rivalry existed between the Livingstons and Clintons, and great jealousy and suspicion were entertained between both the Livingstons and Clintons and Colonel Burr. Each had their warm personal friends, and those friends partook more or less of the feelings and prejudices of their leaders. A set of candidates, therefore, who were apparently particularly friendly to either of these leaders would have been coldly supported by the others. With a view to render these jealousies and collisions obnoxious, and to bring the whole Democratic party heartily into action, Governor Clinton was placed at the head of the ticket; Brockholst Livingston, the most talented member of the Livingston family, was also made a candidate";[63] and also, in order to call out the Revolutionary feelings and sympathies of the electors, the name of General Gates was placed on the list. Burr's troubles, however, now began, for it was easy work to draw up a list of good names, but quite a different matter to get their owners to agree to stand. This difficulty, after an immense amount of trouble, was at last triumphantly overcome by this clever "machine politician"; and upon the night of the second of May, 1800, this hardly-contested election terminated in a victory to the Republicans by a majority of nearly five hundred votes.

A victory which meant the election of a Republican president in the winter of this year, a fact which no person could realise better than the discomfited great Federalist leader, who vainly endeavoured, while smarting under his bitter disappointment, to induce the governor to call an extra session of the old Legislature (whose term of service had still eight weeks to run), for the purpose of changing the mode of choosing presidential electors. He begged Jay to save the country from falling into the hands of "an atheist in religion and a fanatic in politics," as he very uncharitably designated the Republican candidate for the presidency, the celebrated Virginian, Thomas Jefferson. The governor was, however, too honest and patriotic a man to be misled by Hamilton's sophistry, and his letter remained unanswered, to be found among Jay's papers after his death, bearing the following honourable endorsement in the governor's handwriting: "Proposing a measure for party purposes, which I think it would not become me to adopt."

The result of the poll had barely become known, when the Republican leaders at Philadelphia were discussing whom to put forward as vice-president. The candidate would have to be found in New York, as with that State rested the power of determining the choice of president; and the names of three persons were mentioned, namely, those of Chancellor Livingston, Governor Clinton, and Colonel Burr. The members of Congress who composed this conference, "not knowing the wishes of the majority of their Democratic friends in New York, requested Mr. Gallatin to communicate with them, and ascertain their views. Mr. Gallatin, in pursuance of this request, wrote to Commodore Nicholson of New York, and requested him to converse frankly and freely with the gentlemen who had been named as candidates, and to consult other friends and inform him of the result of his inquiries."[64]

Meanwhile Burr's friends were losing no time in actively pushing his candidature for the coveted post. For on the fifth of May, only three days after the result of the poll in the city of New York had become known, Mr. Matthew L. Davis, one of that scheming politician's most trusted lieutenants, wrote to the above-mentioned Mr. Gallatin as follows:

> I believe it is pretty generally understood that Mr. Jefferson is contemplated for President. But who is to fill the Vice-President's chair? I should be highly gratified in hearing your opinion on this subject; if secrecy is necessary, you may rely

on it; and, sir, as I have no personal views, you will readily
excuse my stating the present apparent wishes and feelings of
the Republican party in this city. It is generally expected that
the Vice-President will be selected from the State of New York.
Three characters only can be contemplated, viz. Geo. Clinton,
Chancellor Livingston, and Colonel Burr. The first seems averse
to public life, and is desirous of retiring from all its cares and
toils. It was therefore with great difficulty he was persuaded to
stand as candidate for the State Legislature. A personal interview at some future period will make you better acquainted
with this transaction. In addition to this, Mr. Clinton grows
old and infirm. To Mr. Livingston there are objections more
weighty. The family attachment and connection; the prejudices
which exist not only in this State, but throughout the United
States, against the name; but, above all, the doubts which are
entertained of his firmness and decision in trying periods. You
are well acquainted with certain circumstances that occurred
on the important question of carrying the British treaty into
effect. On that occasion Mr. L. exhibited a timidity that never
can be forgotten. Indeed, it had its effects when he was a candidate for governor, though it was not generally known.[65] Colonel
Burr is therefore the most eligible character, and on him the
eyes of our friends in this State are fixed as if by sympathy for
that office. Whether he would consent to stand I am totally
ignorant, and indeed I pretend not to judge of the policy farther than it respects this State. If he is elected to the office of
V. P., it would awaken so much zeal and pride of our friends in
this State as to secure us a Republican governor at the next
election. If he is not nominated, many of us will experience
much chagrin and disappointment. If, sir, you do not think it
improper, please inform me by post the probable arrangement
on this subject. I feel very anxious.[66]

The above letter plainly shows what apt pupils Burr had in the art
of political intrigue; or what is most likely, this master leader in "burrow-
ing underground" dictated the epistle himself! For having just gained the
New York elections, which foreshadowed a New York vice-president—
and even the presidency itself probably, by means of a little unscrupulous
manipulation, of which Burr was quite capable, as after events sufficiently

proved—by the combined aid of the Clintons and Livingstons, the Burrites without loss of time made strenuous efforts to throw over their allies, in the hope of obtaining the prize of victory for their own leader. Gallatin's correspondent, Commodore Nicholson, another Burrite, also hastened to inform his son-in-law, that Chancellor Livingston's deafness "presented an insuperable barrier to his nomination."[67] And having thus summarily disposed of the claims of the chief of the Livingston party to his own satisfaction, he proceeded to settle as positively those of George Clinton, by asserting that he (Clinton) would rather not accept the nomination, as "his age, his infirmities, his habits and attachment to [a] retired life, in his opinion, exempt him from active life." He furthermore stated that Clinton considered "Colonel Burr is the most suitable person, and perhaps the only man"; and he adds significantly, "but his name must not be played the fool with."[68]

But the friends of Mr. Clinton, when the success of these manoeuvres became apparent in the nomination of Burr for the vice-presidency by the Republican caucus, flatly denied their leader had ever refused to allow his name to be put forward; in fact the still hale veteran was anxious for the office, as after events proved, and roundly accused Commodore Nicholson of having substituted Burr's name for that of Clinton in his letter to Gallatin, at the request of that artful intriguer.[69] Colonel Burr obtained his point but at a heavy cost, for by his underhand conduct in this business he mortally offended the Clinton and Livingston families. This was soon to become evident, for when the political control of the State was transferred from the Federal to the Republican party by the elections held in 1800 and 1801, the spoils of office fell to the latter, and these were in the gift of the Council of Appointment. Now up to the autumn of the year 1801, the governor alone exercised the power of originating nominations, but the Constitutional Convention held in the month of October in that year, for the special purpose of settling the controversy which had arisen regarding the relative powers of the governor and Council of Appointment respecting nominations for office, and to consider the expediency of altering the Constitution in regard to the number of senators and assemblymen, unanimously decided that the Council of Appointment had equal powers of nomination with the governor.

The Republican majority having obtained a settlement of the latter important point in accordance with their wishes, proceeded at once to make full use of the power thus placed in their hands, by deposing the present occupants of the various State offices, and filling their places with their own adherents, on the principle thus early practised by Republican as well as Federalist politicians, that to the victors belong the spoils"; a doctrine, said to have originated in Jefferson's removal of Federalists from office during his first administration. But the odium by rights attaches to both the great political parties, for nothing can be sadder to the admirers of that rugged Revolutionary veteran John Adams, than the knowledge that *the very last hours of his political power* were spent in making Federalist nominations to official positions, and sending them into the Senate, which was as rapidly confirming them, so that the new president should be unfairly hampered by these partisan appointments![70]

Colonel Burr was now to reap the reward for his selfish conduct in the matter of the vice-presidency, for the Council of Appointment, composed of members of the Clinton and Livingston parties, completely ignored his friends in the distribution of the offices, which were divided among their own adherents. Chancellor Livingston, as we shall shortly see, was to be provided for by a national appointment, but State offices were conferred on the following members and connexions of the family. Edward Livingston became Mayor of New York; Morgan Lewis, Chief Justice; Doctor Tillotson, Secretary of State; and General Armstrong, United States Senator. The first of these gentleman was the chancellor's youngest brother, while the others had all married daughters of this house. Brockholst Livingston and Smith Thompson,—the latter's wife was a Livingston, —were appointed Justices of the Supreme Court.[71] A strong proof of how much their public services were appreciated by their fellow-citizens.

While Edward Livingston had already had conferred on him by Jefferson the office of United States Attorney for the district of New York, concerning which, Bayard, a Federalist member of Congress for Delaware, thus refers in his attack upon the Republican appointments in the House of Representatives:

> I shall add to the catalogue but the name of one more gentleman, Mr. Edward Livingston of New York. I knew well—full well I knew—the consequence of this gentleman. His means were not limited to his own vote; nay, I always considered more than the vote of New York within his power. Mr. Livingston has been made the Attorney for the district of New York; the road of preferment has been opened to him, and his brother has been raised to the distinguished place of Minister Plenipotentiary to the French Republic.[72]

It is, nevertheless [to quote the words of the industrious historian of New York political parties], but an act of simple justice, in this place, to add that the gentlemen belonging to the Livingston family who received these appointments were all of them men of high character for talents, and in all respects well fitted for the offices to which they were respectively appointed. Edward Livingston was not only competent to execute properly the duties pertaining to the mayoralty,[73] but all will now admit that his talents qualified him for any office within the control of the people of the state or nation. The reports of the Supreme Court of this State are enduring monuments of the learning and abilities of both Brockholst Livingston and Smith Thompson. As a man of genius Livingston was unquestionably the superior of Thompson; but for legal acumen, clearness of perception, and logical powers of mind, there are few if any men, in this or any other country, who can excel Judge Thompson.[74]

The natural result of these appointments was a complete breach between the majority of the Democratic or Republican party in this State, represented by the Clintons and Livingstons, and that smaller portion which recognised the vice-president as its leader. The Clintons especially were very bitter in their denunciations of their former ally, and with the encouragement of De Witt Clinton, James Cheetham— whom Burr's biographer designates "a scurrilous dog of an Englishman, who began life as a hatter, and who knew as much of American politics as De Witt Clinton chose to tell him"[75]—savagely attacked Burr in the columns of the *American Citizen*; while his friends retaliated in kind on the Clintons and Livingstons in their newspaper, the *Morning Chronicle*.

But not content with the publicity thus afforded to his disgraceful vituperations, Cheetham carried on the attack in a series of pamphlets,—one of these being entitled *A View of the Political Conduct of Aaron Burr*,—in which the vice-president of the United States was openly accused of being an unfit person to occupy such an exalted position. Burr personally disdained to defend his reputation against Cheetham's calumnies, but as some of his friends more clearly foresaw that his downfall was foredoomed, unless some means should be taken to clear his character in the eyes of the public, a writer, styling himself "Aristides," came to the vice-president's rescue, and published a pamphlet in his leader's defence. In this smart but scurrilous *Examination of the Various Charges exhibited against Aaron Burr*,

Esq., the private, as well as the public, characters of the principal members of the Clinton and Livingston families were shamefully vilified. According to this pamphleteer the Livingstons "practised with unlimited success" the maxim,

Rem facias; rem
Si possis recte; si non, quocunque modo rem.[76]

The writer, however, was far too sweeping in his denunciations of the most distinguished men belonging to the Democratic party in the State, for his statements to be taken seriously by his readers. People wondered for a time who the writer could be—as the secret was well kept for several years; and then, "Aristides" and his pamphlet,[77] were both forgotten in the final political downfall of Burr, on that fatal July morning, when, upon the duelling ground at Weehawken, his great rival, Hamilton, the victim of a false code of honour, fell mortally wounded by the vice president's pistol shot.

Notes

1. Some of the more violent Sons of Liberty at the time of the Stamp Act riots, belonged to a secret organisation known as Vox Populi; vide letter from Judge Robert R. Livingston to General Monckton, dated New York, 8 November, 1765.
2. In a letter to his brother Robert of the Manor, dated Trenton, 17 December, 1781, Governor Livingston had written, "By the blessing of God, and the instrumentality of General Washington and Robert Morris, I hope we shall drive the devils to Old England before next June."
3. The governor's effigy was not actually burnt, but that of a member of the Council was.
4. Under the title of "The Primitive Whig."
5. Mrs. Livingston, however, died a year before her husband. Her death took place on the 17th July 1789, and his upon the 25th of July 1790. Their remains were interred in the burial-ground attached to the Presbyterian Church at Elizabethtown; but during the winter of 1790, their son Brockholst had them removed to his family vault in New York.
6. Robert R. Livingston to John Jay, New York, 25th January, 1784.
7. A letter dated 29th November, 1783, quoted from in Chapter XIII.
8. Governor Livingston to Dr. John Beatty, 19th February, 1784.
9. Governor Livingston to President Huntington, 29th October, 1779.
10. Robert R. Livingston to John Jay, Clermont, 30th July, 1784.
11. This was the British colonial governor, who must not be confounded with the American governor of the same name.
12. An original printed copy of this proclamation is in the author's possession; also original copies of similar proclamations, issued by Lieut.-Gov. James De Lancey in 1752 and 1757, and by Lieut.-Gov. Cadwallader Colden in 1762. A facsimile of the

one issued in 1757 will be found facing this page. These printed broadside proclamations were issued for distribution among the tenantry.

13. H. Van Rensselaer to "Cozin" Robert Livingston, Claverack, 11th August, 1753.

14. From a report furnished by Lieut.-Gov. De Lancey to the Lords of Trade in 1757,
it appears that the only iron furnaces of any account in the province at this date,
were those owned by Robert Livingston, whose iron works at Ancram had produced, in the seven years between 1750–1756 inclusive, over three thousand tons
of iron."

15. From a report furnished by Lieut.-Gov. De Lancey to the Lords of Trade in 1757,
it appears that the only iron furnaces of any account in the province at this date,
were those owned by Robert Livingston, whose iron works at Ancram had produced, in the seven years between 1750–1756 inclusive, over three thousand tons
of iron."

16. It is not generally known that the original draft of the Declaration. also contained
the words "*Scotch and other* foreign mercenaries, etc.," in the clause denouncing the
invasion of the colonies by British and German troops. The words in italics were,
however, deleted in committee to save the blushes of the Scotch members present.

17. Governor Livingston to Samuel Allinson, Morristown, 25 July, 1778.

18. George Bancroft, History of the Formation of the Constitution of the United
States of America, vol. i, pp. 232, 233.

19. For Governor Livingston's views concerning the paper currency, see the commencement of this chapter.

20. According to the records of the Council of Revision, the members present on this
occasion, were Governor Clinton, Chancellor Livingston, Chief Justice Morris,
and Justices Yates and Hobart. Three days were spent in discussing the clauses of
this bill and each other's objections. Justice Hobart, however, was not present on
the first day.

21. The credentials of the New Jersey delegates are dated 18 May, 1787, "and of our sovereignty and independence the eleventh." The Convention had met at Philadelphia
on the fourteenth of this month.

22. Known as the "New Jersey Plan"; while the one in favour of a strong central government was known as the "Virginia Plan."

23. Mr. Livingston *was* personally in favour of a "national government," but as the
majority of the delegates of any State would control the vote of that State, he could
easily have been outvoted by his fellow-delegates.

24. Letter, dated 12 February, 1831, from Mr. Madison to Mr. Sedgwick, the author of
The Life of William Livingston.

25. The author of this work is, perhaps, prouder of his descent from one of the signers
of the Constitution, than he is of his descent from a signer of the Declaration of
Independence.

26. This Philip Livingston must not be mistaken for "the Signer" who died in 1778. He
was, apparently, the eldest son of Peter Van Brugh Livingston, generally known as
"Gentleman Phil."

27. The origin of Mr. Joseph Chamberlain's well-known paraphrase "Learn to think
imperially."

28. New Hampshire was daily expected to give its adherence; and as this would make
the ninth State, the Constitution would then be the government of these nine
States, whatever the remaining four might decide to do.

29. Hamilton (John C.), *History of the Republic of the United States,*— edition 1858—
vol. iii, pp. 483, 484. Cf. Elliot's *Debates,* vol. ii, pp. 208–216.

30. The following is the order in which the several States ratified the Federal Constitution: Delaware, Pennsylvania, New Jersey, Georgia, Connecticut, Massachusetts, Maryland, South Carolina, New Hampshire, Virginia, New York, North Carolina, and Rhode Island.

31. Robert R. Livingston to the Marquis de Lafayette, Clermont, 17th September 1788.

32. Governor Livingston to Mr. Houston, 22 December 1786.

33. Governor Livingston to Mr. Elijah Clarke, 17 February 1787.

34. Governor Livingston's autograph acceptance of this, his last, re-election, dated 2 November 1789, and addressed to "The Honorable the Legislative Council and General Assembly of the State of New Jersey in Joint-Meeting," is in the author's possession. He died upon the 25th July 1790.

35. *Life of William Livingston*, p. 449.

36. James Madison to Thomas Jefferson, 27th May 1789.

37. George Washington to Robert R. Livingston, New York, 31st May 1789.

38. Namely, Alexander Hamilton and John Jay. The former was subsequently appointed Secretary of the Treasury; and the latter Chief Justice of the Supreme Court.

39. Namely, Mr. John C. Hamilton, whose ponderous work of filial devotion (entitled, *History of the Republic of the United States as traced in the Writings of Alexander Hamilton and his Contemporaries*) is thus scathingly referred to by Mr. James Parton in his *Life of Thomas Jefferson:* "And have we not a lumbering pamphlet, in seven volumes octavo, designed to show that George Washington was Punch, and Alexander Hamilton the man behind the green curtain, pulling the wires and making him talk? We have. It weighs many pounds avoirdupois. But we must rule out extremes and frenzied utterances, and endeavour to estimate this gifted and interesting man as though he had no worshippers, no rivals, and no sons."

40. Hammond's *Political History of New York*, and Parton's *Life of Aaron Burr*.

41. Hammond, Political History of New York, vol. i, p. 107.

42. William Livingston, upon the death of his friend in 1757, wrote "a funeral eulogium" in his honour; and upon the marriage of his son to the amiable Mrs. Provost in 1782, a member of the Livingston family wrote a letter of congratulation to the happy bridgeroom, in which he made use of the fanciful expression, "May Love be the time-piece in your mansion, and Happiness its minute-hand."—Quotation from letter from William S. Livingston to Colonel Aaron Burr, dated 10th July, 1782.

43. John Adams to James Lloyd, Quincy, 17th February, 1815.

44. *Life of Aaron Burr*, vol. i., pp. 168–170.

45. Sparks's *The Writings of George Washington*, vol. x, pp. 404, 405. Jay's nomination by Washington as Envoy Extraordinary and Minister Plenipotentiary to Great Britain had been confirmed by the Senate, after some opposition from the Republican senators, on the 19th April, or ten days prior to Washington's above offer of the post of Minister to France. So carefully did Chief Justice Jay guard the secret of his having had the refusal of the French Mission, that his son even appears to have been unaware of it, as he does not mention it in his biography of his father.

46. Sparks's *The Writings of George Washington*, vol. x, p. 406.

47. James Monroe to Robert R. Livingston, May 9, 1794. Original letter in the possession of Mr. Fred. M. Steele of Chicago, to whom the author is indebted for a copy. This letter completely disposes of Mr. J. C. Hamilton's assertion that Mr. Livingston, having declined, wished to be asked again.

48. *History of the Republic*, vol. vi, p. 8

49. Hamilton (John C.), *History of the Republic*, vol. vi, pp. 254–257. Mr. Hamilton, of course, insinuates the chancellor grossly abused Washington for his conduct in regard to this treaty, but the letter quoted from in the text shows Washington himself never thought so. According to Mr. M'Master (*History of the People of the United States*, vol. ii, p. 245) Brockholst Livingston was "Decius," and Chancellor Livingston "Cato" only.
50. Washington to Robert R. Livingston, Philadelphia, 20th August, 1795.
51. Washington to Edmund Randolph, Mount Vernon, 29th July, 1795.
52. Letter dated 25th August, 1795, as quoted in John C. Hamilton's *History of the Republic*, vol. vi, p. 282.
53. Son of Governor Livingston, and the Lieutenant-Colonel Henry Brockholst Livingston of the War of Independence.
54. Hammond *Political History of New York*, vol. i, p. 106.
55. *Pennsylvania Magazine*, vol. vii, pp. 486, 487, and Hunt, *Life of Edward Livingston*, p. 54. Mr. Hunt's account, however, gives an erroneous idea of Mr. Livingston's conduct on this occasion.
56. M'Master, *A History of the People of the United States*, vol. ii, pp. 381, 382.
57. An exception was certainly made in Burr's case, but then Alexander Hamilton was a popular hero, and Burr had shot him out of spite and in cold blood.
58. Hammond, *Political History of New York*, vol. i, pp. 90, 113, 114.
59. Edward was nearly eighteen years the younger of these two talented brothers. In later years he became secretary of state under President Andrew Jackson; and of whom we shall have more to relate in another chapter.
60. For this speech see *American Oratory*, pp. 122–131.
61. Parton, *Life of Andrew Jackson*, vol ii, p. 18.
62. Parton, *Life of Aaron Burr*, vol. i, p. 247.
63. Hammond, *Political History of New York*, vol. i, pp. 135, 136.
64. Hammond, *Political History of New York*, vol. i, pp. 137, 138. Commodore Nicholson was Mr. Gallatin's father-in-law.
65. This treacherous attack upon Chancellor Livingston is a clear indication how much Burr dreaded his influence with the Republican party in Congress. The statement as to his "timidity" over the British treaty, evidently means Mr. Livingston's refusal to stoop to the abuse of Washington, that was so freely indulged in by the Burrite faction on that occasion.
66. Matthew L. Davis to Gallatin, New York, 5th May, 1800.
67. Hammond, *Political History of New York*, vol. i, p. 138.
68. James Nicholson to Albert Gallatin, Greenwich Lane, 7th May, 1800.
69. Hammond, *Political History of New York*, vol. i, pp. 138, 139.
70. Morse, *Thomas Jefferson*, pp. 209, 218. Parton, *Life of Aaron Burr*, vol. i, p. 295. It was not, however, until Andrew Jackson's time (1829–1837), that this doctrine was fully acted upon as regards *national* appointments.
71. Hammond, *Political History of New York*, vol. i, pp. 172–181. Judge Brockholst Livingston, whom Mr. Hammond styles "the most talented member of the Livingston family," was promoted by Jefferson on the 10th November, 1806, to be an associate justice of the Supreme Court of the United States.
72. As quoted by Mr. Henry Adams in his *History of the United States during the First Administration of Thomas Jefferson*, vol. i, p. 295.
73. The mayoralty of New York City is said to have been worth ten thousand dollars a year at this date, and so was more prized than many of the State offices. Now the mayors are elected by the people.

74. Hammond, *Political History of New York*, vol. i, pp. 180, 181.

75. Parton, *Life of Aaron Burr*, vol. i, p. 307.

76. The above lines are from Horace's *First Epistle to Maecenas* (Book I, lines 65, 66); and the meaning conveyed by them is equivalent to the Quaker's advice to his son on starting in business, which was to the effect, so the story goes, that he was to make money, honestly if possible, but at any rate to make money!

77. The author of this libellous pamphlet was Burr's intimate friend, William P. Van Ness; and among other statements made in it derogatory to the Livingstons, is one to the effect, that a youthful member of this family was given to vaunting that "to be born of the name of Livingston was a fortune."

CHAPTER XV

Concerning the Mission of Robert R. Livingston of Clermont to France, and his Negotiations with Napoleon Resulting in the Louisiana Purchase.

"Ce n'est point seulement la Nouvelle-Orléans que je veux céder, c'est toute la colonie sans en rien réserver. Je connais le prix de ce que j'abandonne, et j'ai assez prouvé le cas que je fais de cette province, puisque mon premier acte diplomatique avec L'Espagne a eu pour objet de la recouvrer. J'y renonce donc avec un vif déplaisir. Nous obstiner à sa conservation serait folie. Je vous charge de négocier cette affaire avec les envoyés du congrés. N'attendez pas même l'arrivée de M. Monroe: abouchez-vous dès aujourd'hui avec M. Livingston; mais j'ai besoin de beaucoup d'argent pour cette guerre, et je ne voudrais par la commencer par de nouvells contributions."

Napoleon Bonapartb to M. Barbé-Marbois,
11th April, 1803.[1]

IT is a relief to leave the scene of local party warfare, degraded by the gross personal abuse of such men as Cheetham and Van Ness, for the larger and more honourable field of national employment, which was now open to Chancellor Livingston by the election of the Democratic Jefferson to fill the presidential chair. These two statesmen had been friends, ever since the time they had both sat on the historical committee which had drafted the Declaration of Independence; and even before Jefferson was formally declared to be the president-elect he had opened up a correspondence with Livingston concerning his desire to have his old friend a member of his cabinet.[2]

It was on the 14th of December, 1800, when it had been pretty accurately ascertained that the next president would be chosen by the Republican party, that Jefferson—who already regarded himself as sitting in the presidential chair—wrote, to his old Revolutionary colleague, a long letter, in which, after first of all referring diplomatically to his correspondent's pet hobby the steam engine, and inquiring about some recent discovery of mammoth bones in the State of New York—a discovery which deeply interested "the philosopher of Monticello,"—he broached the subject, which, at that particular moment, was of more absorbing interest to the writer than all the steam engines or mammoth bones in the world! To quote, however, his own words:—

> But I have still a more important subject whereon to address you. Tho' our information of the votes of the several states be not official, yet they are stated on such evidence as to satisfy both parties that the republican vote has been successful. We may therefore venture to hazard propositions on that hypothesis without being justly subjected to raillery or ridicule. The Constitution, to which we are all attached, was meant to be republican, and we believe it to be republican according to every candid interpretation. Yet we have seen it so interpreted and administered as to be truly what the French have called it, a *Monarchie masqué*.[3] So long, however, has the vessel run on in this way, and been trimmed to it, that to put her on her republican tack will require all the skill, the firmness, and the zeal of her ablest and best friends. It is a crisis which calls on them to sacrifice all other objects, and repair to her aid in this momentous operation. Not only their skill is wanting, but their names also.
>
> It is essential to assemble in the outset persons to compose our administration, whose talents, integrity, and revolutionary name and principles may inspire the nation at once with unbounded confidence; impose an awful silence on all the

maligners of republicanism; suppress in embryo the purpose avowed by one of their most daring and effective chiefs, of beating down the administration.[4] These names do not abound at this day. So few are they, that yours, my friend, cannot be spared from among them without leaving a blank which cannot be filled. If I can obtain for the public the aid of those I have contemplated, I fear nothing. If this cannot be done, then are we unfortunate indeed! We shall be unable to realise the prospects which have been held out to the people, and we must fall back into monarchism for want of heads, not hands, to help us out of it. This is a common cause, my dear Sir, common to all republicans. Tho' I have been too honorably placed in front of those who are to enter the breach so happily made, yet the energies of every individual are necesary, and in the very place where his energies can most serve the enterprise. I can assure you that your colleagues will be most acceptable to you; one of them, whom you cannot mistake, peculiarly so. The part which circumstances constrain me to propose to you is the Secretaryship of the Navy. These circumstances cannot be explained by letter. Republicanism is so rare in those parts which possess nautical skill, that I cannot find it allied there to the other qualifications. Tho' you are not nautical by profession, yet your residence, and your mechanical science qualify you as well as a gentleman can possibly be, and sufficiently to enable you to choose under-agents perfectly qualified, and to superintend their conduct.

Come forward then, my dear Sir, and give us the aid of your talents, and the weight of your character towards the new establishment of republicanism: I say for its new establishment; for hitherto we have seen only its travestie. I have urged thus far, in the belief that your present office would not be an obstacle to this proposition. I was informed, and I think it was by your brother, that you wished to retire from it, and were only restrained by the fear that a successor of different principles might be appointed. The late change in your Council of Appointment will remove this fear.[5]

After some further remarks as to the expenses attending the holding of such an office, and on the custom of general entertainment introduced under Washington's first administration, which had now been abandoned for a simpler style of living, Jefferson winds up his lengthy letter by saying:

> I have been led to make this application before official knowledge of the result of our election, because the return of Mr. Van Benthuysen, one of your electors and neighbours, offers me a safe conveyance, at a moment when the post offices will be peculiarly suspicious and prying. Your answer may come by post without danger, if directed in some other handwriting than your own. . . . P. S. You will be sensible of the necessity of keeping this application entirely secret until formal declaration in February, of who is President, shall have been made.[6]

A few days after Jefferson had written tins letter, it became known that he and Burr had tied for president, and that therefore, in accordance with the then law ruling presidential elections, the decision as to which of these candidates should be chosen to fill this office devolved upon the House of Representatives. For the next two months the country was distracted over this "Tie question"; as it was not until the 17th of February, 1801, after a continuous sitting of seven days, and on the thirty-sixth ballot, that Jefferson was legally declared elected, whereupon the vice-presidency, of course, fell to Colonel Burr, to that artful schemer's bitter disappointment, who all along had been in hopes of getting the higher office.

Some weeks before this date, however, Chancellor Livingston had declined the future president's flattering offer of the Secretaryship of the navy; and Jefferson in acknowledging his letter of refusal, writes:[7]

> Your favour of January 7th came duly to hand. A part of it gave me that kind of concern which I fear I am destined often to meet. Men possessing minds of the first order, and who have had opportunities of being known, and of accquiring confidence, do not abound in any country, beyond the wants of the country. In your case, however, it is a subject of regret, rather than of complaint, as you are in fact serving the public in a very important station.

This last letter was written the day before the result of the final balloting for president was known; but a week later, and a few days before his inauguration, the president-elect again writes to his friend, and offers him.

this time the post of minister plenipotentiary to France, which he begs him to accept so that his talents may "be employed on the broader scale of the nation at large," and not, as hitherto, confined to his own "particular state."[8]

As Jefferson's French sympathies were well known, and agreed with those entertained by Mr. Livingston for that nation, he accepted this office in the spirit in which it had been tendered by the great Republican leader, though he had refused the nomination to this identical post at the hands of President Washington seven years before. Also "the hope of acquiring such information on agriculture and the arts as would be useful to his fellow-citizens," was a motive that influenced him on this occasion to accept a foreign mission.[9] In this object he was not disappointed, for at Paris he met another "visionary" like himself, who firmly believed that boats could be built to be successfully propelled by steam. This meeting led, a few years later, to the construction of the first successful American steamboat, and thus the acceptance of this French mission by Chancellor Livinsgton "gave immortality to Fulton."[10] In order to accept this office Mr. Livingston had to resign the chancellorship, which he had held for nearly a quarter of a century. It was not, however, until the autumn of this year, that he received his final instructions from the president, and sailed for France, where he landed some time in the month of November.[11]

There was one drawback to Livingston's appointment on this important mission, for he still suffered from that complaint which, as already mentioned, had been successfully used as an excuse by the Burrites to prevent his nomination by the Republican caucus for the office of vice-president. In connection with this unfortunate ailment, his old friend Gouverneur Morris, a former minister to France under Washington's administration, and a leading Federalist, relates the following good story in a letter written to Livingston himself, soon after that gentleman had taken over the charge of the American mission at Paris. After thanking Livingston for a letter he had just received from him, he proceeds to give his correspondent an outline of American politics since his departure, in which he makes some candid and amusing remarks upon some recent and contemplated acts of his old colleague's new Republican friends.

> The chief [he then goes on to say] seems to me in a wretched plight. He is in the hard necessity of giving offices to the unworthy, and turning good officers out to make room for them. He will soon be completely entangled in the meshes of

his own folly. Your appointment is not a favourite thing among them. When the Beau Messenger returned, he said the French thought it very extraordinary, that, to succeed a minister who could not *speak* their language, we had sent one who could not *hear* it. This will give what doctors call a symptomatic indication, for though straws and feathers be light things, they show which way the wind blows.[12]

Mr. Livingston was accompanied on his mission by his two sons-in-law, Lieutenant-Colonel Edward P. Livingston and Robert L. Livingston, as members of his staff. The former in writing to his sister Christina (Mrs. J. N. Macomb) gives an interesting account of society in Paris at this important period, when Bonaparte was planning to become Emperor of France; and, therefore, this letter is of historical interest.[13] In it, he writes:—

"Since my last letter to you I have been amusing myself with the novelties which this place affords. . . . You have often heard, I presume, of the society of this place, and as an instance of it the number of theatres here is always spoken of. This is true that the French is a more lively character than that of most nations of Europe, but I do not find that great levity which is attributed to them, nor do I perceive that very great difference in them which we should suppose. The higher circles here at present live in a style of luxury and extravagance, perhaps not inferior to the old Court. The morals of Paris have never been remarkable, it cannot therefore be supposed they are much improved. Few of the ministers or great men here are married, but they all have mistresses, whose style of living, dress, etc., is exceedingly superb. They make a great show at the public places, and at all the parties given by the ministers and officers of Government, and have a considerable influence. As these examples are so conspicuous, those of the same character, though not in such elevated spheres, are admitted into most societies, so that characters are not much enquired into. It is true that these persons are not admitted at Madame Bonaparte's, on account of the dislike the First Consul appears to have for them, but everywhere else, and, particularly, are collected at the parties of the Second Consul, which is the most fashionable society here, and without doubt the most brilliant circle that Europe can produce. There is however to be found those, who disliking this company form a circle in some measure distinct from them, at least in their private society, of these we have been able to obtain a very agreeable circle of acquaintances, as the affability of their manners and their well-known politeness makes them charming acquaintances, and particularly so for strangers. The contrast between this country and England is in that particular very striking.

"It is not very easy here to enter into society without engaging in it so much as to border upon dissipation, for when you are once introduced into the world, the amusements and parties succeed each other so rapidly that nothing but indisposition or a feigned one can keep you out of the vortex. Besides our private engagements we have 4 every decade on [or] in every 10 days with the officers of Government, and which it is expected that some of the family will attend, these consist of concerts, sometimes balls and always cards; you there meet all the fashionable people, all foreigners of distinction, which makes it very agreeable, and when the rooms are so crowded that you cannot move, it is then called extremely delightful. The principal amusement of the middling classes of people is the theatre, on this account 13 or more are open here in the winter, there is as you may suppose a very great difference in their merits; three or four are generally very good, and well regulated. The Opera is what most pleases me, as the late dinner hours prevent your going to the play until very late, and the dancing and decorations being in so superb a style, please those who are not capable from ignorance of the language of enjoying the wit of their Comedies. I have seen one French Tragedy, but I fancy I shall not see many more of them as I do not think they excel in that way. I believe I have already mentioned to you the superior dancing of the French ladies, and that those who excel in that way have almost excluded others, who have not time or inclination to devote half of their lives to it, from the pleasure of it, particularly in large companies. . . ."

The new American minister to the French Republic had arrived in Paris at a most momentous and critical period in the history of the two countries. For the first rumours he had heard on landing informed him of the cession of Louisiana and the Floridas by Spain to France. He thereupon went to the notorious Talleyrand, the Minister of Foreign Affairs, for information, who coolly informed him that "it had been a subject of conversation, but nothing concluded"; though the Spanish treaty was not only actually signed, but its contents known to the American minister in London. Livingston, however, soon ascertained the true facts of the case in spite of Talleyrand's duplicity, but his notes and remonstrances remained unanswered by that most shifty of diplomatists.[14] The contemplation of a French military colony on their borders, naturally gave rise to much excitement in America; and even the peace-loving president so far forgot himself, as to appear willing to risk a war with France, rather than put up with such a neighbour. And on the 18th of April, 1802, he writes to Livingston a long despatch, in which he emphatically declares "the day that France takes possession of New Orleans fixes the sentence which is to restrain her for ever within her low-water mark. It seals the union of two nations, who, in conjunction, can maintain exclusive possession of the ocean. From that moment we must marry ourselves to the British Fleet and nation."[15] Bold words to come from a man whose favourite phrase was "Peace is our passion," and whose distrust of the British Government was notorious.

A few months later, however, he appears to have discovered that threats of this nature, unless backed by deeds, were not likely to make much impression on a man of the First Consul's disposition, for in another letter to his minister at Paris, dated 10th of October in this year, he announces his intention of managing matters as follows:

> We shall so take our distance between the two rival nations as remaining disengaged till necessity compels us, we may haul finally to the enemy of that which shall make it necessary. We see all the disadvantageous consequences of taking a side, and shall be forced into it by a more disagreeable alternative; in which event we must countervail the disadvantages by measures which will give us splendour and power, but not as much happiness as our present system. We wish therefore to remain well with France; but we see that no consequences, however ruinous to them, can secure us with certainty against the extravagance of her present rulers. I think therefore that while we do nothing which the first nation on earth would deem crouching, we had better give to all our communications with them a very

mild, complaisant and even friendly complexion, but always independent; ask no favours, leave small and irritating things to be conducted by the individuals interested in them, interfere ourselves but in the greatest cases, and then not push them to irritation. No matter at present existing between them and us is important enough to risk a breach of peace; peace being indeed the most important of all things for us, except preserving an erect and independent attitude.[16]

This letter, as a recent American historian truly remarks, "would have perplexed any European diplomatist."[17] But Jefferson's passion for peace did not extend beyond his Cabinet; Congress was getting irritable over the delay in the settlement of the New Orleans difficulty regarding the right of deposit, hitherto permitted to their traders, but which was now threatened to be withdrawn; while the Western States, being more immediately concerned in the free navigation of the Mississippi, were loudly clamouring for war. Meanwhile Livingston in Paris was not idle, and he continued energetically to press the First Consul by all the means at his disposal to come to a friendly settlement with the United States, but so far without receiving the slightest encouragement. He also about this time presented Talleyrand with "a very able memorial, shewing by conclusive arguments, that the cession of the province to the United States would be a measure of wise and sound policy, conducive not less to the true interests of France than to those of the Federal Union."[18]

The French Minister of Finance, who was soon to take part in these negotiations, thus records Mr. Livingston's exertions at this period:

> M. Livingston, ministre des États-Unis à Paris, avait depuis plusieurs mois suivi cette affaire avec chaleur. Il avait alors remis au ministre des affaires étrangères, un mémoire dans lequel les raisonnements étaient appuyés d'insinuations presque menaçantes. Il ne s'y bornait pas à demander la cession de la Nouvelle-Orléans, il proposait aussi que la France cedât les vastes contrées qui sont au nord de la rivière des Arkansas, à la rive droite du Mississippi. Mais ses ouvertures étant restées sans réponse.[19]

The French Minister of Foreign Affairs, however, still gave no sign, for Bonaparte, the First Consul, had not yet relinquished all hopes of founding anew French colonies in North America; but as Shakespeare aptly puts it,

> There's a divinity that shapes our ends.
> Rough-hew them how we will.[20]

And Mr. Livingston was shortly to experience the truth of this saying.

For upon Easter Sunday, the 10th of April, 1803, Bonaparte, after attending the religious ceremonies usual to that day, summoned to his presence two of his ministers, who had had personal experience of the United States, of whom M. Barbé-Marbois, Minister of Finance, was one. To these gentlemen, the First Consul explained, in his customary vehement manner when discussing political affairs, that he had nearly decided upon selling Louisiana to the United States. The principal reason he gave for this sudden change in his plans, was the one so ably enunciated by Mr. Livingston in his memorial, that upon the next outbreak of hostilities between France and England, it would at once fall into the latter power's hands owing to her naval supremacy; and none knew better than Bonaparte himself how soon this event was likely to occur.[21] Having heard what these two ministers had to say for and against his scheme, the First Consul dismissed them, without, however, letting them know what he had finally decided upon doing in the matter.

But at daybreak on the following morning Bonaparte sent for Barbé-Marbois, and informed him that he was determined to "renounce Louisiana"; and he forcibly emphasised his remarks by saying:

> Ce n'est point seulement la Nouvelle-Orléans que je veux céder, c'est toute la colonie sans en rien réserver. Je connais le prix de ce que j'abandonne, et j'ai assez prouvé le cas que je fais de cette province, puisque mon premier acte diplomatique avec L'Espagne a eu pour objet de la récouvrer. J'y renonce donc avec un vif déplaisir. Nous obstiner à sa conservation serait folie. Je vous charge de négocier cette affaire avec les envoyés du congrès. N'attendez pas même l'arrivée de M. Monroe: abouchez-vous dès aujourd'hui avec M. Livingston; mais j'ai besoin de beaucoup d'argent pour cette guerre, et je ne voudrais pas la commen cer par de nouvelles contributions.[22]

But before proceeding to relate how Mr. Livingston received this wel-come but unexpected proposal from the First Consul, it will be as well to explain Bonaparte's reference to the expected arrival of Mr. Monroe in Paris. This gentleman's appointment as special envoy to assist Livingston in his negotiations arose in this way. The president's position in regard to this affair, as we have already noticed, was a very delicate one. On the one hand, in spite of his bluster about an alliance with England, he had no real wish to go to war with France; while on the other hand, he had to conciliate the Western States in view of the next presidential election. And when, almost immediately after he had written his last quoted letter to Livingston, the right of deposit at New Orleans was actually withdrawn, even the peace-loving president discovered that "something sensible" had become necessary.[23] The "something sensible" resolved itself into the nom-ination of a minister extraordinary to aid Mr. Livingston in buying New Orleans; not that Jefferson for one moment distrusted the resident minis-ter's capabilities, but as he explained in a despatch to that gentleman, dated 3d February, 1803:—

> The late suspension by the Intendant of New Orleans of our right to deposit there, without which the right of navigation is impracticable, has thrown this country into such a flame of hostile disposition as can scarcely be described. The Western country was peculiarly sensible to it, as you may suppose. Our business was to take the most effectual pacific measures in our power to remove the suspension, and at the same time to per-suade our countrymen that pacific measures would be the most effectual and the most speedily so. The opposition caught it as a plank in a shipwreck, hoping it would enable them to suck the Western people to them. They raised the cry of war, were intriguing in all quarters to exasperate the Western inhabit-ants to arm and go down on their own authority, and possess themselves of New Orleans. . . . As a remedy to all this, we determined to name a minister extraordinary to go immedi-ately to Paris and Madrid to settle the matter. This measure being a visible one, and the person named peculiarly popular with the Western country,[24] crushed at once and put an end to all further attempts on the legislature. From that moment all has been quiet. . . . The measure was, moreover, proper from another cause, we must know at once whether we can acquire

New Orleans or not. We are satisfied nothing else will secure us against a war at no distant period, and we cannot pass this season without beginning those arrangements which will be necessary if war is hereafter to result. For this purpose it was necessary that the negotiator should be fully possessed of every idea we have on the subject. . . . With this view, we have joined Mr. Monroe to yourself at Paris, and to Mr. Pinckney at Madrid, although we believe it will be hardly necessary for him to go to this last place. . . . The future destinies of our country hang on the event of this negotiation and I am sure they could not be placed in more able or more zealous hands. On our part we shall be satisfied that what you do not effect cannot be effected. Accept therefore assurances of my sincere and constant affection and high respect.[25]

To those who were not in Jefferson's secrets, the nomination of Mr. Monroe as minister extraordinary, was regarded as an intentional slight put upon the resident minister in France by the Republican Government, and Livingston's old friend Gouverneur Morris certainly so considered it. He thus gives vent to his feelings on the subject, in a letter written to his friend some few weeks after Monroe's departure; but it must be borne in mind, that though Mr. Morris was far from being a narrow-minded man, he was a strong Federalist, and therefore politically opposed to the government then in power.

I did not write to you by Mr. Monroe [he says in this letter], because he and I are not on such terms of intimacy as to ask his care of a letter, because I did not put one in his care, and because I wished you to judge of things, without any bias from comments on my part. Before this arrives you will have made your own interpretations. You will have seen, too, that your brethren of the Corps Diplomatique consider Mr. Monroe as the efficient and confidential man. Not being in the confidence of our Cabinet, I cannot account for a conduct, which, in every point of view, is so strange. Setting aside the sacrifices you have made to promote the cause, which brought them into power, I cannot help thinking, that your rank in society, the high offices you have held, and, let me add, the respectable talents with which God has blessed you, all require more delicacy on the part of your political friends than has on this occasion been exhibited. It is possible, that I am unjust to Mr. Monroe, but really I consider him as a person of mediocrity in every respect.

Just exceptions lie against his diplomatic character, and taking all circumstances into consideration, his appointment must appear extraordinary to the Cabinets of Europe. It is itself a most unwary step, and will lower our government in public estimation. I was, therefore, just so much the more vexed at it on your account. I trust it will not be pretended, that the application of money could not be as safely entrusted to your care and intelligence, as to those of Mr. Monroe. The pretext, that he is only joined with you in the commission, is mere pretext, and every discreet man with you will naturally consider him as the principal, the chief, and in fact the sole Minister.[26]

The Senate having confirmed Monroe's nomination, he set sail for France on the 8th of March 1803, and reached Havre exactly a month later, when Bonaparte was at once informed of his arrival by the telegraph.[27] The news of the special American envoy having landed in France, may have hastened the First Consul's determination to sell Louisiana, for as we have seen, at the very moment Monroe was leaving Havre for Paris, M. Barbé-Marbois had received his master's instructions to settle matters with Mr. Livingston, *without waiting for his colleague's arrival*. Livingston, however, was as yet totally unaware of the change that had taken place in the First Consul's plans, and on the very day that Bonaparte had summoned his ministers to Saint Cloud to be informed of his decision, the American minister,—who had also received intimation of Monroe's arrival at Havre,—wrote a letter of welcome to his colleague, in which, after congratulating him on his safe arrival, he says, "We have long and anxiously waited for you. God grant that your mission may answer your and the public expectation. War may do something for us, nothing else would. I have paved the way for you, and if you could add to my memoirs an assurance that we are now in possession of New Orleans, we should do well."[28] Within twenty-four hours all was changed, and Livingston could not be blamed for wishing that his colleague had been detained some little time longer on his voyage.

The First Consul entertained a highly favourable opinion of Livingston, and from a contemporary English eyewitness of the official reception, held by Napoleon Bonaparte in honour of his being appointed

First Consul for life, during the summer of the previous year, we learn, that upon this occasion, among "so many representatives of nations, and noble strangers from every country who had collected to pay their respects to the First Cousul of France, now established as the sole head of the government for life," he noticed "the American ambassador, Mr. Livingston, plain, and simple in manners and dress,—representing his republic with propriety and dignity." And in this gentleman's interesting description of this historical event, he further mentions the particular attention Napoleon paid to the American minister; for he says:

> We reached the interior apartment, where Bonaparte, First Consul, surrounded by his generals, ministers, senators, and officers, stood between the second and third consuls, Lebrun and Cambacérèes, in the centre of a semicircle, at the head of the room. The numerous assemblage from the *Salle des Ambassadeurs*, formed into another semicircle, joined to that at the head of which stood the First Consul.
>
> Bonaparte, of a small, and by no means commanding figure, dressed plainly, though richly, in the embroidered consular coat—without powder in his hair—looked, at the first view, like a private gentleman, indifferent as to dress, and devoid of all haughtiness in his air. The two consuls, large and heavy men, seemed pillars too cumbrous to support themselves, and during the levee, were sadly at a loss what to do,—whether the snuffbox or pocket handkerchief was to be appealed to, or the left leg exchanged for the right. The moment the circle was formed, Bonaparte began with the Spanish ambassador, then went to the American, with whom he spoke some time, and so on, performing his part with ease and very agreeably.[29]

Talleyrand, and not Barbé-Marbois, however, startled Livingston on the eleventh of April 1803, by asking him somewhat abruptly whether his government "wished to have the whole of Louisiana," and, if so, what they were prepared to pay for it; but when the latter pressed his questioner for something more definite, and mentioned the sum of twenty million francs, provided the claims of American citizens against Prance for the losses inflicted by her cruisers were also paid, the French Foreign Minister as usual became evasive, said it was too low an offer, and inferred "that he did not speak from authority, but that the idea had struck him." Mr. Livingston, thereupon, informed him, he could not proceed further in the negotiations until he had had an opportunity of consulting Mr. Monroe.[30] But just before the arrival of the special American envoy in Paris, Livingston had another interview with Talleyrand, but with no better result, as the French minister, while trying to get his opponent to commit himself as to naming a higher price, coolly declared "that his proposition was only personal."[31] On the afternoon of this day—the twelfth—Mr. Monroe arrived at his destination, when he was surprised to learn from his colleague of the hints dropped by Talleyrand, as to the readiness of the French Government to sell not only New Orleans, but the whole of Louisiana.

The next day was spent by the two American envoys in examining Mr. Livingston's papers and comparing notes, and in the evening the latter gave a dinner in his apartments in honour of his colleague, at which Monroe was present. As Mr. Livingston was doing the honours of the table, he saw M. Barbé-Marbois strolling in the garden before his windows. He, thereupon, sent him a message by Colonel Livingston, requesting the pleasure of his company, whereupon that gentleman joined the party just as coffee was being served. In the course of the conversation that took place after his entrance Mr. Livingston mentioned to the French Finance Minister Talleyrand's peculiar conduct of the last two days in reference to the negotiations for the cession of Louisiana, but as such a discussion could not well be carried on in such company, M. Baibé-Marbois invited his host to come to the Treasury Office after the party had broken up, and there talk the whole matter over together, without any risk of interruption; Barbé-Marbois hinting at the same time that he knew something of the matter.

It was midnight before Mr. Livingston left the Treasury Office to return to his own house, but before he parted from the French minister, the terms of the sale of Louisiana by France to the United States, had been practically agreed upon between these two statesmen. During this interview, when the question of the price to be paid by the United States came to be discussed, M. Barbé-Marbois informed the American minister that the First Consul had said to him, "Well, you have the charge of the Treasury; let them give you one hundred millions [francs], and pay their own claims, and take the whole country," though he knew well enough half this amount would have satisfied Bonaparte. Seeing by Mr. Livingston's face that he was surprised at so extravagant a price being named, he at once remarked "that he considered the demand exorbitant and had told the First Consul that the thing was impossible, and that the United States had not the means of raising that amount." Whereupon, still according to M. Barbé-Marbois, "the Consul told him they might borrow it."[32]

"I now plainly saw," says Livingston in his despatch to the Secretary of State, from which these particulars are derived, "the whole business— first the Consul was disposed [to sell]; next he distrusted Talleyrand on account of the business of the supposed intention to bribe, and meant to put the negotiation into the hands of Marbois, whose character for integrity is established. I told him that the United States were anxious to preserve peace with France; that for that reason they wished to remove them to the west side of the Mississippi; that we would be perfectly satisfied with New Orleans and the Floridas, and had no disposition to extend across the river; that of course we would not give any great sum for the purchase."

After some further fencing, the French Finance Minister lowered his terms to sixty million francs, with estimated claims to the amount of twenty millions more, and pressed Livingston to agree to this lesser sum; warning him, at the same time, of the danger of delay when dealing with a man of the First Consul's disposition. "You know," he added, "the temper of a youthful conquerer; every thing he does is as rapid as lightning; we have only to speak to him, as opportunity presents itself, perhaps in a crowd, when he bears no contradiction. When I am alone with him, I can speak more freely, and he attends; but this opportunity seldom happens, and is always accidental." Livingston, however willing to close the business, there and then, could not do so without consulting his colleague, as his instructions never contemplated the purchase of the whole of Louisiana.

But on his return home he sat down, late as it was, and wrote a long despatch to Madison, which he wound up by saying:

> As to the quantum, I have yet made up no opinion. The field open to us is infinitely larger than our instructions contemplated, the revenue increasing, and the land more than adequate to sink the capital, should we even go the sum proposed by Marbois,—nay, I persuade myself that the whole sum may be raised by the sale of territory west of the Mississippi, with the right of sovereignty, to some power in Europe, whose vicinity we should not fear. I speak now without reflection and without having seen Mr. Monroe, as it was midnight when I left the Treasury Office, and it is now near three o'clock. It is so very important that you should be apprised that a negotiation is actually opened, even before Mr. Monroe has been presented,

in order to calm the tumult which the news of war will renew, that I have lost no time in communicating it. We shall do all we can to cheapen the purchase; but my present sentiment is that we shall buy.[33]

After some further haggling over the price the American envoys finally agreed to pay eighty million francs, which was to include the claims of American citizens, estimated at twenty millions. Mr. Monroe was presented to Bonaparte on the first of May, when he and Livingston dined at the Tuileries, and on the following day the treaty, antedated to the 30th of April, was signed. The separate convention, respecting the settlement of the American claims, however, was not signed until about a week later, when it was also antedated like the Treaty of Cession.[34] As soon as they had concluded their labours, the plenipotentiaries rose and shook hands; when Livingston expressing the general satisfaction said:

We have lived long, but this is the noblest work of our whole lives. The treaty which we have just signed has not been obtained by art, or dictated by force; equally advantageous to the two contracting parties, it will change vast solitudes into flourishing districts. From this day the United States take their place among the powers of the first rank; the English lose all exclusive influence in the affairs of America. Thus one of the principal causes of European rivalries and animosities is about to cease. However, if wars are inevitable, France will have one day in the New World a natural ally, increasing in strength from year to year, and which nothing can prevent from becoming powerful and respected on all the seas of the globe. The United States will re-establish the maritime rights of all the world, which are now usurped by a single nation. These treaties will thus be a guarantee of peace and concord among commercial states. The instruments which we have just signed will cause no tears to be shed; they prepare ages of happiness for innumerable generations of human creatures. The Mississippi and Missouri will see them succeed one another, and multiply, truly worthy of the regard of Providence, in the bosom of equality, under just laws, freed from the errors of superstition and the scourges of bad government.[35]

But not even Livingston, with all his optimism regarding the future of this newly-acquired territory, could foresee all the immense advantages his country was to secure in later years through the purchase of Louisiana—the occupation of which territory by the Americans was to give them in time the claim to, and ultimate possession of, the whole continent between the Gulf of Mexico and the Pacific Coast! A recent American historian—not over-friendly to Mr. Livingston—in his account of this treaty says, in reference to the troubles which subsequently arose in regard to the settlement of the claims of American citizens against France, and which were assumed by the United States under the above-mentioned convention:

> Livingston's troubles did not end there. He could afford to suffer some deduction from his triumph; for he had achieved the greatest diplomatic success recorded in American history. Neither Franklin, Jay, Gallatin, nor any other American diplomatist was so fortunate as Livingston for the immensity of his results compared with the poverty of his means. Other treaties of immense consequence have been signed by American representatives,—the treaty of alliance with France; the treaty of peace with England, which recognised independence; the treaty of Ghent; the treaty which ceded Florida; the Ashburton treaty; the treaty of Guadeloupe Hidalgo,—but in none of those did the United States Government get so much for so little. The annexation of Louisiana was an event so portentous as to defy measurement; it gave a new face to politics, and ranked in historical importance next to the Declaration of Independence and the adoption of the Constitution,—events of which it was the logical outcome; but as a matter of diplomacy it was unparalleled, because it cost almost nothing.[36]

When Gouverneur Morris heard of the purchase of Louisiana, he wrote a cordial letter of congratulation to Livingston, in which, after remarking that some of his Federalist friends were not over-pleased at his declaring publicly his approval of a treaty, negotiated by their political opponents, he expressed it as his firm opinion, that this successful termination to his correspondent's negotiations with the French Government had saved his own.

To tell you an important truth, my friend [he wrote], you have saved that administration who, in return, will never forgive you for performing, without orders and without powers, such great public service. Your conduct is a satire on theirs, for you have gained what they did not dare to ask. Had the bargain been disagreeable to those States, by whom the President expects to be re-chosen at the next election, you might have been disavowed, but it secures the Western States, quiets the Southern, and is consequently popular. It might have been generous and manly in the President [he goes on to say] to have told Congress, that his Minister in France, forming a just estimation of that extensive country, had, before the arrival of his colleague with powers and instructions, in a manner highly honourable to himself prepared the way, and seized the favourable moment to conclude an important negotiation, in consequence of which they had in a few days not only realised his expectations, but exceeded his hopes. You have seen the communication actually made. When it was read in my presence, I was obliged to bite my tongue pretty hard to prevent it from telling the true state of that important transaction. It seems, however, to be pretty well understood, though I have been silent, not thinking myself authorised to embroil you with the chiefs of your own party, whatever may be my opinion of your true interest. If I am rightly informed, offence is taken. Vanity has certainly been wounded, because confidants must know the facts, and vanity is the leading trait of a certain character. You will learn from your friends here how *they* stand at headquarters, and whether your services have strengthened *their* interest. It seems to be a prevailing opinion that the Clinton party have exclusively the ear of our President as to what regards this State [New York], and it is presumed that his arrangements are taken with them for the next election. You tell me you will be out next spring; but will you have permission to return? Unless my observation has deceived me, it will, if granted at all, be granted with reluctance.[37]

As subsequent events conclusively proved, this keen and caustic observer of human nature was perfectly correct in his prognostications.[38] For Livingston, on his return to America, found himself neglected, as his friend had predicted; while Jefferson's protégé and neighbour, the Virginian Monroe, derived the entire political credit to be obtained from this peaceful diplomatic triumph. Mr. Monroe was undoubtedly a fortunate man, for, thanks to the "Virginia Dynasty," he became Secretary of State under Madison in 1811, and less than six years afterwards was elected to succeed him in the presidency.[39] Monroe's Secretary of State, and also his successor in the occupation of the White House, was John Quincy Adams, who had been trained from a youth upwards as a diplomatist under the eye of his father, the celebrated Revolutionary statesman, and whose opinion therefore, as to which of these two American plenipotentiaries the credit of the Louisiana Purchase should properly belong, must carry great weight. It is, therefore, satisfactory to know that he, who certainly was not biassed in favour of Livingston, used publicly to declare that "the credit of the acquisition of Louisiana, whether to be considered as a source of good or evil, is perhaps due to Robert R. Livingston more than to any other man." And these words, be it noted, were used in a speech delivered in Boston, on the 27th of September 1836, in the honour of James Madison, Jefferson's Secretary of State at the time of the purchase.[40]

That Mr. Adams thought highly himself of this diplomatic achievement, is proved by his styling it in the above eulogy "the great and imperishable memorial of the administration of Jefferson." He had, also, in another eulogy, delivered also at Boston some five years previously upon the life and character of Livingston's fortunate colleague, James Monroe, used these words in reference to the former's share in negotiating this successful treaty:

> He [Monroe] was joined in the Commission Extraordinary, with Robert R. Livingston, the Resident Minister Plenipotentiary from the United States to France, well known as one of the most eminent leaders of our Revolution. . . . Mr. Livingston had, many months before, presented to the French Government a very able memorial, shewing by conclusive argument, that the cession of the province to the United States would be a measure of wise and sound policy, conducive not less to the true interests of France than to those of the Federal Union.[41]

On the 30th of June 1804, General Armstrong, Livingston's brother-in-law, was appointed to succeed him as resident minister at Paris, and Jefferson appears, at one time, to have entertained the idea of transferring the latter to the Court of St. James's. For Rufus King, the late minister to that Court, after his return home during the previous summer, in the course of a conversation with Mr. Gallatin, the Secretary of the Treasury, asked who was to be his successor. To which Mr. Gallatin replied, "Either Mr. Livingston or Mr. Monroe." Whereupon Mr. King remarked, "Mr. Livingston would do very well, his deafness excepted, which is a strong objection"; and he went on to inform the secretary that "his British Majesty asked him twice who would be sent, and expressed his satisfaction in case Mr. Livingston was the man; but when he saw Mr. Monroe's name announced in the newspapers for that mission, he inquired particularly of his character, and asked him [Mr King], whether he had not been opposed to him in politics. Upon being answered that those differences of politics had only been shades of opinion, and that Mr. Monroe was a man of great probity and integrity, 'Well, well,' his Majesty replied, 'if he is an honest man he will do very well.'"[42]

But at the very time this conversation was being held in America, Mr. Monroe had decided the question himself by proceeding to London; and had actually been presented to George III., as Rufus King's successor, the day before Mr. Gallatin, in New York, had forwarded a report of his conversation with Mr. King to President Jefferson. Monroe's reason for crossing the Channel without special orders from his government, was that being warned by Napoleon not to proceed to Madrid as he should have done, and as he had intended doing; and being also accredited to the Court of St. James's in case his mission should require his presence there, he had decided to fill in his time by occupying this post until the Spanish ministers had got over their vexation at the cession of Louisiana to the United States.

Previous to his being relieved by General Armstrong, Mr. Livingston paid a brief visit to London, which he appears to have undertaken for the purpose of sounding the English Government, as to the possibility of arranging a peace between that country and France. He had apparently crossed the Channel in the expectation of finding Mr. Fox, with whom he had become acquainted in Paris, Foreign Minister; and Napoelon, who had all his plans laid for being proclaimed Emperor, probably had hinted to Livingston that if England were prepared to make the first overture in that direction he would be willing to receive it favourably. However, as it happened, Livingston on his arrival in London found the "Great Commoner" still at the head of the government, and thus nothing came of his mission;[43]

but it is worth recording what Pitt and his biographer—Earl Stanhope—
have to say in regard to this incident.

Athwart these warlike preparations [says Lord Stanhope]
came one faint gleam of peace. Mr. Livingston, Minister from
the United States to France, arrived in London. All his leanings were to Fox, all his overtures to that statesman. But Fox
thought it his duty to lay before the Government the information which he had thus received. Accompanied by Grey he
called upon Pitt in Downing Street, on the 5th of June [1804].
Immediately after they had taken leave, Pitt put down in writing what had passed, for the information of his colleagues.

MEMORANDUM

June 5, 1804.

The purport of the communication made me by Mr. Fox
and Mr. Grey was that Mr. Livingston had expressed to them
his opinions respecting the possibility of peace between this
country and France. That he had taken particular care to dis-
claim any authority or commission on the subject, but that his
opinions were chiefly founded on conversations with Joseph
Bonaparte some time since, and more recently with Talleyrand
and Marbois. From Joseph Bonaparte he had only collected generally that there was a disposition in the French Government
to peace. From the two others he understood that the French
Government would expect some arrangement about Malta,
such as had been before proposed—probably its being garri-
soned by Russia; and that on the point of our relinquishing it
they would not give way; but that they should be ready to consent to withdrawing their troops from Switzerland and Holland,
and to provide for the independence of both those countries
by the guarantee of other Powers, and that guarantee as general as possible, and that they would also agree to the restoration of Hanover. That some idea had been mentioned of some
guarantee in return against our making further acquisitions
in India; but Mr. Fox observed that it had not been explained
what Power there was that could enter into such guarantee, and

rather hinted that he imagined on that account they might not mean farther security than our assurance of a system of moder-ation. They added, to questions, which I put, that nothing had been said with respect to providing for the security of Holland or Switzerland, by any arrangement for the defence of either in the first instance, by fortresses or auxiliary troops, or by anything beyond the guarantee suggested; but Mr. Grey stated that he understood the basis proposed was to provide for their independence, and that the mode of doing so would, he con-ceived, be considered as matter of subsequent discussion. They further added that Mr. Livingston understood that it would be expected that the first overture of a disposition to treat would be made either directly or indirectly on our part; and that they would be extremely disposed to receive it, and that the present moment [with a view to Bonaparte's new dignity] was thought a favourable one. That they had mentioned to Mr. Livingston that the detention of the English in France might be one obsta-cle to any such overture; and Mr. L. had expressed a strong opinion (but merely as an opinion of his own, and not founded on his conversations) that on any indication of a favourable disposition here towards an overture, they would be glad to take the opportunity of releasing the prisoners, as their detention was generally disapproved in France.

Mr. Fox also said that in the course of conversation Mr. Livingston had expressed a great readiness to do anything in his power towards facilitating a negotiation, and thought himself capable of being of considerable use. Mr. Fox rather intimated a belief that the object of Mr. L. coming here was to bring about some explanation, and that it was generally supposed to be so in France; and he seemed to think that he possibly was prepared to have said more if he had found the administration composed as he perhaps expected when he left France. I thanked Mr. Fox and Mr. Grey for the communication, without expressing any opinion on any part of it, and only informed them that I should report what they had told me to the King's Ministers.

W. P.[44]

For my part [the English Prime Minister said to his friend and confidant, Mr. Rose], I think no good consequences can

result from this communication. If France had really any serious intention of putting an end to the war the new Emperor
would have found some less exceptional channel of communication than through a man whose hostile disposition to this
country has been so strongly and so lately manifested.[45] His
public character at that Court, too, makes him an unfit instrument for the purpose.[46]

To this expression of opinion on the part of Mr. Pitt, Lord Stanhope
adds the remark: "The doubts of Mr. Pitt on this occasion seem to have
been justly founded. No good consequences ensued; and the overture of
Mr. Livingston was only, I conceive, a *Will of the Wisp.*"[47]

Here Lord Stanhope's prejudices against the United States' representative in Paris have evidently somewhat blinded his judgment, for a few
months later Napoleon personally opened negotiations, regarding a cessation of hostilities, with George III. direct;[48] and there is no reason for supposing, that if Mr. Livingston had been able to have carried back with him
to France some definite offer from the English Government, negotiations
resulting in the then termination of the war might not have taken place. It
is most improbable that Mr. Livingston would have undertaken this journey, unless he had had something more to go upon than the casual conversations of Joseph Bonaparte and the two French ministers. But Napoleon
at this date, with the Imperial crown at last within his grasp, apparently,
though wishing for peace with England, did not care to give his enemies
the opportunity of saying that he feared the English; and hence his reason
for taking advantage of Livingston's services on this occasion. If Mr. Fox
had been Foreign Minister, his mission would most probably have had quite
a different result.

After Mr. Livingston had been relieved of his duties in the French
capital, he did not return home at once, but travelled about so as to see
something of Europe. It was upon his return to Paris after the completion
of this tour, that he took his final leave of the Emperor Napoleon, who
presented him, as a mark of his personal esteem, with a gold snuff-box on
which was painted the donor's portrait, the work of the celebrated French
miniaturist Isabey, and which is still in the possession of Mr. Livingston's
descendants. The Emperor had also, when First Consul, liberally aided
the American minister in his endeavours to promote the usefulness of
the recently founded American Academy of Fine Arts, by presenting it
with some valuable paintings and rare prints. Mr. Livingston was the

principal founder of this Academy, and took great interest in adding to its various collections, and after his return to New York he became its president.[49]

Notes

1. Barbé-Marbois, *Histoire de la Louisiane*, pp. 298, 299. Monsieur Barbé-Marbois was the French Minister of Finance.
2. Jefferson and Livingston were much about the same age, the former having been born on the 2nd April, 1743, and the latter on the 27th November, 1746. They were the two youngest members of the above committee.
3. One of the heaviest charges made against the Federalists by the Republican party, was that of wishing for the re-establishment of a monarchical régime in America. Hamilton, at least to judge by his speeches, would not have been so very averse to such a form of government, as he honestly dreaded entrusting the people with too much political power.
4. Alexander Hamilton is evidently meant by this remark.
5. This refers to Mr. Livingston's office as Chancellor of the State of New York.
6. Thomas Jefferson to Chancellor Livingston, Washington, 14 December, 1800. From the original letter kindly lent me, with others, by the late Mr. Robert E. Livingston of New York. The writer had a curious habit of hardly ever using capital letters when commencing a fresh sentence. In the above extracts the necessary capitals have therefore been inserted. This letter will be found printed in full in *Jefferson's Writings*, vol. iv, pp. 337–340; also in Randolph's *Memoirs of Thomas Jefferson*, vol. iii, pp. 450–452. Chancellor Livingston's papers are unfortunately much scattered, and thus, the author has been unable to get access to a large number of his letters, which he understands are still in existence, and not to be found printed in any collection.
7. Thomas Jefferson to Chancellor Livingston, Washington, 16 February, 1801. Original letter. This letter is *not* printed in *Jefferson's Writings*, or in Randolph's *Memoirs*.
8. The same to the same, 24th February, 1801. Original letter. This letter is to be found in *Jefferson's Writings*, but not in Randolph's *Memoirs*.
9. *Vide* Mr. Livingston's preface to his *Essay on Sheep*, printed by order of the State Legislature in 1809.
10. Adams (Henry), *History of the United States*, etc., etc. vol. i, p. 112. An account of Fulton's first steamboat, named after Mr. Livingston's home, the *Clermont*, will be found in the succeeding chapter.
11. His appointment as minister plenipotentiary was officially confirmed on the 2d October, 1801.
12. Gouverneur Morris to Robert R. Livingston, Washington, 20th March, 1802. Livingston's predecessor at Paris, was Mr. William V. Murray of Maryland. Who is meant by the "Beau Messenger" the author is unable to say.
13. Letter dated Paris, 23d February, 1802. The original is in the possession of Mr. John Navarre Macomb of Chicago, Ill., a grandson of Christina Macomb.
14. Adams (Henry), *History of the United States*, etc., etc., vol. i, p. 409.
15. Jefferson to Robert R. Livingston, Washington, 18th April, 1802. Original letter. This is to be found printed in full in the works previously referred to. Unless otherwise stated to the contrary, this remark also applies to future letters from Jefferson

to Livingston. The author of the Declaration of Independence had evidently not lost his taste for high-sounding phrases!

16. Jefferson to Robert R. Livingston, Washington, 10 October, 1802. Original letter.
17. Adams (Henry), *History of the United States*, etc., etc., vol. i, p. 423.
18. Adams (John Quincy), *An Eulogy on the Life and Character of James Monroe*, p. 59.
19. Barbé-Marbois, *Histoire de la Lousisiane*, p. 249.
20. *Hamlet*, act v, scene 2.
21. A month previous to this date, Livingston had been an eyewitness to a scene in Madame Bonaparte's drawing-room between the First Consul and Lord Whitworth, the English ambassador, at which the former, in his usual arrogant way, taxed the English nation with wishing for war; and when the ambassador stated in reply that what the English people wanted was peace, Bonaparte impetuously retorted, "I must either have Malta or war!" *Vide* Adams (Henry), *History of the United States* etc., etc., vol. ii, p. 19.
22. Barbé-Marbois, *Histoire de la Louisiane*, pp. 298, 299.
23. Jefferson to Monroe, Washington, 13th January, 1803.
24. Mr. Monroe, as Governor of Virginia, and a prominent leader of the Republican party, had great influence in the Southern and Western States, which Mr. Livingston, as a citizen of one of the Northern States, did not possess. This was the Mr. Monroe, who had accepted the mission to France in 1794, after it had been declined on that occasion by Mr. Livingston.
25. Jefferson to Robert R. Livingston, Washington, 3d February, 1803. Original letter.
26. Gouverneur Morris to Robert R. Livingston, Morrisania, 23d April 1803.
27. The system of signalling then in use in France had been brought to a high state of perfection.
28. Livingston to Monroe, Paris, 10th April 1803.
29. Trotter, *Memoirs of the Latter Years of the Right Honourable Charles James Fox*, pp. 258–266. Mr. Trotter was secretary to Mr. Fox, the celebrated British statesman, who was also present at this reception.
30. Livingston to Madison, Secretary of State, Paris, 11th April 1803. This does not quite agree with M. Barbé-Marbois' statement that "Les conférences commencérent le même jour [11 Avril] entre MM. Livingston et Barbé-Marbois, à qui le premier consul confiait cette négociation." (*Histoire de la Louisiane*, p. 301.) But as his account was published in 1829, while Mr. Livingston's letter was written immediately after the above interview with Talleyrand, it is apparent M. Barbé-Marbois' memory, owing to lapse of time, must have misled him in this instance.
31. Livingston to Madicon, Paris, 13th April 1803.
32. *Histoire de la Louisiane*, p. 299. See also Livingston's letter to Madison of the 13th April 1803.
33. Livingston to Madison, Paris, 13th April 1803. Should be by rights dated 14th, as it was written in the early morning hours of that day.
34. Adams (Henry), *History of the United States*, etc., etc., vol. ii, p. 42. By signing this treaty the American envoys exceeded their instructions; for they were sent to negotiate for the purchase of New Orleans and the Floridas, whereas they bought New Orleans and the whole territory on the west bank of the Mississippi, instead of that on the left bank! The latter, however, was now so closed in by the United States, that Spain was glad enough to cede the Floridas to that government sixteen years later.
35. Barbé-Marbois, *Histoire de la Louisiane*, pp. 333, 334. The following is this gentleman's description of Mr. Livingston:—"M. Livingston, chancelier de L'Etat de New

York, avait été membre du congrès et ministre des affaires étrangères. Il était chef d'une de ces familles patriciennce qui, par d'ancions services, une conduite honorable et une grande fortune bien employée, sont l'ornement des États auxquels elles appartiénnent."—*Ibid.*, p. 303.

36. Adams (Henry), *History of the United States of America during the First Administration of Thomas Jefferson*, vol. ii, p. 48. In previous quotations from this work, which was published in 1889, it has been referred to under a shorter title. In these two volumes will be found an interesting and readable account of the above treaty, and of the constitutional difficulties arising from this purchase, which was ratified by the United States Government on the 31st October 1803.

37. Gouverneur Morris to Robert R. Livingston, Morrisania, 28th November 1803.

38. That Mr. Morris was a keen, and generally correct, observer of the political events of his day, is also proved from another remarkable forecast he made in the same letter, regarding Napoleon's threatened invasion of England:—"I agree with you [viz. Livingston]," he writes, "in the opinion, that the late negotiation was conducted miserably on the part of Britain. But mark how the affairs of this world run. The King's Ministers, having bungled themselves into a miserable peace, bungled themselves out of it into an expensive war, and have thereby roused the national spirit depressed before; and now it is well within the circles of probabilities, that events, to which they are but solemn witnesses, may get them gloriously through the contest, and place their country foremost in the rank of nations." Certainly, the rising fortunes of Napoleon, soon to be Emperor, did not blind this clever critic to the fact that England, and not France, would be the ultimate winner!

39. Monroe owed his election solely to the fact that the slave States were determined, if possible, to have the presidents Southern men.

40. *An Eulogy on the Lift and Character of James Madison* etc., etc. Delivered by John Quincy Adams at Boston on the 27th September 1836. By his praise of Livingston on this occasion, Mr. Adams gave great offence to some of Monroe's admirers, which he duly records in his voluminous Diary, under date 9th December 1836.

41. *An Eulogy on the Life and Character of James Monroe* etc., etc. Delivered by John Quincy Adams at Boston on the 25th August 1831.

42. Gallatin to Jefferson, New York, 18th August 1803.

43. The Right Honourable George Rose, Joint Paymaster-General, and friend and confidant of Mr. Pitt, records in his Diary, under date 17 May [1804]: "I learned from Mr. Pigott, one of the Bank Directors, that Mr. Livingston was arrived from Paris with powers (as generally believed) to treat of peace; the report adding, that he came in the expectation of finding Mr. Fox Secretary of State for Foreign Affairs, with whom he hoped he could successfully negotiate. The funds rose 1 per cent, on the news."—*Diaries of Mr. Rose*, vol. ii, p. 136.

44. Earl Stanhope, *Life of Pitt*, vol. iv, pp. 199–201.

45. Mr. Livingston's strong opposition to the Jay Treaty was well known in London, also his pronounced French leanings. On hearing of his arrival in England, Mr. Pitt told Mr. Rose, he could place no confidence in such "a violent Republican" and hater of England. Mr. Rose, whereupon, according to his own account, expostulated with his chief, and assured the Prime Minister, he (Rose) had been privately informed that Mr. Livingston was not so inimical to their country as was commonly reported to be the case, and that it would not do to let Mr. Fox understand that he would not listen to any peace overtures from that quarter. Hence Mr. Pitt's subsequent interview with Fox and Grey, and the long memorandum drawn up by

the Prime Minister for submission to his Cabinet.—*Diaries of Mr, Rose*, vol. ii, pp. 136 *et seq.*

46. *Diaries of Mr. Rose*, vol. ii, pp. 151, 152.
47. *Life of Pitt*, vol. iv, p. 202.
48. "On January 2nd, 1805, a month after his coronation as Emperor, Napoleon wrote to George III. proposing peace, as neither nation had anything to gain by war."— The *Cambridge Modem History (Napoleon)*, vol. ix, p. 244.
49. Clarkson, Clermont or Livingston Manor, pp. 116, 117. The Lift and Correspondence of Rufus King, vol. iv, p. 449.

CHAPTER XVI

CONCERNING THE FIRST STEAMBOAT, THE "CLERMONT," AND HOW ROBERT R. LIVINGSTON "GAVE IMMORTALITY TO FULTON."

"He [Chancellor Livingston] built the first steamboat, and gave immortality to Fulton."

ADAMS (HENRY), *History of the United States.*

AS we have seen in the previous chapter, when Jefferson wrote to Chancellor Livingston offering him a seat in his Cabinet, he referred to his correspondent's pet hobby "the steam-engine."[1] Nearly two years previous to this, Mr. Livingston had given Jefferson a very full and interesting account of this steam-engine, of which the boiler was constructed of wood.[2] The designer of this primitive engine had, for some years past, taken a great deal of interest in the application of steam for motive power; and, like some other enthusiasts in America, had endeavoured to put his theories into practice.[3] For this purpose he had engaged an Englishman, one Nesbet or Nisbet, to construct a steamboat at a place south of Tivoli on the Hudson, not far from his home, now known as De Koven's Bay. This experimental boat was of thirty tons burden and was to be propelled by a steam-engine, but it turned out a failure when put to the test of a trial trip, and Chancellor Livingston abandoned all further experiments for the time being.[4]

Before this boat had disappointed his expectations, Mr. Livingston had applied to the State Legislature for "the exclusive right and privilege of navigating all kinds of boats, which might be propelled by the force of fire or steam, on all waters within the territory or jurisdiction of the State of New York, for the term of twenty years from the passing of the act; upon condition that he should within a twelvemonth build such a boat, the mean of whose progress should not be less than four miles an hour." As a reason why the Legislature should grant his request, Mr. Livingston stated in the above application, "that he was possessed of a mode of applying the steam-engine to propel a boat on new and advantageous principles; but that he was deterred from carrying it into effect, by the uncertainty and hazard of a very expensive experiment, unless he could be assured of an exclusive advantage from it, should it be successful." Mr. Livingston's friend Dr. Mitchell, one of the city representatives in the House of Assembly, introduced the bill, and "Upon this occasion," wrote its sponsor to one of Fulton's biographers, "the wags and the lawyers in the house were generally opposed to my bill. I had to encounter all their jokes, and the whole of their logic. One main ground of their objection was, that it was an idle and whimsical project, unworthy of legislative attention."[5] It met also with much derisive treatment in the Senate, where "it was a standing subject of ridicule throughout the session, and whenever there was a disposition to indulge in a little levity, they would call up the steamboat bill, that they might divert themselves at the expense of the project and its advocates." It was, however, passed by the New York Legislature in March 1798, only to lapse through the failure of Mr. Livingston's experimental boat, as already mentioned.[6]

Then came Mr. Livingston's acceptance of the French mission, and it was during his residence in Paris, that he first made the acquaintance of Robert Fulton, then engaged in his torpedo experiments, which invention he was anxious to dispose of to the French Government. In the American minister, the inventor Fulton found another enthusiastic believer in the immense benefits that would be conferred on America, with her extensive navigable inland waters, if steam could be successfully applied so as to take the place of sails, in the propelling of boats. Fulton lacked the necessary funds for his experiments, and these were provided by Mr. Livingston, who could also assist his protégé with practical advice, owing to his own experience and labours in the cause of steam navigation. Fulton, thereupon, built a model steamboat, which he experimented with on the Seine. This little boat was, however, only a partial success, but it led to its inventor finding out his mistakes, and, in time, ultimately triumphantly overcoming his initial difficulties?[7]

Among Chancellor Livingston's papers are several relating to his connection with Fulton in his steamboat experiments.[8] But such experiments run into money; and before Mr. Livingston left France for America he arranged with Fulton to continue to assist him in his experiments by advancing a further sum, sufficient to cover the latter's estimated cost of the construction of a larger and more powerful boat. Whereupon an agreement was drawn up, in which it is stated:—"Whereas the said Livingston and Fulton have for several years past separately tried various mechanical combinations for the purpose of propelling boats and vessels by the power of steam engines; and conceiving that their experiments have demonstrated the possibility of success, they hereby agree to make an attempt to carry *their invention* into useful operation, and for that purpose enter into partnership." This agreement, which was signed upon the 10th of October, 1802, clearly proves that the experimental steamboat was the *joint invention* of Livingston and Fulton, and that the former's assistance to the latter was not solely confined to the financing of the experiments as is the popular idea. And while Livingston returned to his native country, Fulton went to England to superintend the manufacture of an engine for this boat, at the works of Messrs. Boulton and Watt, of Birmingham. This caused some delay, so that Fulton did not, himself, return to America until some time after his partner in this enterprise, and his engine did not reach New York until still later.

Very soon after his arrival in that city, Robert Fulton commenced the building of the first successful American steamboat in accordance with the first article of the partnership deed, which stipulated "that a passage boat moved by the power of a steam engine shall be constructed at New York, for the purpose of navigating between New York and Albany, which boat shall not exceed 120 feet in length, 8 feet in width, nor draw more than 15 inches water. That such boat shall be calculated on the experiments already made, with the view to run 8 miles an hour in stagnate water, and carry at least 60 passengers, allowing 200 pounds weight to each passenger." This boat was built at the shipyard of Charles Brown on the East River, and was launched early in the spring of 1807. The engine from England having then arrived was put on board, and in August she was completed, and was moved by her machinery across to the Jersey shore. The *Clermont*, as she was called after the senior partner's family seat on the Hudson, was 130 feet long, 16 1/2 wide, and seven feet deep, and measured

160 tons by the custom-house regulations then in force. The engine had a steam cylinder 24 inches in diameter and a stroke of 4 feet. The boiler was 20 feet long, 7 feet deep, and 8 feet wide. The wheels were 15 feet in diameter, with floats 4 feet long, and a dip of 2 feet.

It was upon Sunday, the 9th of August 1807, that Fulton first tested the capabilities of his new boat, and on the following day he wrote an account of this preliminary trial trip to Mr. Livingston at Clermont. In this letter he says:

> Yesterday about 12 o'clock I put the steamboat in motion first with a paddle 8 inches broad 3 feet long, with which I ran about one mile up the East River against a tide of about one mile an hour, it being nearly high water. I then anchored, and put on another paddle, 8 inches wide $ feet long, started again, and then, according to my best observations, I went 3 miles an hour, that is two against a tide of one; another board of 8 inches was wanting, which had not been prepared I therefore turned the boat and ran down with the tide . . . and turned her round neatly into the berth from which I parted. She answers the helm equal to anything that ever was built, and I turned her twice in three times her own length. Much has been proved by this experiment. First, that she will, when in complete order, run up to my full calculations. Second, that my axles, I believe, will be sufficiently strong to run the engine to her full power. Third, that she steers well, and can be turned with ease.

And he jubilantly continues, after giving some further particulars concerning the working of the engine, and some contemplated alterations to the paddles: "Yesterday, I beat all the sloops that were endeavouring to stem tide with the slight breeze which they had; had I hoisted my sails I consequently should have had all their means added to my own. Whatever may be the fate of steamboats for the Hudson, everything is completely proved for the Mississippi, and the object is immense." In this letter he also mentions that he expects his contemplated "corrections, with the finishing of the cabins, will take me the whole week, and I shall start on Monday next at 4 miles an hour."[9]

Fulton was as good as his word, for on Monday, the 17th of August, at one o'clock in the afternoon he started the *Clermont* on her first trip to Albany,[10] which place she reached, after calling at Mr. Livingston's seat on the way, at five o'clock in the afternoon of the following Wednesday, the distance run being about one hundred and fifty miles; actual steaming time thirty-two hours, equal to a mean speed of near five miles an hour. On his return in her to New York, Fulton wrote at once the following short account of the voyage to the editor of the *American Citizen*:—

> Sir,
>
> I arrived this afternoon, at four o'clock, in the steamboat from Albany. As the success of my experiment gives me great hopes, that such boats may be rendered of great importance to my country, to prevent erroneous opinions, and give some satisfaction to the friends of useful improvements, you will have the goodness to publish the following statement of facts.
>
> I left New York on Monday, at one o'clock, and arrived at Clermont, the seat of Chancellor Livingston, at one o'clock on Tuesday—time, twenty-four hours; distance, one hundred and ten miles. On Wednesday I departed from the Chancellor's, at nine in the morning, and arrived at Albany at five in the afternoon—distance, forty miles; time, eight hours. The sum is one hundred and fifty miles in thirty-two hours—equal to near five miles an hour.
>
> On Thursday, at nine o'clock in the morning, I left Albany, and arrived at the Chancellor's at six in the evening: I started from thence at seven, and arrived in New York at four in the afternoon—time, thirty hours; space run through, one hundred and fifty miles—equal to five miles an hour. Throughout my whole way, both going and returning, the wind was ahead: no advantage could be derived from my sails: the whole has therefore been performed by the power of the steam-engine.
>
> I am, Sir, your obedient servant,
>
> Robert Fulton.[11]

On the following day—the 22nd of August—Fulton wrote a hasty note to Mr. Livingston, to let him know of his safe arrival back in New York, in which he says, "I arrived here yesterday afternoon at 4 o'clock, thus performing the voyage from Albany in 30 hours; this will do."[12] A week later he wrote again, giving some interesting particulars as to his future plans; for having proved by his trial trip that the *Clermont* was a success, he was now engaged in fitting her out for the regular packet service between New York and Albany. This letter runs as follows:—

Saturday, the 28th [29th?] August, 1807.[13]

DEAR SIR:—On Saturday I wrote you that I arrived here on Friday at four o'clock, which made my voyage from Albany exactly thirty hours. We had a little wind on Friday morning, but no waves which produced any effect. I have been making every exertion to get off on Monday morning, but there has been much work to do—boarding all the sides, decking over the boiler and works, finishing each cabin with twelve berths to make them comfortable, and strengthening many parts of the iron work. So much to do, and the rain, which delays the caulkers, will, I fear, not let me off till Wednesday morning. Then, however, the boat will be as complete as she can be made—all strong and in good order, and the men well organised, and, I hope, nothing to do but to run her for six weeks or two months. The first week, that is, if she starts on Wednesday, she will make one trip to Albany and back. Every succeeding week she will run three trips—that is, two to Albany and one to New York, or two to New York and one to Albany, always having Sunday and four nights for rest to the crew. By carrying for the usual price there can be no doubt but the steamboat win have the preference, because of the certainty and agreeable movements. I have seen the captain of the fine sloop from Hudson. He says the average of his passages have been forty-eight hours. For the steamboat it would have been thirty certain. The persons who came down with me were so much pleased that they said, were she established to run periodically, they never would go in anything else. I well have her registered and everything done which I can recollect. Everything looks well, and I have no doubt win be very productive.

Yours Truly,
Robbrt Fulton.

You may look for me Thursday morning about seven o'clock. I think it would be well to write to your brother Edward to get information on the velocity of the Mississippi, the size and form of the boats used, the number of hands and quantity of tons in each boat, the number of miles they make against the current in twelve hours, and the quantity of tons which go up the river in a year. On this point beg of him to be accurate.

In reference to Mr. Fulton's remark in the above letter, as to "the persons who came down with me"; here is a copy of the entry in the "captain's book," giving the names of the passengers, and the passage money paid, on this return trip from Albany to New York:—

List of Passengers on board the North River steamboat from Albany to New York, August 21, 1807.

	Dollars.
Captain Thomas Hunt..	7
Monsieur Parmentoo Monsieur Mishaud...........................	13
Mr. D. E. Tyle...	6
Captain Davies..	1
	27
Mr. Fulton	— [14]

Owing to the usual unforeseen delays, the *Clermont* did not leave New York, on her first passage as a regular packet, until Friday, the 4th of September, or a couple of days later than Fulton had anticipated. So he evidently did not share the sailor's superstition regarding that day of the week. She carried on this journey her full complement of passengers; the fare for the whole distance, as far as Albany, being seven dollars.[15] At the termination of the voyage, the following paper was drawn up, and signed by those passengers who had travelled the whole distance in her, and was published in the number of the *Albany Register* of Tuesday, 8th September, 1807:—

On Friday morning at 18 minutes before seven o'clock, the north river steam boat left New York; landed one passenger at Tarrytown (25 miles), and arrived at Newburgh (63 miles) at 4 o'clock in the afternoon; landed one passenger there, and arrived at Clermont (100 miles), where two passengers, one of whom was Mr. Fulton, were landed at 15 minutes before a o'clock in the morning: and arrived at Albany at 37 minutes past it o'clock, making the whole time *twenty-eight hours and forty-five minutes*; distance, 150 miles. The wind was favourable, but light from Verplank's point to Wappinger's creek (40 miles); the remainder of the way it was ahead, or there was a dead calm. The subscribers, passengers on board of this boat, on her first passage as a packet, think it but justice to state, that the accommodations and conveniences on board exceeded their most sanguine expectations.

SELAH STRONG,	GEORGE WETMORE,
G. H. VAN WAGENEN,	WILLIAM S. HICKS,
THOMAS WALLACE,	J. BOWMAN,
JOHN Q. WILSON,	J. CRANE,
JOHN P. ANTHONY,	JAMES BRAIDEN,
DENNIS H. DOYLE,	STEPHEN H. ROWAN.

ALBANY, SEPT. 5, 1807.[16]

One of the above passengers, then only a youth, but in later years to become a judge and outlive all his fellow passengers on this journey, used to be fond of relating his experiences on this trip, and how one of his Quaker friends tried to prevent him from embarking, by accosting him as he was going on board, with "John, will thee risk thy life in such a concern? I tell thee she is the most fearful *wild fowl* living, and thy father ought to restrain thee!"[17]

There is no necessity to follow further in these pages, the somewhat chequered career of "Fulton's Folly," as the new steamboat had been derisively called by the incredulous, before its talented constructor had proved that the steam-engine could be successfully applied as a motive power in the navigation of the Hudson, except to remark that like most successful inventors, neither Fulton nor Livingston reaped much pecuniary benefit from their joint labours in the cause of science. For though they built other and more powerful steamers, and though the New York Legislature, during the following year, passed a law prolonging "for five years, the exclusive privilege of Mr. Livingston and Mr. Fulton for each additional boat that they should establish, provided that the whole time should not exceed thirty years from the passing of the law," most unscrupulous attempts were made by some unprincipled persons to deprive them of the just reward of their public-spirited enterprise.[18]

Chancellor Livingston, as he is usually designated, though no longer occupying that position, spent the few remaining years of his life at Clermont, where he devoted his attention to agricultural pursuits, in which he took great and intelligent interest. He was also a very successful rearer of sheep, and it was he who introduced the celebrated Merino breed from

Rambouillet in France, into the United States. He was also the author of an *Essay on Agriculture*, and an *Essay on Sheep*. By a resolution of the New York State Legislature, passed in March, 1809, a thousand copies of the latter essay were printed at the public expense for gratuitous distribution.[19] It ran into a second edition, and the notorious William Cobbett published an English reprint of this last issue in 1811, the editor's preface to which, is dated from the "State Prison, Newgate, Wednesday, 3rd April 1811."[20]

The "Sage of Clermont," as he has been styled by a contemporary writer,[21] died at his seat on the Hudson, on the 26th February, 1813, in the sixty-seventh year of his age, and was buried in the old family vault at Clermont. Within recent years, namely during the summer of 1877, "a tablet of black marble, with a large gilt bronze medallion portrait of the Chancellor's face, cast from the statue made by order of the Legislature of the State of New York by the sculptor E. D. Palmer, of Albany," has been erected in St. Paul's Church, Tivoli, by his grandsons, the late Clermont and Robert E. Livingston. This tablet "enumerates, in concave letters of gold," most of the public offices held by the Chancellor,[22] whose private character is thus described by one who knew him intimately:—

> In Mr. Livingston, to the proud character of integrity, honour, and disinterestedness, were added the mild, yet ennobling features of religion. An inquiring believer in its truth, an exemplar of its gentle effects on the character, he daily sought its consolations, and strengthened his pious resolutions in the rich inheritance it promises. He was devoted to the Protestant Episcopal Church from an enlightened preference of its doctrines and discipline. . . . His person was tall and commanding, and of patrician dignity. Gentle and courteous in his manners, pure and upright in his morals. His benefactions to the poor were numerous, and unostentatious. In his life without reproach, victorious in death over its terrors.[23]

Mr. Palmer's statue of Chancellor Livingston, under the provision of the Act of Congress, entitling each State to have the statues of two of its most prominent citizens placed in the Capitol at Washington, is to be found in this Valhalla of American statesmen:

> The Chancellor is represented standing erect, his form mantled by his robe of office, which falls in graceful folds from

his broad shoulders. The right hand bears a scroll inscribed "Louisiana," suggestive of his great diplomatic achievement, which secured for the United States the immense area of territory now [1876] comprised within the boundaries of the six States of Louisiana. Arkansas, Missouri, Iowa, Minnesota, and Kansas.[24]

Vanderlyn's portrait of Robert R. Livingston is now in the possession of the New York Historical Society, to which institution it was presented by Mrs. Thomson Livingston in 1876, and another by Gilbert Stuart is at Clermont.

Robert R. Livingston, fresco in Senate wing corridor in US Capitol. Theodor Horydczak Collection, Library of Congress, Prints and Photographs Division, Public Domain.

By his wife Mary, only daughter of John Stevens Esq. of Hunterdon, New Jersey,[25] Chancellor Livingston had two children, both daughters:—

1. Elizabeth Stevens, born 5th May, 1780; she married 20th November 1799, her kinsman Edward Philip Livingston, fourth son of Philip Philip Livingston of Jamaica, West Indies.[26] Her husband, settling in New York, became a naturalised citizen, and was Lieutenant-Colonel New York Militia, Aide-de-Camp to Governor Clinton, and private secretary to Minister Livingston at Paris 1801; Judge of the Court of Common Pleas 1804: Senator in the New York State Legislature from 1808 to 1813; under the new constitution, from 1833 to 1834, and from 1838 to 1839. He was elected lieutenant-governor of the State in 1830; being alien-born he was not eligible for the higher office of governor. He died on the 3rd November 1843, and the present owner of Clermont, to whom this work is dedicated, is his grandson. Mrs. Edward P. Livingston died on the 10th June 1829.

2. Margaret Maria, born nth April, 1783, in Philadelphia. She married 10 July, 1799, also a kinsman, Robert L. Livingston, son of Walter Livingston, Teviotdale, and private secretary to Minister Livingston, 1801. Mrs. Livingston died 8 March, 1818, and her husband on 7 January, 1843.

Notes

1. Thomas Jefferson to Robert R. Livingston, 14th December 1800.
2. Robert R. Livingston to Thomas Jefferson, 26th January 1799.
3. Notably Rumsey, Fitch, and Stevens. The latter was Chancellor Livingston's brother-in-law.
4. Clarkson, *Clermont or Livingston Manor*, pp. 121, 122. Lossing, *The Hudson*, p. 169. Brunel, the great French engineer, afterwards the constructor of the Thames Tunnel, then a very young man, is said to have been associated with the projectors of this steamboat; *vide Quarterly Review*, vol. xix, p. 354.
5. Colden, *Life of Robert Fulton*, p. 145.
6. *Ibid.*, pp. 144–146.
7. The following works contain accounts of these experiments,— namely Clarkson's *Biographical History of Clermont or Livingston Manor*, and the various biographies of Robert Fulton by Colden, Renwick, Knox, and Peyton F. Miller. Cf. also Munsell's *Annals of Albany*, vol. vi.
8. For the loan of these original letters and papers, the author is indebted to the late Mr. Clermont Livingston, the father of the present owner of "Clermont."
9. Robert Fulton to Robert R. Livingston, New York, Monday, the 10th August 1807. Original letter, which bears the New York postmark of same date.
10. None of the biographers of Fulton, most strange to say, give the correct date of the first trip to Albany and back.

11. As printed in Colden's *Life of Robert Fulion* (pp. 174, 175). Mr. Colden gives no date to this letter, but comparing it with the one written by Fulton to Mr. Livingston on the following day, is sufficient proof that it must have been written on Friday, the 21st August, 1807.

12. Robert Fulton to Robert R. Livingston, New York, August the 21st, 1807. Original letter, wrongly dated in his hurry "21st," should be 22nd. Bears New York postmark of latter date.

13. Robert Fulton to Robert R. Livingston, Saturday, the 28th August, 1807. Wrongly dated again, as the last Saturday in August in this year fell on the 29th. As this letter is copied from Knox's *Life of Robert Fulton*, pp. 113–115; and not having seen the original, though said by this writer to have been in the possession of Mr. Clermont Livingston, the author cannot give the postmark in this case.

14. As copied for the author by the late Mr. Clermont Livingston.

15. Munsell, *Annals of Albany*, vol vi, p. 23.

16. Munsell, *Annals of Albany*, vol. vi, pp. 23–25.

17. Namely Mr. John Q. Wilson.

18. Colden, *Life of Robert Fulton*, p. 181. For further particulars relating to Mr. Livingston's connection with Fulton, the author begs to refer his readers to the various biographies of this gifted man; who married 7 January, 1808, Harriet, a daughter of Walter Livingston of Teviotdale and who died on the 24th February, 1815, from the effects of a chill. He was buried in the Livingston family vault in Old Trinity Church, New York. The author has to thank Mrs. Sutcliffe, a great granddaughter of Robert Fulton, for the date of his marriage.

19. Clarkson, *Clermont or Livingston Manor*, pp. 81–85.

20. *Vide* copy in the British Museum Library.

21. Spafford, *Gazetteer of the State of New York*, published in 1813.

22. The above particulars are derived from an article describing this tablet, contributed by the late Mr. T. S. Clarkson to the *Daily Republican* of 12th July, 1877.

23. *An Address delivered on the Anniversary of the Philolexian Society of Columbia College*, May–15, 1831. By John W. Francis, M.D. Robert R. Livingston graduated from this College (then King's) in 1765.

24. De Peyster, *A Biographical Sketch of Robert R. Livingston*. read before the New York Historical Society, 3 October, 1876. A photograph of this statue faces this page.

25. According to Miss Jay—*The Descendants of James Alexander*— the above John Stevens was the son of another John Stevens, "who came to America in 1698 as law officer for the Crown, and Surveyor-General of New Jersey, where he purchased large tracts of land; his wife was a Campbell of noble descent." John Stevens, junior, married Elizabeth Alexander, a younger sister of Peter Van Brugh Livingston's wife. There were two children of this marriage—(1) John Stevens, whose experiments in steam navigation have been referred to; and (2) Mary, wife of Chancellor Livingston. They were married on the 9th September, 1770.

26. A list of Philip P. Livingston's children will be found in the Appendix.

CHAPTER XVII

CONCERNING EDWARD LIVINGSTON OF CLERMONT, JURIST AND SECRETARY OF STATE.[1]

"Great men are the guide-posts and landmarks in the State."
EDMUND BURKE.

OF Judge Robert R. Livingston of Clermont's numerous family, its two most talented members were the eldest and youngest sons. The eldest son's career has already been related, and now it is the turn of the youngest, Edward, the Benjamin of the flock. According to the record in his father's Bible, he was born at the old Clermont mansion, on the 28th of May 1764, and was therefore nearly eighteen years younger than his eldest brother, the chancellor. In spite of this great difference in their ages, which at the date of the death of the elder brother found the younger in the prime of life, there was a remarkable similarity in their respective political careers. They both took part in wars against Great Britain, the elder in the War of Independence, the younger in the War of 1812; the one became secretary of foreign affairs under the Continental Congress, the other secretary of state—the equivalent office in the Union—under President Jackson; the former was minister to France during the first Republic, and the latter minister to the same country during the reign of Louis Philippe, the "Citizen King"; and both, while holding the latter office, had to deal with the claims of American citizens against the French Government.

Edward inherited his father's sweetness of disposition, of whom, his friend William Smith, "the historian," was accustomed to say, "If I were placed on a desert island, with but one book and one friend, that book should be the Bible and that friend Robert R. Livingston."[2] His biographer relates, as a proof of Edward's amiability of temper at a very early age, that "when he was about eight years old, he was charged with violent conduct. The accusation was brought by one of his sisters to their mother. 'Then go in the corner,' said Margaret Beekman, 'I am sure you have been very naughty, or Edward would not have done so.'"[3] His first tutor was a Dutch clergyman, known as Dominie Doll. This gentleman was a widower, and with his only daughter, lived for some years under Judge Livingston's hospitable roof. After his father's death, Edward was placed for a short time at a school in Albany, and from there was transferred to Esopus—now Kingston in the County of Ulster. This place is situated on the west bank of the Hudson, and eighteen miles from his home at Clermont on the other side of the river. He was now under the charge of his former tutor, Dominie Doll, who, after his patron's death, had established a school at this place. Every Saturday the youthful scholar walked the long eighteen miles which separated him from his home, to return in the same manner every Monday. In after years, he attributed the good health, which sustained him through a life of great mental activity, to the habit and love of walking which he ever afterwards retained.

Edward had not been long settled at Esopus, when his studies were interrupted by the advance of General Vaughan's expedition on that town; which, on account of its being the temporary capital of the newly formed State of New York, was marked out by the British leaders for destruction. On receipt of the news of the advance of the British flotilla, the Dominie removed his school from the doomed town of Esopus to the neighbouring village of Hurley, where the State Government had also taken refuge. Edward, then only thirteen years of age, never forgot these acts of vandalism, by which, not only his schoolmaster's home was destroyed, but also his own birthplace and his brother's residence. In after life, some twenty years later, when a member of the House of Representatives, in an eloquent speech against Great Britain, he asked how he could be expected to be friendly to a nation, which had indulged in such acts of barbarity!

Considering the difficulties which beset the path of an American student in those stormy times, it is a wonder that Edward Livingston ever attained the amount of knowledge, which fitted him to fill, in later years, the high offices which he held under the Federal and State Governments. In 1779 he was entered a junior at Nassau Hall, Princeton, which college had been re-opened in that year, after some years' suspension caused by the war. The president of Princeton College, during the time that young Edward was a student there, was Dr. Witherspoon, one of the signers of the Declaration of Independence for New Jersey. He graduated from Princeton in 1781, when he returned to his home of Clermont, which had been rebuilt under his mother's energetic supervision.[4]

But Margaret Beekman was not only of an energetic nature herself, but was determined that the war still raging should not interfere with the plans she had formed for her youngest son's further education; and in a letter, written to John Jay, during the following year, she says: "My Edward passed through his College education last fall, and except a little jaunt with me to Boston last winter, he has applied himself to learning the French language under Mr. Tetard who, with a German refugee minister, I took in the house to teach him German. He is master of the French, and reads and understands the other." In this same letter, this patriotic woman also writes, "I sigh for the evacuation of our capital, when shall we meet? You can have no idea of the sufferings of many, who from affluence are reduced to the most abject poverty, and others who die in obscurity."[5]

As it was to be still some months before the British evacuated the city of New York, Edward went to Albany where he commenced to study law in the office of John Lansing, afterwards the second of the New York chancellors. But after the departure of the royal troops, Mrs. Livingston moved with her family from Clermont to her town house in New York, and in this city Edward continued his studies until January 1785, when he was admitted to practise as an attorney. During his four years of study, which were devoted principally to mastering the intricacies of the civil law, he had plenty of leisure for devoting to less serious occupations, and he was well known in the fashionable world of New York as "Beau Ned," owing to the scrupulous attention he paid to his dress.

The following lines, written by himself about this period, give a good description of his various tastes and occupations:

> On Edward's table, emblem of his head,
> See cards and pamphlets, plays and law books spread.

> Here lies a plea, begun with special care,
> Ending with "Stanzas on Augusta's Hair."
> Gilt poets there with ancient classics mix;
> The "Attorney's Guide" lies close to "Scapin's tricks";
> Lo! in the midst, a huge black-lettered book
> With dust begrimed, yclepèd Coke.
> Memento-like the Gothic volume lies,
> And still "Remember you 're a lawyer!" cries;
> Alas! unheeded cries, its voice is drown'd
> By frolic's pleasure's more attractive sound;
> She bids her roses in his fancy blow,
> And laughing cries, "Remember you 're a beau."

His legal studies—and in spite of his love for a gay life he was a most industrious worker—did not prevent him also from falling in love; and on the fly-leaf of his Longinus he wrote, early in this period, the following lines:

> Longinus, give thy lessons o'er;
> I do not need thy rules;
> Let pedants on thy precepts pore,
> Or give them to the schools.
> The perfect beauty which you seek,
> In Anna's verse I find;
> It glows on fair Eliza's cheek,
> And dwells in Mary's mind."

The three ladies here celebrated were the daughters of Mr. Charles M'Evers, a New York merchant, and well known for their beauty and accomplishments. The eldest, Mary, was Edward's choice, and they were married on the 10th of April 1788. Her sister Eliza, in the following year, became the wife of John R. Livingston, an elder brother of the bridegroom.

In December, 1794, he was returned from the city of New York, as a member of the fourth Congress of the United States; and from this period dates his appearance in public life. He was re-elected, in 1796 and 1798, to the two following Congresses. He first took his seat in the House of Representatives at Philadelphia on the 7th of December 1795. To quote the words of Mr. Gilpin, in an address delivered before the American Philosophical Society in 1843, Edward Livingston "during the six years he remained in Congress, maintained a position equally distinguished by the ability that marked his views on all public questions, and the enlightened and candid spirit which he evinced in the discussions of a period when those differences were first developed, that presently assumed a character more ardent and limits more defined. United in political opinions with Madison, Gallatin, Giles, and Macon, he bore a conspicuous share in the debates and the public measures which they approved of or opposed; and he came at once to be considered as a leading member of the party to which he attached himself."

One of his earliest speeches was made on behalf of American seamen, who were always liable to impressment by the captains of British men-of-war, owing to the difficulty such men had of proving that they were citizens of the United States. By his advocacy of their claims for redress he overcame the apathy of the Government on the subject, though not without experiencing strong opposition from the Federalist representatives in the House, who loudly complained that the young Republican member, by his conduct on this occasion, "had thrown obloquy on the Government." Which accusation Edward Livingston referred to in the following remarks, made by him when the report of the Committee on this Bill was before the House:

> On the introduction of this business into the House, it was said that a young member had thrown obloquy on the Government. I uttered nothing but facts. I said that the distressed American seamen had for five years looked in vain for relief. The Government may have had prudential reasons for its conduct. I thought it time, however, the subject was attended to. It is true, I am young; but I am not inattentive to the public business, and I shall always hold it my duty to persevere in such measures as appear to me calculated to promote the public good; nor shall I be deterred from engaging in a business because it may not have been attempted before, for that principle would shut out all improvement.

The Republican party, of which Edward Livingston was an ardent member, was at this period strongly opposed to the foreign policy of the

Government, which, as has been mentioned in a previous chapter, they considered grossly subservient to Great Britain; and many things were said and done, by the more hot-headed of the Republicans during this time of excitement, as to which some of them must have been heartily ashamed in later years, when party passions had had time to cool. Mr. Livingston, who had only been three months in his seat when the House was called upon, in March 1796, to make the appropriation required to carry into effect the treaty with Great Britain, led the attack upon the Government, by submitting a resolution calling upon the president "to lay before this House a copy of the instructions to the Minister of the United States who negotiated the treaty with the King of Great Britain, communicated by his message of the first of March, together with the correspondence and other documents relative to the said treaty." When the motion came up for discussion five days later—7th of March—he added to the resolution the words, "excepting such of said papers as any existing negotiation may render improper to be disclosed."[6]

In the debate that ensued regarding the constitutional powers of the House with respect to treaties, Mr. Livingston took a prominent part. A speech of his, delivered on the 19th of March, occupied nearly the whole day, and Mr. Hunt describes it as "a wonderful performance for so young a man, and a statesman so inexperienced." Not until the twenty-fourth of this month did the committee divide on his resolution, when it was adopted by a vote of sixty-two yeas to thirty-seven nays, and Messrs. Livingston and Gallatin were then sent to carry the resolution to the president, who received them courteously, and said, "He would take the same into consideration." Washington took a week to consider, and when his reply was at last delivered to the House of Representatives on the thirtieth, it was an explicit refusal, "on the ground that to admit a right in the House to make such a demand would be the establishment of a dangerous precedent." Thereupon, the House in a passion, passed two resolutions. One disclaimed the wish to have "any agency in making treaties." The other maintained that, when a call was made on the president for information, the representatives were not bound to state for what purpose it was wanted.[7] In the discussion that followed as to granting the necessary appropriation, Mr. Livingston took no part, but voted in the final division, with the minority, against its being acceded to.

Edward Livingston (1764–1836). The Miriam and Ira D. Wallach Division of Art, Prints and Photographs: Print Collection, New York Public Library Digital Collections, Public Domain.

In the second election of Edward Livingston to Congress he beat his opponent, Mr. James Watson, by a majority of 550 votes, though the latter's cause was warmly advocated by Alexander Hamilton, who would gladly have excluded from the House the talented young Republican lawyer.

One of the reasons given by the Federalist handbills in favour of their candidate, was the absurd one that his opponent had so little sympathy with the people as to drive a chariot; which coming from a party, whose leaders were notoriously adverse to trusting these very people with a share in the government of the country, certainly did not credit the voters of New York with much common-sense. Moreover, the force of this argument was much impaired by the retort of the Republican journals that Mr. Watson also drove a chariot. So that as far as the chariot question was concerned, it was a case of Hobson's choice with the electors, who on this occasion preferred the Republican to the Federalist owner of this mark of aristocracy!

Even in those early days of his political career, Edward Livingston had become a recognised leader of the growing Democratic party in his native State, and a French traveller of note,[8] then on a visit to the United States, has recorded under the head of "Personages who deserve particular mention" in New York, the names of only three men—Hamilton, Burr, and Edward Livingston; and he gave to the last the most extended notice of the three, styling him "one of the most enlightened and most eloquent members of Congress in the party of the opposition." In the new Congress, Mr. Livingston was to give still further proofs of his oratorical powers, by his denunciation of the two notorious measures introduced by the Government during the session of 1798, known as the Alien and Sedition Laws. It was on the nineteenth of June in this year that he made his celebrated speech against the Alien Bill—a speech which was immediately "printed on satin, and hung up in thousands of the taverns and parlours of the Democratic States," while its author was deluged with petitions for its repeal, to be presented at the next session.[9]

Mr. Livingston's third election to Congress occurred in April 1798, two months before he had made his powerful and popular demonstrations against the Alien and Sedition Bills. On this occasion his majority was not so large as in the preceding election, but if it had taken place after, instead of before, his great speech, he would probably have been returned unopposed. He continued to hold a leading position among the orators of the Republican party, though, in this, the sixth Congress, he had not such an opportunity afforded for his powers of debate, as in the preceding one. He, however, ably held his own in a debate arising from the demand for the extradition of a murderer, one Jonathan Robbins, by the British Government, in which a question arose as to the legality of the president's interference with the judiciary in the exercise of its functions in the case of extradition under a treaty, when the subject of it is in custody. This debate is famous for the great speech made by the celebrated John Marshall of Virginia in defence of President Adams's action in this matter.

It was upon this House of Representatives that the duty devolved of making the selection between Jefferson and Burr for the presidency, owing to the Tie difficulty referred to in another part of this work;[10] and frantic attempts were made by the Federalists—in their excessive anxiety to ruin Jefferson's chances—to induce Edward Livingston to cast his vote for Burr, but without success. And upon the seventeenth of February 1801, Mr. Jefferson's election was secured on the thirty-sixth ballot, when some of the Federalist members, seeing there was little hope of their being able to detach votes from Jefferson, gave in to the inevitable, though with a bad grace, and by casting blank ballots gave him the necessary majority of States.[11] With this event, Mr. Livingston's career in Congress dosed for a time, as he did not offer himself for re-election to the seventh Congress;

and it was not until nearly a quarter of a century had elapsed, that he again entered the House, as the member from the first district of Louisiana in the eighteenth Congress.

Within the same month which witnessed the inauguration of his great Republican leader, Edward Livingston lost his dearly beloved wife from an attack of scarlet fever, concerning which heavy bereavement he made the following entry in his family Bible:

> On the 13th of March 1801, it pleased Heaven to dis-
> solve an union which for thirteen years it had blessed with its
> own harmony, with an uninterrupted felicity rarely to be met
> with; formed by mutual inclination in the spring of life, it was
> cemented by mutual esteem in its progress, and was terminated
> by a stroke as sudden as it was afflictive.

This was the commencement of a series of domestic and public afflictions which were "destined in all their circumstances to try to the utmost the strength of his philosophy."[12] For so true is it, that

> When sorrows come, they come not single spies, But in
> battalions.[13]

Livingston's active mind, however, quickly turned to work as a solace for his domestic sorrow; and he therefore gladly accepted from Jefferson the post of Attorney of the United States for the district of New York; while a few months later, his public duties were still further increased, by his nomination by the Council of Appointment of his State to the office of Mayor of the city of New York, in the place of its late Federalist occupant.[14] The holding of two such offices at the same time—the one under the General Government, and the other under that of the State—excited no comment in those days; and the mayoralty of New York Was then esteemed one of the highest prizes in the gift of the Council of Appointment, so much so, that De Witt Clinton in 1803, resigned his seat in the Senate of the United States in order to accept it.[15]

As mayor, Mr. Livingston had earned a reputation for rigid impartiality and honesty, in the administration of his duties as first magistrate, which, with his uniform politeness and courtesy of manners, had made him honoured and respected by his fellow-citizens, before the outbreak of the great scourge of cholera during the summer of 1803, when his unselfish and noble conduct during that terrible visitation still further endeared him in their affections. To quote the words of Mr. Parton in reference to the behaviour of Edward Livingston upon this occasion:

During the prevalence of the yellow fever in New York, in 1803, the conduct of the Mayor was all that it could be of daring and humane. He kept a list of all the infected houses, and visited them every day saving lives that have not yet all run their course.[16] At length his own turn came. He was prostrated with the fell disease. "Then," he used to say, "I received the reward of what I had done for the people. As soon as it was known that I was in danger, the street in which my house was situated was blocked by the crowd." Young people strove for the privilege of watching by his bedside, and every delicacy the city afforded was sent in to him. He recovered to find himself a defaulter to the general government to the amount of fifty thousand dollars, through the misconduct of his subordinates. He resigned both his offices; gave up his property; left his home; And did what Aaron Burr ought to have done, but had not the moral strength to do; he went to New Orleans, and began again the practice of the law at the bottom of the ladder.[17]

It was indeed a sad awakening for a man of his talents and political prospects, to find them all blasted by the mis-conduct of a man in whom he had trusted.[18] His misfortune naturally gave the discomfited Federalists a welcome opportunity for rejoicing over the fall of such a prominent Republican politician; while the leaders of his own party were as much, selfishly, disgusted and alarmed, that such an opportunity should have been afforded to their hated rivals. Gallatin, Jefferson's new Secretary of the Treasury, especially took it much to heart; and in a letter to his chief, written before Mr. Livingston had had time to realise the full extent of his losses, he says:

I received last night a private letter from New York, in which E. Livingston's defalcation is spoken of as a matter of public notoriety in that city. I suspected as much from the last letter from Gelston and answered rather angrily . . . A resignation or removal must unavoidably follow, and I apprehend an explosion.[19]

The president also long bore Edward Livingston, a personal grudge for this affair which was to bear bitter fruit in after years, until Jefferson, shortly before his death, at last, tardily recognised, that this much maligned victim of over-confidence in his subordinates had been too hastily and harshly judged.[20] So liable are public characters to be thoughtlessly condemned—

> Who pants for glory, finds but short repose;
> A breath revives him, or a breath o'erthrows.[21]

Finding that his private fortune was not sufficient to meet the claim of the Government, then roughly estimated at about a hundred thousand dollars, he voluntarily admitted judgment in favour of the United States for that amount, and at the same time conveyed all his property to a trustee for sale, that the proceeds might be applied to the payment of this debt. And to quote the words of Mr. George Bancroft, the late eminent historian:

> Without a word of complaint, crimination, or excuse, he at once devoted his inheritance, his acquisitions, the fruits of his professional industry, to the discharge of his obligation to the Government, and, for near a score of years, gave himself no rest till he had paid it, principal and interest, without defalcation.[22]

Mr. Livingston, says Mr. Hunt, seldom in after-life made any allusion to the particulars of this unhappy affair, but some five years later, when he was engaged in a public controversy with the president,—Mr. Jefferson,—concerning his rights to lands at New Orleans—known as "The Batture Controversy"—he published a pamphlet in his own defence in which he thus referred to this painful incident:

> It is time that I should speak. Silence now would be cruelty to my children, injustice to my creditors, treachery to my fame. The consciousness of a serious imprudence, which created the debt I owe the public, I confess it with humility and regret, has rendered me perhaps too desirous of avoiding public obser-vation,—an imprudence which, if nothing can excuse, may at least be accounted for by the confidence I placed in an agent, who received and appropriated a very large proportion of the sum, and the moral certainty I had of being able to answer my call for the residue whenever it should be made. Perhaps, too, it may be atoned for in some degree by the mortification of exile, by my constant and laborious exertions to satisfy the claims of justice, by the keen disappointment attending this deadly blow

to the hopes I had encouraged of pouring into the public treasury the fruits of my labour, and above all by the humiliation of this public avowal.[23]

Mr. Livingston also resigned both his public offices; but as the pestilence was still raging in the city, he offered to continue to discharge his duties of mayor until the subsidence of the epidemic. Governor Clinton, in acknowledging the receipt of his letter resigning the mayoralty, and while thanking him for his offer to remain in charge, postponed accepting his resignation until he found Livingston could not be induced to retain this office. It was then offered to the governor's talented nephew, De Witt Clinton, who resigned his seat in the United States Senate in order to accept it. When it was publicly known that he had definitely decided to retire from the mayoralty, he received from all sides expressions of regret and sympathy, which must have softened somewhat his feelings of bitter disappointment at this abrupt termination to his natural hopes of political advancement. In the parting address, delivered to him by the Common Council of the city, these expressions of regret at losing him as mayor, and sympathy for him in his misfortunes, found full vent. It concludes with these words:

> We must indeed be destitute of feelings of men, if we could witness, without regret, the period which dissolves a connection endeared by so many ties. We look in vain for consolation to the future. Yet you have so marked the path of duty that inferior abilities, if guided by attentions as pure, may follow the steps traced by your wisdom, and for a time preserve the impulse which your energy has produced. While we cherish this hope, the memory of your example will direct our conduct and animate our zeal in the discharge of our respective functions. Be assured, Sir, that our attachment to your person and gratitude for your services will endure with the recollections of your virtues, and that you bear with you our lasting regret and esteem, and our prayers for your prosperity and happiness.[24]

The year in which this unexpected misfortune happened to Mr. Livingston, was the one which witnessed the sale of Louisiana by France to the United States, in which transaction his elder brother, the chancellor, had acted as the principal negotiator on the American side. This "blessed arrangement," as the Marquis de Lafayette called the transference of Louisiana to the country, whose independence he had helped to secure,[25] opened to Edward Livingston a prospect of a fresh field for his talents, "where the French language, with which he was familiar, was the one chiefly spoken, and where the civil law, whose principles he had mastered and admired, was the basis of jurisprudence. He felt sure that he could in time effect his deliverance by professional exertions at New York; but there the progress would be too slow for his patience, while there existed a reasonable chance of a more speedy rescue elsewhere." He, therefore, at the close of this year, within two months after retiring from the mayoralty, embarked as a passenger on board a vessel bound to New Orleans. His children, whom he devotedly loved, he left in New York in the care of his brother, John R. Livingston, whose wife was a sister, of his own deceased wife; while all the funds he took with him to make this new start in life "consisted of about one hundred dollars in gold, and a letter of credit for one thousand dollars more."[26]

Edward Livingston landed at New Orleans on the 7th of February 1804, after a passage of six and a half weeks, where he at once, with his usual energy, set to work to retrieve his shattered fortunes. His name and his letters of introduction procured for him a hearty welcome to the city of his adoption, and he "at once became conspicuous at the New Orleans Bar, which has from that time to the present produced a surprising array of men of mark. Moreau, Lislet, and Brown and Livingston and Mazureau and Derbigny and Workman and Duncan explored the sources of the Roman and Spanish and French laws at that early period. Ready money was rarely to be had in those days for the services of an advocate, but liberal payments in lands were made instead, and in this way Mr. Livingston acquired title to real estate afterwards of value to his family. But his circumstances were not without pressing cares and anxiety, and the harassments which followed him to New Orleans weighed heavily upon his mind."[27]

A few weeks after his arrival in this city, he wrote a letter to his sister, Mrs. Garretson, in which he says:

> My profession and other circumstances have given me a very extensive acquaintance in the province; and the impressions I have received are very favourable to the character of the inhabitants. They are, in general, hospitable, honest, and polite, without much education, but with excellent natural abilities, and, in short, people with whom a man, who had nothing to

regret, might pass his life as happily as can be expected in any part of this uncertain world. . . . It now seems decided that I must be separated from all the friends of my early life for an uncertain length of time; from some of them most probably for ever. This is an idea I did not wish to entertain; but circumstances have forced me to contemplate it, until I have become enabled to regard it, if not with composure and tranquility, at least with the resignation arising from necessity. The labours of a great portion, if not the whole of my life, are now pledged to others, for I much fear the losses on selling real estate will leave a large deficiency in the fund appropriated for my debts. I must make this up, and as I have a better prospect of effecting it here than at New York, I am in justice bound to remain. The separation from my children is the hardest trial; but I cannot, without the greatest injustice to Julia, take her from the truly maternal protector she has found; and I must try the effects of the summer climate before I will indulge myself with the society of my little Lewis, whose education I can myself direct.[28]

From the interesting, but very untrustworthy and scandalous, reminiscences of Mr. Vincent Nolte, a German merchant, who came in contact with Mr. Livingston during his residence in New Orleans some few years later, but who evidently bore the talented lawyer a grudge for his treatment of him during the siege of that city by the British in 1814–15, we learn that even he regarded Mr. Livingston as infinitely superior in talents to any of his fellow-citizens, for he mentions him as "a man of remarkable intellectual powers and real talent."[29] Though in accordance with his love for relating scandalous stories of those persons who happened in any way to thwart the plans of "this lively but most mendacious writer,"[30] he rakes up all the rumours at that time afloat in the Creole city to the detriment of Mr. Livingston. But, as Mr. Parton truly remarks in referring to Mr. Nolte's gossip, he "is a man who is incapable by nature of uttering, because he is incapable by nature of knowing, the unadulterated truth."[31]

Mr. Livingston during the year following his settlement in New Orleans was entrusted by the Court with the drawing up of a new code of procedure, so as to simplify the existing practice, which was a medley of the civil and Spanish law. This is a strong proof of the leading position he had at once assumed among the lawyers of this city. He performed the work promptly; and when he had been in Louisiana but little over a year, the Legislature adopted an entire system of practice proposed and framed by him. This was so simple in its working that Mr. Livingston, in describing it in a letter to the English publicist, Jeremy Bentham, written some years later, gave the following anecdote as a proof of its easy acquirement by a stranger to the new system:

> When I was pursuing my profession at New Orleans [says Edward Livingston], a young gentleman from one of the common-law States came there. He had been admitted to the bar in his own State, and was, of course, entitled to admission in ours, if found by examination sufficiently versed in our laws; he had studied them, and was ready to undergo the examination, but expressed to me his regret that a long time must elapse before he could make himself master of the routine of practice, with which, in our system, he was entirely unacquainted, and, asking to be admitted into my office until that could be effected, requested me, with much solicitude, to tell in what period I thought he might, with great diligence, be enabled to understand the rules of practice, so difficult to be acquired according to the common law. I answered that it was not very easy to calculate to an hour, but as he was engaged to dine with me the next day, at four, I thought I could initiate him in all the mysteries of the practice before we sat down to dinner; nor was there any exaggeration in the statement. What will your articled clerks, tied for seven years to an attorney's desk, say to this?[32]

Mr. Livingston had not long been a resident of New Orleans when he met, at one of the unostentatious public balls at which the primitive Creole society of Louisiana amused themselves, the lady who was to be his second wife. She was Madame Louise Moreau de Lassy, the beautiful young widow of a retired French officer, and the elder of the two daughters of Monsieur Jean D'Avezac de Castera, a once rich Creole planter of St. Domingo, ruined by the revolt of the slaves in that island, in which two of his sons were killed. M. D'Avezac escaped, but only to die at Norfolk, Virginia, of yellow fever, and broken-hearted at the ruin of this flourishing colony. Madame Moreau returned to the island where her mother had remained in the hope of better days; but finding the insurrectionists were triumphant, she was persuaded to accompany some members of her family in their flight. After some narrow escapes from capture by the revolted negroes, in which the aged grandmother and a faithful slave were shot, the fugitives were successful in getting on board a British frigate, which was cruising off the island in the hope of assisting such of the planters and their families who could reach the coast.

To quote from Miss Hunt's charming *Memoir of Mrs. Edward Livingston* from which these particulars are derived:

> Mr. Livingston was thirty-nine years of age, Madame Moreau nineteen. They became interested in each other at first sight. It was fortunate that he understood French, for she could not speak a word of English. He soon discovered that beauty and grace were not the only gifts which nature had showered on the young widow. She at once appreciated the intellect and good-ness which characterised Mr. Livingston. They were married on the 3rd of June 1805. One of Madame Moreau's young cousins was married on the same night to Edgard Montégut, a nephew of the Spanish Marquis de Casa Calvo. The two marriages were celebrated in the chapel of the old Ursuline Convent on Conde Street now the archiepiscopal residence, and one of the oldest buildings in Louisiana. The marriage took place at midnight, with only a few friends present, owing to the recent death of Madame Moreau's aunt. The place, the hour, and the circum-stances were solemn. The altar shone with tall lighted candles; the windows of the chapel were thrown wide open, to admit the soft breezes laden with the perfume of June flowers; behind the grating were heard the sweet chants of the unseen cloistered Ursulines. The brides were both young and beautiful, one sur-passingly so. No one who ever saw Mrs. Livingston could forget her. The Abbé—later Bishop de L'Espinasse—who performed the ceremony delivered a touching and eloquent address, in which he dwelt upon the vicissitudes through which the refugees had passed, and upon the haven of rest they had now found.[33]

Edward Livingston was now blessed again with "A home," as he wrote to his sister, Mrs. Tillotson, soon after his marriage, "and a wife who gives it all the charms that talents, good temper, and affection can afford"; but his heart still yearned after his beloved children, for in the same letter he laments the fact that his new home "is situated at a distance from my family, and in a climate to which I cannot, without imprudence, bring my children."[34] His worldly prospects were also steadily improving, his income was increasing yearly, and he had acquired several valuable properties in landed estate, either by purchase or in payment for his professional services.

> One of the earliest of these acquisitions was a property on the shore of the Mississippi, adjacent to the city, called the Batture de Ste. Marie, which alone—but for an unlooked-for and most untoward, as well as unjust and illegal opposition, which he was destined to meet at the hands of his former friend, the President of the United States, whose election when trembling in the balance, as we have seen, his vote and steady conduct had helped to decide,—an opposition yielded in aid of local jealousies and temporary prejudice—would have made real, at an early day, his dream of independence. This opposition gave rise to a long and bitter controversy—a controversy most interesting in itself, and one which brought into full play the genius and the character of Livingston.[35]

As this now historical controversy, however, cannot in these days be of much interest to the general reader, all that is necessary to say here in reference to it, is that the crucial point of the question in dispute, was whether the riparian owners of land on the banks of the Mississippi, in the city of New Orleans or its suburbs, had the right to possess the alluvion deposited in front of the banks, known locally as a *batture*—as rightly claimed by Livingston; or whether this alluvion was public property—as alleged was the case by Jefferson. The controversy commenced in November 1807, by the President's high-handed proceedings in giving instructions that an order should be issued from the office of the Secretary of State to the Marshal of the district of New Orleans, "to remove immediately by the civil power any persons from the Batture Ste. Marie who had taken possession since the 3d of March,"[36] and was continued for several years. Not content with having thus despotically acted in his official capacity, in regard to this dispute, of such vital importance to Mr. Livingston's interests, Mr. Jefferson after his retirement from the presidency, actually went out of his way to attack his former friend in a pamphlet, "bristling with vituperation and ridicule of his adversary." Mr. Livingston's biographer gives the following account of the reasons that possibly influenced the late president to publish, in 1812, the above pamphlet.[37]

Years went by [says Mr. Hunt] and Mr. Jefferson passed out of office. Mr. Livingston had resumed the more even tenor of professional life, and had made advances in public estimation. The litigation of the cause against the Marshal at New Orleans was approaching a decision.[38] There was a manifest modification of the popular sentiment with respect to the merits of the case. It now occurred to the ex-president that if the judgment of the Court should be pronounced in Livingston's favour, and followed by acquiescence on the part of the public of New Orleans, his own conduct would require careful explanatory treatment to make it appear at all excusable. It would then be clear that, acting upon *ex parte* representations, and refusing to hear both sides, he had forcibly invaded the rights of a citizen, because he had the physical power to do so, and because it happened to be a case in which his own sentiments had been in unison with those of a mob. The result of this kind of reflection was that he furbished, at leisure, the notes and arguments which he had before prepared for the use of counsel, left it all bristling with vituperation and ridicule of his adversary, and printed the whole for circulation through the country in 1812[39]

When Mr. Livingston read this laboured self-vindication of Mr. Jefferson, he at once saw the opportunity thus afforded him, and in his brilliant reply, published some few months later, he utterly demolished his famous opponent's arguments.[40] So ably written was Mr. Livingston's reply, that the editor of the *American Law Journal*—in which it was printed as an answer to Mr. Jefferson's pamphlet, which also appeared, reprinted with additional notes, in the same volume—describes it as being "emphatically a *réplique sans réponse.*"[41] While that celebrated lawyer, James Kent, a former fellow-student of Edward Livingston, and then Chief-Justice of the State of New York, wrote to him after reading his answer:

If I had any doubt of your title to the batture after reading Jefferson's pamphlet, your reply has completely removed it. I purchased the reply as soon as I heard it was to be procured, and before the one you were so kind as to intend for me came to hand, and a more conclusive argument I never read. Permit me to assure you that I have sympathised with you throughout the whole of the controversy, as I took a very early impression that you were cruelly and shamefully persecuted, and that, too, by the executive authority of the United States. I am more and more confirmed in this opinion, and Mr. Jefferson has richly merited all the reproach and indignation which your pamphlet conveys. I never doubted in the least (it would have been impossible) that his interference summarily under the Act of Congress was unauthorised; but as I read but once his book on the title, and did not examine his authorities, but assumed them to have been fairly cited, I was left in perplexity and doubt, and had not leisure to sit down to a re examination of the subject. When your reply came, I read it eagerly, and studied it thoroughly, with a re-examination of Jefferson as I went along; and I should now be as willing to subscribe my name to the validity of your title and to the atrocious injustice you have received, as to any opinion contained in Johnson's Reports. This last pamphlet is the ablest work with which you have hitherto obliged the public, and it gives you new and increasing claims to their consideration.[42]

This case was still before the courts and his principal debt as yet unpaid, when the war between England and the United States broke out in 1812. This unfortunate and deplorable war still further postponed the hoped-for relief from his heavy burden, as until the claim against him by the Government was finally adjusted, he must continue to devote his labours to securing this much desired object, and while this war lasted his resources for paying it were, for the time being, completely paralysed. It was some months, however, before the inhabitants of New Orleans were themselves to experience the horrors of war; and as they had been left so long undisturbed, the majority of them entertained the fond delusion that Great Britain intended to leave them in peace. Even when, in the month of September, 1814, a note of warning was received from Jean Lafitte,— the much traduced Baratarian privateersman and smuggler chieftain,—the principal American officials still remained incredulous, and showed their appreciation of that bold smuggler's patriotism in declining the British commander's bribes to aid him in his approaching invasion of the State of Louisiana, and in hastening to warn the authorities at New Orleans of these overtures, by despatching an expedition to capture the Baratarian stronghold on the Gulf of Mexico. This was duly executed, and so, instead of being rewarded for his patriotism, as his conduct richly deserved, Lafitte found himself treated as an outlaw and pirate by those very people whom he had refused to betray![43]

There was one man, however, in New Orleans who thoroughly believed in the good faith of the Baratarian chiefs—the brothers Lafitte—as he had acted as their legal adviser, and had thus gained a correct insight into their true character. This man was Edward Livingston, who, as soon as the authorities had made public the communications received from Jean Lafitte,—"the blacksmith of St. Philip Street, New Orleans, miscalled the pirate of the Gulf of Mexico,"[44] fully comprehended the importance of his warning, and at once summoned a meeting of the citizens to be convened at Tremoulet's coffee-house to concert measures for the defence of their threatened city, and to counteract the effects of the British proclamation to the inhabitants of Louisiana, a copy of which had been included in the above officially scouted communications. This meeting was held on the 15th of September, and, says Mr. Parton:

> "Mr. Livingston upon taking the chair, presented a series of spirited resolutions, breathing union and defiance, and supported them by a speech of stirring eloquence. They were passed by acclamation. A Committee of Public Defence, nine in number, with Edward Livingston at its head, was appointed, and directed to prepare an address to the people of the State. The meeting adjourned; and the spirit that was to save the city began to live in the hearts of the people. The address of the Committee of Public Defence, written by the master-hand of the chairman, was soon promulgated, and contributed powerfully to rouse the apathetic and discordant community.
>
> This address, considering the circumstances, was really a masterpiece of composition. With all the requisite swell and animation of style, it was chiefly an artful appeal to self-interest, a play upon the fears of the slow and incredulous Creoles; "fellow-citizens," began the concluding and clinching paragraph, "the navigation of the Mississippi is as necessary to two millions of our western brethren as the blood is to the pulsation of the heart. Those brave men, closely attached to the Union, will never suffer, whatever seducing offers may be made to them—they will never suffer the State of Louisiana to be subject to a foreign power, and should the events of war enable the enemy to occupy it, they will make every sacrifice to recover a country

so necessary to their existence. A war ruinous to you would
be the consequence. The enemy, to whom you would have the
weakness to yield, would subject you to a military despotism,
of all others the most dreadful; your estates, your slaves, your
persons would be put in requisition, and you would be forced at
the point of the bayonet to fight against those very men whom
you have voluntarily chosen for fellow-citizens and brethren."[45]

Upon the 2d of December 1814, General Jackson, to whom the defence
of Louisiana had been entrusted by the United States Government, rode into
the city of New Orleans. Edward Livingston was among the first to welcome
the celebrated Indian fighter, who was shortly to gain fresh laurels in his
contest with a far more powerful enemy than the savages he had hitherto
encountered—an enemy fresh from their victories over the French in the
Peninsular campaigns of Wellington. In his reply to the welcome of the governor, the general briefly "declared that he had come to protect the city, and
he would drive their enemies into the sea, or perish in the effort. He called on
all good citizens to rally around him in this emergency, and, ceasing all differences and divisions, to unite with him in the patriotic resolve to save their city
from the dishonour and disaster, which a presumptuous enemy threatened to
inflict upon it. This address was rendered into French by Mr. Livingston. It
produced an electric effect upon all present. Their countenances cleared up.
Bright and hopefill were the words and looks of all who heard the thrilling
tones, and caught the heroic glance of the hawk-eyed General."[46]

One of Jackson's first acts was to appoint Edward Livingston to be one
of his aides. They had met in Congress some years before, and they now
renewed a friendship which was to last for the remainder of their eventful
lives. For as General Jackson's biographer emphatically declares: "Edward
Livingston plays a first part in the career of Andrew Jackson. They met
upon the threshold of their public life, and it so chanced that at each of
the three great crises of Jackson's life Edward Livingston was by his side,
always his able, his faithful, his eloquent ally."[47] From the pen of the same
vivid writer, we obtain the following interesting description of the good
effect the general's arrival had upon the inhabitants of New Orleans, and
also what erroneous ideas Creole society had entertained as to his personal
appearance and manners:

Jackson has come! There was magic in the news. Every
witness, living and dead, testifies to the electric effect of the

General's quiet and sudden arrival. There was a truce at once to indecision, to indolence, to incredulity, to factious debate, to paltry contentions, to wild alarm. He had come, so worn down with disease and the fatigue of his ten days' ride on horseback that he was more fit for the hospital than the field. But there was that in his manner and aspect which revealed the master. That will of his triumphed over the languor and anguish of disease, and every one who approached him felt that the man for the hour was there. He began his work without the loss of one minute. The unavoidable formalities of his reception were no sooner over than he mounted his horse again, and rode out to review the uniformed companies of the city. These companies consisted then of several hundred men, the *élite* of the city-merchants, lawyers, the sons of planters, clerks, and others, who were well equipped, and not a little proud of their appearance and discipline. The General complimented them warmly, addressed the principal officers, inquired respecting the numbers, history, and organisation of the companies, and left them captivated with his frank and straightforward mode of procedure.

The new aide-de-camp, Mr. Livingston, as he rode from the parade ground by the General's side, invited him home to dinner. The General promptly accepted the invitation. It chanced that the beautiful and gay Mrs. Livingston, the leader of society then at New Orleans, both Creole and American, had a little dinner-party that day, composed only of ladies, most of whom were young and lively Creole belles. Mr. Livingston had sent home word that General Jackson had arrived, and that he should ask him to dinner,—a piece of news that threw the hospitable lady into consternation. "What shall we do with this wild General from Tennessee?" whispered the girls to one another; for they had all conceived the idea that General Jackson, however becomingly he might comport himself in an Indian fight, would be most distressingly out of place at a fashionable dinner-party in the first drawing-room of the most polite city in America. He was announced. The young ladies were seated about the room. Mrs. Livingston sat upon a sofa at the head of the apartment, anxiously awaiting the inroad of the wild fighter into the regions sacred hitherto to elegance and grace.

He entered. Erect, composed, bronzed with long exposure to the sun, his hair just beginning to turn grey, clad in his uniform of coarse blue cloth and yellow buckskin, his high boots flapping loosely about his slender legs, he looked, as he stood near the door of the drawing-room, the very picture of a war-worn noble warrior and commander. He bowed to the ladies magnificently, who all rose at his entrance, as much from amazement as from politeness. Mrs. Livingston advanced towards him. With a dignity and grace seldom equalled, never surpassed, he went forward to meet her, conducted her back to her sofa, and sat by her side. The fair Creoles were dumb with astonishment. In a few minutes dinner was served, and the General continued, during the progress of the meal, to converse in an easy, agreeable manner, in the tone of society, of the sole topic of the time, the coming invasion. He assured the ladies that he felt perfectly confident of defending the city, and begged that they would give themselves no uneasiness with regard to that matter. He rose soon from the table and left the house with Mr. Livingston. In one chorus, the young ladies exclaimed to their hostess, "Is *this* your backwoodsman? Why, Madame, he is a prince!"[48]

It was principally owing to Mr. Livingston's intercession in their behalf that General Jackson was induced, on taking command of the army defending New Orleans, to accept the proffered services of the Baratarians—whom he had styled in one of his earliest proclamations, a "hellish banditti"; but he never had any reason to repent of having done so, as they acquitted themselves to that commander's entire satisfaction.

Such confidence had Edward Livingston [continues Mr. Parton] in the honour and humanity of the Baratarian chiefs, that he had assigned to Pierre Lafitte the charge of his beloved wife and child. If the British should succeed in penetrating the lines, Pierre, whose post was at Fort St. John, two miles above the city, was to hasten to Livingston's residence, and convey to a place of safety, in a little chaise that stood ready for the purpose, Mrs. Livingston and her daughter, then a beautiful child of seven, afterwards famous as Cora Livingston, the belle of Washington, in President Jackson's day. It is pleasant to know that the grim and steadfast warrior, amid all the hurly-burly of the siege, found time to love and caress this little girl, and win her heart. She sat in his lap and played around his high-splashed boots, at headquarters, while he was busied in the affairs of his great charge.[49]

The general also soon found his volunteer aide-de-camp was simply invaluable to him, from his knowledge of the mixed population he had come to defend; so that Mr. Livingston's time during the British siege of New Orleans was fully occupied in attending to his new duties. While his youthful son, Lewis, who had recently came to reside with his father, was appointed by Jackson to the post of assistant-engineer under Major Latour, with the rank of captain. But there is no need to enter here into a detailed description of the fighting which now ensued, and which resulted in the defeat of the veterans of the Peninsular War by the raw and untrained American militia. But then Jackson was a host in himself, and his frequent boastful assertion, "I will smash them—the redcoats—so help me God!" turned out no empty boast after all, as the gallant Pakenham found to his cost, when, on the 8th of January 1815, he fell mortally wounded while leading his Highlanders in a vain attempt to storm the American intrenchments.

At the commencement of the fighting round New Orleans, cotton bales had been used in constructing some of these rough intrenchments; and Mr. Nolte, who served as a volunteer in the American army, relates the following anecdote in connection with these historical cotton bales, which he gives as an appropriate illustration of Mr. Livingston's quickness at repartee. Mr. Nolte, it appears, had recognised from the marks on some of the bales that were being taken out of a ship lying in the river for this purpose, that these particular bales were his own property, and he naturally felt vexed at their being put to this use. But to quote his own words:

> Adjutant Livingston [he says], who had been my usual legal counsel at New Orleans, that same evening inspected Battery No. 3, where the men were arranging some bales. I was somewhat vexed at the idea of their taking cotton of the best sort, and worth from ten to eleven cents, out of a ship already loaded and on the point of sailing, instead of procuring the cheaper kind, which was to be had in plenty throughout the suburbs of the city, at seven or eight cents, and said as much to Livingston. He, who was never at a loss for a reply, at once answered, "Well,

Mr. Nolte, if this is your cotton, you at least, will not think it any hardship to defend it."[50]

Jackson was a born fighter, but no scholar, so upon Livingston devolved the duty of drawing up most of his orders and proclamations, and even Mr. Nolte admits that the general could not have entrusted the duty to better hands. General Jackson's famous address to the militia of New Orleans, which was read to the troops after the review held on the 18th December, was one of Mr. Livingston's compositions, and he had also the task assigned him of reading it to them upon this historical occasion, which he executed "with an energy and emphasis worthy of the impassioned words he spoke."[51] After the disastrous failure of the British general to carry the American intrenchments on the 8th of January, the impetuous Jackson wished to follow up his brilliant victory by pursuing the retreating enemy, and cutting them off from their ships.

> Before taking a decisive step, however, [says Mr. Parton], he called an informal council of officers, and asked their opinion of the scheme. They opposed it with one accord. "What do you want more?" said Edward Livingston. "Your object is gained. The city is saved. The British have retired. For the pleasure of a blow or two, will you risk against those fearless troops your handful of men, composed of the best and worthiest citizens, and rob so many families of their heads?"

The general, finding that the opinion of his advisers was against this advance, did not persist, but continued to harass the British, by "cannonade in the daytime," and by "hunting parties" during the night.[52]

The wisdom of this advice was soon apparent, for a few days later the British troops retired to the shelter of their shipping, without any further fighting of any consequence, and Jackson's army returned in triumph to New Orleans. Both Mr. Livingston and his son escaped unharmed, and from a letter of the boy captain to his aunt, Mrs. Montgomery, dated ad February 1815, is taken the following passage, describing the reception accorded to the victorious army and its general by the grateful Creoles of Louisiana:

> Was there ever a finer sight, or a more affecting one, than that which presented itself to our view on the 23rd ultimo,

when the main body of the army, mostly composed of fathers of families returned, with their brave and modest leader, General Jackson, at their head, amidst the acclamations of an immense multitude of old men, women, and children (the only ones who did not share in the dangers of the field), who all hailed them as the saviours of their country and themselves. . . . On the 24th, the General, accompanied by all his staff, proceeded to the Cathedral, where a grand *Te Deum* was to be sung. On the public square, facing the building, was erected a triumphal arch. On both sides of this, a few steps back, were stationed our best-looking troops; and in front of these, nearest to the arch, were to be seen eighteen young ladies, dressed in the same apparel, and each representing one of the States. In the middle of the arch there were two little children, standing on two thrones, erected on both sides, between the columns of the arch. Each held a crown in her hand; General Jackson easily found out who they were for; his modesty suffered, but he was obliged to submit. He passed through the arch and was crowned, amidst the huzzas of the Americans and acclamations of the French, who did not cease to repeat, "Vive Jackson! *Vive notre Vive notre Générall*"[53]

On the 4th of February, Mr. Livingston, Mr. Shepherd, and Captain Maunsel White were sent by Jackson on a mission to the British fleet to arrange for a further exchange of prisoners, and for the return of the slaves of some of the planters, who had been carried off to the ships by the English in their retreat. At the time of this visit of the American Commissioners to the British fleet, the latter was on the point of sailing, in order to make a second attack upon Fort Bowyer, at Mobile Point. The commissioners were consequently detained on board, much against their wish, but the English commanders were afraid if they were permitted to return, they would warn Jackson of the intended expedition. They were, however, treated with the greatest respect by all the British officers; but they had the mortification of witnessing the surrender of the fort to the combined British naval and military forces on the eleventh of the month.

The capitulation was so arranged, [says the author of *Jackson and New Orleans*] as to enable some of the naval command-ers to get up a drama which might add to the importance of the achievement. A great dinner was given on the occasion, on board the *Tonnant*, at which Admiral Codrington took the head of the table, and the Americans were seated on his right. After a sumptuous repast, and as the dessert and wines were brought on the table, the cu tains of the cabin were drawn aside, and a full view of Fort Bowyer was presented to the company at the very moment when the American flag descended the staff, and that of Great Britain, ascending under a salute of artillery, waved in its place. "Well, Colonel Livingston, you perceive," remarked Admiral Codrington, "that our day has commenced," pointing to the British flag. "Your good health," replied Mr. Livingston, touching glasses with the exultant Briton; "we do not begrudge you that small consolation."

Small it proved, indeed, as the opening fortunes of the British were suddenly closed by an event which occurred on the 13th, just two days after the surrender of Fort Bowyer. On that day Mr. R. D. Shepherd was standing on the deck of the *Tonnant*, conversing with Admiral Malcolm, a gentleman of the most amiable and genial manners, when a gig approached with an officer, who, coming aboard the *Tonnant*, presented to the admiral a package. On opening and reading the contents, Admiral Malcolm took off his cap and gave a loud hurrah. Then turning to Mr. Shepherd, he seized his hand, and grasping it warmly, exclaimed, "Good news! Good news! We are friends. The *Brazen* has just arrived outside, with the news of peace. I am delighted!' Adding in an undertone, "I have hated this war from the beginning."[54]

Mr. Livingston and his companions returned to General Jackson on the nineteenth, but the latter could not consider the news of peace they brought with them authentic until it had been confirmed by his own Government. Edward Livingston's long and unexplained absence from home had naturally greatly alarmed his family. Connected with this delay Mr. Parton relates the following anecdote. To understand the story it is necessary to know that the "Mitchell" mentioned in it, was Major Mitchell, a British officer:

The major being the highest in rank among the English prisoners, was popularly regarded as a kind of hostage, whose presence assured land treatment to the American prisoners in the hands of the British. Fearful would be the fate of Major Mitchell, thought the multitude, if the American prisoners came to any harm. The General calling one day upon Mrs. Livingston, as was often his custom, found her in some concern for the safety of her absent husband. Her little daughter, too, began to whimper—

"When are you going to bring back my father, General? The British will kill my father, and I shall never see my father any more," said the child, sobbing.

The mighty man of war stooped down, and, patting the little girl upon the head, consoled her thus—

"Don't cry, my child. If the British touch so much as a hair of your father's head, I 'll hang Mitchell I"

This was enough for the logic of childhood. The little girl dried her tears, and had no more fear for her father's safety.[55]

Before leaving New Orleans, General Jackson had his portrait painted on ivory as a miniature, by a French artist, which he presented to Edward Livingston, with an expression of the sentiments which inspired the gift written upon a slip of paper inserted in the frame, Livingston fully reciprocated the general's sentiments of friendship and esteem, and in a letter written by the former to one of his sisters at this time, he says.

We have just parted with our great and good General, and his departure has left a gloom on every countenance and a void in every heart, except a few who envied his glory, or did not dare to partake in his dangers. I have been with him from the time of his arrival, and am proud to think that I obtained his friendship and confidence. He presented me on his departure, with a picture, which I shall leave as an honourable memorial to my son.[56]

These two friends were to meet again eight years later in Washington; the one as a member of the New Orleans or First District of Louisiana in the House of Representatives, the other as a newly chosen senator from Tennessee.

In 1820 Mr. Livingston once more entered public life as a member of the Lower House in the Louisiana Legislature, where he at once became

conspicuous by his talents and activity. He was the most energetic member
of a commission appointed for the purpose of codifying the civil law of the
State. His labours on this commission so impressed the Legislature with
his special aptitude for this work, that in the following year he was elected
by joint ballot of the General Assembly of Louisiana to revise the entire
criminal law of the State.

> For such a task, [says his biographer] no man ever had more
> complete or more comprehensive qualifications. He was fifty-
> seven years of age, and in the prime of intellectual strength. He
> had studied profoundly, and during most of his life, the Roman,
> English, the French, and the Spanish laws. He was master of all
> the languages in which those laws are written and treated. The
> variety of his professional business had made him as familiar with
> the practical working as with the theory of each system. He had
> had some judicial experience in a court of both civil and crimi-
> nal jurisdiction. His miscellaneous acquirements and general cul-
> ture were such, in extent and variety, as have rarely, if ever been
> excelled by any man of ordinary and active pursuits. He had an
> unusual knowledge of men in every condition, and of all charac-
> ters, and especially a thorough acquaintance with the peculiar
> people directly interested. Philanthropy was the basis of his own
> nature, and a keen interest in the affairs of humanity and society
> had given direction to much of his reading and reflection.

In March 1822, the year following his appointment, he submitted
to the Assembly his preliminary report, which the Legislature ordered to
be printed,—one thousand copies in French and one thousand copies in
English,—and the cost of same to be defrayed out of the contingent fund
of the State; and that one thousand dollars be paid to the author towards
the compensation to be allowed him on the completion of his labours.[57]
For the next two years Mr. Livingston devoted himself heart and soul to
this great object; but when he had given the final touches to the draft of
his completed work, he met with a disaster which, if he had been a weaker
man, would have led to his throwing up the arduous task in sheer despair!
To quote from Mr. Hunt's sympathetic account of this catastrophe:

> He had given the final, lingering touches to the draft of
> his work. An engrossed copy, for the printer, had been made.

One night he sat up late to finish the task of comparing the two papers. That task was done, and with it the great mental undertaking. Relieved of a long-borne and heavy, though not distasteful burden, he went to sleep. An alarm of fire awoke him. He rushed to the room where he had left his papers. Both draft and copy were reduced to ashes. The next morning he sat down to the work of reproducing the vanished structure. He was then sixty years of age. In two years more the reproduction was complete,—a phoenix of what had been destroyed.[58]

Mr. Livingston was strongly in favour of the total abolition of capital punishment, and the substitution of imprisonment for life in its place. In his preliminary report he says:

> I approached the inquiry into the nature and effect of this punishment with the awe becoming a man who felt, most deeply, his liability to err, and the necessity of forming a correct opinion on a point so interesting to the justice of the country, the life of its citizens, and the character of its laws. I strove to clear my understanding from all prejudices which education or early impressions might have created, and to produce a frame of mind fitted for the investigation of truth, and the impartial examination of the arguments on this great question. For this purpose, I not only consulted such writers on the subject as were within my reach, but endeavoured to procure a knowledge of the practical effect of this punishment on different crimes in the several countries where it is inflicted. In my situation, however, I could draw but a very limited advantage from either of these sources; very few books on penal law, even those most commonly referred to, are to be found in the scanty collections of this place, and my failure in procuring information from the other States is more to be regretted on this than on any other topic on which it was requested. With inadequate means, but after the best use that my faculties would enable me to make of them; after long reflection, and not until I had canvassed every argument that could suggest itself to my mind, I came to the conclusion that the punishment of death should find no place in the code which you have directed me to present. In offering this result, I feel a diffidence which arises, not from any doubt of

its correctness —I entertain none—but from the fear of being thought presumptuous in going beyond the point of penal reform at which the wisdom of the other States has hitherto thought proper to stop; and from a reluctance to offer my opinions in opposition to those (certainly more entitled to respect than my own) which still support the propriety of this punishment for certain offences. On a mere speculative question, I should yield to this authority; but here I could not justify the confidence you have reposed in me were I to give you the opinions of others, no matter how respectable they may be, instead of those which my best judgment assured me were right.[59]

Mr. Livingston then goes on to deal very exhaustively, in spite of the drawbacks he mentions, with this important question, from the standpoint "that the end of punishment is the prevention of crime." His proposed substitute for the death penalty, however, would not be regarded by an educated person as a less terrible alternative, for it was nothing less than solitary confinement for life, which is thus graphically described in his Code:

A gloomy cell; inscriptions recording the nature of the crime and the intensity of the punishment; so much of mystery as excites the imagination; real suffering enough to deter when the veil is withdrawn, not so much as to enlist the feelings of the community and make them arraign the cruelty of the law: perfect security from escape; a gradation in the discipline to show, by strong features, the different degrees of atrocity of the crime; such are the characteristics of the punishments substituted for that of death now inflicted for the different species of capital homicide. These convicts are considered, for many purposes, to be made as much dead to the world as if no commutation of their former punishment had been made; their property is divided among their heirs; they are buried in their solitary cells, and their epitaph is contained in the inscription that records their crime, and the daily renewal of its punishment. Their existence is preserved by the policy of the law, for reasons which it has proclaimed; and, although, they are kept within the reach of the pardoning power, yet that policy will be counteracted by any remission of the sentence, the case of acknowledged innocence alone excepted.[60]

In verity, a living death; and it is strange Mr. Livingston did not realise that madness lay that way!

Owing to his views regarding the abolition of capital punishment, much conservative opposition was aroused as to the adoption of his Code by the Louisiana Legislature; but the novel and humane alterations advocated by him in the treatment of criminals under detention, in the reform of prison discipline, and in the administration of penal justice, gained for its author world-wide fame.

Victor Hugo [to quote Mr. Hunt's words] wrote to him, "You will be numbered among the men of this age who have deserved most and best of mankind." Villemain declared that the proposed system of penal law, "was a work without example from the hand of any one man." Jeremy Bentham proposed that a measure should be introduced in Parliament to print the whole work for the use of the English nation. Taillandier wrote: "The moment approaches when the Legislature of Louisiana will discuss the proposed codes, prepared with so much care by Mr. Livingston; we hope that his principles will be adopted, and that State endowed with the noblest body of penal laws which any nation has hitherto possessed."

The new law-giver received every kind of evidence of the general appreciation in which his labours were held. From reviews and journals, and from the leading contemporary writers upon jurisprudence, there was a strong current of exalted, almost unqualified, praise. Many of the most prominent statesmen of the world wrote to him in terms of appreciative commendation. He received autograph letters upon the subject of his work from the Emperor of Russia[61] and the King of Sweden. The King of the Netherlands sent him a gold medal, with a eulogistic inscription. The Government of Guatemala translated one of his codes,—that of Reform and Prison Discipline,—and adopted it word for word. In his honour, the same Government gave to a new city and district forming a part of its territory the name of Livingston.

But perhaps nothing can more strikingly illustrate the position which Livingston now held before the country and the world than the fact that, at a time when his debt to the Government remained wholly unpaid, and thus while the original cause of Jefferson's prejudice against him was still outstanding in all its force,—a cause which, in ordinary circumstances, would have increased its fruits, like accumulations of interest,—the latter, from his retirement at Monticello, closed a long letter to him with the following assurance: "Wishing anxiously that your great work may obtain complete success, and become an example for the imitation and improvement of other States, I pray you to be assured of my unabated friendship and respect!"[62]

In July 1822, Mr. Livingston was unanimously elected to represent the First District of Louisiana in the eighteenth Congress. He was afterwards twice re-elected, so that he sat in the House of Representatives during six consecutive sessions, commencing with that one which opened in December, 1823. Thus, after the lapse of nearly a quarter of a century, he returned to the chamber in which his early triumphs had been achieved. To his friend Du Ponceau he wrote:

The unanimous voice of my fellow-citizens sends me to Congress, where I very much fear, however, I shall be of no use. So long retired from public affairs, I am an utter stranger to the politics of the day, and my old-fashioned Republican ideas, I fear, will find the less favour, because, so far from being weakened by my age and experience, they every day require new force.

At Washington, Livingston met his old friend General Jackson, whom he had not seen since their parting at New Orleans eight years previously. It was Livingston, so it is said, who first suggested to the victorious general the idea of his standing for the presidency; but though fresh from his military triumphs when this proposal was made to him, the modest general scouted the suggestion as being "simply ridiculous."[63] But in 1822 the enemies of "King Caucus,"—that powerful organisation which had for the past twenty years secured the election of presidents favourable to the "Virginia Dynasty,"—hailed with delight the announcement that General Jackson had been nominated by the Legislature of Tennessee as an independent candidate for the presidency. The favourite candidate on this occasion of the Congressional Caucus was William H. Crawford of Georgia, but there was a split in the camp, and altogether there were "six Richmonds in the field" during the presidential campaign of 1824. When the votes of the Electoral College were counted, it was found, that though Jackson stood at the head of the four candidates finally put forward, he had not received the requisite majority, and that John Quincy Adams, and not Crawford, came next. Therefore, like in the great "Tie" case of a quarter of a century before, the choice between Andrew Jackson, Adams, and Crawford, the three highest on the list, devolved upon the House of Representatives. The result being that Adams was elected, on the first ballot, by the votes of thirteen States against seven for Jackson, and only four in favour of Crawford—the regular Caucus nominee.[64]

Edward Livingston worked hard for his friend during the above election, and also during the one four years later, when Jackson was triumphantly placed in the chair. These two elections destroyed the prestige of the Congressional Caucus system of nominations for the presidency; but, as Mr. Parton states with truth, "the breaking down of the Caucus system was not the unmixed blessing which it was hoped it would be."[65] Livingston's congressional duties had necessarily detained him in Washington and in the north, and had thus prevented him from seeing much of his constituents during these years. His political opponents took advantage of his absence to oppose his re-election in 1828, and, owing to this cause, were able to secure his defeat.

At least, so thought his friend General Jackson, who, upon hearing the result of this election, at once wrote to Livingston to express his regret at hearing the news.

> I sincerely regret [he says] to hear you have lost the election. . . . I was fearful of this, when I read your letter and found you had not returned to New Orleans. Two speeches to your constituents would have given you a large majority. Your absence, combined with the system of detraction, by the supporters of the administration, which was unsparingly wielded against you, gulled the people, and defeated your election. Your friends will think they will be able to elect you to the Senate of the United States; but unless you visit New Orleans in the fall, you will be beaten. Your enemies have wielded your absence against you, and will still use it to your injury. You must visit

your friends this fall to succeed, when we will expect to see you as you pass, with your family, at the Hermitage, to whom present Mrs. J. and my salutations.[66]

Though he would have liked to have retained his seat in the House, Mr. Livingston scorned to go out of his way to make concessions to the popular clamour for his presence in New Orleans, while he considered he was better attending to the interests of his constituents by remaining in Washington. He, however, as it turned out, actually gained by the loss; as at its next session, the Legislature of Louisiana elected him a Senator of the United States, in spite of Jackson's fears as to the result; which event took place on the same day that his friend entered upon his duties as president. The latter, at once, as was to be expected, desired to employ the newly-elected senator in his Administration. But at this time he had in his gift, no place, for which the senatorship could be exchanged, as clear matter of advancement; and no place, the duties of which were better suited to Mr. Livingston's tastes. He was offered by Jackson the choice of any one of the seats in his Cabinet, with the exception of the Secretaryship of State, which had been promised to Mr. Van Buren of New York; and upon his declining to accept this offer, the president urged his friend to go on a mission to France, as Minister Plenipotentiary, for the purpose of obtaining from the French Government, an indemnity for the spoliations which had been committed upon American vessels, under the authority of the Berlin and Milan decrees of Napoleon. The acceptance of this mission—which was more suitable to Livingston's talents than any seat in the Cabinet, other than the one already appropriated—being dependent on a prompt departure for Paris, and it being then impossible for Mr. Livingston to fulfil this condition, he was obliged also to decline this post.[67]

A few months before taking his seat in the Senate, Mr. Livingston came into the possession of Montgomery Place, the beautiful estate of his eldest sister, the widow of General Montgomery. This lady had intended to have made Edward Livingston's son, Lewis, her heir; but this promising young man having predeceased her, she diverted the bequest to the father. To this lovely retreat on the Hudson, Mr. Livingston retired in March, 1831, where he was soon joined by his family, and he was anticipating with pleasure the prospect of spending the next few months in the relaxation of gardening, in which he took great interest, when his plans for thus passing a quiet summer in the society of his beloved wife and daughter were unexpectedly dispelled by the receipt of the following letter, which was marked "*Strictly Confidential*":

> MY DEAR SIR: We wish to see you here at the earliest practicable moment, on an affair of deep interest. The President will be obliged if you will start the day after you receive this, under circumstances which will serve to avoid speculation by preventing its being known that your destination is Washington. That may probably be best done by giving out that you are going to Philadelphia. The President desires me to say to you, that he will test your adaptation for the service that may be required of you by the secrecy and despatch of your movements on this occasion. Lest you may have left town, I send a copy of this to our friend Bowne, who knows only that he is to see that you get it, and that he is to say nothing about it, an injunction which he will be sure to observe. Make my best respects to the ladies, and believe me to be,
>
> Very truly yours,
M. VAN BUREN.
>
> WASHINGTON, April 9, 1831.

Mr. Livingston obeyed the summons, observing the secrecy and haste enjoined, though wondering what the reason could be to warrant such precautions being needed. On his arrival at Washington, he learned to his surprise that Jackson intended dissolving his Cabinet, and that he was wanted to succeed the secretary of state. The following letter to his wife, written immediately after his arrival at the seat of Government, explains the position of affairs:

> Guess until you are tired, my dear Louise, and you will not hit on the cause of my summons to this place. An offer is made to me of a place that would be the object of the highest ambition to every politician,—it is pressed upon me with all the warmth of friendship, and every appeal to my love of Country. Yet it makes me melancholy, and, though, I have not refused, I have not accepted. In short, to keep you no longer in suspense, I am offered the first place in an entire new Cabinet, with the exception of the P[ost] M[aster] G[eneral]. V[an] B[uren] has taken the high and popular ground, that being a candidate for

the Presidency he ought not to remain in the Cabinet, when all measures will be attributed to intrigue and made to bear upon the President. He has, therefore, prevailed on the President to accept his resignation. I have, in an interview I have just had, requested time for consideration. The suddenness of the offer, my private arrangements, and, as a conclusive argument, the state of your health, which might, perhaps, oblige me to make a voyage.

This last was answered ingeniously enough. Davezac[68] should have leave to meet you at any port to which you might sail, and conduct you to Paris. At last, it was put on the footing that I should have as much time for deliberation as the present incumbent would consent to remain in office, but with a smart slap on the knee, "My friend Livingston, you must accept." And so we parted. I shall make no promise until we meet. The selection, I think, except the first place, a good one. E[dward] L[ivingston], Secretary of State; H. L. White, War; M'Lane, Treasury; Woodbury, Navy; Attorney-General, not decided as yet. All this is a profound secret, not even communicated to C[ambreleng].[69] Therefore, give not the slightest hint, even to him. In addition to the reluctance to give up my independence, I have serious doubts of my ability to fill the office with credit. I know nothing of the details; the political intrigues would worry me; in short I am perplexed. I must remain here, I think, until Tuesday.[70]

After returning home, and talking the matter over with Mrs. Livingston, whom he was in the habit of consulting in all his affairs, he finally decided to accept the president's offer. Mr. Livingston was back at Washington on the 5th of May, and on the 24th of this month took over the charge of the State Department. He did not enter on the duties of this high office with a light heart; and, in a letter to Governor Roman of Louisiana, resigning his senatorship, he declared, that "in exchanging a situation which he had always thought more independent than any in the Government, for one of greater labour, more responsibility, and greater exposure to obloquy and misrepresentation, he had neither consulted his interest nor ease, and still less his ambition, which was before perfectly satisfied but that he yielded to the wishes of those who, forming, he feared, a too favourable opinion of his powers, thought he could be more useful to the nation in the station to which he had been called."

While in a letter to his wife, written after he had been a month in office, he says:

> Here I am, in the second place in the United States—some say the first; in the place filled by Jefferson and Madison and Monroe, and by him who filled it before any of them, my brother[71]; in the place gained by Clay at so great a sacrifice; in the very easy-chair of Adams; in the office which every politician looks to as the last step but one in the ladder of his ambition; in the very cell where the great magician, they say, brewed his spells. Here I am, without an effort, uncontrolled by any engagements, unfettered by any promise to party or to man; here I am! and here I have been for a month. I now know what it is; am I happier than I was? The question is not easily answered.[72]

It was during Mr. Livingston's occupation of the State Department that the President was brought into conflict with the "Nullifiers" of South Carolina—the predecessors of the Secessionists of thirty years later—owing to the strong opposition aroused in the Southern States to the new Tariff Act introduced in 1832 by the National Government. Jackson, impulsive as usual, was determined to stamp out any treason to the United States, so, instead of foolishly allowing the Nullification or Secession movement time to spread, as happened under President Buchanan's weak Administration in 1860, he at once took every precaution to nip it in the bud. He now, as in his old campaigning days of eighteen years before, relied upon the pen that had served him so well at New Orleans when fighting a foreign foe. To his secretary of state, therefore, he entrusted the drawing up of the celebrated Proclamation, issued on the 10th of December, 1832, in which the president firmly warned the Nullifiers of what the consequences would be if they persisted in their folly.

The original draft of this historical document, says Mr. Hunt, "is entirely in Livingston's handwriting, much amended by erasures and interlineations, according to his invariable habit in all but epistolary compositions." Mr. Hunt then goes on to say:

> Having read the obviously candid but somewhat vague statement communicated by Major Lewis to Mr. Parton,[73] to the effect that General Jackson, on examining Mr. Livingston's draft, informed the latter that he had not correctly understood

his notes in some particulars, and that certain parts of the paper must be altered, which was accordingly done by the Secretary, I compared the actual Proclamation, word for word, with the draft in Livingston's handwriting, in order to see what were the corrections which had been thus suggested. There is no variation between them, except some verbal amendments such as so painstaking a writer would have been sure to make while reading the printer's proof, and except one change of materiality in the paragraph next to the last.[74]

In his instructions to Mr. Livingston, the president wrote: "Let it [the proclamation] receive your best flight of eloquence, to strike to the heart and speak to the feelings of my deluded countrymen of South Carolina. The Union must be preserved without bloodshed, if this is possible; but it must be preserved at all hazards and at any price."[75] The letter from which this extract is taken, accompanied a rough draft from the president containing his proposed concluding sentences for this proclamation, which, Mr. Hunt declares, were not used by the secretary, though "the thoughts they embody appear here and there in the closing paragraphs."[76] This celebrated State document is far too lengthy to produce here, but the following lines from one of its most eloquent passages deserve special recognition:

Look on this picture of happiness and honour, and say WE, TOO, ARE CITIZENS OF AMERICA! Carolina is one of these proud States; her arms have defended, her best blood has cemented the happy Union! And then add, if you can without horror and remorse, This happy Union we will dissolve; this picture of peace and prosperity we will deface; this free intercourse we will interrupt; these fertile fields we will deluge with blood; the protection of that glorious flag we renounce; the very name of Americans we discard. And for what, mistaken men—for what do you throw away these inestimable blessings! For what would you exchange your share in the advantages and honour of the Union? For the dream of separate Independence,—a dream interrupted by bloody conflicts with your-neighbours, and a vile dependence on a foreign power. If your leaders could succeed in establishing a separation, what would be your situation? Are you united at home! are you free from apprehension of civil discord, with all its fearful consequences? Do our neighbouring republics, every day suffering some new revolution, or contending with some new insurrection,—do they excite your envy? But the dictates of a high duty oblige me solemnly to announce that you cannot succeed. The laws of the Unitde States must be executed. I have no discretionary power on the subject; my duty is emphatically pronounced in the Constitution. Those who told you that you might peaceably prevent their execution have deceived you; they could not have been deceived themselves. They know that a forcible opposition could alone prevent the execution of the laws; and they know that such opposition must be repelled. Their object is disunion: but be not deceived by names: disunion, by armed force, is TREASON.

According to General Jackson's principal biographer, "the proclamation was viewed at the North with an enthusiasm that seemed unanimous, and was nearly so. The Opposition press bestowed the warmest encomiums upon it. Three days after its appearance in the newspapers of New York, an immense meeting was held in the Park, for the purpose of stamping it with metropolitan approval. Faneuil Hall in Boston was quick in responding to it, and there were Union meetings in every large town of the Northern States. In Tennessee, North Carolina, Virginia, Maryland, Delaware, Missouri, Louisiana, and Kentucky, the proclamation was generally approved as an act, though its extreme federal positions found many opponents."[77] There is no doubt that the strong Union feeling running through this proclamation took the Southern politicians by surprise.

> One short week [wrote Mr. Clay on the day the document appeared] produced the message and the proclamation—the former ultra on the side of State rights, the latter ultra on the side of consolidation. How they can be reconciled I must leave to our Virginia friends. As to the proclamation, although there are good things in it, especially what relates to the Judiciary, there are some entirely too ultra for me, and which I cannot stomach. A proclamation ought to have been issued weeks ago, but I think it should have been a very different paper from the present, which, I apprehend, will irritate instead of allaying the excited feeling.

Owing, however, to the president's firmness, resort to force became unnecessary, and the celebrated historian, Mr. Bancroft, thereupon remarks on this incident:

Once more the conflicts of party turned on the question of
the preservation of the Union. A spurious aristocracy claimed
a right for every State which they could rule, to nullify the laws
of the United States to such an extent as would have made the
Constitution like a ship at sea, water logged, and at the mercy
of every wave of political cupidity or passion. The salvation of
the country turned on the right interpretation of the principles of democracy. Jefferson, its early leader, was no more; but
Madison lived long enough to expound its acts and resolutions
of former days; and Jackson, as President of the United States,
having Livingston as his adviser, gave authority to that exposi-
tion. Who that looks back upon those days does not rejoice
that the chief magistrate was Jackson, and that his adviser was
Edward Livingston, who to the clearest perceptions and the
firmest purpose added a calm conciliating benignity and the
venerableness of age, enhanced by a world-wide fame.[78]

On the 29th of May, 1833, Mr. Livingston resigned the office of secretary of state, receiving on the same day from the president, the appointment of Envoy Extraordinary and Minister Plenipotentiary to France. The
reason for this change of offices was the critical phase that had arisen in
the negotiations between the two countries, regarding the settlement of
the losses sustained by American citizens during the wars of Napoleon.
The French Government, by the treaty of 4th July, 1831, had agreed to
pay to the United States the sum of five millions of dollars, in six annual
instalments, in satisfacton of these claims, and the first of these instalments became due on the 2nd of February, 1833. Jackson's Administration,
considering the affair as settled, and strangely overlooking the important fact that the French Chamber of Deputies had not voted the requisite appropriation, had sold to the Bank of the United States a draft for
the amount of the first instalment, drawn upon the French Minister of
Finance. Whereupon the bank sold the draft to parties in England, who,
in due course, presented it to the French Treasury for payment, when it
was protested, owing to the Chamber not having voted any money for this
purpose.

At this important crisis, the United States was only represented at
the French Court by a *chargé d'affaires;* Mr. Rives, the late American minister, having returned home in 1831, after concluding the above-mentioned
treaty. The president, fully recognising the gravity of the situation, and

irritated by the supposed insulting conduct on the part of the French Government, turned at once to his old friend and councillor, as the most likely person in his Cabinet to get him out of this unexpected difficulty. Hence Livingston's resignation of the secretaryship of state, and his acceptance of the French Mission.[79] Popular rumour, after the return of Mr. Rives, had assigned the vacant post to Mr. Livingston, some months before the neglect of the French Government to fulfil its obligations had led to the latter's consenting to go to France, which, for a man at his advanced age— then just entering his seventieth year,—was no light task to undertake.

More than a twelvemonth before his actual appointment his friend John Randolph of Roanoke had warmly urged his acceptance of this important mission, in the following characteristic passage in the postscript to a letter written in March, 1832:

> If General Jackson does not kill the bank, the bank will kill him.[80] Let me conjure you to lay this matter at heart, and accept, not the Chiltern Hundreds, but the mission to France, for which you are better qualified than any man in the United States. In Mrs. Livingston, to whom present my warmest respects, you would have a most able coadjutor. *Dowdies*, dowdies won't do for European Courts—Paris especially. There and at London the character of the Minister's lady is almost as important as his own. It is the very place for her. There she would dazzle and charm; and surely the *salons* of Paris must have far greater attractions for her than the Yahoos of Washington. If I had not lost the facility of speaking French by long disuse, I should like it of all things.[81]

The month previous to his appointment as envoy extraordinary to France, Mr. Livingston's beloved daughter Coralie—better known by her pet name of Cora—was married to Mr. Thomas Pennant Barton of Philadelphia. son of Dr. Benjamin F. Barton, author of the first American work on botany.[82] Knowing how devotedly attached Mr. and Mrs. Livingston were to their only child,[83] the president two months later, appointed the bridegroom to the post of secretary to the French Legation, so that the newly married couple might accompany the bride's parents to Prance. General Jackson, who had known Mrs. Barton since her early childhood, when at New Orleans, "amid all the hurly-burly of the siege, he had found time to love and caress this little girl, and win her heart," sent her her husband's commission, accompanied with the following graceful expression of his wishes for their mutual happiness:

> MY DEAR CORA,—Your kind letter with that of your husband were duly received. I have postponed a reply until I could enclose to you his commission as Secretary to the French Legation, which I now do, and request that you present it to him, with your hand, and with a tender of my high regard. I hope to have the pleasure of seeing you and Mr. Barton before you sail for France. Should I be disappointed in this, permit me to assure you both, that wheresoever you may travel, you take with you my kind wishes and prayers for your health, prosperity, and happiness.
>
> I remain, with great respect, your friend,
>
> ANDREW JACKSON.[84]

WASHINGTON, June 4, 1833.

Mr. Livingston and his companions sailed from New York on board the *Delaware* man-of-war, on the 14th of August in this year, and arrived at Cherbourg on the twelfth of the following month, after a most agreeable voyage of twenty-eight days. On his arrival at Paris, the new American minister presented his credentials to the king, who received him with marked cordiality. For Louis Philippe never forgot the hospitable treatment he had received from members of the Livingston family and their fellow-countrymen while an exile in the United States; and he was never tired when talking to Americans, of referring to his youthful adventures in the western parts of their great continent. Mr. Livingston's fame as a publicist had also already made his name familiar to Parisian literary circles, and in the spring of the year in which he arrived in France, he was elected Foreign Associate of the Institute of France, a distinction which has always been sparingly conferred, which few Americans have received, and which can only be obtained through the double merit of genius and industry.

> The king's answer to my address [wrote Mr. Livingston to his Government] was long and earnest. I cannot pretend to give you the words of it, but, in substance, it was a warm expression of his good feeling towards the United States for the hospitality he had received there. As to the Convention, he said, "Assure your Government that unavoidable circumstances

alone prevented its immediate execution, but it will be faithfully performed. Assure your Government of this," he repeated;
"the necessary laws will be passed at the next meeting of the
Chambers. I tell you this not only as king but as an individual
whose promise will be fulfilled."

Unfortunately, Louis Philippe, unlike Napoleon, had not the power
to enforce his wishes upon his ministers, much less so upon the members
of the Chamber of Deputies; so that at the next session of the Chambers
held during the following year, the bill appropriating the money due to the
United States could not obtain the necessary majority, even his Minister of
Finance voting against it. The king was sincerely annoyed at the rejection
of this bill, and expressed his vexation to the American minister. He even
went so far as to hint, in his confidential conversations with Mr. Livingston,
that he considered it would be advisable for the President of the United
States to insert a passage in his next message which should show that the
American Government was in earnest in the matter, and was resolved to
insist upon the prompt payment of the indemnity.[85]

Mr. Livingston duly communicated the tenor of these conversations
to his Government, and anxiously awaited the result. "From this you may
imagine," he wrote towards the close of this year (1834), "the anxiety I shall
fed for the arrival of the President's message. On its tone will depend very
much, not only the payment of our claims, but our national reputation for
energy."[86] Jackson, nothing loath, eagerly took the hint, and in his message of
December, 1834, after reciting the whole history of the affair in full and plain
terms, proceeded bluntly to recommend that, in the event of no provision
being made for the payment of the debt at the approaching session of the
French Chambers, Congress should pass a law "authorising reprisals upon
French property." According to Mr. Parton, President Jackson's own Cabinet
considered the allusions to France in his message, "needlessly irritating and
menacing, but the General would not consent to abate a word of them. 'No,
gentlemen,' he exclaimed one day, during a Kitchen Cabinet discussion of the
message, 'I know them French: they won't pay unless they 're made to.'"[87]

News of the contents of this message reached France early in January
1835; and, it is related, also on the authority of Mr. Parton,

The French king, alive to all the importance of the subject,
was so anxious to obtain the message at the earliest moment,
that he sent a courier to Havre to await the arrival of the

packet, and convey the document to Paris. Louis Philippe, therefore, received the message before it reached the American ambassador, and was the first man in Paris who read it. I am enabled to state [continues this author], that the king read the message with much surprise, but more amusement. He thought it a capital joke. He was amused at the interpretation put upon the advice he had given Mr. Livingston. The language of the message, which a Tennessean deemed eminently moderate and dignified, sounded in the Cabinet of the Tuileries like a fiery declaration of war. Upon the whole, however, the king was pleased and satisfied with the message, because he thought it calculated to produce the effect upon the deputies which he desired it should produce.

Though the "Citizen King" was satisfied, it was far otherwise with the Parisians when the news became public property; and their newspapers, of all shades of opinion, vehemently denounced the message as a gross insult to France. The excitement was increased when, shortly afterwards, American newspapers arrived, containing, to Mr. Livingston's intense disgust and annoyance, the extracts from his confidential correspondence, referring to his private conversations with the king. The latter had to bend before the storm he had unwittingly raised; and to quiet the popular clamour, the French minister resident in Washington was immediately recalled, and Mr. Livingston was informed that passports were at his disposal. At the same time, however, a bill was introduced in the Chamber of Deputies by the Minister of Finance proposing to pay the money, provided the Congress of the United States should pass no hostile act in accordance with the president's threatening message.

On receiving the communication, conveying the above information of the intentions of the French Government, from the Comte de Rigny, the Minister of Foreign Affairs, Mr. Livingston's first impression was that he ought to demand his passports and leave France; but after reflection, he decided it was his duty to await instructions from his own Government, before taking such a pronounced step, though his own personal inclinations were in favour of that course. Meanwhile he wrote a most able paper, addressed to the Minister of Foreign Affairs, in which he pointed out that the French people had interpreted the message erroneously, that it was written to heal, not to widen the breach; and that the president had used no words which could be construed as insulting to a brave and high-spirited nation, with whom he sincerely wished to remain in peace. Fortunate it was for the two nations that the American minister in Paris at this critical juncture was a person who possessed the entire confidence of General Jackson; as there is no doubt it was mainly owing to Mr. Livingston's prudent and praiseworthy conduct on this occasion that war was avoided.[88]

That Mr. Livingston rightly gauged the position of affairs at Washington is proved by the fact, that on the 14th of January, 1835, the Senate, *without one dissentient voice*, passed a resolution to the effect, "That it is inexpedient, at present, to adopt any legislative measures in regard to the state of affairs between the United States and France." His conduct was officially approved by his Government as wise and patriotic; and he was also informed, if he *had* chosen to follow his inclination and abandon the mission, and had quitted France with the whole legation, that course would not have surprised or displeased the president. He was instructed at the same time, should the Chambers again reject the Appropriation Bill, to leave France in a United States man-of-war, with all the legation; but, if the appropriation should be made, to retire either to England or Belgium, leaving Mr. Barton as *chargé d'affaires*, and there await further instructions.

On the 18th of April, the Chamber of Deputies did pass the bill, coupled, however, with the proviso that the payment should not be made, until the French Government should have received satisfactory explanations of the terms used by the president in his annual message. This unexpected *dénoûment* was not provided for in Mr. Livingston's instructions, and he was therefore obliged again to rely upon his own judgment. This time he decided to demand his passports, which having received, he embarked at Havre, with his wife and daughter, on board the *Constitution* frigate, on the 5th of May, and arrived in New York on the twenty-third of the following month. His son-in-law, Mr Barton, was left behind as *chargé d'affaires*. Mr. Livingston personally would have preferred remaining a little longer in Europe, only he was afraid that such a proceeding on his part would have been misconstrued by the French Government.

He thus states his reason for returning direct to the United States, in a letter written to his brother-in-law, the American *chargé d'affaires* at The Hague, when on the eve of sailing from Havre.[89]

> I was very happy, my dear Davezac [he wrote], to find that you saw the condition annexed to the law providing for the

payment of the indemnity in the light I do, and approve of my return. The necessity for this movement disappointed me, for I wished very much to pass some time with you, and afterwards in England; but this was impossible after the refusal to pay, for such in effect is the annexation of a degrading condition. My stay in Europe would be considered as evidence of a desire to resume my mission. . . . We have been here four or five days, waiting the arrival of the frigate from Cherbourg, where she went to take in water. She is just returned, and we embark to-morrow.

Mr. Livingston, always anxious to avoid hurting the susceptibilities of a sensitive and high-spirited people like the French, whenever it was possible to do so without loss of dignity to the Government he represented, had, before leaving Paris, officially informed the French Ministry that the president had approved the pacific interpretation of his message, which he (Livingston) had given to it in his note of the previous January. "This he considered," says Mr. Parton, "and General Jackson considered was more than equivalent to the apology which the Chamber of Deputies demanded." The Chamber, moreover, never obtained any further satisfaction from the sturdy old soldier, and after some further diplomatic fencing, and the offer from Great Britain of her mediation, the French Government, in the spring of 1836, paid the four instalments then due without any reservation,[90] and thus this awkward dispute was at last brought to a satisfactory conclusion.[91]

Though Mr. Livingston returned to America without having fulfilled the object of his mission to France, his conduct, under these trying circumstances, met with the cordial approval of his own Government and fellow-countrymen; so that on landing in New York he received quite an ovation, and public dinners were given in honour of a minister who had so worthily upheld the dignity of his country in a foreign land. But the late Envoy Extraordinary to the French Court did not long survive his return home. One of his last political acts was to tone down the president's special message to Congress of the 15th January, 1836, regarding the French dispute, which General Jackson had the good sense to submit to his old friend's judgment. A few days after the delivery of this message, Mr. Livingston left Washington for New York, where he passed the remainder of the winter, until milder weather found him once more at his beautiful home on the Hudson. He had only been installed at Montgomery Place a few weeks, "when a sudden and violent illness terminated his life on the 23rd of May,

1836, within five days of his seventy-second birthday."[92] His remains were laid in the family vault at Clermont; and "a plain tablet, placed by his wife and daughter in the Dutch Reformed Church at the village of Rhinebeck, bears a simple inscription, describing him as 'a man, for talents equalled by few, for virtues surpassed by none.'"[93]

Few men have left a purer reputation behind them than the subject of this chapter. Honours were paid to his memory, not only in his own country, but also abroad. The Government of Guatemala ordered the observance of a public mourning, to mark their appreciation of the services rendered by the late celebrated jurist in the cause of humanity; while M. Mignet, the eminent French historian, at the close of a long oration devoted to a review of his life and character, delivered before the Academy of the Institute of France, on the 30th of June, 1838, declared that, "By the death of Mr. Livingston, America has lost her most powerful intellect, the Academy one of its most illustrious members, and Humanity one of her most zealous benefactors."[94]

By his first marriage Mr. Livingston had three children, two sons and a daughter, all of whom died in his own lifetime, unmarried; and as Mrs. Barton also died childless, Edward Livingston's family is now extinct. His widow survived him by nearly a quarter of a century, dying at Montgomery Place, on the 24th of October, 1860, at the advanced age of seventy-eight years.[95]

Notes

1. The author, in this chapter, has departed from his usual custom of writing from the original authorities direct, as in Edward Livingston's case, his life has been so fully dealt with by the late Mr. C. H. Hunt, that it would be superfluous for him to take this trouble. Moreover, the author of the *Life of Edward Livingston*, which was published in 1864, had access to sources of information some of which are not available to the present writer. Though Mr. Hunt's work is the main authority, other authors have also been made use of, wherever anything of interest could be found relating to the subject of this sketch.
2. Clarkson, *Clermont or Livingston Manor*, p. 38.
3. Mrs. Margaret Livingston is usually referred to in family anecdotes by her maiden name. To save more references than are absolutely necessary, the authority for statements in this chapter, unless otherwise noted, is Mr. Hunt's work.
4. The year following the burning of Clermont, Mrs. Livingston started the rebuilding of her home. Among Governor Clinton's papers is a letter from her son, the chancellor, dated 2 May, 1778, requesting exemptions from enlistment for six mechanics, required by his mother for work on the new house.
5. Mrs. Margaret Livingston to John Jay, Claremont, 21 April 1782, The Hon. John Jay was at this date American minister at Madrid.

6. M'Master, A History of the People of the United States, vol. ii, pp. 266, 267.
7. Ibid., p. 276.
8. Le Duc de Larochefoucauld-Liancourt.
9. Parton, Life of Andrew Jackson, vol. ii, p. 18. By this bill it was provided the president might order dangerous or suspected aliens to depart out of the territory of the United States.
10. See Chapter XV.
11. Upon the 17th February 1801, Albert Gallatin wrote to his wife: "We have this day, after 36 ballots, chosen Mr. Jefferson President. Morris of Vermont, withdrew; Craik, Dennis, Thomas, and Baer put in blank votes; this gives us ten States. The four New England States voted to the last for Mr. Burr. South Carolina and Delaware put in blank ballots in the general ballot box; that is to say, they did not vote. Thus ended the most wicked and absurd attempt ever tried by the Federalists. . . ." Adams (Henry), Life of Albert Gallatin, p. 262.
12. Hunt, Life of Edward Livingston, pp. 89, 90.
13. Hamlet, Act. IV, Scene v.
14. Appointed 10th August 1801, and installed fourteen days later. The Mayors of New York, since the year, 1833, are elected by the people.
15. Hammond, Political History of New York, vol. i, p. 197.
16. Mr. Parton wrote the above in 1859.
17. Parton, Life of Andrew Jackson, vol. ii, p. 19. As this writer was also the author of a well-known Life of Aaron Burr, his praise of Edward Livingston is of more than ordinary value.
18. Mr. Hunt says the confidential agent who robbed Mr. Livingston was a Frenchman by birth. Life of Edward Livingston, p. 103.
19. Gallatin to Jefferson, 16th June 1803. Adams (Henry), Writings of Albert Gallatin, vol. i, p. 122. Mr. Adams also appears to have imbibed Mr. Gallatin's prejudices against Edward Livingston, for in his Life of Albert Gallatin, as well as in his History of the United States, he always refers to the defalcations of Mr. Livingston, without a word of explanation as to how they had been caused!
20. Hunt, Life of Edward Livingston, pp. 183, 294, et seq.
21. Pope, Epistles of Horace, Epistle I, Book ii.
22. Preface by George Bancroft to Hunt's Life of Edward Livingston, dated "New York 14th November 1863." When the claim was finally adjusted, it was found to amount to the sum of $43,666.21; but at the date of the last payment to the Government twenty-three years later, it had reached, with the accumulations of interest, the large total of $100,-014.89. The Government took over in final settlement of this claim in 1826, some lots in the city of New Orleans, the property of Mr. Livingston, which realised when sold, some six thousand dollars more than the balance then due. So that the Government actually, in the long run, made a profit out of this "defalcation." Hunt, Life of Edward Livingston, pp. 104, 310.
23. Hunt, Life of Edward Livingston, p. 103.
24. Ibid. pp. 106, 107.
25. In June 1803, Lafayette wrote to Edward Livingston: "Bernadotte is returned from Rochelle, where he was to embark, and his mission I consider as happily ended by the blessed arrangement for Louisiana. With all my heart I rejoice with you on this grand negotiation, which. both as a citizen and a brother, must be not less pleasing to you than it is to me." Bernadotto-to be later on King of Sweden-had been charged by Napoleon with a mission to the American Government, and Lafayette had given him a letter of introduction to his friend Edward Livingston.

26. Hunt, *Life of Edward Livingston*, pp. 108, 110.
27. Miss Hunt's *Memoir of Mrs. Edward Livingston*, pp. 29, 30. This was his second wife, of whom mention will soon be made in the text.
28. Hunt, *Life of Edward Livingston*, pp. 113, 114.
29. Nolte, *Fifty Years in both Hemispheres* (second edition), p. 88.
30. Hunt, *Life of Edward Livingston*, p. 200(note).
31. Parton, *Life of Andrew Jackson*, vol. ii, p. 20.
32. *Works of Bentham*, vol. xi, p. 52, as quoted by Mr. Hunt.
33. *Memoir of Mrs. Edward Livingston*, pp. 17–21.
34. Edward Livingston to Margaret Tillotson, 10th August 1805.
35. Hunt, *Life of Edward Livingston*, p. 115.
36. On the 3d March 1807, Congress had passed a law, "designed to protect the public lands from encroachments by the class since called 'squatters,' and its passage was several months before the question of title to the Batture was presented to the Government." *Hunt, Life of Edward Livingston*, p. 173, (note).
37. This pamphlet is entitled, *The Proceedings of the Government of the United States in Maintaining the Public Right to the Beach of the Mississippi, Adjacent to New Orleans, against the Intrusion of Edward Livingston. Prepared for the Use of Council*. By Thomas Jefferson, Published at New York in 1812, and reprinted, with additional notes at Baltimore two years later, in the fifth volume of *The American Law Journal*. This volume also contains Mr. Livingston's able reply. The author has in his possession the copy originally presented to John Randolph by Robert L. Livingston.
38. On the 4th August 1813, namely the year following the publication of Mr. Jefferson's pamphlet, Mr. Livingston was successful in obtaining a decree from the United States Court at New Orleans re-instating him in possession of the disputed property. Unfortunately this decision did not terminate this weary lawsuit, and Mr. Livingston in the end was most unjustly deprived of the greater portion of his undoubted rights to this Batture.
39. *Life of Edward Livingston*, pp. 142, 143.
40. *Entitled An Answer to Mr. Jefferson's Justification of his Conduct in the Case of the New Orleans Batture*. By Edward Livingston.
41. Preface to volume five of the *American Law Journal* (being the second of a new series), edited by John E. Hall, Counsellor at Law in the Supreme Court of the United States.
42. Chief Justice James Kent to Edward Livingston, Albany, 13th May 1814.
43. Parton, *Life of Andrew Jackson*, vol. i, pp. 580–590.
44. Walker, *Jackson and New Orleans*, p. 61.
45. Parton, *Life of Andrew Jackson*, vol. ii, pp. 20, 21.
46. Walker, *Jackson and New Orleans*, pp. 17, 18.
47. Parton, *Life of Andrew Jackson*, vol. ii, p. 17.
48. Parton, *Life of Androw Jackson*, vol. ii, pp. 29–31. Mr. Parton says ho was indebted for this pretty story to one of the ladies present at this dinner party.
49. *Life of Andrew Jackson*, vol. ii, p. 120. Cora Livingston was born during the eclipse of 1806; and in announcing her birth to one of his sisters, the fond father poetically wrote: "God has given me so fair a daughter, that the sun has hidden his face"; *vide* Mrs. Wharton's *Social Life in the Early Republic*, p. 227.
50. *Fifty Years in both Hemispheres*, p. 216. Mr. Walker says the story that Jackson's defences were composed chiefly of cotton is a vulgar error, as it was found when the intrenchments mentioned in the text were under fire, the bales soon got knocked out of position by the enemy's balls, and also, owing to its inflammable nature,

caught fire as well. So that the Americans very quickly got rid of their cotton-bale fortifications. *Jackson and New Orleans*, pp. 260–262.

51. Parton, *Life of Andrew Jackson*, vol. ii, p. 63.
52. *Life of Andrew Jackson*, vol. ii, pp. 235, 236. Cf. Nolte, *Fifty Years in both Hemispheres*, pp. 204, 224.
53. Hunt, *Life of Edward Livingston*, pp. 201, 202.
54. Walker, *Jackson and New Orkans*, pp. 391–395.
55. Parton, *Life of Androw Jackson*, vol. ii, pp. 303, 304. Another version of this incident is to the effect, that Jackson swore he would hang this officer "as high as Haman," if Mr. Livingston was harmed by the British. Mrs. Wharton, *Social Life in the Early Republic*, p. 257.
56. In Mr. Hunt's biography is an excellent engraving of this miniature, with a facsimile of General Jackson's lines of dedication, which are as follows: "Mr. E. Livingston is requested to accept this miniature as a mark of the sense I entertain of his public services, and a token of my private friendship and esteem.

> "ANDREW JACKSON."

"Headquarters, N. Orleans, May 1st, 1815." *Life of Edward Livingston*, p. 208.
57. Entitled, *Project of a New Penal Code for the State of Louisiana*. By Edward Livingston, member of the House of Representatives from the Parish of Plaquemines. The copy of the above report in the author's possession, was printed in London, under the above title, in 1824. A eulogistic review of this English edition is to be found in the *Westminster Review* for January, 1825.
58. *Life of Edward Livingston*, pp. 257, 258. This happened on the 14th November 1824, at No. 66, Broadway, where Mr. Livingston lodged with his family during the recess of Congress.
59. *Project of a New Penal Code*, etc, (London edition), pp. 38–40.
60. *A System of Penal Law for the State of Louisiana*. By Edward Livingston, pp. 341, 342.
61. The Czar Nicolas. His letter, which is written in French, and dated from "Moscow, le 31 Août, 1826," will be found printed in full in Mr. Hunt's work.
62. *Life of Edward Livingston*, pp. 274–281.
63. Parton, *Life of Andrew Jackson*, vol. ii, p. 350, and vol. iii, p. 30.
64. Hammond, *Political History of New York*, vol. ii, pp. 187–190. Parton, *Life of Andrew Jackson*, vol. iii, pp. 50–66. Mr. Adams's election was secured by Mr. Clay, the fourth candidate, using his influence in his favour. Mr. Clay was afterwards appointed Secretary of State by Mr. Adams.
65. *Life of Andrew Jackson*, vol. iii, p. 30.
66. Andrew Jackson to Edward Livingston, 2d August, 1828.
67. Parton, *Life of Andrew Jackson*, vol. iii, p. 174. Hunt, *Life of Edward Livingston*, pp. 326–329.
68. Auguste Davezac, then United States *chargé d'affaires* at The Hague, was Mrs. Livingston's brother.
69. Churchill C. Cambreleng, a representative in Congress from New York, 1821 to 1839.
70. Hunt, *Life of Edward Livingston*, pp. 356–359. Cf. Miss Hunt's *Memoir of Mrs. Edward Livingston*, pp. 97–99. The above letter is headed "Washington, Saturday night."
71. Namely, Chancellor Livingston, who was the first Secretary of Foreign Affairs, during the War of Independence, from 1781 to 1783. See *ante*, Chapter XIII.
72. Hunt, *Life of Edward Livingston*, pp. 359–362.
73. *Vide* his *Life of Andrew Jackson*, vol. iii, p. 466.

74. *Life of Edward Livingston*, p. 380.
75. President Jackson to Secretary Livingston, 4 December, 1832.
76. *Life of Edward Livingston*, p. 373.
77. Parton, *Life of Andrew Jackson*, vol. iii, pp. 469, 470.
78. *Vide* Mr. George Bancroft's Introduction to Mr. Hunt's *Life of Edward Livingston*.
79. Parton, *Life of Andrew Jackson*, vol. iii, pp. 561–567.
80. This refers to General Jackson's *bitt noire*, the Bank of the United States.
81. Hunt, *Life of Edward Livingston*, p. 382 (footnote).
82. Miss Hunt, *Memoir of Mrs. Edward Livingston*, p. 110.
83. The three children of Mr. Livingston's first marriage had all died young.
84. Miss Hunt, *Memoir of Edward Livingston*, pp. 110, 111 (footnote). Cora Livingston was a noted belle in Washington society. Mr. Josiah Quincy has recorded of her in his diary, that "Burke's famous apostrophe to the Queen of France is none too good for the Queen of American Society in 1826"; *vide* Mrs. Wharton's *Social Life in the Early Republic*, p. 227.
85. Parton, *Life of Andrew Jackson*, vol. iii, p. 568.
86. Sumner, *Andrew Jackson*, p. 344.
87. *Life of Andrew Jackson*, vol. iii, pp. 569, 570. The "Kitchen Cabinet" was the nickname bestowed by the Opposition on some of Jackson's old cronies, who were popularly supposed to be most in the spreident's confidence.
88. In reference to the above-mentioned note to the Comte de Rigny, Mr. Hunt says: "Livingston now felt a keen anxiety to hear an approval of his conduct by the President and people at home, for which he was obliged to wait until late in March. Under date of the 8th of that month, Mr. Van Buren wrote to him: 'Mr. Forsyth met me this morning at the President's with your last letter to de Rigny, and we went through it very deliberately. I could not express myself too strongly for the opinion I really entertain of its merits. . . . The General, as well as Forsyth, was delighted with it. ' " *Life of Edward Livingston*, p. 400.
89. Letter dated Havre, 4 May, 1835.
90. Curiously enough, only quite recently—in 1906—the author's wife received a small sum out of these "spoliation claims," as a descendant of an American citizen who had been a sufferer from these depredations. Certainly, the United States Government cannot be accused of undue haste in the settlement of these claims!
91. The above account of this dispute over the Treaty of 1831 is derived from Hunt's *Life of Edward Livingston*, pp. 386–422; Parton's *Life of Andrew Jackson*, vol. iii, pp. 561–579; and Sumner's *Andrew Jackson*, pp. 343–348.
92. Miss Hunt, *Memoir of Mrs. Edward Livingston*, p. 143.
93. Hunt, *Life of Edward Livingston*, p. 432.
94. M. Mignet's *Notice sur Livingston* was, in 1872, reprinted, as an Introduction to a French version of Edward Livingston's great work on the criminal code, entitled *Exposé d'un Systéms de Législation Criminelle*, etc., and edited by M. Charles Lucas of the Institute of France.
95. Further particulars of this lady and her daughter, Mrs. Barton, will be found in Miss Hunt's *Memoir of Mrs. Edward Livingston*, published in 1886.

CHAPTER XVIII

CONCERNING SOME LIVINGSTON MANSIONS AND THEIR HISTORICAL ASSOCIATIONS.

"O, call back yesterday, bid time return!"
                    SHAKESPEARE, *King Richard II.*

"My love to the whole household of Liberty Hall."
        —*John Jay to Kitty Livingston,* St. Ildefonso, Spain,
                            18 September, 1780.

IN the previous chapters, we have been enabled to trace the successive generations of Livingstons through three centuries by their public actions; but now, when we would like to close this narrative with some particulars concerning their daily home life, how they wooed and won their wives, and matters of a similar nature, we unfortunately find the authentic material available far too scanty for our purpose. Here and there, some interesting family letter has been preserved among a mass of public correspondence, but these alas! are as few and far between, as a well of water in a thirsty desert! From what we have been able to glean from various sources, worthy of record, is, however, given here.

We know the men made good husbands and fathers, and the women good wives and mothers; and we know also, from the records in their family bibles, and in the baptismal registers of their parish churches, that they nearly all lived up to that scriptural precept, which ex-president Roosevelt evidently considers should be the highest duty of the modern American citizen! We also, certainly know, through his own quaint confession, that the father of the first American Livingston was a laggard in love, and that it took him "nine months seeking," and "urgent prayer," in which the good lady was obliged to join, before this ardent lover was satisfied *"anent that business."* However, it is satisfactory to know, that having at last made up his mind, and got "marriage affection to her," it was of a very deep and permanent nature There is a tradition, still preserved in the family, relating to the marriage of this worthy's youngest son, Robert, to the widow Van Rensselaer, that this lady's first husband, on his death-bed, had foretold her second nuptials with the gallant Scot. The maiden name of the fair widow was Alida Schuyler, and the families of Livingston and Schuyler were, a few years later, to be again united by marriage, when Robert's nephew and name sake, who had followed his uncle to America, took as his bride, Alida's niece Margaretta.

According to a lady historian, Philip the elder Robert's son and heir, was "dashing and gay," and went about "breaking hearts promiscuously." Certainly, from his portrait, he appears to have been better endowed that way than either of his forebears; but we very much doubt Mrs. Lamb's authority for this aspersion on his good fame, as Philip married young, and even if he did cross the Kissing Bridge, more than once, with a fair companion, doubtless the Dutch maidens were not averse to paying the customary toll to such a good looking cavalier. Then we get a tantalising glimpse, all too brief, of the dashing Philip's grandson and namesake, who accompanied another Philip, his friend Schuyler, one evening in September of the year 1753, to the theatre, then a novelty in New York, to see *The Conscious Lovers* performed by a company of play actors just out from England. But we must let young Philip Schuyler, to whom we are indebted for this graphic insight into the social life of New York a hundred and fifty years ago, speak for himself; only explaining that the writer was then only in his twentieth year, and that the letter was addressed to his great friend at Albany, "Brom" Ten Broeck. These two youthful Albanians, were in later years, to make their mark in the history of their native province.

Philip Schuyler had only that day—20th of September, 1753—arrived from Albany by water, and had landed at Ten Eyck's Wharf at one o'clock in the afternoon; and this is his description of how he spent the rest of the day:

The same evening I went to the play with Phil [Livingston].[1] You know I told you before I left home that if the players should be here I should see them, for a player is a new thing under the sun in our good province. Philip's sweetheart went with us. She is a handsome brunette from Barbados, has an eye like that of a Mohawk beauty and appears to possess a good understanding. Phil and I went to see the grand battery in the afternoon, and to pay my respects to the governor, whose lady spent a week with us last spring, and we bought our play tickets for eight shillings apiece, at Parker and Weyman's printing office in Beaver Street on our return. We had tea at five o'clock, and before sundown we were in the theatre, for the players commenced at six. The room was quite full already. Among the company was your cousin Tom and Kitty Livingston,[2] and also Jack Watts, Sir Peter Warren's brother-in-law. I would like to tell you all about the play, but I can't now, for Billy must take this to the wharf for Captain Wynkoop in half an hour. He sails this afternoon. A large green curtain hung before the players until they were ready to begin, when, on the blast of a whistle, it was raised, and some of them appeared and commenced acting. The Play was called *The Conscious Lovers*, written you know by Sir Richard Steele, Addison's help in writing the *Spectator*. . . . But I said I could not tell you about the play, so I will forbear, only adding that I was not better pleased than I should have been at the club, where last year I went with cousin Stephen, and heard many wise sayings which I hope profited me something. . . . But I must say farewell, with love to Peggy, and sweet Kitty V. R. if you see her?

Here the curtain not only falls before the players, but also between us and the audience in a most provoking manner. As, even the name of the handsome Creole with an eye like a Mohawk beauty, has not come down to us. We can quite imagine, however, at the stir she must have made among the elderly ladies with the spectators that evening, and can hear them whispering together behind their fans—"the bold eyed minx!", as her male companions were heirs to two of the largest landed estates in the province. But whether she married or not is unknown;

except that she did not become the wife of Philip Livingston, of whom the next mention made, is the following mournful entry in his father's family bible:

> On the 20th of February 1756, at seven o'clock in the evening fell asleep in the Lord my dear beloved mother Catharina Livingston, and her remains were brought up in my sloop by my brothers John, Philip, and William, on the first of April; and on Saturday the 3rd of April, 1756, between two and three o'clock in the afternoon fell asleep in the Lord my beloved son Philip, and was on the 5th of April together with his grandmother laid in my vault in the church.

Philip Schuyler more fortunate than his friend Phil Livingston lived to marry *his* sweetheart, Catharine Van Rensselaer, who will live forever in Knickerbocker annals as "Sweet Kitty V. R."; and to become in later years, the well-known Revolutionary general.

It is recorded, that many heads of families in New York were much perturbed in their minds, over the arrival in their city of this company of English actors and actresses, and swore that they would not countenance such folly, whatever the governor and his worldly hangers-on might do. But these good citizens had evidently not consulted their wives and daughters before making their rash vow, as it is also duly recorded in the annals of the time, that few of them were missing, from among the audience when the "large green curtain" rang up! But one notable New Yorker certainly was not present, and that was Phil Livingston's uncle William, who was far too conscientious a man to yield on a question of principle, and also too much committed by his attacks on the follies of the time, in the columns of his paper—the *Independent Reflector*—to be seen in such frivolous company. Yet this stern moralist, when his children grew up, took great pleasure in encouraging them in their simple amusements, and after he had moved into New Jersey, there were few merrier households in the whole of the thirteen colonies than that of "Liberty Hall."

Liberty Hall, now Ursino, Elizabeth, NJ, built in 1773. Library of Congress, Prints and Photographs Division, Public Domain.

It was under this happy roof, before civil war came to throw a gloom over it, that the youthful Alexander Hamilton made his first appearance on the continent of America; and hither also resorted many of the youth of New York, including another notable statesman to be, John Jay, who wooed and won at Liberty Hall, a daughter of the house for his bride, the beautiful Sarah, who certainly could not have taken after her father as regards personal appearance. It seems strange, that William Livingston—whom John Adams so bluntly describes in his journal, on meeting him in 1774—the year in which his daughter became Mrs. John Jay—as "a plain man, tall, black, wears his hair,[3] nothing elegant or genteel about him"—should have been the father of two such handsome children, as his daughter Sarah and his son Brockholst undoubtedly were, according to their portraits. That Adams' description was no libel on William Livingston's personal appearance is borne out by the latter's portrait, and also by his own unflattering description of himself, as "a long nosed, long chinned, ugly looking fellow." His other children may also have been good-looking for what we know?

Probably they got their good looks from their mother, whose portrait has not come down to us.

From some family letters still preserved among the public correspondence of the Honourable John Jay, and which the editor of the latest edition of these papers has very wisely included in those printed,[4] we learn that John Jay had proposed to the fair Sally in January, 1774, and that having first obtained her father's consent to their marriage, had thereupon informed his own parents. Mr. and Mrs. Jay at once gave theirs also, though at this time neither of them had seen their future daughter-in-law, owing to the confidence they had in their son's prudence, which satisfied them as to "the propriety of his choice," to quote from Mr. Peter Jay's letter of concurrence to Sarah's father. From other letters in the same valuable collection, we are able to gather further interesting particulars concerning Mrs. John Jay and her immediate family circle, during the troublous times so soon to follow upon the wedding of this young couple, which took place in the spring of this year.

The earliest of these is from a young lady friend of Sarah, who had been invited to be one of the bridesmaids, but had been prevented from accepting. This lady was Miss Maria Eliza Philipse of Philipseborough, who, in a letter congratulating the bride, writes:

> It was no small mortification to me in not having it in my power to accept of the kind invitation by cousin Kitty Livingston[5] of being one of the bridesmaids. I own that I had flattered myself with the pleasing expectation of being one of the number. Had it not been for my papa (who thought the weather too warm for me to be in town) I should have realised all those pleasures of which I had formed such a delightful idea. The being with my dear Mrs. Jay would have been my principal inducement, and spending with her some hours as agreeable as those I enjoyed at Elizabethtown. But apropos—Mama and I were a little jealous at your stopping twice at Collo. Cortlandt's and not once at Philipseborough, you being such a prodigious favourite. However we all hope soon to be favoured with a visit from you and Mr. Jay.

From now on John Jay was to be often separated from his wife, owing to bis public duties at the Continental Congress and the Provincial Convention; and on the formation of the new government he was appointed

Chief Justice of the Supreme Court of the State of New York. His parents had to abandon their home at Rye, owing to the advance of the British troops, and seek a safer asylum further north; while Sarah's old home— Liberty Hall—was also being constantly threatened by destruction, as already related in a previous chapter.[6] In a letter from John Jay to his sister-in-law, Kitty Livingston,—a prime favourite of his,—dated Philadelphia, 27th February, 1779, he makes reference to a report "that the enemy have visited Elizabethtown, and burnt her father's house." This report was, however, as regards the burning of the house, untrue, though it was entirely due to Sarah's mother and sisters, who bravely clung to their beloved home, and thus were able, on more than one occasion, to avert, by their personal intercession with the British officers, the fate of many of their neighbours' homesteads. In the above letter, John Jay alludes to similar losses which had befallen him and his family, but he adds: "They never have, and I hope never will, cost me an hour's sleep."

It was on the visit of the British soldiers to Elizabeth-town on this occasion, undertaken for the purpose of capturing Sarah's father, that her sister Susan showed so much bravery and coolness. Finding Governor Livingston was not at home, the British officer in command demanded his papers. As it happened the governor's correspondence with Congress and General Washington was in a box in the parlour. This box Miss Susan persuaded the officer was her own private property, and at her request he very gallantly put a guard over it, whereupon the artful young woman pointed out to the officer some drawers filled with papers of no value, with which they departed—so the story says—in great glee! According to the *New Jersey Gazette* of March 3d, 1779, which contained an account of this raid, "the officers in general behaved with great politeness, and exerted themselves in preventing the soldiers from plundering." On a corrected report of these proceedings reaching Philadelphia, John Jay wrote at once to his wife: "I wish to know the particulars of Susan's convention with Lord Cathcart. It is said she had the advantage of him in the treaty, and displayed much fortitude as well as address on the occasion. Pray how did John Lawrence fare? We hear he was in the house and was made a prisoner? Did they release or carry him off?"[7]

About eighteen months after this raid Liberty Hall was again in the possession of the British troops for a brief period, and again it was owing to the fact of Mrs. Livingston and some members of her family being in occupation, that it was spared from destruction. On this occasion Susan presented the Honourable Cosmo Gordon, who commanded the first battalion of the Guards on this expedition, with a rose in acknowledgment of his chivalry in protecting her home from the fate which was dealt out to some of the neighbouring villages by these same troops. On their return journey the British had to fight their way through Elizabethtown, and it appears that this humane officer was unfortunately wounded in the thigh from a bullet, said to have been fired by a militia man hiding in one of Governor Livingston's fields. At least, this was the version which gained credit in New York City, then in the occupation of the British, and which led to a fair and indignant loyalist, writing the following account of this incident for insertion in Rivington's *Royal Gazette;* in which paper it duly appeared on the 29th of June, 1780:

MR. PRINTER,

By inserting the underwritten paragraph, you will oblige a customer and loyal subject, though humane herself, thinking that lenity may go too far. Your new female correspondent expects to see your obedience to-morrow. 'T is true in every particular. We are informed, from undoubted authority, that on the return of the British allies, detached on the expedition to Springfield in the Jersies, last Friday, the 23d instant, the Hon. Lieutenant-Colonel Cosmo Gordon, commanding the first battalion of British Guards, received at the head of the brigade, a ball on the upper part of his thigh from the fields of the back part of the house of the rebel Governor Livingston; most probably his own servants, or tenants, keeped up the fire which struck the very person who in the morning made a civil visit, with three or four of the officers of the corps, and received a rose from Miss Susan L., as a pledge of protection, and a memorandum of a request of a safe-guard to save the house from a fate the well-known sins of the father made it justly merit; though even at that period inhabited by two ladies, so amiable in appearance as to make it scarcely possible to suppose they are daughters of such an arch-fiend as the cruel and seditious proprietor of the mansion. It is a well-known fact, that there was a guard to protect the house, during the continued fire on the columns from the fields all around, and that the vermin followed the royal troops from the vicinity of the Congress governor's house, keeping a continual galling fire, till the rear passed the orchard in Elizabethtown, and the advanced Jager videttes awed them back to their grateful and humane master's house and farm.

NEW YORK, June 29, 1780.

But it was from the partisan bands that most danger arose, as these men, on both sides, were not over scrupulous, plunder being their chief object; and as we have seen in a previous chapter,[8] the leader of one of these notorious corps, Ensign Moody, had even offered a reward of two hundred guineas for the capture of the obnoxious governor. These constant alarms, at last, even told upon the nerves of these brave women, so that the daughters went on visits to their relatives or friends in safer districts, while the mother remained all alone at what she considered to be her post of duty. Susan, the eldest daughter, went on a visit to her uncle Robert of the Manor, as is proved by the following extract from a letter to the latter, written by the governor, then at Trenton, on the 17th of December, 1781:

> DEAR BROTHER, I hear that your very numerous family is going to be increased by the addition of one of mine. I fear S[usan] will be troublesome to a house so overrun with company as yours. But my poor girls are so terrified by the frequent incursions of the refugees[9] into Elizabethtown, that it is a kind of cruelty to insist on their keeping at home, especially as their mother chooses rather to submit to her present solitary life than to expose them to such disagreeable apprehensions. But she herself will keep her ground to save the place from being ruined, and I must quit it to save my body from the provost in New York; so that we are all scattered about the country. But by the blessing of God, and the instrumentality of General Washington and Robert Morris, I hope we shall drive the devils to Old England before next June.

Mrs. Livingston did not reside the whole year round at Liberty Hall, as even she, courageous woman as she was, found it absolutely necessary to be absent for short periods, so as to obtain some relaxation from the strain imposed upon her by this solitary life, but she never ventured far away from her threatened home. Her eldest daughter, Susan, before visiting the Manor, had been staying for some time with John Jay's father, then living at Poughkeepsie. She had taken with her on this visit, her little nephew Peter, then nearly six years of age, whom her sister Sarah had to leave behind, when she accompanied her husband on his mission to Spain in October, 1779. The child was a great pleasure to both his grandfathers; and Governor Livingston kept up a constant correspondence with his little grandson. "He prints all his letters," writes Mrs. Livingston to her daughter Sarah, "so that my dear little Peter can read them for himself." It is not surprising, however, that the grandfather had them printed, as his handwriting is said to have been so notoriously bad, that whenever Washington received a despatch from the "war governor" of New Jersey, he was accustomed to summon his staff together to assist him in the deciphering of it.[10]

Sarah Jay had also her adventures, though not like her mother and sisters caused by the incursions of British troops or loyalist refugee bands, but in her case arising out of the elements, as the American 36 gun frigate, *Confederacy*, in which she and her husband,—accompanied by her brother Colonel H. Brockholst Livingston, as her husband's private secretary,—sailed for Spain, was dismasted in a storm. But we will let Mrs. Jay describe this disaster in her own words, in a letter to her mother, dated

On Board of the *Confederacy*, 12 December, 1779.

About 4 o'clock in the morning of the 7th of November, we were alarmed by an unusual noise upon deck, and what particularly surprised me was the lamentations of persons in distress. I called upon the captain to inform me of the cause of the confusion that I imagined to prevail; but my brother desired me to remain perfectly composed, for that he had been upon deck but half an hour before, and left everything in perfect security. Perfect security! vain words! Don't you think so? And so indeed they proved; for in that small space of time we had been deprived of nothing less than our bowsprit, foremast, mainmast, and mizzen-mast; so that we were in an awkward situation, rendered still more so by a pretty high south-east wind and a very rough sea. However, our misfortunes were only begun. The injury received by our rudder the next morning served to complete them, as we were ready to conclude. The groans that distressed me were uttered by two men who had suffered from the fall of the masts; one of them was much bruised, and the other had his arm and hand broken; the former recovered, but the latter, poor fellow! survived not many days the amputation of his arm.

Will it not be painful to my dear Mama to imagine to herself the situation of her children at that time? Her children did I say? Rather let her imagine the dangerous situation of more than three hundred souls, tossed about in the midst of the ocean in a vessel dismasted and under no command, at a season too that threatened inclemency of weather. And would you for a moment suppose me capable of regretting that I had for a time bid adieu to my native land, in order to accompany my beloved friend? Would you have despaired of ever embracing your affectionate children? or would you have again recommended them to Him who appointed to the waters their bounds. Who saith unto the waves thus far shalt thou go, and to the winds, peace be still! Mama's . nown piety and fortitude sufficiently suggest the answer to the two latter queries; and to the former it becomes me to reply. I assure you that in no period of our distress, though ever so alarming, did I once repine, but incited by his amiable example, I gave fear to the winds, and cheerfully resigned myself to the disposal of the Almighty.[11]

Sarah Van Brugh Livingston (1756–1802), wife of Hon. John Jay. The Miriam and Ira D. Wallach Division of Art, Prints and Photographs: Print Collection, New York Public Library Digital Collections, Public Domain.

The disabled ship fortunately was in West Indian waters when this disaster occurred, and shortly after the date of Mrs. Jay's letter to her mother reached St. Pierre, Martinique, from which port they took passage in the French frigate *Aurore* to Cadiz. While they were in Spain, correspondence, both with Congress and the various members of their respective families, was a matter of difficulty, and also of uncertainty as to whether the letters would ever reach their destinations, owing to the vigilance of the British cruisers. Some of the letters which did reach the hands of the persons for whom they were intended, have been preserved, and are of considerable interest. Sarah's younger sister Kitty was evidently the member of the family in America, on whom the Jays depended most for news from home, always anxiously looked forward to by those abroad, especially in times such as these. As John Jay, in thanking this sister-in-law on one occasion, writes: "You are really a charming correspondent as well as a charming everything else. We have had more letters from you than from all our other friends in America put together"; and the lively Kitty Livingston certainly richly deserved the compliment.

In one of her letters, from Philadelphia, where she was spending the winter of 1779–80 with her friends the Morrises, written the day after Christmas, after giving her brother-in-law full particulars concerning military movements, and the position of Washington's army, then in winter quarters in New Jersey, she touches on gayer matters, such as entertainments and dances. For if gallant British officers could dance and flirt with fair loyalists in the city of New York, why should not equally brave American and French officers follow the redcoats' example in Philadelphia, with as fair rebels for partners? Certainly Miss Kitty had no objection, and she goes on to give an account of their various amusements:

> As the General does not meet Mrs. Washington here, she sets out early to-morrow for camp. We had yesterday a Christmas dinner in compliment to her at the Chevalier's.[12] Next Thursday he gives a ball to thirty Ladies; to-morrow evening we have a second at Mrs. Holker's. His Excellency intends having concerts once a week at his house; he entertains very generally and with Elegance. I have seen him wear a suit of clothes of the Countess de la Luzerne's work, which does that lady great honour. Last Thursday the assemblies commenced, and there are private dances once a week; to-morrow evening there is one at the City tavern.

Not bad for rebel Philadelphia, with all the necessities of life at unheard of prices, and the army starving in their winter quarters! But these brave women,—worthy wives, sisters, and sweethearts of the men who perished with Montgomery amid the winter snows of Canada; or, who, under the reckless Arnold, stormed the British entrenchments at Saratoga, or, learned, under the greatest leader of them all, Washington, to beat the picked regiments of Britain in the open field, and to bear with fortitude the miseries of Valley Forge and Morristown,—knew that by attending these harmless entertainments, they were showing their French allies and the world at large, that fair America was not to be cast down because their country was engaged in a life and death struggle with mighty England.

As a proof of how enormously Continental money had depreciated at this date, Chancellor Livingston, in a letter to Governor Clinton, written also from Philadelphia, just a month earlier than Kitty's letter to John Jay, says, "I am sorry to tell you that money has fallen below any thing that you can suppose. I need give you no other proof of it than by telling you that I this day[13] paid £537 [of] this money for a plain suit of cloaths, £21 for plain buttons to a servant's coat and putting them on, and 26 dollars for sawing a cord of wood; grain and country produce have even risen beyond foreign articles."

Charming Kitty Livingston was evidently a great favourite wherever she went, and the Chevalier, a great admirer of hers, one day laughingly assured her that he was positive, that her sister Mrs. Jay would so far conform to Spanish customs as to paint her face, and go to places of amusement on the Sabbath; and he offered to back his opinion with a wager. This Kitty, nothing loath, gaily accepted; and thereupon at once wrote to her sister,

> Do you know that I am trading on your stock of firmness; and if you are not possessed of as much as I suppose you to be I shall become bankrupt, having several wagers depending that you will not paint nor go to plays on Sundays. The Chevalier is not to be convinced that he has lost his bet to me, till Mr. Carmichael informs him you do not paint. Mr. Witherspoon informed me that he was questioned by many at Martinique if you did not?[14]

Sarah Jay, writing from Madrid in reply, jokingly hopes "the bets depending between you and the Chevalier are considerable, since you are entirely entitled to the stake, for I have not used any false colouring, nor have I amused myself with plays or other diversions on Sundays."[15] The Chevalier, we learn from a letter from Kitty's hostess—Mrs. Robert Morris—to Mrs. Jay, paid up like a man:—"The Chevalier," she writes, "acquiesces in the loss of his bet; he presented Kitty with a handsome dress cap, accompanied with a note acknowledging your firmness."[16]

It was about this time, that Mrs. Montgomery, the widow of General Montgomery, then on a visit to her brother's, the chancellor's, family, in New Jersey, wrote also to Mrs. Jay, and among other items of news, informs her cousin that the chancellor had recently been blessed with a daughter; and adds "as this girl is designed for your boy, whom I admire extremely, I can only pray that she may cement our families in a still closer union."[17] This little baby girl, the chancellor's eldest daughter, did not, however, ultimately marry Peter Jay, but, instead, her cousin Edward P. Livingston of Jamaica, West Indies, whose grandson now owns the chancellor's home— "Clermont." In the same letter Mrs. Montgomery refers to the craze for duelling, which had become so fashionable among the American and French officers:

> Yesterday when informed from Camp of the Death of your Cozin William Alexander Livingston,[18] who received his death from a Mr. Steeks [sic] in a Duel, there was buried at the same time in like circumstances a Mr. Peyton from Virginia. You may judge how fashionable duelling is grown when we have had five in one week, and one of thems so singular that I cannot forbear mentioning it. It happened between two Frenchmen, who were to stand a certain Distance and march up and fire when they pleased. One fired and missed; the other reserving fire till he had placed his Pistol on his antagonist's forehead, who had just time to say, *Oh mon Dieu, pardonna moy*, at the same time bowing, when the Pistol went off with no other mischief but singeing a few of his hairs. Tell Harry[19] to beware of engaging in a quarrel with the Dons in Spain. This duelling is a very foolish way of putting oneself out of the world.

Mrs. Montgomery's account of William Alexander Livingston's death is confirmed by Lewis Morris, junior, evidently an eye-witness of this fatal duel; for in a letter to his father, General Lewis Morris, dated from "The Camp, English Neighbourhood, August 2, 1780," he says, "Peter Van Brook's son, William A. Livingston, was killed in a duel yesterday, by Lt. Stakre, the Butcher's son, and the day before Captain Peyton of Col Moylan's Regt., by Adjutant Overton of the same. Fatal business this." There is nothing to explain the reason for this duel, or the presence of young Livingston in the American camp,[20] as twelve months previously he had been a prisoner in the hands of Governor Trumbull of Connecticut, who had written to his uncle, Governor Livingston, an old friend of the Connecticut governor, as to his disposal? Which drew from Governor Livingston a characteristic reply, dated "Raritan, 23 August, 1779," in which, after thanking his friend for his kindness to his nephew, he continues,

> I think you was perfectly right in refusing his request to go into New York. He was certainly a British subject at the time of his capture; and if his name does not stand too much in his way, we may get a good American in exchange for him. Indeed I am sorry that a single individual of his name should chuse to be such a subject. But all families are liable to have degenerate members. Even Adam's had its Cain; that of Isaac its Esau; and among the twelve Apostles there was at least one traitor.

As Sarah's father increased in years, he also increased greatly in corpulence[21]; and Mrs. Montgomery noticed this alteration in his figure, for she tells his daughter in the same letter, "I saw your father well and very fat a very few days since. Your Mama is gone to live at Elizabethtown with her family." This was after one of this lady's short absences from Liberty Hall, and just before the British troops passed through Elizabethtown in the summer of this year, as already recorded. In reference to this incident, Mr. Robert Morris in a note to John Jay, dated Philadelphia,. 6 July, 1780, says, "Kitty stayed the winter with us, and went into the Jersies in May or beginning of June. Mrs. Livingston about this time moved with the family to Elizabethtown, and was there when Mr. Knyphausen[22] came out the other day. At first the family were treated politely, but after a while they found it necessary to leave that place, being threatened hard by the *Brutish*, as our soldiers now call the British.''

Susan also wrote to her sister Sarah, on the 21st October, 1780, telling her news of their youngest brother John Lawrence (Johnny), who had recently joined the *Saratoga* as midshipman, and whose sad and mysterious end was shortly to cause his family such bitter grief. She also mentions that "next month I expect the favour of a visit from Nanny and Cornelia Van

Home. I shall endeavour to persuade Nanny to desert his Majesty's banners and to turn *Rebel* and join us. If I succeed I shall merit the united thanks of the officers of the American army for gaining so fine a girl to our party."

Kitty was back in Philadelphia during the summer, autumn, and winter of 1781–2, on another visit to Mr. and Mrs. Robert Morris, while Susan went to Poughkeepsie and then to her uncle's manor on the Hudson, as already mentioned. On the 19th of October, 1781, Robert Morris sends John Jay "Kitty's picture by Mr. Du Simitière," a Frenchman then residing at Philadelphia. But Kitty's visit on this occasion was sadly spoilt, by her increasing anxiety as to the fate of her youngest brother Johnny, of whom, and his vessel the *Saratoga*, no news had been heard for several months. On Mr. Matthew Ridley arriving in Paris in December, he writes to Jay: "We left Philadelphia 20th October. . . . Miss K. Livingston well but under great anxiety for her brother, Mr. John Livingston, who went out in the *Saratoga*, and has not been heard of."

Susan had taken Sarah's little boy with her to Poughkeepsie, where they stayed with Mr. Jay's father, then in rapidly failing health. John Jay was pleased that his boy should be with his grandfather, but feared the trouble of having visitors might worry his father in his state of health. He therefore wrote to his friend Egbert Benson, for his assistance in finding the child some suitable home in the neighbourhood. In this letter, dated Madrid, 8 December, 1781, he informs Benson, that "Harry Livingston, Jr., has been so kind as to write a letter to Mrs. Jay, and for which we are much obliged to him. I wish, however, he had been as particular about my father as about my son." He then asks his correspondent whether he cannot manage to get Harry Livingston to take charge of his son, and let him go to school with his own children, and still spend some hours with his grandfather every day, but not to continue to live with him. Of Mrs. Harry Livingston, Jay writes, "she is an excellent woman, and in my opinion a *rara avis in terra*." Harry Livingston, Jr., evidently means Major Henry Livingston of Poughkeepsie,[23] a son of Henry Livingston, County Clerk of Dutchess, and grandson of Gilbert Livingston, the elder Robert's fourth son. He would have been at this date in his thirty-fourth year. This Harry Livingston married twice, but the lady who gained such high praise from John Jay must have been his first wife, Sarah Wells, daughter of the Rev. Benjamin Wells.

Whether the little Peter went to reside with the Harry Livingstons is not stated, but the old grandfather was fast fading away, and apparently the child was still living with him, when the latter died on the following

17th of April. As in a letter to Mrs. John Jay from her mother—"to my dear child of my heart"—written from Elizabethtown four days after old Mr. Jay's death, but before Mrs. Livingston had heard the news, this lady says: "Your dear little son is a great comfort to me; he is amiable, and has the love and esteem of all that know him. He is not yet returned from a visit to his grand pappa Jay, where he went last August accompanied by his aunt Susan. . . . Mr. Jay is declining fast." In the same letter Mrs. Livingston gives the news of the capture by the British of John Jay's elder brother: "Sir James Jay has been one of my family since the first of February. . . . Last Monday morning, he left us with an intent to be back in two days, but unfortunately he was taken off from Mr. Syclar's [Arendt Schuyler's] and carried into the king's lines where he is at present."

On the same day—21st April, 1782—as Sarah's mother wrote to her from "Liberty Hall," Mrs. Margaret Livingston, the chancellor's mother, wrote to Sarah's husband from "Claremont," and tells him that his great friend, her son Robert, had just paid her a visit. Whereupon the proud old grandmother loudly sings the praises of the baby granddaughter;—"his little Bess you would be delighted with was you to see her; you can't think what a little cherub she is; her temper the finest you can imagine. But I think I hear his Excellency tell his sweet Lady sitting near—'Let an old woman a writing or talking about a favourite grandchild and she will be so profuse, etc.'" The writer refers in the same letter to the misery the war was causing to everyone; "I sigh," she declares, "for the evacuation of our capital, when shall we meet? You can have no idea of the sufferings of many who from affluence are reduced to the most abject poverty, and others who die in obscurity." And in the usual woman's postscript she adds: "I forgot to tell you that your son grows a very fine boy."

John Jay in his reply, dated Paris, 26 August, 1782, where he had recently arrived with his wife from Spain, having been appointed one of the American Peace Commissioners by Congress, "hopes the Chancellor may have a son equally promising, for Claremont has my best wishes that it may administer affluence to every succession of wise and good possessors." This hope, however, as regards the chancellor having a son was never realised, as his next, and last child, was also a daughter. But these two daughters, when they grew up, both married Livingston cousins, so that the chancellor's home and surname were retained in the family.

Lieut-Col. Brockholst Livingston did not proceed to Paris with his relatives, the Jays, but sailed for home with despatches for the Continental

Congress. Unfortunately, ill luck followed him also on the homeward journey, as the vessel, on which he was a passenger, was captured by a British
cruiser and taken into New York. From Chancellor Livingston, who had
been appointed by Congress Secretary of Foreign Affairs during the previous year, Jay received the following particulars of the capture of his brother-
in-law and the loss of his despatches:

> Your last despatches by Colonel Livingston did not come to
> hand, the vessel in which he sailed was taken and carried into
> New York. He destroyed his letters. He was immediately com-
> mitted to the Provost, where he met with your brother,[24] who
> had been sometime confined there. On the arrival of General
> Carleton, which was a few days after, both were liberated on
> their *paroles*, so that Mr. Livingston can give no intelligence of
> any kind. Carleton spoke to him in the most frank and unre-
> served manner, wished to see the war carried on, if it must be
> carried on, upon more generous principles, than it has hitherto
> been.[25]

This gallant and humane officer, the former Governor of Canada
and afterwards Lord Dorchester, gave his late prisoner a letter for his
father Governor Livingston, on the question of reprisals; in which he said:
"Colonel Livingston will have the pleasure of placing this letter in your
Excellency's hands. His enlargement, sir, has been the first act of my command, being desirous, if war must prevail, to render its evils as light as
possible to individuals."[26] This was the commencement of a courteous correspondence of some length, between the newly appointed British commander at New York and his neighbour, the American governor of New
Jersey.

The war was now hastening to a close, and the British government
had sent Sir Guy Carleton to New York, as the most suitable officer to
facilitate the necessary withdrawal of the British troops, as soon as ever
the terms of the Peace were settled in Paris. The Definitive Treaty of Peace
was finally signed upon the 3rd of September, 1783, and upon the following 25th of November, the city of New York was evacuated by the British
troops; and four days later Chancellor Livingston gaily writes to Jay:

> Dear John, I am two letters in your debt, and am conscious
> that I shall make an ill return for them in offering you this

product of a midnight hour, after a day spent in the fatigue of business and ceremony that our present situation exacts. But having just been informed by Mr. Platt that he sails tomorrow morning, I cannot permit him to go without offering you my congratulations on an event which you have so greatly contributed to bring about, the evacuation of this city by the British on Tuesday last. Our enemies are hardly more astonished than we are ourselves, and than when you will be when you hear that we have been five days in town without the smallest disturbance; that the most obnoxious royalists that had sufficient confidence in our clemency to stay had not met with the least insult. Their shops were opened the day after we came in, and Rivington himself goes on as usual. *The State of New York Gazette* is as well received as if he had never been printer to the king's most excellent majesty. So that your friends in Europe will find their apprehensions ill-founded, and that the race of Tories will not, after all, be totally extinct in America. Perhaps by good training and by crossing the breed frequently (as they are very tame), they may be rendered useful animals in a few generations.

The Jays returned to America during the following summer, and Liberty Hall was once more a happy home,— under whose roof, as in the days before the war, were welcomed visitors from all parts, including General and Mrs. Washington,—still a shadow hung over the meeting between Sarah and her long separated family, owing to the total absence of news as to the fate of the dearly-beloved younger brother. Governor Livingston still clung to the hope that his son was a prisoner in some distant part of Europe; and this belief was further unhappily strengthened by a rumour that Johnny was, with some other members of the crew of the *Saratoga*, detained in confinement at Algiers, and made to work on the fortifications of that seaport. In his distress, the unhappy father appealed to his son-in-law for assistance to clear this mystery up, who at once instituted enquiries, and in his letter in answer to that of his father-in-law, Jay writes:

The last list of the *Saratoga's* officers and men was carefully examined by Mr. Remsen this morning.[27] It is dated the 20th of December, 1780, and noted to have been received in the office the 9th February, 1781. There are no such names as Reynolds and Minor in it. The *Saratoga* is with great probability supposed to have been lost on the 18th of March, 1781, about four o'clock in the afternoon of that day. One of the lieutenants, who had been put in a prize, parted from her a little before that time, and left her in full chase of a sail, the wind coming on so exceedingly violent that the prize before mentioned was obliged to take in her sails. The lieutenant, I am told, is persuaded that the *Saratoga*, whose captain was venturous and full of ardour was then lost. Besides it would be very extraordinary, indeed, that a young gentleman of talents should be for years working in Algiers, and that openly on the fortifications, and there meet with this Blinckhorn, and Reynolds, and Minor, and yet never be able to convey intelligence of himself to any of the Christian consuls or captives, or to the regency of the country. He knew I was in Spain, and that we had ministers also at courts at peace with Algiers, and must soon have learned that among other friendly nations the French had a consul there. I will nevertheless cause copies of your letter to be transmitted to the French and English consuls at Algiers, for although Blinckhorn's story appears to me to deserve no credit, yet in cases of this kind no pains should be spared to remove doubts.

In a letter, written a few months after the evacuation of New York by the British, Governor Livingston makes allusion to his bad handwriting, and to the fact that one of his daughters was accustomed to act as his amanuensis:

> My principal secretary of state [he writes to Mr. Kempe, late royalist Attorney-General of the Province of New York], who is one of my daughters, is gone to New York to shake her heels at the balls and assemblies of a metropolis, which might as well be more studious of paying its taxes, than of instituting expensive diversions. I mention this absence of my secretary to atone for the slovenly hand-writing of this letter, and my enclosed certificate, because she is as celebrated for writing a good hand as her father is notorious for scribbling a bad one.[28]

The absent daughter was most probably Kitty, who, during the follow-ing month was married at Liberty Hall to Matthew Ridley of Baltimore.[29]

Before saying a final farewell to Liberty Hall there are some anec-dotes worth repeating concerning its owner, who, as we have seen, was a man lacking ambition, though by the force of circumstances and his own patriotic wish to be of service to his country, he had been placed in such a prominent position during the War of Independence. Now, however, that peace had come, he was only too glad, like Cincinnatus, to resume the simple country life he had been deprived of all these years. In a letter to Monsieur de Marbois, the French Minister to the United States, dated 24th September, 1783, he expresses his delight at this welcome change in his mode of living. "Thanks to heaven," he writes, "that the times again permit me to resume my favourite amusement of raising vegetables; which, with the additional pleasure resulting from my library, I really prefer to all the bustle and splendour of the world." He was singularly free from affectation, and one of the anecdotes concerning him is related by Mr. Sedgwick, who says:

> He was accustomed to work in his garden like a common labourer; and a Jerseyman who came to see him for the first time, on business, was told by a person occupied with a spade, and looking very like a gardener, that he should be called. The applicant seated himself in the parlour, and when the governor entered, was somewhat surprised to find that the gardener was, with the addition of only a coat, the high dignitary whom he had ventured to approach.

Two French travellers have also left on record their impressions of Governor Livingston. The Marquis de Chastellux who visited Trenton in November 1781, before the conclusion of the war, mentions in his *Travels in North America in 1780–1782:*—"I had scarce alighted from my horse, before I received a visit from Mr. Livingston, Governor of the Jerseys. He is an old man, much respected, and who passes for a very sensible man. He was pleased to accompany me in a little walk I took before dinner, to examine the environs of the town, and the camp occupied by the Americans before the affair of Prince Town." The other Frenchman, who passed through New Jersey seven years later, remarks on his republican simplicity: "You may have an idea," he writes in one of his letters, "of this respectable man, who is at once a writer, a governor, and a ploughman, on learning that he takes pride in calling himself a New Jersey farmer."[30]

One of his favourite relaxations was fishing, and about this date, namely after the war, he received a letter from one of his grandsons relating to this sport, and with all a boy's enthusiasm tendering his grandfather some advice. This brought a jocular reply from the grandsire, who wrote: "I hope you do not believe that grandpapa wants any instructions from a West Chester man how to catch *fresh water fish*. Why he understands it better than he does the affairs of government."

We had nearly omitted to mention that during the stay of Governor Livingston's daughters in the neighbourhood of General Washington's headquarters, the commander-in-chief, who generally had Mrs. Washington with him, always gave them a hearty welcome to his family circle; and to his favourite Kitty, he wrote from the camp, Valley Forge, on the 18th March 1778:

> General Washington having been informed lately of the honour done him by Miss Kitty Livingston in wishing for a lock of his hair, takes the liberty of inclosing one, accompanied by his most respectful compliments.[31]

The girls also had near relatives among the officers there, one of these being Major-General Lord Stirling, their uncle, and another, their youthful cousin Henry Philip Livingston, an officer in Washington's Corps of Guards, and who became captain of the same in December 1778. General Greene was also a great friend of theirs, and in one of her letters to her sister Sarah, Kitty loudly sings the praises of her favourite general.[32] This friendship was fully reciprocated by General Greene, who, in writing to his wife on one occasion says: "I am now at Lord Stirling's seat, in a most agreeable family of Governor Livingston's. There are three young ladies of distinguished merit, sensible, polite, and easy. Their manners are soft and engaging; they wish much to see you here, and I wish it too."[33] They had also another great friend at headquarters, namely their old playmate Alexander Hamilton, Washington's pet aide-de-camp whom the wicked Tory newspapers, who, as we well know, respected no one on the "rebel" side, irreverently dubbed "Mrs. Washington's Tom Cat."

When General Washington became the first President of the United States of America in 1789, his wife remained at home at Mount Vernon, until her husband had become settled in his new surroundings at New York, then the Capital. When he was ready to receive her, Mrs. Washington travelled by way of New Jersey and slept one night at Liberty Hall, and upon the following morning Governor Livingston accompanied her to Elizabethtown Point, where she was met by her husband, the President, and embarked with great ceremony in his state barge for New York.

One more anecdote concerning the family at Liberty Hall. As already mentioned, Mrs. Jay was the beauty, and in a medallion portrait still preserved, in which her hair is done up according to the French fashion of the time—*àla* Marie Antoinette—she bears a certain resemblance to that unhappy queen. When she accompanied her husband to Paris on his appointment as one of the Peace Commissioners, they went on one occasion to the theatre, and at their entrance the audience rose en masse mistaking Mrs. Jay for their queen, then at the height of her beauty.[34]

Clermont, built in 1730 by Robert, son of the first Lord of the Manor. Historic American Buildings Survey, Library of Congress, Prints and Photographs Division, Public Domain.

We must now say a final farewell to Liberty Hall and cross the river to Clermont where stands the second Livingston residence built on the Manor, the oldest now existing. As has been already mentioned in Chapter X, Clermont was the south-westerly portion of the Manor bequeathed by the first lord to his second surviving son, Robert, who built his house about 1730 directly upon the banks of the Hudson River and literally within a stone's-throw of the water. In front rise the Catskills seemingly from the river's shore, though really about seven miles distant. The banks here are seventy feet high, affording a most charming view over a beautiful lawn which is lined with immense locust trees from one of which, still standing, a limb was shot by a gun from the frigate when the house was burnt in 1777 by the British.[35]

This old house has been the centre of so much that concerned the Livingston family, that some anecdotes which have come down to us are sure to be of interest to the many descendants of Judge Robert, and his wife Margaret Beekman. The following narrative has been taken entirely from Mrs. Delafield's *Biographies of Francis and Morgan Lewis*, and *A Group of American Girls*, by Helen G. Smith.

The first owner of Clermont was, as we have seen, a picturesque figure, retaining the costume worn by men of his rank at the period when he retired from an active part in the world's affairs, and never afterwards laying it aside. His only child, the Judge, was to him the light of his eyes and the joy of his heart. The most perfect confidence existed between them. In both, religion was the ruling principle. They were both gentle in their temper and affectionate in their dispositions, both were inflexible where their duty was concerned. Robert was adored by his grandchildren, and the Clermont sisters were fond of relating instances of his liberality towards them. Were they about to make a trip to town, he would put a note in their hands saying, "For your ribands my dears," and he admitted that he liked to see ladies well dressed, and thought brocade more becoming than chintz.

Mrs. Church, a daughter of General Schuyler, the belle of her day, never visited Clermont without asking to see the old gentleman, even if indisposition confined him to his room. She said: "No one flatters me as much to my taste as he does."

On the outbreak of the war he expressed a wish to go to Boston. His son asked: "Father, what could you do there?" He replied: "If I stopped a bullet, I might save a better man." The story of his death has already been told in a previous chapter.

After hostilities commenced, his heir, Judge Robert R. Livingston, left his town house, and removed his large family to Clermont, this trip in those days being no trifling undertaking. The cabin of a sloop had to be engaged, the berths furnished with bedding; crockery, knives, forks, etc., must be provided, and provisions cooked to last several days; it was almost as much trouble as furnishing a small house. We, now, can hardly realise the discomforts of travelling when it took a week to reach Albany from New York by road, and when for half the year the roads were unsafe for carriages on springs, and the taverns, such as they were, were few and far between.

"The connection between the Judge and his wife was one of those blessed unions sometimes permitted lest the world should forget that marriage was instituted in Paradise." So writes Mrs. Delafield. This happy bond was severed upon the Judge's death in 1775, and then Clermont and the large estates descended to his heir, Chancellor Robert R. Livingston. As he at this time was busily engaged in public affairs, he left the whole control of the property in the hands of his mother, who survived her husband, and lived as mistress of Clermont for twenty-five years.

The burning of the house in 1777 has already been mentioned, but the widow, undaunted, soon began the rebuilding, for in a letter of November 19, 1778, we find her stating to Governor Clinton that she requires "many hands," "such as masons, carpenters, brick burners, stone and lime breakers and burners," showing that all the materials were taken from the place itself, for with the outside world at that time there was practically no communication.

She followed exactly the plan of the former house in rebuilding, the height of the ceilings being twelve feet, which was considered remarkable in a period when wood and open fireplaces were the only means of producing heat.

Since her time many additions have been made to the old house beginning in 1803 when a north wing was built, but the interior of the main house has never been changed. A quaint, dark wood staircase winds up from the long centre hall, and on the first floor are seen the well proportioned rooms, old mahogany doors in beautifully carved doorways, and fine old fireplaces, in one of which still remains a curious iron fireback, decorated with the Royal British arms at a time when the fleur-de-lys of France were still among the quarterings! The library, with bookcases running nearly to the ceiling, contains many valuable and curious books. Some of the old portraits are yet to be found in the house.

The oldest is the one of the Rev. John Livingston, painted as a young man, undoubtedly before he was ordained, and when, as he himself has told us, he was fond of dress. It is a panel picture now very dark with age. Another curious one is of young Henry Beekman, whose early death left his sister sole heiress of the vast Beekman estate, and another is that of a sweet faced lady in velvet and satin gown, whose exact identity cannot be determined, but who is thought to be Margaret Howarden, the wife of Robert of Clermont.

Here, too, is one of Gilbert Stuart's best works, the portrait of Chancellor Robert R. Livingston, familiar to many from the numerous copies amongst the members of the family, as well as from its reproduction upon one of the commemorative stamps of the Louisiana Purchase.

The domestic life at Clermont must indeed have been complicated, and one marvels at what Margaret Beekman Digitized accomplished in the management of the estate, the care of her household, and the education of her children.

The work of the kitchen, garden and farm was done by slaves, who at Clermont were either inherited or born on the place. Their work of course saved their mistress manual labour, but not the necessity of perpetual supervision and instruction. She could not be well served unless she herself was well skilled in the mysteries of pantry, dairy, kitchen and poultry yard. The upper servants were drawn from the tenant class, who as a rule paid their rent in produce or labour, rather than in money.

It is related that Mrs. Livingston once offered freedom to a slave woman of ungovernable temper, on condition that she would leave forever. The answer was an indignant refusal: "I was born on the place and have as good a right to live here as you have. I do not want to be free."

Thanksgiving Day had not then become a national institution, so Christmas was the great holiday of the year. Then Madam sat in her drawing-room, a table near her, on which lay piles of Madras handkerchiefs, rows of knives, bags of silver coin, etc. Then all her servants came and wished her "Merry Christmas" and received a present in return. Great preparations were made in the kitchen for the winter, all hands were busy pickling beef and pork, curing hams, preparing sausages. The good housewife had always well filled shelves of mince-meat, cheese and preserves, and apples were plenty, and the buckwheat cake regularly appeared at a Knickerbocker breakfast. As soon as the river was free from ice, the shad made their appearance, then calves and lambs were due, and wild ducks and geese flew northwards, so by spring there would be nothing to complain of in the way of fare.

Mrs. Livingston's house was well known to judges making their circuit, to lawyers and members of the Legislature on their way to and from Albany. Indeed her reputation for hospitality was so far famed, that one day a Lutheran minister, of the name of Hardwick, presented himself at her door, and said that he had come from New York to die under her roof, the hour of his departure being close at hand. He related that in an illness forty years before, it had been disclosed to him that he should die at a certain hour forty years after. This time had now come.

Chancellor Livingston, who was then at home, wished to divert his mind until the fatal hour had passed, and an elder of the Lutheran Church, living near, came in his carriage and implored Hardwick to spend the day with him. The old naan refused to leave Clermont, and soon mounted the stairs, pausing on the landing to look at the clock, and remarking he had not long to live. He passed into his bedroom and lay down on his bed, and as the clock struck the appointed hour of twelve, he expired. This story, says Mrs. Delafield, is an extraordinary instance of the effect upon the mind, of a long cherished idea, at a time when the body is enfeebled with age.

The education of her younger children was a serious difficulty for Mrs. Livingston. Schools were generally closed during the war, and it was difficult to find the right man as tutor. Finally she was fortunate in procuring the services of Dominie Doll, a learned minister, capable also of teaching the German language. By another good chance she obtained an excellent music master, who taught the children to play upon the spinet. She was herself a French scholar, so no doubt she taught that herself to her children, when other aid was not to be had.

Churches, as well as schools, were usually closed at that time, but a connection of Mrs. Livingston's writes from Clermont to a friend in town: "We read the Bible every Sunday; here it is on every dressing-table, the first book opened, read as the preparation for the day." To quote Mrs. Delafield's words: "A large family grew up in the intellectual and moral atmosphere of Clermont, not one of whom lived in vain."

One wonders where this large household disposed itself, for the mansion, though of good size, would not seem spacious enough to shelter all the children, attendants, teachers, friends, and relations, who seem ever to have been welcomed there. Mrs. Livingston felt so sorry that Dominie Doll's only child should be away from him, that when the long, cold winter set in, she sent for the girl, to make one of the Clermont household!

At another time she heard of an orphan girl, Miss Le-Touche, whose family she had known, being left without protection when the

British occupied New York. She at once sent for her and made her a permanent member of the family until she married Stephen Duponceau of Philadelphia, a friend of the Chancellor.

"The Marquis de Lafayette," says Mrs. Delafield, "was soon domesticated in the family of Mrs. Robert Livingston. He tried to persuade Edward to run away with him to Europe. 'We will write,' he said, 'from the other side to be forgiven. I will adopt you for my brother and you shall have every advantage of education that Europe can afford.' My uncle said that it was a great temptation, but he thought of his mother and resisted."

It was Mrs. Livingston's habit to leave the drawing-room, and spend some time in reading and in correspondence before retiring. She always seems to have kept abreast of the times, and her opinion had weight with those in public affairs. Shortly before the delegates who declared New York State independent met at Kingston, a number of the most influential Republicans met at Clermont to consider, among other questions, who should be the first governor. A valid objection to every person was raised until Mrs. Livingston proposed George Clinton. Her suggestion was received with acclamation: "He is the man! Why did not we think of him at once?"

After the war was over, Mrs. Livingston again took possession of her house in Queen, now Pearl Street, New York. It was the habit of her children with their families to pass with her every evening not otherwise engaged. The members of the bar, gentlemen on their promotion and foreigners of distinction were not backward in seeking admission to a salon where they were received with hospitality.

This remarkable woman died suddenly in June, 1800, falling backward while sitting at the head of her table in the dining-room at Clermont. All of her children had settled within a few hours' drive of Clermont, and many of these homes are still in the possession of their descendants.

It has already been said that the chancellor allowed his mother to continue as mistress of Clermont, after the property became his in 1775. Had the case been in England, he would undoubtedly have built for her a smaller house on the estate, which would have been known as the Dower House. Instead of doing this, however, after the war, in 1783, he built for himself a new home, of an original and very beautiful design, about a quarter of a mile south of the old house, and approached from it by an avenue of locust trees, unrivalled in America.

As the chancellor grew more and more prominent, this new house, which was also called Clermont, came to be equally well known with the original Clermont, and in latter days this has caused some confusion, which now, however, has been remedied by the present owner of both houses, who designates the later building as Arryl House, and retains it merely as a curiosity, upon his Clermont estate.

The life of the chancellor at his well beloved home has already been spoken of, but we may quote one or two accounts of the style of living of this gentleman of a bygone age.

The house was built in the form of a capital H, and the projecting wings in front were united by an elevated terrace, which was filled with orange, lemon, and myrtle trees. A conservatory ran the whole length of the house on the south side. In this greenhouse the dinner and supper tables were set on great occasions, the tables being so constructed that the largest and most ornamental of the plants rose from their centre. Two head gardeners took charge of the greenhouse and flower garden. The men servants were negroes. The butler, old and grey-headed, Mrs. Delafield says she has often seen walking slowly through the halls looking and behaving as if the charge of the whole establishment rested on his shoulders.

When the chancellor came back from France he brought with him many pieces of interesting furniture, tapestries and silver plate, which had been obtained from returning *tmigrés*, who were glad to sell to the wealthy American, and one of his young relatives describes how Cousin Chancellor would walk about among the young people, relating the history of each piece, which would prove as interesting as any story book. But perhaps they enjoyed best of all the splendid library, containing more than six thousand books, besides quantities of pamphlets. Books not only in English and the learned languages, but in Spanish and French, both of which tongues the chancellor read and spoke with ease.

Arryl House was nearly always filled with guests, and these were among the most distinguished persons of our own country, as well as such foreigners who visited our shores. Many a bearer of an ancient and honoured name of the old French noblesse was here received and sheltered for months, and even years, for the chancellor used to say "he loved all Frenchmen for the sake of those who had fought for us."

The chancellor was fond of riding, and was on horseback a great deal, but when he made calls he drove in a great gilded coach drawn by four horses. It would hardly seem as if the owner of Clermont maintained a style of living quite in consonance with the strictly republican principles which he had hazarded all to gain.

At his death[36] he bequeathed Clermont and the greater part of its estate, to his elder daughter Elizabeth, wife of Edward Philip Livingston. Upon his death, Clermont with about 2000 acres passed to his eldest son, Clermont, and upon his death to his only son John Henry Livingston, the present owner, who is the sixth in direct descent living within the old walls.

Arryl House and its grounds, the chancellor left to his younger daughter, Margaret Maria, the wife of Robert L. Livingston. This place was inherited by their son Montgomery Livingston, and on his death without heirs, it passed out of the family for a period of about fifty years. But now, at the time of writing—anno 1908—the house and about 200 acres of land have been purchased by the owner of Clermont, thus re-uniting both historic properties after a separation of nearly a century.

Margaret Maria, the chancellor's younger daughter, was said to be very beautiful. Kotzebue, the German dramatic poet, saw her in Paris with her father, and he speaks of her in his memoirs as the youngest sister of Venus.

In 1824, the Marquis de Lafayette made his triumphal journey through the United States. He proceeded immediately up the Hudson to Staatsburgh to the home of General Lewis, who had married Gertrude, a sister of Chancellor Livingston. From there he went on to Clermont where a grand fête to the tenantry, and review of the county militia took place. Marshall Grouchy, who was watching the affair from a window at Arryl House, lost his balance and fell out, breaking his arm. In the evening there was a great ball given, which Lafayette opened with Mrs. Montgomery. With this last picture of a beautiful and historic estate we will turn from Clermont to some of the other houses built upon the manor.

The original Manor House, built by Robert Livingston, the elder, and first lord, in 1699,[37] no longer exists; only the site of it now remains. The exact date and the cause of its destruction are apparently unknown. Probably it ceased to be used as the Manor House after the death of the third proprietor, namely towards the close of the eighteenth century, when the estate was subdivided among his heirs, but it is strange no authentic information concerning its destruction is on record.[38] The last Lord of the Manor's eldest surviving son, Colonel Peter R. Livingston, who would have been the sole heir under the entail, if that had not been abolished when the province became independent of the mother country, had commenced to build for himself during his father's lifetime a house which he intended to complete as a grand Manor House. "He built the basement and the first story, consisting of a fine large hall, with parlour and dining-room opening out of it from one end, and four good rooms, two on each side of the hall. The war ended, the entail done away with, his father devised his estate to his eight children, Peter R., Maria, Walter, Robert C., Catharine, Alida, John, and Henry. Peter R., disappointed, put a roof on his unfinished house, as it is seen to-day, the colonial staircase leading up to—an attic! With comparatively small means this city-bred man and his wife Margaret, a daughter of James Livingston of New York City, a son of Robert, 'the nephew,' settled 'down' to their changed conditions. They called their house 'The Hermitage' and as such it is known to-day, standing solidly in spite of a century of neglect, a peculiar building; but it is no longer in the possession of the family. There Colonel Peter R. Livingston died on the 15th of November, 1794."[39]

About two miles north of the old Manor House at the extreme end of the Manor where it is bounded by the little creek called the Wachankassik is another one of the old 18th century Livingston places, the only one now remaining except Clermont which still belongs to a Livingston. This is Oak Hill. The house was built by John Livingston, one of the sons of the 3rd Lord of the Manor in the last decade of the 18th century.

Before deciding where to place his house he climbed up one of the tallest oak trees with which the place was covered and thus determined its site. Oaks were always here preserved and still abound. Until very recently two very large ones, each about five feet in diameter, stood in front of the house and no doubt it was one of these that John Livingston climbed.

The situation of the house is unique, certainly not surpassed by any other in the Manor.

Placed upon a height rising direct from the Hudson just where the river bends towards the south-west the view is unimpeded over the water for quite ten miles, while in front one gains a view of the Catskills very different from that seen from any other part of the Manor.

The house has, for its period, very high ceilings, so much so that when John Livingston was building it, his family protested, saying "John, you will freeze"; and very natural it was thus to protest when one considers the difficulty at that time of heating a house in winter.

Here may be seen one of the old firebacks from the Manor House marked R. M. L., the initials of Robert and Mary Livingston, third Lord and Lady of the Manor.

Here also are the original portraits of Robert first Lord of the Manor and of Alida, his wife, as well as much of the old family furniture and many pieces of the family silver.

John Livingston bequeathed Oak Hill to his youngest surviving son Herman who married, December 8 1821, Sarah Lawrence Hallett of that well known Long Island family.

Mrs. Livingston's quiet unruffled intrepidity quite equalled the well known, easily excitable but fearless nature of her husband. One day entering her dining-room she found a man stealing the silver from her sideboard. Without a moment's hesitation she walked direct to him and taking the silver out of his hands said: "How dare you come into my house? Leave instantly," which the thief did, to be caught later as he was endeavouring to pawn some of the smaller pieces which he had concealed in his pockets. When asked afterwards whether she was not frightened Mrs. Livingston replied: "I was so angry at seeing any one dare to come thus into my house that I did not think of being afraid."

The time of their marriage was a period of great gaiety and hospitality throughout that countryside, which included not only Oak Hill, Teviotdale, The Hill, The Hermitage, and Clermont in the Manor, but also further south the estate of John Swift, son of Robert Cambridge Livingston and that of Robert Tillotson whose mother was Margaret, a sister of Chancellor Livingston. To show how little wind and weather were then regarded the late Herman Livingston often told the story of a dinner given by his wife and himself. Upon the day appointed there set in a furious snow-storm, so severe that it seemed doubtful whether any one of the expected guests would venture out. However, all arrived with the punctuality which was customary in those days, all, except Mr. Charles Dale, who had married Harriet, daughter of Walter Livingston and widow of Robert Fulton. Scarcely had dinner been announced and the guests seated at the table when Mr. Dale was heard arriving. Mr. Livingston met him in the hall. Lowering his voice, Mr. Dale said: "They are all here? Supposing no one else would venture out in such a storm I merely drove over to laugh at you for giving a dinner with no guests, but they are all here." "Yes," replied the host, "all but you." "And I shall soon be there," rejoined Mr. Dale, and was ushered in 'mid the laughter of the guests, glad to turn upon one who thought none but himself could face the storm.

Mr. and Mrs. Herman Livingston's happy married life lasted nearly forty-seven years until Mrs. Livingston's death September io 1868, a blow from which her husband never recovered. On the 9th of May, 1872, he gladly followed her. They had three children.

John Henry, the eldest, died unmarried.

Cornelia, the second child, married Clermont Livingston of Clermont and died in 1851, leaving one daughter, Mary, and one son, John Henry, the present proprietor of Clermont.

Herman Thong, the youngest, married Susan Bard Rogers and became upon the death of his father the owner of Oak Hill. He in his turn bequeathed that estate to his eldest son Herman, the present proprietor, the fourth generation of the family living at Oak Hill.[40]

There are other beautiful places in the neighbourhood such as "The Hill" and "Montgomery Place," which, however, are no longer owned by members of the Livingston family, but the latter, once the home of Edward Livingston and his daughter Mrs. Thomas Barton, will eventually revert to a member of the family, Maturin Livingston Delafield, great-great-grandson of Judge Robert R. Livingston.

"The Hill," a fine mansion, was built by Henry Walter, one of the sons of Walter Livingston of Teviotdale; it got its name from its position "on a high hill dominating the whole surrounding country." Here Henry Walter Livingston and his wife Mary, whose maiden name was Allen, a granddaughter of Chief Justice Allen of Pennsylvania, and known in the New York society of her day as "Lady Mary" from her charming manners, entertained their friends and visitors in quite a regal manner, as his widow continued to do after Henry Walter's death. Among foreign visitors of distinction, who at various times were welcomed under their hospitable roof, were Louis Philippe, afterwards King of France, Joseph Bonaparte, ex-king of Spain, and the Marquis Lafayette. In connection with the visit of the ex-king of Spain, the late Bishop Kip relates the following anecdote in his *New York Society in the Olden Time:*

> Thither came Joseph Bonaparte, the ex-king of Spain, who remained several days with a suite of forty persons. At the moment of his departure, when all the equipages were drawn up at the grand entrance, and Mrs. Livingston was making her adieux on the marble piazza, the princess, his daughter, called for her drawing materials. It was supposed that she wished to sketch the view, which extends for sixty miles around. But those who looked over her page discovered that it was the *chatelaine* she was sketching.

Like Louis Philippe, the ex-king of Spain never forgot his hospitable entertainers in a foreign land; and to quote Bishop Kip again:

How vivid were Joseph Bonaparte's recollections of this visit may be drawn from the fact that when, years afterwards, he was dying in Florence, hearing that a lady of this family was in the city, he sent for her to his bedside. He talked to her about her mother, and ended with the remark: "Your mother should have been a queen!"[41]

Notes

1. Mr. Bayard Tuckerman in his recent *Life of General Philip Schuyler* (edition 1898, p. 40), inserts "Livingston" in brackets after "Phil," so he must have seen the original letter, and thus been able to identify this "Phil"; while Dr. Benson Lossing, in his *Life of Philip Schuyler* (edition 1872, p. 68), who also prints this letter, does not give the surname. Mr. Tuckerman apparently, judging from his index, considers this Philip Livingston was the Philip, afterwards known as "The Signer." The context, however, shows that Schuyler's friend must have been about his own age, while "The Signer" at this date was a married man getting on to the forties. The only Philip Livingston who fits the date for age, and in other respects, is Philip, the eldest son of Robert, third Lord of the Manor, who was born in February 1734, and thus Schuyler's junior by a few weeks. This young man must have been just fresh from Harvard, at the date of Schuyler's visit to New York, as from a letter of his father's still in existence, he refers to his son Philip having entered Cambridge College in August 1751. Philip died, unmarried, in April 1756.
2. Probably the youngest daughter of Philip Livingston, second Lord of the Manor, born in April, 1733; and therefore only a few months older than her nephew, the Philip referred to above.
3. Meaning he did not wear a wig, like other men of his class.
4. *The Correspondence and Public Papers of John Jay*, edited by Henry P. Johnston.
5. An elder sister of Sarah.
6. Chapter XIII.
7. John Lawrence was Governor Livingston's youngest son. At the date of the above raid he was only sixteen years of age.
8. Chapter XIII
9. Namely, the partisan bands of New Jersey Loyalists.
10. Governor Livingston could, however, apparently write distinctly enough when he chose, or had the leisure; because, a letter of his, dated a November, 1789, acknowledging his last re-election as governor, and which is now in the author's possession, is perfectly legible.
11. Mr. E. S. Maclay in his *History of the United States Navy from 1775 to 1901*, vol. i, p. 146, says the rigging had got in a slack condition owing to the change from a cold to a warm climate.
12. Chevalier de la Luzerne, at this date representing France at the Continental Congress.
13. Namely the 30th November, 1779.
14. Letter dated 10th July, 1780. Mr. Carmichael was John Jay's official secretary.
15. Letter dated 1st December, 1780.
16. Letter dated 12th July, 1781.
17. Letter dated 6th September, 1780.

18. Third son of Peter Van Brugh Livingston, and therefore Sarah Jay's first cousin. He was only in his twenty-third year when killed in this duel.

19. Lieutenant-Colonel Henry Brockholst Livingston had already fought a duel during the Burgoyne campaign.

20. The author, in referring to this duel in his former work, was under the impression that William Alexander Livingston was an American officer, but he has been unable to discover any proof of this, though he has traced the career of nearly every Livingston who held a commission during the war. See Appendix A.

21. In early life he was so tall and thin that he was known as the "whipping post."

22. Lieutenant-General Baron von Knyphausen, who during Sir Henry Clinton's absence from New York was in command of the British troops. He was a man of fine personal appearance, and commanded the German contingent in the British army. His lack of knowledge of the English language and of geography was, however, a source of amusement to the English officers, who used to relate the following anecdote concerning his voyage out to America. The voyage happened to be an unusually protracted one, and one night while playing whist, General Knyphausen suddenly turned to the captain of the vessel and said, with an air of much sincerity, "Captain, ain't we hab sailed past America?"

23. See his military record under Appendix A.

24. Namely Sir James Jay, whose capture has already been referred to.

25. Dated Philadelphia, 9 May, 1782.

26. In a long letter to Washington relating his experiences, and the reason for giving his parole, Colonel Livingston states he left Madrid on the 7th February, sailed from Cadiz, on the nth March, and was captured on the 25th April. Letter dated Elizabethtown, 16 June, 1782. *Correspondence of the American Revolution*, vol. iii, pp. 517–522.

27. Letter dated New York, 25 January, 1790.

28. Letter dated Elizabethtown, 3 March, 1787.

29. The marriage took place on the 14th April, 1787. Their married life was a very short one, as Mr. Ridley died on the 13th November, 1789, at the age of forty. The widow married again, her second husband was her kinsman John Livingston of Oak Hill. Her elder sister Susan did not marry until 1794. Her husband was the Hon. John Cleve Symmes, an old friend of the family. She was his third wife. For list of all Governor Livingston's children, their marriages, etc., see Appendix.

30. As quoted by Mr. Sedgwick from Brissot's *Travels*, Letter VI.

31. Mrs. Ellet's *The Women of the American Revolution*, vol. ii, p. 118.

32. Kitty Livingston to Mrs. Jay, Philadelphia, 18 October 1781.

33. Greene, *Life of Nathanael Greene*, vol. i., p. 356.

34. Mrs. Wharton, *Social Life in the Early Republict* p. 35.

35. See Chapter XIII.

36. Chancellor Livingston's total landed estates in Dutchess, Columbia, Ulster, and Delaware counties aggregated 300,000 acres. As soon as was possible after his father's death, he gave to each of his three brothers 30,000 acres, and to each of his six sisters 20,000 acres.

37. On "A map of the Towns of Livingston, Germantown and Clermont in the County of Columbia" printed in 1798, it appears marked as "Manor House Built in 1699," so it must have still been in existence in that year. *Doc. Hist. New York*, vol. iii, p. 498. Mr. G. W. Schuyler says that there was an earlier house built in 1694. *Colonial New York*, vol. i, p. 275.

38. To Mrs. Harold Wilson the author is indebted for the following particulars:—"The first Livingston Manor House was built in 1699 by the first proprietor, on the side

of the hill, a short distance from the mouth of Roeloff Jansen's Kill, which empties into the Hudson at this point. The last Lord of the Manor left the Manor House and that portion of his estate to his eldest grandson Robert Thong Livingston, who built the new house, now standing, early in the nineteenth century, as he died December 20th, 1813. He married, November 15th, 1787, Margaret, daughter of John Livingston and Catherine De Peyster of New York City. The present house stands on the brow of the hill, just above the site of the first Manor House. I know of no reason for removing the old Manor House except for the great improvement in situation. This is a good sized ordinary house, and commands a fine view of the Hudson River for miles up and down. The Catskill Mountains loom opposite, about eight miles distant from the western shore. Robert Thong Livingston put in his new house the mantelpieces, door casings, and firebacks from the large open fireplaces of the old house."

In regard to "The Hill," this lady writes in the same letter:—"Walter Livingston, second son of the last Lord of the Manor, died in 1798. His son Henry Walter built the fine house, originally known as 'The Hill,' in the year 1801,1 believe. Henry Walter died in 1810. His widow lived there and died in 1855. After the death of Henry Walter, the place was always called 'Widow Mary's Place.' "

39. From information also kindly supplied by Mrs. Harold Wilson of Columbia county, New York.

40. An illustrated article entitled "Oak Hill on Livingston Manor" was contributed by Miss Marion Harland to the *Home Maker* in June and July, 1889.

41. *New York Society in the Olden Time*, p. 22. The author's father, the late Jasper Livingston, when quite a young man, was a visitor at some of these family mansions on the Hudson about the above period. His paternal uncle, Lieutenant-Governor Edward P. Livingston, was then the owner of "Clermont"; and the Henry Walter Livingstons were connections of his through his mother, as Henry Walter's daughters Ann and Cornelia married brothers, his maternal half-uncles Anson and Carroll. The author's fourth daughter is named "Cornelia" after the late Mrs. Carroll Livingston, and *her* husband, though a Dutchman, is descended on *his* mother's side from Judge Robert R. Livingston of Clermont. Thus the intermarriages still keep on!

CHAPTER XIX

CONCERNING THE HERALDRY OF LIVINGSTON.

"Arms of Descent or Paternal Arms are those which belong
to one particular family, and distinguish it from others, and
which it is unlawful for any other family to assume. The inher-
itance of such in the third generation constitutes a Gentleman
in right of blood, in the fourth a Gentleman of Ancestry—a
position which the mere possession of money or title is powerless to procure."

—WORTHY, *Practical Heraldry.*

FOR the student of family history, the "noble science of Heraldry" must
always possess a great fascination. By its aid he is materially assisted in
his researches, when groping for genealogical proofs of ancestors who lived
in those "brave days of old," when the *sword* was mightier than the pen,
and its knightly owner could no more sign his name, than can the "illiterate voter" of the present day. For, as an eminent authority on Scottish
heraldry says with truth:

In Scotland, as in Wales, where surnames are comparatively
few in number, Armorial Bearings afford no inconsiderable
assistance in authenticating Genealogies and in distinguishing
the various branches of a widely extended Clan. Unaided by
the characteristic symbols of the Herald, and in the absence

of an estate to serve as a designation, who, for example, could ever comprehend the endless ramifications of the families of Douglas. Campbell, or Scott?[1]

To which list, Mr. Seton might well have added the family of Livingston, whose ramifications are as extensive as in the case of any of those he mentions. According to the same reliable authority, "the introduction of both Arms and Surnames into Scotland is usually assigned to the reign of William the Lyon (1165–1214)."[2]

The seals attached to ancient charters and other documents form the most authentic, as well as the earliest, record of armorial bearings in Scotland. These naturally, owing to their composition, have suffered greatly from the destructive ravages of time. Fortunately, however, there are still some of the earlier Livingston seals in existence, some of which have been included in Mr. Henry Laing's valuable catalogues[3]; while others have been brought to the author's notice by his learned friend, the late Mr. Joseph Bain.[4] The earliest Livingston documentary seal now in existence, as far as is known, is that of Sir Andrew de Livingston, Sheriff of Lanark, appended to a Homage Roll, dated 28th August 1296. This, however, is evidently not heraldic. It is thus described by Mr. Bain in his list of Homage Seals: "Lozenge shape; a wolf (?) passant to sinister, a tree behind; 'S'ANDREE D'LEVINGISTON MIL.'" The next in order of date in same list, is that of Sir Andrew's kinsman, Sir Archibald de Livingston, Sheriff of Linlithgow, also not heraldic. This is attached to an indenture of the 12th February 1301–2, by which its owner agrees to keep the town and sheriffdom for King Edward I, with ten men-at-arms for twenty marks until Pentecost. This seal, which is much worn, is thus catalogued by Mr. Bain:—"A fragment of his seal remains—a Bacchante (?) with a thyrsis in her left hand; flattened and defaced."[5] Apparently, judging from his seal, Sir Archibald must have been a worshipper of Bacchus; and that he was fond of wine is proved by another document of about the same date, in which it is recorded that Walter, Bishop of Chester, was charged by Edward I, to see that this worthy knight was supplied with "two tuns of wine and 20 qrs. of wheat, whenever he asks it," to make up for "his victual lost at sea."[6]

THE ARMS OF LIVINGSTON OF LIVINGSTON

FROM THE ARMORIAL DE BERRY
A. D. 1450-1455

FROM THE MS. OF SIR DAVID LINDSAY
LYON KING AT ARMS, A. D. 1542

THE ARMS OF LIVINGSTON OF CALLENDAR

FROM THE ARMORIAL DE BERRY
A. D. 1450-1455

FROM THE MS. OF SIR DAVID LINDSAY
LYON KING AT ARMS, A. D. 1542

THE ARMS OF LIVINGSTON OF DRUMRY

THE ARMS OF LIVINGSTON OF WEMYSS

FROM THE ARMORIAL DE BERRY
A. D. 1450-1455

FROM THE MS. OF SIR DAVID LINDSAY
LYON KING AT ARMS, A. D. 1542

Though the above Sir Archibald also took the oath of allegiance to the English king, his seal is not now to be found appended to his particular Homage Roll. We, however, now come to the first authentic armorial Livingston seal. This is that of Sir William Livingston, the founder of the House of Callendar, and is attached to the Treaty of Peace—as well as to the ratification of the same—between England and Scotland in October 1357, which settled the ransom of David II; who had been defeated and taken prisoner by the English at the battle of Durham or Neville's Cross,—17th October 1346. The original documents, which the author has seen, are still preserved in the Public Record Office, London. This seal, which is also somewhat defaced bears on a shield the well-known three cinquefoils within the double tressure, flowered and counter-flowered, surrounded by an inscription, which reads—"S'Will[elm]i [De] Levi[n]giston."[7]

How the Livingstons came to adopt the three cinquefoils for their family arms will probably now, at this late date, never be known. These are also borne in Scotland by the ancient, and now ducal, House of Hamilton, with which the Livingstons came to be connected in later years,—with this distinction, however, that while the Livingston arms are *Argent, three cinquefoils gules*, those of Hamilton are *Gules, three cinquefoils pierced ermine*; while a third old Scottish family, that of Fraser of Lovat, bear on an *Azure field three cinquefoils* (or *fraises*) *argent* for their paternal coat; and yet another, Borthwick, Lord Borthwick, *Argent, three cinquefoils sable*. The former, of these two last charges, appears on the quartered arms of the Marquis of Huntly, and on those of the now extinct Earldom of Wigton, through ancient alliances between scions of these two great Houses and heiresses of the Fraser family.

The double tressure, flowered and counter-flowered, "First by Achaius borne"—

> From his steed's shoulder, loin, and breast,
>   Silk housings swept the ground,
> With Scotland's arms, device and crest,
>   Embroider'd round and round.
> The double tressure might you see,
>   First by Achaius borne,
> The thistle and the fleur-de-lis,
>   And gallant unicorn—[8]

which surrounds the rampant lion of Scotland on the Royal Arms, was formerly only permitted to be borne by a subject, who was either descended from daughters of the royal family, or who had merited well of his king and country, "as a special additament of honour."[9] There is no reason to believe that Sir William Livingston could claim descent from royalty, so the probability is that this "additional honour" was bestowed on him by King David II, when that monarch dubbed him a knight banneret for valiant services rendered under the royal standard during his disastrous invasion of England in 1346.[10]

It will be seen from the above description that the Livingston paternal coat,—three red cinquefoils on a silver field,—like all *ancient* Scottish armorial bearings, such as the "chequered fess of the Stewarts and Lindsays, the crowned heart and mullets of the Douglases, the inescutcheons of the Hays, the cinquefoils of the Hamiltons, the saltire and chief of the Bruces, the crescents of the Setons, the fleurs-de-lis of the Montgomeries, the garbs of the Cumins, the pale of the Erskines, the engrailed cross of the Sinclairs, and the boars' heads of the Gordons,"[11] is beautiful from its simplicity. For, as an old epitaph has it,

Plain Coates are noblest, though ye vulgar eye
Take Joseph's for the best in Herauldry.[12]

Which is in accordance with the old French armorial rule: *"Qui porte le moins est le plus."*[13]

The technical blazon of the Livingston coat-of-arms is: *Argent, three cinquefoils gules, within a double tressure, flowered and counterflowered with fleurs-de-lis, vert.* Owing to the marriage of Sir William Livingston, the owner of the above seal, to the heiress of the Callendar estates, his descendants quartered his wife's paternal arms with their own. There is, however, apparently, no seal bearing the quartered arms of Livingston and Callendar, still in existence, of earlier date than the middle of the fifteenth century. The best specimen of an early seal bearing these arms, among Mr. Laing's casts in the British Museum, is that of James, the eldest son of Sir Alexander Livingston of Callendar, Keeper of the King's Person during the minority of James II. This James Livingston was in later years to become the first Lord Livingston of Callendar. This really beautiful little seal is thus described in Mr. Laing's *Descriptive Catalogue of Ancient Scottish Seals:* "Couché. Quarterly, first and fourth, three cinquefoils within a double tressure flowered and counterflowered, for Livingston; second and third, a bend between six billets, for Callendar. Crest on a helmet with mantlings, two serpents nowed [viz. knotted]. Inscription on a scroll—'S Jacobi De Levyg-ston.'"[14]

In Sir David Lyndsay's well-known heraldic manuscript, executed in 1542, the arms of "Levyngstoun, Lord of Callendar," are correctly emblazoned as "First and Fourth, *Argent, three cinquefoils gules, within a double tressure, flory and counterflory, vert*, for Livingston; Second and Third, *Sable, a bend between six billets or*, for Callendar." But in an older manuscript, the work of a French Herald—*The Armorial de Berry* (1450–1455) now in the possession of the Bibliothèque Nationale de France at Paris, there are some curious variations in the above blazon, probably due to the author's ignorance of Scottish heraldry, namely the tressure in the Livingston quarters is *azure* instead of *vert*; while for the *Bend between six billets or*, of Callendar, is substituted a *Bend chequy or and sable*.[15] From these manuscripts we also learn that the original Livingstons of that ilk—long extinct in the male line—always retained their simple paternal coat—*Argent, three cinquefoils gules*—without the double tressure, which is, apparently, entirely restricted to the descendants of Sir William Livingston of Callendar, knight banneret.[16] It seems a pity, however, that the junior, though ultimately more noble and historical line of Callendar, could not also have retained this simple but effective blazon. A cadet of this branch, that of Kilsyth, certainly did drop the maternal Callendar quarter, retaining that of Livingston only, with the. double tressure.[17] This latter coat was also that borne by the Livingstons of Drurnry and of Wemyss.[18]

But the different blazons of the various titled and untitled branches of the family in Scotland need not be referred to further here, this chapter being confined to tracing the history of the armorial bearings so far as they concern the American Livingstons, and their right to bear these, as cadets of the House of Callendar. And though we have already alluded to this interesting subject in a previous chapter,[19] still it is as well to deal with it again in this place, as so much ignorance still exists as to what were the proper arms of Robert, the first Lord of the Manor of Livingston. This state of ignorance is proven by the fact that, for more than two centuries, most of his descendants have borne arms, containing a spurious quarter, to which they certainly are *not* entitled.

The origin of the quarter complained of was as follows.[20] In the year 1698[21] Robert Livingston, the founder of the most notable branch of the American family, wrote to his brother, William, then residing in Edinburgh, to procure for him the necessary papers to prove that the writer was a native of Scotland, after the union of the kingdoms, so as to be able to refute the charge of alienism brought against him by his political opponents in New York, on account of his Dutch training, owing to his having spent his early years at Rotterdam, with his exiled father. The results of his brother's inquiries are contained in a letter, dated Edinburgh, 13th December 1698.[22] In this letter William Livingston sends his brother a description of his "proper coat of armes," in which the first, third, and fourth quarters are correctly blazoned,—with the exception that gillyflowers are given in the place of cinquefoils in the Livingston quarters,[23] but for the second quarter, instead of the Callendar arms, the writer gives the following charges: "2nd Quarterly, first and last, Gules, a chifron [chevron] argent, a rose betwixt two Lyons counter-rampant of the field; 2nd and 3rd Argent, three martlets gules, the name of Hepburn of Waughteen [Waughton]."

The reason assigned by the writer of this letter—who must have obtained his information from the Lyon Office—for the introduction of this Hepburn quarter into their family arms, was their descent from William, fourth Lord Livingston, whose "wife was daughter to Sir Patrick Hep-bum of Waughteen," and, presumably, an heiress. On the other hand, the Scottish peerage writers state, this lady was the daughter of Adam Hepburn, second Lord Hailes. The truth is, however, that she was not the daughter of either of these members of the Hepburn family, but as the author has pointed out in his previous work,[24] her father was Alexander Hepburn of Quhitsum or Whitsome, a younger son of the first Lord Hailes.[25] These mistakes probably arose from the fact that, at this date, the end of the fifteenth and the commencement of the sixteenth century, there were *three* matrimonial alliances contracted between the families of Livingston and Hepburn—three Livingston sons marrying three Hepburn daughters.

Firstly, that contracted between William, Master of Livingston—afterwards fourth Lord Livingston—and Agnes, daughter of the above Alexander Hepburn of Whitsome, as is proved by an action the father of the bride brought against the bridegroom's father, James, third Lord Livingston, in 1501, to recover a thousand marks as damages for the non-fulfilment of his obligation to infeft the young couple in "forty pound land."[26] Secondly, between Magister Alexander Livingston of Dunipace and Elizabeth, elder daughter and co-heiress of Sir Adam Hepburn of Craggis (brother to Patrick, first Earl of Bothwell) who fell at Flodden in anno 1513—"qui obiit in servitio et sub vexillo regis ultimo defuncti in campo bellico apud Northumberland," so runs the clause in a charter referring to his decease.[27] Sir Adam's son-in-law also lost a kinsman in this same battle, namely William Livingston, third Laird of Kilsyth,[28] who also fell "sub vexillo regis," in that fierce fight around their ill-starred king, James the Fourth, where, in the stirring lines of Sir Walter Scott:—

> The English shafts in volleys hail'd,
> In headlong charge their horse assail'd,
> Front, Bank, and rear, the squadrons sweep
> To break the Scottish circle deep,
> That fought around their king.
>
> . . . .
>
> No thought was there of dastard flight,
> Link'd in the serried phalanx tight,
> Groom fought like noble, squire like knight,
> As fearlessly and well.[29]

This Magister Alexander Livingston was the grandfather of the: John Livingston, the younger, of Dunipace, one of the Rev. Alexander Livingston's fellow-commissioners in March, 1590.[30] Curiously enough, another daughter of this Sir Adam Hepburn of Craggis, Helen, was married, "after banns," in the: parish church of Bolton, 3rd November 1510, to her kinsman Sir Patrick Hepburn of Wauchton, when the parties produced a dispensation by the Archbishop of St. Andrews permitting the marriage to take place, in spite of the fact that the bridegroom and bride "were related within the third and fourth, or fourth and fourth degrees of consanguinity."[31] This is interesting from the fact that the father of this Sir Patrick Hepburn of Wauchton or Waughton, is evidently the person referred to in the letter sent to America, as the father-in-law of William fourth Lord Livingston. The third marriage between a Livingston and a Hepburn was that of Marion, the elder sister of the Agnes Hepburn who married the above William, Lord Livingston; her husband was Patrick Livingston of Castlecary.[32]

But the extraordinary part of the whole affair connected with the assumption of this erroneous quarter, is that the writer of the letter containing this misleading information, should have known what his correct armorial bearings were, as these were actually engraved on the seal he used to secure this very letter[33]! It is, however, interesting to know that William Livingston's informant considered that William, the *fourth* Lord Livingston, was the father of the ancestor killed at Pinkie Field in 1547—whom he calls

"Robert"[34]— and *not* Alexander, the *fifth* lord, as stated by some writers on the family. In one part of his former work, the author certainly criticised this statement[35] but this was before his later researches, notably the discovery of the Colzium House charters, which have led him to alter his opinion as to this. He wishes further to emphasise the fact again in this place, that he never has doubted "the descent of the New York Livingstons from the old Barons of Callendar," as some person shave erroneously concluded from certain remarks made by him in the *Livingstons of Callendar*, but only was puzzled *as to which of these Barons was the actual ancestor.*[36]

Fortunately, the right of the American Livingstons to the use of the coat-armour of the Scottish House of Callendar, rests on a far more solid foundation than that afforded by the above letter, and is quite unquestionable.[37] Their right to bear the family arms is derived from the fact that there are still in existence armorial seals used by the *three immediate Scottish ancestors* of the first American Livingston—namely those of his great-grandfather, grandfather, and father; and that the earliest in date of these—anno 1560—was used by its owner in the actual presence of, and with the express sanction of the then head of the family, William the sixth Lord Livingston of Callendar, as is proved by the latter's signature and seal being attached to the same document.[38] This then is proof positive that the armorial bearings used by the Reverend Alexander Livingston, Rector of Monyabroch, on this occasion, were his "proper seal," as they are deliberately stated to be in this charter.

It is seldom indeed, that such an authoritative proof as to the right of a Scottish cadet to the family coat-armour, dating back so far, can be produced nowadays, as the system of Heraldic Visitations in use about this period in England, did not extend into Scotland[39]; and at this time, moreover, there was no official Register of Scottish Arms, which dates from an Act of the Scottish Parliament in 1672—over a century later,—and which required everyone "to enter his armes within a year and a day."[40] This Act, it is needless to state, was not strictly enforced, and as far as it concerns the Rev. John Livingston, the last of these three Scottish ancestors, it only became law the year of his death, and ten years after his banishment from his native land.

In a previous chapter[41] we have alluded to the similarity of the inscriptions on the seals of the chief and the rector, as regards the spelling of their surname, so there is no need to refer to this again, but in reference to the unusual mark of cadency, namely the *single* cinquefoil, used on the latter's seal, the following quotation from Mr. Seton's learned work on Scottish Heraldry is of great interest:

> The practice of altering the *number* of charges, either by way of diminution or increase, prevails to some extent among the French and other Continental nations, but is of very rare occurrence in Scottish Heraldry. In his *Jurisprudentia Heroica*, Christyn mentions the bearings of the House of Clermont Tallart, in Dauphiny, viz: two silver keys in saltire, on a red field, adding that the family of Chatto, as a cadet, carried only a *single key* in bend. On the other hand, according to Pont, the Scottish family of Sydserf, originally from France, carried argent, a fleur-de-lis, azure; while Sydserf of Ruchlaw appears from the Lyon Register, to bear *three* of these charges on a similar field. In like manner, the ancient arms of the Turnbulls of Bedrule, and also of Minto, consisted of a single bull's head, erased, sable; but "of late," to use the language of Nisbet, "Those of this name multiply the heads to three."[42]

The Rev. John Woodward also remarks on this practice in his *Heraldry British and Foreign*, where he says: "Diminishing the Number of Charges of the same kind is an expedient for differencing seldom if ever practised in Great Britain, but it is one of which there are examples in Foreign Heraldry."[43]

The Reverend Alexander Livingston's son, the minister of Lanark, also used the quartered arms of Livingston and Callendar on his seal, but in the former quarters he carried the usual number of cinquefoils within a *single* tressure.[44] This evidently confirms the foreign origin of his father's seal, or else why should the son have not continued to have thus differenced his paternal arms? The difference as to the *tressure* may have been unintentional,[45] as it is not repeated in the arms borne by the latter's celebrated son, the Rev. John Livingston of Ancrum.[46] Though the senior *male* lines in Scotland have all been extinct for some time; and though *the line of male descent* evidently now lies with the descendants of the Reverend Alexander Livingston of Monyabroch, still, as a matter of strict heraldry, his descendants should have continued to have borne their family arms with a mark denoting they were cadets of the ancient House of Callendar.[47]

Not content, however, with altering their paternal coat-of-arms by the addition of a fabulous quarter, the American Livingstons have also adopted a distinct crest and motto of their own. In this possibly they have a greater show of reason, as it was to commemorate his narrow escape from shipwreck, when on a voyage to England in 1695, that led Robert, the first Lord of the Manor of Livingston, to adopt as his crest and motto: a "ship in distress" in lieu of the well-known "demi-savage," and *Spero Meliora* for *Si Je Puis*.[48] These again were still further altered by Robert of the Manor's grandson, William Livingston, afterwards the first Governor of the State of New Jersey: the crest to a "ship under full sail," and the motto to *Aut Mors out Vita Decora*; a maxim which the owner of this latter crest and motto certainly nobly acted up to. Mr. William Livingston thus characteristically relates his reason for these alterations, in a letter written to a kinsman many years afterwards:

> My grandfather [he wrote] altered the crest and motto of the family arms, the former into a ship in an adverse wind, the latter into *Spero Meliora*. These have since been retained by all the family except myself, who not being able, without ingratitude to Providence, to wish for more than I had, changed the former into a ship under full sail, and the latter into *Aut Mors aut Vita Decora*.[49]

The armorial bearings to which this crest and motto belonged were those used after the Declaration of Independence, as the temporary great seal of the State of New Jersey under its new constitution, "until another could be procured."[50] Certainly a strange vicissitude in the history of the family coat-armour!

The family crest, however, unlike the quartered arms of Livingston and Callendar, which are the same to-day as they were, when emblazoned over five centuries ago; on the shields of their knightly owners, has gone through a Darwinian system of evolution before appearing in its present form of a demi-savage, wreathed round the head and waist with laurel, holding in his right hand a club, and in the left a serpent, which is twisted about his arm. The earliest Livingston seals, unfortunately, only give the shield without the crest, which first appears above the arms of the celebrated Sir Alexander Livingston of Callendar, Justiciar of Scotland, and Keeper of the King's Person during the minority of James II,[51] and those of Sir James Livingston, his eldest son, afterwards created a Lord of Parliament by this same monarch.[52] The crest on these seals is two serpents nowed, namely knotted together towards the right. This crest is fully shown on the latter beautifully engraved seal. It was also borne in olden time by members of the junior line of Kilsyth.[53] These two snakes continue to appear, in a slightly different form—namely, as "two demi-snakes embowed"—on the seals of the earlier Lords of Callendar, until as late as the middle of the sixteenth century, when they disappeared in that particular form, from the family arms.[54] The latest seal bearing this crest is that of William, sixth Lord Livingston, the patron of the Rev. Alexander Livingston of Monyabroch, and which is attached to the deed of the 15th of March 1560–1.[55] Thirty years later, this same nobleman had adopted as his crest, "a demisavage, holding with both hands a club sinister bendwise in front."[56] The exact date of the adoption of the present form of crest is unknown, but it only needed a slight alteration in the holding of the club, and the retention of one of the original snakes, to complete the evolution. The two savage supporters first make their appearance on the seal of James, third Lord Livingston (A.D. 1499),[57] and these probably led to the adoption of the demi-savage as a crest by his descendants, in the place of their more ancient cognisance of the two snakes.

The origin of the old family motto—*Si Je Puis*—is wrapped in mystery! It does not appear on any of the old seals, nor in any of the Registers of Arms prior to that of Workman's (*circa*, 1565), where the spelling of it has much puzzled the compiler. He has tried three separate ways— "Cevs ave plvis," "Cevs ave plase," and "Seys a pais," which evidently shows he could not have been much of a French scholar.[58] It is quite possible, owing to the date of its first appearance, and the difficulty experienced by this heraldic authority to arrive at its true meaning, that this motto may have been adopted by William, sixth Lord Livingston, when in France, a few years before the date of Workman's manuscript. It was, however, subsequently used by the chiefs of the House of Livingston, the attainted Earls of Linlithgow; as well as by another titled branch, that of the Earls of Newburgh, which earldom is now in the possession of a Roman nobleman, Prince Giustiniani-Bandini, and which is, moreover, the only Livingston title now in existence! The only motto as yet discovered on any early Livingston armorial seal is that of the House of Kilsyth—now also attainted and extinct. This motto is *Spe Expeclo*, and figures on the seal of Sir James Livingston of Kilsyth (A.D. 1647), on a scroll above the helmet, in the place where the crest should be.[59]

We will now close this article on the family heraldry, with a list of the various mottoes used by the different branches of Livingstons:

The Lords Livingston of Callendar .... *Si Je Puis.*
The Earls of Linlithgow .... ditto.
The Earls of Newburgh .... ditto.
The Earls of Callendar .... *Et Domi Et Foris.*
The Viscounts of Kilsyth .... *Spe Expecto.*
The Viscount of Teviot .... *Ce Que Je Puis.*
Sir William Livingston of Culter (temp. 1565) .... *Si Dieu Plaist.*
Sir James Livingstone of Westquarter (temp. 1673) .... *Si Possim.*
Sir Thomas Livingstone of Bedlormie and Westquarter ...... *Si Je Puis.*
The Fenton-Livingstones of Westquarter .... ditto.
The Livingstone-Learmonths .... *Si Possim.*
Les Comtes de Leviston .... *Pro Rege Et Patria.*
The descendants of Guillaume de Livingston .... *Leviston Fortis Æquus.*
David Livingstone of Balrownie[60] .... *Nativum Retinet Decus.*
William Livingstone, merchant, Aberdeen .... *Fortis Et Æquus.*
Alexander Livingstone of Countesswells .... *Si Je Puis.*
The American Livingstons .... *Si Je Puis.*

Spero Meliora.

Aut Mors Aut Vita Decora.[61]

Though a novice m the "noble science," the author hopes that the above account of the family arms will be found of some little use by those descendants of the ancient House of Livingston, who take an interest in the heraldry of their ancestors; and he also trusts that he has been successful in proving that the *correct* armorial bearings of the American Livingstons are the quartered arms of Livingston and Callendar *alone*, without the objectionable *second* quarter complained of above, and with the cinquefoil "of auld" restored to the original paternal coat, in place of the un-heraldic, and modern, gillyflower. Surely it ought to be a matter of pride to members of the family on the other side of the Atlantic, that their right to bear arms which date back to the middle of the fourteenth century, and have figured honourably in the history of Scotland, is so unquestionable[62]! And even to-day in republican America, their armorial bearings are publicly honoured, by being sculptured above one of the dormer windows in the State Capitol at Albany.[63]

The author, in conclusion, wishes to emphasise the late Lord Lindsay's statement that "Every British gentleman entitled to bear coat-armour is noble, whether titled or not,"[64] by quoting the following very apt remarks on this subject from the Reverend John Woodward's *Heraldry British and Foreign:*

> A subject of the British Empire, if he be a gentleman of coat-armour, and resident abroad, ought always to assert his *nobility*. He is legally a *noble* in the continental sense of the term, and he does wrong not only to himself, but to others similarly situated, if through a false idea of modesty, or through ignorance, he repudiates that nobility to which he is fully and legally entitled. This was better understood in former days.... A British gentleman of coat-armour is usually at least the equal, and in nine cases out of ten the social superior, of the Counts and Barons whom he meets with at home or abroad, even if they happen to be the heads of their families, and not (as is much more frequently the case) cadets more or less remote, who are careful to retain their courtesy title and the use of the coronet.[65]

Notes

1. Seton, *The Law and Practice of Heraldry in Scotland*, p. 9.
2. *Ibid.*, p. 191.
3. The late well-known Edinburgh seal engraver. He published, in 1850, *A Descriptive Catalogue of Ancient Scottish Seals*, which was followed, sixteen years later, by a supplemental volume. His collection of casts of ancient Scottish seals is now in the British Museum. The author has sulphur copies of all the Livingston casts in this collection, but some of the seals listed in Mr. Laing's catalogues, unfortunately, are not to he found among these casts, such as that of the Rev. John Livingston of Ancrum. *Supplemental Catalogue* No. 649.
4. Also quite recently (in 1904) Mr. W. R. Macdonald, Carrick Pursuivant, has published a very interesting work—*Scottish Armorial Seals*—which contains some Livingston seals not mentioned in Mr. Laing's catalogues.
5. *Calendar of Documents Relating to Scotland*, etc., vol. ii., 198, 327, 548.
6. *Calendar of Documents Relating to Scotland*, Document No. 1268
7. *Ibid.*, vol. iii. pp. 305, 306. A much better specimen, than either of those in the Record Office, was found by Mr. Henry Laing loose among the Melrose charters, and is included in his collection of casts at the British Museum. Sir William Livingston was one of the Scottish Commissioners who negotiated the above Treaty of Ransom, and his eldest son, Patrick, is named among the noble hostages. It was twelve years previous to the above date—namely in 1345—that Sir William Livingston had been granted by King David, the estate of Callendar.
8. Scott's *Marmion*, Canto IV, Stanza VII.
9. Nisbet, *System of Heraldry*, vol. i, p. 180. Seton, *Scottish Heraldry*, pp. 447–451.
10. In a safe conduct from King Edward III, dated 7th December 1347, he is styled "Willelmus de Levingston bannerettus." *Fædera*, vol. v, P. 597.
11. Seton, *Scottish Heraldry*, pp. 152, 153.

12. Cussans, *Handbook of Heraldry*, p. 157.
13. Woodward, *Heraldry British and Foreign*, vol. ii., p. 51.
14. No. 534 in the above Catalogue. This seal was copied by Mr Laing from an original attached to a deed, in H. M. General Register House, Edinburgh, of the year 1445. As a contrast to this handsome seal, there is another in same collection (No. 645 in Supplemental Catalogue), and of the same period, very coarsely executed, in which the first and fourth quarters bear the Callendar arms, and the second and third those of Livingston, or the reverse of the correct method of quartering these arms. This seal belonged to James Livingston's unfortunate younger brother, the Alexander Livingston of Dunipace, who was beheaded for high treason in 1450. Apparently, Sir Alexander the father of these brothers used a similar seal to that of his younger son, though he certainly erred in so doing; *vide* seal described by Mr. Bain as appended to an instrument dated 18th September 1449. *Cal. Doc. Scot.* vol. iv, p. 246.
15. Stodart, Scottish Arms, vol. i, plate 6.
16. The Lyndsay Manuscript is now in the possession of the Advocates' Library, Edinburgh. Copies of this beautiful heraldic work have been twice executed in facsimile, namely in 1822 and 1878. Three of the Livingston arms emblazoned in this manuscript, as well as three from the Armorial de Berry, will be found reproduced on the plate at the commencement of this chapter. It will be noticed in the arms from the Lyndsay Manuscript, that the cinquefoils are drawn "pierced," but it is not customary to blazon them thus nowadays.
17. A copy of a seal bearing these arms—*circa* 1518—with the addition of a mullet to denote cadency, is among the Laing casts at the British Museum.
18. See arms on plate at commencement of this chapter.
19. See Chapter I.
20. The Rev. Beverley R. Betts of Jamaica, New York, in a very interesting review of Mr. E. de V. Vermont's America Heraldica (published in 1886), contributed to the New York Genealogical and Biographical Record for January, 1887, drew attention to this erroneous quarter. On reading this article, the author of this work confirmed Mr. Betts' able criticism in the following number of this periodical, and in consequence of these articles, Mr. de Vermont had the blazon of the Livingston arms corrected accordingly.
21. See Chapter VI.
22. A copy of this letter will be found in the Appendix (No. LIV.) of *The Livingstons of Callendar.*
23. This is, however, a very unsatisfactory innovation from an heraldic as well as artistic, point of view, though popular at that date. Nisbet thus refers to this substitution in his *System of Heraldry* published in 1722, which he rightly condemns. "The Livingstons, Earls of Linlithgow," he states, "have been sometimes in use, with their descendants, to turn the cinquefoils to gillyflowers, upon what account I cannot learn, if not upon the saying of Gerard Leigh, that cinquefoils being sanguine, represent the stock-gillyflowers; but others more knowing, prefer the cinquefoil, as more anciently used in armories, and more military, as Guillim who disparages the gillyflower in his *Display* as an effeminate figure. The family of Linlithgow have disused the gillyflower and taken again the cinquefoil; but their cadets have, in our new Register, gillyflowers recorded in place of cinquefoils."
24. *Livingstons of Callendar*, p. 32, note 52.
25. In the new edition of Douglas' Peerage, now in course of publication, under the able editorship of the present Lyon, King of Arms, this error has also been corrected, in the account of "Hepburn, Earl of Bothwell."

26. *Livingstons of Callendar*, p. 33, note 32.
27. Charter dated 25 October, 1513. *Register of the Great Seal of Scotland.*
28. *Livingstons of Callendar*, p. 159, note 19.
29. *Mannion*, Canto VI, Stanza xxxiv.
30. See Chapter I.
31. *Laing Charters* (in University of Edinburgh) No. 278.
32. For notice of this marriage the author is indebted to Sir James Balfour Paul's new edition of Douglas' *Peerage*, vol. ii, p. 144.
33. Namely Livingston and Callendar quarterly. From information kindly supplied by Mr. Johnston Livingston, the owner of the original letter.
34. The late Mr. Joseph Bain was entirely in favour of this descent, see *Livingstons of Callendar*, pp. 651, 652, note 30.
35. *Livingstons of Callendar*, p. 32.
36. See also Preface to the present work, in which evidence is given that the name of the ancestor killed at Pinkie should be James and not Robert.
37. It is a decided pity that Robert Livingston of the Manor did not send his brother the £7 or £8, the estimated cost of his "Birth Brief," as it would have been of great interest to have possessed the then Lyon Herald's opinion in fuller detail.
38. See Chapter I. This charter is printed in extenso in the original Latin, and a translation, in Appendix No. XXXI of The Livingstons of Callendar.
39. In 1592 (or thirty-two years later than the date of the above charter) the Scottish Parliament did pass an Act authorising such a system of Heraldic Visitations throughout the realm, "in order to distinguish the arms of the various noblemen and gentlemen and 'thaireftir to matriculat thame in thair buikis and regesteris'"; says the present Lyon King of Arms, Sir James Balfour Paul, in an Introduction to his *Ordinary of Scottish Arms*; but this Act was practically never put into use. In the disturbed state of Scotland in those days the enforcing of such an Act would have been a matter of great difficulty.
40. In reference to the Act of 1672, the present Lyon King of Arms says, "The Register constituted by the above Act still continues to be the 'Public Register of all Arms and Bearings in Scotland,' and no persons of Scottish descent whose arms are not registered in it have a right to armorial bearings unless they can prove that they represent families whose arms are known to have been in existence previous to 1672," *vide* his Introduction to *An Ordinary of Scottish Arms* (edition, 1903) p. xiv. This authority also says in reference to this Act, in the Preface to his latest edition, that of 1903: "There are many families in Scotland who can prove that they had a right to Arms previous to the commencement of the compilation of the Register in 1672, but whose ancestors did not obtemper the order contained in the Act of Parliament of that year, to give in their Arms to be recorded by the Lyon. For the sake of heraldic accuracy and to prevent mistakes in future, it certainly seems desirable that such families should now do what then ought to have been done, and so legally constitute their right to ensigns armorial. It is not in their case a question of setting a new grant, but simply of getting the old arms put on record."
41. See Chapter I.
42. *The Law and Practice of Scottish Heraldry*, pp. 100, 101.
43. *Heraldry British and Foreign* (edition, 1896) vol. ii, p. 51.
44. For facsimiles of these two seals see plate at commencement of this work. Mr. Laing evidently had not come across the Rev. Alexander Livingston's seal, but a copy of that of the son's is among his casts at the British Museum, and is described in his *Catalogue.*

45. Mr. Seton mentions the following examples of *single* tressures, but does not refer to that of the Rev. William Livingston: "As exhibiting instances of the single tressure (flory)," says Mr. Seton, "we may mention the seals of William Livingston of Balcastell (1469), David, William, and John Charteris (1474–1584), and Sir James Hamilton of Finnart (1532)." *Law and Practice of Scottish Heraldry*, pp. 447, 448. Cf. Laing's *Descriptive Catalogue*, Nos. 172, 173, 174, 403, and 535.

46. No. 649 in Laing's *Supplemental Catalogue*, but unfortunately not to be found in his collection of casts at the British Museum; thus the author has been unable to obtain a facsimile of it. This is Mr. Laing's description of this seal: "A signet, with the shield quarterly, Livingston and Callendar; above the shield are four Hebrew characters, Ebenezer? From a letter to the Earl of Lothian, dated 39th July 1648." This nobleman was the patron of the living of Ancrum.

47. This applies also, of course, to his living descendants. The Lyon Office claim that all Scottish arms should be registered with them; and that in the case of cadets, their arms should be "matriculated," with "due and proper marks of difference to show their position of cadency in the male line of the family." The rule in Scotland, moreover, is to confine each matriculation to "the heir-male of the particular cadet who matriculated," but these changes never amount to "a material alteration," *vide* Fox-Davies' *Heraldry Explained*, pp. 23, 24. In a numerous family, however, this would mean a lot of matriculations!

48. Robert of the Manor was, however accustomed to use a signet ring with three gilly-flowers within a single tressure; while his eldest son and heir John, who died within his father's lifetime sealed a letter, dated 13 July 1713, with two different seals; one like his father's above mentioned signet, and the other a ship with main and foresail only set, and bearing the motto *Spero Meliora*. The latter seal is the earliest known specimen of the altered crest now in existence, and differs somewhat from the dismasted ship commonly used by later members of the family. From information kindly supplied the author by Mr. Johnston Livingston of New York.

49. Sedgwick, *Life of William Livingston*, p. 52.

50. According to a resolution passed by the New Jersey Legislature after its independence was declared: "That the seal at arms of his Excellency William Livingston should be deemed, taken and used, as the great seal of the State until another could be procured." Mulford, *History of New Jersey*, p. 431.

51. Bain, *Calendar of Documents relating to Scotland*, vol. iv, p. 246. This seal, which is much defaced, is attached to a document dated 18th September 1449.

52. Laing, *Descriptive Catalogue of Ancient Scottish Seals*, No. 534, (A.D. 1445).

53. *Ibid.*, No. 535 (A.D. 1469).

54. *Ibid.*, No. 536 (A.D. 1499); and No. 539 (A.D. 1556).

55. See facsimile on plate at commencement of this volume. This is the same seal as Laing's No. 539 (A.D. 1556).

56. Laing, *Supplemental Catalogue*, No. 651 (A.D. 1590). In Workman's *Heraldic Manuscript* (*circa*, 1565) this nobleman's crest is thus blazoned: "Lord Levinston— as L. Lord of Callendar; crest—a demi-savage wreathed with leaves, and with branches behind his shoulders, holding in his dexter hand a club in bent sinister. " The snakes, according to this manuscript, became additional supporters, as these are given as "two naked savages, holding clubs over their shoulders, and on each side of the shield two serpents entwined and erect." Stodart, Scottish Arms, vol. ii, p. 99.

57. Laing, *Descriptive Catalogue*, No. 536.

58. Stodart, *Scottish Arms*, vol. ii, p. 99.

59. Laing, *Descriptive Catalogue*, No. 541.

60. A cadet of Dunipace, and so are the next two on the list.

61. For authorities see *Livingstons of Callendar*, pp. 655, 656.

62. Mr. Fox-Davies, the author of several recent works on heraldry, in his last publication, a little handbook entitled *Heraldry Explained*, says, on page 29, that to possess the right to bear arms which "date from before about 1600, is something to be exceedingly proud of."

63. There are six dormer windows in all. Above the other five are carved the arms of Stuyvesant, Schuyler, Jay, Clinton, and Tompkins. *Heraldry in England and America*, by Mr. George R. Howells.

64. See quotation at head of Chapter I.

65. Edition 1896, vol. i, p. 15. The words in *Italics* are so printed by Mr. Woodward.

APPENDICES

APPENDIX A

A LIST OF LIVINGSTONS WHO HELD COMMISSIONS IN THE AMERICAN ARMY AND NAVY DURING THE WAR OF INDEPENDENCE A.D. 1775–1783

GOVERNOR LIVINGSTON of New Jersey, in a long ode to General Washington, contributed to the *New Jersey Gazette* in March, 1778, under the pen-name of Hortentius, enthusiastically wrote:

> Then with one voice thy country call'd thee forth,
> Thee, WASHINGTON, she call'd:—with modest blush,
> But soul undaunted, thou the call obey'd,
> To lead her armies to the martial field.
> Thee, WASHINGTON, she call'd to draw the sword,
> And rather try the bloody chance of war
> In virtue's cause, than suffer servile chains,
> Intolerable bondage! to inclose
> The limbs of those whom God created free.
> Lur'd by thy fame, and with thy virtues charm'd,
> And by thy valour fir'd, around thee pour'd
> AMERICA's long-injur'd sons, resolv'd
> To meet the veteran troops who oft had borne
> BRITANNIA's name, in thunder round the world.[1]

The Livingstons, including the governor himself, were not backward in their willingness to meet "the veteran troops" of Britain in the field, and the following list is a proof of that fact. It is doubtful whether any other family in the Thirteen Colonies, contributed so many of its members to the patriot army and navy. At Saratoga there were seven, probably eight, officers of the name under General Gates, including three who commanded regiments in the field, namely:

> Colonel Henry Beekman Livingston, commanding the 4th New York Line;
> Colonel James Livingston, commanding an Additional Battalion of the New York Line;
> Lieutenant-Colonel Henry Livingston, commanding the Manor of Livingston, or Tenth Albany Militia Regiment;
> Lieutenant-Colonel Richard Livingston, of Colond James Livingston's Regiment;
> Major Henry Brockhoist Livingston, aide to General Arnold;
> Captain Abraham Livingston, of Colond James Livingston's Regiment;
> Lieutenant Gilbert James Livingston, of Colond Cortlandt's Regiment;

and the doubtful one, Lieutenant Gilbert R. Livingston, whom Governor Clinton recommended on the 19th September, 1777 for a staff appointment to Brigadier-General Ten Broeck, who had the command of the New York Militia regiments in the American Army. Owing to their number, and the similarity of the initials of two of these officers, writers on the military history of the War of Independence, have often been misled as to the identity of the Livingston combatants. Thus, Captain Henry Beekman Livingston is declared by some historians, to have assisted at the capture of Fort Chambly in October, 1775, and to have been voted a sword of honour by Congress for that feat of arms,[2] when it was Major (afterwards Colonel) James Livingston who should have that credit, and the sword of honour was presented to Henry Beekman Livingston because he was the bearer of General Montgomery's despatches announcing the surrender of Montreal. He is also stated by the same authorities to have been aide to General Schuyler in 1776, when this officer was his cousin, of the similar initials, Major Henry Brockhoist Livingston. Again, the officer commanding the garrison at Verplanck's Point at the time of Arnold's treason is declared by Dr. Lossing to have been Colonel Henry Livingston of the Manor[3] while the late Mr. Streatfeild Clarkson considered he was Colond Henry Beekman Livingston,[4] when he was neither of these two officers, but Colonel James Livingston of Chambly renown. Then Mr. H. B. Dawson, a very careful writer, in his account of the capture of Fort Montgomery in October, 1777,[5] says the Lieutenant-Colonel Livingston, who was sent by Governor George Clinton to meet the British flag, and who was subsequently taken prisoner when the British stormed the fort, was Henry Livingston, when his name was William Smith Livingston, second-in-command of Samuel B. Webb's Connecticut Regiment. It is unnecessary, however, to record further and similar errors, those given are sufficient to prove the necessity of this List. The author, however, does not claim that his List is perfect by any means, nor does he deny that he is also liable to error, but he hopes, if any are discovered, he may be informed, so that they may be corrected. However, as he has gone, wherever possible, to the original authorities, he does not think he has committed any error of importance. In some cases, where he has been unable to consult the original authorities himself, he has been indebted for information to the following works[6]:

(1) *New York in the Revolution as Colony and State*, edited by Mr. James A. Roberts. This volume contains those New York Muster Rolls which are still in existence in the State Archives at Albany. Its value, however, as a work of reference, is sadly spoilt by the omission of dates. Not a single date is given!

(2) *Historical Register of Officers of the Continental Army during the War of the Revolution*, by Mr. F. B. Heitman. This work, owing to its having only recently (1908) been placed in the British Museum Library, was therefore consulted after the author had practically finished his researches. It contains some particulars as to dates of commissions not to be found elsewhere, and also the names of two officers unknown to the writer. Naturally, Mr. Heitman's list is not so complete in militia officers, and he has committed some errors, such as confusing Henry Beekman with his cousin Henry Brockhoist, and also with Henry Livingston, Junior; and stating that Lieutenant-Colonel Richard Livingston was the officer taken prisoner at Fort Montgomery; also some of his dates are evidently wrong.

(3) *The Navy of the American Revolution*, by Charles Oscar Paullin. To this work the author is indebted for the addition of Lieutenant Muscoe Livingston.

In regard to the parentage of the various officers, these have in the case of the lesser known men given some trouble to ascertain, and in many cases would have been impossible, considering that so many contemporary members of this numerous family bore similar Christian names, but for the fact, at this period, that it was the custom of the younger branches to distinguish themselves from one another by the addition of the initial of their father's Christian name after their own. This idea, and a very useful one, was apparently started by Judge Robert R. Livingston of Clermont. Thus we have Henry P. Livingston, meaning Henry, the son of Philip Livingston "The Signer"; Henry G. Livingston = Henry, the son of Gilbert Livingston; Gilbert J. Livingston = Gilbert, the son of James Livingston, and so on.

For some particulars concerning Captain Henry P. Livingston of General Washington's Guard, the author must also acknowledge his indebtedness to Dr. Carlos E. Godfrey's interesting monograph on that Corps, published in 1904. He is also indebted for some original letters, journals, diaries, etc., to such useful publications as the *American Historical Review*, *Magazine of American History*, and kindred works, which all receive due notice whenever made use of.

CONTINENTAL OR REGULAR ARMY

I

HENRY BEEKMAN LIVINGSTON, SECOND SON OF JUDGE ROBERT R. LIVINGSTON OF CLERMONT. BORN 9 NOVEMBER, 1750.

Commissions

Captain, Fourth (Dutchess) New York Regiment, 28 June, 1775[7] nominated Major, 28 February, 1776[8]; elected Lieutenant-Colonel, Second New York Regiment, 8 March, 1776[9]; Colonel, Fourth Regiment, 21 November, 1776[10]; resigned, 20 November, 1778[11]; resignation accepted by Continental Congress, 13 January, 1779.[12]

After the war, commissioned Brigadier-General of New York Militia[13] and admitted an Original Member of the Society of the Cincinnati.[14]

War Service

Canadian Expedition under General Montgomery until occupation of Montreal, 13 November, 1775, as bearer of the despatches announcing the surrender of that place, was presented by Continental Congress with a sword of honour, 12 December, 1775, and recommended by General Schuyler for promotion, "out of respect to his family as well as his own merit," 21 February, 1776[15]; on special service, Long Island July-September, 1776[16]; recommended by General Washington for promotion, "he having upon every occasion exhibited proofs of his ability and zeal for the service," 8 October, 1776[17]; Saratoga (both battles) September-October, 1777[18]; at the second of these battles—7 October, 1777—General Arnold attributed "great part of our success to the gallant part he and his corps acted in storming the enemy's works, and the alertness and good order they observed in the pursuit"[19]; sent by General Gates on a mission to Sir Henry Clinton in New York, October-November, 1777[20]; Valley Forge, 1777—1778[21]; Monmouth or Freehold, 28 June, 1778[22]; Quaker Hill, Rhode Island, in which battle "he behaved with great spirit," according to General Sullivan's despatch to Congress, 29 August, 1778.[23] He resigned, as noticed above, soon after the last campaign, but from the correspondence of Governor George Clinton, he appears soon to have tired of an inactive life at Philadelphia, for on 20 August, 1780, he wrote to the governor asking to be employed "in the interesting operations intended against New York." These came to nothing, but in the following October, when Sir John Johnson made one of his destructive raids into northern New York, Clinton entrusted him with the command of some levies sent to reinforce the militia in Tryon County. On 16 April, 1781, he again offered his services "as an officer in one of the new regiments" then being raised for the defence of the frontiers, but nothing seems to have come from this second application.[24]

II

HENRY BROCKHOLST LIVINGSTON,[25] A YOUNGER SON OF GOVERNOR WILLIAM LIVINGSTON OF NEW JERSEY. BORN 25 NOVEMBER, 1757.

Commissions

Staff rank of Major in the Continental Service and Aide-de-Camp to General Schuyler, prior to 21 February, 1776[26]; Lieutenant-Colonel, 4 October, 1777.[27]

After the war, an Original Member of the Society of the Cincinnati.[28]

War Service

His first experience was as a gentleman volunteer in a boat cutting-out expedition under his uncle, Colonel Lord Stirling, in January, 1776, when that officer captured the British transport *Blue Mountain Valley*.[29] Northern campaign, 1776, 1777, when he served as aide to General Schuyler, and volunteer aide to Generals St. Clair and Arnold.[30] Under the latter he took part in the Battle of Freeman's Farm, 19 September, 1777.[31] Prior to this engagement, he had been the bearer of despatches to Continental Congress, announcing the success of Brigadier Stark at Bennington, 16 August, 1777; when it was proposed "that Major Livingston, aide to General Schuyler, who brought to Congress an account of the late success of Brigadier Stark, be presented with a commission of lieutenant-colonel." Owing to the requisite majority of votes, required in cases of promotion, not being obtained, "the question was lost," and it was, "after debate ordered to be expunged, and the matter referred to the Board of War."[32] New England dislike of General Schuyler was evidently the reason why the question of promotion was shelved on this occasion. Major Livingston also got into trouble with General Gates, owing to his championship of General Arnold, to whom he ascribed "the sole honour of our late victory"[33]—that of the 19th September. He, therefore, left the camp for Albany, on the twenty-sixth of that month, to rejoin his old commander, Schuyler.[34] Eight days later the Continental Congress promoted him to "the rank of lieutenant-colonel as a reward for his merit and services in the American army."[35] He was granted leave of absence to accompany his brother-in-law, John Jay, as his private secretary, on his mission to Spain, 15 October, 1779.[36] Returning to America he was captured at sea, 25 April, 1782, and confined in the Provost at New York, until the arrival of Sir Guy Carleton a few days later, who at once released him on his parole.[37]

III

HENRY LIVINGSTON, JUNIOR, THIRD SON OF HENRY LIVINGSTON, CLERK OF DUTCHESS COUNTY.

BORN 13 OCTOBER, 1748.

Commission

Major, Third (Ulster) New York Regiment, elected 2 August, commissioned 28 August, 1775.[38]

War Service

In Canada under General Montgomery, siege of St. Johns, and until occupation of Montreal. Returned home December, 1775, and retired from the service.[39]

IV

ROBERT G. LIVINGSTON, JUNIOR, ELDEST SON OF ROBERT GILBERT LIVINGSTON, SENIOR, NEW YORK MERCHANT.

BAPTISED 2 APRIL, 1749.[40]

Commission

Colonel, and Deputy Adjutant-General to the Northern Army under General Schuyler, 23 August, 1775.[41]

War Service

Unknown, apparently did not serve any length of time.
[See also under Militia No. VI.]

V

HENRY G. LIVINGSTON, SECOND SON OF THE ABOVE R. G. LIVINGSTON, SENIOR.

BAPTISED 1 MAY, 1754.

Commission

Captain, Fourth (Dutchess) Regiment, 28 June, 1775.[42]

War Service

Apparently declined the commission, as there is no record of acceptance or service with this regiment.
[See also under Militia No. VII.]

VI

GILBERT R. LIVINGSTON (SOMETIMES DESIGNATED GILBERT R. G. LIVINGSTON), THIRD SON OF ROBERT GILBERT LIVINGSTON, SENIOR.

BAPTISED 27 SEPTEMBER, 1758.

Commission

Ensign, First (New York) Regiment, 24 February, 1776, did not accept this commission, but volunteered for service in Canada with Colonel Wind's New Jersey Regiment[43]; Ensign, Third (Ulster) Regiment, October, 1776[44]; Second-Lieutenant, 21 November, 1776.[45]

War Service

In Canada, 1776; no record of other service. On the 19th September, 1777, Governor George Clinton sends him to General Ten Broeck, commanding New York Militia under General Gates, with a warm letter of recommendation for the post of Brigade Major on that general's staff, so he may have been present at the final battle of Saratoga.[46]

VII

GILBERT J. LIVINGSTON, SON OF JAMBS LIVINGSTON, SHERIFF OF DUTCHESS COUNTY.

BORN 14 OCTOBER. 1758.

Commissions

Ensign, Second (Albany) Regiment,——1776[47]; Second Lieutenant, 21 November, 1776[48]; First Lieutenant, 28 June, 1779[49]; resigned 1 February, 1780.[50]

War Service

Not specially mentioned, but he must have been present with his regiment (Colonel Cortlandt's) at Saratoga, etc. On the 1 February, 1780, he was one of several New York Line officers, who placed their resignations in General Washington's hands, because they found it impossible to support themselves and their families on their pay, owing to the alarming depreciation of the currency.[51]

[See also under Militia No. VIII.]

VIII

ROBERT H. LIVINGSTON, FOURTH SON OF HENRY LIVINGSTON, CLERK OF DUTCHESS COUNTY.

BORN 25 OCTOBER, 1760.

Commission

Second Lieutenant 2nd Continental Artillery, 29 June 1781.[52]

War Service

Served to June, 1783.[53]

[See also under Militia No. IX.]

IX

JOHN R. LIVINGSTON, THIRD SON OF JUDGE ROBERT R. LIVINGSTON OF CLERMONT.

BORN 13 FEBRUARY, 1755.

Commission

Captain, Fourth (Dutchess) Regiment, 28 June, 1775.[54]

War Service

Did not accept the commission.

[See also under Militia No. V. and COMMISSARIAT DEPARTMENT No. III.]

X

JAMES LIVINGSTON, A GRANDSON OF ROBERT LIVINGSTON, THE NEPHEW.

BORN 27 MARCH, 1747.

Commissions

Raised a Regiment of Canadian Refugees, with local rank of Major, under General Montgomery, in the autumn of 1775[55]; Continental Congress appointed him Colonel of same, 8 January, 1776[56]; on failure of Canadian Expedition, Congress granted him permission to raise and command an additional Battalion of NewYork Line, 15 August, 1776.[57]

War Service

Canadian Expedition under General Montgomery, 1775; with Major Brown captures Fort Chambly, 18 October, 1775[58]; siege of Quebec, 1775—1776[59] relief of Fort Stan-wix or Schuyler on the Mohawk River under General Arnold, August, 1777[60]; Saratoga (both battles), September-October, 1777[61]; commanded garrison at Verplanck's Point at date of Arnold's treason, when the shot from his four pounder caused the British sloop-of-war *Vulture* to slip her berth, which led to Major André having to return by land, and thus, to his capture, September, 1780[62]; was retired, on the reduction of his regiment, 1 January, 1781.[63] On 8 March, 1785, Congress "*Resolved,* that the eminent services he had rendered the United States in Canada previous to his receiving a commission, entitle him to the pay of colonel from the time of his joining the American army in Canada, and the paymaster in the settlement of his accounts, is hereby directed to make such allowance from that time."[64]

XI

RICHARD LIVINGSTON, AN ELDER BROTHER OP COLONEL JAMES LIVINGSTON.

BORN 19 OCTOBER, 1744

Commission

Lieutenant-Colonel in his brother's regiments.

War Service

See No. X. Resigned 2 November, 1779.[65]

XII

Abraham Livingston, Younger Brother of Colonel Jambs Livingston.

Born 1754.

Commission

Captain in his brother's regiments.

War Service

See No. X. Retired 1 January, 1781.[66]
[See also under Militia No. X.]

XIII

Henry P. Livingston, Youngest Son of Philip Livingston "The Signer."

Baptised 26 March, 1760.

Commissions

First Lieutenant, Commander-in-Chief's Guard, popularly known as General Washington's Life Guards, 2 June, 1777[67]; Captain of same, by Resolution of Continental Congress, 4 December, 1778.[68]

War Service

Battle of Brandywine, 11 September, 1777[69]; Germantown, 4 October, 1777; Monmouth, 28 June, 1778; on furlough from November, 1778, until 26 March, 1779, when he resigned.[70]

XIV

William Smith Livingston, a Great Grandson of Robert Livingston "The Nephew," and Nephew and Godson of Chief Justice William Smith, "The Historian". Born 27 November, 1755.

Commissions

[For his earlier commissions see under Militia No. XI.]

Lieutenant-Colonel of Samuel B. Webb's Additional Connecticut Continental Regiment, 11 January, 1777.[71]

War Service

Stationed on the Hudson River under General Putnam, 1777. Just before the British attack on Fort Montgomery, 6 October, 1777, he had occasion to visit Governor Clinton, who detained him there[72]; and thus, though his regiment was not engaged in the defence of that fort, he was the officer employed by Governor Clinton to meet the British flag, and on the British storming the fort he was taken prisoner.[73] Prisoner of war in New York and on Long Island[74]; escapes from the prison-ship *Martel* in December, 1777.[75] Makes a claim on the State of New York for loss of horse and equipment for $300, 15 May, 1778; Governor Clinton endorses the certificate, 20 May, 1778.[76] In command of Colonel Webb's re-organised regiment[77] at Battle of Quaker Hill, Rhode Island, where he was slightly wounded, and praised by General Greene for his gallantry, 29 August, 1778.[78] Resigns his commission 10 October, 1778.[79] On the 6th April, 1779, he was admitted, after taking the usual oaths, to practise as an attorney-at-law in all courts of record in the State of New Jersey.[80]

[See also under MILITIA No. XL]

MILITIA, LOCAL LEVIES, AND MINUTE MEN

I

WILLIAM LIVINGSTON, SEVENTH SON OF PHILIP LIVINGSTON, SECOND LORD OF THE MANOR. BORN NOVEMBER, 1723.

Commissions

Second Brigadier-General of New Jersey Militia, 28 October, 1775[81]; Governor, Captain-General, and Commander-in-Chief in and over the State of New Jersey and Territories thereunto belonging, Chancellor and Ordinary of the same, 31 August, 1776.[82]

War Service

His governorship lasted during the war, and until his death in 1790. He was of great assistance to Washington in providing him with reinforcements and information during his campaigns.

II

PETER R. LIVINGSTON, ELDEST SURVIVING SON OF COLONEL ROBERT LIVINGSTON, THIRD LORD OF THE MANOR.[83] BORN 27 APRIL, 1737.

Commission

Colonel, Manor of Livingston, or Tenth Albany Regiment of Militia, 20 October, 1775.[84]

War Service

Apparently none; as member of the New York Convention, and for some time president of the same, he was fully occupied in civil duties. It was on account of this lack of military knowledge, that General Ten Broeck, in the summer of 1778, objected to his being appointed to the command of the expedition to Unadilla.[85] It was his younger brother Henry who commanded the Manor Regiment at Saratoga. He is said to have resigned his commission on 21 September, 1780.[86]

III

ROBERT R. LIVINGSTON, JUNIOR, ELDEST SON OF JUDGE ROBERT R. LIVINGSTON OF CLERMONT. BORN 27 NOVEMBER, 1746.

Commission

Lieutenant-Colonel, Manor of Livingston Regiment, 20 October, 1775.[87]

War Service

None, as he was fully occupied by his duties as member of Continental Congress, Chancellor of the State of New York, etc. His military duties therefore devolved on Major Henry Livingston of same regiment (see No. IV).

IV

HENRY LIVINGSTON, YOUNGEST SON OF COLONEL ROBERT LIVINGSTON, THIRD LORD OF THE MANOR. BORN 8 JANUARY, 1752.

Commissions

First Major, Manor of Livingston Regiment, 20 October, 1775; acting Lieutenant-Colonel prior to 25 October, 1776[88]; Lieutenant-Colonel, 28 May, 1778.[89]

After the war, Lieutenant-Colonel of Militia in Columbia County, 30 September, 1786; Brigadier-General of the same, 9 October, 1793; and Major-General of the Militia of the State, 9 February, 1810.[90]

War Service

In August, 1777, he was sent in command of the Manor Regiment by General George Clinton to reinforce General Gates[91], and he fought at Saratoga in General Ten Broeck's Brigade of New York Militia. On 14 October, 1777, he accompanied Colonel Wilkinson, General Gates's Adjutant-General, when he was sent to meet General Burgoyne's flag of truce.[92] In October, 1780, he commanded the little American garrison of militia—of whom only sixty men were fit for duty—at Fort Edward, which post he is said to have saved by a stratagem from being attacked by the British, when they, during this month, raided northern New York from Canada.[93] Owing, however, to his men refusing to remain at this exposed post after their time of service had expired, he was compelled to evacuate Fort Edward and retire to Albany.[94] On his arrival there, he was appointed a member of a court-martial summoned to try three spies, two of whom were hanged by orders of this court.[95] In July, 1781, he wrote to Governor Clinton asking to be employed again on active service in the forthcoming campaign against New York.[96] This application came to nothing, as the governor in his reply pointed out he could not employ him out of his own district, which was in the north of the State.[97] In the autumn of this year he served under Lord Stirling, then in command at Albany.[98]

V

JOHN R. LIVINGSTON.
[In Continuation of No. IX. Continental Army.]

Commission

First Major, Manor of Livingston Regiment, prior to 15 January, 1777, on which date he resigned his commission in favour of Samuel Ten Broeck.[99] John R. Livingston must have succeeded his cousin Henry Livingston on that officer's promotion to lieutenant-colonel in place of Robert R. Livingston (see under Nos. III and IV.)

War Service

Apparently none.
[See also under COMMISSARIAT No. III.]

VI

ROBERT G. LIVINGSTON, JUNIOR.
[In Continuation of No. IV. Continental Army.]

Commission

Major of Minute Men, Dutchess Co., 17 October, 1775.[100] On 23 August, 1776, General Ten Broeck recommends him to the New York Convention for promotion to the rank of Colonel of Militia, but nothing seems to have come of this recommendation.[101] In January, 1777, he was arrested as a "suspect" by order of the Rhinebeck Committee of Safety, tried, condemned, and sent to Ulster gaol. He demanded a rehearing, when it was ordered he should be reprimanded, and upon taking the oath of allegiance, he was discharged.[102]

War Service

None.

VII

Henry G. Livingston.
[In Continuation of No. V. Continental Army.]

Commissions

Captain of Fusiliers in Colonel John Lasher's Regiment, First New York Independents, 14 September, 1775[103]; voted in favour of his regiment being incorporated in the Continental Army, 29 January, 1776[104]; Brigade-Major and aide-de-camp to Lord Stirling, 12 August, 1776[105]; recommended by Brigadier-General McDougall for promotion to the rank of Lieutenant-Colonel in McDougall's old regiment—First New York Line—"as General Washington wishes to see him provided for," but the senior officers objected to his being promoted over their heads, so nothing came of this recommendation, 7 November, 1776.[106]

War Service

Battle of Long Island, 27 August, 1776, in which Lord Stirling and most of his command were captured. Granted a royal pardon by Lord Howe, on Christmas Day, 1776; escapes from New York City and joins General George Clinton, before whom he takes the oath of allegiance to the United States of America, 14 February, 1777, and to whom he delivers up the royal pardon.[107]

VIII

Gilbert J. Livingston.
[In Continuation of No. VII. Continental Army.]

Commission

Captain in the Levies under Colonel Weissenfels, Colonel Malcom, and Colonel Pawling.[108] [No dates given.]

War Service

Unknown.

IX

ROBERT H. LIVINGSTON.
[In Continuation of No. VIII. CONTINENTAL ARMY.]

Commission

Lieutenant in Colonel Graham's Levies.[109] [No date given.]

War Service

Unknown.

X

ABRAHAM LIVINGSTON.
[In Continuation of No. XII. CONTINENTAL ARMY.]

Commission

Captain in Colonel Willett's Levies.[110] [No date given.]

War Service

Unknown.

XI

WILLIAM SMITH LIVINGSTON.
[In Continuation of No. XIV. CONTINENTAL ARMY.]

Commissions

Fourth Lieutenant of Fusiliers in Colonel Lasher's Regiment, 14 September, 1775; votes against his regiment being incorporated in the Continental Army, 29 January, 1776[111]; Major, 24 June, 1776[112]; aide-de-camp to General Greene, 16 August, 1776.[113]

[For further commissions see under No. XIV. Continental Army.]

War Service

Long Island, August, 1776; as General Greene was prevented by illness from being in the field on the date of the battle, probably Major Livingston was not present either.[114]

[For further war service see under No. XIV. as above.]

XII

JOHN LIVINGSTON, FIFTH SON OF COLONEL ROBERT LIVINGSTON OF THE MANOR. BORN 21 FEBRUARY, 1750.

Commission

Aide-de-camp to Governor Clinton, April, 1778.[115]

War Service

Accompanies Governor Clinton in pursuit of Sir John Johnson and his raiders, May, 1780.[116]

XIII

ROBERT JAMES LIVINGSTON, A YOUNGER BROTHER OF WILLIAM SMITH LIVINGSTON. BORN 5 NOVEMBER, 1760.

War Service

Though this young patriot of sixteen years held no commission in the American Army, still, as he was severely wounded in the cause of American liberty, he deserves to have his name included in the list. The following particulars are derived from Mr. Maturin L. Delafield's interesting article on *The Descendants of Judge William and Mary Smith*[117]:—

He had prepared himself for and had probably matriculated at the College of New Jersey, when the British troops overran the State. Young Livingston, but sixteen years of age, accidentally learned that the American army was in motion and was secretly moving upon the enemy. He left home to join the vanguard of the Americans, and fell severely wounded at the victory of Trenton (26 December 1776). Tradition states he was wounded in the first onslaught, and that for a few moments he was in the power of the Hessians, by whom he was roughly used. A lady, whose name unfortunately has not been preserved, had the lad removed to her house, sent for his mother and kept them until he could be carried in safety to his home at Princeton.

An anonymous correspondent to the *Magazine of American History*,[118] declares that this lady's name was Mistress Beckie Coxe, and that when she died, and was buried in the churchyard of St. Michael's at Trenton, some members of the lad's family attended her funeral.

ARMY COMMISSARIAT DEPARTMENT

I

WALTER LIVINGSTON,
THIRD SON OF COLONEL ROBERT LIVINGSTON OF THE MANOR
BORN 27 NOVEMBER, 1740.

Commissary of stores and provisions for the Department of New York, 17 July, 1775[119]; Deputy Commissary General prior to November, 1775[120]; resigned this office, 7 September, 1776, because of a dispute with the Commissary General, who had sent another Deputy Commissary to the Northern Army who had declined to recognise Mr. Livingston as his superior officer; Continental Congress accepted his resignation, 14 September, 1776.[121]

II

ABRAHAM LIVINGSTON, A SON OF PHILIP
LIVINGSTON, "THE SIGNER"
BAPTISED 3 JULY, 1754.

Commissary of Provisions to the New York troops, 16 February, 1776[122]6; on 10 May, 1776, received the thanks of Continental Congress for "voluntarily resigning a contract which might have been so profitable to him,"[123] appointed in December, 1776, together with William Turnbull, "agents to repair to the eastern states for the purpose of purchasing and collecting clothing for the use of the army[124];" in 1780, while acting as

Continental agent in the Southern States, he was captured by the British and confined as a prisoner of war at Charleston, S. C.[125] Here he appears to have settled, and to have died, unmarried, prior to 25 September, 1782.[126]

III

JOHN R. LIVINGSTON
[In continuation of No. IX. CONTINENTAL ARMY and No. V. MILITIA.]
Army agent for the purchase of clothing for the New York troops, 3 October, 1776.[127]

NAVY

I

JOHN LAWRENCE LIVINGSTON,
YOUNGEST SON OF GOVERNOR WILLIAM
LIVINGSTON OF NEW JERSEY
BORN 15, JULY 1762.

Commissions

His father obtained for him a midshipman's commission in the spring of 1780, "from a view to the public interest, which requires our navy to be officered by the children of respectable families."[128]

War Service

He sailed in the *Saratoga*, a vessel named after General Gates's victory over Burgoyne, and made one or two successful short cruises in her. In a letter from his sister Kitty to another sister, Mrs. John Jay, dated July 10, 1780, she writes "Brother Jack has received a summons to his duty on board the *Saratoga* (as senior midshipman), the ship being shortly to sail on a cruise."[129] In another letter, this time from Susan Livingston to Mrs. Jay written in October of same year, she refers to a report that the *Saratoga* had taken three prizes, and that their brother's share of the prize money should amount to near "twenty thousand pound."[130] But a year later, the *Saratoga* was missing, to the great grief of Governor Livingston and his family, and no reliable news was ever received as to her fate. What evidence there was pointed to the ship having capsized in a squall, while chasing a sail on the 18 March, 1781. It was years, however, before the distracted father gave up all hope of ever seeing his sailor son again.[131]

II

Muscoe Livingston

Parentage unknown; but evidently related to Governor Livingston of New Jersey, who took an interest in his career, and asked for a naval appointment on his behalf, 27 August, 1779. This the Marine Committee of Continental Congress declined to entertain, on the plea "that it is not eligible to employ Mr. Muscoe Livingston in the way he proposed."[132] Two years later, his name is again before the Committee of Congress, as recommended for the appointment of Lieutenant in the United States Navy by the Board of Admiralty, but, on the 20th July, 1781, they report "that appointment of Muscoe Livingston as Lieutenant be postponed."[133] Subsequently he obtained the commission.

Commission

Lieutenant, no date given.[134]

War Service

Unknown.

Addenda

As the author has been unable to trace the parentage of the two officers, of whom particulars are given below, derived from Mr. Heitman's *Register;* and as there is nothing to indicate, as in the case of Muscoe Livingston, that they are descendants either of Robert Livingston of the Manor, or of Robert Livingston, the Nephew, he has not included them in the above list.

Army

I

James Livingston (Pa.) Lieutenant and Regimental Quartermaster of Flower's Artillery Artificer Regiment 1777—.

II

Robert Livingston (Va.) Ensign, 5th Virginia, November, 1776; taken prisoner at Trenton, 26 December, 1776; 2nd Lieutenant, 1 April, 1777; transferred 3d Virginia, 14 September, 1778; 1st Lieutenant—1779, and served to—. In service March, 1780.[135]

CONTINENTAL ARMY

HENRY BROCKHOLST LIVINGSTON

See page 517

As a confirmation of the statement, that this officer was aide-de-camp to General Schuyler in 1776, and *not* Henry Beekman Livingston, the following extract is given from Alexander Graydon's *Memoirs*, who, then, a captain in a Pennsylvania regiment, was sent on a mission to that general in May 1776:—"We were much indebted upon this occasion, to the polite attentions of Mr. Brockhoist Livingston, who was at this time one of the aides-de-camp of General Schuyler."[136]

JAMES LIVINGSTON

See page 523

That Colonel James Livingston served under General Arnold at the relief of Fort Stanwix, is confirmed, unexpectedly, by the discovery of an original letter of his, addressed to General Gates from German Flats, on 21 August 1777, the day upon which General Arnold held his council of war at that place.[137]

MILITIA

WILLIAM SMITH LIVINGSTON

See page 533

According to Mr. Stryker, this officer, as aide-de-camp to General Greene, was present at the Battles of Trenton and Princeton, and was wounded in the latter engagement.[138]

ROBERT JAMES LIVINGSTON

See page 534

In reference to this young volunteer, Mr. Stryker states he joined the Hunterdon County Militia as a private, just prior to the battle of Trenton, and that he was "afterwards an ensign in the Fifth Virginia Regiment,"[139] but he does not state his authority. If this is correct, it would settle the identity of the Robert Livingston of Virginia in Mr. Heitman's *Register*.[140]

Notes

1. Printed in full in *Documents Relating to the Revolutionary History of New Jersey*, Second Series, vol. ii, pp. 135–137.
2. Drake, *Dictionary of American Biography*, p. 555. Appleton's *Cyclopedia of American Biography*, vol. iii, p. 745. Strangely enough, Mr. Heitman, in his *Register of the Continental Army*, has fallen into the same errors, and also Mr. John Schuyler in the *Society of the Cincinnati of New York*, p. 251.
3. *Field Book*, vol. i, p. 720 (note).
4. *Clermont or Livingston Manor*, p. 150.
5. *Battles of the United States*, vol. i, p. 338.
6. Acknowledgment is rendered, wherever use has been made of these authorities, and full references are always given, whether the source of information is original or not.
7. Force, *American Archives*, Fourth Series, vol. iii, p. 25.
8. By the New York Provincial Congress. *Journals*, vol. i, p 328.
9. A certificate signed by Chas. Thomson, Secretary to the Continental Congress, dated 8 March, 1776, is worded as follows:—"Henry B. Living" ston is elected lieutenant-colonel of the 2nd battalion of New York forces, and by the order in which he stands, takes rank of Lieut.-Col. Wiesenfels and Lieut.-Col. Cortlandt, appointed on the same day." *Correspondence of the Provincial Congress, 1775–1777*, vol. ii, p. 412.
10. *Calendar Historical Manuscripts War of Revolution*, vol. ii. p. 35.
11. *Journals of Congress* (original edition), vol. iv, p. 668.
12. *Ibid.*, vol. v, p. 21.
13. Information supplied by the Adjutant-General's office, Albany, New York.
14. Schuyler, *Society of the Cincinnati of New York*, p. 251.
15. *American Archives*, Fourth Series, vol. iii, pp. 1596, 1602, 1603, and 1950; vol. iv, p. 380. Richard Smith's *Diary* in *American Historical Review*, vol. i, p. 296. *Journals of Provincial Congress*, vol. i, p. 328.
16. *American Archives*, Fifth Series, vols. i and ii. Washington's letter, naming him for this duty, is dated 14 June, 1776, and is printed in *Magazine of American History*, vol. iii, p. 117.
17. *American Archives*, Fifth Series, vol. ii, p. 948.
18. Wilkinson, *Memoirs*, vol. i, pp. 239, 270. *Correspondence of the American Revolution*, vol. i, p. 427. *George Clinton's Public Papers*, vol. ii, p. 225. *Benedict Arnold at Saratoga*, p. 3.
19. *Correspondence of the American Revolution*, vol. ii, pp. 550–553. Quoted by Chancellor Livingston in a letter to General Washington, dated 14 January, 1778.
20. *George Clinton's Public Papers*, vol. ii, 517.
21. *Ibid.*, vol. ii, pp. 605, 606.
22. *The Army Correspondence of Colonel John Laurens*, pp. 193–199.

23. Dawson, *Battles of the United States*, vol. i, pp. 439–441. *Life of Nathanael Greene*, vol. ii, pp. 129–131.
24. *George Clinton's Public Papers*, vol. vi, pp. 127, 317, 318, 322, and 785. The letter of 16 April, 1781, as printed in this correspondence, is signed "Henry Livingston," but the address—"Philadelphia"—and the nature of the contents, indicate Colonel Henry Beekman Livingston as the writer.
25. Owing to his initials being the same as the preceding officer, some writers on the War of Independence, have been unable to distinguish the one from the other.
26. *American Archives*, Fourth Series, vol. vi, p. 416.
27. *Journals of Congress* (new edition), vol. viii, p. 769.
28. Schuyler, *Society of the Cincinnati of New York*, p. 250.
29. Hatfield, *History of Elisabeth, New Jersey*, pp. 421–425. *American Archives*, Fourth Series, vol. iv, pp. 837, and 1658.
30. Sedgwick, *Life of William Livingston*, p. 237. *Correspondence of the American Revolution*, vol. ii, pp. 511–515.
31. Arnold, *Benedict Arnold at Saratoga*, p. 3.
32. This expunged resolution of Congress is printed for the first time, in Mr. W. C. Ford's edition of the Journals, now in course of publication. This is by far the best edition issued, and is moreover, fully indexed, but some of the Livingston references are incorrect. *Journals of Congress*, under date as August, 1777, vol. viii, p. 665.
33. Henry Brockhoist Livingston to General Schuyler, Camp, Bemis's Heights, Sept. 33, 1777. Arnold, *Life of Benedict Arnold*, p. 180.
34. The same to the same, 26 September, 1777; also Colonel Varick to General Schuyler, dated 25 September. *Life of Benedict Arnold*, pp. 183, 184.
35. *Journals of Congress* (new edition), vol, viii, p. 769.
36. *Journals of Congress* (original edition), vol. v, p. 385.
37. Henry Brockhoist Livingston to General Washington, Elizabethtown, 16 June, 1782. *Correspondence of the American Revolution*, vol. iii, pp. 517–532.
38. *American Archives*, Fourth Series, vol. ii, p. 1813; vol. iii, p. 25.
39. His Journal of his military experiences from 25 August to 22 December, 1775, is still preserved, and is printed in *The Pennsylvania Magazine of History and Biography* for the year 1898. He left Montreal,, on his return, on 17th November, 1775.
40. Date of birth unknown; when unable to give this, the date of baptism, whenever possible, is inserted instead.
41. *Journals of New York Provincial Congress*, vol. i, p. 177. In place of Mr. Duer who was unable to accept.
42. *Calendar Historical MSS. War of Revolution*, vol. i, p. 107; vol. ii, p. 41.
43. *Ibid.*, vol. ii, p. 53. *American Archives*, Fifth Series, vol. i, p. 646.
44. *American Archives*, Fifth Series, vol. ii, p. 997.
45. *Calendar Hist, MSS. War of Revolution*, vol. ii, pp. 34, 49, and 53.
46. *Public Papers of George Clinton*, vol. ii, pp. 337, 338.
47. *Calendar Hist. MSS. War of Revolution*, vol. ii, p. 53. Mr. Heitman says he was Ensign, 3rd New York, 1 September, 1776.
48. *Calendar Historical MSS. War of Revolution*, vol. ii, p. 34.
49. Heitman, *Historical Register Officers Continental Army*, p. 266.
50. *George Clinton's Public Papers*, vol. v, p. 480. Mr. Heitman gives date of resignation as 5 April, 1780. Probably date of its acceptance(?)
51. *George Clinton's Public Papers*, vol. v, p. 480.
52. *New York in the Revolution as Colony and State*, p. 63. Heitman's *Register*, p. 367.

53. Heitman's *Register*, p. 267.
54. *Calendar Historical MSS. War of Revolution*, vol. ii, p. 41.
55. A good account of James Livingston's services in aiding General Montgomery with his regiment of refugees, will be found in Mr. Justin H. Smith's *Our Struggle for the Fourteenth Colony*, who quotes from the original authorities very fully.
56. *American Archives*, Fourth Series, vol. iv, p. 1636.
57. *American Archives*, Fifth Series, vol. i, p. 1609 and vol. ii, PP. 1221 et seq.
58. *American Archives*, Fourth Series, vol. iii, p. 1132.
59. Justin H. Smith, *Our Struggle for the Fourteenth Colony*, vol. ii, pp. 74 *et seq.*
60. *Gates's Manuscript Papers*, quoted from by Arnold, *Life of Benedict Arnold*, p. 155; and Washington Irving, *Life of Washington* (original edition), vol. iii, p. 184. According to some writers the Colonel Livingston, who served under General Arnold at the relief of Fort Stanwix, was Colonel Henry Beekman Livingston, but the latter officer only reached General Gates's camp on the 21 August, 1777, the date on which Arnold and his colonels held their council of war at German Flatts on the Mohawk.
61. Wilkinson, *Memoirs*, vol. i, pp. 239 *et seq.*
62. *Washington's Writings*, vol. vii, p. 139. *Magazine of American History*, vol. xxi, pp. 71–74.
63. Heitman's *Register*, p. 367.
64. *Journals of Congress* (original edition), vol. x, p. 71.
65. Heitman's *Register*, p. 267.
66. Heitman's *Register*, p. 266.
67. Godfrey, *The Commander-in-Chief's Guard*, pp. 43, 307.
68. *Journals of Congress*, vol. iv, p. 498.
69. A letter of his, addressed to his father, "The Signer," describing this battle, fell into the hands of the British, who had it published in the *New York Gatetie*, This newspaper erroneously described the writer as being Henry Brockhoist Livingston, "son of the usurped governor of New Jersey." *New Jersey Archives*, Second Series, vol. 1, pp. 483,484.
70. *The Commander-in-Chirfs Guard*, pp. 68, 307.
71. *Correspondence and Journals of S, B. Webb*, vol. i, p. 217.
72. *Ibid.*, vol. i, p. 230.
73. *George Clinton's Public Papers*, vol. ii, pp. 380–404.
74. *Narrative of Major Abraham Leggett*, pp. 17–22.
75. *Pennsylvania Magazine of History and Biography for year 1879*, p. 173. *Ibid., for year 1898*, pp. 502–503.
76. *George Clinton's Public Papers*, vol. iii, pp. 90, 311.
77. Colonel Webb, and a great part of his regiment, had been taken by the British, in his attempt to land on Long Island, 10 December 1777.
78. *Life of Nathanael Greene*, vol. ii, p. 129. In the *American Historical Review*, vol. v, pp. 719, 720, there is printed a letter from Major Huntington of this regiment, dated 21 September, 1778, in which he says: "Colonel Livingston had left the regt. and rode over to the left, to see how the action went on, and in his absence received a slight wound."
79. *Correspondence of Samuel B. Webb*, vol. ii, p. 264.
80. *New Jersey Archives*, Second Series, vol. iii, p. 259.
81. *Minutes of Provincial Congress, New Jersey*, p. 246.
82. Sedgwick, *Life of William Livingston*, pp. 204, 305.

83. Previous to the War of Independence, the third Lord of the Manor had held a commission, under the crown, as "Colonel of the Regiment of Militia in the Lordship and Manor of Livingston," which had been conferred on him by the royalist governor, Tryon, ad July, 1772; and he was usually addressed by this title during the rest of his life, though the command of his regiment was transferred to his son Peter R. by the Provincial Congress, as stated above, in October, 1775. The third Lord had previously held a captain's commission in the provincial militia for many years. His colonel's commission, in an excellent state of preservation, is in the possession of Mrs. Harold Wilson.

84. *American Archives*, Fourth Series, vol. iii, p. 1121. *Calendar Historical MSS. War of Revolution*, vol. i, pp. 174, 175.

85. *Public Papers of George Clinton*, vol. iii, pp. 513–518.

86. Hough, *Northern Invasion of 1780*, p. 117 (note).

87. *American Archives*, Fourth Series, vol. iii, p. 1121. *Calendar Historical MSS. War of Revolution*, vol. i, pp. 174, 175.

88. *Calendar Historical MSS. War of Revolution*, vol. i, pp. 174, 175, 506.

89. The original commission "To Henry Livingston, Junior, Esq., Lieutenant-Colonel of the Regiment of Militia in the Manor of Livingston in the County of Albany, whereof Peter R. Livingston is Colonel," signed by Governor George Clinton, Poughkeepsie, 28 May, 1778, is in the possession of Mrs. Harold Wilson.

90. From information kindly supplied by the Adjutant-General's Office, Albany, New York.

91. *Public Papers of George Clinton*, vol. ii, pp. 267–268.

92. Wilkinson, *Memoirs*, vol. i, pp. 268–274 and 299.

93. Mr. F. B. Hough gives the following account of this incident in his *Northern Invasion of October, 1780*, p. 123:—"The invading troops approached Fort Edward, but were probably prevented from making an attack by a stratagem of Colonel Livingston, who commanded there. Hearing of the incursion of the enemy he wrote a letter to Captain Sherwood, on the morning of the day in which Fort Anne was surrendered, saying he was very strong and would support that garrison if attacked. He gave this letter to a messenger, who he had little doubt would carry it to the enemy, which he is presumed to have done, and thus to have saved that post from the fate which had befallen the others."

94. Governor Clinton to General Washington, Albany, 18 October 1780. In a footnote to this letter Mr. Hough says the officer in command of Fort Edward was "Colonel James Livingston of the Continental army." *Northern Invasion*, pp. 108–110. This, however, cannot be correct as at this date Colonel James Livingston was in command of Verplanck's Point on the lower Hudson. Moreover, Governor Clinton in a letter to General Greene, 14 October, 1780, plainly states, "We have not a single Continental troop there [namely north of Albany], and our whole dependence is in the militia, and this to oppose a very formidable body of regular troops." *Ibid.*, pp. 96, 97. Besides, all the references to the commander of Fort Edward indicate he was Lieutenant-Colonel Livingston of the New York militia. Cf. *Public Papers of George Clinton*, vol. vi, pp. 288–307.

95. *Public Papers of George Clinton*, vol. vi, p. 334.

96. Henry Livingston to Governor Clinton, Manor Livingston, 3 July, 1781. *Public Papers of George Clinton*, vol. vii, p. 56.

97. Governor Clinton to Henry Livingston, Poughkeepsie, 6 August, 1781. *Ibid.*, p. 57.

98. Duer, *Life of William Alexander, Earl of Stirling*, p. 226.

99. *Journals of Provincial Congress*, vol. i, p. 772. Samuel Ten Broeck had held the commission of Second Major since 20 October, 1775.
100. *Calendar History MSS. War of Revolution*, vol. i, p. 164.
101. *American Archives*, Fifth Series, vol. i, p. 1133.
102. Judge Jones, *History of New York during the Revolutionary War J* vol. ii, pp. 407, 408.
103. *Calendar Historical MSS. War of Revolution*, vol. i, p. 143.
104. *Ibid.*, vol. i, pp. 333, 334. The voting resulted in a tie, so the regiment did not join the regular army.
105. Appointed by General Washington. *American Archives*, Fifth Series, vol. i, p. 915.
106. *Calendar Historical MSS. War of Revolution*, vol. ii, p. 15. *American Archives*, Fifth Series, vol. iii, p. 558.
107. *Calendar Historical MSS. War of Revolution*, vol. i. pp. 669–671. *Public Papers of George Clinton*, vol. i, pp. 594, 595.
108. *New York in the Revolution as Colony and State*, pp. 70, 74, 82.
109. *Ibid.*, p. 79.
110. *New York in the Revolution as Colony and State*, p. 87. Heitman, *Register*, p. 266.
111. See under No. VII, MILITIA. The cousins voted on opposite sides.
112. "Chosen by a majority of votes of the first Battalion as Major, in preference to Captain Jno. Roosevelt." John Varick, Jun., to Captain Richard Varick, New York, 25 June, 1776. *New York City during American Revolution*, p. 75.
113. *American Archives*, Fifth Series, vol. i, pp. 916, 1138.
114. Greene, *Life of Nathanael Greene*, vol. i, p. 205.
115. *Public Papers of George Clinton*, vol. iii, p. 156.
116. *Livingstons of Callendar* (original letter quoted), p. 414.
117. Printed in the *Magazine of American History*, vol. vi, p. 277.
118. Printed in the *Magazine of American History*, vol. vii, p. 65.
119. Ford's *Journals of Congress*, vol. ii, p. 186.
120. *Ibid.*, vol. iii, p. 340.
121. *American Archives*, Fifth Series, vol. ii, pp. 220, 221, and 1339.
122. *American Archives*, Fourth Series, vol. v, p. 270.
123. *Journals of Congress*, vol. ii, pp. 164, 167.
124. *Ibid.*, vol. iii, p. 87.
125. 119 *Ibid.*, vol. vi, p. 152.
126. *New York Genealogical and Biographical Record*, vol. iii, p. 32.
127. He and Abraham P. Lott were appointed by the New York Congress, and were allowed two and a half per cent, commission on their purchases. *American Archives*, Fifth Series, vol. iii, p. 218.
128. Sedgwick, *Life of William Livingston*, p. 345. The above quotation is from a letter of Governor Livingston to his cousin, the Chancellor, dated 19 April, 1780.
129. *The Correspondence and Public Papers of John Jay*, vol. i, pp. 376, 377.
130. *Ibid.*, p. 376 (note). Of course, depreciated Continental currency is meant.
131. *Ibid.*, vol. ii, p. 162; vol. iii, pp. 383 *et seq.*
132. *Journals of Congress* (original edition), vol. v, p. 360.
133. *Naval Records of the American Revolution*, 1775–1783, pp. 181, 182.
134. Paullin, *The Navy of the American Revolution*, p. 509. He is No. 75 on Mr. Paullin's List of Lieutenants.
135. *Historical Register of Officers of the Continental Army*, p. 267.
136. *Memoirs of a Life passed in Pennsylvania* (edition 1811) p. 129.

137. To the courtesy of Mr. Kelby, the librarian of the New York Historical Society, the author is indebted for his discovery of this letter among the Gates's MSS. in the possession of that institution.
138. Stryker (William S.) *The Battles of Trenton and Princeton*, pp. 292, 348.
139. *Ibid.*, p. 194.
140. See Addenda II., to this Appendix, p. 538.

APPENDIX B

FAMILY OF THE REV. JOHN LIVINGSTON OF ANCRUM[1]

THE Rev. John Livingston was born at Kilsyth, Stirlingshire, Scotland, 21 June, 1603; married at Edinburgh, in the West Church, 23 June, 1635, Janet, eldest daughter of Bartholomew Fleming, of the old Scottish family of that name, of which the then head was the Earl of Wigton, who, with his eldest son, Lord Fleming, was present at the wedding. Mr. Livingston died at Rotterdam, Holland, between 14 and 21 August, 1672. Mrs. Livingston was born at Edinburgh, 16 November, 1613, and died at Rotterdam, 13 February, 1693–[14], and was buried in the French Church in that city.

They had the following children:—

I   John, born at Iron-furnace of Milton, Ireland, 30 June, 1636; died at Stranraer, Scotland, 8 January, 1639; buried in Inch Churchyard.

II   William, born at Lanark, 7 January, 1638; married Ann Veitch, 23 December, 1663; died at Edinburgh, and interred in the Greyfriars Burial-Ground, 12 June, 1700.[2]

III   Bartholomew, born at Stranraer, 3 September, 1639; died 24 September, 1641; buried in Inch Churchyard.

IV   Agnes, born at Stranraer, 20 September, 1640; died 17 October, 1641; buried in Inch Churchyard.

V   Marion, born at Stranraer, 10 October, 1642; married Rev. John Scott, minister at Hawick, 28 September, 1658; died at Hawick in July, 1661 or 1667(?) and buried in Hawick Churchyard.

VI   Janet, born at Stranraer, 28 September, 1643; married Andrew Russell, merchant in Rotterdam, Holland; died in August, 1696.

VII   John, born at Stranraer, 20 August, 1644; died at same place in October, 1645, and buried in Inch Churchyard.

VIII Agnes, born at Stranraer, 18 August, 1645; married David Cleland, Chiruigeon; died—.

IX   James, born at Stranraer, 22 September, 1646; married apparently twice; his second wife, Christian Fish, 15 August, 1683; died at Edinburgh and interred in Greyfriars Burial-Ground, 4 June, 1700.[3]

X   Joanna, born at Stranraer,— September, 1647; died at Ancrum in October, 1648, and buried in Ancrum Churchyard.

XI   Barbara, born at Ancrum, 21 June, 1648; married James Miller or Millar, merchant; died —.

XII   John, born at Ancrum, 24 June, 1652; died at same place, 12 October, 1652, and buried in Ancrum Churchyard.

XIII Andrew, born at Ancrum, —August, 1653; died 7 February, 1655, and buried in Ancrum Churchyard.

XIV   Robert, born at Ancrum, 13 December, 165–4.[4]

XV   Elizabeth, born at Ancrum, 7 January, 1657; died at Rotterdam, Holland, 31 October, 1666, and buried in the Zuiden Churchyard.

Notes

1. From the Family Record in Mr. John Henry Livingston's manuscript copy of Rev. John Livingston's *Autobiography*, collated with the one formerly in the possession of the late Mr. Van Brugh Livingston and with additional particulars derived from contemporary letters and journals owned by Mr. Johnston Livingston.

2. From Register of Interments in Greyfriars Burial-Ground, Edinburgh, A.D. 1658– 1700. His brother James had been interred eight days before him in same graveyard.

3. James was the father of Robert Livingston, "The Nephew," who must have been the son of the *first* marriage—mother's name unknown.

4. The first Lord of the Manor of Livingston, see Appendix C.

FAMILY OF ROBERT LIVINGSTON, FIRST LORD OF THE MANOR OF LIVINGSTON[1]

ROBERT LIVINGSTON, the youngest son of the Rev. John Livingston of Ancrum, was born at that place, 13 December, 1654; married, 9 July, 1679, in the Presbyterian Church, Albany, New York, Alida, daughter of Philip Pieterse Schuyler and Margarita Van Schlechtenhorst (only daughter of the celebrated director of Rensselaerwyck), and widow of Rev. Nicholas Van Rensselaer. Mr. Livingston died 1 October, 1728,[2] and was buried in the family vault on the Manor. Mrs. Livingston was born 28 February, 1656, and died 27 March, 1729. They had the following children:—

I   Johannes or John, born 26 April, 1680; married (1) at New London, Connecticut, in April, 1701, Mary, only child and heiress of Fitzjohn Winthrop, Governor of Connecticut; she died 8 January, 1713, on the Livingston Farm, Mohegan, near New London, and was buried at New London ; (2) Elizabeth, daughter of Mrs. Sarah Knight, October, 1713; she died 17 March, 1735–[6], and was buried alongside his first wife in the burial-ground, New London. Colonel John Livingston died 19 February, 1720.[3] He had no children by either marriage.

II Margaret, born 5 December, 1681; married, 20 December, 1700, Colonel Samuel Vetch or Veitch, formerly of the Darien Company, and afterwards first English governor of Annapolis Royal. She died in June, 1758.

III Johanna Philippina, born 1 February, 1683–[4]; died 24 January, 1689–[90].

IV   Philip, born 9 July, 1686. The second Lord of the Manor.[4]

V   Robert, born 24 July, 1688; married Margaret Howarden, at the Reformed Dutch Church, New York City, 11 November, 1717; died 27 June, 1775. He was the first proprietor of Clermont.

VI   Gilbert or Hubertus, born 3 March, 1689–[90]; married, 22 December, 1711, Cornelia Beekman; died 25 April, 1746.[5]

VII   William, born 17 March, 1692 [? N.S.]; died 5 November, 1692.

VIII   Johanna, born 10 December, 1694; married Cornelius Gerrit Van Home.

IX   Catharine, born 22 May, 1698; died 6 December, 1699.

Notes

1. From Robert Livingston's Family Bible, with some additions from other contemporary sources, and collated with the late Mr. Henry Brace's manuscript genealogy of the Livingston Family, kindly lent the author by Mrs. Harold Wilson.
2. He is said by some authorities to have died at Boston, Mass., *vide Musgrave's Obituary*, Harleian Society's Publications, vol. xlviii, and Allen's *American Biographical Dictionary* (edition 1857).
3. According to *Musgrave's Obituary* he died "in America," while some writers say he died in England. Probably "New England" is meant (?).
4. For further particulars and list of his children see Appendix D.
5. For list of Gilbert's children see Appendix F.

APPENDIX D

FAMILY OF PHILIP LIVINGSTON, SECOND LORD OF THE MANOR[1]

PHILIP LIVINGSTON was born 9 July, 1686; married 19 September, 1707, Catharine, daughter of Peter Van Brug (or Brugh) and Sarah Cuyler. Mr. Livingston died 4 February, 1748–[9] or 15th new style. Mrs. Livingston was baptised 10 November, 1689, and died 20 February, 1756 [N.S.]. They had the following children:—

I   Robert, born 16 December, 1708. Third Lord of the Manor.[2]

II   Peter Van Brugh, baptised at Albany, 3 November, 1710.[3]

III   Peter, baptised at Albany, 20 April, 1712; died young.[4]

IV   John, baptised at Albany, 11 April, 1714; married 3 December, 1742, Catherine, daughter of Abraham de Peyster and Margaret Van Cortlandt; died 1788.

V   Philip, born 15 January, 1716, [? O.S.]. "The Signer."[5]

VI   Henry, baptised at Albany, 5 April, 1719; died in Jamaica, W. I., February, 1772.

VII   Sarah, baptised at Albany, 7 May, 1721; died — October, 1722.

VIII William, born 8 November, 1723. Governor of New Jersey.[6]

IX   Sarah, baptised at Albany, 7 November, 1725; married 1 March, 1748, William Alexander, titular Earl of Stirling; died — March, 1805.

X   Alida, baptised at Albany, 18 July, 1728; married (1) 26 September, 1750, Henry Hansen of Harlem; (2) Colonel Martin Hoffman, 26 September, 1766. She died in February, 1790.

XI   Catherine, baptised at Albany, 15 April, 1733; married 18 April, 1759, Aiderman John Lawrence of New York; died —.

Notes

1. Authorities: Peter Van Brugh Livingston's *Manuscript Genealogy of 1769*, etc., etc., *vide Livingstons of Callendar*, pp. 407, 408. This, as well as the succeeding lists, also collated with Mr. Brace's manuscript.
2. For list of his children see Appendix E.
3. See Appendix G.
4. According to Mr. Brace Nos. II and III should be reversed.
5. See Appendix H.
6. See Appendix I.

FAMILY OF ROBERT LIVINGSTON, THIRD LORD OF THE MANOR[1]

R OBERT LIVINGSTON was born 16 December, 1708[2]; married (I) Maria, daughter of Walter Thong, or Tong, and granddaughter of Rip Van Dam, President of the Council, 20 May, 1731. Mrs. Livingston was born 3 June, 1711, and died 30 May, 1765. He married (2) Gertrude, daughter of Kiliaen Van Rensselaer and Maria Van Cortlandt, and widow of Adonijah Schuyler. She was born 1 October, 1714, and died —. No issue.

The children of Robert Livingston and Maria Thong were:

I Catharine, born at Albany, 4 August, 1732; died 25 November, 1732.
II Philip, born at New York, 9 February, 1733–[4]; died unmarried, 3 April, 1756.
III Sarah, born at New York, 23 April, 1735; died 4 September, 1745.
IV Peter R., born 27 April, 1737.[3]
V Maria, born 29 October, 1738; married, 21 October, 1759, James Duane, afterwards one of the New York delegates in Continental Congress, etc.; died 6 May, 1821.
VI Walter, born 27 November, 1740; married in 1769, Cornelia, daughter of Peter Schuyler and Gertrude Schuyler; died 14 May, 1797. His wife was baptised 26 July, 1746, and died in 1822. Walter Livingston was member of Provincial Congress, 1775. Member of Assembly 1777, 1778, 1779. Speaker 1778, 1779. Member of Continental Congress 1784. Commissioner of United States Treasury 1785, etc.[4] He built "Teviotdale" in Columbia County.

VII   Robert, better known as Robert Cambridge,[5] born 26 December, 1742; married, 22 November, 1778, Alice, daughter of John Swift; died 23 August, 1794.

VIII Catharine, born 22 December, 1744; married, in 1766, John Paterson; died May, 1832.

IX   Sarah, born 16 February, 1745–[6]; died 11 May, 1749.

X   Alida, born 15 December, 1747; married Valentine Gardiner; died September, 1791.

XI   Margarita, born 16 February, 1748–[9]; died 22 June, 1749.

XII   John, born at New York, 21 February, 1749–[50]; married (1) Mary Aim, daughter of Jacob LeRoy and Cornelia Rutgers, 11 May, 1775; (2) Catharine, daughter of Governor Livingston of New Jersey, and widow of Matthew Ridley, 3 November, 1796. John Livingston died at Oak Hill, Columbia Co., 24 October, 1822.

XIII Hendrick, or Henry, born at New York, 8 January, 1752–[3]; died, unmarried, 26 May, 1823.

Robert Livingston, Third Lord of the Manor, died November, 1790.

Notes

1. From the record in his Family Bible, with additions from other authentic sources. Cf. *Livingstons of Callendar*, pp. 416–418.
2. Robert Livingston gives, in nearly all cases, dates according to the new, as well as old, style of reckoning. In the above list the old method is adhered to.
3. See Appendix K.
4. See also under Chapter XIII and Appendix A.
5. So called because he was a graduate of Cambridge University, and to distinguish him from the numerous other Roberts.

APPENDIX F

FAMILY OF GILBERT LIVINGSTON, FOURTH SON OF ROBERT LIVINGSTON, FIRST LORD OF THE MANOR[1]

GILBERT LIVINGSTON was born 3 March, 1689–[90][2]; married 22 December, 1711, Cornelia, daughter of Colonel Henry Beekman and Johanna de Loper, who was born 18 June, 1693,[3] and died 24 June, 1742. Gilbert Livingston died at Kingston, N. Y., 25 April, 1746. He was a member of the General Assembly, Clerk of the County of Ulster, and a lieutenant-colonel of militia. Under his father's will he inherited one-seventh part of the Saratoga patent. It was on this land that General Burgoyne surrendered to General Gates in October, 1777.[4] They had the following children:—

I   Robert Gilbert, born 11 January, 1713; married 3 November, 1740, Catharine, daughter of John McPheadres and Helena Johnson; died 27 October, 1789.

II   Henry, baptised at Kingston, N. Y., 29 August, 1714,[5] married Susanna, daughter of John Conklin and Joanna Storm; died 10 February, 1799.

III   Alida, baptised at Kingston, N. Y., 20 May, 1716; married (1) 24 November, 1737, Jacob, son of John Rutsen and Catharine Beekman; (2) Henry son of Hendrick Van Rensselaer and Catharine Van Brag; died —.

IV   Gilbert, born —; died —;

V   Gilbert, born—; married Joy Dorrell of Bermuda. In 1769 he was a lieutenant in the British army.

VI Johannes[6], baptised at Kingston, N. Y., 5 October, 1720; died unmarried, October, 1739.

VII Johanna, born 28 August, baptised at Kingston, N. Y., 9 September, 1722; married 28 May, 1748, Pierre Van Cortlandt, member of Assembly, and later President of the Council of Safety, and first Lieutenant-Governor State of New York; died 16 September, 1808.

VIII William, baptised at Kingston, N. Y., 23 August, 1724; died unmarried.

IX Philip, baptised at Kingston, N. Y., 26 June, 1726; died unmarried.

X James, baptised at Kingston, N. Y., 7 April, 1728; married Judith Newcomb; died —.

XI Samud, baptised at Kingston, N. Y., 1 February, 1730; died unmarried.

XII Cornelius, baptised at Kingston, N. Y., 30 April, 1732; died unmarried.

XIII Catharine, baptised at Kingston, N. Y., 21 July, 1734; married Thomas Thom[7]; died —.

XIV Margaret, baptised at Kingston, N.Y., 23 June, 1738; married 17 October, 1764, Peter Stuyvesant, grandson of Governor Stuyvesant; died —.

Notes

1. From information kindly supplied by Mrs. Montgomery Schuyler, and collated with Mr. Brace's manuscript genealogy, and that of Peter Van Brugh Livingston of 1769.
2. According to record in his father's Bible.
3. Mr. Brace gives 18 July, 1695, as the date of Cornelia Beekman's birth.
4. Schuyler (G. W.), Colonial New York, vol. i, p. 287.
5. Born 8 September, 1714, according to Gunn's Memoirs of Rev. John H. Livingston p. 35. New style of reckoning probably meant (?)
6. Johanna according to Mrs. Montgomery Schuyler.
7. Stephen Thorne, according to the Manuscript Genealogy of 1769.

APPENDIX G

FAMILY OF PETER VAN BRUGH LIVINGSTON[1]

PETER VAN BRUGH LIVINGSTON the second son of Philip
Livingston, second Lord of the Manor of Livingston, was born at
Albany, N. Y., and baptised 3 November, 1710[2]; married (1) Mary, eldest
daughter of James Alexander, member of Council and Surveyor General
of the Province of New Jersey. She was born 16 October, 1721, and died
27 September, 1769; (2) Mrs. Ricketts. Peter Van Brugh Livingston died in
1793. The children of Peter Van Brugh Livingston and Mary Alexander
were:—

I   Philip, usually known as "Gentleman Phil," born 3 November, 1740;
married, 7 October, 1790, in New York, Cornelia, daughter of David
Van Home and Anne French[3]; died May, 1810.

II   Mary, baptised at New York, 27 May, 1742; died in infancy.

III   Catharine, baptised 2 October, 1743; married, 20 April, 1762, Nicholas
Bayard, Alderman of New York[4]; died 2 November, 1775.

IV   James Alexander, baptised 10 October, 1744; died —.

V   Mary, baptised 29 October, 1746; married, 11 June, 1772, Captain
John Brown, 60th Regiment or Royal Americans; died —.

VI   Peter Van Brugh, born 31 March, 1753; married Susan Blondel or
Blundel; died —.

VII   Sarah, born 30 April, 1755; married 24 March, 1777, Captain James
Ricketts, 60th Regiment or Royal Americans; died in 1825.

VIII William Alexander, born 10 February, 1757; killed in a duel 1 August,
1780.

IX   Susan, born 23 March, 1759; married (1) John Kean of South Carolina, 27 September, 1786; (2) Count Julian Ursino Niemcewiez, a polish patriot, aide to Kosciuzko, 2 July, 1800; died 14 May, 1833.

X   Elizabeth, born 20 June, 1761; married Monsieur Otto, French consul and minister in United States; died 17 December, 1787.

XI   James Alexander, born 27 July, 1763; died young.

XII   Ann, born 14 September, 1767; died young.

Notes

1. Mostly derived from his own *Manuscript Genealogy of 1769*, and Miss Jay's *Descendants of James Alexander*, printed in *New York Genealogical and Biographical Record*, vol. xii. Cf, *Livingstons of Callendar*, pp. 503–505.
2. According to Mr. Brace he was Philip's third son, but in his own manuscript genealogy Mr. P. V. B. Livingston states he was the second.
3. A correction in Mr. Brace's manuscript reads: "Catherine, dau. of Philip Van Horne and Elizabeth Ricketts."
4. Another correction in Mr. Brace's genealogy reads: "William, son of Samuel Bayard and Margaret Van Cortlandt." Nicholas is, however, in accordance with Mr. P. V. B. Livingston's own manuscript.

APPENDIX H

FAMILY OF PHILIP LIVINGSTON, "THE SIGNER"[1]

PHILIP LIVINGSTON, the fifth son of Philip Livingston, second Lord of the Manor, was born 15 January, 1716[2]; married 14 April, 1740, Christina, third daughter of Dirck Ten Broeck (Recorder and Mayor of Albany) and Margarita Cuyler. She was born 30 December, 1718, and died 29 June, 1801. Philip Livingston died at York, Penna., 12 June, 1778. They had the following children:—

I   Philip Philip, born at Albany, N. Y., 28 May, 1741 [O.S.]; settled in Jamaica, W. I., before the Revolution, and married Sarah Johnson of the Parish of St. Andrew in that island 29 June, 1768; died at New York, 2 November, 1787. Mrs. Livingston was born 23 March, 1749, and died at New York, 6 November, 1802.[3] Philip P. Livingston was a member of Assembly, Jamaica, W. I.

II   Dirck, or Richard, born 6 June, 1743; died unmarried.

III   Catharine, baptised 25 August, 1745; married (r) Stephen Van Rensselaer, New York, 23 January, 1764; (2) Dominie Eilardus Westerlo, 19 July,. 1775; died 17 April, 1810.

IV   Margaret, baptised at New York, 25 October, 1747; married, at Kingston N. Y., 30 July, 1776, Thomas Jones M.D. of New York; died 17 January, 1830.

V   Peter Van Brugh, baptised at New York, 13 March, 1751; died unmarried in Jamaica, W. I.

VI   Sarah, born at New York, 7 December, 1752; married at Kingston New Church, 26 November, 1775, Rev. John H. Livingston D.D.;

died at New Brunswick, N. J. 29 December, 1814. The Rev. John H. Livingston, a son of Henry Livingston and Susan Conklin, was born at Poughkeepsie, N. Y., 30 May, 1746, and died at New Brunswick, 20 January, 1825. He was a celebrated divine and president of Queen's College, New Brunswick, and in 1829, his biography was written by the Rev. Alexander Gunn D.D., "at the request of the Reformed Dutch Church in America."

VII   Abraham, baptised at New York, 3 July, 1754; died unmarried, at Charleston, S. C., in 1782. He was Commissary to the American Army, etc., during the War of Independence.

VIII Alida, baptised at New York, 3 August, 1757; died unmarried.

IX   Henry, or Henry P., baptised at New York, 26 March, 1760; died unmarried. He was Captain in General Washington's Life Guard.[4]

Notes

1. Authorities: *Manuscript Genealogy of 1769*; Baptismal Registers, Dutch Reformed Church, New York City; Miss Ten Broeck Runk's *The Ten Broeck Genealogy*; and Mr. Brace's manuscript.
2. The year is a little doubtful, should be evidently old style of reckoning, or 1717, new style, as Professor Pearson gives the date of baptism as January, 1717. *Collections on the History of Albany*, vol. iv, p. 143.
3. For list of their children see Appendix L.
4. See under Chapter XIII. and Appendix A.

APPENDIX I

Family of William Livingston, Governor of New Jersey[1]

WILLIAM LIVINGSTON was born in November, 1723, and was the seventh son of Philip Livingston, second Lord of the Manor; baptised at Albany, 8 December, 1723; married about 1745, Susanna, daughter of Philip French, and Susanna Brockholies [or Brockhoist]; died at Elizabethtown, N. J., 25 July, 1790. Mrs. Livingston was baptised at New York, 19 June, 1723, and died also at Elizabethtown, N. J., 17 July, 1789. A *Memoir of the Life of William Livingston*, by Theodore Sedgwick, Jun., was published in 1833.[2] Their children were:—

I   A son, born in 1746; died in infancy.

II A son, born in 1747; died in infancy.

III Susanna, born in 1748; married 10 September, 1794, John Cleve Symmes of New Jersey, Colonel of Militia, 1775. Member of State Convention, 1776, associate justice of the Supreme Court of New Jersey in 1777, and a judge of the Supreme Court of the new North-West Territory in 1786. She was his third wife. She died —.

IV Catharine, born 16 September, 1751; married (1) Matthew Ridley of Baltimore, 14 April, 1787; (2) John Livingston of Oak Hill, 3 November, 1796; died 8 December, 1813. Her second husband was the fifth son of Robert, third Lord of the Manor, and she was his second wife. This second marriage took place at Governor John Jay's official residence, Government House, New York City.

V   Mary, born 16 February, 1753; married 27 May, 1771, James Linn; died —.

VI   William, born 21 March, 1754; married Mary Lennington; died 1817.

VII   Philip Van Brugh, baptised at New York, 28 July, 1755; died unmarried.

VIII   Sarah Van Brugh, born 2 August, 1756; married 28 April, 1774, John Jay, Chief Justice of the State of New York, 1777, Minister to Spain, 1779, one of the American Commissioners who signed the Treaty of Peace with Great Britain in 1783, Chief Justice of the Supreme Court of the United States, 1789, etc.; died at Bedford, N. Y., 28 May, 1802.

IX   Henry Brockholst, born in New York, 25 November, 1757; married (1) Catharine, daughter of Peter Keteltas and Elizabeth Van Zandt, 2 December, 1784; (2) Ann, daughter of Gabriel Henry Ludlow, and Ann Williams; (3) Catharine, daughter of Edward Seaman and widow of Captain John Kortright; died 18 March, 1823, at Washington D. C.[3]

X   Judith, born 30 December, 1758; married John Watkins; died 7 July, 1843.

XI   Philip French, born 1 September, 1760; drowned at Hackensack, N. J.

XII   John Lawrence, born 15 July, 1762; lost at sea 18 March, 1781, with the *Saratoga* man-of-war.[4]

XIII   Elizabeth Clarkson, born 5 April, 1764; died young.

Notes

1. His career has been fully treated in Chapters XII, XIII, and XIV.
2. William Livingston was accustomed to say in his later days, "Of children I have had to the number of these United States." Sedgwick, *Life of William Livingston*, p. 446. For authorities see *Livingstons of Callendar*, pp. 494–502.
3. For his career see Chapters XIII, XIV, and Appendix A.
4. See Appendix A.

APPENDIX J

FAMILY OF JUDGE ROBERT R. LIVINGSTON OF CLERMONT[1]

ROBERT R. LIVINGSTON, the only child of Robert Livingston, first proprietor of Clermont, was born in August, 1718, and baptised on the thirty-first of that month. He married at New York, 8 December, 1742, Margaret, only daughter and heiress of Colond Henry Beekman of Rhinebeck and Janet Livingston, second daughter of Robert Livingston, the Nephew.[2] She was baptised at Kingston, N. Y., 1 March, 1724, and died in June, 1800. Judge Livingston died at Clermont, 9 December, 1775.[3] Their children were:—

I   Janet, born 27 August, 1743; married Richard Montgomery (afterwards the celebrated American general of the Revolution, who fell in the assault of Quebec, night of 31 December, 1775), 24 July, 1773; died 6 November, 1828.

II   Catharine, born 20 February, 1745; died 29 April, 1752.

III   Robert R., born 27 November, 1746; married 9 September, 1770, Mary only daughter of John Stevens of Hunterdon, N. J.; died 26 February, 1813. The well-known Chancellor.[4]

IV   Margaret, born 6 January, 1749; married 22 February, 1779, Dr. Thomas Tillotson of Maryland, Physician and Surgeon-General Northern Department during the Revolutionary War, and later, Secretary of State, New York, etc.; died at Rhinebeck, N. Y., 19 March, 1823.

V   Henry Beekman, born 9 November, 1750; married 11 March, 1781, Ann Hume, daughter of Dr. William Shippen and Alice Lee, of

Philadelphia; died 5 November, 1831, at his residence in Columbia Co., Colonel of Fourth New York Line during War of Independence.[5]

VI   Catharine, born 14 October, 1752; married 30 June, 1793, Rev. Freeborn Garrettson; died 14 July, 1849.

VII   John R., born 13 February, 1755; married (1) Margaret Sheafe of Boston, in 1779; (2) Eliza, daughter of Charles McEvers and Mary Bache, 30 May, 1789. The latter was a younger sister of his brother Edward's wife. John R. Livingston died in September, 1851.

VIII Gertrude, born 16 April, 1757; married 11 May, 1779, Morgan Lewis, a son of Francis Lewis, a Signer of the Declaration of Independence. He was aide to General Gates and Quarter-Master General of the Northern army in 1776; later Chief Justice State of New York 1801–4, Governor 1804, Quartermaster-General United States Army 1812, etc. Mrs. Morgan Lewis died 9 March, 1833.[6]

IX   Joanna, born 14 September, 1759; married her cousin Peter R. Livingston, a great grandson of Robert Livingston, the Nephew. He was Member of New York Assembly and Speaker, 1823. State Senator, 1820–22; 1826–29; President of the Senate, 1828, etc. She died 1 March, 1829.

X   Alida, born 24 December, 1761; married 19 January, 1789, John Armstrong, aide and adjutant-general to General Gates during the War of Independence. He was subsequently United States Senator for New York, 1801; Minister to France, in succession to his brother-in-law, Robert R. Livingston, 1804; Brigadier-General, United States Anny, 1812; and Secretary of War, 1813. Mrs. Armstrong died 24 December, 1822.

XI   Edward, born 28 May, 1764; married (1) Mary McEvers, elder sister of his brother John's second wife, 10 April, 1788; (2) Louise Moreau de Lassy, née D'Avezac de Castera, 3 June, 1805; died 23 May, 1836, at Montgomery Place, Dutchess Co., N. Y.[7]

Chancellor Livingston, the eldest son of Judge Robert R. Livingston, by his wife Mary Stevens, had the following children:—

I   Elizabeth Stevens, born 5 May, 1780; married 20 November, 1799, Edward Philip Livingston, of Jamaica, W. I.; died 10 June, 1829. Edward Philip Livingston was Lieutenant-Colonel of New York Militia and aide-de-camp to Governor George Clinton, 1 September, 1801[8]; Private Secretary to his father-in-law, Minister Livingston on his mission to France same year; State Senator 1808–12; 1822–4; 1838–9;

Lieutenant-Governor, 1830, etc. He died at Clermont, 3 November, 1843.[9]

II   Margaret Maria, born 11 April, 1783; married 10 July, 1799, Robert L. Livingston, third son of Walter Livingston of Teviotdale, Columbia Co.; died 8 March, 1818. Robert L. Livingston, who was also private secretary to his father-in-law in France, 1801–3, was baptised at Linlithgow, Columbia Co., 6 May, 1775, and died 7 January, 1843. His portrait is in the possession of his descendant Mr. Howard Clarkson, of Holcroft.

Notes

1. Compiled from record in his Family Bible and particulars furnished by his descendants, collated with Mr. Brace's manuscript genealogy.
2. See Appendix M.
3. For particulars of his life, see Chapters X and XI.
4. See Chapters XIII to XVI inclusive.
5. See Chapter XIII and Appendix A.
6. For an account of General Morgan Lewis and his family, see Mrs. Delafield's *Biographies of Francis and Morgan Lewis*, published in 1877.
7. For his career see Chapter XVII, also Hunt's *Life of Edward Livingston*, published in 1864.
8. Original commission still preserved at Clermont.
9. See Appendix L.

APPENDIX K

FAMILY OF COLONEL PETER R. LIVINGSTON[1]

COLONEL PETER R. LIVINGSTON was born 27 April, 1737 [O.S.]; married 6 June, 1758, Margaret, third daughter of James Livingston of New York. He died 15 November, 1794. His wife was born 4 July, 1738, and died 31 July, 1809. Their children were:—

I   Robert Thong, born 4 April, 1759; married 15 November, 1787, Margaret, daughter of John Livingston and Catharine de Peyster; died 20 December, 1813.

II   Mary, born 19 October, 1761; died 11 July, 1775.

III   James Smith, born 29 July, 1764; died 20 October, 1765.

IV   Peter William, born 9 May, 1767; married 13 November, 1793, Elizabeth, daughter of Gerard William Beekman and Mary Duyckinck; died 11 February, 1826.

V   Margaret, born 3 June, 1768; married 20 December, 1795.[2] John de Peyster, son of Volckert Peter Douw and Anna de Peyster; died 21 January, 1802.

VI   James Smith, born 24 May, 1769; married Mary Price[3]; died 11 January, 1839.

VII   Moncrieff, born 2 December, 1770; married (1) in 1790, Frances Covert; (2) Catharine Thom; died 22 December, 1853.

VIII   Walter Tryon, born 24 January, 1772; married (1) Eliza Platner; (2) Elizabeth McKinstry, 29 July, 1798; died 24 September, 1827.[4]

IX   John Lafitte, born 9 December, 1773; died 25 April, 1776.

X   William Smith, born 4 November, 1779; died 4 January, 1795.

XI   Mary Thong, born 25 July, 1783; married (1) at Albany, N. Y., 2 May, 1805, Alexander, eldest son of William Wilson, of the township of Clermont, Columbia Co., who was born 29 October, 1783, and died 15 August, 1805. (2) George Crawford of Hudson, N. Y., 23 July, 1808; she died 3 January, 1821. George Crawford married, as his second wife 27 October, 1821, Eliza B., second daughter of Walter Tryon Livingston. She was born 8 June, 1794, and died 8 September 1836. George Crawford married as his third wife 1 June, 1837, Maria, daughter of David Van Ness of Dutchess Co. He died 29 October 1841.

Notes

1. Compiled from the record in his Family Bible as supplied the author by Mr. Fredk. M. Steele of Chicago, Ill., after collation with Mr. Brace's manuscript.
2. Date given by Mr. Brace, according to record in Bible—"November 1796."
3. Name uncertain, so given in Holgat"s *American Genealogy*, p. 163.
4. So in Mr. Brace's manuscript. Holgate has December as the month.

FAMILY OF PHILIP PHILIP LIVINGSTON OF JAMAICA, W.I.[1]

PHILIP PHILIP LIVINGSTON was born 28 May, 1741 [O.S.]; married Sarah Johnson of the Parish of St. Andrew, Jamaica, W. I., 29 June, 1768; Mr. Livingston died 2 November, 1787, in New York City; Mrs. Livingstone was born 23 March, 1749 [O.S.], and died, 6 November, 1802, in New York City. Their children were[2]:—

I   Philip Henry, born 30 October, 1769; baptised by the Rector of Kingston, Jamaica, W. I., 26 November, 1769; married Maria, daughter of Walter Livingston, 8 May, 1788; died December, — 1831. Mrs. Livingston died, — August, 1828, in New York City.

II   George, born 14 October, 1771; baptised 6 January, 1772; died —.

III Catherine, born 13 October, 1772; baptised 6 January, 1773; married John Sanders, 13 October, 1796, at New York; died, 20 March, 1819, at St. Mary's, Jamaica; Mr. Sanders died in Jamaica, — December, 1818.

IV   Christina, born 26 September, 1774. at New York, baptised by the Rev. Mr. John Livingston, 18 November, 1774; married Mr. J. N. Macomb, 29 March, 1797; died 24 August, 1841, at Esperanza.

V   Sarah, born 29 February, 1776, at Kingston, Jamaica, W. I., baptised 16 June, 1776; died 12 April, 1797, in New York.

VI   Henry, born 13 May, 1777; baptised at Kingston, Jamaica, 8 June, 1777; died in Jamaica, being about 4 years of age.

VII   Edward, usually known as Edward P., born 24 November, 1779; baptised at St. Andrew's Parish, Jamaica, by the Rev. Mr. John Poole, 6 January, 1780; married Elizabeth Stevens, eldest daughter of Chancellor Robert R. Livingston of Clermont, 20 November, 1799; died 3 November, 1843. Mrs. Elizabeth Stevens Livingston died 10 June, 1829.[3]

VIII Jasper Hall, born 3 December, 1780; baptised at St. Andrew's Parish, Jamaica, 24 April, 1781; married Eliza, born 15 February, 1786, eldest daughter of Judge Brockholst Livingston, by his first wife, Catharine Keteltas, 14 July, 1802, at New York; died 9 August, 1835, in Jamaica. Mrs. Livingston died at London, England, 25, October, 1860.[4]

IX   Washington, born 6 July, 1783; baptised at Kingston,. Jamaica, 15 September, 1783; died in Jamaica, about ten months after his birth.

X   Maria Margaret, born in New York, 30 December, 1787; died 3 September, 1791.

Notes

1. As the only son of "the Signer," who married and left issue, and as some of his children intermarried with their American cousins, the author considers this family record worth printing here. Having settled in Jamaica, W. I., prior to the War of Independence, Philip Philip Livingston remained a British subject.
2. Abbreviated from the Family Register in the Livingston Bible in the possession of Mr. O. I. Cammann Rose, of Geneva, N. Y., kindly copied for me by Mr. John N. Macomb, Jun., of Branchport, Yates Co., New York, in 1889. The full record will be found in *The Livingstons of Callendar*, Appendix No. LIX. *Cf. Ibid.*, pp. 477, 478.
3. Mr. John Henry Livingston, the present owner of Clermont, to whom this work is dedicated, is a grandson of Edward Philip and Elizabeth Stevens Livingston.
4. The author is a grandson of this marriage; while his wife is a granddaughter of Judge Brockholst Livingston and his third wife, Catharine Seaman. The dates and places of death of Mr. and Mrs. Jasper Hall Livingston, as well as some particulars concerning Mr. Edward P. Livingston are derived from other authentic sources of information.

APPENDIX M

FAMILY OF ROBERT LIVINGSTON, "THE NEPHEW."[1]

ROBERT LIVINGSTON, the Nephew, was born in Scotland; he was a son of James Livingston of Edinburgh, an elder brother of Robert Livingston, first Lord of the Manor, and came out to America, to join his uncle, in 1687. He married 26 August, 1697, Margarita, daughter of Pieter Philipse Schuyler and Engeltje Goosense Van Schaick. She was born in November, 1682. Robert died 21 April, 1725, and was buried in the Dutch Church, Albany, N. Y. Their children were:—

I   Engeltje, baptised Albany, 17 July, 1698; married 3 January, 1734, Johannes, son of Hendrick Van Rensselaer and Catharina Van Brug; died — February, 1747 (buried at Albany, 23 February).

II James, baptised Albany, 21 December, 1701; married New York, 18 May, 1723, Maria, daughter of Jacobus Kierstede and Elizabeth Lawrence; died—.

III Janet, baptised Albany, 24 November, 1703; married Henry, son of Henry Beekman and Johanna Lopers, widow Joris Davidsen; died in 1724.

IV Peter, baptised Albany, 6 January, 1706; married at Albany 30 November, 1728, Zelia, daughter of Henry Holland and Jennie Schley. He was killed by Indians while buying furs near Seneca Lake.

V   John, baptised Albany, 6 March, 1709; married 6 September, 1739, Catryna, eldest daughter of Dirck Ten Broeck and Margarita Cuyler. John died at Stillwater, N. Y., 17 September, 1791. His wife was born 11 September, 1715, and died at Stillwater, N. Y. 6 April, 1802.[2] Three of their sons Richard, James, and Abraham were officers in the American Army during the War of Independence.[3]

Notes

1. After Chapter V had gone to press, the author was furnished by Mr. Fredk. Steele of Chicago, with some further particulars concerning "the Nephew's" family, and so he has embodied these in the above list.
2. According to Miss Runk's *Ten Broeck Genealogy*, p. 58, Mrs. Catryna Livingston was born 1 September, 1715, died at Albany, 6 April, 1801.
3. See under Chapter XIII and Appendix A.

LIST OF AUTHORITIES

A S regards original and manuscript sources of information in private hands, the author has been much indebted to the Livingston (Kilsyth) Charters and other documents at Colzium House; the manuscript copies of the Rev. John Livingston's Autobiography, and the various journals, letters, and other family papers and records in the possession of the Rev. John's descendants in America; which have all been of the very greatest service to him in the compilation of this volume. In his former work, *The Livingstons of Callendar*, the writer has already thanked the owners of these family papers by name; but he now begs to thank them again, one and all, most heartily, as without their welcome aid, much important and original information could never have been obtained.

The author has had searches also made among the various unpublished Scottish Registers and Records preserved in H. M. Register House, Edinburgh—such as the *Registers of Sasines, Inquisitions, Testament Records*, etc., etc.—from which many important facts, hitherto unknown have been gleaned. Fortunately for him, the voluminous manuscripts relating to the early history of New York, now in the custody of the Public Record Office, London, were copied and printed at the expense of that State about half a century ago[1]; and thus, in this case, he has been saved much trouble and expense. Out of curiosity, however, he has himself examined several of Robert Livingston, the first settler's original letters, which are to be found in this valuable collection of early American documents.[2] They are for the most part written in a clear legible hand, and are in a good state of preservation.

Printed Works (and Manuscripts not Mentioned above)

A

Acts and Proceedings of the General Assemblies of the Kirk of Scotland, 1560–1618.
Adams (E. F.), The Works of John Adams.
Adams (J. Q.), An Eulogy on the Life of James Monroe (1831).
—— An Eulogy on the Life of James Madison (1836).
Adams (Henry), Life of Albert Gallatin.
—— Writings of Albert Gallatin.
—— History of the United States during the First and Second Administrations of Thomas Jefferson.
Adams (John Quincy), Memoirs.
American Oratory.
Allen's, American Biographical Dictionary.
Anderson (James), The Ladies of the Covenant.
Anderson's, The Scottish Nation.
Almon's, Remembrancer for 1779.
American State Papers—Foreign Relations.
American Law Journal—vol. v.
American Manuscripts in the Royal Institution (Hist. MSS. Com).
Anton (Rev. Peter), Kilsyth; A Parish History.
Appleton's Cyclopædia of American Biography.
Aristides, An Examination of the Various Charges against Aaron Burr.
Armorial de Berry.
Archives of Rotterdam—Register of Deaths (MS).
Arnold (J. N.), Life of Benedict Arnold.
—— Benedict Arnold at Saratoga.

B

Booke of the Univer sail Kirk of Scotland.
Baillie (Rev. Robert), Letters and Journals.
Bannister (Saxe), Writings of William Paterson, Founder of Bank of England.
Balfour (Sir Jas.), Annales of Scotland.
Burke (Sir Bernard), Dormant, Abeyant, Forfeited, and Extinct Peerages of the British Empire.
Blair (Mr. Robert), Memoirs of the Life of (1754 edition).
——, —— (Wodrow edition).
Beattie (Rev. Jas.), History of the Church of Scotland during the Commonwealth.

Burton (J. H.), *The Scot Abroad.*

Bancroft (George), *History of the United States of America.*

Bryant and Gay, *Popular History of the United States of America.*

Burnet (Bishop), *History of his Own Times.*

Belknap, *History of New Hampshire.*

Biography of the Signers of the Declaration of Independence.

Belisle, *History of Independence Hall.*

Bushnell (C. J.), *Crumbs for Antiquarians.*

Bancroft (George), *History of the Formation of the Constitution of the United States of America.*

Barbé-Marbois, *Histoire de La Louisiane.*

Bowring, *Works of Bentham.*

Bain (Joseph), *Calendar of Documents Relating to Scotland.*

Buccleuch (*Duke of*), *Manuscripts of* (Hist. MSS. Commission).

Brace (Henry), *Ten Broeck Family.*

—— *Livingston Genealogy* (MS.).

Barrett (Walter), *The Old Merchants of New York.*

Breck (Samuel), *Historical Sketch of Continental Money.*

Bolton (C. W.), *History of the County of Westchester.*

C

Chambers, *Biographical Dictionary of Eminent Scotsmen.*

Cleland, *Annals of Glasgow.*

Calderwood, *History of the Kirk of Scotland.*

Calendar of State Papers—Domestic—1638–9.

Calendar of Treasury Papers, 1556–1696.

—— *1702–1707.*

—— *1708–1714.*

Calendar Home Office Papers Geo. III, 1773–1775.

Calendar State Papers—Ireland—1625–1632.

Calendar Clarendon Papers.

Clarendon State Papers.

Collections of the Massachusetts Historical Society.

Carlyle (Thomas), *Oliver Cromwell's Letters and Speeches.*

Cunningham, *The Church History of Scotland.*

Clarkson (Matthew), *The Clarksons of New York.*

Clarkson (T. S.), *History of Clermont or Livingston Manor.*

Collections of the New York Historical Society.

Congress (Continental), Journals of.
Congress (Continental), Secret Journals of.
Chastellux (Marquis de), *Voyages dans l'Amérique, Septentrionale, en 1780, 1781, 1782.*
Catalogue of Columbia College.
Cooper (Rev. M.), *History of North America* (1789).
Colden (C.), *Life of Robert Fulton.*
Cussans, *Handbook of Heraldry.*
Carlisle, Earl of, Manuscripts (Hist. MSS. Commission).
Carrington (H. B.), *Battles of the American Revolution.*
Cortlandt Van (Philip), *Autobiography of* (Mag. Am. History, May, 1878).

D

Darien (The) Papers. (Bannatyne Club).
Delafield (Mrs. Julia), *Biographies of Francis and Morgan Lewis.*
Duer (W. A.), *Life of Lord Stirling.*
Drake, *American Biography.*
Dexter, *Biographical Sketches of the Graduates of Yale College.*
Dawson (H. B.), *The Sons of Liberty in New York.*
—— *Battles of the United States.*
—— *New York City during the American Revolution.*
Davis (M. L.), *Memoirs of Aaron Burr.*
Durand (John) *New Materials for the History of the American Revolution.*
Doyle (J. A.), *The English in America.*
Dwight, *Biographical Sketches of the Graduates of Yale College, 1701–1745.*
Duyckinck, *Cyclopaedia of American Literature.*
Dartmouth, Earl of, Manuscripts of (Hist. MSS. Commission).
Diary of Alexander Brodie of Brodie, A.D. 1652–1680 (Spalding Club).

E

Extracts from the *Registers of the Presbytery of Glasgow prior to* 1601.
Elliot's *Debates on the Federal Constitution.*
—— *The Madison Papers.*
Ellet (Mrs.), *Queens of American Society.*
Ellis (Sir Henry), *A General Introduction to Domesday Book.*
Edinburgh, University of, *A Catalogue of the Graduates.*

F

Ferrier (Rev. William), *Life and Correspondence of the Rev. John Carstairs.*
Force (Peter), *American Archives*—Fourth and Fifth Series.
Frothingham, *The Rise of the Republic.*
Ford (P. L.), *A List of the Members of the Federal Convention of 1787.*
Flanders, *Lives and Times of the Chief Justices of the Supreme Court of the United States.*
Francis (Dr. John W.), *An Address Delivered on the Anniversary of the Philolexian Society of Columbia College.*
—— *Old New York.*
Fox-Davies (A. C.), *Heraldry Explained.*
Fortescue (Hon. J. W.), *A History of the British Army.*
Ford (W. C.), *The Writings of George Washington.*
Fœdera.

G

Gordon (James), *History of Scots Affairs, 1637–1641.*
Gillies (Dr.), *Historical Collections relating to Remarkable Periods of the Success of the Gospel, etc.*
Gunn, *Memoirs of the Rev. John H. Livingston.*
Grant (Mrs.), *Memoirs of an American Lady.*
Gordon (Dr.), *Rise, Progress, and Establishment of the United States of America.*
Griswold, *The Republican Court.*
Gilman, *James Monroe.*
Graydon (Alexander), *Memoirs* (edition 1846).
Godfrey (Carlos E.), *The Commander-in-Chief's Guard.*
Greene (G. W.), *Life of Nathanael Greene.*
Gentleman's Magazine for 1775 and 1776.
Gilpin (H. D.), *Biographical Notice of Edward Livingston.*

H

Hunt (C. H.), *Life of Edward Livingston.*
Hamilton, *Description of the Sheriffdoms of Lanark and Renfrew.*
Hunt's Merchant's Magazine.
Howell's State Trials.

Holgate (J. B.), *American Genealogy.*

Hildreth, *History of the United States.*

Hutchinson, *History of the Province of Massachusetts Bay.*

Hatfield, *History of Elizabeth, New Jersey.*

Hammond, *Political History of New York.*

Hunt (Miss), *Memoirs of Mrs. Edward Livingston.*

Hamilton (J. C.), *History of the Republic of the United States as Traced in the Writings of Alexander Hamilton.*

Howell (G. R.), *Heraldry in England and America.*

Hastings (Hugh), *Public Papers of George Clinton.*

Historic New York.

Harleian Society's Publications (vol. xlviii.).

Historical Magazine.

Hough (F. B.), *The Northern Invasion of October* 1780.

Heitman (F. B.), *Historical Register of the Continental Army, 1775–1783.*

I

Irving (Washington), *Life of Washington.*

J

Jones (Judge), *History of New York during the Revolutionary War.*

Jay (William), *Life of John Jay.*

Johnston (H. P.), *Correspondence and Public Papers of John Jay.*

—— *Observations on Judge Jones' Loyalist History of New York.*

Jefferson (Thomas), *Proceedings of the Government of the United States against Edward Livingston.*

Johnston (G. H.), *Scottish Heraldry Made Easy.*

Jamaica, Island of, *Registers of Deeds, Wills, and other Public Records* (MSS.).

K

Kirkton, *History of the Kirk of Scotland.*

Kip (Bishop), *New York Society in the Olden Time.*

Knox, *Life of Robert Fulton.*

Kingsford (W.), *History of Canada.*

Kidd (Captain), An Account of the Proceedings in Relation to.

King (C. R.), *Life and Correspondence of Rufus King.*

L

Livingston (Rev. John), *Autobiography* (editions 1727, 1754, 1773, 1845, and 1848).

Livingston (Rev. William), *Conflict in Conscience of a deare Christian, etc.*

Livingston (John Henry), *Clermont and the Livingstons of Clermont* (MS).

Livingston (Robert R.), *Essay on Sheep.*

Livingston (Edward), *An Answer to Mr. Jefferson, etc.*

—— *Project of a New Penal Code for the State of Louisiana.*

—— *A System of Penal Law for Louisiana.*

Livingston (E. B.), *The Livingstons of Callendar.*

Laing (Henry), *A Descriptive Catalogue of Ancient Scottish Seals.*

Laing (Henry), *A Supplemental Catalogue of Ancient Scottish Seals.*

Lossing (Benson J.), *The Book of The Hudson.*

—— *Life and Times of Major-General Philip Schuyler.*

—— *History of New York City.*

—— *Pictorial Field Book of the Revolution.*

Lamb (Mrs.), *History of the City of New York.*

Lanman, *Dictionary of the United States Congress.*

Lyman (T.), *The Diplomacy of the United States.*

Lucas (Charles), *Exposé d'un Système de Législation Criminelle, etc.*

Lindsay (Sir David), *Heraldic Manuscript.*

Lindsay (Robert), of Pitscottie, *Chronicles of Scotland.*

Lodge (C. B.), *The Story of the Revolution.*

—— *Alexander Hamilton.*

—— *The Works of Hamilton.*

Lamont, *Diary.*

Laing Charters—the University of Edinburgh.

Le Maistre, *Notice Généalogique sur La Famille de Livingston.*

Larochefoucauld – Liancourt (Duc de), *Voyage dans les États Unis de l'Amerique fait en 1795–1797.*

Laurens (Col. John), *Army Correspondence of, in the Years 1777–1778.*

Lawrie (Sir Archibald C.), *Early Scottish Charters prior to A.D. 1153.*

M

Miscellany of the Wodrow Society.

Miscellany of the Maitland Club.

Munimenta Alme Universitatis Glasguensis.

M'Crie (Rev. Thos.), *Sketches of Scottish Church History.*
—— *Memoirs of Mr. William Veitch and George Brysson.*
Mackintosh, *History of Civilisation in Scotland.*
Mackenzie (Sir George), *Memoirs.*
Magazine of American History.
Musgrave's *Obituary.*
Munsell (Joel), *Annals of Albany.*
—— *Collections of Albany.*
Moore (F.), *Diary of the American Revolution.*
Mulford, *History of New Jersey.*
M'Master, *History of the People of the United States.*
Morse, *Thomas Jefferson.*
Mignet (Monsieur), *Notice sur Livingston.*
Maclay (E. S.), *History of the United States Navy 1775 to 1881.*
Macdonald (W. R.), *Scottish Armorial Seals.*

N

Northern Notes and Queries.
Nicoll (J.), *Diary.*
New York, *Colonial Documents of.*
—— *Journals of Assembly.*
—— *Journals of Legislative Council.*
—— *Journals of Assembly* (State).
—— *Journals of Provincial Congress, 1775–1777.*
—— *Calendars of Historical Manuscripts Relating to the War of the Revolution.*
—— *Civil List.*
—— *Baptismal Records, Dutch Church.*
New Jersey, *Archives of State of.*
—— *Official Register of Officers in the Revolutionary War.*
—— *Minutes of the Provincial Congress.*
—— *Collections of the Historical Society of.*
—— *Selections from Correspondence of.*
New England Historical and Genealogical Register.
New York Genealogical and Biographical Record.
Nolte, *Fifty Years in both Hemispheres.*
Nisbet, *System of Heraldry.*
New York, *Muster Rolls of Provincial Troops, 1755–1764.*
Naval Record of the American Revolution (Library of Congress Publication).

O

O'Callaghan (E. B.), *Documentary History of New York.*
—— *Marriage Licenses of the Province of New York.*
Origines Parochiales Scotiæ (Bannatyne Club).
Original Letters Relating to the Ecclesiastical Affairs of Scotland (Ibid).

P

Paullin (C. O.), *The Navy of the American Revolution.*
Patten (Master), *The Expedition into Scotland, etc.*
Pearson (Professor), *Genealogies of the First Settlers of Albany.*
Parton (James), *Life of Aaron Burr.*
—— *Life of Thomas Jefferson.*
—— *Life of Andrew Jackson.*
Pellew, *John Jay.*
Paul (Sir James Balfour), *An Ordinary of Scottish Arms* (edition 1903).
—— *The Scots Peerage* (In course of publication).
Peyster De, *Biographical Sketch of Robert R. Livingston.*
Pennsylvania Magazine of History and Biography.

Q

Quarterly Review (vol. xix).

R

Rait (R. S.), *Five Stuart Princesses.*
Register of Ministers, Exhorters, and Readers (Maitland Club.)
Register of Interments Greyfriars Burying Ground, Edinburgh, 1658–1700.
Registers of the Privy Council of Scotland.
Register of Arms (Lyon office, Edinburgh).
Ragman Roll.
Roberts (J. A.), *New York in the Revolution as Colony and State.*
Randolph, *Memoirs of Thomas Jefferson.*
Row (Rev. John), *History of the Kirk of Scotland,* 1558–1637.
Rothes, *Relation of Proceedings Concerning the Affairs of the Kirk of Scotland,*
    1627–1638.
Reid (Dr.), *History of the Presbyterian Church in Ireland.*
Rose (Hon. George), *Diaries and Correspondence of.*

Renwick, *Life of Robert Fulton.*
Runk (E. Ten Broeck), *The Ten Broeck Genealogy.*

S

Scott (Hew), *Fasti Ecclesiœ Scoticanœ.*
Select Biographies (Wodrow Society).
Statistical Account of Scotland.
Selections from the Registers of the Presbytery of Lanark, 1623–1709. (Abbotsford Club).
State Tracts of William III.
Scots Magazine (1773).
Sedgwick (Theodore), *Life of William Livingston.*
Stevens (Rev. William), *History of the Scottish Church in Rotterdam.*
Schuyler (G. W.), *Colonial New York.*
Smith (W.), *History of New York.*
Sutherland (Josiah), *Deduction of the Title to Manor of Livingston.*
Schuyler (John), *Society of the Cincinnati in New York.*
Sumner, *Andrew Jackson.*
Sabine (Lorenzo), *Biographical Sketches of Loyalists during the Revolutionary War.*
Stevens' *Colonial Records, New York Chamber of Commerce.*
Schaack Van (H. C.), *Life of Peter Van Schaack.*
Sparks (Jared), *Library of American Biography.*
—— *Diplomatic Correspondence of the American Revolution.*
—— *Works of Benjamin Franklin.*
—— *The Writings of George Washington.*
—— *Life of Gouverneur Morris.*
—— *Correspondence of the American Revolution.*
Smith (E. M.), *Documentary History of Rhinebeck.*
Stanhope (Earle), *Life of Pitt.*
Stodart, *Scottish Arms.*
Stevens (J. A.), *Benedict Arnold and his Apologists* (Mag. Am. Hist., April, 1880).
Seton (George), *Law and Practice of Heraldry in Scotland.*
Smith (J. H.), *History of Dutchess County.*
Spofford, *Gazetteer of the State of New York.*
Street, *The Council of Revision.*
St. Memin Collection of Portraits.
Smith (Justin H.), *Our Struggle for the Fourteenth Colony.*

T

Taylor (Rev. W. M.), *The Scottish Pulpit.*
Tuckerman (Bayard), *Life of General Philip Schuyler.*
Trotter, *Memoirs of the Latter Years of Ri. Hon. Charles James Fox.*

V

Veitch (Mr. William), *Memoirs.*
Vermont (E. de V.), *America Heraldica.*

W

Winthrop Papers (Coll. Mass. Hist. Soc., Fifth Series).
Wodrow (Rev. Robert), *History of the Sufferings of the Church of Scotland.*
—— *Analecta.*
Washington (H. A.), *Jefferson's Writings.*
Wilkinson (General James), *Memoirs of my own Times.*
Walker, *Jackson and New Orleans.*
Whitelocke (Sir Bulstrode), *Memorials of English Affairs.*
Worthy, *Practical Heraldry.*
Wharton (Mrs. A. H.), *Social Life in Early Republic.*
—— *Martha Washington.*
—— *Through Colonial Doorways.*
—— *Salons Colonial and Republican.*
—— *Heirlooms in Miniatures.*
Wharton (Dr. Francis), *Revolutionary Diplomatic Correspondence of the United States.*
Westminster Review (1825).
Woodward (Rev. John), *Heraldry British and Foreign* (edition 1896).
Webb (Samuel B.), *Correspondence and Journals.*

Notes

1. Under the lengthy title: *Documents Relative to the Colonial History of the State of New York Procured in Holland, England, and France.*
2. The English government is also now having these American documents calendared in their series of *Colonial State Papers.*

INDEX

NUMBER ONE

Livingstons only, arranged alphabetically in accordance with their Christian names, the maiden names of the wives being inserted within parentheses, with a special list (A) of these at end of Index; while list (B) contains the names of men married to Livingston daughters. The figures within parentheses give the year of birth. The capital letters P. I. and S. refer respectively to Preface, Introduction, and Sketch of Scottish House of Callendar. An asterisk* before a name denotes a descendant from Robert Livingston, "The Nephew." The author has endeavoured to make this Index as clear and correct as possible, but as it has been compiled whilst on a journey there may be some errors and omissions.

A

Abraham (1754), fourth son Philip, "The Signer," 211, 493, 501, 516.

*Abraham (1754), Captain, 74, 214, 278, 476, 484, 491, 527.

Agnes, wife Sir John Livingston of Callendar (Douglas), S.

Agnes, wife James, third Lord Livingston (Houston), S.

Agnes, wife William, fourth Lord Livingston (Hepburn), S., 5, 460, 461.

Agnes, Lady, wife Alexander, fifth Lord Livingston (Douglas), 5.

Agnes, wife William, sixth Lord Livingston (Fleming), S., 3, 5, 29.

Agnes (1585), wife Rev. William Livingston (Livingston), 17.

Agnes (1640), eldest dau. Rev. John Livingston, 503.

Agnes (1645), third dau. Rev. John Livingston, 49, 504.

Alexander, son Thurstan, S.

Alexander, Sir, of Callendar, Guardian of King James II., of Scotland, S., 448, 464.

Alexander, younger son of above, S., 468.

Alexander, second son James, first Lord Livingston, S.

Alexander, fifth Lord Livingston, Guardian of Mary, Queen of Scots, P., S., 3–5, 462.

Alexander, seventh Lord Livingston, first Earl of Linlithgow, Guardian of Princess Elizabeth Stuart, S., 5, 10, 15, 20.

Alexander, second Earl of Linlithgow, S.

Alexander, second Earl of Callendar, S.

Alexander, third Earl of Callendar, S.

Alexander, Sir, brother to Viscount Teviot, S.

Alexander (about 1530), Rev. of Monyabroch, P., S., 1–11, 461–463, 465.

Alexander, of Falkirk, 18.

Alexander, of Dunipace, 460–461.

Alexander, of Countesswells, 466.

Alexander, of Treptow, Pomerania, 11.

William (1754), third son of above, 212, 228, 518.

William Alexander (1757), fourth son Peter V. B. Livingston, 431, 452, 514.

*William Smith (1755), Lieutenant-Colonel, 214, 222, 226, 232–233, 246, 247, 306, 477, 485, 486, 492, 493.

William Smith (1779), youngest son Colonel Peter R. Livingston, 523.

Z

*Zelia, wife Peter Livingston (Holland), 526.

(A)

MAIDEN NAMES OF LIVINGSTON WIVES

Alexander, Mary, 513.
Beekman, Cornelia, 512.
Beekman, Elizabeth, 522.
Beekman, Margaret, 519.
Blondel, Susan, 513.
Callendar de, Christian, S.
Conklin, Susanna, 511.
Covert, Frances, 522.
D'Avezac de Castera, Louise, 520.
De Peyster, Catharine, 507.
Dorrell, Joy, 511.
Douglas, Lady Agnes, 5.
Douglas, Agnes. S.
Douglas, Lady Mary, S.
Fish, Christian, 504.
Fleming, Agnes, 5.
Fleming, Janet, 5.
French, Susanna, 517.
Gordon, Lady Elizabeth, S.
Hallett, Sarah Lawrence, 449.
Hay, Lady Helenor, S.
Hay, Lady Margaret, S.
Hepburn, Agnes, 460.
Hepburn, Elizabeth, 460.
Hepburn, Marion, 461.
Holland, Zelia, 526.
Houstoun, Agnes, S.
Howarden, Margaret, 506.
Johnson, Sarah, 515.
Keteltas, Catharine, 518.
Kierstede, Maria, 526.
Knight, Elizabeth, 505.
Lennington, Mary, 518.
Le Roy, Maty Ann, 510.
Livingston, Agnes, 17.
Livingston, Barbara, 11.
Livingston, Catharine, 510.

Livingston, Cornelia, 450.
Livingston, Eliza, 525.
Livingston, Elizabeth Stevens, 520.
Livingston, Joanna, 520.
Livingston, Margaret, 522.
Livingston, Margaret Maria, 521.
Livingston, Maria, 524.
Livingston, Sarah, 516.
Ludlow, Ann, 518.
Makgowin, Janet, 2.
McEvers, Eliza, 520.
McEvers, Mary, 520.
McKinstry, Elizabeth, 523.
McPheadres, Catharine, 511.
Newcomb, Judith, 512.
Platner, Eliza, 523.
Rogers, Susan Bard, 450.
Schuyler, Alida, 505.
Schuyler, Cornelia, 509.
Schuyler, Margarita, 526.
Seaman, Catharine, 518.
Sheafe, Margaret, 520.
Shippen, Ann Hume, 519.
Somervell, Nicolas, 18.
Stevens, Mary, 519.
Swift, Alice, 510.
Ten Broeck, Catryna, 526.
Ten Broeck, Christina, 515.
Thong, Maria, 509.
Thorn, Catharine, 522.
Van Brugh, Catharine, 507.
Van Horne, Cornelia, 514.
Van Rensselaer, Gertrude, 509.
Veitch, Ann, 503.
Weir, Marion, 18.
Winthrop, Mary, 505

(B)

MEN MARRIED TO LIVINGSTON DAUGHTERS

Alexander, William, General (Lord Stirling), 507.
Armstrong, John, General, 520.
Barton, Thomas Pennant, 407.
Bayard, Nicholas, 513.
Beekman, Henry, Colonel, 526.
Brown, John, Captain, 513.
Cleland, David, 504.
Crawford, George, 523.
Dale, Charles, 449.
Douw, John de Peyster, 522.
Duane, James, 509.
Fulton, Robert, 365.
Gardiner, Valentine, 510.
Garrettson, Freeborn, Rev., 520.
Hanson, Henry, 507.
Hoffman, Martin, 507.
Jay, John, 517.
Jones, Thos., Dr., 515.
Kean, John, 514.
Lawrence, John, 508.
Lewis, Morgan, General, 520.
Linn, James, 518.
Livingston, Alexander, Rev., 11.
Livingston, Clermont of Clermont, 450.
Livingston, Edward P., 520.
Livingston, John, of Oak Hill, 517.
Livingston, John H., Dr., Rev., 516.
Livingston, Jasper Hall, 525.
Livingston, Philip H., 524.

Livingston, Peter R., Colonel, 522.
Livingston, *Peter R., 520.
Livingston, Robert L., 521.
Livingston, Robert Thong, 522.
Livingston, William, Rev., 17.
Macomb, John Navarre, 524.
Miller, James, 504.
Montgomery, Richard, General, 519.
Niemcewiez, Count, 514.
Otto, Monsieur, 514.
Paterson, John, 510.
Ricketts, James, Captain, 514.
Ridley, Matthew, 517.
Russell, Andrew, 504.
Rutsen, Jacob, 511.
Sanders, John, 524.
Scott, John, Rev., 503.
Stuyvesant, Peter, 512.
Symmes, John Cleeve, 517.
Thorn, Thomas, 512.
Tillotson, Thomas, Surgeon-General, 519.
Van Cortlandt, Pierre, 512.
Van Horne, Cornelius, 506.
Van Rensselaer, Henry, 511.
Van Rensselaer, Johannes, 526.
Van Rensselaer, Stephen, 515.
Vetch, Samuel, Colonel, 505.
Watkins, John, 518.
Westerlo, Eilardus, Dominie, 515.
Wilson, Alexander, 523.

INDEX

NUMBER TWO

GENERAL

Capital letters P. I. and S. refer respectively to Preface, Introduction, and Sketch of Scottish House of Callendar.